MACRO ECONOMICS

We work with leading authors to develop the strongest educational materials in economics, bringing cutting-edge thinking and best learning practice to a global market.

Under a range of well-known imprints, including Financial Times Prentice Hall, we craft high quality print and electronic publications which help readers to understand and apply their content, whether studying or at work.

To find out more about the complete range of our publishing please visit us on the World Wide Web at: www.pearsoned.co.uk

MACRO ECONOMICS

Manfred Gärtner

University of St Gallen, Switzerland

FT Prentice Hall
FINANCIAL TIMES

An imprint of Pearson Education

Harlow, England • London • New York • Boston • San Francisco • Toronto
Sydney • Tokyo • Singapore • Hong Kong • Seoul • Taipei • New Delhi
Cape Town • Madrid • Mexico City • Amsterdam • Munich • Paris • Milan

Pearson Education Limited
Edinburgh Gate
Harlow
Essex CM20 2JE
England

and Associated Companies throughout the world

Visit us on the World Wide Web at:
www.pearsoned.co.uk

First published 2003

ISBN 0273-65163-3

British Library Cataloguing-in-Publication Data
A catalogue record for this book can be obtained from the British Library.

Library of Congress Cataloging-in-Publication Data
Gärtner, Manfred.
Macroeconomics / Manfred Gärtner.
p. cm.
Includes bibliographical references and index.
ISBN 0-273-65163-3 (pbk.)
1. Macroeconomics. I. Title.

HB172.5 G365 2003
339--dc21 2002069213

10 9 8 7 6 5 4 3 2
07 06 05 04 03

Typeset by 25 in Sabon 10/12.
Printed and bound in Great Britain by Ashford Colour Press Ltd, Gosport.

FOR DAVID, CHRIS, KAI,
DENNIS AND LOU

BRIEF CONTENTS

List of case studies and boxes xv

Preface xvii

1 Macroeconomic essentials 1
2 Booms and recessions (I): the Keynesian cross 33
3 Money, interest rates and the global economy 61
4 Exchange rates and the balance of payments 88
5 Booms and recessions (II): the national economy 111
6 Enter aggregate supply 137
7 Booms and recessions (III): aggregate supply and demand 166
8 Booms and recessions (IV): dynamic aggregate supply and demand 192
9 Economic growth (I): basics 221
10 Economic growth (II): advanced issues 251
11 Endogenous economic policy 287
12 The European Monetary System and Euroland at work 308
13 Inflation and central bank independence 340
14 Budget deficits and public debt 372
15 Unemployment and growth 401
Appendix: A primer in econometrics 434

Index 451

CONTENTS

List of case studies and boxes xv
Preface xvii
Publishers acknowledgements xxi

1 MACROECONOMIC ESSENTIALS 1
1.1 The issues of macroeconomics 1
1.2 Essentials of macroeconomic accounting 6
1.3 Beyond accounting 20
Chapter summary 25
Exercises 26
Recommended reading 28
Appendix: Logarithms, growth rates and logarithmic scales 29

2 BOOMS AND RECESSIONS (I): the Keynesian cross 33
2.1 The circular flow model revisited: terminology and overview 38
2.2 Income determination: a first look 43
2.3 Income determination: a second look 47
2.4 An intertemporal view of consumption and investment 50
Chapter summary 55
Exercises 56
Recommended reading 58
Applied problems 58

3 MONEY, INTEREST RATES AND THE GLOBAL ECONOMY 61
3.1 The money market, the interest rate and the *LM* curve 62
3.2 Aggregate expenditure, the interest rate and the exchange rate: the *IS* curve 68
3.3 The *IS-LM* or the global economy model 73
Chapter summary 83
Exercises 83
Recommended reading 85
Applied problems 85

4 EXCHANGE RATES AND THE BALANCE OF PAYMENTS 88
4.1 Globalization 89
4.2 The exchange rate and the balance of payments 91

4.3 Back to *IS-LM*: enter the *FE* curve 95
4.4 Equilibrium in all three markets 102
Chapter summary 106
Exercises 107
Recommended reading 108
Applied problems 109

5 BOOMS AND RECESSIONS (II): the national economy 111
5.1 Fiscal policy in the Mundell–Fleming model 112
5.2 Monetary policy in the Mundell–Fleming model 115
5.3 The algebra of monetary and fiscal policy in the Mundell–Fleming model 121
5.4 Comparative statics versus adjustment dynamics 122
5.5 Adjustment dynamics with expected depreciation 124
5.6 When prices move 127
5.7 Today's exchange rate and the future 130
Chapter summary 132
Exercises 133
Recommended reading 134
Applied problems 134

6 ENTER AGGREGATE SUPPLY 137
6.1 Potential income and the labour market 138
6.2 Why is there unemployment in equilibrium? 144
6.3 Why may actual output deviate from potential output? 158
Chapter summary 161
Exercises 162
Recommended reading 163
Applied problems 164

7 BOOMS AND RECESSIONS (III): aggregate supply and demand 166
7.1 The short-run aggregate supply curve 167
7.2 The aggregate demand curve 168
7.3 The *AD-AS* model: basics 176
7.4 Policy and shocks in the *AD-AS* model 180
Chapter summary 188
Exercises 189
Recommended reading 190
Appendix: The algebra of the *AD* curve 190

8 BOOMS AND RECESSIONS (IV): dynamic aggregate supply and demand 192
8.1 The aggregate-supply curve in an inflation–income diagram 193

8.2 Equilibrium income and inflation: the *DAD* curve 194
8.3 The *DAD-SAS* model 195
8.4 Inflation expectations 198
8.5 The *DAD-SAS* model at work 201
Chapter summary 214
Exercises 215
Recommended reading 216
Appendix: The algebra of the *DAD* curve 216
Appendix: The genesis of the *DAD-SAS* model 216
Applied problems 218

9 ECONOMIC GROWTH (I): basics 221
9.1 Stylized facts of income and growth 221
9.2 The production function and growth accounting 224
9.3 Growth theory: the Solow model 230
9.4 Why incomes may differ 232
9.5 What about consumption? 234
9.6 Population growth and technological progress 238
9.7 Empirical merits and deficiencies of the Solow model 243
Chapter summary 247
Exercises 248
Recommended reading 249
Applied problems 249

10 ECONOMIC GROWTH (II): advanced issues 251
10.1 The government in the Solow model 252
10.2 Economic growth and capital markets 255
10.3 Extending the Solow model and moving beyond 264
10.4 Poverty traps in the Solow model 267
10.5 Human capital 271
10.6 Endogenous growth 275
Chapter summary 280
Exercises 281
Recommended reading 283
Appendix: A synthesis of the *DAD-SAS* and the Solow model 283
Applied problems 285

11 ENDOGENOUS ECONOMIC POLICY 287
11.1 What do politicians want? 288
11.2 Political business cycles 290
11.3 Rational expectations 293
11.4 Policy games 295
11.5 Ways out of the time inconsistency trap 299
Chapter summary 303

Exercises 304
Recommended reading 305
Applied problems 306

12 THE EUROPEAN MONETARY SYSTEM AND EUROLAND AT WORK 308
12.1 Preliminaries 309
12.2 The 1992 EMS crisis 312
12.3 Exchange rate target zones 319
12.4 Speculative attacks 324
12.5 Monetary and fiscal policy in Euroland 328
Chapter summary 333
Exercises 334
Recommended reading 335
Appendix: The two-country Mundell–Fleming model 336
Applied problems 338

13 INFLATION AND CENTRAL BANK INDEPENDENCE 340
13.1 Inflation, central bank independence and the EMS 341
13.2 Supply shocks and central bank independence 350
13.3 Disinflations and the sacrifice ratio 357
13.4 Lessons for European monetary union 365
Chapter summary 367
Exercises 368
Recommended reading 369
Applied problems 370

14 BUDGET DEFICITS AND PUBLIC DEBT 372
14.1 The government budget 373
14.2 The dynamics of budget deficits and the public debt 374
14.3 Maastricht, the fisc and the central bank 388
14.4 What is wrong with having deficits and debt? 392
14.5 Does monetary union need budget rules? 393
Chapter summary 397
Exercises 398
Recommended reading 399
Applied problems 399

15 UNEMPLOYMENT AND GROWTH 401
15.1 Linking unemployment and growth 401
15.2 European unemployment 404
15.3 Persistence in the *DAD-SAS* model 420
15.4 Lessons, remedies and prospects 423
Chapter summary 429

Exercises 429
Recommended reading 431
Applied problems 431

APPENDIX: A PRIMER IN ECONOMETRICS 434
A.1 First task: estimating unknown parameters 435
A.2 Second task: testing hypotheses 437
A.3 A closer look at OLS estimation 439
Appendix summary 449
Exercises 450
Recommended reading 450

Index 451

LIST OF CASE STUDIES AND BOXES

Case studies

1.1	Germany's current account before and after unification	12
2.1	Income vs leisure time in France and the USA	42
2.2	How to pay for the war: Great Britain in 1940	49
3.1	Liquidity traps and Japan's prolonged recession	80
4.1	Italy's current account before and after the 1992 EMS crisis	98
5.1	The 1988 Asia crisis	118
6.1	Ford's focus: an experiment in efficiency wages	153
7.1	International evidence on the quantity equation and the *AD* curve	183
8.1	Quantity equation, Fisher equation and purchasing power parity: international evidence	211
9.1	Growth accounting in Italy	229
9.2	Income and leisure choices in the OECD countries	241
10.1	National incomes during the Second World War, east and west of the Atlantic	256
11.1	Who wanted the euro? The role of past inflations	302
12.1	German unification as a tug of war	313
13.1	New Zealand's Reserve Bank Act: a case from down under	343
14.1	The rise and fall of Ireland's public debt	384
14.2	Who wanted the euro? The role of government debt	390
14.3	Lessons from the Belgium–Luxemburg monetary union	396
15.1	US vs European job growth: cutting the 'miracle' to size	425

Boxes

1.1	GDP as a measure of total output or income	11
1.2	Working with graphs (part I)	22
2.1	Actual income, potential income and steady-state income: Great Britain in 1933	37
3.1	What is money?	62
3.2	Money versus interest rate control	66
3.3	Working with graphs: (part II)	69
3.4	Exchange rates	71
3.5	Money supply vs interest control in a changing world	77
4.1	Traditional vs new balance of payments terminology	94
4.2	Interest rates, default risk and the risk premium	101
4.3	The *IS-LM-FE* model in a different dress	104
4.4	Endogenous and exogenous variables	105
5.1	The Mundell–Fleming model under capital controls	115
6.1	A flow model of the labour market	157
9.1	The mathematics of the Cobb–Douglas production function	228

10.1 An illustration of the income and distribution effects of globalization 262
10.2 Labour efficiency vs human capital: an example 275
12.1 Convergence criteria in the Maastricht Treaty 319
12.2 The Pact for Stability and Growth 332
13.1 The *SAS* curve under fixed and flexible exchange rates 347
14.1 Seignorage vs inflation tax revenue 387
A.1 The coefficient of determination: R^2 443

PREFACE

What makes the book unique?

This text was shaped by its aim to turn the usual priorities in macroeconomics instruction upside down. Here, the ultimate goal is not simply to teach macroeconomic theories and concepts, with real-world applications sprinkled in for motivation and excitement; rather, students work through this book towards an understanding of the macroeconomic issues and challenges facing the world economy and individual countries. Macroeconomic concepts are taught only as they serve this end. Instead of dwelling on such topics as 'the life-cycle versus the permanent-income explanation of consumption behaviour', or elaborating on 'fifty ways to motivate the aggregate supply curve', this book devotes more space than any other macro text to issues of political economy: why do policy-makers make the choices they do and how are these affected by different institutional settings?

An original item not found in other intermediate texts is the *Primer in Econometrics* placed in an optional appendix at the end of the book. Its purpose is to underscore the point that macroeconomics is about the real world. While this is already stressed by the examination of numerous case studies throughout, this appendix goes one step further by conveying an intuitive understanding of basic statistical concepts used in data analysis. Applied-problem sections after each chapter provide opportunities to put these concepts to work, discussing *recent research*, guiding through *worked problems*, and making students embark on *small projects* of their own. Such early hands-on experience with econometric work, when combined with a user-friendly software package, may give students the orientation and motivation for the more serious statistical work to come later in the curriculum.

Content

The text's main body comprises 15 chapters. The first half of the book is fairly conventional, amounting to a streamlined, no-frills introduction to the macroeconomic concepts that are useful for discussion of contemporary macroeconomic issues in the world economies. Essential macroeconomic concepts are introduced in the context of the circular-flow-of-income model. Then students are led via the Keynesian cross, the *IS-LM*, the Mundell–Fleming and the aggregate demand–aggregate supply model to a fully dynamic aggregate demand–aggregate supply framework for analysing short- and medium-run macroeconomic issues. Chapters on the supply-side topics of unemployment and growth round out this conventional set of tools.

Chapters 10 and 11 extend the tool-box into areas that most intermediate macroeconomics textbooks barely mention in passing. The first refines and extends the Solow growth model (introduced in Chapter 9) for a discussion of human capital and poverty traps, and concludes with a discussion of endogenous growth. Under the heading 'Endogenous economic policy' Chapter 11 then shows that politicians may steer the economy along courses not considered optimal from society's viewpoint, and how institutions should be shaped to reduce this danger.

The remainder of the book explores issues from the heart of European and global monetary and economic integration. All major topics are addressed in chapters on inflation, monetary unions, budget deficits and the public debt, and unemployment.

Learning features

The book has a user-friendly design, featuring margin notes and definitions that emphasize important concepts. Exercises geared towards each chapters's central ideas consolidate the acquired knowledge. An extensive and innovative use of graphs facilitates access and enhances learning success. Every chapter contains one or more case studies that apply core concepts to recent experiences in Europe and in other parts of the world.

What courses does the book accomodate?

The organization of the book gives instructors various options:

- Primarily, the text is designed for courses in *undergraduate or intermediate macroeconomics* that on the one hand insist on providing a sound theoretical foundation, but on the other also want to make a point of emphasizing *applications* in the form of case studies or even, if so desired, elementary statistical work.
- The book's first half can also be used for a *short course in macroeconomic theory* whenever time does not permit working through a large 500–800 page macroeconomics text which has become the standard.
- Also, the book readily accommodates courses in *Economic policy* and *Applied macroeconomics*. Such courses may be organized around an appropriate selection from the several dozen case studies and empirical applications. Conveniently, as deemed necessary, students can be referred to the required theoretical tools in the same textbook.
- Finally, the book accommodates *European studies courses* that can be organized around the applied topics discussed in the second part of the book. Here also, should it be necessary to freshen up or expand previously acquired theoretical knowledge, such material is readily available in the same textbook.

Prerequisites

Ideally, students should approach this book with a *Principles of economics* course under their belt. The formal mathematical requirements are mild: anything close to the most basic mathematics training in high school should do. In fact, most of the formal manipulations are optional and either shown in margin notes or in separate sections that supplement graphical arguments.

I am quite confident, though, that the book can also be adopted and used successfully if a principles course is missing and algebraic manipulations are avoided altogether. A host of case studies, some brief, some quite elaborate, provide ample ammunition for keeping up motivation, and the big payoff waits in the later chapters of the book.

Finally, and though it may sound frivolous: I believe that the book is even suited for self-study. The acquired knowledge will definitely be more fragile and lack depth compared with what can be achieved under the guidance of an experienced instructor. But it should provide an up-to-date first foundation for informed discussion of today's national and global macroeconomic issues.

A text for Europe – and beyond

Reflecting my own roots, expertise and work environment, this text has a strong European flavour. The supplied box of tools and concepts has thus been clearly assembled with an eye to enhancing the understanding of key issues surrounding European economic and monetary integration. But the potential of these tools to explain macroeconomic problems is a lot more universal than this might imply. While institutions may vary around the world, and one region may face quite different challenges than another, the basic concepts needed to understand and analyze macroeconomic issues remain surprisingly similar. The tools assembled here, therefore, not only served me well when teaching open economy macroeconomics in Europe, but also when lecturing in Africa and Asia. This personal experience is underscored by the fact that almost a third of roughly 100 adoptions of this text's predecessor, *A Primer in European Macroeconomics*, originated from outside Europe.

Acknowledgements

This brings me to the people I want to thank for their contributions to whatever merits this text may have. In the very first place, these are my students. Most of all, teaching teaches the teacher. Students' questions and curiosity constantly force me to refine explanations, and in the process very often make me understand things better myself. In the same vein, I thank my colleagues at the University of St Gallen, who over the years allowed me to tap their expertise, experience and creativity in joint teaching ventures. Special thanks to Jörg Baumberger, to whom I owe the idea for the case study derived from Keynes' *How to Pay for the War* in Chapter 2.

I doubt that the book would have been written if it were not for Pradeep Jethi. Then commissioning editor, he lured me into this project at an annual conference of the European Economic Association, in Maastricht of all places. I want to thank him, and the professionals currently with Pearson Education who helped and guided me in preparing the current, thoroughly extended and more comprehensive text: Bridget Allen (pre-press manager), Anita Atkinson (senior editor), Jill Birch (freelance copy editor), Catherine Newman (acquisitions editor) and Abigail Woodman (development editor).

More than any previous book of mine, this one could not nearly be what it is without the help and the enthusiasm of the people working with me at the time it was written. While the contributions of Monika Bütler, Philipp Harms,

Adrienne Schaer and Martin Peter to this text's forerunner still show, Frode Brevik and Caroline Schmidt provided invaluable support in updating data and devising new case studies and exercises. Christian Busch joined them with the proofreading and excelled in programming most of the interactive online material that augments the textbook.

I have also benefited from the reviews commissioned by Pearson Education. Both those that offered applause and encouragement, and those that were more reserved or even critical of certain aspects helped shape the book into a better teaching tool.

The mere writing of a textbook may mostly happen at the desk. But the enthusiasm, the creativity and the discipline that are so essential for such a project come from beyond office doors. In this respect I owe much more to my wife Louise and to our children Dennis, Kai, Chris and David than they can possibly know.

A companion website accompanies MACROECONOMICS by Manfred Gärtner

Visit the *Macroeconomics* website at **http://www.booksites.net/gartner** to find the following valuable teaching and learning materials:

- a **website for students,** hosted at **http://www.fgn.unisg.ch/eurmacro**. It includes material ranging from bread-and-butter features like online tests, link collections or macroeconomic dictionaries in a dozen languages to state-of-the-art items including a data bank with macroeconomic time series for many countries, along with a graphing module, and a macroeconomic tutorial with many animations and interactive models.
- a downloadable **instructor's manual** including chapter overviews, solutions to the end-of-chapter exercises, and accompanying PowerPoint slides.

PUBLISHER'S ACKNOWLEDGEMENT

We are grateful to the following for permission to reproduce copyright material:

Figures 9.6 and 12.1 from *Economics*, Prentice Hall Europe, (Case, Fair, Gartner and Heather, 1999), by permission of Pearson Education Limited.

CHAPTER 1

MACROECONOMIC ESSENTIALS

WHAT TO EXPECT After working through this warm-up chapter, you will know:

1. What **macroeconomics** is all about, and how it relates to microeconomics.
2. All you need to know about **national income accounting**, including government budgets and the balance of payments.
3. What the **circular flow model** is, how to use it and what its limitations are.
4. How **money** fits into the macroeconomy.
5. Why economists need to use **models**, and why these simplified pictures of the real world are useful.
6. How to work with **graphs**.

1.1 THE ISSUES OF MACROECONOMICS

Economics is about how people use time and tools to produce what other people want to buy – and about the sometimes intricate choices that must be made and the things that can go wrong.

Microeconomics studies individual entities such as consumers or firms.

Macroeconomics studies the whole economy from a bird's-eye perspective.

The two major subdisciplines of economics are microeconomics and macroeconomics. **Microeconomics** looks in great detail at how individuals make choices – as consumers, as employees, as entrepreneurs, as investors, or even as politicians. **Macroeconomics** looks at the big picture, at the way things are and how they develop after we add everything up, in the whole economy or in large segments or sectors of the economy. Of course, microeconomics and macroeconomics cannot lead separate lives. What happens in the macroeconomy must be the result of all the individual decisions analyzed and explained in microeconomics. This is why the search for the *microfoundations of macroeconomics* ranks high on today's research agenda. However, to model all the choices of millions of different people and show how they interact to generate specific macroeconomic outcomes is simply not feasible. It probably never will be. Inevitably, at some point we have to resort to simplifications or abstractions: either by assuming, say, that all individuals are alike, which is what so-called *representative agents models* do; or by postulating relationships between macroeconomic variables which are *ad hoc* in the sense that they only *proxy* the outcomes of individual choices, but nevertheless seem to work well in many real-world situations.

The foremost single measure of how an economy performs is the aggregate level of *income*. Presenting the world at a glance, Figure 1.1 gives an overview of this variable by classifying countries according to income per capita, which is total income divided by population. Huge differences in per capita incomes exist. At the high end are the industrialized countries with annual incomes per head of $20,000 to $40,000. Lowest are a number of countries in sub-Saharan Africa with average annual per capita incomes of barely $100. To make matters worse, the world's poorest countries do not seem to be growing very much – if at all. In stark contrast, the Asian 'tigers' – Hong Kong, Singapore, South Korea and Taiwan – have been growing at or near double-digit percentage rates throughout the 1980s and much of the 1990s. Other Asian nations, China most notably, seem poised to copy this miracle. At such growth rates incomes double in less than ten years.

Incomes given in Figure 1.1 are *nominal incomes*, i.e. incomes expressed in currency (here US dollars) at current prices. If you want to compare incomes between countries, nominal incomes may not be the best data to look at. Neither should we rely on nominal income as an indicator of how a country's income evolved over time.

Measuring income growth over time in a single country is the simpler problem. Note that nominal income is prices P times real income Y, that is $P \times Y$. Now consider that US nominal income grew by 24% from $P_{1994} \times Y_{1994} = \$25,860$ in 1994 to $P_{1998} \times Y_{1998} = \$32,175$ in 1998. This does

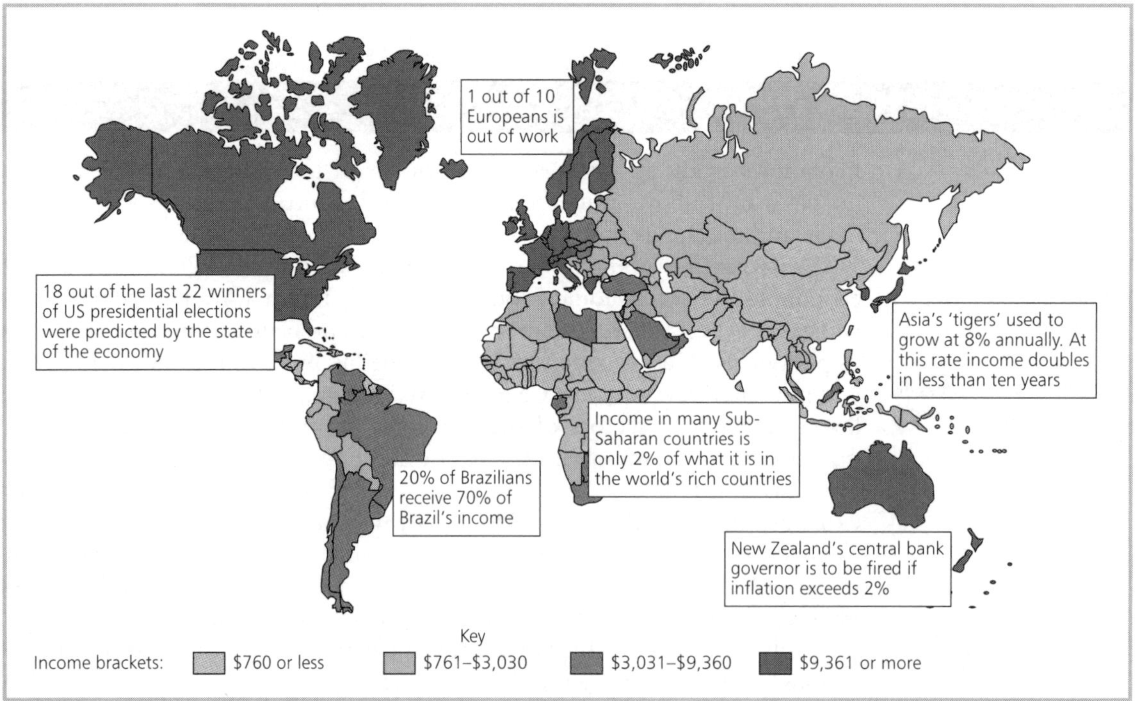

Figure 1.1 The map shows the huge differences that exist in the per capita incomes of the world's nations. Other important macroeconomic variables and issues are reported in boxes: economic growth, unemployment, inflation, the distribution of income and the close link between the economy and politics.
Source: *World Bank Atlas*, 2000, The World Bank.

not necessarily mean that US citizens could buy 24% more goods and services in 1998 than they could in 1994. Possibly, the increase in nominal income might have been entirely due to a 24% rise in prices, with no real improvements in the purchasing power of US incomes at all. Of course, this has not really been the case. In fact, US prices rose by 10% from an index value of, say, 1 in 1994 to 1.1 in 1998. To obtain 1998 real income (expressed in 1994 prices), we need to divide 1998 nominal income by the 1998 price level and multiply by 1994 prices: $Y_{1998} = (P_{1998} \times Y_{1998})/P_{1998} \times P_{1994} = 32{,}175/1.1 \times 1 = \$29{,}240$. So while nominal income rose by 24%, real income grew by only 13%.

Similar issues, with one added complication, arise when comparing incomes between countries. Noting that per capita income in 1998 was $29,240 in the United States but $39,980 in Switzerland would only permit a meaningful comparison of purchasing power if one dollar bought the same in Switzerland as in the United States. Although $10 buys 4 Big Macs at $2.50 each in the US, you need $14.60 to buy the same (at $3.65 each) in Switzerland. This price difference may have two causes: At 6.30 Swiss francs Big Macs may simply be expensive in local currency; or the dollar may be undervalued, meaning it takes too many dollars to buy a Swiss franc. Our current knowledge does not put us in a position to sort this out. All we know is that a dollar buys fewer Big Macs in Switzerland than in the United States, and that we need to take this into account when comparing Swiss income to US income.

Table 1.1 summarizes our Big Mac example. Column 2 shows that in 1998 nominal income per capita in Switzerland was more than $10,000 higher than in the United States. In Poland it was a tenth of Switzerland's. Taking into account the level of prices relative to the United States, the picture changes substantially. In Switzerland, $39,980 buys what only $26,876 buys in the United States. So Switzerland's *real income* per capita is slightly lower than America's. Prices in Poland are half as high as in the United States, and a third of what they are in Switzerland. Therefore, in terms of real income, Poland performs much better than it seems to perform in terms of nominal income.

Empirical note. World-wide the richest countries, with 15% of the population, make some 80% of world income. The poorest countries, with 57% of the population, make 5% of world income.

A statistical *average*, which is what income per capita is, is one thing. The actual *distribution of income* may be quite another story. In Brazil, to give one example, the richest 20% of the population earn almost 70% of the nation's aggregate income. The poorest 20% earn as little as 2%. In Europe, high average incomes conceal that almost one in ten of those who want to work do not find a job. Good unemployment insurance and social security have so far prevented high *unemployment* from showing up in a deteriorating distribution

Table 1.1 Nominal and real income in 1998. The second column shows *nominal income*. Because prices differ substantially between countries (third column), *real income*, the amount of goods that income can buy, turns out quite differently, as shown in the fourth column.

	Nominal income (per capita, in $) *PY*	Price level (relative to US price level) *P*	Real income (in US purchasing power) *Y*
Poland	3,910	0.52	7,543
Switzerland	39,980	1.49	26,876
United States	29,240	1	29,240

of income. But welfare states are struggling and are quickly scaling down the role of the government.

In the United States the results of eighteen out of the twenty-two presidential elections preceding 2004 could have been predicted simply by looking at how the economy was doing, as measured by key indicators such as income growth and inflation. This implies a close link between macroeconomic performance and all the other (and, you may argue, more important) things in life, not only because all these other things typically cost money, but because a precondition for being in power – and thus being able to realize one's dream, ideology or vision, in whatever field – is a satisfactory economic performance.

New Zealand's government made the headlines in the 1990s by putting a clause in the employment contract of its central bank governor that threatens him with the sack if he allows inflation to exceed 2% annually. This reflects a serious concern for *inflation*, the rate at which prices grow. Many other

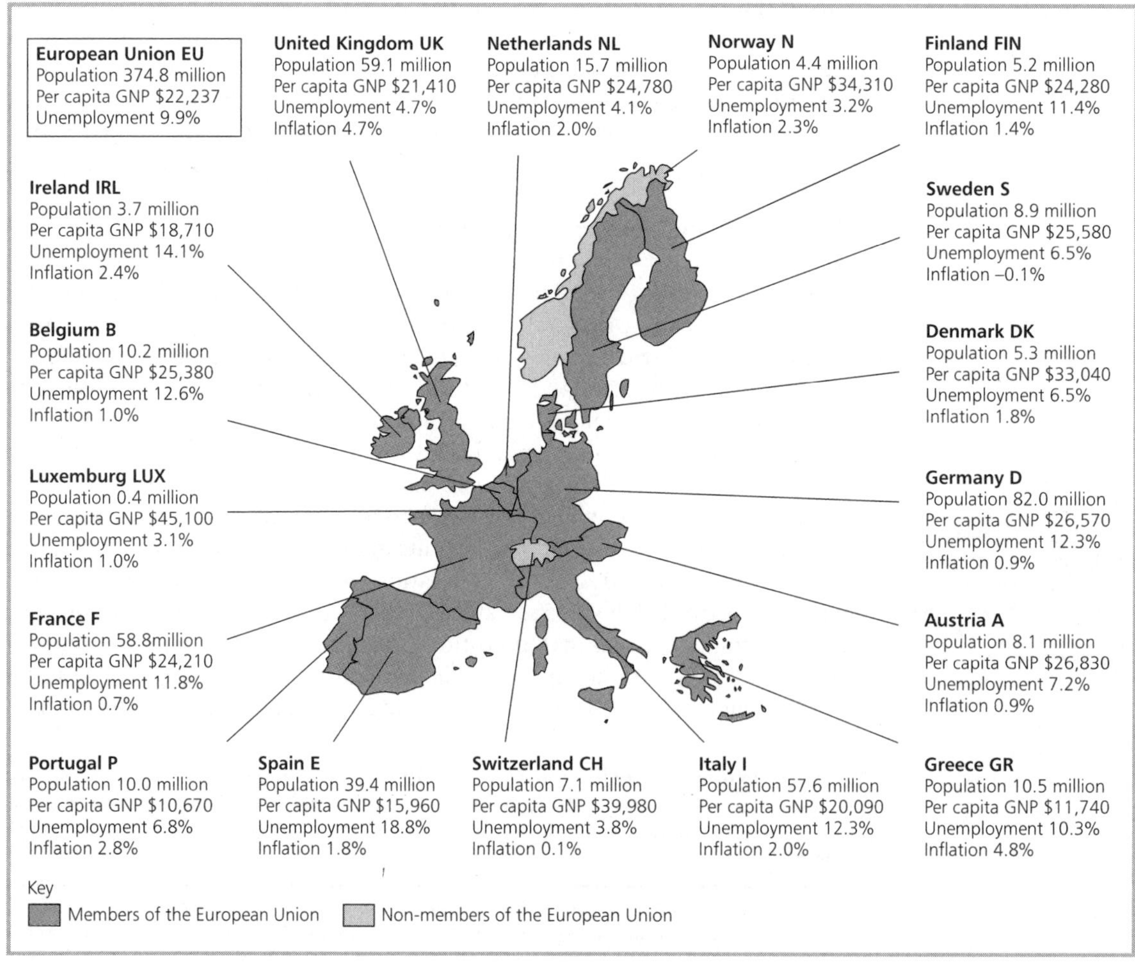

Figure 1.2 The map provides 1998 data on the countries of Western Europe that form the European Union, or that had completed negotiations before choosing not to join. GNP is a measure of a country's total income. Country names are followed by shorthand abbreviations that are used in the text.
Source: IMF, *International Financial Statistics*, and *World Bank Atlas*, 2000.

nations share this concern, which points to inflation as a third important variable in the macroeconomic context.

The world abounds with economic challenges and puzzles. These differ from one part of the world to another, and they must be viewed in the context of different institutions, cultures and historical backgrounds. Despite this, a set of macroeconomic principles and concepts exists which can, applied wisely, be brought to bear on a variety of different issues. This book sets out to assemble such a basic macroeconomic tool kit. While it focuses on and emphasizes what is needed to understand and discuss the experiences and prospects in one part of the world, the European Union and its neighbours, the perspective is global, as indicated by the range of issues, case studies and data.

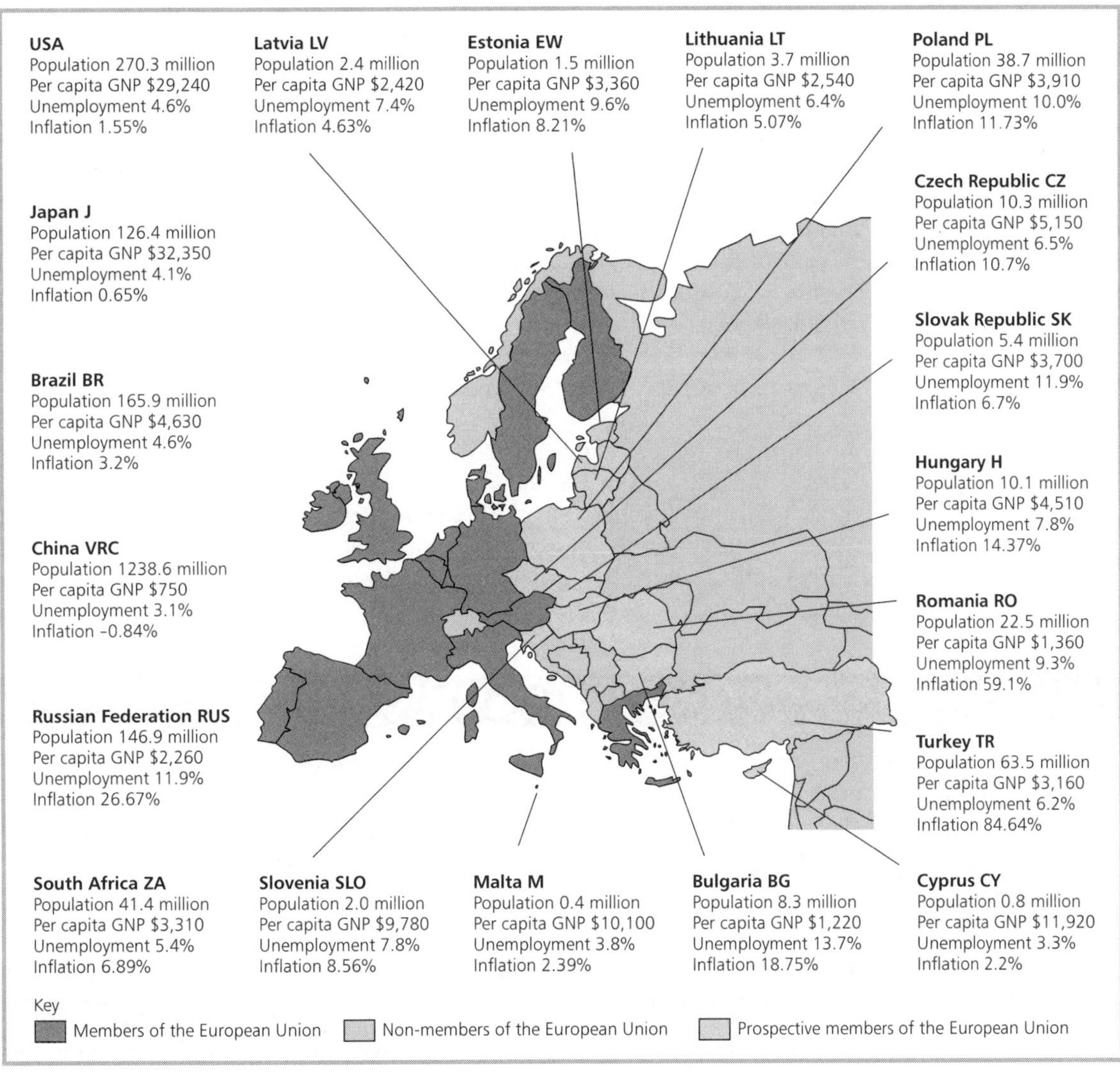

Figure 1.3 This map provides basic 1998 data on prospective EU members and some other countries for reference.
Source: IMF, *International Financial Statistics*, and *World Bank Atlas*, 2000.

The *European Union* grew out of economic and political integration efforts that started half a century ago. At the turn of the millennium it comprises the fifteen member states shown in blue in Figure 1.2. Figure 1.2 also provides some basic information on the member states' economies plus the economies of Norway and Switzerland, whose governments had embarked on an integration path before voters rejected that option.

While European countries appeared reasonably homogeneous in terms of per capita income from the world-wide perspective given in Figure 1.1, the more detailed information included in Figure 1.2 reveals some notable differences. These are not only the obvious differences in size and population, but also in the standardized macroeconomic performance data mentioned earlier. Nominal per capita income, as measured by gross national product (GNP – see Box 1.1), in Luxembourg is four times as high as in Greece or in Portugal. Unemployment ranges from a tolerable, by current standards, 3.1% in Luxembourg to an alarming 18.8% in Spain. Inflation is currently a minor problem, remaining below 3% in most countries. It is the highest in Britain and Greece, with inflation rates of 4.7 and 4.8%, respectively.

A look beyond the current borders of the EU not only shows that greater Europe is a lot more diverse than its Western part, but also that with the imminent accession of many new countries, the EU itself will have to cope with much more economic diversity for many years to come. Figure 1.3 gives a flavour of this by providing basic data for countries considered potential EU members. To put this into global perspective, a number of other countries are added.

While unemployment does not differ much from what we currently see in Western Europe, per capita income is much lower in most candidate nations. Only in Cyprus, Malta and Slovenia do per capita incomes merge with the lower end of EU per capita incomes marked by Greece and Portugal. Most other candidates are in the income range of Brazil, South Africa or Russia, though still much higher than China. Inflation is still a serious problem in some of the countries shown here, particularly in Bulgaria, Romania and Turkey, all of which are still well in the double digit range of annual price increases.

1.2 ESSENTIALS OF MACROECONOMIC ACCOUNTING

Factors of production are all resources used in the production of goods and services: labour, capital goods such as machines, and natural resources such as oil.

The focal point of macroeconomics is the level of income. Incomes are paid out to **factors of production** that are employed by firms to produce goods and services. This output is then put on the market for people to buy. The two major things that can go wrong in this process are as follows:

- Firms may not use all available production factors to produce output, thus leaving factors idle in the form of *unemployment* or slack.
- People may not want to buy all that is being produced, that is *demand may fall short of output*.

Economists have analyzed economies very much in terms of these two failures: underutilization of production factors and/or insufficient (or excessive) demand. These will also be major themes in subsequent chapters of this book, as they lie at the heart of most prominent macroeconomic issues such as unemployment and inflation.

Before embarking on our task to assemble a set of macroeconomic tools and concepts for analyzing these and other macroeconomic issues, we need to clarify some essential terminology and techniques.

The circular flow of income and spending

We start by looking at how economists measure income, and at how they divide it into useful components to facilitate subsequent efforts to understand what determines income and what makes it change. For this purpose we employ a preliminary stylized picture (or 'model') of the economy: the image of continuous circular flows. This model, which we begin to build in Figure 1.4, identifies the key actors (or sectors) of an economy, and then proceeds to describe and measure the interaction between them.

Suppose there are only two actors, *households* and *firms*. In an economy without money – economists call this a *barter economy* – households and firms would interact through a continuous flow of real transactions. Households furnish firms with labour (and usually also capital goods like machines and buildings, or land). Firms use these factors of production, or *resources*, as they are also called, to produce goods (and services). These goods flow back to the households, constituting compensation for having supplied the factors of production.

It would not be very efficient if pizzerias were to compensate pizzaiolos with margaritas and calzones and if Alfa Romeo were to pay employees with a brand new Alfa 147 every six months. In modern economies, firms pay households with money for using the factors of production. This relieves pizzaiolos of a tedious search for Alfa Romeo workers with just the right craving for pizza. Therefore, in the upper half of the graph given in Figure 1.5, an appropriate amount of euros, pounds or kronas flows back to the households, completing this transaction. In the lower half, households spend their money incomes on the goods produced and put on the market by the firms. So in the end the counter-clockwise circular flow of real transactions between households and firms remains intact. It is now complemented by an outer

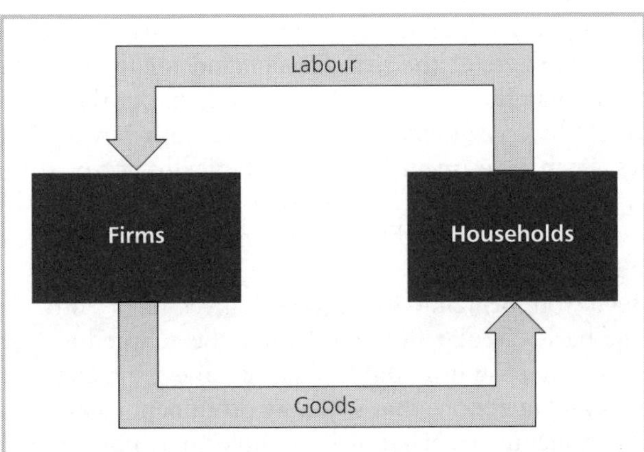

Figure 1.4 The circle shows that households furnish firms with production factors such as labour, and receive goods and services produced by firms in return. (Please excuse us for describing something that flows around four corners as a circle!)

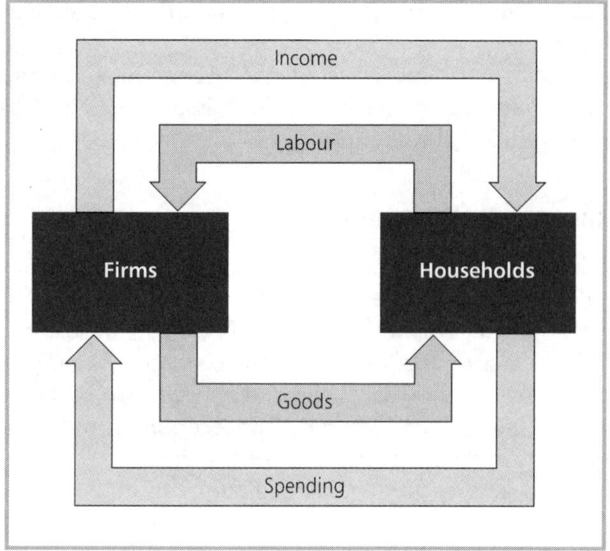

Figure 1.5 The outer circle shows that the inner real flow of labour and goods is financed by a monetary flow of income payments from firms to households and of households' spending on the firms' goods.

circle flowing clockwise which records the payments streams that compensate for the goods received and for the labour provided.

The outer circle has an important advantage over the inner one: it is easier to measure, since all transactions are denominated in the same measuring units. This is not true for the inner circle. Typically, both the factors of production and the goods produced are very heterogeneous and cannot simply be added up. Economists therefore focus on the outer circle of income and spending to measure aggregate economic activity.

An important point to note is that one person's spending – flowing from right to left in the lower part of the outer circle – is another person's income, received after completion of the upper part of the outer circle. So all spending must add up to the same amount to which all incomes add up. Total production or **aggregate output**, the value of all goods and services produced by firms, may therefore be measured either by adding up all incomes, or by adding up all expenditures.

The *expenditure approach* measures **aggregate output** as the sum of all spending. The *income approach* adds up all incomes instead.

Figure 1.5 provided a very simple first picture, and there are a number of complicating factors. For example, consumers may not, and typically do not, spend all their income. As Figure 1.6 illustrates, if households save €20 out of an income of €100, only €80 arrives at the firms in demand for their goods. The €20 *leaks* out of the circular flow system. On the other hand, the firms' products are not only bought by consumers. The pizza place may buy an Alfa and offer home deliveries. Such *investment demand* is typically not paid for out of current income (in fact, firms have no income) but is financed by borrowing money from banks. In this light, investments take the form of **injections** into the income circle.

Figure 1.6, with its focus on bringing savings and investment into the picture, illustrates how the basic circular flow model may be adapted to take into account complications that arise in reality. We now take a big step and introduce all those leakages and injections that will play prominent roles in the remainder of this book. First, income received by households may not arrive at

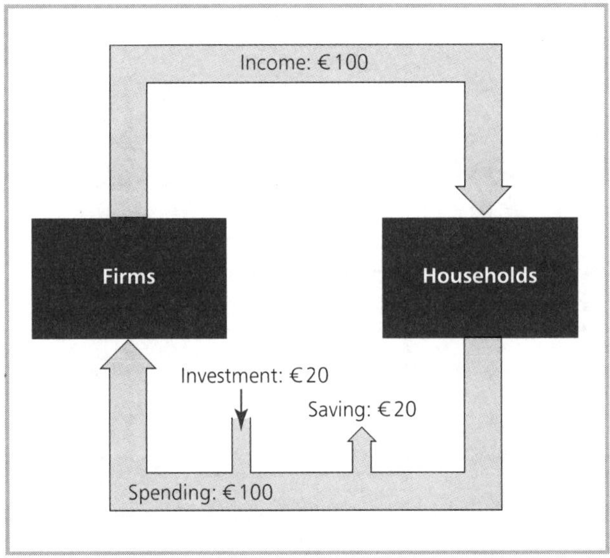

Figure 1.6 If households save part of the income that they receive from firms, income leaks out of the circular flow. If firms buy investment goods that are not directly being financed out of current income, spending is injected into the circular flow.

the firms as demand for three main reasons:

1 *People save*. We have noted this point already. If people save part of their income, their consumption expenditures fall short of what they have produced and received as income. *Saving* may thus be viewed as a *leakage* of income out of the circular flow system.
2 *Governments levy taxes*. The taxes that governments levy on citizens are a part of income which is prevented from turning into demand – another leakage.
3 *People buy foreign goods*. Income earned at home which is used to buy goods produced in a foreign country constitute a third leakage of income from the domestic circular flow system.

But there is also more than one reason why demand from outside the circular flow may be directed towards domestic output. In fact, each of the leakages described above has a counterpart representing an *injection* into the circular flow:

Note. In economics the term **investment** describes purchases of capital goods. This differs from the popular use of the word which calls purchases of financial assets (say, stocks) out of savings '(financial) investments'.

1 *Firms invest*. As noted, firms build or buy new production facilities, new machines, distribution networks and so on. These investments are typically financed via credit from banks or credit markets in general.
2 *Government spending*. Government spending on such things as public consumption, infrastructure or transfers represents an injection from the outside into the income circle.
3 *Foreigners buy our goods*. If residents of foreign countries decide to buy domestically produced goods, this represents a last injection of demand into the circular flow.

Figure 1.7 depicts the improved *circular flow of income* that allows for these six categories of *leakages* and *injections*. Note that we build on the outer, clockwise flow of income and spending introduced in Figure 1.5 and refined in Figure 1.6. For the sake of clarity we will now refrain from identifying firms

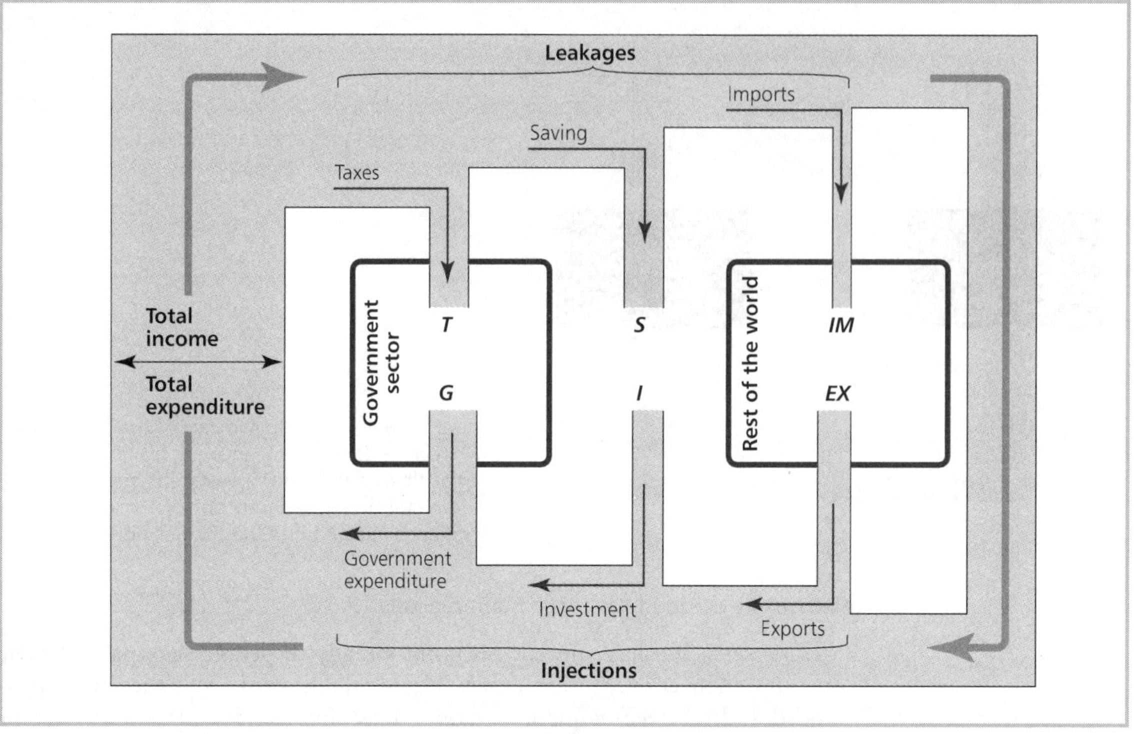

Figure 1.7 This diagram proceeds from the insight that all spending arrives somewhere else as income. In order for income to create an equivalent level of spending, all leakages out of the circular flow, given in the upper part of the circle, must be balanced by an equal amount of injections, given in the lower segment. Pairing leakages and injections in a meaningful way gives the circular flow identity $(T - G) + (S - I) + (IM - EX) = 0$, which always holds. Data for Britain in 1998 are (in £billion): $T = 145.5$, $S = 140.1$, $IM = 246.7$, $EX = 236.5$, $I = 141.7$ and $G = 154.1$. Total income, the width of the stream, was 856.
Source: Eurostat.

and households in the circle. (To include them would complicate the picture since, for example, both firms and households buy imports which would entail separating out their respective imports.)

Leakages of spending are shown in the upper part of the 'circle', injections of spending in the lower part. Only if the sum of all leakages equals the sum of all injections does total expenditure (measured at the end of the lower leg of the circle) exactly match total income (measured at the outset of the upper leg). But wouldn't leakages match injections only by pure chance? The answer is *no*. Quite the contrary: in the end, when we add everything up, leakages and injections always match. Why is that?

Suppose that initially, with the amount of investment planned by firms, injections would fall short of leakages. Then spending tends to fall short of supplied output, and firms must add unsold output onto their existing stock of inventory. Whether they like it or not, they are being forced to 'demand' that part of output themselves which they cannot sell. In the opposite case, if demand exceeds output, either firms must draw down their existing inventory, or, if that is not feasible, that part of demand which exceeds supply remains unsatisfied.

Now let investment not only be the purchase of machines, but also the addition to stocks of inventory (which are classified as capital goods). Then the forced changes of inventory described in the previous paragraph always render investment just enough to make injections equal to leakages. So the bottom line is that, if investment is understood to include inventory changes, the leakages and injections always balance, and *the following equation holds at all times*:

$$(S - I) + (T - G) + (IM - EX) = 0 \tag{1.1}$$

BOX 1.1 GDP as a measure of total output or income

How do modern economies measure total income (or output)? Usually it is done by means of a concept called *gross domestic product (GDP). Nominal GDP* evaluates all final goods and services produced in a country at current market prices. If 100 pizzas and 5 Alfas are produced in a given calendar year at prices of €10 and €30,000, respectively, GDP is $10 \times 100 + 30{,}000 \times 5 =$ €151,000. Important things to watch out for are the following:

- *Only count final products.* If Alfa Romeo buys tyres from an external supplier to put on its cars, you would not want to count tyres twice – once when Alfa Romeo buys them and again when consumers buy an Alfa, the price of which, of course, includes the cost of tyres. As indicated, one way to avoid double counting is by including *final products* only. Another way is to count only the *value added* at each stage during the production process.
- *Only count current production.* If the original Alfa owner resells her car next year, this obviously does not represent output and income generated during that period.

GDP increases, first, if more pizzas and/or Alfas are being produced, and second, if prices rise. Table 1 illustrates these two possibilities.

In 2002 nominal GDP is €151,000. *Real GDP* does not evaluate output in terms of current prices, but in prices in a given year. In terms of what nominal GDP buys in 2002, real GDP in 2002 of course is also €151,000. In 2003 nominal GDP has risen to €182,000. Since prices are the same as in 2002, real GDP has also risen to €182,000: the buying power of nominal GDP is at what €182,000 would have bought in 2002. Finally, in 2004 nominal GDP is at €244,000. But the increase is only due to price increases. Production quantities are the same as in 2003. This leaves real GDP unchanged at €182,000.

Sometimes total income is also measured as *gross national product (GNP).* The difference between the two concepts is that GDP refers to incomes generated within the geographical boundaries of a country, no matter by whom. Instead, GNP measures the incomes generated by the inhabitants of a country, no matter in what country. So if a Spaniard living in Barcelona owns Lufthansa stocks, the annual dividends she may receive are included in Germany's GDP, but in Spain's GNP. For most countries the difference between GDP and GNP is small. We will usually think of GDP when talking about total income or output.

Table 1 An illustration of nominal and real GDP

	Pizzas		Alfas			
Year	Price	Quantity	Price	Quantity	Nominal GDP (in €)	Real GDP in prices of 2002
2002	10	100	30,000	5	151,000	151,000
2003	10	200	30,000	6	182,000	182,000
2004	20	200	40,000	6	244,000	182,000

Note. It is more common to call $EX - IM = NX$ net exports or, as an approximation, the *current account (CA)*.

Note that we have paired each leakage with an injection so as to yield a meaningful total, and to comply with Figure 1.7: $S - I$ is domestic private net savings; $T - G$ is public net savings (called the budget surplus), measuring the interactions between the domestic economy and the government sector; $IM - EX$ are net imports, the country's balance of trade in goods and services with the rest of the world.

As we shall see in subsequent chapters, the circular flow identity is an extremely effective gadget in any trained economist's tool-box. But it can also be very misleading if used in an uninformed way, that is without resolving the ambiguities in cause and effect that are often present in macroeconomics.

One example of such uninformed use would be to rearrange equation (1.1) so as to yield

$$I = S + T - G + IM - EX \tag{1.2}$$

and then conclude that in order to raise what is perceived to be insufficient investment by 10 billion, all the government must do is raise taxes by 10 billion.

A look back at Figure 1.7 reveals that this recommendation naively assumes that increasing the tax leak leaves all other leakages and all injections except I unaffected, thus forcing investment to rise with taxes. Without an economic

CASE STUDY 1.1 Germany's current account before and after unification

Germany's traditional current account surpluses, which had culminated at 4.8% of GDP in 1989, disappeared after unification. In the first full calendar year after the two Germanies had merged the current account dropped from a regular surplus into a deficit the size of about 1% of GDP (see Figure 1(a)).

The circular flow model and the identity of leaks and injections, $S - I + T - G + IM - EX = 0$, provides a first clue as to what had happened. First note, however, that while we are treating the current account *CA* and net exports *NX* as synonyms in Chapter 1, and throughout most of the text, this is only an approximation. The main difference between the two aggregates in reality is that the current account also includes transfers across borders that are not related to the export and import of goods and services. Examples are: aid to developing countries; a Turkish family living in Germany sending money to their parents in Ankara; or the contributions of the German government to international organizations such as NATO, the United Nations, or the European Union. Since such things also constitute leakages out of the circular flow of income, the current account is actually a more precise measure of a country's net leakages to the rest of the world than net exports.

It is often argued that the dramatic shift in Germany's current account was the result of rising government budget deficits triggered by public investment in East Germany's infrastructure and transfer payments to the East. This interpretation is often motivated by comparing West Germany's last full budget in the year before unification, 1989, with the years that followed. This implies that unification drove a more or less balanced government budget into deficit by some 3% of GDP. Panel (b) in Figure 1 shows that this is a misleading story. The year 1989 is clearly atypical, given that the budget had been in deficit for years before and exceeded 2% of GDP in 1988 already. Ignoring 1989 as exceptional, unification increased the budget deficit only by about one percentage point from 2% to 3% of GDP.

In terms of the circular-flow identity: while the increase of the budget deficit $G - T$ may have caused the current account to deteriorate, its magnitude of one percentage point only partly explains the change in the current account by some 5 percentage points. What seems to have mattered much more is the change in private net savings $S - I$ documented in panel (c) of Figure 1. While private savings exceeded investment by some 6% of GDP before unification, this difference dropped to

➤

Case study 1.1 continued

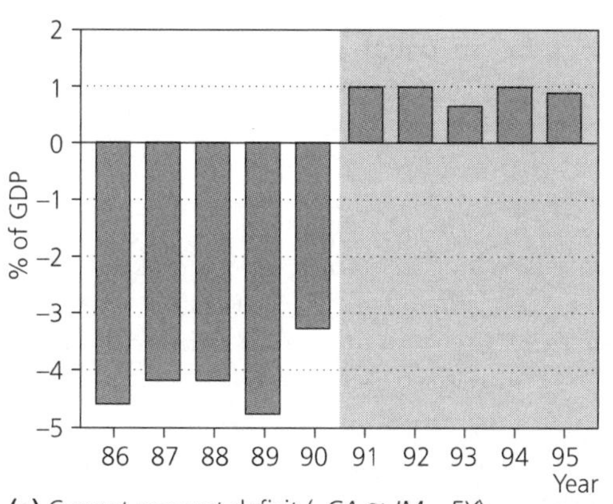

(a) Current account deficit ($-CA \cong IM - EX$)

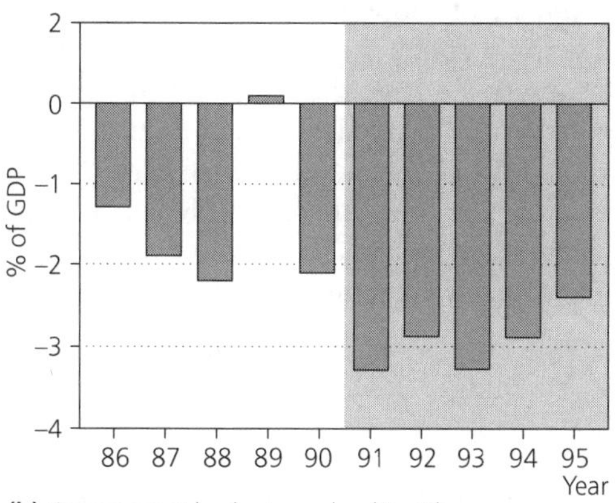

(b) Government budget surplus ($T - G$)

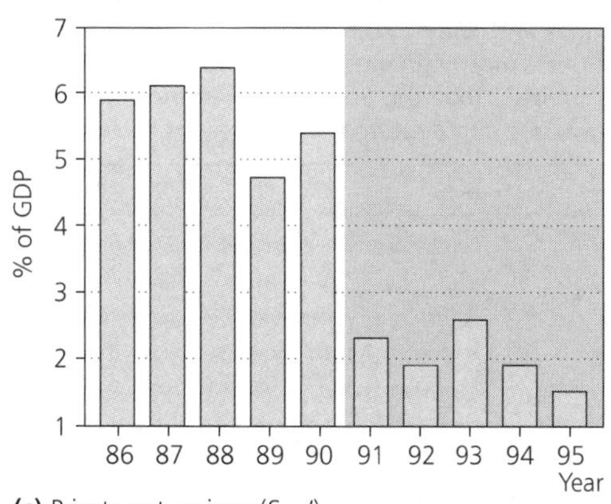

(c) Private net savings ($S - I$)

Figure 1

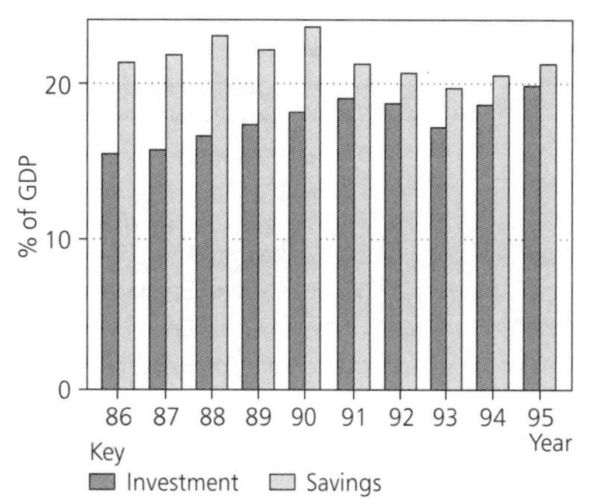

Figure 2

about 2% after unification. This accounts for the remaining change in the current account that was not explained by the change in the government budget deficit.

Of course, the change in private net savings also reflects government policies towards the eastern part of Germany. Net savings did not fall because savings fell, but because investment increased due to investment bonus packages put into action by the Kohl government. Figure 2 shows that savings were still about the same in 1995 as they had been ten years earlier, while investment had risen by about 4 percentage points.

Using stylized, rounded numbers for the time before and after unification Table 1 summarizes the observed changes: the current account deficit ($-CA \cong IM - EX$) rose from −4% to +1%. One percentage point of this reflects the change in government spending behaviour, that is, the increase of the budget deficit from 2% to 3% of GDP. The remaining 4 percentage points (that is, the remaining 80%) of the change in the current account reflect the change in net private savings, which dropped from 6% to 2% of GDP.

Table 1 Injections and leakages before and after German unification. Rounded averages for indicated subperiods as % of GDP

	$S - I$	+	$T - G$	+	$IM - EX$	=	0
1986–90	6%	+	−2%	+	−4%	=	0
1991–95	2%	+	−3%	+	1%	=	0

understanding of what determines the decisions of investors, consumers, exporters and importers, other equally valid (or invalid) interpretations would be the following:

- Raising taxes reduces savings by an equal amount (since equation (1.1) could be rearranged to yield $S = I - T + G - IM + EX$) but leaves investment unaffected.
- Raising taxes reduces imports (from $IM = I - S - T + G + EX$).
- Raising taxes raises exports (from $EX = S - I + T - G + IM$).

What sets these assertions apart is which variables are held fixed and which ones we allow to change after we changed T. Each version was arbitrary. Without an understanding of how investment, savings, import and export decisions are being made, there is no way of telling what will actually happen after a tax increase. It is possible that several of the other leaks and injections may change after T rises. To complicate things further, even the width of the circular flow stream, which measures the income level, may be affected by the tax increase.

So if it is to be used in the context of economic analysis, the circular flow equation needs to be combined with thorough economic reasoning. This will be enlarged upon in subsequent chapters. As it is, the circular flow identity only provides a glimpse at some key structural properties of a country's economy.

National income accounts report data for GDP and its components.

Actual numbers for the components of the leakages and injections combined in equation (1.1) and other related variables are assembled in the **national income accounts** of a country. Table 1.2 presents the sums involved, expressed as percentages of GDP. While country experiences differ, there are some common threads in the data:

- Most countries still run sizeable budget deficits. Governments spend more than they receive.

Table 1.2 The circular-flow identity in numbers (1999, as % of GDP). The data decompose the circular-flow identity for a set of industrial countries. To permit comparability, aggregates are given in percentages of GDP. The data report similarities and differences between countries. Consider Portugal and Spain. Both countries run virtually the same goverment budget deficit. In Spain this is mostly financed by private domestic savings (first column). What sets the two cases apart is that the Spanish government runs into debt against its own citizens, but Portugal runs into debt against the rest of the world.

	$S - I$ in %	$T - G$ in %	$EX - IM$ (or $NX = CA$) in %
Belgium	5.0	−0.9	4.1
Denmark	−1.0	2.8	1.8
France	6.0	−2.4	3.6
Germany	4.3	−2.2	2.1
Greece	−5.7	−2.1	−7.8
Ireland	18.7	2.5	21.2
Italy	6.3	−2.3	4.0
Luxembourg	10.7	1.5	12.2
Netherlands	8.0	−1.6	6.4
Portugal	−4.1	−2.0	−6.1
Spain	1.7	−1.6	0.1
UK	−1.0	−0.1	−1.1
USA	−4.2	1.7	−2.5

Source: Eurostat.

- In the majority of countries private savings exceed private investment. This is one way of financing the government budget deficit (or syphoning off the net injections coming from the government sector). Instead of savings being passed on to firms for investment spending, they go to the government for financing the deficit.
- Most countries shown here export more than they import. Exceptions are Greece, Portugal, the United Kingdom and the United States. In those countries the net injection from the private and government sectors (the excess of $I + G$ over $S + T$) is neutralized by a net leakage of spending to other countries. Other countries may appear to refrain from buying our export goods with all the money they receive for our imports from them, but instead lend part of that money to our government and/or firms to finance the national deficit.

Discussion of the *twin deficits* haunting the US economy in the 1980s and 1990s offers ample real-world examples of uninformed use of the circular flow identity, which the above stylized example attempted to discredit. To some, the US budget deficit causes the current account deficit, and therefore it has to be removed (based on $EX - IM = S - I + T - G$). To others, Japanese and EU import restrictions cause the current account deficit, which in turn forces the US government budget into deficit (based on $T - G = -S + I + EX - IM$). A third view is that neither is true. Rather, insufficient private savings in the United States drive the current account into deficit (based on $(EX - IM) = (S - I) + (T - G)$). Again, while there may be a grain of truth in all three explanations, no judgement is possible before we understand how the people who make up the economy make choices.

Money in the circular flow

Figure 1.5 featured a counter-clockwise flow of real factors such as labour and goods, and a compensating clockwise nominal flow of money income (evaluated at today's wages) and spending (evaluated at today's prices). We know that each flow is simply a mirror image of the other. It seems plausible that how labour is linked to income depends on the wage rate, and how goods relate to spending depends on prices. To sharpen our understanding of this we need to introduce **money** into the circular flow model. How does money fit in?

Money is anything that sellers generally accept as payment for goods and services.

Consider the example given in Figure 1.8. Firms only employ one factor of production – labour – to produce one good – cars. Assume this economy produces 6 cars annually, using 24,000 work-hours. Assume 30,000 euros float around in this economy, in notes and coins. To keep the argument simple, let there be no other money (such as bank accounts). Now if those €30,000 are being turned over (meaning that they flow from firms to households and back) 12 times a year, the firms' cash registers add up a total of €360,000. Since this sum represents the payments for 6 cars, the price of a car is obviously €60,000. On the other hand, over the course of a year €360,000 also arrive in the pockets of households as wage incomes, as compensation for 24,000 work-hours. So the hourly wage rate must be €15 per hour. *Nominal income* and spending equals €360,000, while *real income* and spending equals 6 cars.

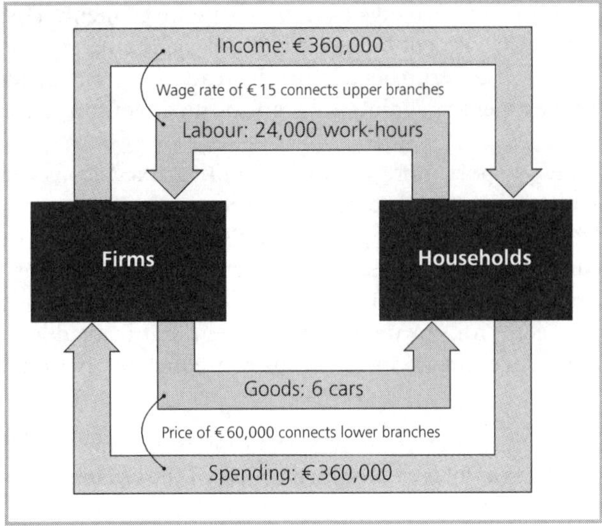

Figure 1.8 Looking at the inner circle first, we assume that firms use 24,000 hours of labour to produce 6 cars. If €30,000 circulates 12 times a year, annual income and annual spending must be €360,000. Hence the wage rate must be €15 per hour and the price of a car is €60,000. Thus, given all the other factors, the supply of money determines goods' prices and nominal wages.

The numerical example discussed here motivates the classical **quantity equation** $M \times V = P \times Y$. It states that the money supply M times the velocity of money circulation V equals nominal income PY (where P is the price level and Y denotes real income). In the example, M increases from €30,000 to €33,000, while we presume V constant at 12. In the first case, this raises P from €60,000 to €66,000, leaving Y unchanged. In the second case, Y rises from 6 to 6.6 at an unchanged price level. It should be obvious that both P and Y may rise, as long as PY = €396,000.

Next, consider the following thought experiment – devised by an economist who later won the Nobel prize. Let a helicopter fly all over our imaginary country, and, little by little, scatter €3,000 in small notes. What are the consequences? If by now €33,000 continue to circulate at the speed of 12 turnovers a year, cash registers will count €396,000, as will wage earners. As regards prices, we consider two extreme cases.

One possibility is that the number of work-hours used in the production process remains at 24,000 hours. This could be because we are operating at the capacity limit, and this leaves output at 6 cars. Then €396,000 of income and spending must be compensation for 24,000 work-hours and payment for 6 cars. So the price of a car must have risen to €66,000, and the hourly wage rate to €16.50. Workers have to work 4,000 hours to earn enough money to buy a car, just as much as before the helicopter mission. Putting this differently, *nominal income*, income in terms of currency, grew by 10% from €360,000 to €396,000. *Real income*, income in terms of what it can buy, is unchanged at 6 cars.

As a second possibility, the increase of nominal spending to €396,000 may induce firms to increase output instead of raising prices. At the original price level, 6.6 cars can be sold. This requires 26,400 work-hours, which, at the going wage rate of €15, produces €396,000 of income. Workers still have to work 4,000 hours to make enough money to buy a car. This leaves the real wage rate, the purchasing power of one hour's work, unchanged at 0.00025 cars. Economy-wide *real income* has increased by 10% to 6.6 cars.

The **aggregate supply curve** indicates how much output firms are willing to produce at various price levels.

Macroeconomists call a graphical picture of how much total or aggregate output is produced at different price levels an **aggregate supply curve**. The first case discussed above is tantamount to postulating a **vertical aggregate supply curve** (see Figure 1.9, panel (a)). Both at a price of €60,000 and at a price of €66,000, 6 cars are being produced. In the second case, producers are ready to produce different numbers of cars at one and the same price level. This is tantamount to postulating a **horizontal aggregate supply curve** (Figure 1.9, panel (b)). We will be looking at aggregate supply curves, their economic

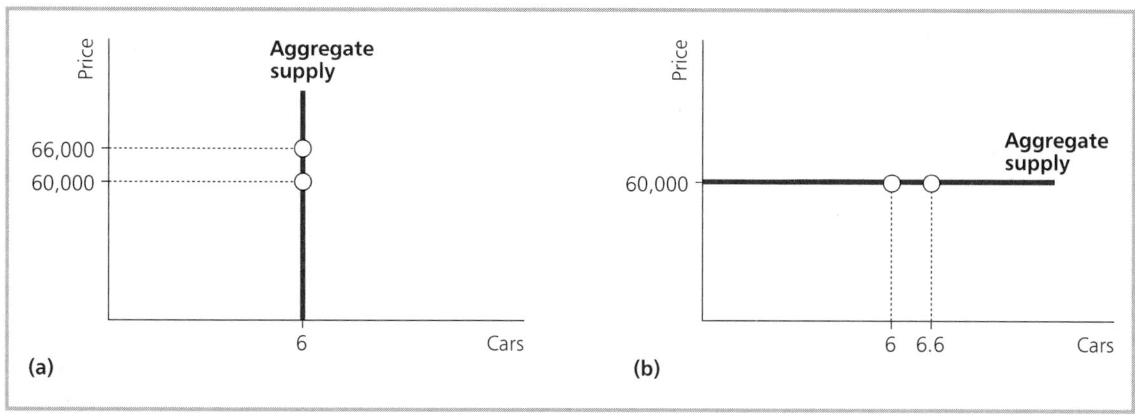

Figure 1.9 This shows two extreme versions of an aggregate supply curve. In panel (a), firms want to supply one specific amount of output only, no matter what the price level does. In panel (b), firms are ready to supply any amount of goods that the market demands at the given price level.

underpinning and slope, in some detail in later chapters. For now the simple but important lesson to be learned from this stylized example is that – with our extreme second case being an exception – the amount of money circulating in the economy directly bears on the price level. So if the supply of money changes, the price level changes. If this continues, we have inflation. Equipped with this tentative understanding we now turn to a brief look at the government budget and the balance of payments.

The government budget and the balance of payments

The **government budget** is primarily a planning instrument. In hindsight it breaks down government receipts and expenditures, and shows how deficits are being financed.

The **balance of payments** records a country's trade in goods, services and financial assets with other countries.

In addition to the national income accounts, which measure the circular flows with leakages and injections, there are two other accounts that macroeconomists need in their elementary tool-box. These are the **government budget** and the **balance of payments**. As Figure 1.7 shows, these two accounts simply trace the interactions between the domestic private sector and the government sector (characterized by the left-hand rectangle) on the one hand, and with other countries (characterized by the rectangle on the right) on the other hand. While the basic data on leakages from and injections into these sectors are already being supplied in the national income accounts, the government budget and the balance of payments break down these numbers in more detail. More importantly, though, they show how *budget deficits* in the first case, and *trade imbalances* in the second case, are being paid for.

The **government budget** has two main purposes: to break up the catch-all variables G and T into more detailed subcategories, and to show how a given budget deficit is being financed. Similarly, the **balance of payments** adds detail to the general notion of exports and imports. But, again, it also traces how a given imbalance between exports and imports is being financed.

The **central bank** is a government agency primarily responsible for supplying the economy with the right amount of money.

Let us start with a look at how governments can finance budget deficits. As is the case for you and me, governments can only spend more than they collect by running up debt (or running down wealth). Unlike private individuals, however, governments have the second option of running into debt with another public or government institution called the **central bank**. So if we denote government debt owed to the private sector by D_{PS} and government debt owed to the central bank (or, actually, to itself) by D_{CB}, a budget deficit must change either or both debt categories:

Here and in the remainder of the book the Greek letter Δ denotes the change of the attached variable over the preceding period.

$$G - T = \Delta D_{PS} + \Delta D_{CB} \tag{1.3}$$

A government budget deficit either changes government bonds holdings by private citizens or by the central bank.

The **balance of payments** records a country's international transactions. Usually these require the purchase or the sale of foreign currency (or foreign money). An exception to this rule is of course the Euro area, where cross-border transactions are done in one currency. The balance of payments is subdivided into three major accounts: the current account CA, the capital account CP and the official reserve account OR. Since purchases of currency must equal sales, the three accounts that make up the balance of payments must add up to zero:

$$\underbrace{CA}_{\text{Current account}} + \underbrace{CP}_{\text{Capital account}} + \underbrace{OR}_{\text{Official reserve account}} = 0 \tag{1.4}$$

The **current account** records goods, services and transfers into and out of the country.

The **current account** records the flow of goods and services across borders that was represented as leakages from and injections into the 'rest of the world' box in Figure 1.7. It measures the net demand for domestic currency which results from the net sales of domestically produced goods and services to the world, hence $CA = EX - IM$. If an American buys a Ferrari, this Italian export invokes the purchase of the appropriate amount of euros by the American customer in exchange for her dollars.

The **capital account** records the flow of financial assets into and out of the country.

The **capital account** records how domestic net holdings of foreign assets (bonds, stocks, securities) *change*. It registers the net demand for the domestic currency which results from the net sales of domestic bonds and other assets to foreigners. If net foreign assets (defined as domestic holdings of foreign assets minus foreign holdings of domestic assets) are denoted by F, then $CP = -\Delta F$. Let a Dutchman buy US government securities (Dutch F rises). In the process he needs to purchase US dollars by selling euros. Hence CP is negative.

The **official reserve account** records the purchases and sales of foreign currency by the central bank.

The **official reserve account** tracks the involvement of the central bank in the foreign exchange market. It measures the net demand for the domestic currency which the sales of currency reserves held by the central bank constitute. Hence, if RES denotes central bank foreign currency reserves, $OR = -\Delta RES$. If the central bank sells \$1 million that it held in its vaults in exchange for domestic currency, reserves fall by \$1 million and a \$1 million net demand for domestic currency results.

Table 1.3 shows the composition of the balance of payments identity for the EU member states, Japan and the USA in 1999. In that year many central banks participated heavily in the foreign exchange market, accumulating or running down foreign currency reserves.

Using the definitions given in the last three sections we may rewrite the balance of payments definition (equation (1.4)) in a way that reveals how the home country finances trade imbalances with the rest of the world:

$$EX - IM = \Delta F + \Delta RES \tag{1.5}$$

Table 1.3 The balance of payments accounts. (1999, in millions of US dollars). Note that while in theory $CA + CP + OR = 0$, this does not hold in reality due to errors and omissions during data compilation.

	CA	*CP*	*OR*
Austria	−5,846	4,913	2,170
Belgium	11,898	−13,310	1,867
Denmark	2,305	7,341	−9,437
Finland	6,940	−4,206	97
France	38,700	−41,800	1,450
Germany	−21,030	−24,910	14,110
Greece*	−4,860	119	4,515
Ireland	898	−2,970	3,116
Italy	11,156	−19,954	8,852
Japan	90,400	−31,111	−76,260
Netherlands	22,064	−18,875	5,094
Portugal	−6,569	9,632	−202
Spain	−5,578	−11,214	22,794
Sweden	5,504	5,961	−3,254
United Kingdom	−19,370	11,520	1,030
United States	−339,090	369,490	8,720

*Greek data for 1997
Source: IMF, *IFS Yearbook 2000*.

If exports exceed imports, this means that traders exercise an excess demand for domestic currency (which they need to buy our exports). This can be balanced either by us accepting – i.e. buying – foreign debt titles (which raises F), or the central bank can supply the required domestic currency, thus running up foreign currency reserves RES.

The similarity between the interpretation of the government budget and of the balance of payments should be evident. Both show how an asymmetry between leakages and injections can be financed, regarding the government sector in the first case, and the rest of the world in the second case. And in both cases two options are available: one involving the market alone, and one involving the central bank.

In real life the central bank does not use helicopters to 'pump' money M into the economy. What really happens may be illustrated by means of a simplified balance sheet, which includes just three items that are essential here (see Table 1.4). The central bank's one liability is the currency it puts into circulation. For our present purposes this is equal to the money supply. Note that bank notes printed in the central bank's basement are not part of the money supply, and not effective economically, as long as the central bank does not put them into circulation.

Assets equal liabilities and are of two kinds: first, government securities – i.e. the amount of government debt held by the central bank C_{CB}; second, currency reserves – i.e. the amount of dollars, yen and other foreign currencies in the central bank's vaults.

Table 1.4 The central bank balance sheet

Assets		Liabilities	
Government securities	D_{CB}	Currency in circulation (money)	M
Currency reserves	RES		

Now D_{CB}, RES and M are obviously closely related. In fact, $M = D_{CB} + RES$. So the two ways to increase the money supply are to buy either government bonds or foreign exchange:

$$\Delta M = \Delta D_{CB} + \Delta RES \tag{1.6}$$

Or, put the other way: if a government budget deficit (unmatched leakages into and injections from the left-hand rectangle in Figure 1.7) is being financed by the central bank buying up government debt, or if the central bank at any time buys government bonds previously held by households, D_{CB} rises and the money supply increases. Also, if the central bank buys foreign currency, be it to finance a current account surplus or for other reasons, RES rises and the money supply increases as well. Our numerical example discussed above indicates that such money supply increases may either raise prices or raise output, or a combination of both. But these issues will be examined in more detail in later chapters.

1.3 BEYOND ACCOUNTING

National income accounts, government budgets and the balance of payments provide indispensable information about the current state of the economy. The macroeconomist's foremost task is to move beyond pure measurement towards a logically coherent understanding of how the variables listed in the previous sections, and other variables not mentioned yet, influence each other. Only then may we hope to link undesirable developments documented in the data, such as a current account deficit, a recession, unemployment or rising inflation, to an underlying cause and then to propose remedies.

The art of simplifying and model-building

A **model** is a simplified, logically coherent story that links economic variables like consumption and taxes to each other.

When addressing this task, economists draw simplified pictures of the real world. These they call **models**. Simplifications are necessary, since anything close to a perfect account of the real world would be too complicated for anyone to understand. On the other hand, the economist's way of making assumptions in order to simplify some problem at hand remains one of the biggest obstacles to a constructive dialogue between economists and non-economists; not so much because these models may often seem complicated, but because they are considered unrealistic, that is, of little relevance for real-world problems. This prejudice against economic theorizing is widespread. We therefore pause briefly here to consider the purpose of simplifying and model-building. Consider the following analogy.

A tourist wonders how to get from Sète to Bocuse-sur-Mer. She is unlikely to launch into space to obtain an unobstructed, realistic view of the world, before setting out to tackle her problem. Even if she did, this would be of little help, since neither town could be seen from up there. What she might do is use a high-performance telescope and focus on southern France. But even this would distort her perspective from reality, as the rest of the world would slip out of sight.

It is more likely that she will obtain a road map of southern France – a cheap and easy-to-use but extremely unrealistic device: it misses many important parts of the world like the Sahara or the Shetland Islands, it shows neither trees nor bushes, ignores the true colours of the Mediterranean Sea and pastures, and its smell is a far cry from the fragrance of *Herbes de Provence*. Yet despite these drawbacks, people seem to find maps – these naive, unrealistic pictures (or, we could say, models) of the world – very useful and buy them by the million every year. Of course, some maps are better than others, and you could get the wrong one for your purpose: a map of the London underground system would be of little help for our traveller, as would be an aerial navigation map or a hiker's map of southern France. But the reason that these maps are useless is not because they are unrealistic, but because they focus on the wrong things for the purposes of our traveller.

For very much the same reason it is perfectly acceptable and even mandatory for economists to build models of the economy that are unrealistic. Under no circumstances should the goal be to include as many features of the real world as possible, that is, to make them as realistic as possible – just as no publisher would cram all the real-world features onto a road map. So in the end no models are too unrealistic or abstract. But there may be models that focus on the wrong features for the problem at hand.

Mathematical models

A **mathematical model** tells its simplified, logically coherent story by means of algebraic equations.

Macroeconomic models come in all shapes and sizes. Some are written in prose. Some are presented in diagrams. Most frequently they are cast in a set of mathematical equations which forces rigour into economists' reasoning. It may seem unnecessarily awkward to express a simple statement like 'the number of tickets for a ferry trip across the English Channel which people want to buy per month falls as the fare increases' by

$$D = a - bP$$

where D = demand for ferry tickets, P = price of a ticket, and a and b are parameters, stand-ins for some positive numbers which we do not exactly know. However, a linear equation like this tells us exactly by how much D falls if P increases. Sometimes we may want to be less specific and write the more general equation

$$D = f(P)$$

where f states that D is a function of P. Dealing with such general functions and stating their properties requires calculus, though we will avoid that unless it is absolutely necessary.

Even models that consist of mathematical equations can be made more transparent and more accessible by transferring them into diagrams. We will do so frequently throughout this text and use purely mathematical reasoning as sparingly as possible.

Empirical tests

Just as the effectiveness of road maps is judged by the ease with which they guide their users to unfamiliar destinations, the quality of an economic model is judged by its potential to help us understand what happens in the real world. Such confrontation of models with reality is attempted in a variety of ways, using both a historical perspective and sophisticated statistical techniques. Most **empirical tests** address either of two questions:

Empirical tests are confrontations of hypotheses (statements) derived from models (or theories) with real-world data or events. They serve to gauge whether a model is useful or not.

- Can the model provide a specific macroeconomic event with a coherent explanation? Examples of such events are the oil price explosions of the 1970s and what they did to unemployment and inflation, German unification and the subsequent crises in the European Monetary System, or the Asian crisis of 1998.

BOX 1.2 Working with graphs (part I)

Graphs are an indispensable tool in economics. Economists use the technique frequently to provide illustrative examples, in dealing with non-economists, and also in teaching, as we will do abundantly in this book.

Lines in a diagram illustrate the relationship between two variables displayed on the axes of the graph, either as it results from behaviour, in equilibrium or by definition. The demand function shown in the text, $D = a - bP$, is one such example. It shows the negative relationship between the demand for ferry passages and the price. The vertical intercept of this line is a. The slope is $-b$, meaning that increasing the price by one unit reduces demand by b units (see Figure 1, panel (a)).

An example of a positive relationship between two variables is the supply function, $S = c + dP$, indicating that the supply of ferry transport rises when the price moves up (panel (b)). The equilibrium condition $S = D$ requires supply to equal demand. In the graph this obtains where both curves intersect (panel (c)). The price equilibrium is $\bar{P}$. Demand and supply are $\bar{D}$ and $\bar{S}$, respectively.

What do we do if our equation proposes a relationship between more than two variables? Suppose the demand function is $D = a - bP + fT$, where T is the price for transport through the Eurotunnel. For these three variables we could draw a three-dimensional (3D) graph, showing the dependence of the demand for ferry transport on the price for ferry transport and, positively, on the price for transport through the Eurotunnel. A 3D graph is often useful to give a visual image of a relationship in the form of a plane, but it is rarely used for analytical purposes. The reason is that as more relationships (planes) are added to such a graph, it tends to become confusing. Also, the technique obviously breaks down as we deal with more than three variables. What is done then is to hold one (or more) variable(s) constant, and only

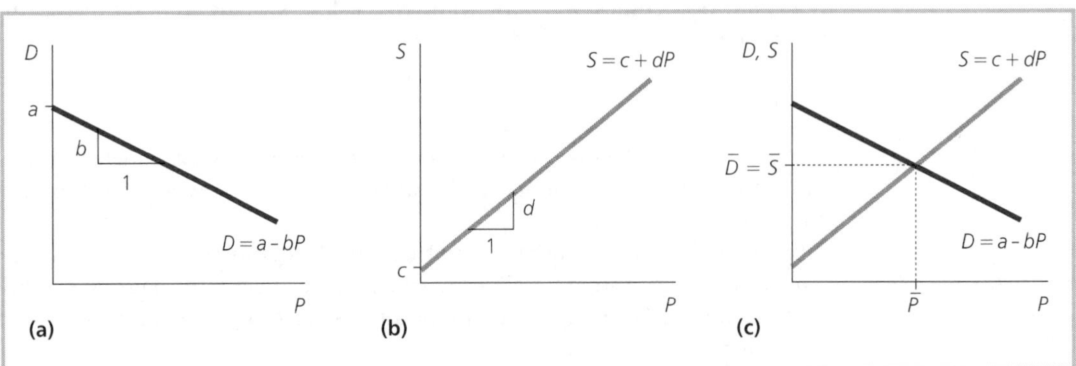

Figure 1

Box 1.2 continued

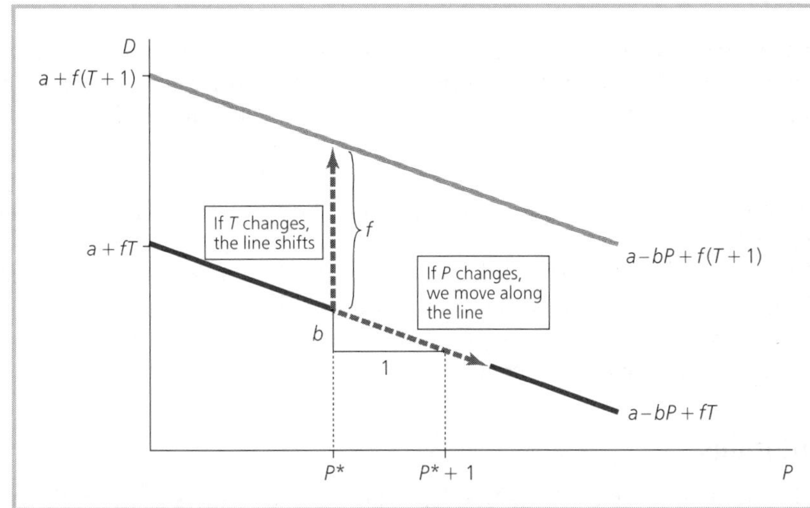

Figure 2

focus on the relationship between the two remaining variables that are permitted to change in a 2D graph. In the Channel passage example we may fix Eurotunnel transport fares at some (arbitrary) level and only trace how demand changes with the price for ferry transport. (Alternatively, we may fix the ferry price at some arbitrary level and then draw a graph of how demand responds to tunnel fares.)

As long as we keep T constant and only vary P, we are moving along the curve. But we may also ask what happens if T changes. This will generate a shift of the curve: at any P demand is different from what it was before, because T is different (see Figure 2). The failure to distinguish between *movements along a curve* and *shifts of a curve* is a frequent source of confusion for those new to using graphical models in economics. Using unspecified position and slope parameters in the equations and in the graphs reflects that we either do not know any exact values of a, b, c and d, or that we would like our result to be robust to changes in those parameters, as long as these remain positive.

Sometimes we may not even know whether the relationship is linear, i.e. a straight line as in panel (a) in Figure 3, or non-linear, i.e. a curve as in panel (b). The latter is probably the more general case. Very often, however, working with more general, bent curves will yield the same qualitative results (that is, variables change in the same direction). Whenever this is the case, we will work with simpler-to-draw straight lines. Knowledge about the non-linearity of a relationship will only be exploited if it does make a difference.

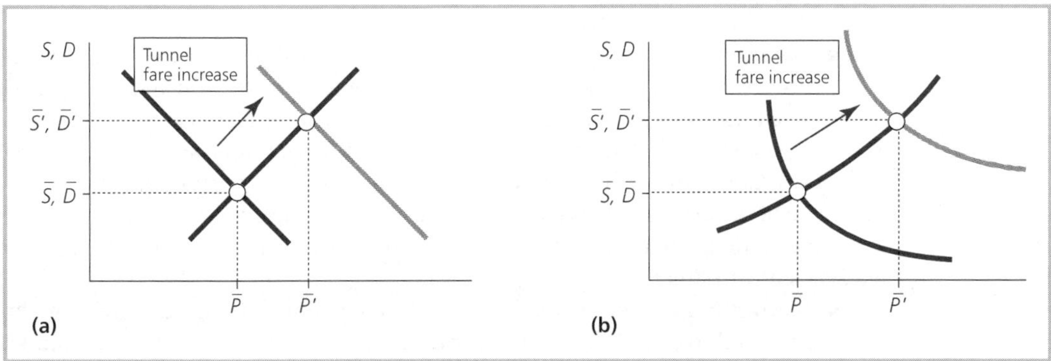

Figure 3

- Are the building blocks, the equations, used in the construction of the model, or the conclusions offered by the model, supported by real-world data?

Statistical techniques for this purpose are provided by the discipline of *econometrics*. A first glimpse at the underlying concepts are offered at the end of the book in the appendix, 'A primer in econometrics'. This material is optional. The book can be studied without using it and the empirical end-of-chapter exercises that illustrate the use of econometrics and provide the opportunity for first hands-on experience. If time permits, however, I strongly encourage you to give them a try.

While the first part of this book emphasizes the development of the concepts and *tools of macroeconomics* and only occasionally looks at empirical questions, the balance shifts increasingly towards the *issues of macroeconomics* as we progress from chapter to chapter.

Institutions

Model-building is an art. Good models ignore those features of the real world that are not relevant for the issue under consideration and focus on the important ones. Economists have become increasingly aware that individuals, whose behaviour they want to explain, are very sensitive to the institutional environment in which they operate. They therefore show a heightened sensitivity to whether the models they want to apply to a specific set of issues take proper account of the relevant institutional background. Because institutions differ – to give one example – labour economists have been using quite different models when studying European labour markets than when looking at the United States. In the United States, with trade unions being very weak, it may be a reasonable approximation to ignore their role and focus on individual behaviour in the wage bargaining process. In Europe trade unions have traditionally been much stronger, and for many countries it may be severely misleading to ignore their role in the centralized bargaining process that has been established.

Other institutional features that are being closely scrutinized are the following:

- The *(international) monetary system*. Are exchange rates flexible, determined in the market, or set by the government and the central bank? Are groups of countries sharing a common currency, or does each country retain its own national currency?
- *Central bank independence*. Does the central bank act on government orders, or can it take its own independent decisions on monetary policy? The importance of this issue is easily seen by looking back at equation (1.3), which showed that one way to pay for excessive public spending that results in a government budget deficit is by making the central bank buy government securities and thus increase the money supply. Or is monetary policy even delegated to some supranational authority such as the European Central Bank?
- *International capital markets*. Borrowing and lending, the investment of financial wealth, has quickly moved beyond national borders onto the global stage. The extent to which a country participates in this process, to which financial assets move freely across borders or meet obstacles,

encouraging or deterring potential investors, has an increasingly important role for a nation's economic prospects.

- *International trade relations as regulated in the new World Trade Organization (WTO)*. Does the presence of this institution and its particular design bear on the issues of whether it is good or bad for a country to protect its industries by using tariffs or non-tariff barriers to trade, or on who benefits and who loses?

While many of these institutions have evolved historically, European integration requires redesigns and another look at old motives.

After these preliminaries we are now ready to assemble a basic set of macroeconomic models. This will eventually carry us a long way towards understanding not only Europe's recent experience, current challenges and ongoing debates of macroeconomic issues, but those in other countries and continents and on a global scale as well.

CHAPTER SUMMARY

This chapter has introduced essential concepts and insights:

- Macroeconomics looks at the big picture, at what things like income, spending, unemployment or inflation look like after we add everything up.
- The circular flow model shows the real and monetary flows between households and firms. It can be enhanced to account for interactions with the government sector and other countries. Leakages out of and injections into this circle always balance. At the core of this 'model' is the identity between income and output on the one hand, and between spending and output on the other.
- Output, income and spending all measure the same thing. Depending on whether we define a country by its geographic boundaries or by its residents, the empirical counterpart of these concepts is gross domestic product (GDP) or gross national product (GNP).
- The central bank is the arm of the government responsible for monetary policy. If the central bank provides the economy with more money, this raises nominal income, which is defined as the price level times real income. Only economic analysis (to be provided in later chapters) will reveal under what circumstances it is more likely for the price level to rise or for real income to rise.
- The national income accounts reveal who buys aggregate output and how aggregate income is spent.
- The government budget records the interaction between the private sector and the government sector. It also reveals how the government finances budget surpluses or deficits.
- The balance of payments records the interaction with the rest of the world. It also reveals how imbalances in the trade of goods and services are being financed.
- Economists work with simplified pictures of the world, which they call models. Models are instrumental in understanding the key economic issues in today's world.

KEY TERMS AND CONCEPTS

aggregate output
aggregate supply curve
balance of payments
capital account
central bank
circular flow model
current account
empirical tests
factors of production
government budget
gross domestic product (GDP)
gross national product (GNP)
macroeconomics
mathematical model
microeconomics
model
money
national income accounts
nominal income
official reserve account
real income

EXERCISES

1.1 Figure 1.2 gives nominal per capita incomes in European countries, expressed in US dollars. Real incomes are as follows:
A 23,145; B 23,622; CH 26,876; D 22,026; DK 23,855; E 15,960; F 21,214; GB 20,314; GR 13,994; I 20,365; IRL 17,991; LUX 36,703; N 26,196; NL 22,325; P 14,569; and S 19,848.
- (a) What is your country's price level relative to the United States price level of 1? (If your country is not included, choose any country.)
- (b) Rank the fifteen EU members according to their price level.

1.2 Which of the following transactions constitute leakages, and which ones injections?
- (a) The home country receives aid from the International Monetary Fund.
- (b) Immigrant workers transfer their salaries to their home countries.
- (c) Domestic firms invest in foreign countries.
- (d) The government raises taxes and uses the proceeds to buy computers abroad.

1.3 Table 1.5 contains data for the Netherlands, Germany and Spain in 1999. All numbers are in billions of US dollars. Fill in the missing numbers, following the logic of the circular flow model.

1.4 You head your country's central bank and must determine the amount of money to circulate next year. You know that every euro circulates four times a year. The statistical office forecasts that production will remain unchanged at 1,000 barrels of whisky (the only good produced in your country) next year.
- (a) What is the slope of the aggregate supply curve if the production of whisky remains constant as forecasted?
- (b) Compute the price of one barrel of whisky if you fix the money supply at €4,000.
- (c) What would be the price of one barrel of whisky if the velocity of money circulation rose to 5 while the money supply remained at €4,000?

Table 1.5

	Saving	Investment	Taxes	Government expenditure	Budget deficit	Imports	Exports	Current account
Netherlands	91			164	6	174	196	
Germany		414	888	874		501	542	41
Spain		127	211		8		154	1

(d) Given the rising velocity of money circulation from (c) and constant production of whisky, how would you fix the money supply if your targeted price level was €5 per barrel of whisky?

(e) What is the price of whisky if output rises to 1,600 barrels in the following year?

1.5 Some time after an increase in the money supply from 50 billion to 100 billion units, the government of country A learns that the price level has increased from 100 to 150 while the velocity of money circulation has remained constant. What does that tell you about the slope of the aggregate supply curve?

1.6 The government of country B plans to spend €10,000 next year. Due to political constraints, taxes cannot exceed €5,000. Eighty per cent of the budget deficit will be financed by issuing government bonds to the private sector, the rest by issuing bonds to the central bank in exchange for money.

(a) Compute the anticipated change in the money supply if neither international trade nor international capital movements take place.

(b) What will be the effect on the price level if real output stays constant at $Y = 10{,}000$ and V at 4?

(c) Compute the anticipated change in the money supply if international trade in goods takes place, but international capital movements are still forbidden. The statistical office forecasts a current account deficit of €3,000.

(d) Can you think of arguments that render the assumption of a constant level of real production (employed above) implausible?

1.7 A country's net foreign assets stand at 500. Next year's exports are expected to be 30, expected imports are 20. The central bank will not intervene in the foreign exchange market. What are the country's net foreign assets by the end of next year?

1.8 Consider Figure 1.10. The graph shows a stylized demand curve for video recorders.

(a) What are the endogenous variables in this model?

(b) The price of a video recorder is 1,500 Swiss francs. What is the quantity demanded?

(c) If the price fell to only one-third of its previous level, what would market demand be?

(d) The supply curve can be described by the following equation:

$$P = 500 + 0.000025 \text{ Quantity}$$

Draw the curve into the diagram in the figure.

(e) Determine the equilibrium price level and the quantity sold graphically.

(f) It becomes unfashionable to waste time in front of the TV. Show how this change of preferences affects market demand. What will be the effect on the equilibrium price level and quantity?

(g) Due to a new technology it becomes cheaper to produce video recorders. How will that affect the diagram above?

(h) The government introduces a tax on video tapes. How will that affect the diagram? What happens if the government introduces an even higher tax on visits to the cinema?

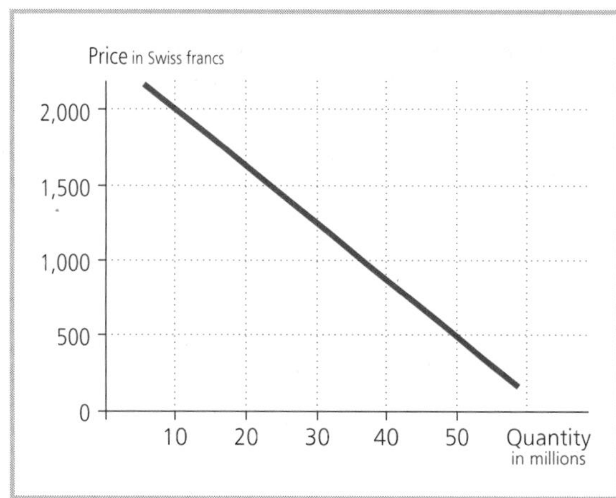

Figure 1.10

RECOMMENDED READING

Data

For macroeconomic data including national income accounts, government budgets and the balance of payments, a good source to start searching are international organizations. The broadest set of countries is covered by the IMF (International Monetary Fund) publications *International Financial Statistics* and *Government Financial Statistics* (Washington DC).

A very good and inexpensive first source and overview on most countries of the world is provided by the World Bank in *The World Bank Atlas* (Washington DC). Standardized data on its twenty-three members are provided by the OECD (Organization for Economic Cooperation and Development) in *Economic Outlook* and *Historical Statistics* (Paris).

Relatively short series on EU member states are published by the European Commission in *European Union* and *Eurostat* (Brussels).

If you do not find what you are looking for in these international publications, you may have to go to national sources. All governments have statistical offices. But beware: definitions and compilation procedures may vary between countries, so data may not be directly comparable.

Economics

If the repetition of concepts in this chapter was too dense on occasion, you may want to go back to a principle text such as David Begg, Stanley Fischer and Rudiger Dornbusch (1994) *Economics*, 4th edn, London: McGraw-Hill, or Karl Case, Ray Fair, Manfred Gärtner and Ken Heather (1999) *Economics*, Harlow: Prentice Hall Europe.

A history of economic thought in a nutshell that you may want to read here, and again after Chapter 10, is given in 'Schools brief: Paradigm lost', *The Economist*, 3 November 1990, pp. 82–3.

Economy

International periodicals that keep you on top of economic developments are *The Economist*, *The Financial Times* and *The Wall Street Journal Europe*. *The Economist* is particularly renowned for high-standard analyses of current economic issues. Also, do not forget the section on the economy in your favourite national newspaper.

Mathematics

If you would like to read up on the few maths tools that I use in this book, the didactically superb classic to be recommended is A. Chiang (1984) *Fundamental Methods of Mathematical Economics*, 3rd edn, Singapore: McGraw-Hill. There you will find it all – and more.

APPENDIX LOGARITHMS, GROWTH RATES AND LOGARITHMIC SCALES

Logarithms

Taking the logarithm of a number or of a variable is nothing mysterious. Just as taking the square root of 9 amounts to picking 3, since $3^2 = 3 \times 3 = 9$, taking the logarithm of 1 to base 5 is zero, since $5^0 = 1$. Economists find it convenient to use Euler's number $e \equiv 2.71828 \ldots$ as the base. Logarithms to the base of e are called **natural logarithms** and are referred to by the shorthand symbol ln. Then, in general terms: the natural logarithm of some number or variable a is the power to which e must be raised to yield a, that is $e^{\ln a} = a$.

Logarithms possess some properties that assist with model-building and the visual display of models and data in graphs. Since we are not interested in the higher mathematics of logarithms, we skip proofs and illustrate the concepts needed by means of numerical examples.

Consider a country's nominal income PY, which is the product of the price level P and real income Y. If $P = 100$ and $Y = 200$, then $PY = 20{,}000$. Now take your pocket calculator, key in 100 for the price level, and press the ln button. This should give you the natural logarithm of 100, that is $\ln 100 = 4.605$. For real income you get $\ln 200 = 5.298$. Now type in nominal income and your calculator gives you $\ln (100 \times 200) = \ln 20{,}000 = 9.903$. What is noteworthy about this result is that obviously $\ln (100 \times 200) = \ln 100 + \ln 200$, since $9.903 = 4.605 + 5.298$. That is, the logarithm of the product PY is the sum of the logarithms of its two components. This result

$$\ln PY = \ln P + \ln Y \qquad \textbf{Property 1}$$

holds generally, as you may check by entering other numbers for P and Y. You may use the above or other numbers to convince yourself that

$$\ln (P/Y) = \ln P - \ln Y \qquad \textbf{Property 2}$$

that is, the logarithm of the fraction P/Y equals the difference between the logarithms of the numerator and the denominator.

A third useful property is

$$\ln X^n = n \ln X \qquad \textbf{Property 3}$$

You may again convince yourself by entering some numbers into your pocket calculator, or you may derive this third property directly from property 1. For n being an integer, X^n may be written as

$$X^n = \underbrace{X \times X \times X \times \ldots \times X}_{n \text{ times}}$$

With the above rules for products, taking the logarithm of this gives

$$\ln X^n = \underbrace{\ln X + \ln X + \ln X + \ldots + \ln X}_{n \text{ times}} = n \ln X$$

What is so great about these results? Assume that you want to know what combinations of P and Y multiply into a given nominal income of 20,000.

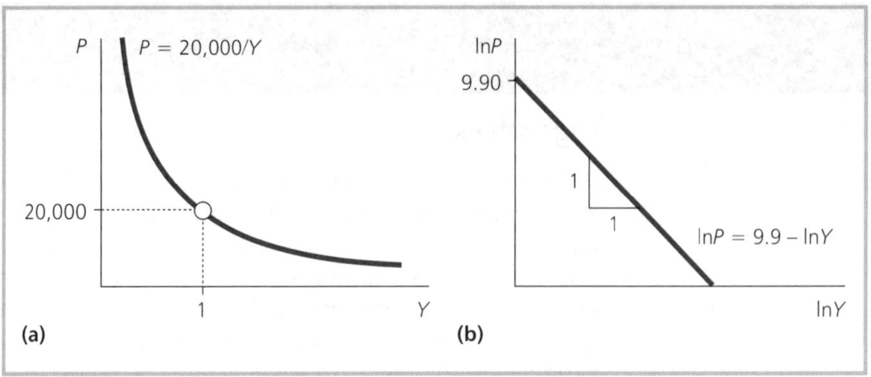

Figure 1.11

After writing $PY = 20,000$ you may solve for P to obtain $P = 20,000/Y$. The graph of this relationship is curved (called a hyperbola) as shown in panel (a) in Figure 1.11. Drawing it is not easy, since the slope is different for each value of Y. Working with it is not easy either: increasing nominal income from 20,000 to, say, 22,000 shifts and turns the line at the same time.

Now take the logarithm on both sides of $P = 20,000/Y$ and you obtain $\ln P = \ln 20,000 - \ln Y$. This new equation is additive and linear (see panel (b)). It intersects the vertical axis at $\ln 20,000 = 9.90$ and has a slope of -1 all over. Working with such a linear graph or model is much more convenient than manipulating a hyperbola.

Growth rates

The growth rate of Y over its previous value Y_{-1} is computed as $(Y - Y_{-1})/Y_{-1}$. Logarithms come in handy when we discuss such growth rates. Let inflation be 10%, or 0.1. As the P column in Table 1.6 illustrates, this means that the price level rises in larger and larger increments: after a change in the price level of 10 units in period 2, the change in period 6 is already 14.64. If P is plotted against the time axis, P turns out to follow a non-linear, accelerating path. This acceleration is not very visible for such short time horizons, but it becomes more and more pronounced as time passes.

Now look at the fifth column in Table 1.6, which gives $\ln P$. The period-to-period changes in the logarithm of P are obviously constant at 0.0953 – and they closely approximate the growth rate of P which is 0.1. The useful property of logarithms suggested by these numbers is that if a variable grows at a constant rate, and thus the variable moves up at an accelerating pace as time

Table 1.6

Time	P	$\Delta P = P - P_{-1}$	$(P - P_{-1})/P_{-1}$	$\ln P$	$\ln P = \ln P - \ln P_{-1}$
1	100			4.605	
2	110	10	0.1	4.700	0.0953 ~ 0.1
3	121	11	0.1	4.7957	0.0953 ~ 0.1
4	133.1	12.1	0.1	4.8911	0.0953 ~ 0.1
5	146.41	13.31	0.1	4.9864	0.0953 ~ 0.1
6	161.05	14.64	0.1	5.0817	0.0953 ~ 0.1

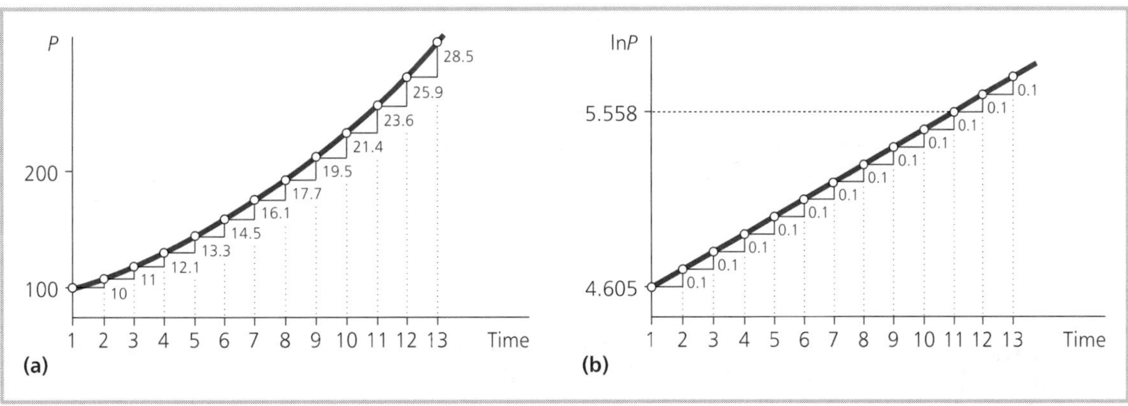

Figure 1.12

progresses (see panel (a) in Figure 1.12), the logarithm of this variable moves up at a constant pace. Thus as time progresses, the logarithm of this variable follows a straight line. The slope of this line closely approximates the growth rate of the variable.

The approximation becomes better as the growth rates become smaller: $(P - P_{-1})/P_{-1} = 0.05$ is approximated by $\ln P - \ln P_{-1} = 0.04879$; at $(P - P_{-1})/P_{-1} = 0.01$ the logarithmic approximation is $\ln P - \ln P_{-1} = 0.00995$. With high precision it only holds for very small growth rates. As a rule of thumb, however, for practical purposes *growth rates smaller than 0.2 may be approximated by the change in the logarithm of the variable under consideration:*

$$\frac{Y - Y_{-1}}{Y_{-1}} \cong \ln Y - \ln Y_{-1}$$

Logarithmic scales

The one major drawback that arises when the logarithm of a variable is measured along the axis instead of the variable itself is that the units of measurement do not have a direct interpretation. To overcome this we may retain the logarithm as the unit of measurement that determines the equidistant tick marks on the vertical axis, but after that translate the logarithms back into original values. This is called **logarithmic scaling**. Figure 1.13

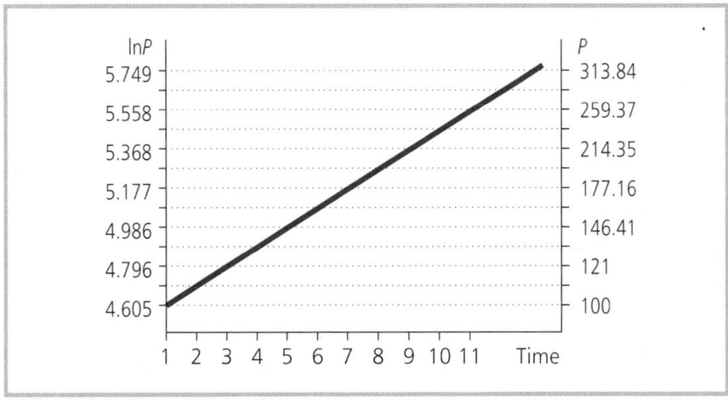

Figure 1.13

illustrates the procedure. The vertical axis on the left measures the logarithm of P. The distance between two tick marks equals 0.0953 units of $\ln P$. The vertical axis on the right translates each value of $\ln P$ back into the corresponding value for P. What happens then, and this is important, is that now one tick mark on the ordinate represents ever larger changes of P as we move up. In fact, equal distances on this vertical axis represent equal percentage increases of 10%. So the distance between 100 and 110 is the same as the distances between 200 and 220 or between 1,000 and 1,100.

To further explore this chapter's key messages you are encouraged to use the interactive online module found at

www.fgn.unisg.ch/eurmacro/tutor/circularflow.html

and many other features hosted at **www.fgn.unisg.ch/eurmacro**

CHAPTER 2

BOOMS AND RECESSIONS (I)
THE KEYNESIAN CROSS

WHAT TO EXPECT After working through this chapter, you will understand:

1 The difference between **steady-state income**, **potential income** and **actual income** and what **booms** and **recessions** are.
2 How **aggregate** (desired) **demand** determines output and income in the short run.
3 How additional government spending may trigger additional private spending via the **multiplier**.
4 That economic decisions are often made on the basis of what people expect to happen in the future rather than on what they observe today.

At the very least, a macroeconomic model should explain why an economy produces a specific volume of goods and services and no other. In terms of the circular flow of income (Chapter 1), this amounts to explaining why the stream of income is exactly as wide as it is. This question is not trivial:

- As Figure 2.1 illustrates, income per capita differs by a factor of 50 between the richest and the poorest countries in the world. Even within the (by world standards) rich set of EU member states, per capita income in the four richest economies is about twice as high as in the four poorest ones.
- Figure 2.2 takes a look at income developments during a full century. In the sample of European and other industrialized countries incomes have typically increased tenfold or more during the 20th century. In Japan income is almost 50 times as high at the turn of the millennium as it was in 1900.

So, *the most important goal of macroeconomics is to develop an understanding of what makes incomes differ between countries, and what makes them grow or fluctuate over time*. One way of simplifying this task is by slicing up the current volume of output into components that are conveniently analyzed separately, because they are determined by different factors. Rather than talking about this in the abstract, consider the development of British GDP since the turn of the 20th century (Figure 2.3).

Visual inspection of the graph suggests a separation of real income into three components:

1 There is a long-run or *secular trend* that connects the pre-First World War path with the path on which Britain has moved since about 1970. On the

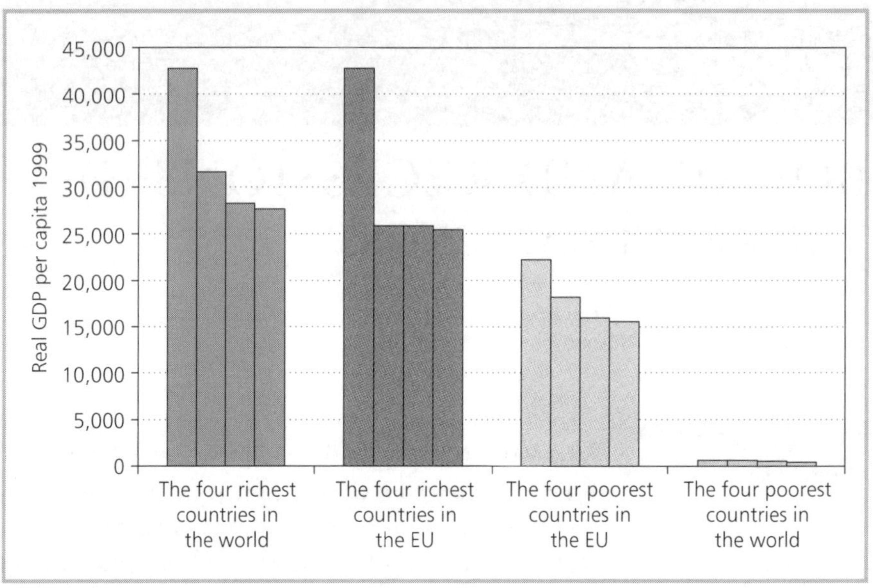

Figure 2.1 This figure shows, along with Figure 2.2, why economists are so eager to understand why countries produce the output and generate the income that they do. Figure 2.1 shows that incomes (here for 1999) between countries may vary by a factor of 50. Figure 2.2 shows that industrialized countries have tripled incomes over the past four decades.
Source: World Bank, *World Development Indicators* 2001.

The **steady-state income** results when all variables, including the capital stock, have adjusted to their desired or equilibrium levels.

secular-trend line, income is in a steady state. **Steady-state income** is the level of income that is generated:

(a) if all factors of production are being used at normal rates, and
(b) if the economy's capital stock is at its long-run equilibrium level (or growth path).

Potential income is the income that can be produced with current labour and capital. The capital stock may or may not have reached its equilibrium level.

2 Displacements from the steady-state income path may occur. Evidently, major displacements strike in the wake of wars. Through a destruction of the private capital stock and public infrastructure, income can fall dramatically below pre-war and desired levels. Rebuilding the capital stock may take decades. Consequently, it also takes decades to bring **potential income,** based on currently *available* capital, back towards steady-state income. The two light grey lines illustrate this convergence of potential income back to steady-state income after the First and Second World Wars. As inferred by the data, these lines postulate linear convergence within forty years.

The **business cycle** refers to recurring fluctuations of income relative to potential income. A **boom** (or expansion) describes rising income (relative to potential income) which culminates in a peak. A **recession** describes declining income (relative to potential income) which bottoms out at a trough.

3 Even during periods for which it appears safe to believe that potential income evolved smoothly, income does fluctuate. These short-run ups and downs are what we mean by the term **business cycle**. From the bird's-eye perspective employed in Figure 2.3 the business cycle is dwarfed by long-run growth and by the shocks to potential output due to the two world wars. Figure 2.4 expands the part of the graph that shows the development of real income during the last twenty years. This demonstrates that economies operate substantially above normal capacity levels during **booms** (which culminate in a *peak*) and below potential income during **recessions** (which bottom out in a *trough*) (see Figure 2.4).

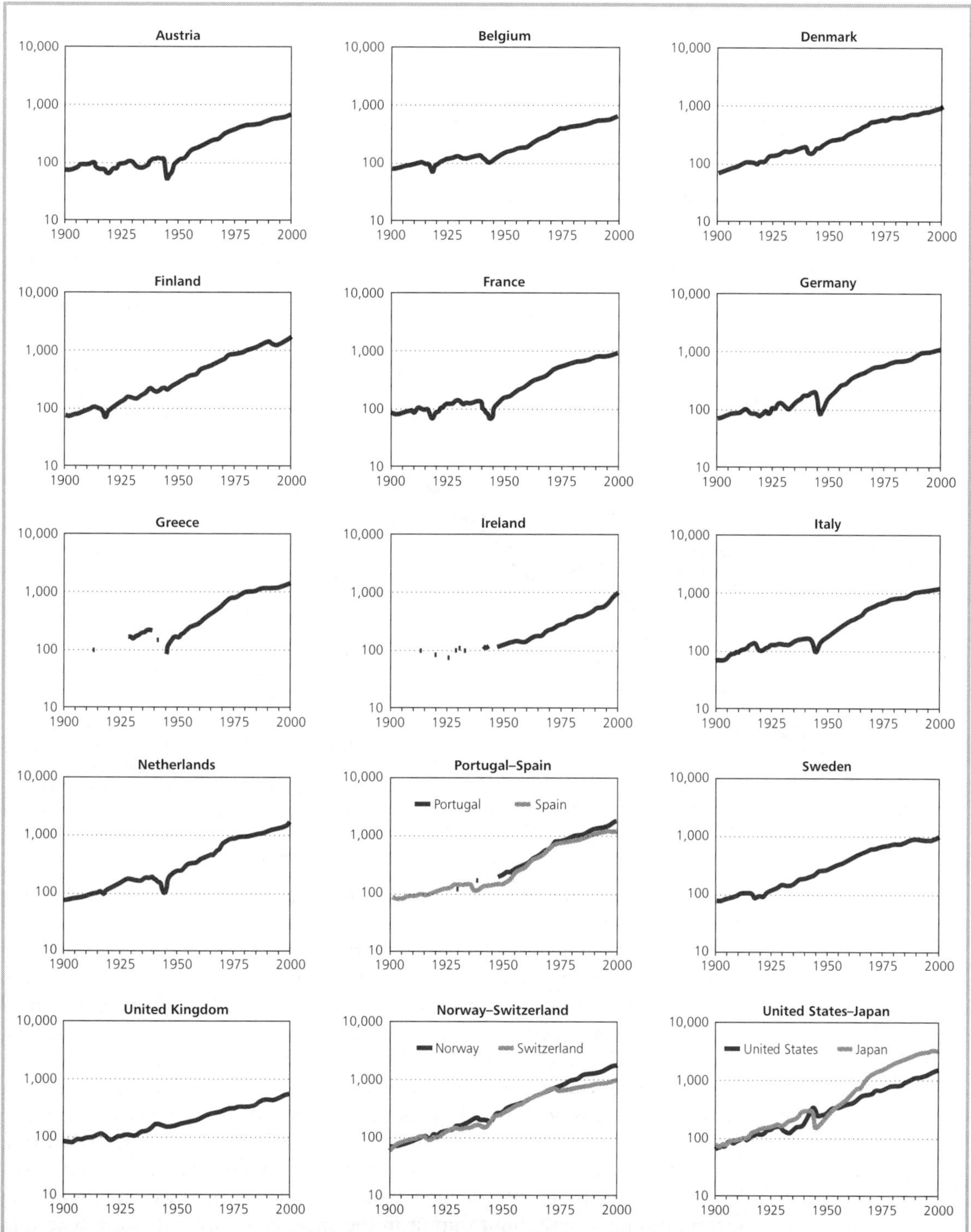

Figure 2.2 Real GDP in Europe and the world, 1900–2000 (1913 = 100).
Source: IMF; A. Maddison (1995) *Monitoring the World Economy, 1820–1992*, Paris: OECD.

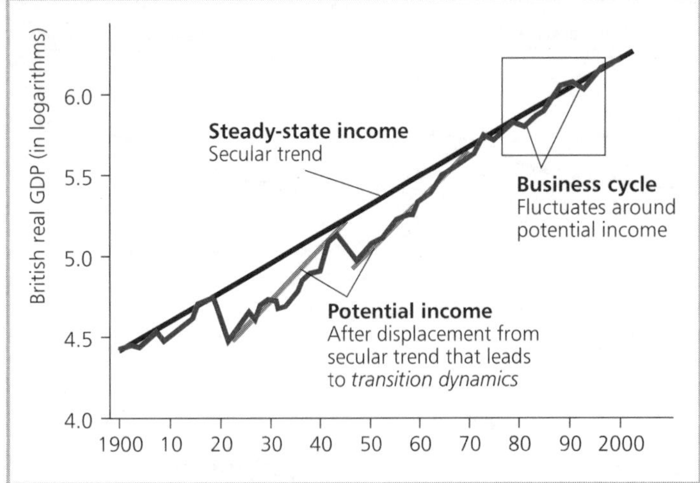

Figure 2.3 By using British real GDP the graph shows that **actual income** may be divided into **steady-state income, potential income** (which may deviate from steady-state income) and the **business cycle** (which is the deviation of actual income from potential income).
Source: A. Maddison (1989), *The World Economy in the 20th Century*, Paris: OECD; IMF: *International Financial Statistics*.

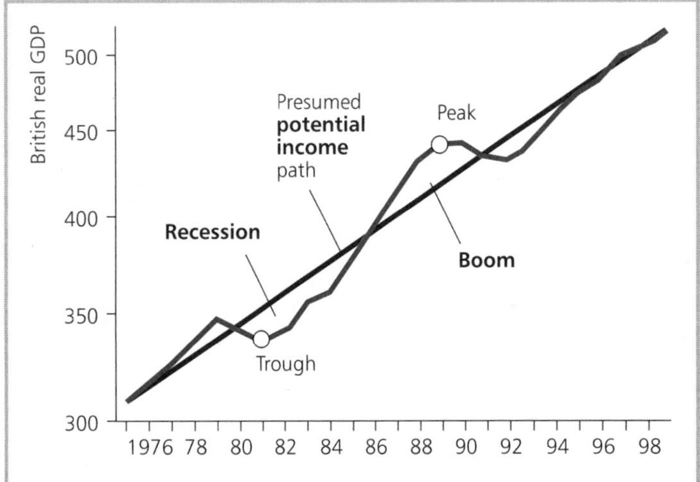

Figure 2.4 Business cycles describe movements of income around potential income. During a **recession** actual income falls below potential income. A **boom** drives actual income above potential income. Extreme values relative to potential income are called **peaks** and **troughs**. Operational definitions of when exactly a recession starts or ends may differ between organizations or countries.
Source: IMF, *International Financial Statistics*.

But why does annual GDP data not reflect the smoothness suggested by the concept of potential income? Why do we observe business cycles when the section of the population eligible for work and the stock of capital goods used in the generation of income change slowly and smoothly? The answer is that in the short run, temporarily, firms freely employ more or less of available capital or labour. Firms operate temporarily below capacity levels, or even beyond normal capacity levels. Why would they do that? Because they experience a drop in the demand for their products and do not want to build up stocks, or because demand is booming above normal levels and they would like to cash in.

So if we want to understand how output and income move in the short run, during **booms** and **recessions**, the key word is **demand**. The production possibilities laid out by the production function under normal use of production factors do not strictly limit output in the short run. Firms do have a certain flexibility to adjust the volume of goods and services produced to the demand that they experience. In this chapter we will take an extreme view. We assume that, at current prices, firms produce exactly the amount of output that is demanded. The short-run *AS* curve is therefore horizontal.

In the long run, however, labour and capital utilization will have to return to normal levels and put a lid on the output that can be produced, no matter what the price level is. This makes the long-run *AS* curve vertical, as we shall see in Chapter 6.

BOX 2.1 Actual income, potential income and steady-state income: Great Britain in 1933

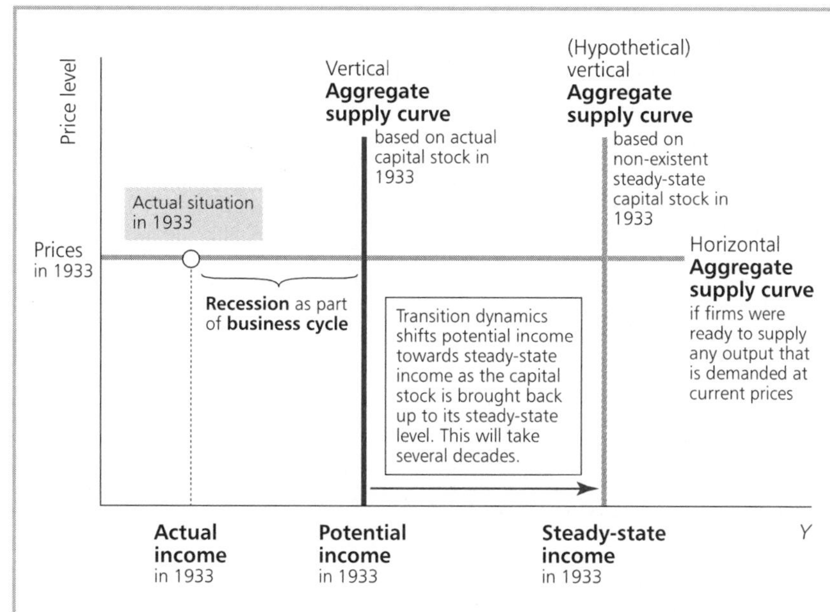

Figure 1

The year 1933 in Great Britain provides a good opportunity to elaborate on the concepts of steady-state income, potential income and actual income. Figure 1 recasts this macroeconomic situation, taken from Figure 2.3 in terms of a price–income diagram. We have already used such a diagram to introduce the concept of aggregate supply curves in the context of the circular flow economy (which produced cars only) in Chapter 1.

Actual income can be taken from Figure 2.3. Combining this with 1933 prices identifies the actual situation in 1933. Britain, like the rest of the world, experienced a severe recession at that time. Hence, actual income is substantially below potential income that might have been produced. Figure 1 features a vertical aggregate supply curve over potential income, postulating that what a country can potentially produce is independent of the price level. The capital stock had not fully recovered from First World War destruction. Hence steady-state income (the income that could have been produced had the First World War not occurred and had the capital stock grown smoothly since then) exceeds potential income. The light blue vertical line marking steady-state income at all price levels marks a reference point or very long-run centre of gravity for the British economy. (We will discuss in Chapter 9, in the context of economic growth, which mechanisms tend to drive an economy, very slowly, towards the steady state.)

The actual situation observed in 1933 demonstrates that firms deviate from potential income, at least temporarily. One way to interpret this is to concede that the vertical aggregate supply curve over potential income does not properly describe aggregate supply in the short and medium run. In the short run, firms respond along a horizontal aggregate supply curve, following demand.

Chapters 2 to 6 focus on the deviations of income from potential income, the analysis of the ups and downs of the business cycle. The discussion of the medium- and long-run reference path, potential income and steady-state income, is left for Chapters 7 to 9.

2.1 THE CIRCULAR FLOW MODEL REVISITED: TERMINOLOGY AND OVERVIEW

We begin by building up some terminology and clarifying key concepts. For that purpose we revisit the circular flow diagram from Chapter 1 (see Figure 2.5).

In an attempt to develop an expression for the total spending (or total demand) which comes back to domestic firms, note that households receive **gross income** Y (top left-hand corner). Payment of taxes reduces this to **disposable income** $Y - T$. After removing savings from the loop we obtain what is left for consumption, i.e. $C = Y - T - S$. Because of the third leakage we have to subtract from this **imports** IM from abroad. Therefore, what remains at the end of the upper segment and what comes around the right-hand-side curve to the lower segment of the income circle is $C - IM$. Adding to this the three demand injections shown in the lower part of the circle gives total spending on domestically produced goods:

$$\text{Total expenditure} = C + I + G + EX - IM \; (= \text{total income})$$

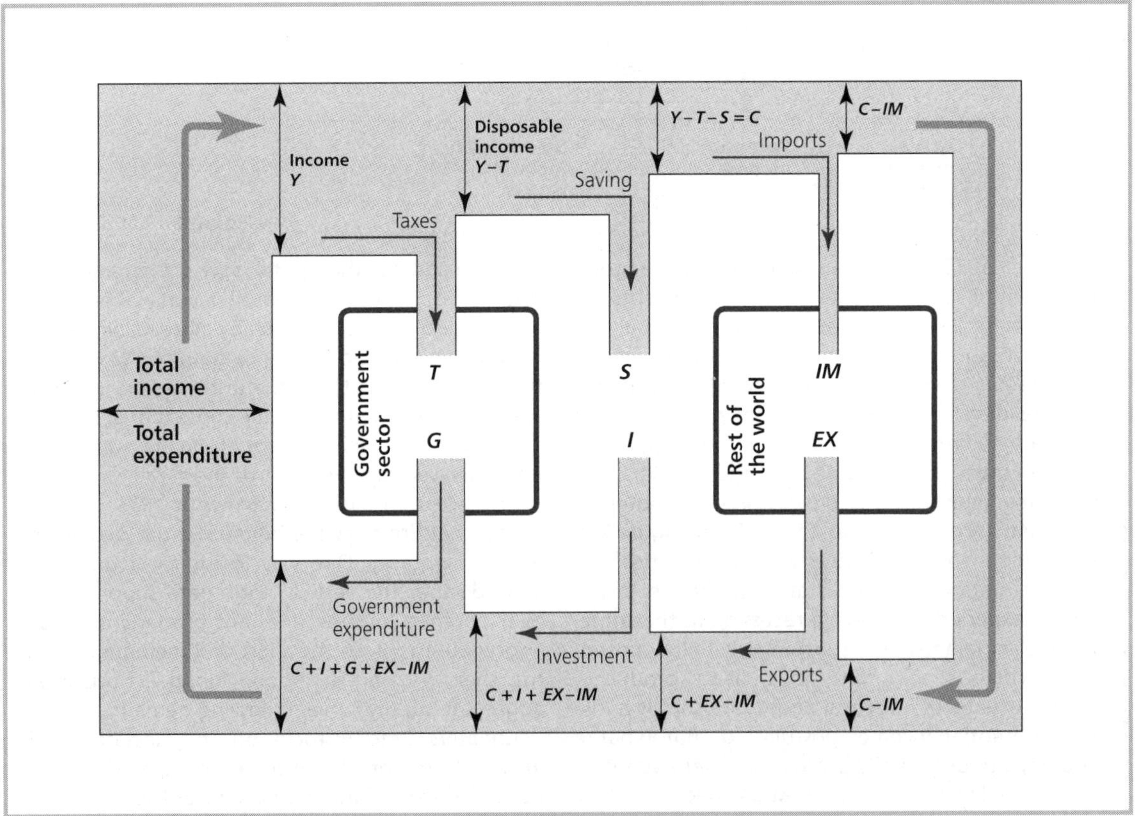

Figure 2.5 The circle begins with income Y on the left. Taxes reduce this to disposable income $Y - T$, and savings to consumption $C \equiv Y - T - S$. Taking away imports leaves $C - IM$. Addition of exports, investment and government expenditure in the circle's lower segment gives total expenditure as $C + I + G + EX - IM$.

The equality between expenditure (or demand) and income is always guaranteed because investment may include an undesired component. To illustrate this crucial point once more, let the rest of the world start to boycott our country, eliminating exports. If other spending plans and taxes remain unchanged we are left with a gap between output and planned expenditure exactly the same size as the former exports. Firms are being forced to close that gap by unplanned investment spending in the form of involuntary inventory build-up (see Figure 2.6).

Aggregate expenditure is the sum of all planned or voluntary spending on domestically produced goods and services.

Actual expenditure is the sum of all categories of demand, including unplanned investment.

Henceforth, the variable I always stands for *planned* investment. *Unplanned* investment is denoted by I^u. The sum of all planned demand is called **aggregate expenditure.** For contrast we call the sum of all demand, planned and unplanned, **actual expenditure.**

So far the circular flow model gives us only a vague understanding of where the level of income might be at any point in time. Even if we knew that desired demand was at 100, income might be at 200 with 100 units of undesired investment, or at 95 with −5 units of undesired investment. Anything can happen.

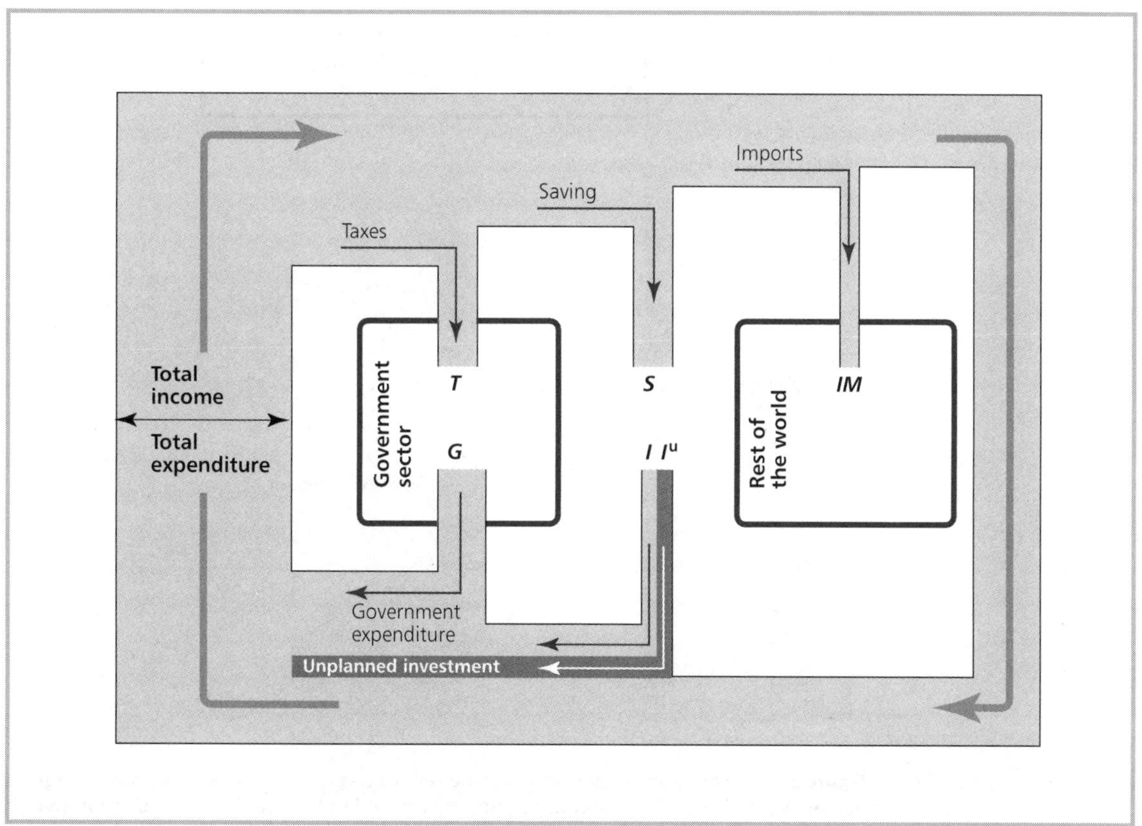

Figure 2.6 Assume that the circular flow has been in equilibrium. If exports drop to zero, income exceeds desired spending by the amount represented by the blue injection. This exactly equals the former level of exports, and must now be demanded *involuntarily* by firms which are being forced to stock up inventory.

In this situation firms can be expected to go to great lengths to avoid having to undertake investments they had not planned and do not want to make. In order to achieve this, they must set output exactly to the level they expect others plan to buy, that is to aggregate expenditure. At this point the economy is in **equilibrium**. Plans work out and do not need to be revised.

Note. The equilibrium concept employed here is a **demand-side equilibrium.** Note that we do not consider where this demand-side equilibrium is relative to potential income or steady-state income. Later on in this book we will do so.

Having a firm grasp of the concepts of actual expenditure, output, income and aggregate expenditure is essential for much of what will be discussed below. For easy reference and for control, Figure 2.7 shows these concepts and how they interrelate. The grey area in Figure 2.7 defines **actual expenditure**. Because it comprises all components of demand, even those that are not planned, it always equals income (or output). The blue column defines *planned expenditure*, which henceforth we call **aggregate expenditure,** as

$$AE = C + I + G + EX - IM \qquad \textbf{Aggregate expenditure} \qquad (2.1)$$

It only equals income if firms succeed in setting output to a level that does not require them to undertake any unplanned investment in the form of undesired inventory changes. They will do everything they can to succeed in this effort.

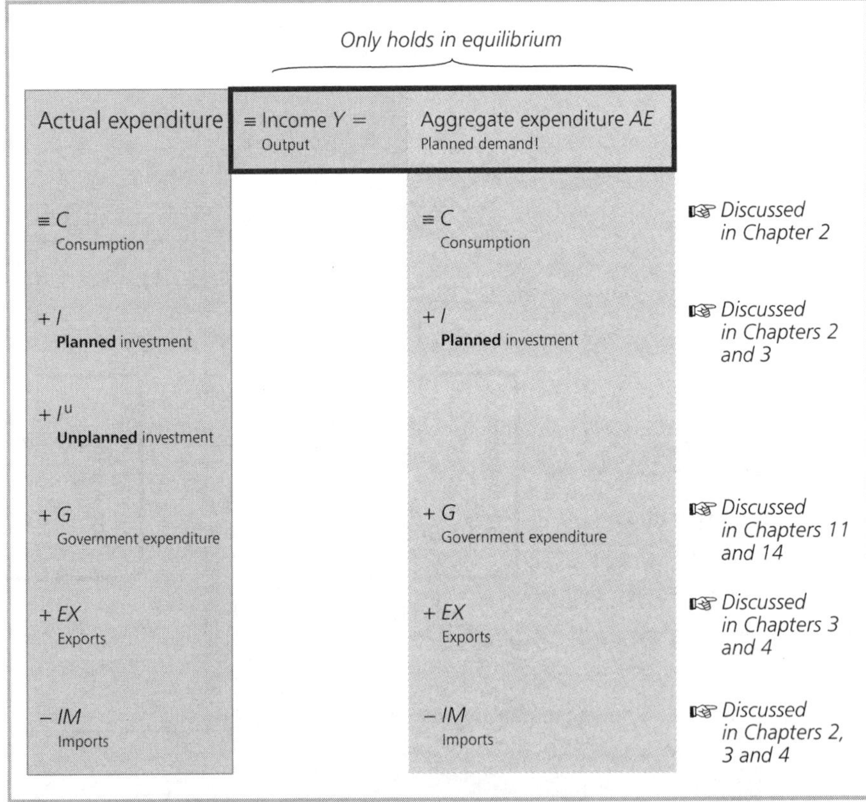

Figure 2.7 The diagram shows how income relates to expenditure. **Income always equals actual expenditure**: this is because if nobody wanted to buy the firms' production (which equals income) voluntarily, the firms would be forced to buy it themselves, having to undertake unplanned investment (first column). **Income equals aggregate (desired) expenditure in equilibrium,** that is, if all spending is as planned, then firms need not change inventories in an undesired way (third column).

Income, therefore, is much more likely to be at the level marked by aggregate expenditure than at any other level. It is therefore crucial to understand what determines the different components of aggregate expenditure. To the right of each expenditure category you find references to where this variable is discussed in this book.

Table 2.1 gives real data for the components of aggregate expenditure that we have just encountered. For most countries the lion's share goes to consumption. It averages almost two-thirds of aggregate expenditure. The rest is divided between government spending, investment (with roughly equal shares) and net exports. The small shares of net exports, which can be negative, camouflage the intense international involvement of those economies shown. To remedy this, the last column *EX* shows export shares as indicators of the openness of economies.

You may well be puzzled by the small shares of the government sector shown in Table 2.1. Isn't everybody complaining about big governments that claim 35%, 40% or 50% of aggregate expenditure? This apparent contradiction is resolved after noting that only government purchases are injections into the circular flow of income. In addition to those purchases, governments pay large sums in transfers, such as social security and unemployment insurance payments. These payments do not represent government demand for goods and services. They are best seen as negative taxes, as something that the government gives to citizens rather than taking it from them. On the aggregate, *transfers paid for by taxes cancel out*: the government takes taxes out of one pocket of the private sector and puts transfers back into the other. Aggregate disposable income is therefore unaffected. For this reason, when we talk about taxes T we mean **net taxes** (gross taxes minus transfers), and G only represents **government purchases** of goods and services. It excludes all transfer payments and interest payments on government debt.

Taxes T in our models are **net taxes**, the difference between all taxes and transfers. Government spending G in our models are **government purchases** of goods and services. It does not include transfers.

Table 2.1 Demand categories in the circular flow model (1999, as % of GDP). Consumption is the dominating category of aggregate expenditure. Investment and government spending follow with shares of about 20% each. The small balance is filled by net exports. This conceals that exports can be sizeable, ranging from 11% in the United States and Japan to 87% in Ireland.

	C	*G*	*I*	*EX* – *IM*	*EX*
Austria	54.5	18.6	26.8	0.1	44.2
Belgium	52.3	14.1	29.5	4.1	72.2
Denmark	49.6	26.8	21.8	1.8	34.5
Finland	48.2	20.1	23.5	8.2	38.7
France	54.2	19.3	22.9	3.6	27.4
Germany	56.0	18.8	23.1	2.1	27.5
Greece	69.0	14.3	24.5	–7.8	16.6
Ireland	47.0	12.1	19.7	21.2	87.2
Italy	59.1	16.3	20.6	4.0	26.3
Netherlands	49.6	14.0	30.0	6.4	55.3
Portugal	62.7	18.6	24.8	–6.1	32.3
Spain	58.8	15.1	26.0	0.1	29.3
Sweden	49.1	26.0	19.1	5.8	45.5
United Kingdom	63.3	18.7	19.1	–1.1	27.2
Japan	60.1	10.4	27.3	2.2	10.9
United States	67.1	14.9	20.5	–2.5	11.2

Source: OECD *Statistical Compendium*

The remaining part of this chapter shows that under reasonable assumptions only one equilibrium level of income exists. The next section introduces some basic concepts by means of a stylized example.

CASE STUDY 2.1 Income vs leisure time in France and the USA

In 1997 GNP in the United States of America stood at $7,783 billion while GNP in France was $1,542 billion. This is a preliminary, raw comparison of incomes, however, which does not take into account a number of factors.

One very important factor is that one US dollar does not buy the same amount of goods in all countries – its purchasing power is not the same. Adjusting for differences in purchasing power, on a common measure French GNP is worth only $1,302 billion. This means that when French people spend $1,542 billion in France (and on imports into France), it buys them only what $1,302 billion would have bought them in the USA. The reason is that prices, expressed in dollars, are some 15% higher in France than in the US.

A second factor we need to take into account are population sizes. With populations of 267.6 million in the USA and 58.6 million in France, per capita GNP was $29,080 in the USA, but only $22,210 in France.

Next consider that a smaller share of the population work in France than in the USA, either because they are not active (meaning they are too young or too old), because they do not want to work, or because they cannot find work. In 1997 employment in France was 22.5 million and in the US it was 130.5 million. This puts output per worker at $59,619 in the US and $57,851 in France.

To push the argument one step further, note that in France workers work an average of 1,656 hours per year, while in America they work 1,966 hours. Thus GNP per hour worked is $34.93 in France, compared with $30.33 worth of output produced in the USA during one work hour.

What is the message in this? We started by noting that US per capita GDP exceeds per capita GDP in France. Thus a standardized 'family' comprising, say, two adults and two children, earns more dollars in the USA than in France. However, fewer persons in the French family work. And those who work do work fewer hours than their US counterparts. So who is better off? The US family, having higher income but little time to spend it? Or the French family, with ample leisure time but less money to spend? It is your decision: since there is an obvious trade-off between income and leisure, it is your preferences that must determine what is right for you or for your country. The point is that comparing the welfare of French and Americans by looking at per capita GDP alone may be just as misleading as comparing it by looking at leisure time alone.

Table 1 Population, employment, work hours and GNP

	France	USA
Total GNP (1997)		
in million dollars	1,541,630	7,783,092
in million international $	1,301,886	7,783,092
Population (1997)	58,617,110	267,644,154
GNP per capita		
in dollars	26,300	29,080
in international $	22,210	29,080
Employment (1997)	22,504,000	130,543,000
GNP per worker		
in dollars	68,505	59,621
in international $	57,851	59,621
Annual work hours per worker	1,656	1,966
GNP per work hour		
in dollars	41.37	30.33
in international $	34.93	30.33

Sources: World Bank Atlas; OECD; ILO.

2.2 INCOME DETERMINATION: A FIRST LOOK

Human behaviour in the circular flow

In a state of equilibrium, desired and actual expenditure must be equal. In order to understand what individuals do desire to spend, we first look at the four components that constitute aggregate expenditure. Let all but one of the expenditure categories be autonomous, that is independent of income or other variables. We may even keep these autonomous spending variables fixed:

$$G = \text{constant} \tag{2.2}$$

$$I = \text{constant} \tag{2.3}$$

$$NX(\approx CA) = EX - IM = \text{constant} \tag{2.4}$$

Equation (2.4) defines net exports $EX - IM$ as NX. As a reminder we state that net exports are a good first approximation for the current account CA in the balance of payments.

The **marginal propensity to consume** says by how much consumption rises if income rises by one unit.

For consumption C we assume that individuals always want to spend a constant fraction c of their income Y (taxes T are assumed to be zero for now); c is the **marginal propensity to consume** and should be taken to be around 0.8:

$$C = cY \qquad \textbf{Consumption function} \tag{2.5}$$

Note. Since we assume that $T = 0$ here, income is either consumed or saved, $Y = C + S$. Hence, equation (2.5) implies the savings function $S = (1 - c)Y$.

Substituting equation (2.5) for C in equation (2.1) gives

$$AE = cY + I + G + NX$$

It shows that aggregate spending is not independent of income, but increases as Y rises. The aggregate expenditure line in Figure 2.8 shows how AE relates to Y and also breaks up aggregate expenditure into its four components.

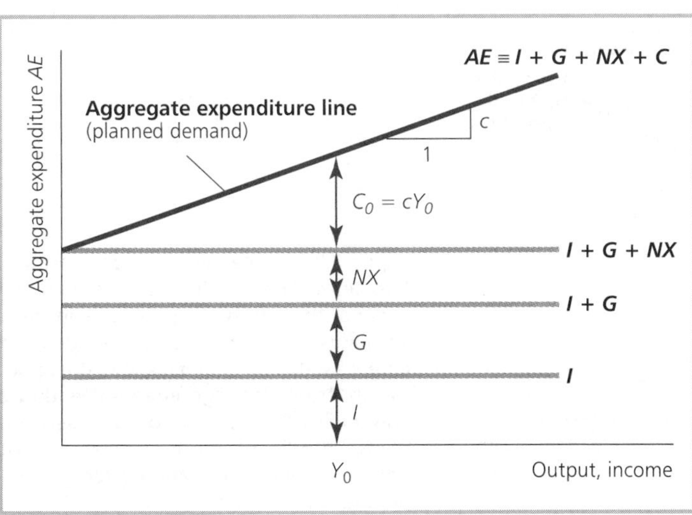

Figure 2.8 Aggregate (or planned or desired) expenditure varies with income. The graph stacks four demand categories. It starts with I, G, and NX, which are all considered independent of income. That makes these lines horizontal. Consumption spending increases with income, with a marginal rate of consumption of c. This gives the aggregate-expenditure line slope c. The line meets the vertical axis at the level of autonomous expenditure.

Equilibrium income

The graphical representation of aggregate expenditure can now be used to determine **equilibrium income.**

Figure 2.9 replicates the aggregate-expenditure line from Figure 2.8. This line has a positive intercept, depicting those components that are immune to income changes. Its slope is positive but smaller than 1, since individuals do not want to consume their entire income, but wish to save a small fraction of it. By contrast, the actual-expenditure line passes through the origin and has slope 1. This is because actual spending always equals income. The two lines intersect at point A, which marks that level of income Y_0 at which actual expenditure is exactly as planned. At higher income levels, actual spending exceeds planned expenditures. At lower income levels, planned spending exceeds actual spending. This type of graph is known as the **Keynesian cross.**

The **Keynesian cross** is a diagram which plots *planned* expenditure against income and *actual* expenditure against income. Equilibrium income obtains where both lines cross.

Since we are currently assuming that firms produce any amount of goods that is demanded, the kind of equilibrium determined by the Keynesian cross is called a **demand-side equilibrium.**

We should note here that if income is initially at the wrong level, i.e. out of equilibrium, it tends to move back towards equilibrium. If Y exceeds Y_0, firms cannot sell all the output they produce. A reasonable reaction would be to reduce output, moving it closer to Y_0. If Y falls short of Y_0, firms realize that they could sell more than they are currently producing, and so increase production.

What if spending plans change?

The derived unique equilibrium income depends on planned spending. An important question to follow from this is, how does equilibrium income change if one of the actors involved revises spending plans?

Assume that the government raises expenditure by ΔG. Then income obviously also rises by ΔG. But this cannot be the end of the story. Households will

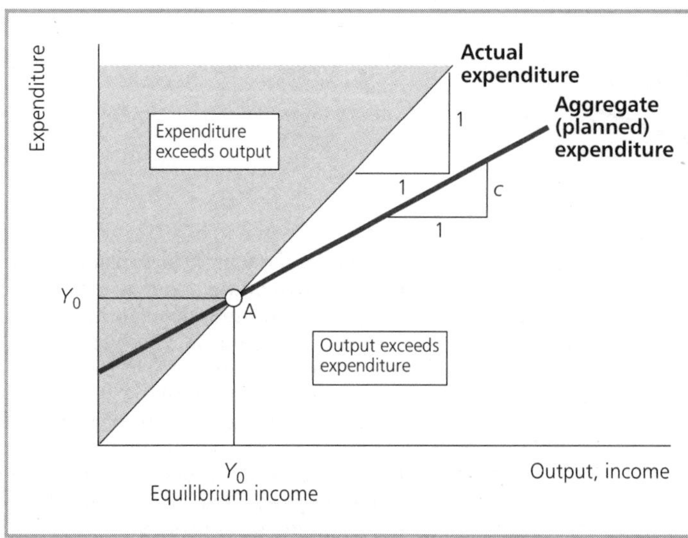

Figure 2.9 The **Keynesian cross** contains two lines. The 45° line measures **actual expenditure** which always equals income. At points above this line, desired demand exceeds output; at points below, the opposite is true. The **aggregate-expenditure** line indicates the sum of all spending plans. Both lines cross in A, meaning that here spending plans are perfectly compatible with income.

want to spend part of this additional income: this added consumer spending again adds to income, which raises consumer spending even further, and so on. This process is complicated and worth looking at in more detail with the help of Figure 2.10 and Table 2.2.

Let the economy initially be in equilibrium at the point labelled A. Now the government increases expenditure per period by one unit ($\Delta G = 1$). We will trace the consequences of this spending increase through a series of fictitious rounds, in order to finally arrive at the cumulative total effect. These rounds may have a time dimension – say, months, because consumers respond to income increases with a lag of one month. Or we may consider the division of the total effect into a number of rounds as simply a conceptional tool to guide the analysis, and the total effect may actually accrue instantaneously thanks to the foresight of firms.

In round #1, one additional unit of government expenditure shifts the aggregate-expenditure line upwards by one unit. This constitutes an increase

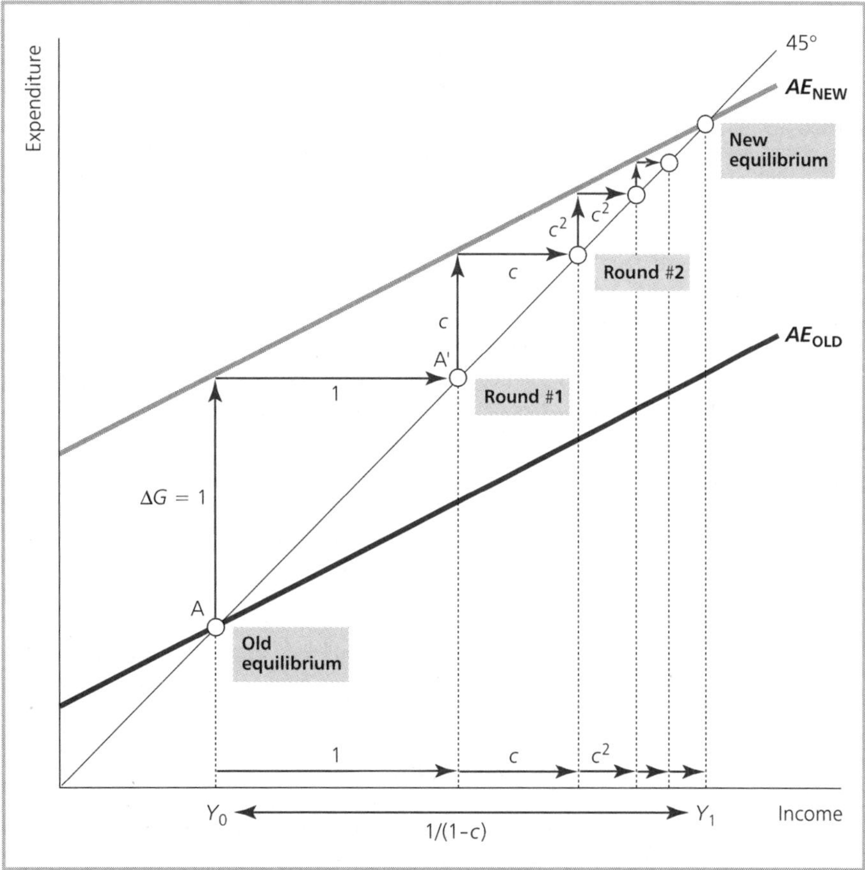

Figure 2.10 If government spending or any other autonomous spending increases by 1, the *AE* line shifts up by 1. Income rises by $\Delta Y > 1$ due to the multiplier effect. The reasoning behind this is that the government's spending increase of 1 not only raises income by 1, leading to point A′. It also induces added consumption of *c*, adding *c* to income. This raises consumption and income by another c^2, and so on. All these effects add up to the **multiplier** $\Delta Y = 1/(1 - c)$.

Table 2.2 Income effects of an increase of government expenditure. The table traces the income gains generated by a one-unit increase in government spending. In round #1, income only rises by 1 as output follows demand. In round #2, individuals want to consume a fraction c out of their income increase experienced in round #1. This raises output and income by c as well, bringing the total effect to $1 + c$ (fifth column). This process continues. The initial demand increase multiplies into more and more additions to demand in subsequent rounds. Note, however, that these additions become smaller and smaller.

Round	ΔG	ΔC	ΔY (this round only)	ΔY (summed over all rounds)
#1	1	0	1	1
#2	0	c	c	$1 + c$
#3	0	c^2	c^2	$1 + c + c^2$
#4	0	c^3	c^3	$1 + c + c^2 + c^3$
⋮	⋮	⋮	⋮	⋮
#237	0	c^{236}	c^{236}	$1 + c + c^2 + c^3 + \cdots + c^{236}$
⋮	⋮	⋮	⋮	⋮

of aggregate spending at the old income level Y_0 by one unit, and also raises income by one unit to $Y_0 + 1$. In round #2, consumers plan to spend the fraction c of their first-round income increase, also raising income by c. By now the total income increase adds up to $1 + c$, and already exceeds the increase in government spending which triggered this process. The process continues, however. In round #3, consumers add a fraction c of their second-round income increase of c to their old level of spending, meaning that they increase consumption by $c \cdot c = c^2$. Income increases by c^2 as well. By analogous reasoning, consumption and income increase by c^3 in round #4, by c^4 in round #5 and so on.

Does this process ever end? Yes and no. With respect to time or rounds, it does go on forever, but the income increases that accrue in each new round will eventually peter out. This is because the marginal propensity to consume c is between zero and one. Raising c to the power of a higher and higher number yields smaller and smaller results. If the second-round effect was $c = 0.8$, the effect in round #11 is already reduced to $c^{10} = 0.107$. This guarantees that the total effect of a one-unit increase of government spending does not grow infinitely large, despite the fact that an algebraic expression for this comprises infinitely many terms:

$$1 + c + c^2 + c^3 + c^4 + \ldots + c^\infty \qquad (2.6)$$

But then how large is the total effect on income? One way to figure this out is by noting that in equilibrium

$$\text{income } Y = \text{aggregate expenditure } AE$$

$$Y = C + I + G + NX \qquad \textbf{Equilibrium condition}$$

Substituting the consumption function (2.5) for C gives

$$Y = cY + I + G + NX$$

Subtracting cY from both sides and dividing by $1 - c$ yields an expression for **equilibrium income** as a function of all autonomous expenditure:

At **equilibrium income** all spending is planned spending (or income equals aggregate expenditure).

$$Y = \frac{1}{1-c}(G + I + NX) \qquad \textbf{Equilibrium income} \qquad (2.7)$$

Maths note. We have hit upon a rule that has many uses in economics: for any parameter $-1 < x < 1$ the series $x^0 + x^1 + x^2 + \ldots$ converges to $1/(1 - x)$ as the exponent grows to infinity. Or, more precisely, $\sum_{i=0}^{\infty} x^i = \frac{1}{1-x}$. As $c^0 = 1$ and $c^1 = c$, the effects listed in equation (2.6) and in Table 2.2 constitute such a series.

Income only changes if either G, I or NX changes:

$$\Delta Y = \frac{1}{1-c}(\Delta G + \Delta I + \Delta NX) \tag{2.8}$$

In our present example we have $\Delta I = \Delta NX = 0$. Substituting this into equation (2.8) and dividing by ΔG gives us

$$\frac{\Delta Y}{\Delta G} = \frac{1}{1-c} \qquad \textbf{Multiplier} \tag{2.9}$$

The **multiplier** measures the income change resulting from a one-unit increase in autonomous expenditure.

An increase of government expenditure (or investment, or net exports) by 1 *multiplies* into an income increase by $1/(1 - c)$. This is why the expression given on the right-hand side is called the **multiplier**. Its numerical value depends on the value of c. For $c = 0.8$ the multiplier is 5. For $c = 0.9$ the multiplier is 10. The verbal explanation is that additional government spending initially makes firms produce just that much more. To be able to do that, they need to employ more labour and pay for it and so income rises. Part of this income returns to the firms as consumption demand. So more labour must be hired and income rises further. When this process comes to a halt, income has risen by the multiplier times the initial increase in government spending.

What has fascinated previous generations of economists (and politicians) about the multiplier is that by raising spending, governments can induce income increases far greater than the initial spending increase. Before we get too excited about this result, however, let me caution that many of the refinements to be discussed in the remaining sections of this chapter and in subsequent chapters will gradually erode the *quantitative* importance of the multiplier.

2.3 INCOME DETERMINATION: A SECOND LOOK

Now that we understand the basic concepts of **equilibrium income** and the **multiplier** we move on to a more realistic scenario. This perspective includes more plausible behavioural and institutional features, and then introduces expectations. We begin by deriving a refined but traditional version of the multiplier.

Disposable income is that part of income left to households after the payment of taxes.

The previous analysis has ignored taxes T. These reduce gross income Y to **disposable income** $Y - T$. Individuals are free only to decide how to split disposable income between consumption and savings. Hence

$$C = c(Y - T) \qquad \textbf{Consumption function} \tag{2.10}$$

In the simplest case, taxes can be thought of as being proportional to income,

$$T = tY \qquad \textbf{Tax equation} \tag{2.11}$$

The **marginal income tax rate** says by how much taxes rise if income rises by one unit. The **average income tax rate** gives the share of taxes on income on average, that is T/Y. In equation (2.11) the marginal and the average income tax rate are the same.

where t is the **marginal and average income tax rate.**

For a first look at imports M, which we shall refine later, let these also be proportional to income.

$$IM = mY \qquad \textbf{Import function} \tag{2.12}$$

where m denotes the marginal propensity to import. We continue to consider the remaining components of demand: I, G and EX exogenous.

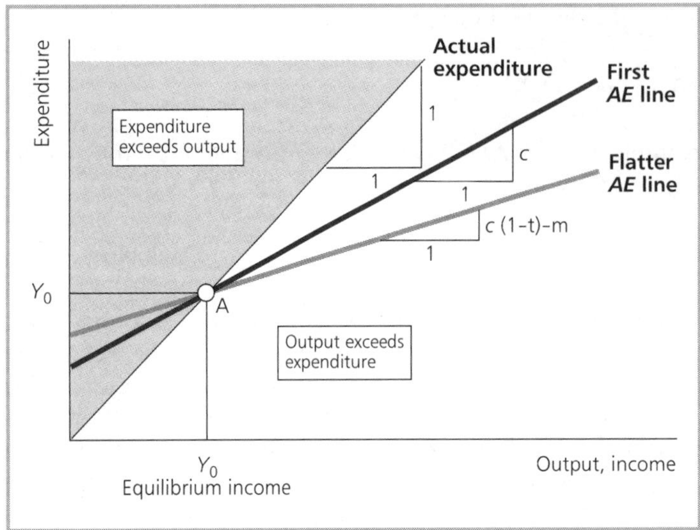

Figure 2.11 If taxes and imports rise with income, the leaks out of the circular flow increase as income rises. Hence, aggregate expenditure does not increase with income as fast as it did in Figure 2.9. This is represented by the flatter *AE* line, which now has slope $c(1 - t) - m$. A flatter *AE* line signals a smaller multiplier effect. (Note that the flatter line is drawn for higher autonomous spending. Otherwise both lines would intersect on the vertical axis, not at A.)

This refined model of aggregate demand yields a much flatter *AE* line than the previous model, as Figure 2.11 illustrates. An equation for the *AE* line is obtained by substituting equations (2.10), (2.11) and (2.12) into (2.1). After collecting terms this gives

$$AE = [c(1 - t) - m]Y + I + G + EX \qquad \textbf{Aggregate expenditure} \qquad (2.13)$$

The slope $c(1 - t) - m$ of the flatter *AE* line is due to two effects. First, income-dependent taxes reduce disposable income to $(1 - t)Y$ even before individuals decide whether to save or consume. Consumption out of each unit of income then is only $c(1 - t)$. Second, m out of each unit of income leaks abroad in payment for imports, so only $c(1 - t) - m$ out of each additional unit of income is used to buy domestically produced goods.

An algebraic expression for equilibrium income in the refined model is obtained by requiring aggregate spending (as shown in equation (2.13)) to equal income. After solving for Y this yields:

$$Y = \frac{1}{1 - c(1 - t) + m}(G + I + EX) \qquad \textbf{Equilibrium income}$$

The new multiplier is obtained by taking first differences, letting $\Delta I = \Delta EX = 0$ and dividing by ΔG:

$$\frac{\Delta Y}{\Delta G} = \frac{1}{1 - c(1 - t) + m} \qquad \textbf{Multiplier} \qquad (2.14)$$

Empirical note. Empirical estimates of multipliers for industrial countries range between values of 1.5 and 3.

Substituting some plausible numbers into the multiplier equations (2.9) and (2.14) illustrates that the achieved refinement has important quantitative consequences. With a marginal propensity to consume of $c = 0.9$, the simple multiplier given in equation (2.9) stands at a value of 10. Now substitute the same value for c into the refined multiplier given in equation (2.14), assume a modest tax rate of $t = 0.2$, let the marginal propensity to import be about one-fifth ($m = 0.22$), and you will arrive at a multiplier of 2.

CASE STUDY 2.2 How to pay for the war: Great Britain in 1940

Many of the tools we encounter in this and subsequent chapters are due to British economist **John Maynard Keynes** (1883–1946), who gave his name to such terms as **Keynesian cross** and **Keynesianism** (for an entire school).

In 1940 Keynes published *How to Pay for the War*. One of the questions raised in this treatise is how Great Britain could meet the economic efforts required by the Second World War without generating inflation. In essence (after streamlining it in some inessential aspects), Keynes's argument runs as follows:

1 Income in 1938 (the latest available data) ran at £5,520 million. *Potential income* was estimated at £6,345 million. So income (output) could increase by $\Delta Y = 6{,}345 - 5{,}520 = £825$ million without risking inflation. (If demand were driven beyond potential income, he assumed, firms would start to raise prices.)

2 How far can government spending be raised without pushing income beyond potential income? The answer is certainly not £825 million! The permitted change of income and therefore the permitted change of government spending are related by the multiplier. We may take the one given in equation (2.14). Letting $m = 0$ (private, income-sensitive imports would be controlled and low during the war), we obtain:

$$\Delta Y = \frac{1}{1 - c(1-t)} \Delta G$$

Knowing that $\Delta Y = 825$, all we need to know to calculate ΔG is c and t.

3 *Assumptions*. Proceeding from the 1938 data $Y = 5{,}520$, $C = 4{,}380$ and $T = 770$, a reasonable guess is to assume that marginal and average consumption and tax rates are the same, that is $c = C/Y = 4{,}380/5{,}520$ and $t = T/Y = 770/5{,}520$.

4 *Result*. Substituting the obtained rates $c = 0.79$ and $t = 0.14$ into the multiplier expression gives a multiplier of 3.15. Letting $\Delta Y = 825$ and solving the multiplier equation for ΔG finally yields $\Delta G = 262$. Therefore, government spending can be geared up by £262 million (in 1938 prices) without triggering inflation. If that doesn't provide sufficient funds, tax rates may have to be raised (if politically feasible), which in turn reduces the multiplier and drives equilibrium income down.

Keynes's assumptions, line of argument and results may also be presented graphically in the context of the Keynesian-cross diagram (see Figure 1).

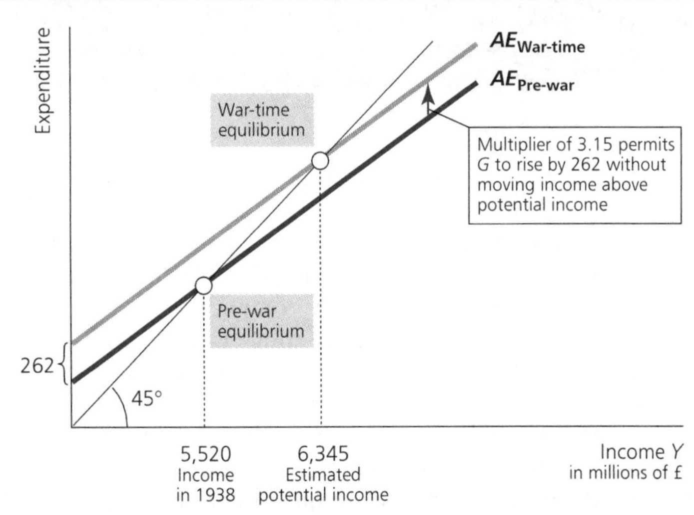

Figure 1

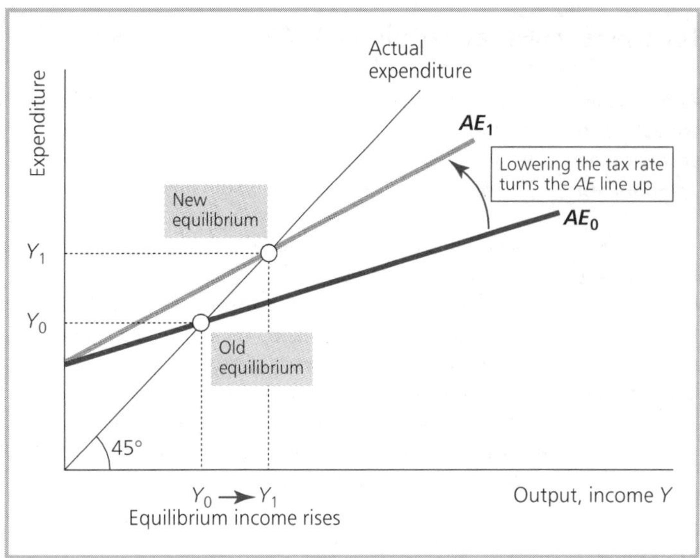

Figure 2.12 If the marginal tax rate is lowered, households retain more disposable income at any level of gross income. Since households spend a constant fraction of disposable income, they spend more at any given level of income. The upward shift of this spending is shown by turning the aggregate expenditure curve from AE_0 into AE_1. With more spending out of given income, equilibrium income is higher.

Therefore, the government's fiscal policies can now influence income via a second channel. If the government decreases the marginal rate of income taxation, disposable income increases, the multiplier increases and the *AE* line becomes steeper (see Figure 2.12). Equilibrium income rises from Y_0 to Y_1.

We conclude this chapter by discussing consumption and investment demand from a more modern *intertemporal perspective*. The payoff will be a first encounter with expectations, which play a prominent role in modern economic analysis, and a first insight into when it is safe to work with the multiplier model, and when not to.

2.4 AN INTERTEMPORAL VIEW OF CONSUMPTION AND INVESTMENT

A second look at consumption

Relationships such as the consumption function $C = cY$ used above are necessarily simplifications, i.e. abstractions of reality. Today's economists agree that individuals make consumption decisions in the context of a rather intricate optimization problem. The approach taken here is that such precise, micro-based consumption behaviour is overly complicated and therefore not practical for many applications. So we will continue to work with simplifications, while trying to foster an understanding of those circumstances under which they break down.

Why is $C = cY$ a simplification? First, people evidently do not consume, say, 80% of their income on their weekly or monthly payday. They realize that the pay covers a given period of work and so spread consumption possibilities more or less evenly over that period. But if people are intelligent enough to realize and do that, wouldn't they apply the same principle if they inherited €1,000,000 at age 21? Assume that you inherited that sum under the condition that you refrained from any other paid work for the rest of your life. What would your consumption spending plan look like? You would probably try to spread consumption possibilities deriving from the inherited fortune over your expected lifetime. Your consumption during the first year after your twenty-first birthday would only be a very small fraction of the inherited million.

These ideas can be generalized. Utility-maximizing individuals will not adjust current consumption to every kink in the development of their income. In much the same way as they do over the course of a month, individuals would like to obtain a smooth consumption path over their lifetime. The restriction is, of course, that they usually cannot spend more than they earn. But because of the possibility of obtaining loans and to save, this need not apply for each period of time, but only over the total lifetime.

Figure 2.13 shows a stylized but fairly typical income pattern over an individual's lifetime (light blue lines). As a rule, income rises during the early stages of a career as the person becomes more productive and experienced. Income then levels out during the later years of the person's career. On retirement, income drops to some fraction of previous income levels, depending on the retirement plan and the amount of private savings.

Ideally, individuals would like to keep consumption fairly constant along a path like the light grey lines in Figure 2.13. However, this may not always be possible, particularly because of the reluctance of banks to extend loans to young people on the mere expectation of higher future income. But it is what individuals would prefer. So to simplify the argument, if we ignore bequests, rule out that individuals die in debt, and ignore interest payments on savings, total (planned) lifetime consumption equals total (expected) lifetime earnings. Consumption per period equals expected lifetime income divided by expected remaining lifetime n:

$$C = \frac{1}{n} Y + \frac{1}{n} (Y^e_{+1} + Y^e_{+2} + Y^e_{+3} + \ldots + Y^e_{+n-1})$$

The superscripts e on each Y in parentheses indicate that individuals do not know this value yet, but have to form an **expectation** of it. Y^e_{+1} is the income

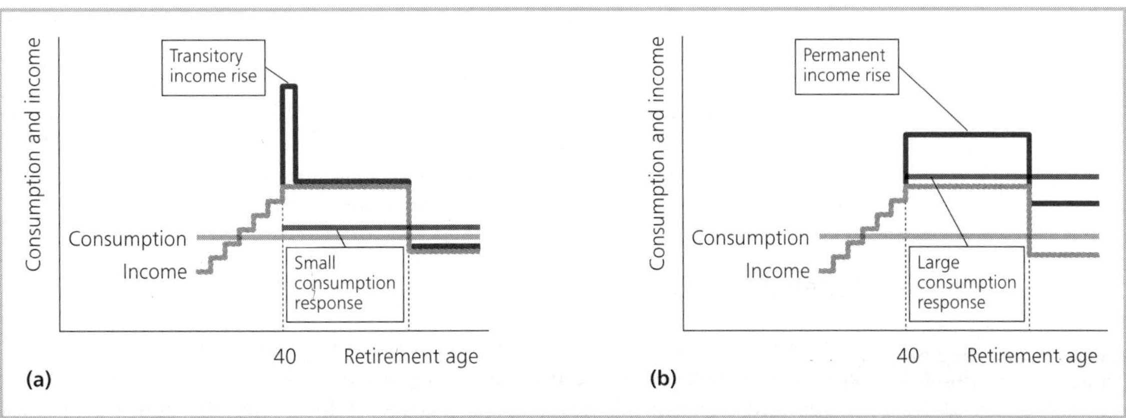

Figure 2.13 Lifetime patterns of income exhibit rising and falling sections as illustrated by the light blue line. The grey line is the attached consumption plan. A perceived transitory income rise (panel (a)) increases consumption by very little. A perceived permanent income rise (panel (b)) results in a large consumption response.

expected one period from today in the future. Note that while the series given in parentheses may represent a complicated time profile of income, it is simply all income expected from tomorrow until we die. For the sake of notational convenience, we may denote this sum of all expected future income by Y_+^e to obtain the more compact consumption function

$$C = \frac{1}{n} Y + \frac{1}{n} Y_+^e \tag{2.15}$$

Now let individuals enjoy an income increase in period 40. The first question to ask is whether or not this was expected. If the experienced income rise is part of the expected lifetime income pattern, there is absolutely no need to revise the lifetime consumption plan, and consumption will not respond at all.

Things are different if income increased unexpectedly, way beyond what the lifetime pattern prescribed (blue lines in Figure 2.13). Then a second crucial question must be asked: will the individual be able to sustain this added stream of income in the future? Or is it purely temporary, windfall income that will not have an impact on expected future income streams?

Empirical note. Empirical studies indicate that the marginal propensity to consume out of permanent income increases is close to 1, say 0.9. Out of transitory income increases, individuals consume much less, between 0.2 and 0.4. This is much more, however, than our theoretical arguments would suggest.

Panel (a) in Figure 2.13 illustrates the case in which the unexpected income bonus is considered to be purely *temporary*. Then expected lifetime income only increases by a very small percentage and the consumption of this period's income bonus is spread out over all the remaining periods of one's life. This is reflected in a very small upwards shift of the consumption path in period 40.

In panel (b), the increase in income is considered to be *permanent*. This shifts the entire pattern of income upward by the observed change of income and the impact on expected lifetime income is very large. The response to this increase is to consume roughly the full amount of the income increase during this period.

The lesson to be learned from this is that *exceptional* (or *transitory*) income, i.e. not expected to accrue regularly, period after period, produces consumption reactions quite different from those to *regular* (or *permanent*) income. Thus, when we apply our models, it is advisable to ask whether individuals consider an experienced income change permanent or transitory. Only in the first case may we expect to observe a substantial increase in consumption demand via multiplier effects.

The above discussion provides a first opportunity to appreciate that economic decisions are made on the basis of what people expect to happen in the future (will income stay up permanently?) rather than what they observe today. This **pivotal role of expectations** will be a recurring theme throughout this book, and is a general characteristic of modern economics.

When do firms invest?

Capital costs are the costs of financing the purchase of capital goods. They equal the interest payment for a loan, or the interest foregone because money was invested and not lent out.

The motive behind investment is to make profits. Profits accrue as the difference between the gross returns generated by a project relative to the invested funds and the **capital costs**, i.e. the costs of financing the acquired capital goods. Figure 2.14 illustrates this basic principle and demonstrates how this cost-benefit calculation by firms determines the volume of investment during a given period.

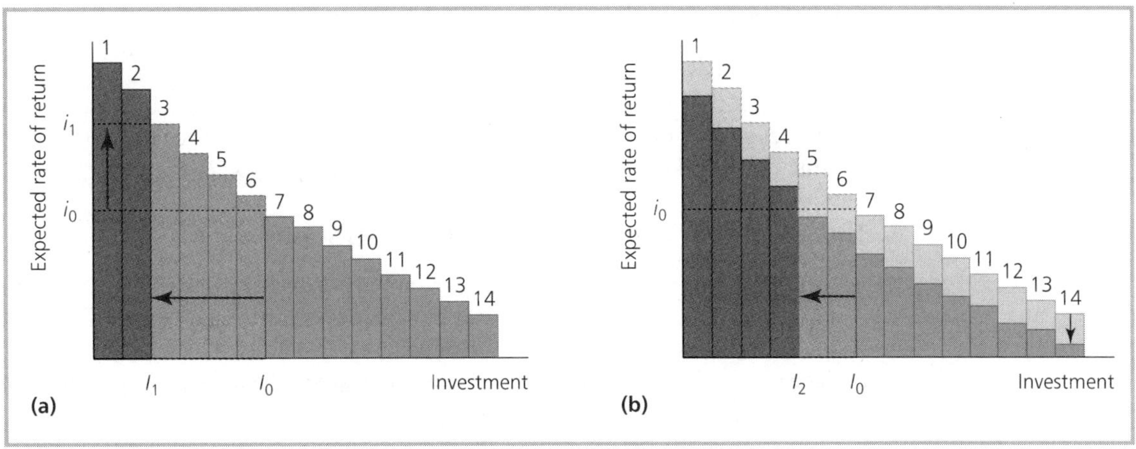

Figure 2.14 Both panels rank investment projects by their expected internal rate of return. Only those projects are realized whose rates of return exceed the interest rate. Panel (a) shows that a rising interest rate reduces investment. Panel (b) shows that falling expected rates of return, due to lower expected future income, reduce investment.

The internal **rate of return** is the revenue generated by a project as a percentage of the invested funds.

At any point in time a very large number of potential investment projects exists. Each project has its own (expected) internal **rate of return.** Both panels in Figure 2.14 rank all projects according to their respective internal rates of return. Each project is represented by a column. The height marks the rate of return expected from this project. The width indicates the project's investment volume to be assigned to the current period.

The internal rate of return represents expected gross profits generated by the project. Only if these exceed capital costs, or the returns from capital had it been put to other uses, will the firm go ahead with the investment project. So for each project the rate of return must be compared with the interest rate at which the firm could borrow or lend (we simplify by assuming that both rates are the same). At an interest rate i_0 only the first six projects have a higher rate of return and will therefore be implemented. All the other projects remain on the drawing board. Total investment at an interest rate i_0 is I_0.

What happens if the interest rate changes? Let i increase to i_1 (panel (a)). Now projects #3, #4, #5 and #6 become unprofitable and will be dropped. Total investment falls to I_1. This holds generally. If capital costs in the economy, as measured by the interest rate, increase, while all other things remain unchanged, investment falls. We may thus assume a negative relationship between investment and the interest rate.

The second factor we identified as a determinant of investment demand is the internal rate of return. Anything that changes this rate affects today's investment. The rate of return to be expected from a project crucially depends on the demand expected during the lifetime of the project. Since we know that demand varies positively with income, if the firm expects aggregate income to be lower in the future, it can expect a lower internal rate of return. Panel (b) illustrates the economy-wide effect. If expected income falls, this decreases the expected internal rates of return of all investment projects. At a given interest rate i_0, formerly feasible projects #5 and #6 now become unprofitable and total investment falls from I_0 to I_2.

Generalization of these arguments gives the investment function

$$I = aY^e_+ - b\,i$$

which states that investment is a function of all expected future income and of the current rate of interest. Current income is not included because it is safe to assume that it takes at least one period for the project to generate any sales.

The Keynesian cross with income expectations

So what are the implications of this for our previous determination of equilibrium income in the circular flow and for the expenditure multiplier? The first result, that a unique equilibrium income level exists and that a neat first attempt to determine it is at the point of intersection between the aggregate demand line and the 45° line in the Keynesian cross, remains intact. The multiplier, however, has lost some of its pervasiveness and must be handled with much more care.

Figure 2.15 draws a distinction between the *AE* line resulting from perceived **permanent income** increases and from perceived temporary or **transitory income** increases. In the first case the line is fairly steep, not only because *c* may be reasonably large, as in previous sections, but because the higher expected future income may also raise investment. An increase in autonomous expenditure (such as government expenditure or exports) then raises income via a significant multiplier. With a perceived transitory income increase, the line is rather flat, particularly if the economy is also very open, with a substantial share of consumption leaking abroad. Then the multiplier effect can be very small, or virtually absent. We must keep these insights in mind when we extend and refine our model in subsequent chapters.

This chapter's analysis has an important **bottom line**: small changes in autonomous expenditure may cause large changes in income. Thus booms and recessions can be triggered by the government changing spending levels, by booms and recessions abroad that affect our exports, or by changes in consumption or investment spending. At the root of the last two effects may be changes in the income tax rate, expectations of income changes in the future or changes in the interest rate.

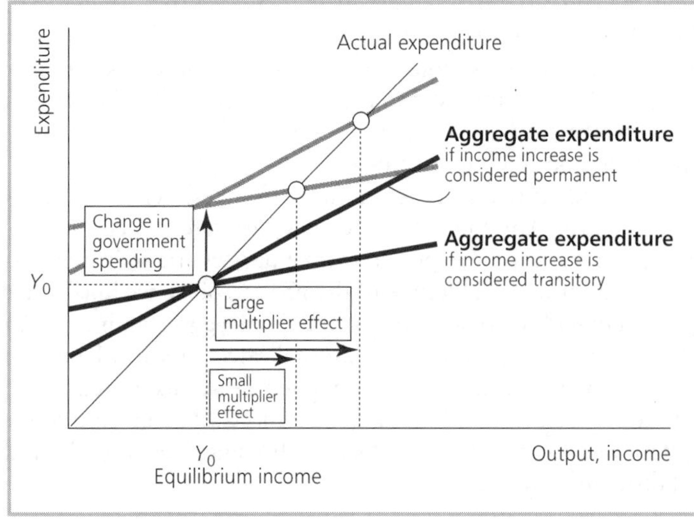

Figure 2.15 For changes of income that are regarded as permanent, the aggregate-expenditure line is very steep. Accordingly, multiplier effects are fairly large. If an income increase is considered transitory, both the slope of the aggregate-expenditure line and the multiplier effect are small.

CHAPTER SUMMARY

- A country's income at a given point in time is determined by the steady-state level of income, the deviation of potential income from steady-state income, and the deviation of income from potential income. The latter is called the business cycle.
- In the circular flow model there exists one equilibrium level of income at which actual spending is exactly as planned. What sets this level of income apart from all other feasible income levels is that firms will try to set production to this very level to avoid having to invest or disinvest involuntarily.
- An increase in autonomous expenditure, such as government purchases, generates an income increase that may vastly exceed the original stimulus. This multiplier effect occurs because the exogenous spending increase raises income and thus induces consumers to spend more and raise income even higher.
- When the multiplier is large, small changes in government expenditure or other autonomous injections or leakages may cause sizeable booms or recessions.
- Factors that reduce the size of the multiplier are high marginal income tax rates and a high marginal propensity to import.
- Consumption does not depend on current income only, but more importantly on expected future income.
- Multiplier effects apply fully only if consumers consider observed income changes to be permanent.
- The multiplier becomes much smaller if observed income changes are considered transitory.
- Investment rises when expected future income rises and when the interest rate falls.

KEY TERMS AND CONCEPTS

actual expenditure
aggregate (planned) expenditure
average income tax rate
boom
business cycle
capital costs
consumption function
disposable income
equilibrium income
government purchases
import function
Keynesian cross
marginal income tax rate
marginal propensity to consume
multiplier
net taxes
permanent income
planned investment
potential income
rate of return
recession
steady-state income
transitory income

EXERCISES

2.1 (a) Trace potential income in Figure 2.3 in the main text.

(b) Consider French real output between 1900 and 1994 as given in Figure 2.16. Add your guess of the paths of steady-state income and potential income to the graph.

2.2 Figure 2.17 displays the evolution of real GDP between 1978 and 2002 for the United States and France.

(a) Try to identify business cycles, marking peaks and troughs on the graphs.

(b) Identify the US position in 1982 in a diagram with prices on the vertical axis and income on the horizontal axis.

(c) Two US economists, Arthur F. Burns and Wesley C. Mitchell, claimed half a century ago that the typical business cycle lasts between six and thirty-two quarters. Does this agree with your findings?

(d) Given the data of the past, what is your forecast for the development of the American and French real GDP for the years to come?

2.3 Consider an economy with the following data (note that I is *planned* investment, which may not coincide with actual investment):

$C = 750 \quad I = 500 \quad T = 0 \quad G = 250$
$NX = 250 \quad Y = 1{,}000$

(a) Is this economy's circular flow in equilibrium in the sense that firms do not have to change inventories involuntarily?

(b) Translate the above data into a diagram with demand on the vertical axis and income on the horizontal axis.

(c) Suppose $C = 0.75Y$. Draw the aggregate-expenditure and the actual-expenditure lines. Identify demand-determined income in equilibrium.

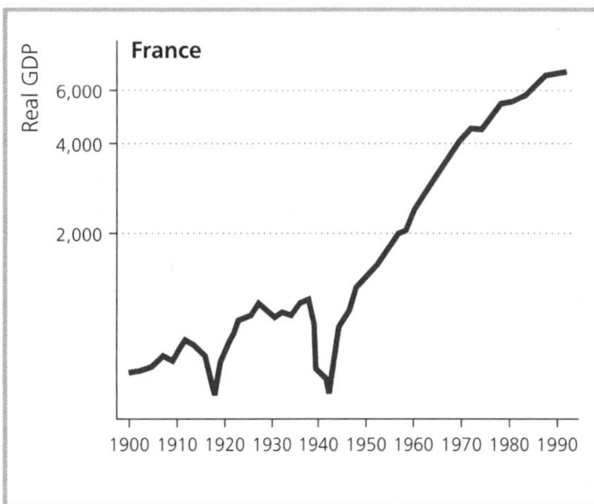

Figure 2.16

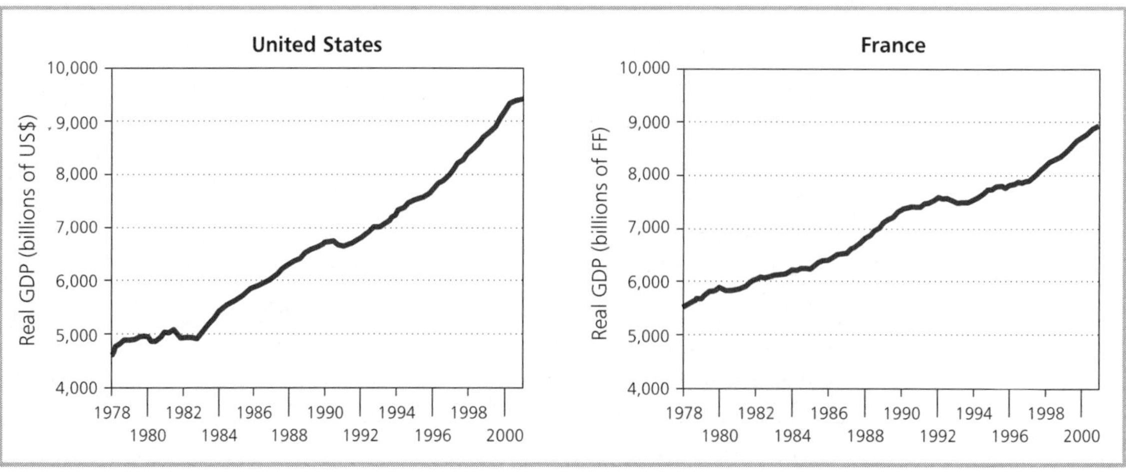

Figure 2.17

(d) What happens to equilibrium income if government expenditure increases by 500 units? Show your result in a graph and verify that it is supported by the multiplier formula of equation (2.9).

(e) Using a graph, show what happens if net exports fall from 250 to 100.

(f) Using a graph, show what happens if the marginal propensity to consume rises from 0.75 to 0.8.

2.4 One effect of German unification was a rise in demand for most European countries' exports. However, the impact differed considerably among European countries, depending on the multipliers that transform an exogenous change in demand into a change in income.

Consider the Netherlands and the United Kingdom. The share of imports in Dutch GDP is 52%, the share of imports in British GDP is 27%. Assume that these average import propensities are also the marginal propensities to import. Assume, further, that for both countries the marginal propensity to consume is 80% and the average tax rate is 30%.

(a) Calculate the effect of an exogenous increase of export demand by 100 units on Dutch and British GDP.

(b) Employ the successive-rounds interpretation of the multiplier. By how much has equilibrium income increased after round #3?

2.5 In the summer of 1991 the German parliament imposed a surcharge of 7.5% on personal and corporate income tax (the so-called *Solidaritätszuschlag*), promising that this tax surcharge would be removed after one year. However, following a decision in March 1993 the solidarity surcharge was reintroduced in January 1995 and was still in effect in 1996. What would you expect aggregate consumption to look like, starting at the first announcement of the solidarity surcharge? Does it make any difference whether individuals believed the government's pledge that the surcharge would be removed after one year?

2.6 Figure 2.18 shows quarterly data for nominal GDP and nominal consumption in France. (Both time series are deviations from a non-linear trend.) What is your interpretation of these time series in the light of the hypothesis that consumption only responds to permanent changes of income?

2.7 Consider the economy of exercise 2.3. However, let investment depend on the interest rate in the following form:

$$I = \bar{I} - b\,i$$

with $\bar{I} = 500$ and $b = 5{,}000$

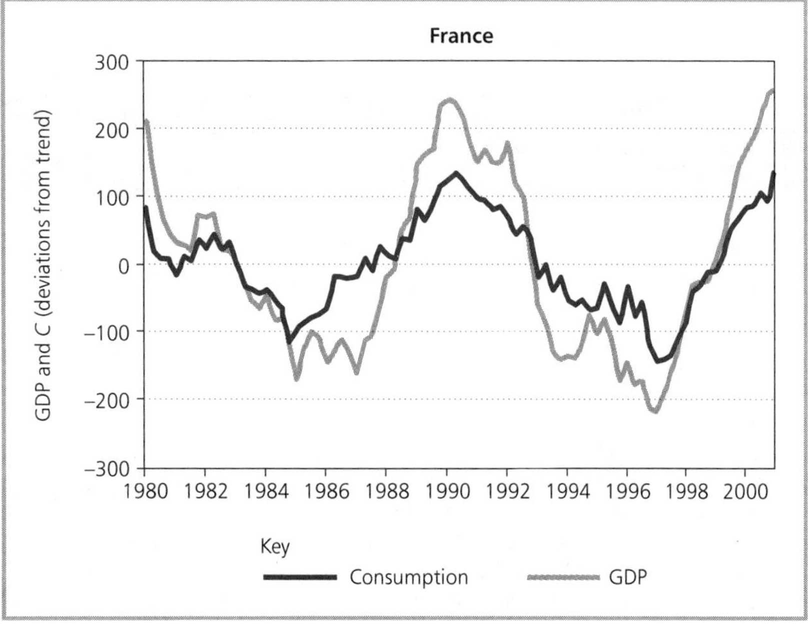

Figure 2.18

(a) Assume that, due to the increasingly pessimistic expectations of investors, autonomous investment decreases from 500 to 300. The interest rate and all other exogenous variables stay constant. Calculate the resulting change in equilibrium income.

(b) At the same time the interest rate decreases from 0.06 to 0.05. Calculate the effect on equilibrium income.

2.8 Consider the economy of exercise 2.7. The government increases expenditure from 250 to 750 (i.e. $\Delta G = 500$). This additional expenditure is financed partly by taxes, which account for 50% of government revenue, and partly by issuing bonds. This sudden appearance of huge quantities of government bonds on the capital market drives up interest rates from 0.05 to 0.06. What is the effect on equilibrium income? Would it have been better to finance the expenditure entirely by taxes?

2.9 Investment decisions not only depend on the interest rate but also on expectations of the future overall economic situation, represented by future GDP.

(a) Through what channels might Y enter the investment decision?

(b) Assume that, to form their expectations about future GDP, investors simply extrapolate today's GDP, that is: $Y^e_+ = Y$. Moreover, assume that these expectations enter the investment function in the following form (note that we neglect the influence of the interest rate):

$$I = \alpha Y.$$

(i) How will this modification affect the multiplier?

(ii) Derive the multiplier for this case, in which Y influences investment.

RECOMMENDED READING

While much of the discussion in this and the next chapter derive from John Maynard Keynes's thinking, his writing is very heavy-going and reading it at this stage may confuse rather than enlighten. The graphical apparatus on which we rely has been introduced by John Hicks (1937) 'Mr. Keynes and the "Classics": A suggested interpretation', *Econometrica* 5: 147–59. Concepts such as the Keynesian cross and the multiplier are discussed extensively in almost every macroeconomics textbook. If you desire a more extended or alternative discussion, consult any introductory or intermediate macroeconomics text.

APPLIED PROBLEMS

SEASONED RESEARCH

Consumption out of permanent and transitory income

One important issue in the context of the simple macroeconomic model discussed in Chapter 2 is whether consumption does respond to all income changes, whether or not individuals consider them transitory or permanent. Addressing this very issue, Michael R. Darby, in 'The permanent income theory of consumption – a restatement' (1974, *Quarterly Journal of Economics* 88: 228–50), looks at the relationship between personal consumption expenditures C, and the permanent component Y^P and the transitory component Y^T of disposable income in the United States. Employing the statistical method of ordinary least square (OLS) described in the Appendix (pp. 434–50) he arrives at the following equation (the numbers in parentheses are absolute t-statistics):

$$C = -1.35 + 0.93Y^P + 0.57Y^T \qquad R^2 = 0.999$$
$$(0.49) \quad (121.6) \quad (3.40)$$

The obtained coefficients suggest that if permanent income increases by one dollar, consumption rises by 93 cents. If the income increase is considered transitory, consumption rises by only 57 cents. According to our rule of thumb that coefficients are significantly different from zero only if they carry absolute t-statistics larger than 2, the constant term is not significant, but the other two coefficients are.

The coefficient of determination called R^2 is high. At 0.999 it suggests that the estimated equation explains US consumption spending very well.

WORKED PROBLEM

Pizza e pasta – consuming in Italy

Table 2.3 contains data on consumption spending C and on disposable income $(Y - T)$ in billion lire for Italy.

As a first step, we want to find out how well these data comply with the simple consumption function $C = c_0 + c_1(Y - T)$. The OLS method yields

$$C = -3{,}764.9 + \underset{(5.11)}{} 0.71(Y - T) \quad \underset{(486.5)}{}$$

$$C = -3{,}764.9 + 0.71(Y - T)$$
$$\quad (5.11) \qquad (486.5)$$

$R^2 = 0.999$ Annual data 1961–91

As in the above example from published research, this even simpler equation explains Italian consumption almost perfectly. The marginal propensity to consume is found to be 0.71. The t-statistic of 486.5 renders this coefficient highly significant.

It can be argued that parts of consumption spending cannot be adjusted to changing income immediately: your summer vacation that has been booked since the previous autumn; high car maintenance costs that can only be reduced by selling the car at a loss; your second daughter who insists on taking ballet lessons just like her older sister, and so on. To allow for such adjustment lags we may suppose that only desired consumption C^* is related to income, that is $C^* = c_0 + c_1(Y - T)$. If desired consumption drifts away from actual consumption, the response of actual consumption only closes a fraction α of this gap. Formally we may write $C - C_{-1} = \alpha(C^* - C_{-1})$. Substituting the above explanation of desired consumption for C^* in the partial adjustment equation yields $C = \alpha c_0 + (1 - \alpha)C_{-1} + \alpha c_1(Y - T)$. Estimating this equation yields

$$C = -1{,}830.6 + 0.22C_{-1} + 0.57(Y - T)$$
$$\qquad (3.07) \quad (6.31) \qquad (25.10)$$

$R^2 = 0.999$ Annual data 1961–91

The autoregressive coefficient (the one in front of C_{-1}) $0.22 = 1 - \alpha$ carries a t-statistic of 6.31, rendering it highly significant. The coefficient of disposable income is also significant, but smaller than in our first estimate above. Note, however, that it represents the product αc_1. Since α is estimated at 0.78, we may compute $c_1 = 0.57/0.78 = 0.73$, which barely differs from the previous estimate. So while the long-run marginal propensity to consume is the same as estimated above, the short-run effect is smaller. If disposable income increases by 100,000L, consumption immediately goes up by 57,000L. This is not the end, however. One period later, consumption goes up by another $0.22 \times 57{,}000 = 12{,}540$L, one period later by another $0.22 \times 0.22 \times 57{,}000 = 2{,}758.8$L, and so on. So while the partial adjustment version of the consumption function estimates the same overall response of consumption as the simple version, it suggests that the response is spread over a longer span of time.

YOUR TURN

Consumption function in first differences

One thing to note in the above study of Italian consumption functions is that both consumption and

Table 2.3

Year	C	$Y-T$	Year	C	$Y-T$	Year	C	$Y-T$
1960	14,561	22,520	1971	43,660	65,960	1982	335,448	475,205
1961	15,919	25,151	1972	47,951	72,136	1983	387,170	553,129
1962	17,967	28,215	1973	58,484	86,914	1984	443,268	634,682
1963	21,017	32,109	1974	73,637	108,296	1985	498,048	706,280
1964	22,784	34,988	1975	85,972	120,875	1986	551,868	782,365
1965	24,366	37,708	1976	106,383	153,198	1987	606,889	858,348
1966	26,873	40,973	1977	129,209	187,982	1988	670,883	953,439
1967	29,767	45,192	1978	150,848	222,825	1989	740,267	1,037,647
1968	31,762	49,082	1979	185,051	275,473	1990	806,593	1,137,230
1969	34,838	54,302	1980	236,603	344,912	1991	881,171	1,231,558
1970	39,992	60,652	1981	284,030	406,106			

disposable income show a clear upward trend during the thirty-one years considered here. This can be a problem. Regressing two heavily trended variables on each other may give a statistically significant result, although the two have nothing to do with each other (a classic example is the negative correlation between the number of telephones and the number of storks during the first half of the 20th century). In an attempt to alleviate this problem we may compute first differences on both sides of the consumption function to obtain $\Delta C = c_1 \Delta(Y - T)$. Please check whether this formulation is supported by the data.

To further explore this chapter's key messages you are encouraged to use the interactive online module found at

www.fgn.unisg.ch/eurmacro/tutor/Keynesiancross.html

and many other features hosted at **www.fgn.unisg.ch/eurmacro**

CHAPTER 3

MONEY, INTEREST RATES AND THE GLOBAL ECONOMY

WHAT TO EXPECT

After working through this chapter, you will understand:

1 Why it is useful to divide the economy into a **goods market**, a **money market** and a **foreign exchange market**.

2 Which variables determine and are influenced by the **interest rate**.

3 Under what conditions the goods market and the money market are in **equilibrium** – separately and simultaneously.

4 How **fiscal** and **monetary policy** affect income in the global economy.

5 More about how to **work with graphs**.

With Athens leading the way by coining silver around 700 years BC, Europe has a long tradition of making economic transactions by using money. The discussion of equilibrium income and the multiplier in Chapter 2 did not really need money. Just as in our first look at the circular flow model in Chapter 1, it was possible to exchange the real thing: labour, goods and services. This analysis yielded important first insights, but was also bound to leave loose ends.

For instance, we found that a crucial determinant of investment was the interest rate. Yet we have no idea what determines the interest rate. It certainly does not move about arbitrarily. In fact, it is what we forfeit if we decide to retain money – coins and notes – in our pockets instead of putting it in an interest-bearing bank account. So understanding the interest rate seems impossible without considering **money**.

Also, the discussion of exports and imports in Chapter 2 remained silent about the exchange rate. This facilitated our first look at equilibrium income and the multiplier. But it needs to be remedied as we move on to a more realistic view. The exchange rate is the price of one country's money in terms of another country's money. So again, we need to bring money into the picture in order to understand **exchange rates**.

The **exchange rate** is the price of one unit of foreign currency in terms of domestic currency.

This and the next chapter pick up these loose ends and tie them together. Step by step we will arrive at a richer picture of the economy which will eventually enable us to discuss many important new questions that Chapter 2's simple multiplier model cannot handle. The knowledge acquired in Chapter 2 will find its way into this extended model. In addition to the goods market, which is all Chapter 2's economy consists of, we will look at the domestic money market in this chapter and at the foreign exchange market in Chapter 4.

3.1 THE MONEY MARKET, THE INTEREST RATE AND THE *LM* CURVE

The notion of a **money market**, in which supply and demand interact, may sound odd. It appears plausible that the central bank controls the **supply of money** by printing and issuing coins and bills. It seems less straightforward to imagine a well-defined **demand for money**. People certainly want as much money as possible! So how can there ever be an equilibrium between a finite supply and an unlimited demand?

At the root of such reservations lies a confusion between wealth and money. **Wealth** has been accumulated through past savings. **Money** is a form of

BOX 3.1 What is money?

There is no simple answer to this question and only in a few cases will the answer to whether or not some asset is money be an unequivocal yes or no. Norwegian kroner will certainly do the trick in Oslo or Trondheim (and maybe even in Copenhagen, but probably not in Florence). A Eurocheque or a Visa card are other options. Both draw on your bank account, and will fail in certain instances. Stocks will only be accepted on rare occasions. Your car, your house? Probably not.

So there is obviously no strict way of telling what is money and what is not. Central bank statistics therefore offer a number of different data series on money, and economists use these as considered appropriate for the problem at hand. The most narrow aggregate includes all coins and bills in circulation plus those that private banks are required to hold as reserves in the central bank's vaults. This aggregate is called the **monetary base**, or **high-powered money**, or simply **M0**. It has the advantage of being under the direct and perfect control of the central bank. Its disadvantage is that it is clearly an incomplete measure of liquidity. Demand deposits (wealth held in bank accounts that can be withdrawn on demand, that is, without prior notice) on which cheques can be written or credit cards used can serve as a means of payment in all but the most trivial or rare situations. **M1** adds demand deposits to M0. **M2** and **M3** widen the spectrum by including assets with successively lower degrees of liquidity.

- M0 (monetary base, high-powered money): currency (coins and bills) in circulation plus cash reserves held by private banks at the central bank.
- M1: M0 plus demand deposits.
- M2: M1 plus savings deposits with unrestricted access plus small-denomination time deposits.
- M3: M2 plus large-denomination time deposits.

As mentioned above, only M0 is under perfect control of the central bank and, hence, classifies as a policy instrument. But the demand deposits included in M1 can be influenced by the central bank, via reserve requirements (the central bank requires private banks to hold a certain fraction of their demand deposits in cash at the central bank), although they are finally determined in the market. Central bank control is even weaker over M2 and M3. So with what justification can we speak of a monetary policy? The key assumption is that there is another **multiplier** m′, a fixed relationship between the control variable M0 and the targeted aggregates (for example, $M1 = m'1 \times M0$). To the extent that this is true, it does not matter too much with which definition of money we work.

Empirically, money multipliers have been found to be relatively stable. Observed changes reflect the financial innovations that have been introduced over the past two decades.

holding wealth. Alternatively, and predominantly, wealth is held in other forms: in interest-bearing bank accounts, as government securities or corporate bonds, stocks, real estate and so on. The advantage of such assets over money is that they offer higher (expected) returns. Then why do people hold any money at all? Because it provides a service which the other assets cannot deliver.

Recall that in Chapter 1 money was defined as anything that sellers generally accept as payment for goods and services. So if individuals hold money, in the first place it is because they need it for transactions in the goods market. The demand for money is basically a demand for the services of money. The main service of money is that it permits or facilitates purchases. Instead of looking at the choice involved in the abstract, consider the following illustration.

To streamline the argument, assume that there are only two assets: money, which yields no interest, and savings accounts which yield a fixed interest per period. Let the economy be represented by one consumer only. She receives income Y_0 once a month, is left with disposable income $Y_0 - T$ after taxes, and regularly consumes $C_0 = c(Y_0 - T)$. Consumption is a **flow variable**, measured from the beginning to the end of a month. Money, by contrast, is a **stock variable**, measured at a particular moment in time. The consumer's money holdings cannot possibly remain constant over the course of a month, as money is being held for the very purpose of getting rid of it in exchange for goods and services. So if we ask how much money the consumer holds, we are talking about *average* holdings during the entire month.

A **flow variable** is measured over a *period* of time. Examples are income, consumption and exports.

A **stock variable** is measured at a *point* in time. Examples are the money supply, the number of workers and the capital stock.

How much money does the consumer hold? Well, she has a large set of choices. One possibility is shown in panel (a) of Figure 3.1. If she decides to go to the bank only once a month, she must obtain money in the amount of consumption C_0. Otherwise she could not carry out her consumption plan. If purchases are spread evenly over the month, her money holdings decline linearly day by day and hit bottom on the evening before the next pay day. The *average* holding of money, or her **demand for money**, is obviously $C_0/2$.

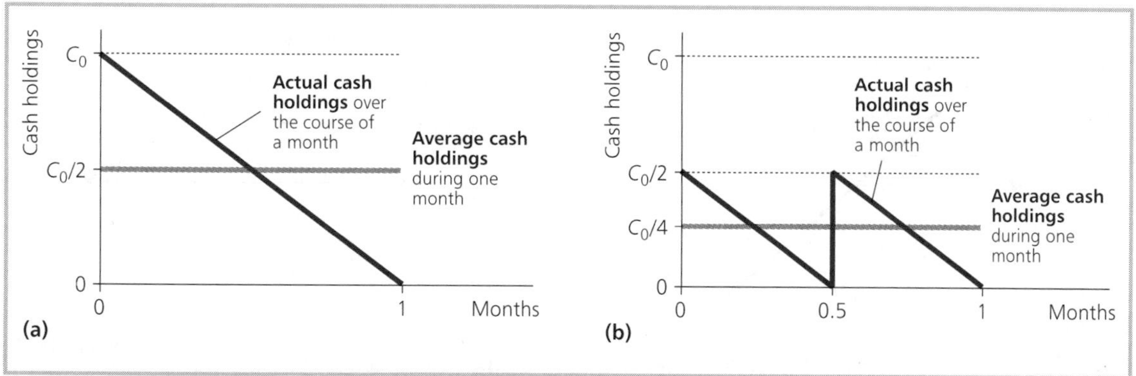

Figure 3.1 With one monthly trip to the bank, all cash (or money) that buys a month's consumption C_0 must be picked up. Cash linearly declines from C_0 to 0 during one month (panel (a)). With two monthly trips to the bank only, cash worth $C_0/2$ must be picked up each time. It declines to 0 in half a month (panel (b)). Average cash holdings equal $C_0/2$ in the first case and $C_0/4$ in the second.

Panel (b) in Figure 3.1 shows a second option. On receiving her salary the consumer may opt for cash withdrawal of half the pay only, depositing the other half in a savings account. In this case she will be out of cash by the middle of the month and must make an additional trip to the bank to withdraw the second half of her salary from the savings account. In this case, average money holdings are easily found to average $C_0/4$. The average demand for money can be reduced further by going to the bank weekly or even daily. A general formula for average money demand is then $C_0/(2n) = c(Y_0 - T)/(2n)$, where n denotes the number of trips to the bank per month.

How often does the consumer go to the bank? This decision must result from a reasoning process that weighs benefits against costs. To hold a lot of money on average carries the *benefit* that withdrawal fees and time losses associated with a trip to the bank or to the cash machine are being kept low. The *costs* of holding a lot of money arise from the interest earnings foregone by not putting part of the income temporarily into the savings account. If the interest rate rises, these costs go up too. Individuals will then respond by going to the bank more often, and by holding less money on average.

Maths note. Solve (3.1) for i to obtain $i = kY/h - L/h$, which defines a surface the height of which is measured in i. Holding Y constant leaves a negative relationship between i and L. Holding i constant leaves a positive relationship between Y and L. The figure below shows vertical slices cut parallel to the L axis.

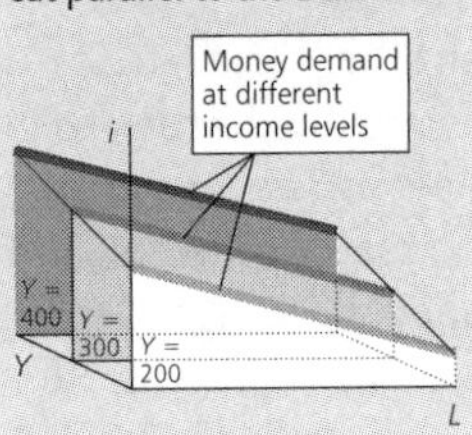

We may combine these insights into a simple money demand equation:

$$L = kY - hi \qquad \textbf{Money demand function} \qquad (3.1)$$

L denotes the demand for money (or liquidity). The first term on the right-hand side of the equation encapsulates the insight that money holdings are positively related to income. The more income received at the beginning of the month, the higher is the volume of planned transactions, and more money must therefore be held at the bank for a given number of trips to the bank. The second term states that the demand for money falls as the interest rate rises. A higher interest rate makes holding money more costly, induces more frequent trips to the bank, and thus causes a lower average demand for money at any given level of income.

Panel (a) in Figure 3.2 illustrates one version of the money-demand function. The line is drawn while holding income constant. The negative slope

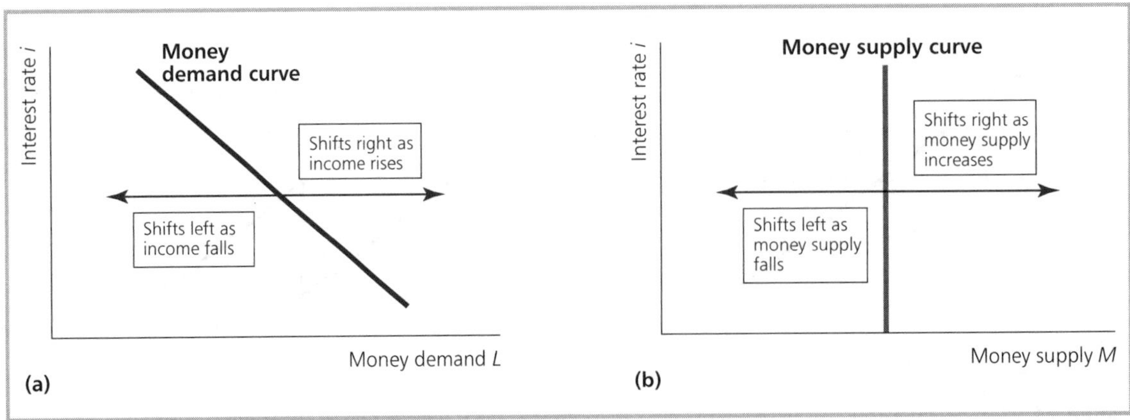

Figure 3.2 Rising interest rates raise the opportunity costs of holding money. Therefore they drive down the demand for money at given income levels (panel (a)). Rising income raises transactions and shifts the money demand curve to the right. The money supply curve is vertical. Changing supply shifts the curve left or right (panel (b)).

indicates that the demand for money rises as the interest rate falls. An increase of income shifts the curve to the right: if the interest rate is fixed at i_0, which fixes the number of trips to the bank, average money holdings needed for transaction purposes must rise as income rises.

No market is complete without supply. The money supply M is determined by the central bank. As we discussed in Chapter 1, the central bank typically controls the volume of currency that circulates in the economy, but also wider monetary aggregates, by sales or purchases of treasury bills (either directly from the government, or from the private sector) or by buying or selling foreign currency. Since this supply of money provided by the central bank does not depend on the interest rate, panel (b) in Figure 3.2 shows it as a vertical line. Monetary policy shifts this vertical line to the left or to the right by changing the money supply.

Are L and M nominal or real variables? Well, when individuals demand money they want to have a certain buying power in their wallet, depending on their real income Y, and on i. So L must be a demand for real money. The money supply M controlled by the central bank is a nominal magnitude. It loses value if the price level rises. In equilibrium the real money demand must equal the real supply of money, $L = M/P$. For the moment, we are assuming the price level to be fixed. And for the sake of convenience we may suppose prices to be fixed at $P = 1$. Then M also represents the real money supply and $L = M$ in equilibrium.

Figure 3.3 merges the money-supply and the money-demand curves and shows how they interact. The figure shows how equilibrium obtains. Only one interest rate i_0 exists at which individuals want to hold the exact volume of money the central bank has decided to provide. If the interest rate is higher than i_0, individuals economize on their money holdings, and supply exceeds demand. At an interest rate below i_0 an excess demand for money exists.

The interest rate i_0 clears the money market only if income equals Y_0. If Y rises to Y_1, desired money holdings increase at any given interest rate. The L

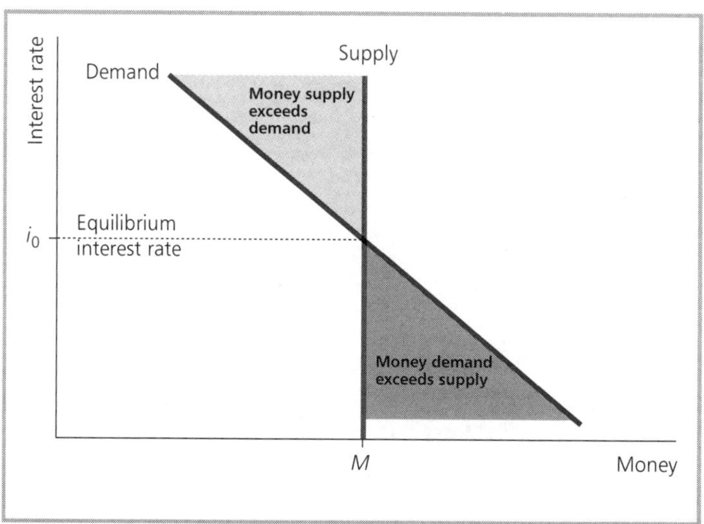

Figure 3.3 Money demand and supply are equal at one interest rate i_0. At higher interest rates there is an excess supply. A lower interest rate generates an excess demand.

curve shifts to the right, reflecting an excess demand at the old interest rate i_0. A rise of the interest rate is required to offset the demand increase caused by the income rise. Only as the interest rate reaches the higher level i_1 is the money market back in equilibrium (see Figure 3.4, panel (a)).

Panel (a) in Figure 3.4 teaches us that money demand can equal a given supply at many different interest rates, provided they are paired with the right income level. If interest rises from i_0 to i_1, thus pushing demand down, income needs to rise from Y_0 to Y_1 to make up for this loss and stimulate demand by the exact amount needed. The equilibrium points A and B can be transferred onto a diagram with i and Y on the axes (panel (b)). All other equilibrium combinations are to be found on a line through A and B. This line is called the ***LM* curve** because it combines all points at which money demand L equals a given money supply M.

The ***LM* curve** identifies combinations of income and the interest rate for which the demand for money equals the money supply.

BOX 3.2 Money versus interest rate control

News on the screen and in papers often speculates on whether the Bundesbank or the Fed will reduce interest rates at some forthcoming board meeting. So, are central banks typically controlling interest rates rather than the money supply? Has our interpretation of *monetary policy* and *money supply control* been misguided? Not really.

Take a second look at the money market diagram with the downward-sloping money demand schedule (Figure 1). Faced with this demand schedule, the central bank's situation is very much like that of a monopolistic firm facing a downward-sloping demand curve for its product. It can either set the volume and accept the price at which the market is willing to buy it, or it may set the price and live with whatever quantity the market is prepared to acquire. The price for holding money is the interest foregone. So either the central bank sets M, making the money supply curve vertical in the grey position, and lets the money demand curve determine i. Or it sets i, making the money supply curve horizontal in the light grey position, and lets the money demand curve determine M. The variant that central banks opt for has been changing over time, for practical and institutional reasons that need not concern us at this chapter's level of aggregation and abstraction. For some pros and cons see Box 3.5.

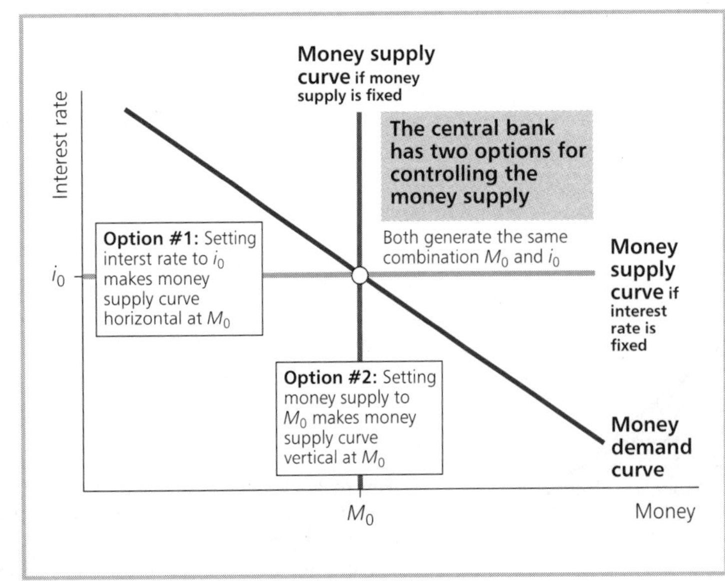

Figure 1

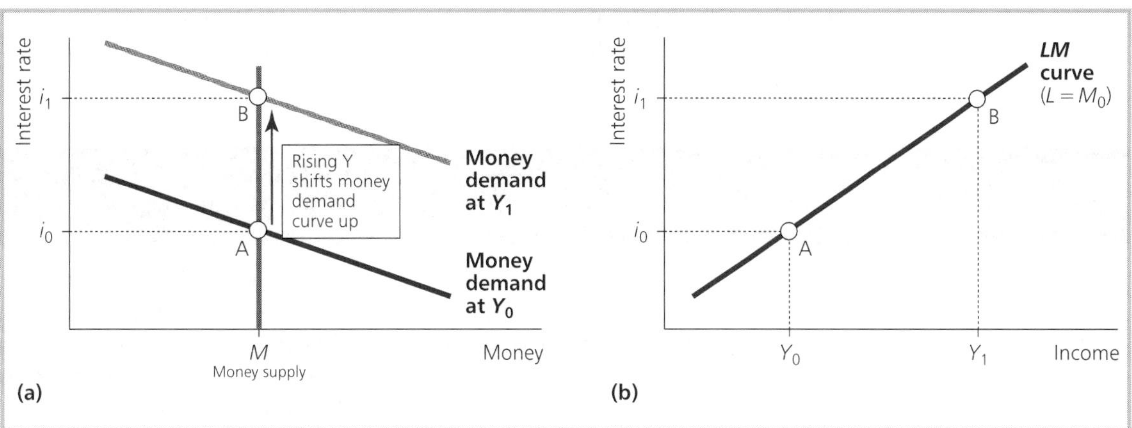

Figure 3.4 Panel (a) shows a vertical money supply and a negatively sloped money-demand curve. Rising income raises money demand at any interest rate, shifting the money-demand curve right. To retain equilibrium, the interest rate must rise to contain money demand at its old level. Transferring points A and B into panel (b) gives two points on the *LM* curve, the money-market equilibrium line.

An algebraic expression for the *LM* curve is obtained by taking equilibrium, that is $M = L$, substituting this into equation (3.1), and solving for i. This gives

$$i = \frac{k}{h}Y - \frac{M}{h} \qquad \textit{LM}\ \textbf{curve} \qquad (3.2)$$

Figure 3.5, panel (a), looks at the demand-and-supply diagram again and shows what an increase in the money supply does to the *LM* curve. A money supply increase shifts the vertical supply curve to the right, forcing the market clearing interest rate down at all given income levels. The result is a shift of the

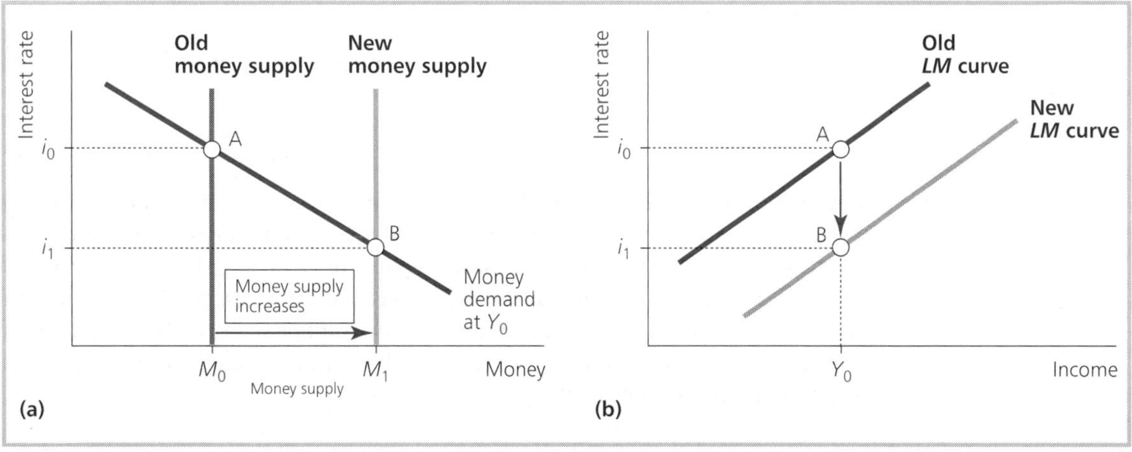

Figure 3.5 In panel (a) the money supply increase shifts the vertical money-supply curve to the right. To retain equilibrium, money demand must be spurred by lowering the interest rate from i_0 to i_1. Transferring points A and B to panel (b) gives two money-market equilibrium points on two different *LM* curves, each one drawn for a different money supply.

LM curve to the right. What actually happens to income and the interest rate still remains unclear and, as we will see, is eventually determined in interaction with other markets.

3.2 AGGREGATE EXPENDITURE, THE INTEREST RATE AND THE EXCHANGE RATE: THE *IS* CURVE

Next we return to the goods market, which was at the centre of the discussion in Chapter 2. We review the components of aggregate expenditure, introduce the exchange rate and state a **generalized equilibrium condition for the goods market** in a form that will eventually allow us to tie up loose ends with the two other markets. This generalized equilibrium condition will be called the *IS* curve.

Reminder. Y^e_+ is a stand-in for all income expected to accrue during future periods. Period incomes may be weighed to reflect time discounting. Then Y^e_+ would be a present value.

Consumption and investment

The earlier discussion of consumption taught us that consumption spending depends on current income and on expected future income:

$$C = c_1 Y + c_2 Y^e_+ \quad \textbf{Consumption function} \quad (3.3)$$

where c_1 may be thought to be relatively small, say about 0.3. The sum of both coefficients, $c_1 + c_2$, is close to 1, say 0.9. So a one-unit increase of current income ($\Delta Y = 1$) that does *not* affect expectations of future income ($\Delta Y^e_+ = 0$) increases consumption by 0.3. The same one-unit increase of current income expected to *last* into the future ($\Delta Y^e_+ = 1$) raises consumption by 0.9.

Investment spending was found to depend on two major factors – expected future income and the interest rate:

$$I = b_1 Y^e_+ - b_2 i \quad \textbf{Investment function} \quad (3.4)$$

For pragmatic reasons, in a continuing effort to keep the analysis transparent, for most of the time we will work with the simpler consumption and investment functions

$$C = cY \quad \textbf{Simple consumption function} \quad (3.5)$$

and

$$I = \bar{I} - bi \quad \textbf{Simple investment function} \quad (3.6)$$

The consumption function (3.5) is compatible with (3.3) if we keep in mind that c is small, i.e. around 0.3 if an observed income change is considered *transitory*, and around 0.9 if income is believed to have changed *permanently*.

Expected future income may be suppressed in the investment function with the argument that its influence on demand is (implicitly) already taken care of in the consumption function, and that the additional effect on aggregate demand via investment is likely to be small.

Exports and imports

When car buyers consider buying either a Peugeot or a Renault, they consider the quality and characteristics of the product, look at the price tag and then

BOX 3.3 Working with graphs: (part II)

I do not recommend learning the slopes of equilibrium curves like *LM* by heart. Neither do I advise memorizing which factor shifts the graph which way. As long as the economic reasoning behind some market equilibrium is understood, slopes and shifts of curves can, in most cases, be worked out by simple thought processes. Algebra or calculus is not necessary.

For example, take the *LM* curve to demonstrate the nature of the thought process. Suppose you forgot how the graph slopes in the *i*/*Y* diagram and how it shifts when the money supply increases. Here is a way out:

The slope of a curve:

1. Pick an arbitrary point A in the *i*/*Y* plane. Assume that A is an equilibrium, i.e. a point on *LM*. (You may safely do that as, without any further information, you are free to position the *LM* curve anywhere in the diagram.) See Figure 1.
2. Move horizontally from A to B. With *i* being the same at A and B, but *Y* being larger at B, the demand for money at B is obviously higher than at A. Thus, as we are holding the money supply constant, B features an excess demand for money. In other words, B is not on *LM*!
3. Starting from B, work out in which direction *i* has to move in order to restore equilibrium. As demand is too high in B, *i* must change so as to reduce money demand via higher opportunity costs, i.e. it must rise. At some point such as C it will have risen just enough to re-establish equilibrium.
4. Now that we have two points A and C on the *LM* curve, we have identified the curve's slope. In fact, we may draw the curve right through A and C.

How does the curve shift?

1. As before, pick an arbitrary point A in the *i*/*Y* plane. Assume that it is an equilibrium point, i.e. it lies on *LM*. See Figure 2.
2. Assume that the money supply has been increased. Since the old money supply equalled demand at A, A must now feature an excess supply of money.
3. Holding *i* constant, work out whether *Y* has to rise or to fall in order to raise money demand and thus re-establish equilibrium. Here the answer is, obviously, that *Y* has to rise. So the new equilibrium point is found east of A – say, at B.
4. As we could have started from any other point on the old *LM* curve and obtained the same qualitative result, we may now conclude that the entire *LM* curve has shifted to the right into the position of the new *LM* curve.

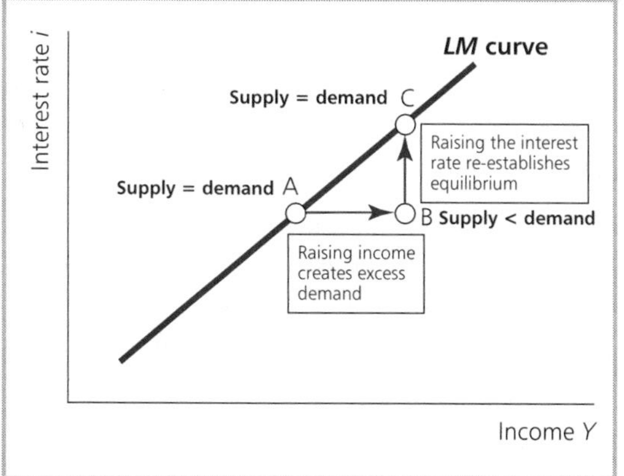

Figure 1

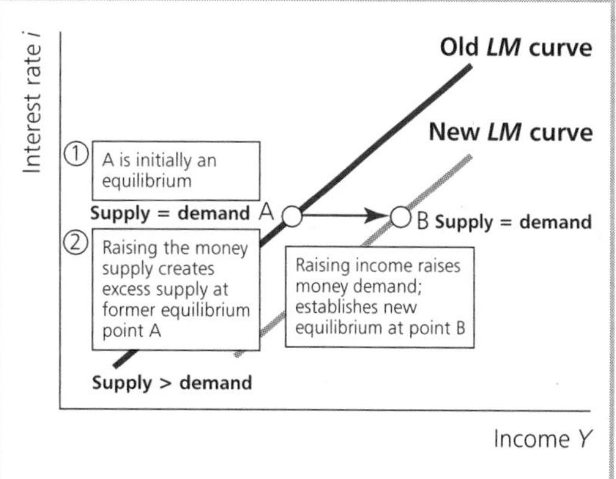

Figure 2

make a choice. If one of the two cars becomes cheaper, other things remaining unchanged, demand for this model will increase.

This also applies in the open economy, at the international level. British imports from France will tend to fall when the price of French products expressed in pounds increases. For the same reason exports from the United Kingdom to France will increase. The price of French cars expressed in British pounds changes whenever the exchange rate changes, even if French car manufacturers keep the euro price constant. Therefore the exchange rate must be a major determinant of the exports and imports of a country.

The **real exchange rate** R is the ratio between the price of a (bundle of) good(s) abroad and at home: $R \equiv EP^{\text{World}}/P$.

Purchasing power parity denotes the exchange rate E^{PPP} that equates prices abroad and at home in domestic currency: $E^{\text{PPP}} \times P^{\text{World}} = P$.

If the **real exchange rate** of the euro falls below **purchasing power parity**, it is cheaper to buy imported goods: French people will buy Rovers rather than Citroëns, enjoy cheddar and cheshire over roquefort and brie, and eventually, although the exchange rate would have to be very low, they may even switch to drinking British wine. Considering all of these factors means that French imports from Britain rise as the exchange rate falls. The opposite occurs if the real exchange rate goes up. Domestic goods gain a price advantage and domestic residents purchase fewer and fewer imported goods and services. These arguments generalize the import function to

$$IM = m_1 Y - m_2 R \qquad \textbf{Import function} \qquad (3.7)$$

making imports not only more dependent on income as stated above, but also on the relative price of domestic and foreign goods as measured by the real exchange rate R.

The export function must be a mirror image of the import function, since our exports are simply the imports of the rest of the world from us. The two determinants of our exports would thus be *world income* and the real exchange rate:

$$EX = x_1 Y^{\text{World}} + x_2 R \qquad \textbf{Export function} \qquad (3.8)$$

The exchange rate affects our exports with a positive coefficient. If our currency *depreciates* against other currencies, other currencies *appreciate* against our currency. This makes our exports cheaper for foreigners and they will want to buy more of them.

The algebra of the *IS* curve

The ***IS* curve** shows those combinations of income and the interest rate for which aggregate expenditure equals income (or output). Its name derives from the fact that in an economy with no government (then $T - G = 0$) and no trade with other countries (then $IM - EX = 0$) the required balancing of leakages and injections $[(S - I) + (T - G) + (IM - EX) = 0]$ obtains if $I = S$.

An equation for the ***IS* curve** is obtained by substituting equations (3.5), (3.6), (3.7) and (3.8) into the goods market equilibrium condition $Y = C + I + G + EX - IM$. Since we would like to obtain an equilibrium condition which can be shown on the $i - Y$ surface along with the LM curve obtained above, we solve the equilibrium condition for i. This yields

$$i = -\frac{1 - c + m_1}{b} Y + \frac{x_2 + m_2}{b} R + \frac{\bar{I} + G + x_1 Y^{\text{World}}}{b} \qquad \textit{IS}\ \text{curve} \qquad (3.9)$$

The negative coefficient in front of Y shows that the curve slopes down. This simply reflects Chapter 2's result that a rise in the interest rate reduces investment and thus lowers equilibrium income. The positive coefficient in front of R signals that a real depreciation stimulates net exports and thus raises equilibrium income. Finally, the coefficients in front of the autonomous

BOX 3.4 Exchange rates

The **nominal exchange rate**, or, for short, the exchange rate, *E* is the price of one unit of foreign currency in terms of domestic currency:

$$\text{Exchange rate} = E = \frac{\text{Swiss francs}}{\text{Swedish kronor}}$$

If the Swiss francs/Swedish kronor exchange rate is 0.125, this means that one Swedish kronor costs 0.125 Swiss francs. This commonly used definition has a *counter-intuitive implication* which may cause confusion for students new to international economics: if Switzerland's exchange rate goes up, the Swiss franc loses value – it *depreciates*. The Swiss need more francs to obtain a given number of Swedish kronor. A falling exchange rate means that the domestic currency is getting stronger – it *appreciates*.

We only speak of *appreciation* and *depreciation* if the exchange rate is moved by market forces. If governments decide to move the franc up to 0.2 against the kronor in a system of fixed exchange rates, the franc is *devalued*. In the opposite case it is *revalued*.

On its own, the nominal exchange rate does not provide any information about the actual buying power of a given amount of money in different countries. It can only do this in combination with information about individual prices or the general price level. If the Volvo S60 sells for 50,000 francs in Switzerland and for 300,000 kronor in Sweden, where is it cheaper? A measure of the relative price level in two countries is the **real exchange rate**:

$$\text{Real exchange rate } R = \frac{E \times P^{\text{World}}}{P}$$

$$= \frac{\frac{\text{Swiss francs}}{\text{Swedish kronor}} \times \text{Swedish price}}{\text{Swiss price}}$$

In the above example, to purchase an S60 costs 50,000 francs in Switzerland, but only $0.125 \times 300{,}000 = 37\,500$ francs in Sweden. This also follows from substituting prices and the exchange rate into the above equation. The real exchange rate of $0.125 \times 300{,}000/50{,}000 = 0.75$ means that the Swiss only pay 75% of what the S60 costs in their home market when they buy the car in Sweden.

In this case, or whenever the real exchange rate is below 1, the Swiss franc is said to be **overvalued**. If the exchange rate is higher than 1, and Swiss franc prices abroad exceed home prices, the franc is **undervalued**.

The exchange rate that equalizes the domestic and the international purchasing power of a currency is called **purchasing power parity**. It is the nominal exchange rate which sets the real exchange rate to a value of 1:

$$\text{Purchasing power parity } E^{\text{PPP}} = \frac{P}{P^{\text{World}}}$$

$$= \frac{\text{Swiss price}}{\text{Swedish price}}$$

In the present example the purchasing-power-parity exchange rate turns out to be $50{,}000/300{,}000 = 1/6$.

Macroeconomists do not usually look at prices for individual goods but at economy-wide price indexes which constitute a representative basket of goods and services.

expenditures indicate that an increase shifts the curve up, and by how much it does so. Equation (3.9) can actually be graphed as an *IS plane*, with the two endogenous variables *i* and *R* on the horizontal axis (see Figure 3.6). The 2D equilibrium line in *i*–*Y* space, the *IS* curve, is obtained by placing a vertical cut through the *IS* plane parallel to the income axis (Figure 3.7).

The *IS* curve depicts the equilibrium income levels from Chapter 2 at different interest rates. While drawing the curve, autonomous expenditures and the real exchange rate are kept constant. Raising either of these moves *IS* up and raises equilibrium income at any given interest rate.

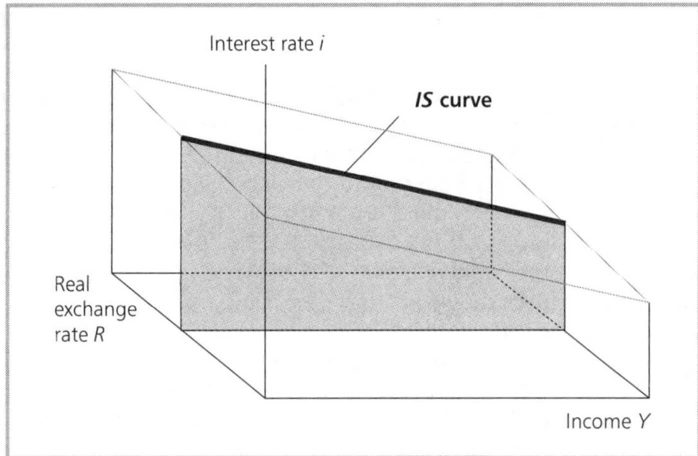

Figure 3.6 All goods market equilibria form a plane in *R-i-Y* space. It slopes up as we move towards the rear (depreciation generates excess demand; to reverse this, the interest rate must rise). The plane slopes down as we move to the right (rising income leads to an excess supply; to eliminate this, the interest rate must fall). Placing a vertical cut parallel to the income axis carves out an equilibrium line (*IS* curve) for a given real exchange rate.

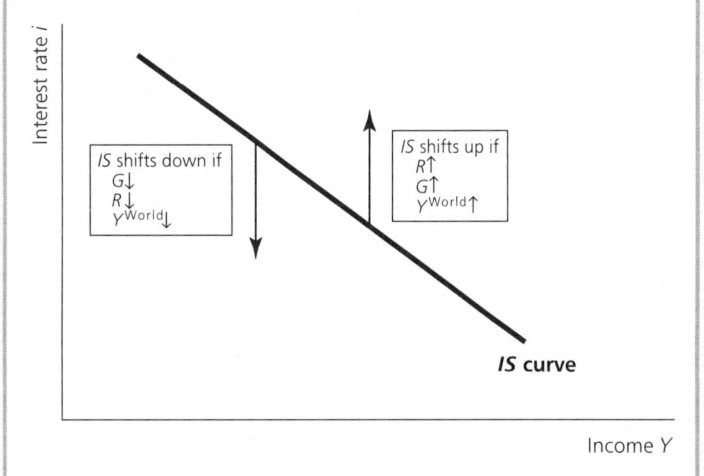

Figure 3.7 The *IS* curve shows all combinations of interest rates and income that make aggregate spending equal to output. It is drawn for given government expenditures, world income and a given exchange rate. As these variables rise, the *IS* curve moves up (or to the right).

Note. We may also draw on the Keynesian cross to derive the negatively sloped *IS* curve:

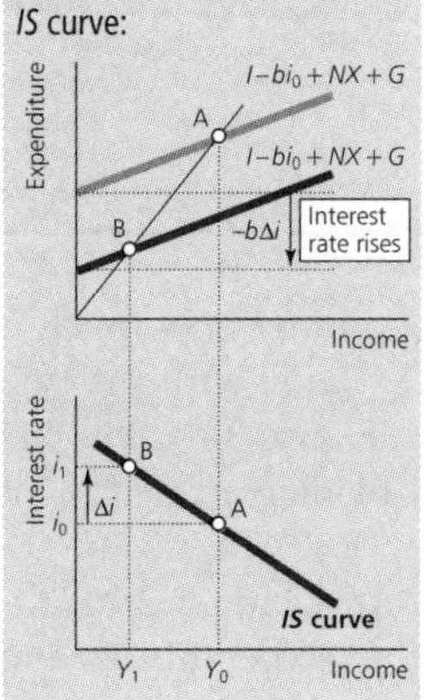

The slope of the *IS* curve depends on the marginal propensity to consume (and to import) (equation (3.9)). The larger c is, the smaller is the numerator in the fraction preceding Y, and the flatter is the line. So when an income increase is considered permanent, meaning that c is large, the *IS* curve looks comparatively flat. For an income increase that consumers classify as transitory, the *IS* curve looks rather steep. The reasoning behind this is that in the latter case an interest rate reduction does stimulate investment and income in the first round, but there will be few of the second- and third-round effects described by the multiplier, since consumers adjust their consumption by only a small amount.

To strengthen understanding of the *IS* curve we may look at it from a different angle by referring back to the circular flow. Figure 3.8 shows this flow again and includes what we know by now about the factors that influence leakages and injections.

Now suppose the interest rate falls. This boosts investment injected into the flow. To maintain equilibrium, i.e. equality between aggregate expenditure and income, income must rise. So when i goes down, Y must go up to keep

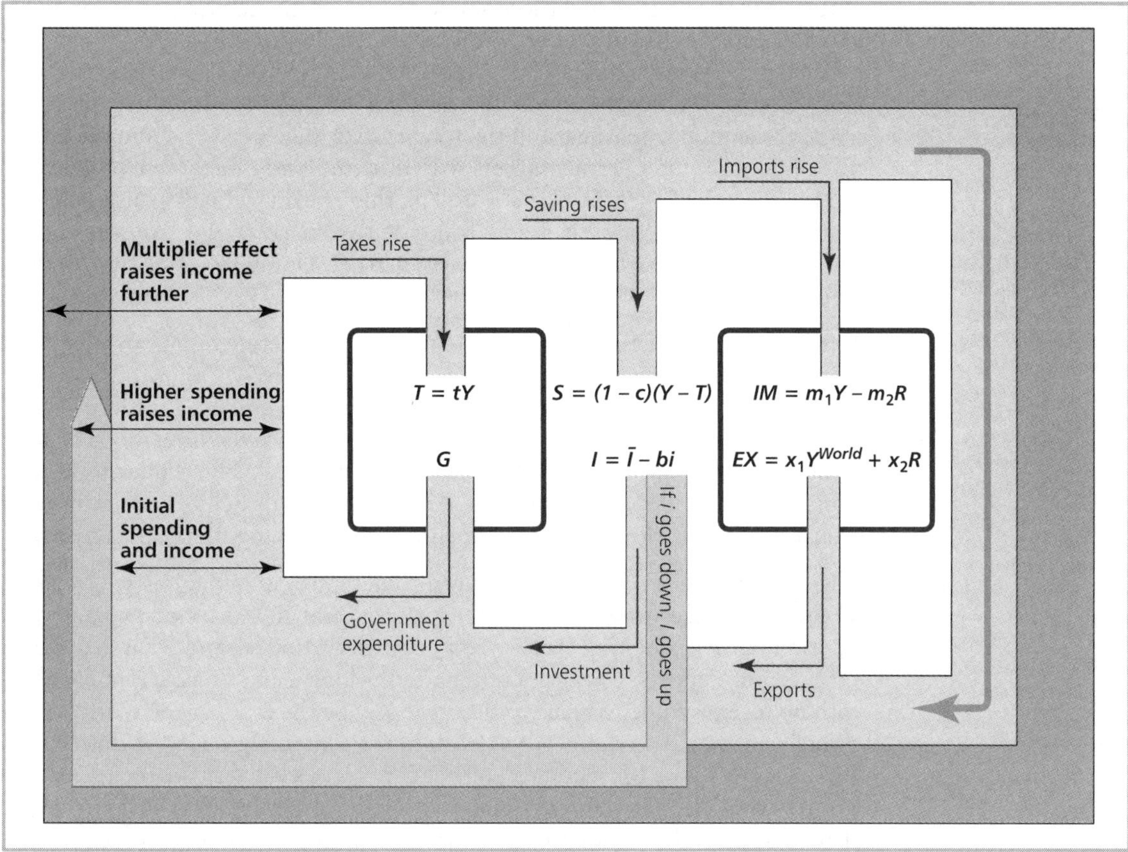

Figure 3.8 This shows how what we learned in this chapter fits into the circular flow diagram. If *i* falls, *I* goes up. *I* increases by the grey segment of the investment injection. This demand rise adds to income. Since this stimulates consumption, second-round effects set in. The fact that leakages also get larger (not shown in graph) ensures that income does not continue to rise forever. Eventually, the stream of income settles into a new width determined by the multiplier. Note that changes of world income, the exchange rate or taxes affect the circular flow in a similar way.

the circular flow (the goods market) in equilibrium. This is reflected in the negative slope of the *IS* curve.

Next, suppose the exchange rate depreciates (rises), with *i* remaining unchanged. Then exports rise (do you remember why?) and imports fall, increasing injections and lowering leakages, respectively. To maintain equilibrium, income must rise. Thus a rise in *R* shifts the *IS* curve to the right (or up).

Similar arguments reveal how changes in *G*, *T* or world income affect the position of *IS*.

3.3 THE *IS-LM* OR THE GLOBAL ECONOMY MODEL

The loose end left over after the discussion of the goods market in section 3.2 is the exchange rate. The exchange rate is determined in yet another market, the foreign exchange market. We postpone the introduction of the foreign exchange market until the next chapter. The reason for this is mainly didactic, but not entirely so.

Recall that our first macroeconomic model of the determination of aggregate income, the Keynesian cross discussed in Chapter 2, comprises only *one* market: the goods market. Eventually, however, we will arrive at a model composed of *three* markets on the demand side of the economy: the goods market, the money market, and the foreign exchange market. Going from one market to three interacting markets will turn out to be a huge step, perhaps too big a step to be taken in one stride. For this reason we will pause here and assemble a macroeconomic model from the two markets we have come across so far, the goods market and the money market. Doing so yields two kinds of benefits:

- It shows us how to handle two markets that operate simultaneously and interact with each other, and thus serves a methodological purpose.
- It generates a model that, while it still has clear limitations, constitutes a substantial improvement over the Keynesian cross. Since the limitations concern international macroeconomic aspects, the model is best understood as a picture of the global economy, as if viewed from a satellite camera in outer space, or of a national economy that does not interact with the outside world.

Regarding the second point we need to accept that as long as we leave the foreign exchange market out of the picture, and thus cannot explain what determines the exchange rate, we cannot properly understand what determines exports and imports. This does not matter as long as we consider an economy with no foreign trade, which would obviously be the case for the world, or the global economy. So whatever we learn in the remaining pages of this chapter will have relevance for income determination on a global scale, on a scale that ignores what happens in individual, national economies. Our insights would also be applicable to isolationist countries that choose not to trade with the rest of the world. But not many such countries exist anymore. Our insights also give us a first, while incomplete and, therefore, imprecise, glimpse of how income is determined in large countries that export only a rather small fraction of their output.

The goods market equilibrium condition for the global economy reduces to $Y = C + I + G$, since $EX = IM = NX = 0$. On substituting the consumption function (3.5) and the investment function (3.6) we obtain a new, global *IS* curve:

$$i = -\frac{1-c}{b}Y + \frac{\bar{I}+G}{b}$$

Global-economy *IS* curve (3.10)

Comparing this to the national-economy *IS* curve given in equation (3.9) shows the following:

- The global-economy *IS* curve is much simpler. The reason is that there are fewer leaks and injections. So everything that determines imports and exports, that is the exchange rate, foreign income, and the marginal propensity to import, drops out of the picture.
- The global-economy *IS* curve has a negative slope, just as the national-economy *IS* curve. The reason for this negative slope is investment behaviour, which is the same in both the global-economy and the national-economy version of the curve.

- The global-economy *IS* curve is flatter. This is a consequence of less income leaking out of the circular flow because there are no imports. Hence, the multiplier is larger. If a falling interest rate now raises investment by a given amount, this translates into a larger rise in equilibrium income than it does with the national-economy *IS* curve.

The graphical *IS-LM* model

Both the *IS* and the *LM* curves show combinations of interest rates and income levels that render the market under consideration in equilibrium. It is thus straightforward to merge the two curves onto one graph to obtain a model of the global economy thought to comprise a goods and a money market. Figure 3.9 does just that.

There are many points in this graph (on the *IS* curve) that render a goods market in equilibrium, such as points A, B and C. And there are also many points (on the *LM* curve) that equalize supply and demand in the money market, such as points A, D and E. But there is only one point, A, at which both markets are in equilibrium at the same time and, hence, the entire global economy is in equilibrium.

At B the goods market alone is in equilibrium. At this level of income, though, the interest rate is much too high to clear the money market. Hence, the demand for money is too low, and we have an excess supply of money. This tends to drive down the price for holding money, which we know is the interest rate.

At D the money market is in equilibrium. But at this interest rate income is much too high to permit a goods market equilibrium. Firms are producing more than consumers, investors and the government want to buy. Responding to this signal of insufficient demand, firms cut down production, making income fall.

At a point such as F we have disequilibrium in both markets. Demand exceeds supply in the goods market as well as in the money market. As a result, there will be upward pressure on the interest rate and rising income. This moves the economy towards and eventually into global macroeconomic

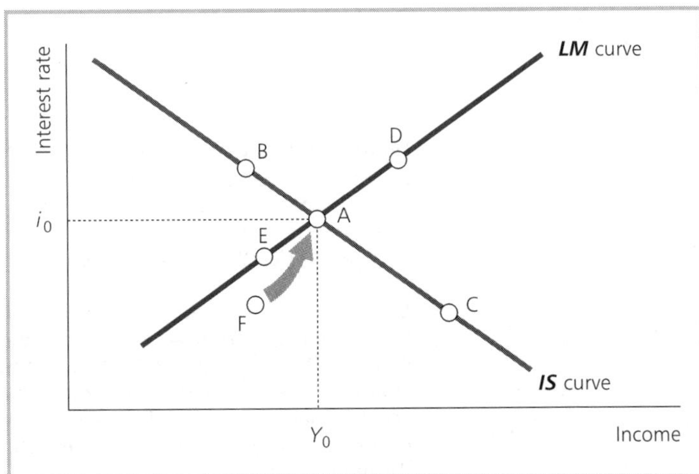

Figure 3.9 While points A, B and C indicate goods market equilibria and A, D and E mark money market equilibria, only point A is an economy-wide equilibrium with both markets being in equilibrium at the same time. At F there is disequilibrium in both markets. The arrow indicates how such a disequilibrium might be removed. Our *IS-LM* model does not really cover this. It only tells where the equilibrium is, not how we get there.

equilibrium point A as depicted by the arrow. Note, though, that this adjustment path is not the only one that could result from our verbal sketch of disequilibrium dynamics. In fact, quite complicated paths are conceivable. We do not go deeper into these, focusing instead on the economy's point of gravity, its equilibrium, and how this can be influenced by policy measures. We should keep in mind, however, that the equilibrium we are looking at is just that, a gravity point, from which the economy may deviate temporarily. It is a highly useful indicator of the direction in which the economy moves, but does not necessarily indicate the economy's exact position at each point in time.

Monetary policy

Monetary policy manipulates the money supply (or the interest rate) to achieve policy goals (such as a rise in income).

By adding the money market to our model we introduced a second policy option for governments and central banks – monetary policy. **Monetary policy** comprises central bank action geared towards steering the money supply. This can happen directly, by purchasing or selling bonds or foreign currency. It can also happen indirectly, by setting interest rates and inducing the market to hold liquidity in the desired amount. Here we use monetary policy as a synonym for direct control of the money supply.

Now suppose the central bank decides to increase the money supply. As we learned from Figure 3.5, this shifts the *LM* curve to the right. The reason is that at any point on the old *LM* curve, such as at A (Figure 3.10), we would now have an excess supply of money in the amount by which the money supply was raised. In order to drive money demand up to the same level, either income must go up or the interest rate must fall, or a combination of the two.

Now, while there are many new i-Y combinations that would render the money market in equilibrium – all points on LM_1 – only the combination i_1-Y_1 at the same time renders a goods market equilibrium. The motor moving the economy from A to B is that once the money supply has increased, shifting the *LM* curve to the right, there is excess supply of money at A. At their current

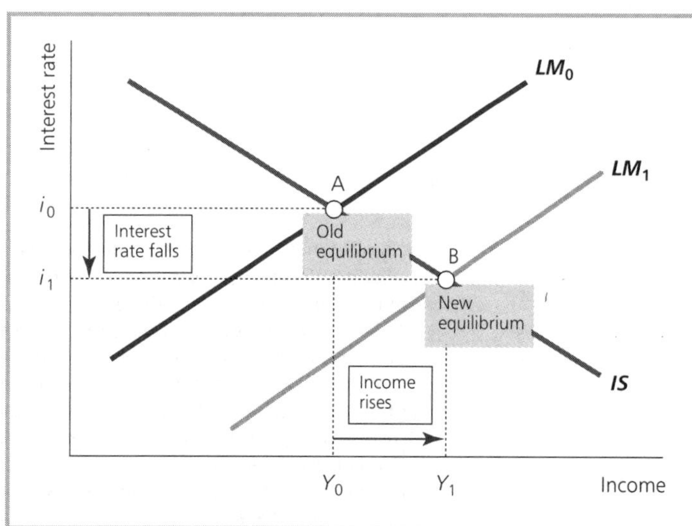

Figure 3.10 When the money supply increases, the *LM* curve shifts to the right, indicating that we need higher income or lower interest rates (or some combination of these effects) to induce people to increase money demand. The slope of the *IS* curve causes the macroeconomic equilibrium to move from A to B. Only the indicated fall in the interest rate and the indicated rise in income will keep the goods market in equilibrium while restoring money market equilibrium after the money supply increase.

BOX 3.5 Money supply vs interest control in a changing world

In Box 3.2 we concluded that it does not really matter whether the central bank uses the money supply or the interest rate as a policy instrument. This is true in a world that does not change. A second look at this issue is required, however, in a world of change and uncertainty.

Suppose the central bank has two options: announce a money supply target at the beginning of the year, and stick with it, no matter what happens, or, announce an interest rate target and stick with it. Further, suppose the world is stochastic, meaning that the *LM* curve or the *IS* curve may shift by themselves. This can happen either because people change their behaviour, which would affect the coefficients of the *LM* or *IS* equations. Or it can happen because there are other factors determining money or goods demand, which our streamlined, simplified equations omitted. The two left-hand panels in Figure 1 look at the situation in which the *IS* curve is subject to change and uncertainty. While it is in the bold position at the beginning of the year, it may end up anywhere in the shaded area bounded by the thin blue lines. The two panels on the right consider change and uncertainty in the money market.

Consider first the policy option of announcing and implementing a specific money supply, as depicted in the two upper panels. On the left, with no uncertainty in the money market, the *LM* curve stays put. As the *IS* curve fluctuates, the economy moves up or down the black segment of the *LM* curve, making income fluctuate modestly within the extremes marked by the vertical dotted lines. On the right, with no change in the goods market,

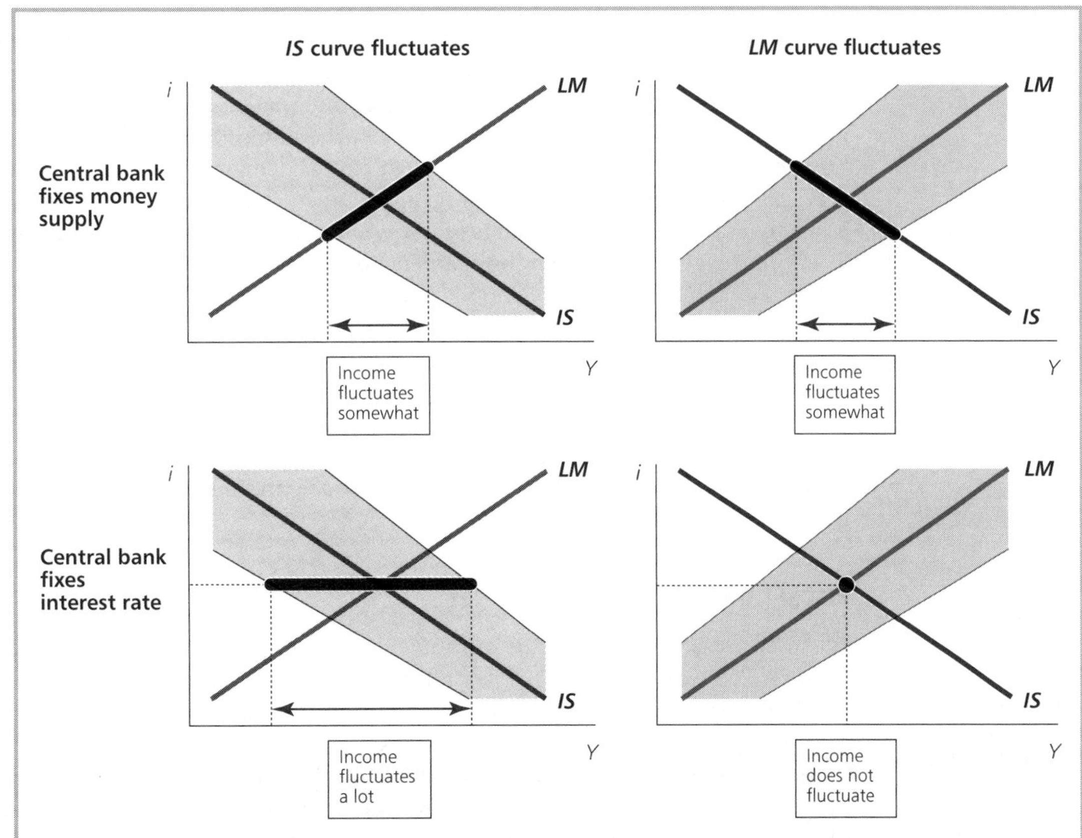

Figure 1

Box 3.5 continued

IS stays put. Changing behaviour on the money markets demand side keep shifting *LM*. Being focused on keeping *M* as planned, the central bank does not do anything about it. The economy moves up and down the black part of the *IS* curve, with income fluctuating moderately within the indicated boundaries.

Next, what happens if the central bank holds the interest rate fixed at the level indicated by the horizontal dotted lines in the two lower panels? On the left, to keep the interest rate unchanged in the face of a downward shift of the *IS* curve, the money supply must be reduced, moving *LM* left. So the negative demand shock in the goods market is fortified by restrictive monetary policy. Income falls a lot. More than it did in the upper left panel when the money supply was fixed. Similarly, in the case of a positive shock to goods demand, the money supply is forced to expand, and income rises a lot. Generally, income must be expected to fluctuate a lot when the goods market is volatile and monetary policy fixes the interest rate. If money demand fluctuates, as in the lower right-hand panel, the money supply must respond in order to keep the interest rate unchanged. This effectively prevents the *LM* curve from shifting at all. It is being kept in the bold position. As a consequence income does not fluctuate at all.

The conclusion from all this is that in a world of change and uncertainty fixing the interest rate and fixing the money supply does not generate the same stability in income. Money supply control always leaves room for income fluctuations, albeit modest ones. Interest rate control is superior if uncertainty and change occur mostly in the money market. It is inferior if the goods market is volatile.

level of income Y_0 individuals do not want to hold the amount of money supplied by the central bank. This drives down the price of holding money, the interest rate. Now the declining interest rate makes investment projects cheaper, so planned investment increases. At the initial level of income Y_0 and an interest rate below i_0 firms perceive an excess demand for their goods and services, thus step up production, raising income. This process continues until a new overall equilibrium obtains at a lower interest rate and higher income.

The potency of monetary policy depends, of course, on the quantitative effects at each link in the reaction sequence. The leverage of monetary policy is greater, the more a given money supply increase drives down the interest rate and the more a given fall in the interest rate stimulates investment. The latter condition refers to the slope of the *IS* curve. As you may easily convince yourself, the steeper the *IS* curve, the smaller is the income increase resulting from a given downward shift of the *LM* curve. If investment was unresponsive to the interest rate, the *IS* curve would be vertical, and monetary policy would not have an impact on income at all.

Fiscal policy in the *IS-LM* model

Fiscal policy manipulates government spending and taxes to achieve policy goals (such as a rise in income).

We are now equipped to refine our understanding of fiscal policy as set out in Chapter 2. **Fiscal policy** comprises all policy measures related to the government budget. At the aggregate level this amounts to government spending and raising government revenue by levying taxes.

As we saw when we discussed the goods market in section 3.2, the *IS* curve moves to the right (or up) when the government increases spending. (The same thing happens when the government reduces taxes.) The reason is that at any point on the old *IS* curve, at a given interest rate and given income, the additional demand exercised by the government creates an excess demand for goods. To restore equilibrium in the goods market, either the interest rate must rise to drive down investment demand and thus make room for higher government purchases, or firms must produce more, raising *Y*. So the new equilibrium must be above and/or to the right of the old one, on a new *IS* curve that has shifted upward, as shown in Figure 3.11.

The new macroeconomic equilibrium is, of course, at point C, where *LM* and the new *IS* curve intersect. But how do we get there? Recall that the *IS* curve is an equilibrium condition. It lists all possible interest rate/income combinations that equate goods supply with goods demand. So as a first step, after *G* has been raised, while the economy is still in *Y*, firms experience an increased demand for their products which they cannot meet. So they decide to increase production, which raises income. The economy moves from A to the right. Now in a second step, because of their higher incomes people want to hold more money than banks can supply at the current interest rate. This excess demand in the money market drives the interest rate up. Both move-

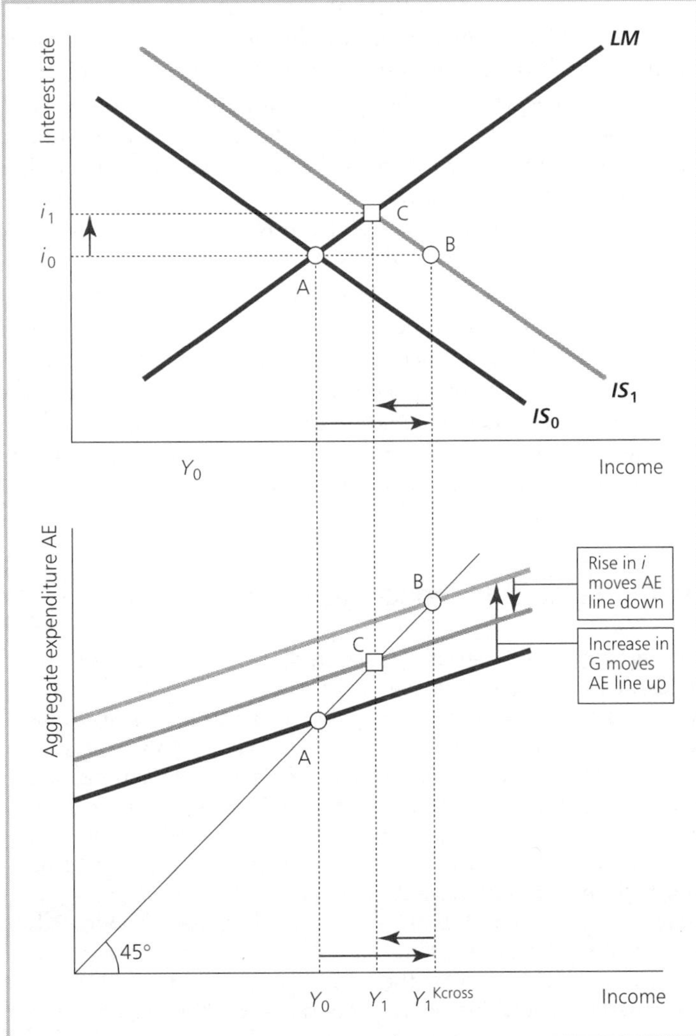

Figure 3.11 The *IS-LM* model rests on the Keynesian cross, but extends this. In the Keynesian cross, an increase in government spending moves the aggregate expenditure line up, moving the economy from A to B. In the *IS-LM* diagram the *IS* curve moves to the right. The same macroeconomic equilibrium B would only obtain if the interest rate did not change. Since money market equilibrium requires the interest rate to rise, investment is driven down and the new equilibrium is in C, where *LM* and the new *IS* curve intersect. In the Keynesian cross this rise in *i* and fall in *I* moves the *AE* line down and the new equilibrium is also at C.

ments – the increase in income and the rise in the interest rate – drive the economy towards and into its new equilibrium at C.

We may deepen our understanding of the effect of fiscal policy in the *IS-LM* model by comparing it with the effect derived in the context of the Keynesian cross in Chapter 2. The lower panel in Figure 3.11 depicts the effect of fiscal policy in the Keynesian cross. The story we told there was that an increase in government purchases G creates excess demand in the goods market. As production expands to meet this new demand and income rises, so does consumption, creating excess demand again. This continues until income has increased by the full multiplier effect which is much larger than the initial rise in G. Investment has not changed, because the interest rate, an exogenous variable in the Keynesian cross, has not changed. At the current interest rate income rises from Y_0 to Y_1^{Kcross}.

How does this effect relate to our analysis of the *IS-LM* model in the upper panel of Figure 3.11? Well, it is a hypothetical effect in this context. It is the income increase needed to restore goods market equilibrium if the interest rate was not permitted to change. This hypothetical equilibrium is given by point B. It again reflects the full multiplier effect of the postulated rise in G on income. Now when the established excess demand in the money market drives the interest rate up, it drives down investment – and equilibrium income – until we arrive at C. In the lower panel the effect of a rising interest rate and falling investment is reflected in a downward shift of the aggregate expenditure line which moves the economy from B back to C.

The fall in income while the economy moves from B to C is called **crowding out**. This expression refers to the fact that when we add the money market to our model economy, an increase in government spending squeezes some investment out of the picture. The effect is a smaller increase in income and, hence, a smaller multiplier. The extent by which government purchases crowd out private investment depends on the slope of the *IS* curve, of course. The steeper the *IS* curve, the less sensitive investment demand is to changes in the interest rate, the smaller is the crowding out effect. Only if the *IS* curve was vertical would there be no crowding out at all and we could enjoy the full multiplier effect.

CASE STUDY 3.1 Liquidity traps and Japan's prolonged recession

Japan's long economic slump experienced during the second half of the 1990s baffled many observers. While the real money supply increased by almost 40% between 1996 and 2000, income rose by a barely observable 3.2%. So contrary to what we have learned from this chapter's analysis, monetary policy in this case does not really seem to have an effect on income worth talking about. Does this mean the *IS-LM* model is of no help in trying to understand Japan's recent slump? One might be tempted to think so. And, in fact, the simple version of the *IS-LM* model developed above fails to account for Japan's experience. A generalized version, however, will provide new insights and an interesting application.

In this textbook most relationships are drawn as straight lines, as is the *LM* curve. This is easy to draw, can be based on simple linear equations, and under most circumstances is a useful approximation of a (possibly) more complicated reality. That is the case in most circumstances, but in extreme situations this is sometimes not so.

Recall that the *LM* curve slopes downwards because, when interest rates go down and bonds lose part of their advantage as a store of value, individuals hold larger shares of their wealth in the

Case study 3.1 continued

form of money. Since bonds lose their dominance as a store of value completely once the interest rate is at (or near) zero, the *LM* curve cannot extend into the region of negative interest rates. To avoid this, the *LM* curve must become flatter as *i* falls, becoming horizontal at or just above a zero interest rate. The existence of a horizontal segment of the *LM* curve does not really matter as long as the *IS* curve intersects *LM* on the upward sloping section. This is the configuration that we have in mind in this textbook. In the unlikely case that the *IS* intersects *LM* where it is flat, we have a problem. Then the economy is in a **liquidity trap**.

The possibility of a liquidity trap is a well-known concept and had been taught to generations of students. However, recent generations of economists considered the liquidity trap to be dead – an academic nicety that did not have any basis in the real world. That is, until US economist Paul Krugman came forward with the suggestion that Japan had fallen into a liquidity trap in the 1990s. Figure 1 sketches Japan's experience according to this argument.

Suppose Japan was in the situation indicated in 1996. Putting this point on the horizontal part of Japan's *LM* curve appears justified by a 1996 interest rate of 0.59%, barely above zero. In the course of the next four years, the nominal money supply rose by some 40%, as did the real money supply, since prices did not change much. This shifted the *LM* curve massively to the right, into the dark blue position. Since the interest rate was already so low that the public was prepared to hold this additional nominal wealth in the form of money, the interest rate could not go down any further. As a consequence, the money supply increase could not stimulate investment demand and income. The economy stayed very much where it was in 1996. Table 1 gives key data for the Japanese economy.

Table 1 Key data for the Japanese economy

	1996	2000
Real GDP (*Y*)	514,852	531,133
Real money supply (*M*/*P*)	163,201	227,210
Price index (*P*)	100.0	101.4
Interest rate (*i*)	0.59%	0.25%

Food for thought

Japan raised government spending several times in order to get out of the recession, with little effect. What might be the cause(s) of this? In the spirit of the quantity equation, we concluded in Chapter 1 that a money supply increase raises nominal income *PY*. In Japan neither *P* nor *Y* rose to a relevant extent. How does this fit in with the quantity equation?

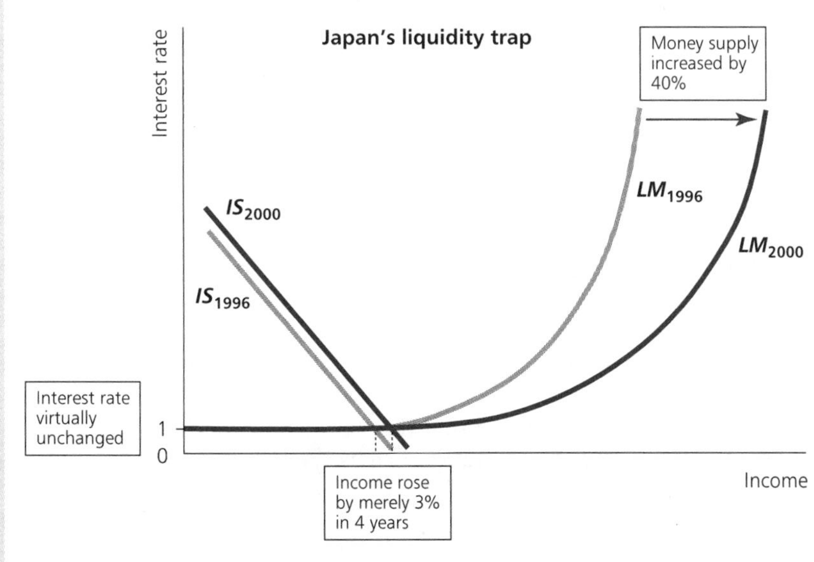

Figure 1

The algebra of the IS-LM model

The *IS-LM* model consists of two markets, the equilibrium lines of which we found out to be:

$$i = \frac{k}{h} Y - \frac{1}{h} M \qquad \textbf{\textit{LM} curve} \qquad (3.2)$$

$$i = -\frac{1-c}{b} Y + \frac{\bar{I} + G}{b} \qquad \textbf{Global-economy \textit{IS} curve} \qquad (3.10)$$

The two endogenous variables, i and Y, are determined simultaneously in both markets. Substituting (3.10) for the interest rate in (3.2) and solving for Y yields

$$Y = \frac{1}{1 - c + bk/h}\left(\bar{I} + G + \frac{b}{h} M\right) \qquad \textbf{Equilibrium income} \qquad (3.11)$$

which says that income goes up either if the government raises spending (or firms increase autonomous investment) or if the central bank expands the money supply. Via

$$\frac{\Delta Y}{\Delta G} = \frac{1}{1 - c + bk/h} \qquad \textbf{\textit{IS-LM} government spending multiplier}$$

we can also see that the government spending multiplier is smaller than it was in the Keynesian cross. The reason becomes clear if we substitute (3.11) into (3.2) to obtain the equilibrium interest rate as

$$i = \frac{k}{(1-c)h + bk}(\bar{I} + G) - \frac{1-c}{(1-c)h + bk} M \qquad \textbf{Equilibrium interest rate} \qquad (3.12)$$

Equation (3.12) reveals that an increase in G not only raises income, but also the interest rate, which exerts a negative effect on investment.

Bottom line

This chapter has refined the discussion of equilibrium income (in the Keynesian cross or in the circular flow model) presented in Chapter 2. The important result for us is that a unique income level exists at which income equals aggregate expenditure. The introduction of the interest rate into the picture links this equilibrium income level to the money supply. This adds monetary policy to the arsenal available to policy makers. Endogenizing the interest rate has deprived the second policy instrument, fiscal policy, of some of its power. Because fiscal policy crowds out private spending, the government policy multiplier is smaller.

It is important to keep in mind that this chapter's *IS-LM* model assumes an economy with no international trade, such as the global economy.

CHAPTER SUMMARY

- The domestic money market is in equilibrium if income and the interest rate assume values that make individuals' demand exactly equal to the amount of money supplied by the central bank.
- Rising income raises the transaction volume per period and, hence, the demand for money. A rising interest rate makes holding money more costly. Hence, it reduces the demand for money.
- The goods market is in equilibrium if income and the interest rate assume values that make aggregate expenditure equal to output produced.
- Aggregate expenditure rises with income (through consumption) and falls as the interest rate rises (through investment).
- The *IS-LM* model is a model of the global economy. If the global money supply rises, interest rates fall and income rises.
- If government spending rises, income increases. Since in this process interest rates go up, there is some crowding out of private investment and, hence, a reduced multiplier.
- Only one macroeconomic equilibrium (defined as simultaneous equilibrium in both markets) exists: income and the interest rate assume one specific value each.

KEY TERMS AND CONCEPTS

crowding out
exchange rate
fiscal policy
flow variable
global economy
IS curve
IS-LM model
LM curve
monetary base
(high-powered money)
monetary policy
money demand function
money market
purchasing power parity
real exchange rate
real money supply
stock variable

EXERCISES

3.1 Which of the following variables are flow variables, and which are stock variables?

(a) A nation's GDP.
(b) A firm's physical assets.
(c) The gold reserves of your country's central bank.
(d) Ferrari Testarossa sales between 1987 and 2001.
(e) Aggregate investment.
(f) British lager consumption per capita in 1999.
(g) The number of Rioja bottles in your cellar.
(h) The profits of your country's central bank in 1996.
(i) The number of Ferrari Testarossa models registered in Lisbon.

3.2 In recent years a number of institutional and technical innovations such as cash machines have made it less expensive to obtain cash. Explain the consequences of this development by using the model of money demand in the text. If this trend continues, will average cash holdings decrease or increase?

3.3 Suppose your bank starts to pay interest on your bank account. Will this decrease or increase your demand for money (defined as M1)?

3.4 Recall the quantity equation from Chapter 1: $M \times V = P \times Y$. In that chapter the velocity of money circulation was assumed to be constant. Is this assumption reasonable in the light of the model of money demand? How would you expect V to change with an increase in the interest rate? Assume that the interest rate remains at its new higher level, with M and Y unchanged. How does this affect the price level?

3.5 How do decreasing transaction costs affect the behaviour of the *LM* curve? (Hint: decreasing transaction costs reinforce the reaction of money demand to a change in the interest rate. Start with the money demand equation and show how transaction costs determine the slope of the money demand function. Then work your way through to Figure 3.5 and decide if – with lower transaction costs – a given increase in money supply leads to a larger or to a smaller shift of the *LM* curve.)

3.6 Consider Table 3.1 which shows monthly exchange rates of the Deutschmark with respect to the English pound, the US dollar and the Danish crown for the first half of 1995. When did the Deutschmark appreciate against the pound and when did it depreciate against the US dollar? When did the Danish crown appreciate against the Deutschmark?

3.7 In Table 3.2 prices for an Italian mid-range car and a man's haircut for both St Gallen (Switzerland) and Stuttgart (Germany) are listed, as well as the Swiss franc/euro exchange rate. Focus on one of the two goods to decide whether the Swiss franc is over- or undervalued. What might explain the apparent difference?

Table 3.2

Average exchange rate in 2002: €1 = 1.6 SFR	Price in Stuttgart (Germany)	Price in St Gallen (Switzerland)
Italian car	€12,500	SFR 23,000
Haircut	€20	SFR 48

3.8 *The Economist* regularly publishes its Big Mac Index. Data on the cost of a Big Mac is gathered in several countries and these prices are then translated into the US dollar price equivalent to produce the index. What are the advantages and disadvantages of using such an index for the purpose of making comparisons?

3.9 (a) What would happen to the slope of the *IS* curve if trade was completely abolished?
(b) What happens to the slope of the *IS* curve if investment only depends on income, but not on the interest rate?

3.10 How do the following changes of exogenous variables shift the *LM* and the *IS* curves? (Note: apply the thought experiment suggested in Box 3.3. Make sure you understand the economic reasoning.)
(a) An increase in money supply.
(b) A decrease in government expenditure.
(c) A decrease in foreign income.
(d) An increase in the foreign price level.

3.11 Suppose the demand-for-money function for three different levels of income looks as shown in Figure 3.12.
(a) What does the *LM* curve look like? It may help to identify points A–D in your new diagram.
(b) What happens to Y and i if income initially is 80, the interest rate is i_0 and the real money supply expands?

Table 3.1

	January	February	March	April	May	June
1 UK pound	2.4119	2.3559	2.2508	2.2206	2.2354	2.2330
1 US dollar	1.5324	1.5018	1.4066	1.3806	1.4077	1.4003
100 Danish Kroner	25.384	25.333	24.965	25.394	25.547	25.617

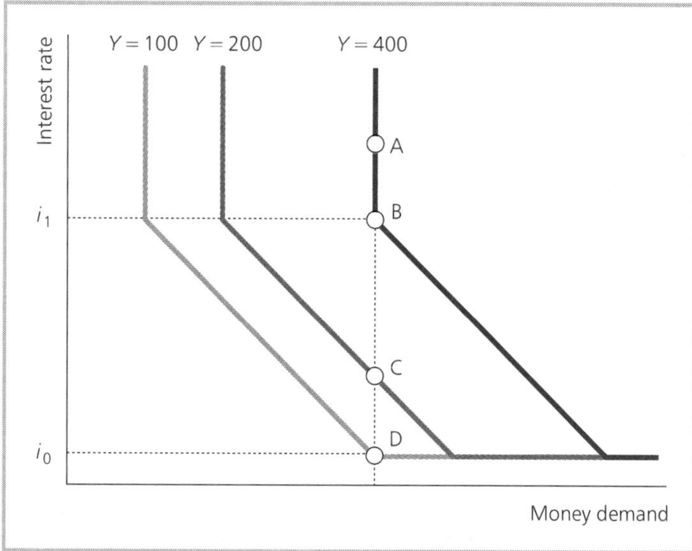

Figure 3.12

3.12 Suppose the central bank and the government cannot agree on the direction of economic policy, so that the government raises spending while the central bank contracts the money supply. Trace in a diagram what happens to income and the interest rate.

RECOMMENDED READING

Half a dozen leading macroeconomists discuss how the concepts on which we built in this chapter fit into current research in 'Symposium: Keynesian economics today', *Journal of Economic Perspectives* 7 (1993).

Also, Jordi Gali (1992) 'How well does the *IS-LM* model fit the postwar US data?', *Quarterly Journal of Economics* 107: 709–38, demonstrates the empirical relevance of the *IS-LM*.

APPLIED PROBLEMS

RECENT RESEARCH

Money demand in the United States

This chapter postulated that the real demand for money L depends on two factors: income Y and the nominal interest rate i. R. W. Hafer and S. Hein ('The shift in money demand: What really happened?', Federal Reserve Bank of St Louis, *Review*, February 1982) assume that income and two interest rates i_C (commercial paper rate) and i_B (bank deposit rate) affect desired real money holdings L^*: $L^* = c_0 + c_1 Y + c_2 i_C + c_3 i_B$. If we assume again that actual money holdings gradually adjust to desired money holdings, $L - L_{-1} = a(L^* - L_{-1})$, we may substitute the above equation to obtain $L = ac_0 + (1 - a)L_{-1} + ac_1 Y + ac_2 i_C + ac_3 i_B$. Estimating this with quarterly data (all measured in logarithms) for the United States gives

$$\underset{(2.8)}{L = -0.61} + \underset{(6.0)}{0.778L_{-1}} + \underset{(2.7)}{0.125Y} - \underset{(3.0)}{0.016i_C} - \underset{(2.1)}{0.032i_B}$$

$R^2_{adj} = 0.976$

quarterly data 1960I to 1973IV

The absolute *t*-statistics given in parentheses show that all the coefficients are significant and have the expected sign. In particular, when income grows or interest rates fall, the demand for money rises. The demand for money seems to respond differently to the two interest rates considered here. As measured by the coefficient of determination of 0.976, the equation's fit is quite high. From $(1 - a) = 0.778$ for the coefficient on $L - 1$ we get $a = 0.222$. Since the coefficient on Y is $ac_1 = 0.125$ this gives $c_1 = 0.56$. So if income grows by 1%, desired money holdings grow by about 0.56%.

WORKED PROBLEM

Investment, interest rates and oil prices in Norway

This chapter showed that investment depends on expected future income and the interest rate: $I = aY^e_+ - bi$. In reality this relationship may not be instantaneous but implies lags, say between the decision to undertake the project to its eventual implementation. We might assume, for example, that this lag is one period, so that this year's investment depends on last year's interest rate and income (assuming that expected income follows actual income). Estimating such an equation for Norway on the basis of annual data for 1979–2000, given in Table 3.3, yields:

$$I = \underset{(3.73)}{109.83} - \underset{(2.20)}{3.76r_{-1}} + \underset{(3.88)}{0.14Y_{-1}} \qquad R^2_{adj} = 0.43$$

(parentheses contain absolute *t*-statistics)

where r is the real interest rate (nominal interest rate minus inflation). The equation supports the hypotheses that higher interest rates drive investment down, while higher income (leading individuals to expect higher income in the future) spurs investment.

When considering how this equation may still be improved or augmented, we may note that the structure of investment spending in Norway is unusual, with some 20% going into North Sea oil fields. The profitability of oil field varies directly with the price at which crude oil can be sold. While, again, investment decisions will be based on expected future oil prices, we may assume that the latter will be positively influenced by the price of oil observed in the recent past. The following equations test this idea by adding the price of oil *OIL*, observed at various lags, to the above equation.

$$I = \underset{(1.88)}{81.97} - \underset{(1.55)}{2.99r_{-1}} + \underset{(3.73)}{0.15Y_{-1}} + \underset{(0.87)}{0.04OIL_{-1}} \qquad R^2_{adj} = 0.42$$

$$I = \underset{(1.32)}{51.00} - \underset{(1.94)}{3.08r_{-1}} + \underset{(4.72)}{0.18Y_{-1}} + \underset{(2.15)}{0.08OIL_{-2}} \qquad R^2_{adj} = 0.52$$

$$I = \underset{(1.05)}{32.39} - \underset{(3.17)}{4.19r_{-1}} + \underset{(6.24)}{0.20Y_{-1}} + \underset{(3.73)}{0.12OIL_{-3}} \qquad R^2_{adj} = 0.66$$

The results indicate that if oil prices influence investment at all, they do so slowly. Only at lags of two or three years is this influence significant, as measured by the *t*-statistic of 2.15 and 3.73, respectively, and the coefficient of determination is significantly improved. One would have to look into the decision processes behind North Sea oil investment to find out whether such lags are realistic.

Table 3.3

Year	Interest rate *i*	Income *Y*	Investment *I*	Oil price *OIL*
1977	–	–	–	223.9
1978	–	–	–	201.3
1979	–	–	–	251.2
1980	−0.63	735.3	198.1	417.1
1981	−1.33	735.9	199.2	455.1
1982	1.83	730.9	199.3	405.5
1983	4.45	747.4	208.2	380.1
1984	5.88	791.5	208.9	384.6
1985	6.91	829.5	205.4	363.2
1986	6.28	794.2	220.7	156.8
1987	4.83	796.4	223.1	161.3
1988	6.27	782.9	222.1	120.0
1989	6.28	799.0	205.0	146.4
1990	6.61	812.9	175.7	172.4
1991	6.45	829.8	171.1	145.9
1992	7.44	834.1	166.1	129.8
1993	4.25	855.3	174.7	113.8
1994	5.73	888.9	183.8	120.4
1995	4.36	928.7	192.5	107.7
1996	4.68	1003.5	213.4	147.1
1997	2.55	1055.0	242.6	128.3
1998	3.09	1044.6	260.8	79.6
1999	3.05	1097.4	244.0	173.1
2000	3.29	1252.7	242.5	–

*All variables in real terms.
Sources: IMF-IFS and Statistics Norway.

YOUR TURN

Swiss money demand

Table 3.4 gives annual data on the real money supply, real income and nominal interest rates for Switzerland, 1970–93.

(a) Check if the data support a money demand function of the form $\log(M/P) = \alpha + \beta \log Y - \gamma i$. Since both M/P and Y exhibit heavy trends (check the plots), you may want to rewrite the equation in terms of changes of the variables and estimate $\Delta \log(M/P) = \alpha + \beta\Delta \log Y - \gamma\Delta i$

(b) Which hypothesis gives a better fit – the hypothesis that the logarithm of real money demand depends linearly on the interest rate, or that the relationship is non-linear? (Hint: Compare the fit obtained for the above equation with the fit of equations of the form $\Delta\log (M/P) = \alpha + \beta\Delta\log Y - \gamma\Delta i^z$, where you raise interest rates to the powers of, say, $z = 2$, $z = 0.5$ or $z = 0.1$.

Table 3.4

Year	*M/P*	*Y*	*i*
1970	49.45	148.53	5.72
1971	52.84	154.88	5.27
1972	56.69	160.24	4.96
1973	53.62	165.30	5.59
1974	50.06	167.25	7.13
1975	48.92	156.02	6.44
1976	51.60	154.71	4.98
1977	53.81	158.36	4.05
1978	60.43	159.30	3.33
1979	63.91	163.18	3.45
1980	57.07	170.33	4.77
1981	51.69	172.78	5.57
1982	50.10	171.18	4.59
1983	52.20	172.90	4.18
1984	52.10	175.96	4.55
1985	50.61	182.49	4.70
1986	51.12	187.72	4.24
1987	53.65	191.53	4.04
1988	59.82	197.08	4.02
1989	54.29	204.69	5.19
1990	49.18	209.40	6.44
1991	47.21	209.34	6.23
1992	45.98	208.70	6.41
1993	49.21	206.92	4.55

To further explore this chapter's key messages you are encouraged to use the interactive online module found at

www.fgn.unisg.ch/eurmacro/tutor/ISLM.html

and many other features hosted at **www.fgn.unisg.ch/eurmacro**

CHAPTER 4

EXCHANGE RATES AND THE BALANCE OF PAYMENTS

WHAT TO EXPECT After working through this chapter you will understand:

1 What **globalization** is and what it means in the context of macroeconomics.

2 What the **balance of payments** is and why it is a mirror image of the **foreign exchange market.**

3 How the **mobility of international capital** affects the equilibrium condition for the foreign exchange market.

4 How the goods market, the money market and the foreign exchange market are put together to form an **open-economy model of the national economy** called the ***IS-LM-FE*** **model.**

Chapter 3's *IS-LM* or global-economy model provides an understanding of the world economy as if viewed from a satellite camera in outer space. Looking at the globe from that vantage point, international borders and national detail disappear and can, therefore, be ignored. In this chapter we start to move in closer, zooming in on the individual country and its national economy, as it interacts with the rest of the world. The degree of a country's interaction with the rest of the world determines to what extent Chapter 3's global-economy model may serve as a first approximation for how a national economy works. If a country's international involvement is relatively moderate, the approximation can be quite good. If the involvement is intense, the approximation may become poor, if not useless.

Following dramatic developments known as **globalization** the world's national economies now interact more intensively than ever before. This makes it mandatory to refine and augment the picture set out in Chapter 3, but we don't need to start from scratch. Our knowledge of the *IS-LM* model continues to be useful for two reasons. First, it explains what goes on in the world that surrounds and influences the individual country; second, it remains an integral part of the national-economy model to be developed in this and the next chapter.

To begin this chapter's discussion we first look at quantitative dimensions of globalization. We then proceed to look at international transactions. Not only how they are being recorded and structured in the balance of payments, but also at their key determinant, the exchange rate, and how it is determined in the foreign exchange market. The *IS-LM* model is then augmented by the foreign exchange market to form a complete model of the national economy.

4.1 GLOBALIZATION

A **closed economy** is an economy that does not trade or interact financially with other countries. The global economy is a closed economy.

An **open economy** trades (goods or assets) with other countries. Most national economies are open economies.

Empirical fact. The US was the world export champion in 2000, selling $1,097 billion worth of output abroad. In second place was Germany ($625 billion) and Japan came third ($450 billion). Total exports from the euro area amounted to $1,148 billion.

Example. A country imports €10 billion worth of produce, prepares oven-ready meals employing €5 billion worth of labour and exports 50% of the meals for €7.5 billion. Then GDP is €5 billion, the import share is 200% and the export share 150%.

The global economy discussed in Chapter 3 is often referred to as a **closed economy**. It neither exports nor imports. By contrast, an economy that trades a lot with other countries is an **open economy**. These days most countries have open economies. Therefore, the national economy model to be developed and analyzed in this and the next chapter is an open-economy model.

A country's openness may have many dimensions. The most frequently used measure of the openness of an economy is the ratio of exports (or imports) to income. Table 4.1 gives export and import shares for the world's largest economies and the euro area.

Interestingly, if you look at the world's two largest economies, Japan and the United States, exports or imports amount to only some 10% of national income. This is still sizeable, but it also means that if we were using Chapter 3's closed-economy model to study these countries, results should not be completely off. This may serve as a justification for using the *IS-LM* model in Case study 3.1 on Japan's liquidity trap. Note, though, that openness is already twice as high for the euro area, still higher or much higher for many individual countries, and increasing worldwide. Figure 4.1 illustrates the latter two points by comparing export ratios for EU members and several other countries in the year 2000 with what they were four decades earlier.

The most striking message in the picture given in Figure 4.1 is the almost universal trend towards more openness. With the perhaps perplexing exception of Japan, where exports seem to have been stagnating relative to income around the 10% mark, all other countries have experienced often dramatic increases in their exports shares. Many countries, including Austria, Belgium, France, Greece, Ireland, Italy, Spain, Sweden and the United States, have more than doubled their export shares. All European countries shown have export shares exceeding 20%. Belgium and Ireland are approaching 100%, which Luxembourg has already exceeded. Such high export shares are only possible if a country serves as a trading hub, by importing goods, then adding value by refining or modifying them, and then exporting them again.

Globalization trends do not only show up in the trade of goods and services. Another, possibly more comprehensive measure of how intensively national economies interact nowadays, is the volume of transactions in the foreign exchange markets. In the year 2000 the equivalent of about $1,500,000,000,000 (yes, that is $1.5 trillion) changed hands in the foreign exchange markets around the world on any average trading *day*. This is 20 times higher than it was in

Table 4.1 Openness indicators, 2000

	Euro area	Japan	United States
Exports as % of GDP	19.4	10.4	11.0
Imports as % of GDP	18.9	8.7	14.7

Source: ECB and IMF

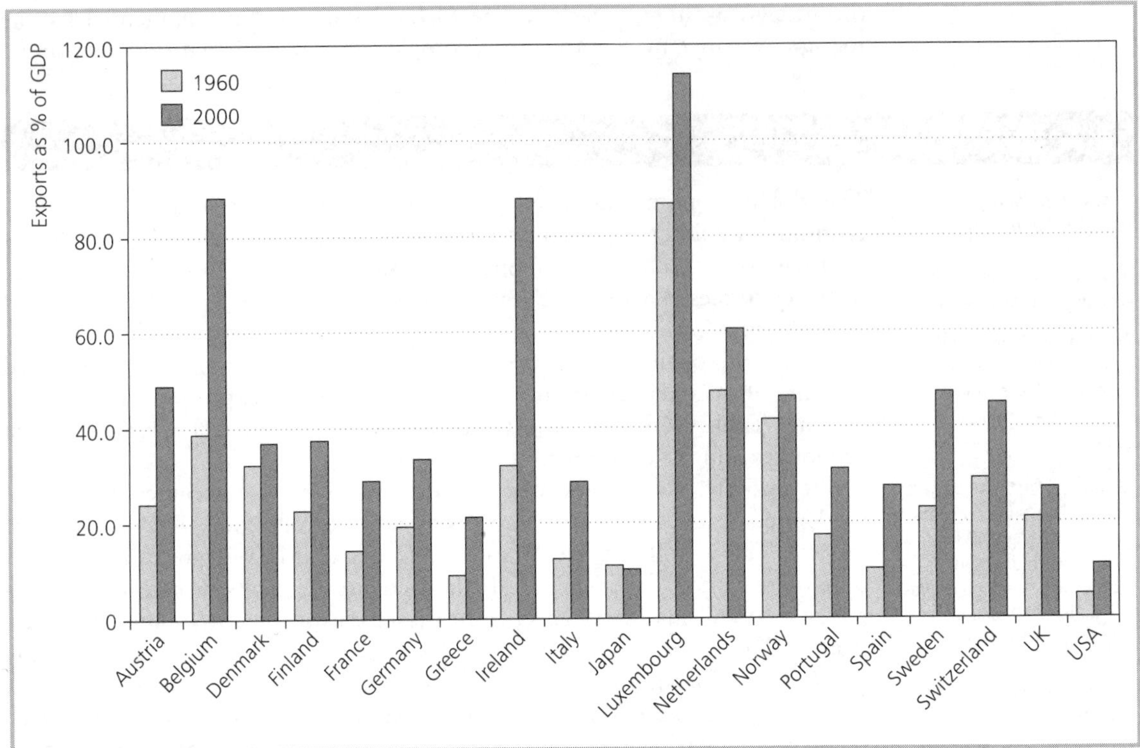

Figure 4.1 The second half of the 20th century is characterized by steadily intensifying cross-border trade. In the countries shown here, exports as a share of income roughly doubled over a period of 40 years. The only exception is Japan. Its economy is less open today than it was back in 1960, and quite surprisingly, the least open economy in this sample of countries by the measure employed here.
Sources: OECD, *Historical Statistics*; IMF; *IFS*.

1980. And to put the number in perspective: world GDP generated in 2000 was about $30 trillion. So one year's worth of world income was spent in the foreign exchange markets within a single month. This is an important insight we should keep in mind because it will prove useful later on.

Motivated by the growing openness of modern economies demonstrated by these statistics, we now turn to the task of tieing up the second loose end left over from Chapter 3. We will do so in two steps. In section 4.2 we first look at the foreign exchange market and the balance of payments, where international transactions take place and are recorded. In this chapter's remaining two sections we will then *model* the foreign exchange market on a level of abstraction similar to the one we worked on when we modelled the goods market and the money market, and then add it to the *IS-LM* model to complete our first macroeconomic model of the national economy.

4.2 THE EXCHANGE RATE AND THE BALANCE OF PAYMENTS

From the beginning of this book we have repeatedly noted that a country's macroeconomic performance depends on, among other things, exports and imports. We saw this when we spelled out the circular flow of income, when we discussed the Keynesian cross, and also when we looked into the goods market and the *IS-LM* curve in Chapter 3. We also noted that a crucial determinant of exports and imports is the exchange rate, since it affects the relative price of goods at home and abroad. While this is an interesting insight, it is of little use as long as we do not know what determines the exchange rate. In principle, the answer is simple. It is supply and demand in the foreign exchange market. We deliberately refrained from adding this market to our model in Chapter 3 so as not to take too big a step at that time. Now, however, the time has come to take a look at the foreign exchange market.

A market brings together potential buyers and sellers of a specific good. And a functioning market generates a price that balances supply and demand, thus clearing the market. The commodity traded in the foreign exchange market is foreign currency, or rather, foreign currencies. There are, in fact, dozens of currencies traded around the clock in the world's currency markets, and each pair of currencies has its market. One that trades euros against yen, one that trades pounds sterling against dollars, one that trades dollars against euros, and so on. We will sidestep the complications arising from this by lumping all foreign currencies – dollars, roubles, shekels, yen and so forth – under the heading foreign exchange. Foreign exchange is, then, simply all currencies other than the domestic currency.

Now when we start thinking about why individuals may want to purchase or sell foreign currency, we need not start from scratch. Luckily, countries began many years ago to record all their international transactions. This record is called the balance of payments. Since any international transaction between countries with their own national currencies requires the purchase and sale of foreign exchange, the balance of payments is at the same time a meticulous record of foreign exchange market transactions. The balance of payments is therefore a mirror image of the foreign exchange market. And the conditions for a balance-of-payments equilibrium are at the same time the conditions for equilibrium in the foreign exchange market. Since this chapter's main aim is to develop an understanding of the foreign exchange market and how it determines the exchange rate, it is worthwhile pausing here and taking a closer look at the balance of payments.

This is not the place to go into the intricate details of balance of payments accounting. After all, we are assembling a macroeconomic model with a high level of abstraction. However, an understanding of the basic mechanisms linking the various balance of payments accounts will be very helpful.

Balance of payments basics

Any transaction that requires a purchase of domestic currency is a credit (positive) item in that country's balance of payments. Any transaction that requires a sale of domestic currency is a debit (negative) item. Since domestic currency can only be purchased if someone else is prepared to sell, the sum of all credit items (of all purchases of domestic currency) must equal the sum of all debit items (sales). This means that the demand for domestic currency always equals the supply of domestic currency, and that the foreign exchange market always clears. This is why the conditions that equalize the balance of payments also equalize the foreign exchange market.

Traditionally, the balance of payments is broken into three subaccounts, as we saw in Chapter 1. The current account *CA* which mainly records cross-border transactions in goods and services, the capital account *CP* which records private financial transactions, and the official reserves account *OR* which records changes in the central bank's foreign exchange reserves.

$$BP = CA + CP + OR = 0 \qquad (4.1)$$

The balance of payments is always zero because of double-entry bookkeeping, as stated above. Therefore, any entry in one of the accounts must be accompanied by an equivalent entry of opposite sign in the same account or one of the other two accounts. Let us look at what this means in practical terms. To do so consider a stylized world with only two countries, Britain and Sweden. Suppose Britain wants to import one Volvo S60 vehicle from Sweden that costs 300,000 kronor. To obtain the 300,000 kronor requested by the Swedish car maker, the UK customer must supply £20,000 at the current exchange rate. In reality, the UK buyer only sees and settles the £20,000 price tag. But since Volvo insists on receiving payment in kronor to pay for Swedish labour and steel, someone must be willing to offer £20,000 in exchange for 300,000 kronor. According to the balance-of-payments identity, this can happen in three distinct ways.

Consider Figure 4.2. Following the rule stated above, the Volvo import shows up as a debit item (that is, with a minus) in Britain's current account. Now who sold 300,000 kronor in exchange for £20,000?

Reality check. Of course, UK importers do not look for UK exporters (or Swedish importers) to buy kronor from, but go to a bank that serves as a middleman. Ignoring this does not affect the substance of the issues.

First, there can be another, balancing transaction in the current account (Figure 4.2, left-hand column). Sweden may import 2,000 Atomic Kitten CDs costing £10 apiece. To pay the British record company, the Swedish importer must acquire £20,000 in exchange for 300,000 kronor. Since this is exactly the amount the UK Volvo importer needs, both transactions, the import and the export, go through as planned. In this case the current account balances. Exports equal imports, i.e. net exports are zero.

A second option shown in Figure 4.2's middle column is that there is a balancing transaction in the capital account. Suppose Swedes want no Atomic Kitten CDs. Then Britain as a whole is unable to pay Volvo in kronor. The only way to import the S60 would be if Volvo did not insist on immediate payment, accepting instead the promise of payment some time in the future. Britain goes into debt to Sweden.

In reality it will not be the UK importer who is in debt to Volvo. Instead, some British institution would go into debt to some Swedish institution or individual. The middle column in Figure 4.2 assumes that a wealthy Swede buys £20,000 worth of UK Treasury bills. Because payment is required in pounds sterling, she offers 300,000 kronor in the foreign exchange market to acquire £20,000. Since this is the exact amount the Volvo importer needs,

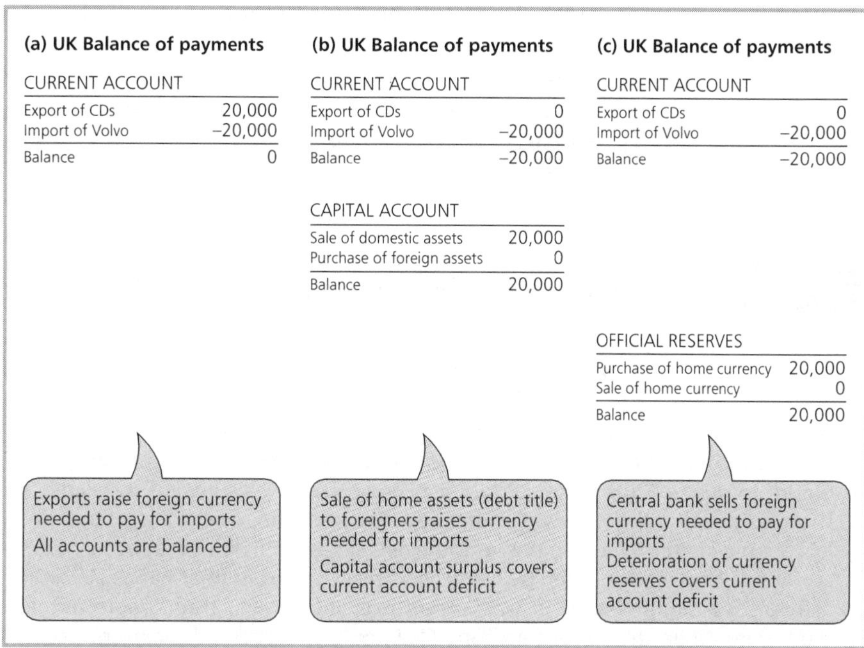

Figure 4.2 To pay for imports from Sweden, Britain needs to acquire Swedish kronor. There are three ways to do so: (a) it can export and accept payment in kronor; (b) it can ask Swedes to lend the required amount of kronor and hand over debt titles instead; (c) it can persuade the Bank of England (or the Sveriges Riksbank) to sell kronor for pounds.

both transactions go through. In this case the item balancing the car import is recorded in the capital account. The current account records a deficit, but the capital account shows a surplus of equal magnitude.

As a third option, which is actually a variant of the second option, the Bank of England could sell 300,000 kronor worth of currency reserves it may hold in exchange for £20,000. In this case, as shown in the right-hand column of Figure 4.2, the current account records a £20,000 deficit, the capital account is balanced, and the official reserves account records a £20,000 surplus.

The advantage of recording private capital flows and the change in official net foreign assets (mostly covering central bank currency reserves) separately is that it reveals at a glance whether foreign exchange market transactions were due to market forces alone, or whether they included the central bank as a buyer or seller. This is important for two reasons.

First, it gives meaning to the notion of balance of payments imbalances, which is actually self-contradictory. How can you speak of a country having a balance of payments surplus when according to equation (4.1) double-entry bookkeeping ensures that the balance of payments is always zero? This is indeed rather unfortunate terminology. What is actually meant by a balance of payments surplus is that the balance of payments, hypothetically, would have been in surplus had the central bank not participated in the foreign exchange market. So according to the numbers given in Box 4.1 on balance of payments terminology, the euro area ran a balance of payments *deficit* in the year 2000. Because if the European Central Bank (ECB) had not sold €17.5 billion worth

The **balance of payments surplus** ($BP^{surplus}$) is defined as $BP^{surplus} = -OR$.

of foreign assets, the demand for euros would have fallen short of its supply in the foreign exchange market. So the **balance of payments surplus** is actually defined as the balance generated by private, non-official involvement in the foreign exchange market. It is equal to the official reserves account with a negative sign.

The second reason why it is useful to know the extent of central bank involvement in the foreign exchange market is that it tells you to what extent

BOX 4.1 Traditional vs new balance of payments terminology

Due to the initiative of international institutions like the IMF and the OECD, economists will have to get used to some new, unfamiliar balance-of-payments terminology. Table 1 is using the euro area's balance of payments with regard to the rest of the world, to describe the major differences between the traditional and the new classification. On the left are the old terms and on the right the new ones currently being implemented by many countries.

There is a slight change in the **current account** definition. While the current account traditionally included transfers not made out of current income, so-called wealth transfers, these will now be recorded in a separate account called the **capital account**. The intention is to clearly separate current income from changes in the stock of assets. Note that this new capital account has nothing to do with the capital account in its traditional definition!

What was formerly called the capital account now obviously needs a new name. It will be called the **financial account**. It includes all the items traditionally recorded in the capital account plus the official reserves balance. Hence, the official reserves account disappears, and there is no longer a distinction between private and non-private financial transactions on this level of aggregation. This information, of course, can still be retrieved from the financial account.

In traditional terminology, the euro area recorded a current account deficit (the sum of all credit items less the sum of all debit items in the current account) of €24.2 billion euros. The capital account was also in deficit by €10.8 billion. The fact that these two deficits were not entirely offset by the official reserves account surplus of €17.5 billion must be due to recording errors and omissions amounting to a statistical discrepancy of €17.5 billion.

Table 1 Balance of payments of the euro area in 2000 (billions of euros)

Traditional classification		Credit	Debit	New classification
Current account: −24.2	Exports of goods	979.1		**Current account: −34.7**
	Imports of goods		926.9	
	Export of services	270.2		
	Import of services		285.5	
	Income received on investments	262.3		
	Income paid on investments		282.5	
	Transfer payments from abroad	66.9		
	Transfer payments to abroad		118.3	
	Net wealth transfers	10.5		**Capital account: +10.5**
Capital account: −10.8	Direct investment		22.8	**Financial account: +6.7**
	Portfolio investment		128.9	
	Financial derivatives		1.1	
	Other investment	142.0		
Official reserves account	Official reserves balance	17.5		
Statistical discrepancy		17.5		**Statistical discrepancy**

Under **flexible exchange rates** $OR = 0$ and the balance of payments reduces to $BP = CA + CP = 0$ or $CA = -CP$.

the price in this market, the exchange rate, was left to market forces alone. If more individuals want to sell euros than are prepared to buy euros, and the central bank jumps in to purchase this incipient excess supply, the resulting exchange rate is obviously a distorted price. A true, undistorted market price only results if the central bank abstains from the foreign exchange market. Thus under an ideal system of flexible exchange rates the central bank does not intervene in the foreign exchanges and the official reserves account is zero.

Real world current accounts and capital accounts

When the central bank refrains from foreign exchange market involvement ($OR = 0$), the capital account is a mirror image of the current account ($CA = -CP$). This property serves as a test of how close a country's actual experience was to an ideal system of flexible exchange rates determined by private market forces.

Note. Errors and omissions are sometimes quite sizeable and may cause CA to not exactly match $-CP$ despite OR being zero.

Figure 4.3 (overleaf) shows current account and capital account balances for 15 countries from 1974 to 2000. If one balance is a perfect reflection of the other, the central bank abstained from the foreign exchanges. This is indeed the case for most countries. A positive current account goes with a negative capital account, meaning that we lend to foreign countries to buy our exports. In the opposite case we borrow from their private citizens so that we can pay for our high level of imports. The less perfectly the capital account mirrors the current account, the stronger must be central bank involvement in the foreign exchange market. This was obviously the case in Switzerland in the 1970s and early 1980s, and in recent years in some European Monetary System member countries such as Italy.

4.3 BACK TO *IS-LM*: ENTER THE *FE* CURVE

The loose end remaining after the discussion of the goods market in Chapter 3 (section 3.2), is the exchange rate. Left to market forces in a system of flexible exchange rates, currency prices tend to move about quite a bit – more than any other macroeconomic variable. While there may be market psychology and speculation involved, a number of strings attach the exchange rate to the set of variables we are focusing on in macroeconomics. This section identifies and formalizes these relationships.

Being the price of one currency in terms of another, the exchange rate, like any price, is determined by supply and demand. Section 4.2 taught us that, being a comprehensive record of a country's residents' international transactions and a mirror image of the foreign exchange market, the balance of payments is an excellent way of identifying and structuring the determinants of currency supply and demand. From the balance of payments identity $BP = CA + CP + OR = 0$ and the insight that under flexible exchange rates, when $OR = 0$, the non-official components of BP do balance, we obtain $CA + CP = 0$ as a condition for **foreign exchange market** equilibrium. We now analyze this condition by first taking isolated looks at each of the two involved accounts, and then putting them together.

In the **foreign exchange market** different currencies are traded for one another.

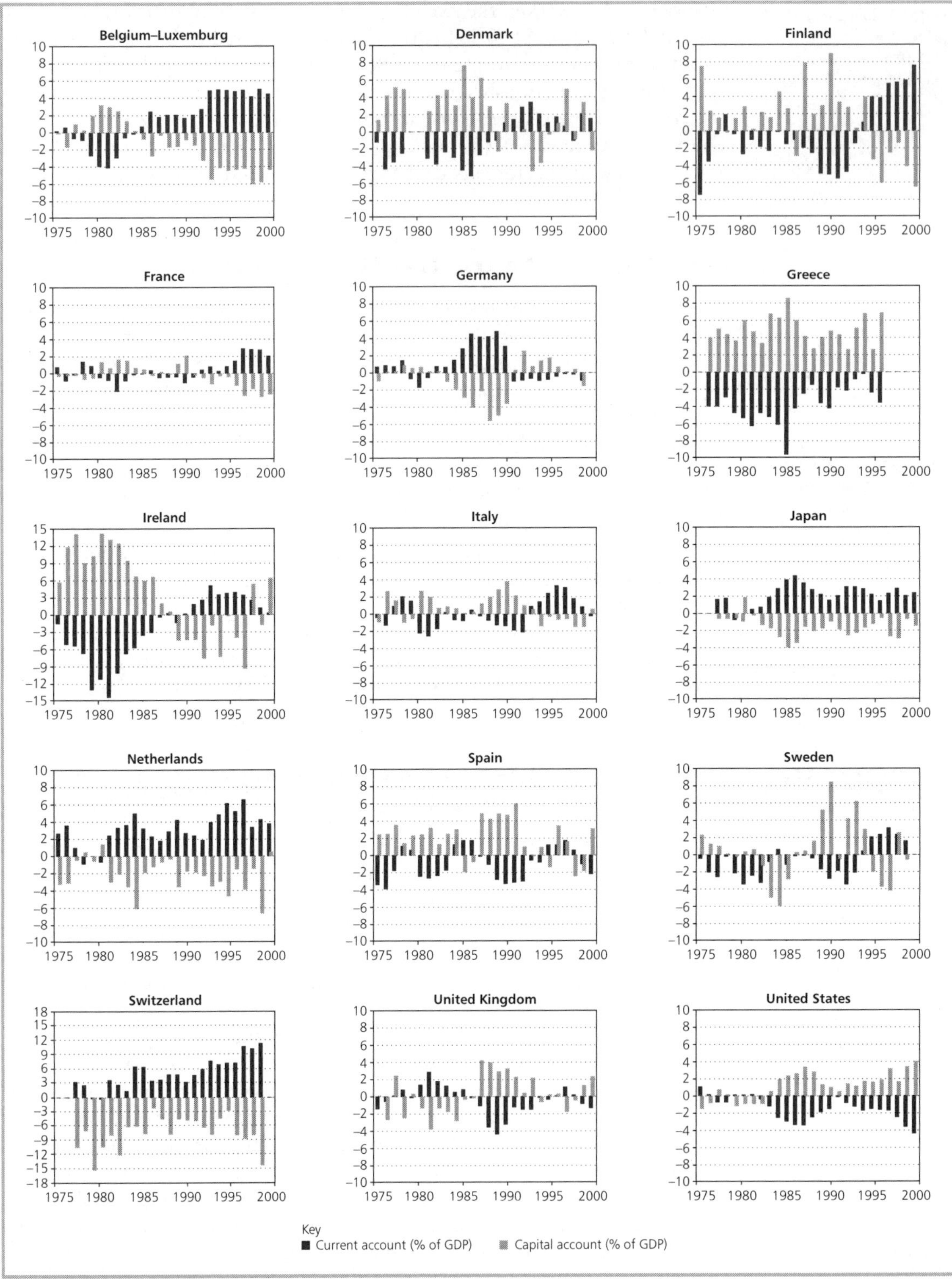

Figure 4.3 Current account and capital account in 15 industrialized countries, 1974–2000.
Source: IMF, *IFS*.

Note. Economists rarely work with 3D graphs. They are used here and below to show where the 2D graphs on the right of Figure 4.4 come from. If you have no problem understanding the 2D graph you can ignore the 3D version.

Maths note. One euro invested at home grows to $1 + i$ euro after one period. If invested abroad it grows to $(1 + i^{\text{World}})(1 + (E^e_{+1} - E)/E)$. Setting this equal to $1 + i$ and subtracting 1 from both sides gives interest parity as

$$i = i^{\text{World}} + \frac{E^e_{+1} - E}{E} + i^{\text{World}} \frac{E^e_{+1} - E}{E}$$

Equation (4.4) simplifies this by ignoring the involved exchange rate gain on the interest payment, which is small under normal circumstances.

An individual is **risk neutral** if he is indifferent between a guaranteed payment of €500, and playing a free lottery in which he can win either €0 or €1,000 with a probability of 50% each.

The **current account** tracks net exports of goods and services. These we already know from the above analysis of the goods market.

$$CA \equiv NX = EX - IM = x_1 Y^{\text{World}} + x_2 R - m_1 Y + m_2 R \qquad (4.2)$$

Figure 4.4, panel (a), shows the current account as a function of income and the interest rate. While the interest rate has no impact on the current account (i is missing from equation (4.2)), CA deteriorates with a factor m_1 as income rises.

For given world income and real exchange rate, only one income level exists which balances the current account. An algebraic expression for this is obtained by letting $CA = 0$ in equation (4.2) and solving for Y. This yields

$$Y = \frac{x_1}{m_1} Y^{\text{World}} + \frac{x_2 + m_2}{m_1} R \qquad \textbf{Current account equilibrium} \qquad (4.3)$$

All points that balance the current account would lie on a vertical line in the i-Y plane. Rising world incomes or real depreciations would shift the CA plane up (see equation (4.2)), thus shifting the $CA = 0$ line in i-Y space to the right (panel (b) in Figure 4.4).

The **capital account** records how capital flows across borders in search of the highest returns. Just as a Londoner's purchase of a Ferrari calls for the purchase of euros, the purchase of bonds issued by the Italian government calls for buying euros as well. So the next question to be addressed is what determines international financial investment decisions.

Investing one unit of capital in the home country gives an annual return equal to the interest rate i. Investing the same amount abroad yields the foreign interest rate plus the percentage change of the exchange rate. If investors are **risk neutral**, they are only then indifferent between having domestic or foreign government's bonds in their portfolio if

$$i = i^{\text{World}} + \frac{E^e_{+1} - E}{E} \qquad \textbf{Capital account equilibrium (Uncovered interest parity)} \qquad (4.4)$$

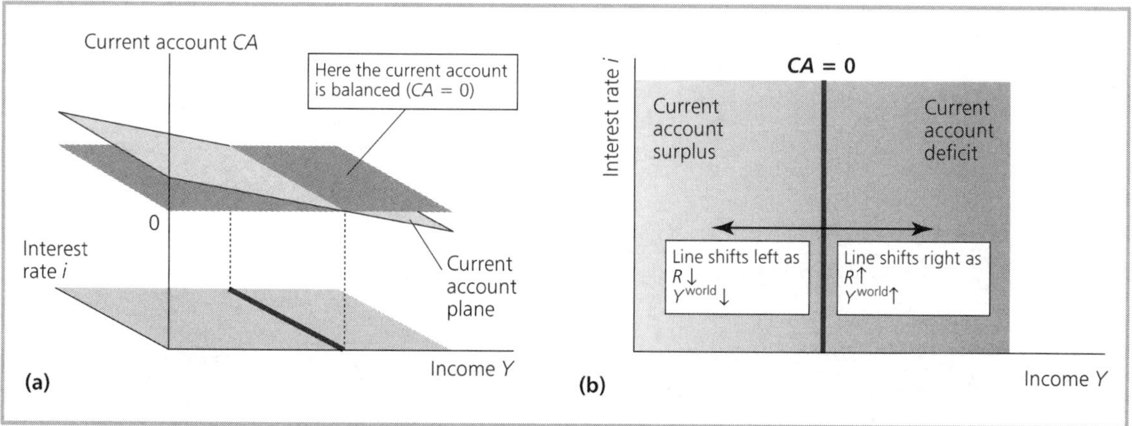

Figure 4.4 The current account worsens as rising income raises imports. The interest rate does not affect *CA*. The current account equilibrium line, therefore, projects as a vertical line onto the *i*-*Y* plane. An exchange rate depreciation or a rise in world income moves the *CA* plane up, shifting the *CA* = 0 line to the right.

CASE STUDY 4.1 Italy's current account before and after the 1992 EMS crisis

In open-economy models of the macroeconomy the exchange rate provides the key link between the monetary sector and the goods market. Changes in policy variables, such as the money supply or the interest rate, affect the exchange rate which, in turn, affect imports and exports and, hence, income.

Whether the assumed effect of the (real) exchange rate on imports, exports and, hence, the current account does indeed have an impact in the real world is often difficult to judge and may require the use of sophisticated statistical techniques. The reason is that imports are not only driven by the exchange rate, but also by domestic income. And exports are not only influenced by the exchange rate, but also by world income. Usually, all these determinants of the current account change all the time, and the movement of one may offset the effects resulting from the movement of another.

A graphic example is provided occasionally when one determinant of the current account changes so dramatically that its effects dominate any effects that may stem from concomitant small changes in the other determinants. This happened after the 1992 crisis in the European Monetary System, when Italy suspended membership in the system and the lira depreciated fast and substantially, relative to the currencies of Italy's trading partners.

Figure 1 shows the effective (that is: trade-weighted) exchange rate for the lira between 1985 and 1995, adjusted for inflation differences. The lira moved up steadily from 1985 through to 1992, making Italy's exports gradually more expensive for foreigners and imports more affordable for Italians. As a result, the current account, which was roughly balanced in the mid-1980s, moved into greater deficit each year – just as the textbook says it should. After 1992 the exchange rate changed its course, depreciating by more than 25% within a short period of time. The turnaround in the current account followed immediately. Within three years the current account deficit of 30 billion dollars (or 40,000 billion lira) in 1992 had become a current account surplus of almost equal size.

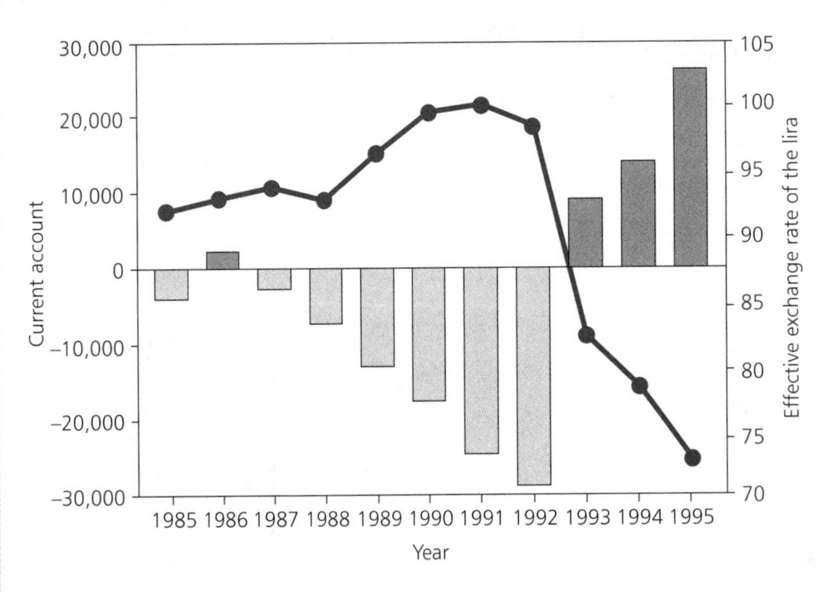

Figure 1

This equation is called the open or **uncovered interest parity** condition. It is uncovered because the return on the right-hand side is not guaranteed, but only an expectation. To keep things simple here, assume that financial investors expect the exchange rate to remain where it is today. Then $E^{e}_{+1} - E = 0$ and (4.4) simplifies to $i = i^{\text{World}}$. If $i > i^{\text{World}}$, investors want to move their wealth into domestic bonds, moving the capital account into surplus. An interest rate deficit, $i < i^{\text{World}}$, moves the capital account into deficit. Thus the capital account is determined by the interest differential:

$$CP = \kappa(i - i^{\text{World}}) \tag{4.5}$$

Figure 4.5, panel (a), shows the capital account as a function of income and the interest rate. Here income has no impact, as it does not feature in equation (4.5). But *CP* deteriorates as the interest rate falls.

In the *i-Y* plane the line that balances domestic and international returns is obviously horizontal at the world interest rate (Figure 4.5, panel (b)). On this line financial investors do not care whether they hold wealth in domestic or foreign bonds and leave their portfolio the way it is. At higher domestic interest rates capital flows in, moving *CP* into surplus. At lower domestic interest rates capital flows out.

The balance of payments or foreign exchange market equilibrium is determined by the interaction of the current account and the capital account. If we merge both planes in one diagram, foreign exchange market equilibrium may obtain when the capital account surplus (deficit) exactly matches the current account deficit (surplus) ($-CA = CP$). Panel (a) in Figure 4.6 depicts the capital account surplus against the current account deficit. It turns out that projecting the line of intersection down onto the *i-Y* plane produces a positively sloped line. This line is repeated in panel (b). The thinking behind its positive slope is that an increase of income stimulates imports, which deteriorates the current account. To match this, we need to export more interest-bearing assets. This is only achieved if a higher interest rate makes those more attractive.

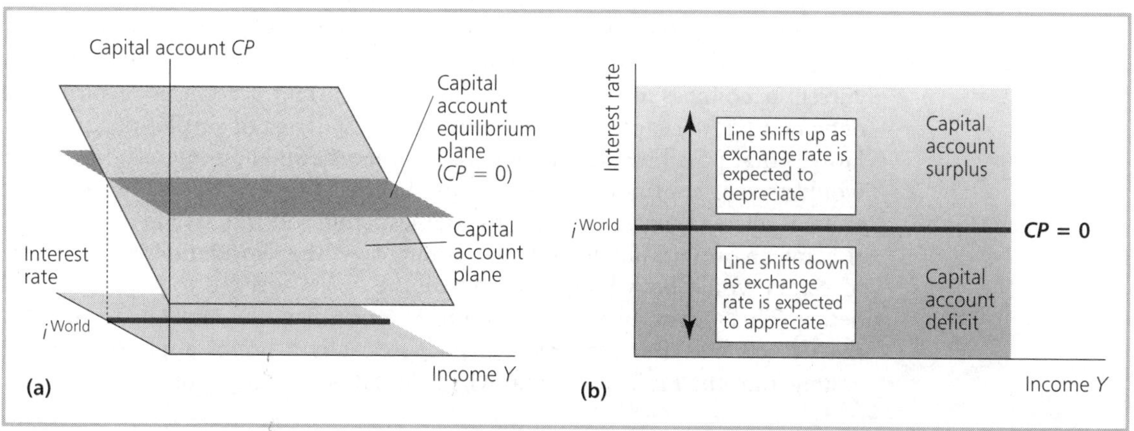

Figure 4.5 The capital account improves as a rising interest rate makes domestic bonds more attractive. Income does not impact on *CP*. The capital account equilibrium line, therefore, projects as a horizontal line onto the *i-Y* plane. An expected depreciation would make domestic bonds less attractive, thus shifting the *CP* = 0 line upwards. Unless stated otherwise, we assume expected depreciation to be zero.

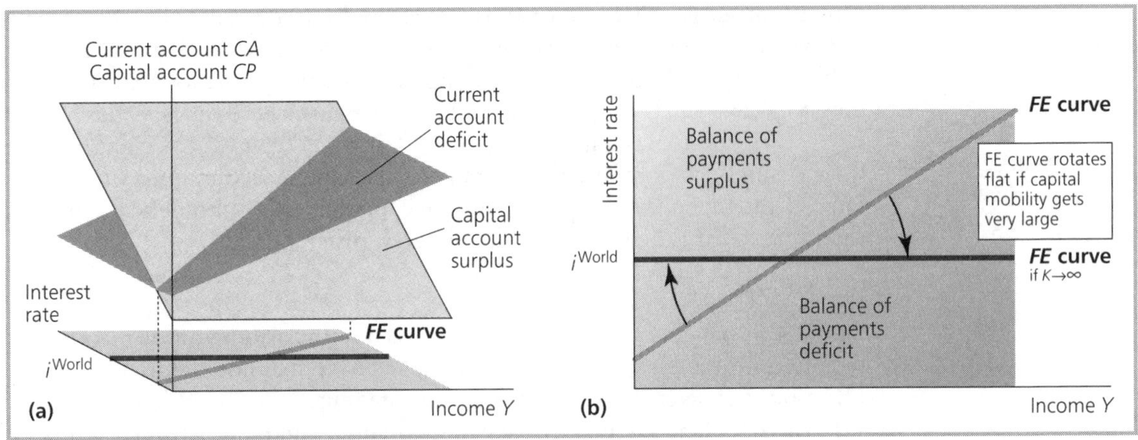

Figure 4.6 In panel (a) one surface measures the current account *deficit*, the other one the capital account *surplus*. When both are equal, the balance of payments and, hence, the foreign exchange market are in equilibrium. The line of intersection between both surfaces projects as a positively sloped line onto the *i*-*Y* surface. If capital mobility increases, the *CP* plane becomes steeper, and the *FE* curve rotates to be flatter.

Empirical note. In 2000 world trade amounted to the equivalent of $7.1 trillion. But $1.5 trillion-worth of foreign exchange changes hands every single day.

There is no question that in today's highly integrated financial markets investors set the pace. Purchases and sales of foreign exchange deriving from the export or import of goods and services amount to some 2% of the transaction volume in the foreign exchange markets. Small differences between domestic and foreign returns lead to a huge reshuffling of international capital which easily dwarfs any existing trade imbalances.

Translating this into our model, the coefficient κ in the capital account equation, which measures investors' reactions to observed excess returns, must be very large. In terms of the *CP* planes in panels (a) of Figures 4.5 and 4.6, these must be very, very steep. The steeper the *CP* plane becomes, the flatter is the accompanying *FE* line. Under perfect capital mobility it is reasonable to assume that it is horizontal, coinciding with the $CP = 0$ line shown previously.

There is a very important difference between the $CP = 0$ line and the nearly horizontal *FE* curve. On the $CP = 0$ line the capital account would be in equilibrium. On the *FE* curve the capital account can only be in equilibrium if the current account is also in equilibrium. If the current account is in surplus or deficit on *FE*, the capital account must feature a deficit or surplus of equal size. How is that possible? Again the reason is that the smallest interest differential would trigger enormous flows of capital across borders. So even if we had a sizeable current account deficit, the domestic interest rate would only need to rise by an infinitesimally small amount over the world interest rate, and investors would be willing to supply all the capital needed to finance the *CA* deficit. This means, of course, that the *FE* curve is not completely identical to the $CP = 0$ line. But for practical purposes it is a useful approximation to assume that the *FE* is horizontal when capital is perfectly mobile.

The algebra of the *FE* curve

The discussion of the foreign exchange market equilibrium line may well be one instance where a little algebra says more than six graphs. The foreign exchange market is in equilibrium when the supply of and the demand for currency balance without central bank intervention, that is when

$$BP = CA + CP = 0 \tag{4.6}$$

Substituting (4.2) and (4.5) into (4.6) gives

$$x_1 Y^{\text{World}} + x_2 R - m_1 Y + m_2 R + \kappa(i - i^{\text{World}}) = 0$$

Solving for the interest rate and collecting terms gives the foreign exchange market equilibrium line

$$i = i^{\text{World}} + \frac{m_1}{\kappa} Y - \frac{x_1}{\kappa} Y^{\text{World}} - \frac{m_2 + x_2}{\kappa} R \qquad \textbf{General } \textbf{\textit{FE}} \textbf{ curve} \tag{4.7}$$

The ***FE* curve** identifies combinations of income and the interest rate for which the foreign exchange market is in equilibrium.

The position of the ***FE* curve** always shifts one to one with the world interest rate. If κ is very large, meaning that capital flows respond very strongly to opening interest differentials, the other coefficients become very small. Thus the slope of the curve becomes very small and neither world income nor the real exchange rate has a relevant impact on the position of the *FE* line. Letting $\kappa \rightarrow \infty$, as we assume henceforth, (4.7) simplifies to

$$i = i^{\text{World}} \qquad \textbf{\textit{FE}} \textbf{ curve} \tag{4.8}$$

BOX 4.2 Interest rates, default risk and the risk premium

The main text assumes that creditors can always be sure that interest payments will be made and loans will be paid off at maturity. So we are talking about bonds with *no default risk*. In such a situation all that financial investors need to do when investing in international bonds is compare interest rates (assuming they do not expect the exchange rate to change).

While this is probably a reasonable first assumption when talking about government bonds in many industrial countries, governments do occasionally default on international loans or interest payments. In the presence of such **default risk** the equilibrium condition for the international capital market changes and thus needs to be reconsidered.

Assume there is no default risk at home. Then one euro invested at home grows to

$$1 + i^{\text{Euro}} \tag{1}$$

after one period. A euro invested in Russia, where default risk is *DR*, can be expected to grow to

$$(1 + i^{\text{Russia}})\left(1 + \frac{E_{+1} - E}{E}\right)(1 - DR) \tag{2}$$

since we need to take into account expected changes in the exchange rate and the possibility of default. Investors are indifferent between investing in Euroland or Russia if these two expressions are the same. Setting (1) equal to (2) and expanding terms this yields

$$\begin{aligned} i^{\text{Euro}} &= i^{\text{Russia}} + \frac{E_{+1} - E}{E} - DR \\ &+ i^{\text{Russia}} \frac{E_{+1} - E}{E} - \frac{E_{+1} - E}{E} DR \\ &- i^{\text{Russia}} DR - i^{\text{Russia}} \frac{E_{+1} - E}{E} DR \end{aligned}$$

If we ignore the final four terms on the right-hand side, which are small under normal circumstances and partly offset each other, this simplifies to

$$i^{\text{Euro}} = i^{\text{Russia}} + \frac{E_{+1} - E}{E} - DR$$

So even if the exchange rate is not expected to change, default risk may drive a wedge between domestic and foreign interest rates. Investors require a higher interest rate (or, more generally, a higher expected return) on Russian assets; a **risk premium** *RP*, which is equal to the default risk in our case. Generally, when expected depreciation is zero, domestic and foreign interest rates are related by

$$i = i^{\text{World}} - RP$$

While we only looked at default risk here, many other things may give rise to a risk premium in financial markets, such as expropriation risk or risk aversion.

4.4 EQUILIBRIUM IN ALL THREE MARKETS

Equilibrium with graphs

We now know how to draw equilibrium lines for the money market, the goods market and the foreign exchange market in the *i*-*Y* plane. Each line yields interesting insights into a particular sector of the economy. But these are not yet sufficient to pin down a unique macroeconomic equilibrium – which is what we are primarily interested in and set out to identify.

If the isolated discussion of individual markets only carried us so far, perhaps we can achieve progress by merging them. Let us construct the macroeconomic equilibrium step by step (Figure 4.7).

Note. We are still assuming that prices are fixed. Then the real exchange rate *R* (see box 3.4) moves one to one with the nominal exchange *E*. In fact, if we let $P = P^{World} = 1$ we may use *E* and *R* interchangeably.

Note that our model contains three endogenous variables that need to be determined: the interest rate *i*, the exchange rate *R* and income *Y*. A good starting point is the *FE* curve. It notes that the only way for the foreign exchange market to be in equilibrium is if the domestic interest rate equals the world interest rate. Next add the *LM* curve. Once the equilibrium interest rate has been determined in the foreign exchange market, the money market equilibrium tells us exactly where equilibrium income Y_0 must be. In Figure 4.7 Y_0 is determined by the point of intersection between the *FE* and the *LM* curve.

What might be puzzling here is that we have determined equilibrium income without even looking at the goods market. How can we be sure that the *IS* curve, the equilibrium condition for the goods market, passes through A? And how can we be sure that the equilibrium conditions stated by *IS* are compatible with the already predetermined levels of *i* and *Y*?

The answer is that there is a whole series of *IS* curves, each for a different exchange rate, and there is always one *IS* curve that passes through A. The underlying exchange rate is the equilibrium exchange rate R_0. But what if the

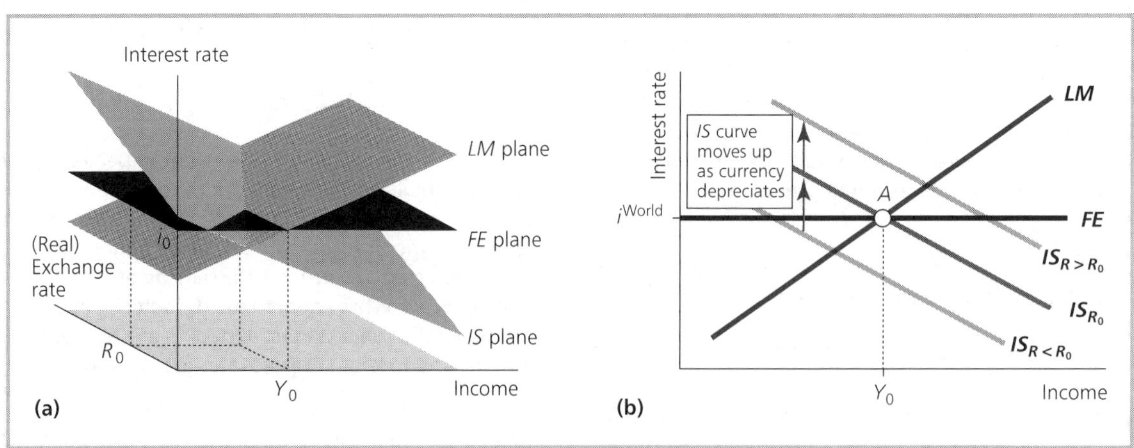

Figure 4.7 Panel (a) shows in 3D that there is only one triplet of endogenous variables, R_0, i_0 and Y_0, that yields an overall equilibrium in all three markets. Panel (b) derives the same result in 2D. The intersection of *FE* and *LM* (both curves are independent of *R*) identifies $i_0 = i^{World}$ and Y_0. *IS* must also pass through this point. This requirement determines *R*.

IS curve is at $IS_{R>R_0}$ because the exchange rate is too high at $R > R_0$, while the interest rate and income are determined by point A? At the given exchange rate, A represents an excess demand for domestic goods, which puts upward pressure on income and upward pressure on the interest rate which eventually drives down the exchange rate and, hence, the *IS* curve. This goes on until *IS* passes through A. But this question will be dealt with in much more detail in the next chapter where the focus will be the interaction between the three markets we have just learned to understand.

The algebra of *IS-LM-FE* equilibrium

The three markets discussed in this chapter constitute the *IS-LM-FE* model. Algebraically, the model consists of three equilibrium conditions for three markets:

$$R = \frac{1 - c + m_1}{m_2 + x_2} Y - \frac{\bar{I} + G + x_1 Y^{\text{World}}}{m_2 + x_2} + \frac{b}{m_2 + x_2} i \qquad \textbf{\textit{IS} curve} \quad (4.9)$$

$$Y = \frac{M}{k} + \frac{h}{k} i \qquad \textbf{\textit{LM} curve} \quad (4.10)$$

$$i = i^{\text{World}} \qquad \textbf{\textit{FE} curve} \quad (4.11)$$

These are the *IS*, *LM* and *FE* curves already discussed. If they look unfamiliar, it is because equations (3.2) and (3.9) have been rearranged so as to show, along with (4.8), the three endogenous variables of the model on the left-hand side. The equilibrium values of R, Y and i are relatively easy to obtain because the model is recursive, meaning that equilibrium values are obtained step by step. We start at the bottom.

1 *The interest rate.* The equilibrium interest rate is determined directly by equation (4.11):

$$i = i^{\text{World}} \qquad \textbf{Equilibrium interest rate}$$

2 *Equilibrium income.* Substitute the equilibrium interest rate into equation (4.10) to obtain equilibrium income as

$$Y = \frac{M}{k} + \frac{h}{k} i^{\text{World}} \qquad \textbf{Equilibrium income}$$

3 *Equilibrium exchange rate.* Now substitute equilibrium income and the equilibrium interest rate into (4.9) to finally obtain the equilibrium exchange rate

$$R = \frac{1 - c + m_1}{m_2 + x_2} \left(\frac{M}{k} + \frac{h}{k} i^{\text{World}} \right) - \frac{\bar{I} + G + x_1 Y^{\text{World}}}{m_2 + x_2} + \frac{b}{m_2 + x_2} i^{\text{World}}$$

Equilibrium exchange rate

Bottom line

This chapter has refined the discussion of equilibrium income by a further step. The one important result still obtaining is that a unique income level

BOX 4.3 The *IS-LM-FE* model in a different dress

The *IS-LM-FE* model comprises three markets which determine three endogenous variables. Under flexible exchange rates these are i, E and Y. When we reduced the 3D graph of this model shown in Figure 4.7 to two dimensions we chose to show i and Y on the two axes, thus relegating E to an invisible role in the background. While this is the traditional choice, we may just as well have chosen to show i and E on the two axes, or E and Y. You often find the latter display in current textbooks, with the valid argument that when the interest rate cannot move under perfect capital mobility, why waste an axis on i? To see what the *IS-LM-FE* model looks like in an E-Y diagram, let us restate the algebraic expressions for the three market equilibrium lines. Letting $P = P^{\text{World}} = 1$, so that $R = E$, equations (4.9–4.11) can be rewritten as

$$E = \frac{1 - c + m_1}{m_2 + x_2} Y - \frac{\bar{I} + G + x_1 Y^{\text{World}}}{m_2 + x_2} + \frac{b}{m_2 + x_2} i \qquad \textit{IS curve} \quad (1)$$

$$Y = \frac{M}{k} + \frac{h}{k} i \qquad \textit{LM curve} \quad (2)$$

$$i = i^{\text{World}} \qquad \textit{FE curve} \quad (3)$$

The positive coefficient of Y in equation (1) indicates that the *IS* curve is a positively sloped line in an E-Y diagram (see Figure 1). The logical reason is that a depreciating exchange rate raises net exports. So firms need to raise output in order to keep the goods market in equilibrium.

Since the exchange rate plays no role in the money market, the *LM* curve is a vertical line in an E-Y diagram. It shifts to the right if the money supply or the interest rate increases.

Equation (3) evidently cannot be displayed in an E-Y diagram since it contains neither E nor Y. In order not to lose the valuable information conveyed by the *FE* curve, equation (3) may be substituted into equations (1) and (2). We then obtain what we may call an IS^* curve and an LM^* curve, goods market and money market equilibrium lines conditional on a simultaneous equilibrium in the foreign exchange market. IS^* and LM^* move up and to the right, respectively, if the world interest rate increases.

It is important to note that the E-Y diagram is only a different way of displaying and manipulating the *IS-LM-FE* model. It is still the same model with the same properties. You may want to check that, and deepen your grasp of the *IS-LM-FE* model at the same time, by taking the results that Chapter 5 derives in the context of the i-Y diagram and replicating them in an E-Y diagram.

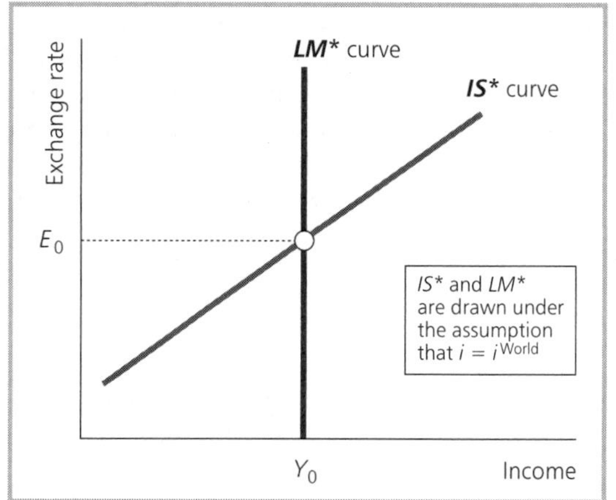

Figure 1

exists at which income equals aggregate demand. Bringing the foreign exchange market into the picture modifies the link between equilibrium income and the money supply and links this income to the world interest rate. Chapter 5 will look at how equilibrium income in the *IS-LM-FE* model is influenced by policy and other factors.

To this end we will need to consider the interaction between the three markets analyzed here. Before moving to this rather demanding task, make sure that you have a clear understanding of the isolated money market (*LM* curve), goods market (*IS* curve) and foreign exchange market (*FE* curve).

BOX 4.4 Endogenous and exogenous variables

The *IS-LM-FE* model provides a good opportunity to illustrate and re-emphasize the distinction between endogenous and exogenous variables, and to show how institutional arrangements change the nature of a variable.

A model always comprises

- *exogenous variables* – their values are determined outside the model, and
- *endogenous variables* – to describe their behaviour is the very purpose of the model.

A model may have an arbitrary number of exogenous variables. But it can only explain as many endogenous variables as it has (independent) equations.

The *IS-LM-FE* model has been reduced to three equations – which take the form of market equilibrium conditions – to explain three endogenous variables. Figure 1 sketches how the exogenous variables have an impact on the three endogenous variables, and how the latter interact.

We must remember here, however, that our initial larger model, with equations explaining other endogenous variables such as consumption, investment, exports, imports and more, has been reduced to three equations by repeatedly substituting equations into each other and thus eliminating these variables. Thus, for example, consumption does not appear any more. But it can be considered a hidden endogenous variable whose equilibrium value is retrieved by substituting equilibrium income into the consumption function.

Institutions and the endogeneity of variables

The above interpretation implicitly assumes that the exchange rate is flexible, determined by market forces. This makes the money supply *M* exogenous, and puts it under the control of the policy-maker.

The roles of the exchange rate and of the money supply are reversed if we move to a system of *fixed exchange rates*. Then the exchange rate becomes exogenous, is set by policy-makers, and the money supply adjusts endogenously. This modifies the model's structure to that shown in Figure 2.

In terms of the representations of market equilibria in the *i-Y* plane, the two institutional scenarios work as shown in panels (a) and (b) of Figure 3.

Under *flexible exchange rates* the positions of *FE* and *LM* are set exogenously. The exchange rate determines the position of *IS*, and endogenously adjusts so as to let *IS* pass through the given point of intersection between *FE* and *LM* (panel (a)).

Under *fixed exchange rates* the positions of *FE* and *IS* are set exogenously. The money supply, which determines the position of *LM*, endogenously adjusts so as to let *LM* pass through the given point of intersection between *FE* and *IS* (panel (b)).

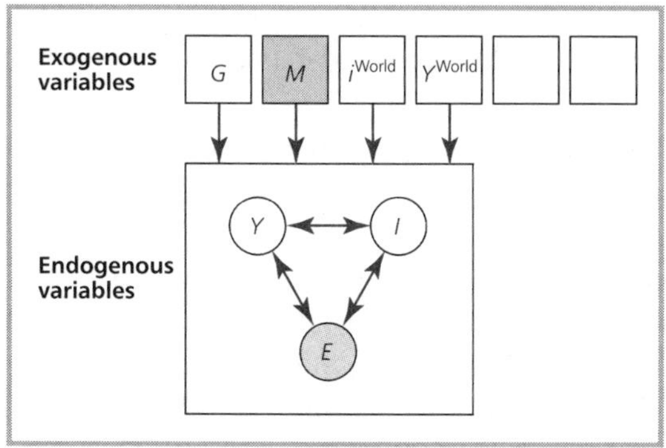

Figure 1 Flexible exchange rates

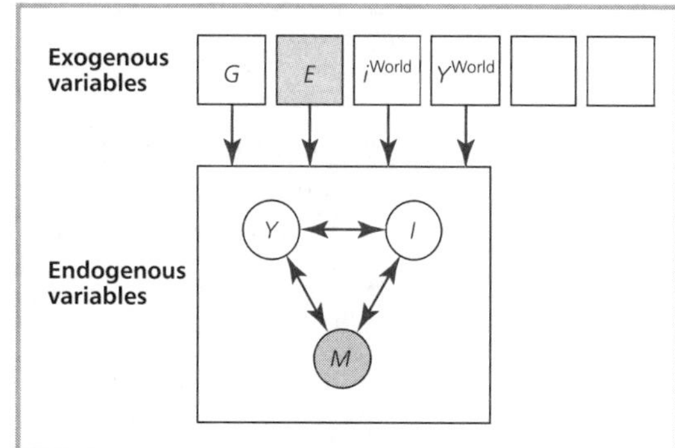

Figure 2 Fixed exchange rates

Box 4.4 continued

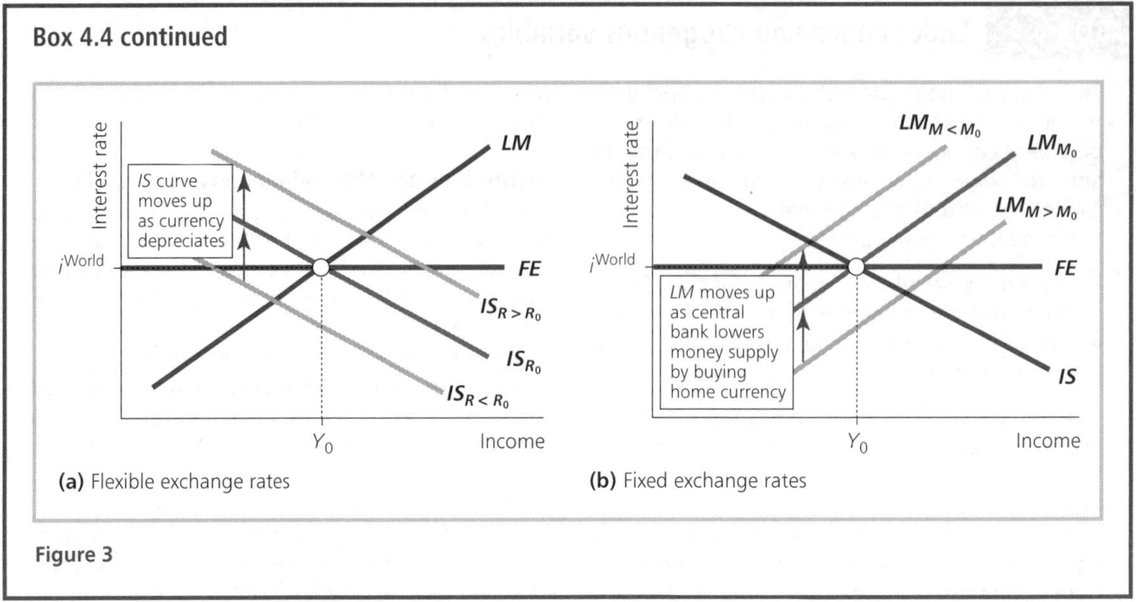

Figure 3

CHAPTER SUMMARY

- Globalization has led to large increases in most countries' exports (relative to income) and in the volumes traded in the world's foreign exchange market.
- The balance of payments is a meticulous record of a country's inhabitants' cross-border transactions. It is useful for macroeconomic purposes as a mirror image of the foreign exchange market. Viewed this way, it helps identify the main motives behind the demand for foreign currency.
- The goods market is in equilibrium if income, the interest rate and the exchange rate assume values that make aggregate demand equal to output produced.
- Aggregate demand rises with income (through consumption), falls as the interest rate rises (through investment), and rises with the exchange rate (through net exports).
- The foreign exchange market is dominated by financial investors. The demand exercised by importers and exporters is negligible in relative volume.
- Equilibrium in the foreign exchange market obtains if domestic assets and foreign assets yield identical returns. If individuals have stationary exchange rate expectations this means that the domestic interest rate must equal the world interest rate.
- Using interest rate parity as the equilibrium condition for the foreign exchange market does not imply that the capital account is balanced. It means that investors are indifferent between holding domestic or foreign assets. Hence, they are ready to finance any current account disequilibrium that might occur.

- Only one macroeconomic equilibrium (defined as simultaneous equilibrium in all three markets) exists. Income, the interest rate and the exchange rate assume one specific value each.

KEY TERMS AND CONCEPTS

balance of payments
capital account
closed economy
current account
FE curve
foreign exchange market
globalization
IS-LM model
official reserves account
open economy
risk neutral

EXERCISES

4.1 How open is your country's economy at present?
(a) as measured by the export ratio
(b) as measured by the import ratio
Use data from *Eurostat*, the OECD or national sources to address this question.

4.2 Suppose an artificial country called Spain recorded the cross-border transactions listed below:

500 Seat Toledos sold to Ireland	€7,500,000
10,000 Atomic Kitten CDs sold in Spain	€150,000
Sergio Garcia flies Air France to New York 10 times, using the Concorde from Paris	€70,000
Franz Beckenbauer spends several golf holidays in Marbella	€40,000
Zinedine Zidane sends cheques home to mom in France	€200,000
Julio Iglesias earns dividend on Microsoft stocks	€1,900,000
Spain's government contributes to EU budget	€1,000,000
Ford acquires office building in Barcelona	€10,000,000
Real Madrid invests in Eurosport TV stocks	€5,000,000
Government pays interest on Spanish government bonds held abroad	€2,800,000

Assemble Spain's balance of payments. Assume there are no statistical discrepancies. What is the current account balance? What are net exports? What is the capital account balance? Is the balance of payments in surplus or deficit?

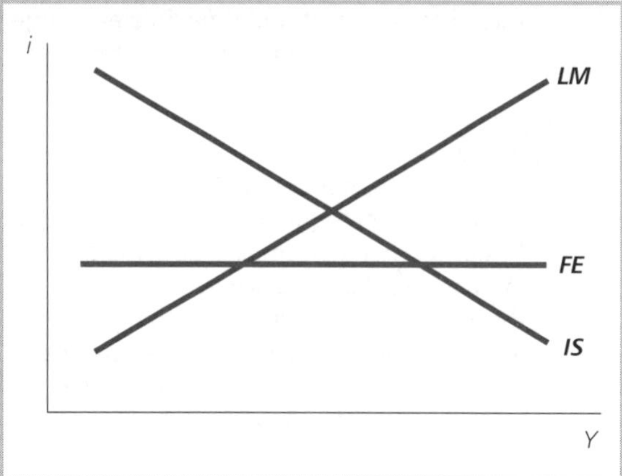

Figure 4.8

4.3 Consider a small open economy that faces the macroeconomic situation as shown in Figure 4.8. Describe the mechanisms that bring about a macroeconomic equilibrium in which all three market equilibrium lines intersect
(a) under flexible exchange rates.
(b) under fixed exchange rates.

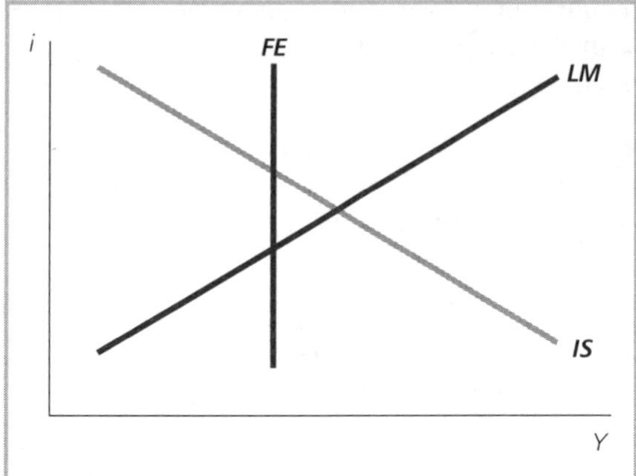

Figure 4.9

4.4 Consider the macroeconomic situation shown in Figure 4.9 in which the *FE* curve is vertical.

(a) Discuss the conditions under which the *FE* curve might be vertical.

(b) Describe the mechanisms that bring about a macroeconomic equilibrium in which all three lines intersect under flexible exchange rates, and under fixed exchange rates.

4.5 Suppose investment is independent of the interest rate and

(a) the *FE* curve is horizontal. Sketch the macroeconomic equilibrium under fixed and flexible exchange rates and describe the mechanisms that help achieve it.

(b) the *FE* curve is vertical. Sketch the macroeconomic equilibrium under fixed and flexible exchange rates and describe the mechanisms that help achieve it.

4.6 Consider an economy that is characterized by constant prices, flexible exchange rates and perfect capital mobility, and where the *IS* and *LM* curves can be written as follows:

$$(LM) \quad M = 0.25Y - 10i$$
$$(IS) \quad i = 0.1(\bar{I} + G + 0.1Y^{World} - 0.4Y + 40R)$$

Initially, the exogenous variables take the following values:

$M = 500$
$i^{World} = 5$
$Y^{World} = 5{,}000$
$\bar{I} = 160$
$G = 200$

(a) Draw the equilibrium curves for the money market, the foreign exchange market and the goods market into an *i*-*Y* diagram.

(b) Compute the equilibrium levels of the interest rate, income and the foreign exchange rate.

(c) If there are no transfers and cross-border factor earnings (meaning that net exports equal the current account) and the capital account runs a deficit of 75, what is the marginal propensity to import?

(d) Suppose the exchange rate is now fixed at 1. What is the resulting money supply?

(e) In (d), to what level does the world interest rate have to move in order to prevent income from changing?

RECOMMENDED READING

A good complement to this chapter might be to read your country's recent balance of payments report published by either the central bank or the government. Examples are:

- Deutsche Bundesbank, *Balance of payments statistics 2001*, Statistical supplement to the monthly report, November 2001, Frankfurt.
- Swiss National Bank, *Swiss balance of payments 2000*, September 2001, Zurich.

APPLIED PROBLEMS

RECENT RESEARCH

Testing uncovered interest parity

Uncovered interest parity introduced in equation (4.4) states that the difference between the domestic interest rate i and the foreign interest rate i^* equals the expected depreciation of the home currency ε^e: $\varepsilon^e = i - i^*$. If depreciation expectations are rational (for more on this see Chapter 8), they should be correct on average: $\varepsilon = \varepsilon^e + \nu$, where ν denotes expectations errors which on average are zero. Substituting the first into the second equation gives $\varepsilon = i - i^* + \nu$. M. Chinn and G. Meredith ('Testing uncovered interest parity at short and long horizons', University of California Santa Cruz, *Working Paper* 2000–01) test this equation by regressing depreciation rates on interest differentials, that is they estimate the coefficients of the equation

$$\varepsilon = \alpha + \beta(i - i^*)$$

If open interest parity holds together with rational expectations the estimate of α should be 0 and β should equal 1. Selected estimation results based on quarterly data for the sample period 1983:I–2000:I are

German mark

$$\underset{(0.003)}{\varepsilon = 0.006} + \underset{(0.180)}{0.851}(i - i^*) \qquad R^2 = 0.40$$

Japanese yen

$$\underset{(0.005)}{\varepsilon = 0.038} + \underset{(0.144)}{0.388}(i - i^*) \qquad R^2 = 0.10$$

British pound

$$\underset{(0.004)}{\varepsilon = -0.003} + \underset{(0.106)}{0.562}(i - i^*) \qquad R^2 = 0.43$$

where standard errors are shown in parantheses. While there is a statistically significant relationship between the interest differential and the rate of depreciation, important differences remain:

- A much larger share of variations in the rate of depreciation can be attributed to variations in the interest differential for the mark and the pound than for the yen. Respective coefficients of determination are 0.40, 0.43 and 0.10.
- The equations estimated for Germany and Japan have significant constant terms, meaning that there is a depreciation tendency unrelated to the interest differential.
- The null hypothesis $\beta = 1$ is rejected for the yen and the pound, but not for the mark. (Example: Testing $\beta = 1$ for the pound yields the t-statistic $(1 - 0.562)/0.106 = 4.13$. Therefore the null hypothesis must be rejected.)

All in all the results are mixed. To the extent that coefficients are not as expected, it remains open to question whether this is due to expectations not being rational or because uncovered interest parity does not hold.

WORKED PROBLEM

Amadeus by the dollar

A country's exports depend on the real exchange rate (as a measure of relative prices) and on the level of income in the destination country. This should also hold for each category of exports. If Austria welcomes American tourists, it exports. Tourists pay for the privilege of enjoying Vienna and the Alps, just as the British pay for Spanish exports of sherry to the United Kingdom. Now consider the data in Table 4.2 on nights spent by US visitors to Austria (NIGHTS), the real exchange rate shilling versus the dollar (SHPER$) and US real GDP (USGDP).

To check whether our export equation explains US tourism to Austria we regress NIGHTS on SHPER$ and USGDP. The result is

$$\text{NIGHTS} = \underset{(1.60)}{-842.7} + \underset{(4.92)}{104.3}\ \text{SHPER\$} + \underset{(3.02)}{0.236}\ \text{USGDP}$$

24 annual observations 1971–94; $R^2_{adj} = 0.50$

Both coefficients are positive as expected, and are significantly different from 0, as the t-values of 4.92 and 3.02 indicate. If the shilling depreciates by one shilling per dollar (at 1987 prices), US tourists spend 104,300 more nights in Austria. If American GDP rises by one billion dollars (at 1987 prices), 236 more nights are being spent in Austria. The coefficient of determination is 0.50, saying that half of the variance in the number of nights spent by US tourists per year is accounted for by changes in the real exchange rate and in US income.

Table 4.2

	NIGHTS (thousands)	SHPER$	USGDP in '87 (billions)
1971	1,774.172	19.18385	2,955.9
1972	1,838.577	17.24196	3,107.1
1973	1,569.763	14.44078	3,268.6
1974	1,339.987	13.99124	3,248.1
1975	1,230.936	13.09453	3,221.7
1976	1,378.784	13.30245	3,380.8
1977	1,428.656	12.36859	3,533.3
1978	1,272.219	11.28735	3,703.5
1979	1,090.836	11.15924	3,796.8
1980	1,332.572	11.53090	3,776.3
1981	1,170.124	14.66295	3,843.1
1982	1,438.524	15.81757	3,760.3
1983	1,740.612	16.61142	3,906.6
1984	2,203.027	18.28409	4,148.5
1985	2,376.876	18.98412	4,279.8
1986	1,408.803	14.01424	4,404.5
1987	1,719.816	11.87747	4,539.9
1988	1,591.663	11.83786	4,718.6
1989	1,697.928	12.97130	4,838.0
1990	2,139.202	11.37000	4,897.3
1991	1,191.496	11.77773	4,867.6
1992	1,526.478	10.97878	4,979.3
1993	1,371.261	11.54847	5,134.5
1994	1,393.102	11.29254	5,342.3

YOUR TURN

Are international interest rates equal?

A key ingredient of the Mundell–Fleming model (to be discussed in the next chapter) is the interest parity condition, stating that interest rates may only differ between countries to the extent by which the exchange rate is expected to change. If the exchange rate is expected to remain where it is currently, the domestic interest rate should equal the world interest rate. To check whether this assumption is a well-guided first guess, consider the money market interest rates for Germany and the Netherlands (annual data) in Table 4.3. Let Holland be the home country and assume that the German interest rate approximates the world interest rate. Check whether the hypothesis $i_{NL} = i_D$ is supported by the data.

Table 4.3

Year	i_D	i_{NL}	Year	i_D	i_{NL}
1980	9.06	10.13	1988	4.01	4.48
1981	11.26	11.01	1989	6.59	6.99
1982	8.67	8.06	1990	7.92	8.29
1983	5.36	5.28	1991	8.84	9.01
1984	5.54	5.78	1992	9.42	9.27
1985	5.19	6.30	1993	7.49	7.10
1986	4.57	5.83	1994	5.35	5.14
1987	3.72	5.16			

To further explore this chapter's key messages you are encouraged to use the interactive online module found at

www.fgn.unisg.ch/eurmacro/tutor/forex.html

and many other features hosted at **www.fgn.unisg.ch/eurmacro**

CHAPTER 5

BOOMS AND RECESSIONS (II)
THE NATIONAL ECONOMY

WHAT TO EXPECT After working through this chapter, you will understand:

1 What the national-economy **Mundell–Fleming model** is, and how it differs from the global-economy model.
2 How **fiscal policy** affects equilibrium income in the Mundell–Fleming model.
3 How **monetary policy** affects equilibrium income in the Mundell–Fleming model.
4 How **demand shocks** in general, including those originating from abroad, affect equilibrium income.
5 The difference between **comparative statics** and **adjustment dynamics**.
6 How things alter if **prices are permitted to change**.

Chapters 3 and 4 made us look beyond the circular-flow and Keynesian-cross representations of the macroeconomy. We saw that proper treatment of monetary and financial aspects, which feature prominently in modern industrial economies, recommends breaking down the open, national economy into three markets: the **goods market**, the **money market** and the **foreign exchange market.** By now we have a clear understanding under what conditions each of these markets is in equilibrium. It also makes perfect sense that a macroeconomic equilibrium is only possible when each individual market is in equilibrium. The national-economy model built in Chapters 3 and 4 is called the ***IS-LM-FE* model,** with obvious reference to its constituent markets. A better known name for it is the **Mundell–Fleming model** after British economist J. Marcus Fleming and Canadian Nobel prize winner Robert Mundell who laid its foundations.

The **Mundell–Fleming model** is a tool for analyzing macroeconomic issues. It comprises the goods market (*IS*), the money market (*LM*) and the foreign exchange market (*FE*). Its simplicity has made it a tool often used in communications between professional and academic economists. Employed wisely, with an informed sense of its limits, the Mundell–Fleming model can be a very powerful tool for understanding the role of aggregate demand in the business cycle.

What Chapters 4 and 5 do with the Mundell–Fleming model echoes the questions that Chapter 2 raised in the context of the Keynesian cross and Chapter 3 within the *IS-LM* framework. In both cases we first determined equilibrium income. Then we showed how equilibrium income responded to changes in autonomous demand or policy instruments via the multiplier. These same two questions, which could be dealt with within a single chapter in the simple models underlying the Keynesian cross and the *IS-LM* model, require one chapter each for the more refined Mundell–Fleming model. Chapter 4 determined the unique equilibrium of the Mundell–Fleming model.

Chapter 5 takes this equilibrium as a starting point. We proceed to ask whether and how equilibrium can be influenced by fiscal and monetary policy, and how one country's equilibrium income may be linked to that of others.

This chapter is designed to sharpen our understanding of the *IS-LM-FE* or Mundell–Fleming model. We will do so

- by reconsidering the effects of **government expenditures**, and of fiscal policy in general and
- by taking a first look at **monetary policy**.

Along the way we will learn to appreciate the important role of the **exchange rate system**. As a recurrent theme we will also discuss the role of **expectations**.

5.1 FISCAL POLICY IN THE MUNDELL–FLEMING MODEL

Fiscal policy manipulates government spending and taxes to achieve policy goals (such as a rise in income).

Fiscal policy comprises all policy measures related to the government budget. On the aggregate level this amounts to government spending and raising government revenue by levying taxes.

In terms of the Mundell–Fleming model, if the government increases expenditures the *IS* curve shifts to the right. The size of this shift is given by the multiplier derived in Chapter 2 (times ΔG). There the interest rate was (implicitly) considered constant, and the multiplier indicated by how much equilibrium income rises after a one-unit increase of government expenditure. As this holds at all interest rates, the *IS* curve shifts exactly by the size of the original multiplier to the right (see Figure 5.1).

If the interest rate actually remains at the level of the world interest rate, and the foreign exchange market equilibrium condition says it must, equilibrium moves from A to B. B is not a money market equilibrium, however. With the interest rate unchanged and higher income than at A, individuals wish to hold more money at B than is being supplied. This excess demand for money puts upward pressure on the interest rate. If we could ignore the *FE* curve, this

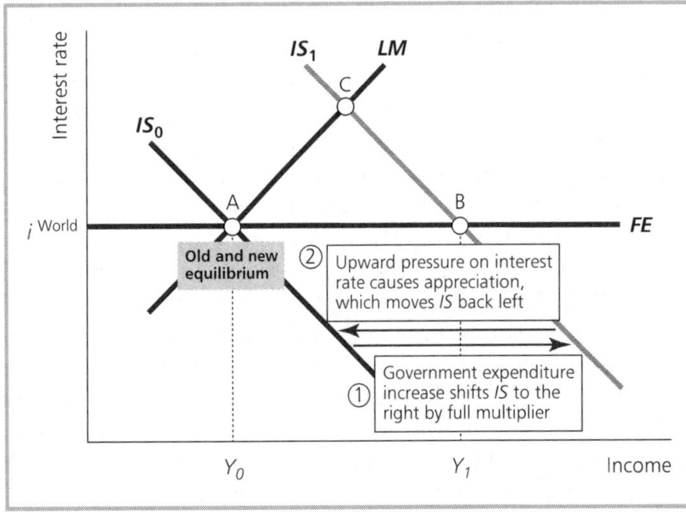

Figure 5.1 (Flexible exchange rates.) A rise in government spending shifts *IS* to the right. Now there is an excess demand for goods in A. As this starts to make income rise, moving along *LM* from A towards C pushes the domestic interest rate beyond the world interest rate. This increases the demand for domestic interest-bearing assets and appreciates the domestic currency. This, in turn, makes domestic goods more expensive, reducing net exports, driving *IS* back towards the left. This continues until *IS* is back at IS_0 and the economy is back at A.

would drive up the interest rate along LM_1 until it reached equilibrium in the money market at C.

But point C is not a foreign exchange market equilibrium. So we will not really move up to C. At the slightest increase of the domestic interest rate, financial investors will want to shift wealth into domestic bonds. For this they need to acquire domestic currency. The result is an *incipient* excess demand for domestic currency. What are the macroeconomic consequences of this? Well, this depends on how the foreign exchange market is organized. Is the exchange rate flexible, left to be determined by the market? Or have governments agreed to set a specific exchange rate (called parity rate) and buy or sell any amount of currency the market wants at that price? We will consider each option separately.

Flexible exchange rates

We speak of a system of **flexible exchange rates** when governments (or central banks) allow the exchange rate to be determined by market forces alone.

Under a system of **flexible exchange rates** the central bank simply ignores the excess demand for domestic currency and leaves things up to the market. So the currency price must change in order to match supply and demand. If financial investors cannot obtain domestic currency at the current price, which is the reciprocal value of the exchange rate, they offer more. This drives *up* the price per unit of domestic currency, and it drives the exchange rate *down*. The domestic currency appreciates. As we know, this has repercussions in the goods market. Domestic goods become more expensive relative to foreign goods and net exports fall. The *IS* curve shifts to the left. During this process C gradually slides down the *LM* curve towards A. This slide cannot come to a halt before A has been reached. Otherwise the domestic interest rate would still exceed the world interest rate, causing the excess demand for domestic currency to continue. Only as *IS* returns to its original position and the economy returns to A are all three markets in equilibrium.

This yields an important insight: under a system of flexible exchange rates and when capital is perfectly mobile across borders, fiscal policy does not give the government leverage over aggregate income. As long as the central bank holds the money supply constant, there will be complete **crowding out**. The exchange rate will be forced to appreciate just enough to reduce net exports by as much as government expenditures increased, leaving aggregate demand unchanged. This means that after G is raised, the composition of demand at point A in Figure 5.1 is different from what it was before. This is also easy to see by looking at the circular flow identity from Chapter 1:

Crowding out occurs when an increase in government spending reduces private spending (such as net exports or investment).

$$\underset{0\ \ 0}{(S - I)} + \underset{0\ \ +}{(T - G)} + \underset{+\ \ -}{(IM - EX)} = 0$$

The line under the identity shows whether a particular variable has increased (+), fallen (−) or remained unchanged (0). Savings has remained the same since it only depends on income, which remains unchanged. Investment is the same because it depends on the interest rate, which remains unchanged. Taxes depend on income and, thus, remain unchanged. Government outlays have increased, which deteriorates the government budget. To compensate for this, the current account must deteriorate as well. At current income and an appreciated currency, imports are higher. Exports are lower because of the appreciation.

Fixed exchange rates

We speak of a system of **fixed exchange rates** when governments (or central banks) announce an exchange rate (the parity rate) at which they are prepared to buy or sell any amount of domestic currency.

In a system of **fixed exchange rates** the exchange rate is set to a particular value by unilateral decision or multilateral agreement on the political level. At this rate the central bank must buy or sell any amount of domestic currency that the market offers or demands. This is tantamount to taking control of the money supply out of the central bank's hands. Figure 5.2 shows what an increase in government expenditures does to income under these conditions.

Again, higher government expenditures shift the *IS* curve to the right, and again the resulting income increase tends to push up the interest rate beyond the world interest rate. Now, however, the resulting excess demand for domestic currency cannot and need not be eliminated by appreciation. Instead, the central bank is obliged to supply just that amount of additional money that would-be buyers cannot find in the market. So two things happen, which did not happen under flexible exchange rates:

1 The exchange rate cannot appreciate, meaning that the *IS* curve cannot shift back. It remains in its new position IS_1.
2 The domestic money supply increases due to the mandatory foreign exchange market intervention of the central bank, shifting the *LM* curve to the right.

The *LM* curve must continue to shift until it intersects IS_1 at B. It cannot come to a halt earlier because this would leave an incipient advantage for the domestic interest rate, creating excess demand for domestic money.

Moving from flexible to fixed exchange rates reverses the roles of fiscal and monetary policy. Under flexible exchange rates monetary policy sets the limit and can enforce a complete crowding out of government expenditure. Under fixed exchange rates fiscal policy is in the driver's seat. The exchange rate regime forces monetary policy to accommodate any government expenditure increase so as to yield the full multiplier effect.

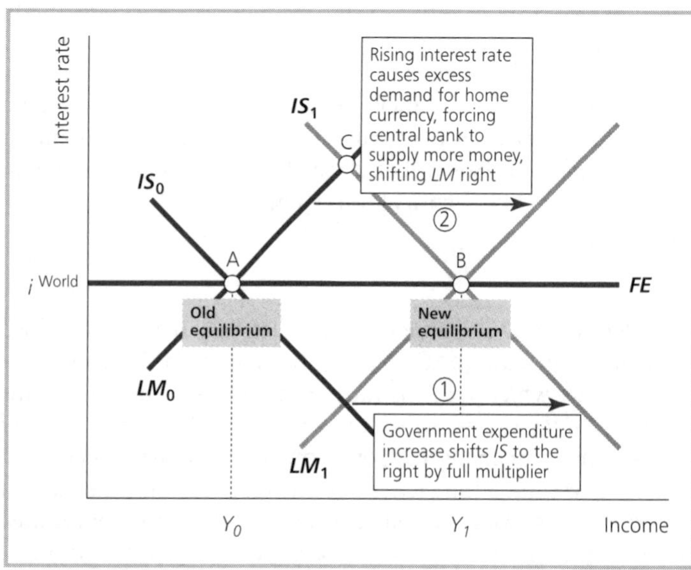

Figure 5.2 (Fixed exchange rates.) The initial rise in government expenditure shifts *IS* to the right. Along with income the demand for money increases, pushing the interest rate up. This makes domestic bonds more attractive, thus raising the demand for domestic currency. The central bank is obliged to supply the requested domestic currency for foreign currency, thus shifting *LM* to the right too. Income rises from Y_0 to Y_1.

BOX 5.1 The Mundell–Fleming model under capital controls

In this book we assume that capital moves unhindered across borders. This describes the current situation quite well in industrial and many other countries. But there are still some countries, mostly in the developing world, that do not permit free movements of capital in and out. In Tanzania, for example, citizens need to submit proof of an import contract and obtain a permit if they want to acquire foreign currency. The purchase or sale of currency is usually not permitted for financial investments. As a consequence the capital account cannot really respond to interest rate differentials. In algebraic terms $\kappa = 0$ in equation (4.5). What does that do to the *FE* curve? This is best seen after solving the general *FE* curve, equation (4.7), for Y to obtain

$$Y = \frac{\kappa}{m_1}(i - i^{\text{World}}) + \frac{m_2 + x_2}{m_1}R + \frac{x_1}{m_1}Y^{\text{World}} \qquad (1)$$

Letting $\kappa = 0$ to signal that capital is not permitted to respond to changes in interest rates, the interest differential drops out of the equation and equation (1) simplifies to

$$Y = \frac{m_2 + x_2}{m_1}R + \frac{x_1}{m_1}Y^{\text{World}}$$

***FE* curve under capital controls** (2)

The *FE* curve under strict capital controls is a vertical line, the position of which is determined by the real exchange rate and world income. The general macroeconomic equilibrium is as depicted in Figure 1.

- Can you explain why *FE* moves right when the real exchange rate depreciates?
- Can this country stimulate income by raising government spending when the exchange rate is fixed?

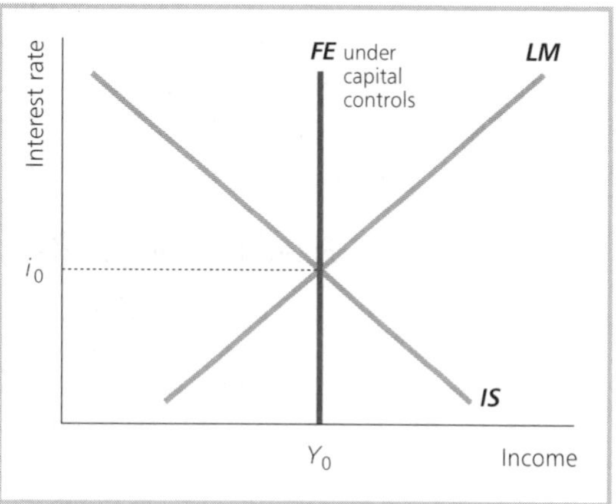

Figure 1

Government expenditure is one autonomous demand factor. Similar results to those derived for government expenditure increases obtain for other variables that affect autonomous demand: taxes, world income, or the autonomous components of consumption, investment, imports or exports.

We now look at the flip side of the coin and check whether the results obtained for government expenditures are confirmed if we analyze the effects of monetary policy directly.

5.2 MONETARY POLICY IN THE MUNDELL–FLEMING MODEL

Monetary policy manipulates the money supply (or the interest rate) to achieve policy goals (such as a rise in income).

Monetary policy comprises central bank action geared towards steering the supply of money. This can happen directly, by purchasing or selling bonds or foreign currency. It can also happen indirectly, as we saw in Chapter 3, by setting interest rates and inducing the market to hold liquidity in the desired amount. Here we use monetary policy as a synonym for direct control of the money supply.

As above, it will prove useful to consider different exchange rate regimes separately.

Flexible exchange rates

An increase of the money supply shifts *LM* to the right. If we could ignore the foreign exchange market equilibrium line, this shift of *LM* would drive the interest rate down, stimulate investment demand and bring the economy to point D. D is not really feasible, however, as it violates the foreign exchange market equilibrium. As soon as domestic interest rates begin to move below the world interest rate, international investors start to move out of domestic bonds. In the wake of this, they try to get rid of domestic currency. The incipient excess supply of domestic currency leads to a depreciation. This makes domestic goods and services cheaper and stimulates net exports. The *IS* curve shifts to the right. This process must go on until IS_1 intersects LM_1 at B (see Figure 5.3).

So our previous result is indeed confirmed. Under flexible exchange rates monetary policy sets the pace. Not only is fiscal policy completely ineffective if used in isolation against the course of monetary policy, but monetary policy is extremely effective at stimulating aggregate demand and income, even if it does not get any help from fiscal policy.

Fixed exchange rates

Under fixed exchange rates the first step is the same. If the money supply is increased via the purchase of domestic bonds by the central bank, the *LM* curve shifts to the right. And again, the increased liquidity tends to drive the interest rate down. As investors get rid of domestic bonds and throw domestic currency on the market, the exchange rate cannot respond. Instead, the central bank is called upon as the 'buyer of last resort'. It is required to take any excess liquidity out of the market which the market does not want to hold. This reduces the money supply, and continues until the money supply is back at its original level. Then the *LM* curve is back in its original position LM_0 and nothing has changed: neither aggregate income or demand, nor the composition of aggregate demand (see Figure 5.4).

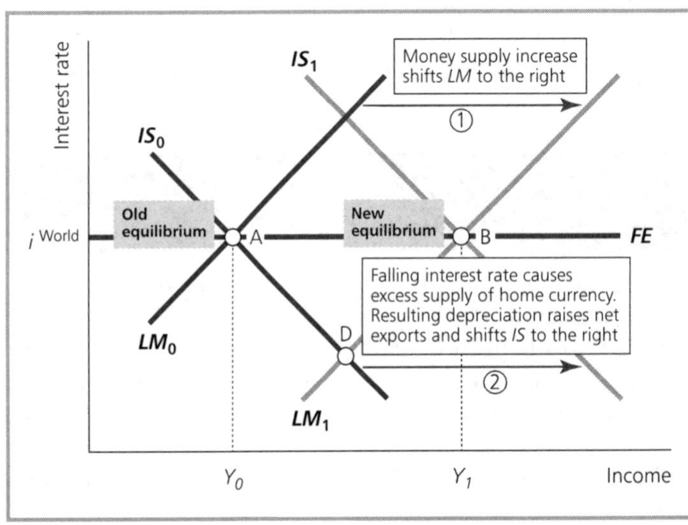

Figure 5.3 (Flexible exchange rates.) A money-supply increase shifts *LM* to the right. This tends to drive down the interest rate along IS_0 towards D. As soon as the interest rate moves below the world interest rate, investors will start to withdraw funds from domestic assets. The exchange rate depreciates, spurring net exports and shifting *IS* to the right. As *IS* reaches IS_1 a new equilibrium obtains in B.

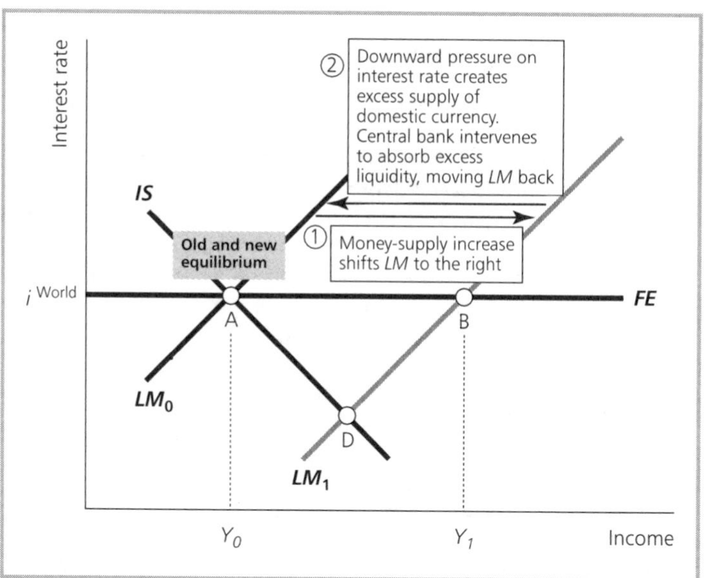

Figure 5.4 (Fixed exchange rates.) A money-supply increase shifts *LM* right. As this tends to push interest rates down, investors withdraw funds from domestic assets. Wanting to move into foreign assets, they sell domestic currency for foreign currency. Under fixed exchange rates the central bank is obliged to sell the requested foreign currency. Since it receives domestic currency as payment, the domestic money supply is reduced, shifting *LM* back left. Eventually we are back at A.

This completes our discussion of fiscal and monetary policy under fixed and flexible exchange rates, and fits right in with the results obtained above. Fiscal policy affects output when exchange rates are fixed. Monetary policy fails because mandatory intervention in the foreign exchange market forces the central bank to sterilize (that means *undo*) any money supply change brought about previously. Under flexible exchange rates, monetary policy can influence income quite effectively. Fiscal policy does not work. The demand added by the government is nullified by complete crowding out via the exchange rate (see Table 5.1).

Table 5.1 Does a policy instrument affect output? Which instrument affects output depends on the exchange rate system. Fiscal policy works when exchange rates are fixed. If they are flexible, full crowding out of net exports occurs via exchange rate appreciation. Monetary policy works when exchange rates are flexible. Under fixed exchange rates, monetary policy is not really available. The obligation to intervene takes money-supply control out of the hands of the central bank.

	Exchange rates system	
Policy instrument	Fixed exchange rates	Flexible exchange rates
Fiscal policy	Yes	No (full crowding out via exchange rate)
Monetary policy	No (forced sterilization through intervention)	Yes

Note: International capital is assumed to be perfectly mobile.

CASE STUDY 5.1 The 1998 Asia crisis

In late 1997 and 1998 many Asian economies suffered a dramatic economic downturn. Figure 1 documents this for four of the largest South-east Asian countries: Indonesia, Malaysia, the Philippines and Thailand. After stunning growth until the mid-1990s, in 1998 incomes contracted by between 5% in the Philippines and 13% in Indonesia.

Industrial countries worried that falling incomes in Asia would reduce demand for their own exports, dragging them into recessions too. Policymakers, therefore, were urged to ease monetary policy to fend off such dangers.

The Mundell–Fleming model helps understand some key features of the Asia crisis. Take the perspective of an industrial country, say France. France's economy before the crisis is at point A in Figure 2. For simplicity, suppose the world consists of France and South-east Asia only. Then i^W is South-east Asia's interest rate and Y^W is Asia's income.

As the crisis hits Asia and Asia's incomes fall, the demand for French exports falls. This shifts France's *IS* curve to the left, which pushes the interest rate and income towards point B. As the French interest rate moves below the world interest rate, however, international investors want to move their wealth out of French assets. This creates an excess supply of French francs. If the exchange rate is flexible, the French franc depreciates relative to Asian currencies. This makes French products more affordable for Asians, so French exports rise again. This shifts the *IS* curve back right, and it continues to do so until *IS* has returned to its original position. French income remains entirely unaffected by the depression in Asia.

Are you happy with this story? Probably not. Two things are particularly unsatisfactory:

- First, if a depreciation of the exchange rate so easily protects us from the fall in Asian incomes, why were the industrial countries so worried in 1998, and why did some even start to ease monetary policy?
- Second, the model says that the French franc *depreciates* and, hence, Asian currencies *appreciate*. In fact, exactly the opposite happened. As Figure 3 shows, all major Asian currencies depreciated substantially in 1997 and 1998: Indonesia's rupiah by more than 500%, but others too, like

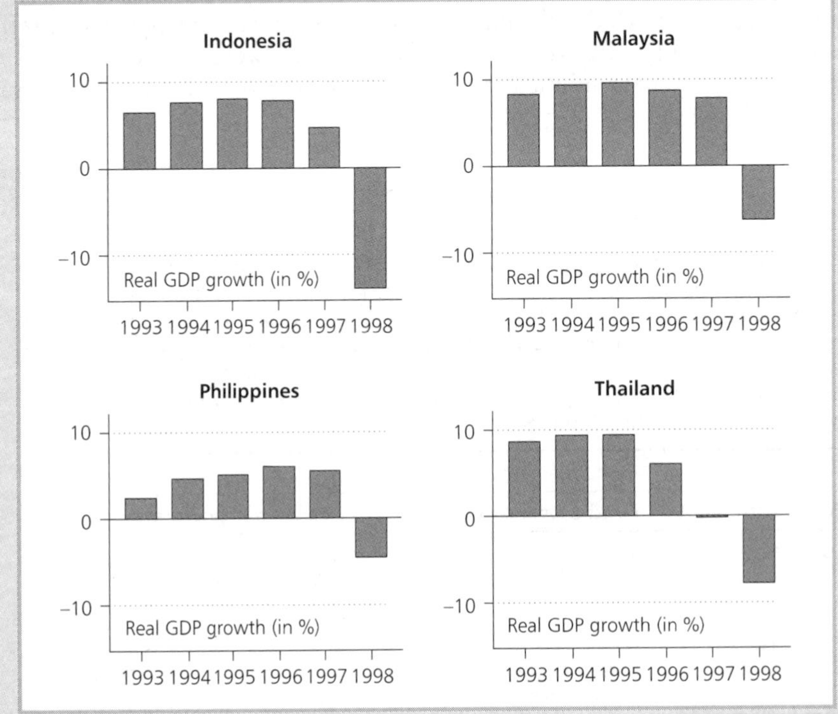

Figure 1

Case study 5.1 continued

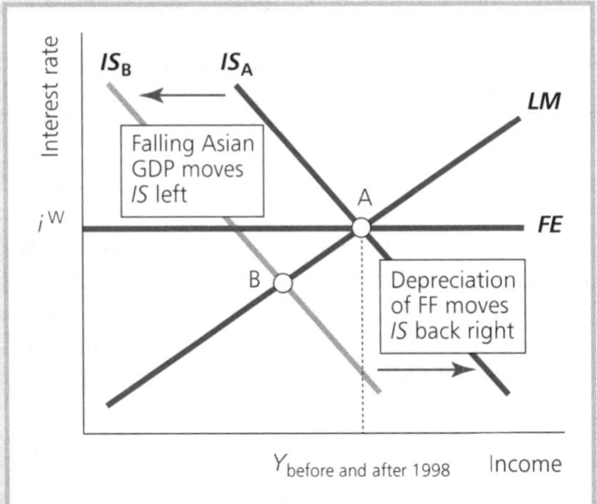

Figure 2

the Thai baht, the Philippine peso and Malaysia's ringgit, by as much as 60%.

So this cannot be the whole story. Let us refine it by looking at the situation more closely.

An important aspect to note is that Asia's crisis not only affected trade but also the international asset markets. Before the crisis, Asia's impressive growth performance had attracted international investment on a grand scale, and, as we can tell with the benefit of hindsight, made investors virtually blind with regard to the underlying risk. This changed rather abruptly in late 1997 and 1998. The dramatic worsening in Asia's overall economic performance, plunging stock markets, political scandals and crises suddenly made investors aware of the high risk involved.

In terms of our model, investors were only willing to hold on to Asian assets if the interest rate (or expected return) exceeded the French interest rate by a risk premium *RP*. If investors see different default risks at home and abroad the international capital market equilibrium condition modifies to $i = i^W - RP$. If French investors are prepared to accept the higher risk perceived in Asian assets only if the expected return is, say, 5% higher than at home, then Asia's interest rate must exceed France's interest rate by 5%. Hence, $i = i^W - 5$. The two interest rates, which were about the same before the crisis, drift apart.

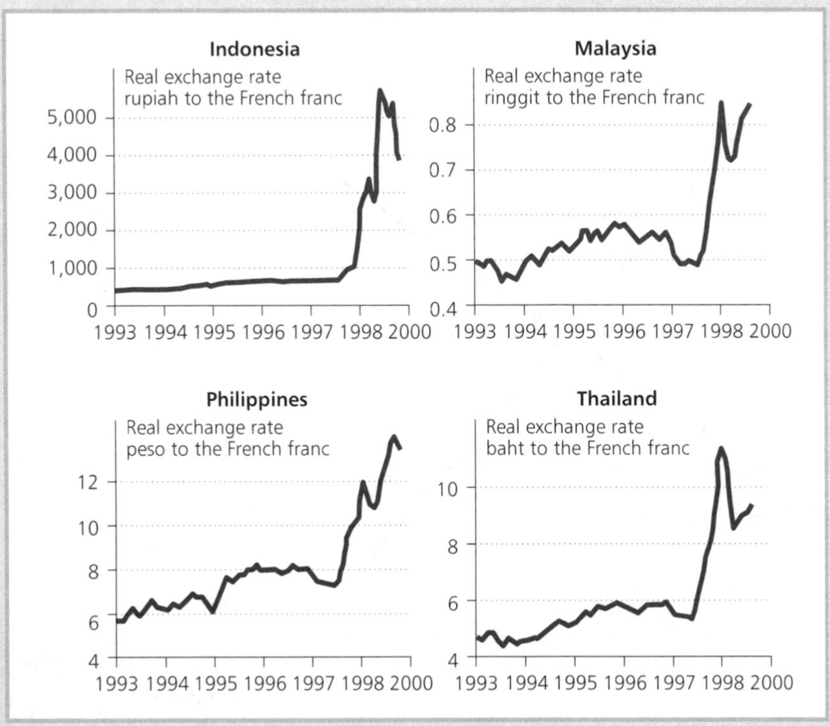

Figure 3

Case study 5.1 continued

The percentage of non-performing loans (i.e. loans that ended in default) is one indicator of riskiness. As seen in Table 1, this percentage was substantially higher in 1998 than it had been in 1997 for all four countries. In the Philippines the increase is only 25%. In the other three countries it is much higher, with Malaysia suffering from a 100% jump upwards. Taking note of this, investors respond by requiring a (higher) risk premium for holding bonds, stocks and other assets in these countries.

How does that fit into the Mundell–Fleming model? Consider Figure 4, in which again we let France's pre-1998 equilibrium be disturbed by the downward shift of the *IS* curve due to falling incomes in and exports to Asia. Now the *FE* curve moves down as well, however, because investors suddenly require a risk premium for holding Asian assets. As long as French interest rates exceed $i^W - RP$, funds flow out of Asia, making Asian currencies depreciate. This shifts the *IS* curve still further to the left, until a new equilibrium obtains in point C at income $Y_{\text{post-1998}}$.

Table 1 Default risk in South-east Asian countries, Non-performing loans as % of banks' assets

	Indonesia	Malaysia	Philippines	Thailand
1997	11	7.5	5.5	15
1998	20	15	7	25

Bottom line

From the perspective of other parts of the world, the real danger from the 1998 crisis in Asia did not come from the fall in Asian incomes. A flexible exchange rate would have taken care of most of this. Much more dangerous was the loss of trust in Asian assets which made Asian currencies depreciate and put exports to Asia in real jeopardy.

Further reading

The ultimate source and bibliography is Nouriel Roubini's web page at www.stern.nyu.edu/globalmacro/asian_crisis/asian_crisis_index.html providing you with what looks like a lifetime's reading – some difficult, some easy – on all aspects of the Asia crisis and on related issues.

Data sources

GDP data are from the Asian development bank. Exchange rates and the price indexes needed to compute real exchange rates are from the IMF. Data on non-performing loans are from Corsetti, Pesenti and Roubini (1997), *What Caused the Asian Currency and Financial Crisis?* Part I: *A macroeconomic overview.* NBER Working Paper 6833, Table 22.

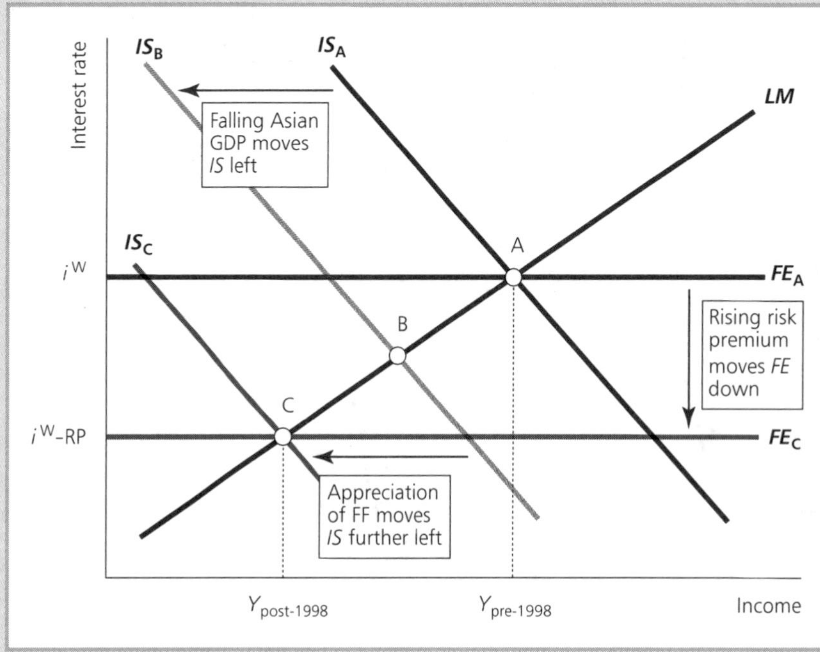

Figure 4

5.3 THE ALGEBRA OF MONETARY AND FISCAL POLICY IN THE MUNDELL–FLEMING MODEL

A little algebra illustrates the policy options more clearly.

Flexible exchange rates

The determinants of equilibrium income under flexible exchange rates have already been derived in Chapter 4. Combining the *FE* curve and the *LM* curve we obtained

$$Y = \frac{M}{k} + \frac{h}{k} i^{\text{World}}$$

Equilibrium income

So there are only two variables that can stimulate output. That is the money supply, which transmits into output changes according to

$$\Delta Y = \frac{1}{k} \Delta M$$

and the world interest rate. Changes in the world interest rate increase output by

$$\Delta Y = \frac{h}{k} \Delta i^{\text{World}}$$

Fiscal policy or other components of autonomous demand do not affect equilibrium income. Any increases in G, $\bar{I}$ or Y^{World} are completely crowded out by exchange rate appreciation. The exchange rate effect can be seen by looking at

$$R = \frac{1 - c + m_1}{m_2 + x_2}\left(\frac{M}{k} + \frac{h}{k} i^{\text{World}}\right) - \frac{\bar{I} + G + x_1 Y^{\text{World}}}{m_2 + x_2} + \frac{b i^{\text{World}}}{m_2 + x_2}$$

Equilibrium exchange rate

which is replicated from Chapter 4, section 4.4.

Fixed exchange rates

Under fixed exchange rates, equilibrium income is obtained by substituting the *FE* curve ($i = i^{\text{World}}$) into (4.9) and solving for Y:

$$Y = \frac{m_2 + x_2}{1 - c + m_1} R - \frac{b}{1 - c + m_1} i^{\text{World}} + \frac{1}{1 - c + m_1}(G + \bar{I}) + \frac{x_1}{1 - c + m_1} Y^{\text{World}}$$

R is now a policy variable controlled by the government. It can raise output via the multiplier

$$\Delta Y = \frac{m_2 + x_2}{1 - c + m_1} \Delta R$$

The money supply is endogenous, that is, outside government or central bank control. Fiscal policy is effective and raises output via the multiplier

$$\Delta Y = \frac{1}{1 - c + m_1} \Delta G$$

which is exactly the one we had already obtained in Chapter 4 (letting taxes be independent of income ($t = 0$)). Finally, both interest and income changes in the rest of the world spill over into the domestic economy via the multipliers

$$\Delta Y = \frac{-b}{1 - c + m_1} \Delta i^{\text{World}}$$

$$\Delta Y = \frac{x_1}{1 - c + m_1} \Delta Y^{\text{World}}$$

5.4 COMPARATIVE STATISTICS VERSUS ADJUSTMENT DYNAMICS

The purpose of the Mundell–Fleming model is to show how equilibrium is affected by policy instruments or other factors which are exogenous to the model. It *compares* equilibria, situations in which the economy has come to rest, in which variables do not change any more and become static. This kind of reasoning is called **comparative static analysis**.

Comparative static analysis looks at how equilibrium positions change after policy changes. It says nothing about whether and how the economy gets there.

Comparative static analysis does not say anything about how long it takes to reach the new equilibrium. Nor does it describe how the endogenous variables evolve as we move from the old equilibrium to the new one. In fact, comparative static analysis does not even indicate whether the new equilibrium will ever be reached, that is whether the equilibrium is **stable**. These are all aspects of the **dynamic analysis** of a model. A thorough treatment of these dynamic aspects calls for the explicit introduction of a time dimension into the model which recognizes that not all reactions take place instantaneously.

If an equilibrium is **stable**, the economy moves towards this equilibrium from all disequilibrium situations.

Dynamic analysis looks at whether an equilibrium is stable, and traces the transition from one equilibrium to another.

We will not make stability an issue here, as this can be shown to apply in the Mundell–Fleming model under reasonable dynamic specifications. Also, we will not spell out an explicit dynamic version of the model, although we will do so in the context of more developed models in Chapters 7 and 8. What we will try to do is develop an intuitive understanding of what transition paths look like.

The first thing to realize is that *some variables are slow while others are fast*. Hence some markets may clear quickly when pushed out of equilibrium and others may take quite some time to adjust.

Empirical note. Multiplier effects take up to two years to materialize fully.

A good rule of thumb is that *prices in financial markets adjust instantaneously*. Examples are the interest rate and the exchange rate. This keeps the money market and the foreign exchange market, where the interest rate and the exchange rate play key roles in equating supply and demand, in equilibrium at all times. In the goods market *output adjusts slowly*. If firms observe an increase or a fall in sales, they need time to gear up or scale down production. Changing production, and, hence, income, may take time to affect consumption. All this adds up to quite a time lag for the multiplier effect to materialize. In a similar vein, following an exchange rate change importers and exporters may need time to get out of existing contracts or business relationships, to find new suppliers or enter new markets.

The crux is that we may expect to be *on* the *LM* curve and *on* the *FE* curve all the time, even while moving from one overall equilibrium to another. We may well be *off* the *IS* curve for extended periods of time, however. If the

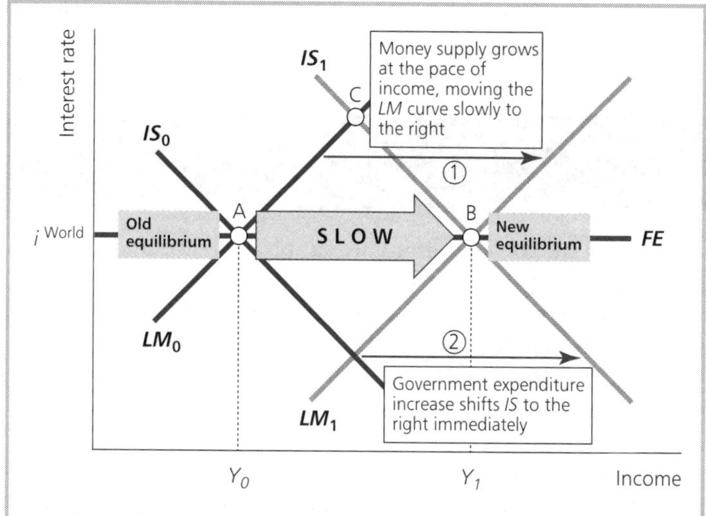

Figure 5.5 (Fixed exchange rates.) Comparative static analysis says that an increase of government spending shifts the economy's equilibrium point from A to B if exchange rates are fixed. Since output (and income) is a slow variable, however, the adjustment from A to B may be slow as well. Temporarily, while firms take measures to gear up production, the goods market remains to the left of IS_1 (the equilibrium line) in disequilibrium.

economy is to the left of *IS*, firms register an excess demand for goods and services and gradually increase output. To the right of *IS*, firms experience insufficient demand and reduce output.

What does this mean in the cases discussed above? Consider the increase of government expenditure under fixed exchange rates. The expenditure increase shifts *IS* out to IS_1 immediately. As long as income does not respond yet, the money market and the foreign exchange market can remain in equilibrium at A, and the goods market registers an excess demand. As income grows a little bit, the demand for money grows a little bit, and the central bank must engineer a corresponding money-supply increase by intervening in the foreign exchange market. This shifts *LM* somewhat to the right, but not into its eventual equilibrium position LM_1 yet. As income continues to grow, it keeps pulling *LM* to the right until all markets finally settle into the new equilibrium point B (see Figure 5.5).

Figure 5.6 contrasts the comparative static with the dynamic effect of a government expenditure increase by plotting both effects along the time axis.

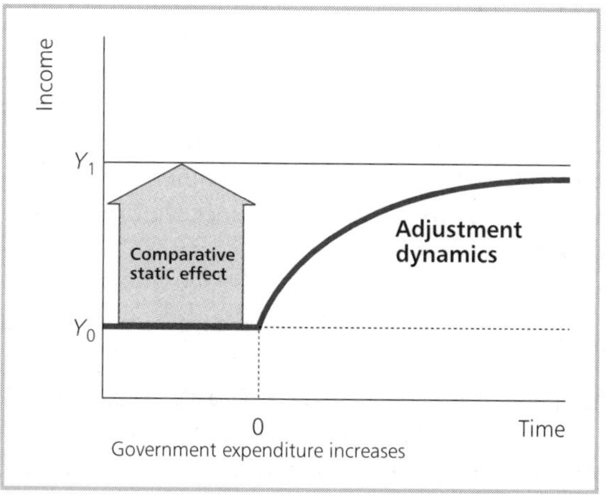

Figure 5.6 (Fixed exchange rates.) This graph shows the time profile of output, after government spending increased. The black line shows the full comparative-static effect, the increase in equilibrium income. Adjustment dynamics is slower, and only gradually approaches the new equilibrium.

The comparative static effect states *where* equilibrium goes. The dynamic adjustment path states *when* output is where, at each point in time.

5.5 ADJUSTMENT DYNAMICS WITH EXPECTED DEPRECIATION

Things become trickier if we consider a money-supply increase under flexible exchange rates. Initially, the money-supply increase shifts *LM* to the right into LM_1 (see Figure 5.8). This means that the new long-run equilibrium moves to B, but also the short-run or temporary equilibrium determined by the intersection between *FE* and *LM*. This requires income to rise. Since this takes time, the economy cannot move out to B immediately. No short-run equilibrium appears feasible!

The solution to this puzzle is hidden in the foreign exchange market equilibrium. When deriving it in Chapter 4 we simplified the uncovered interest parity condition to $i = i^{\text{World}}$ by assuming that individuals expect no depreciation. This is a useful assumption in comparative static analysis, which describes situations where the exchange rate has settled to a constant value. In the context of dynamic adjustment from one equilibrium to another, it is less appropriate. As the exchange rate may move towards a new value, international investors must be allowed to take that into account when allocating portfolios. So equilibrium in the foreign exchange market is given by the equation

$$i = i^{\text{World}} + \frac{E^e_{+1} - E}{E} \qquad \textbf{Uncovered interest parity} \qquad (5.1)$$

As we have already noted, the second term on the right-hand side, expected depreciation, moves the horizontal *FE* curve up or down. Since expectations exercise this pivotal role during dynamic adjustment, we need to take a closer look at how expectations of future exchange rates are being formed.

Exchange rate expectations

A useful way of thinking about exchange rate expectations is in terms of some exchange rate equilibrium E^* and deviations from it. It facilitates the discussion if the exchange rate and the equilibrium exchange rate are expressed in logarithms as e and e^*, respectively. The advantage of this is that the linear difference $e^* - e$ simply proxies the percentage deviation of the exchange rate from equilibrium. If individuals harbour the picture of an inherent tendency for the exchange rate to move towards its equilibrium, depreciation expectations may be formed according to

$$\frac{E^e_{+1} - E}{E} = d(e^* - e) \qquad \textbf{Expected depreciation} \qquad (5.2)$$

The parameter d measures the speed at which the exchange rate is expected to regress to e^*. If $e^* = 10$, $e = 9.9$ and $d = 0.5$, expected depreciation is 0.05 or 5%. Upon substituting equation (5.2) into (5.1) the foreign exchange market equilibrium condition becomes

$$i = i^{\text{World}} + d(e^* - e) \tag{5.3}$$

Equation (5.3) can be drawn as a straight line with slope $-d$ in an i-e diagram. Its position is determined by the world interest rate and the equilibrium exchange rate (Figure 5.7, panel (a)). The message of this line is that the foreign exchange market may be in equilibrium for many different interest rates, if only the interest rate is combined with the right exchange rate. If i falls short of i^{World} this must be made up by an expected appreciation. For this to happen, the exchange rate first has to rise above its equilibrium value. Then investors expect it to appreciate (fall) back towards its equilibrium value.

Panel (b) in Figure 5.7 shows what this implies in the current context of a money-supply increase under flexible exchange rates (compare also Figure 5.8). First, note that at the new static equilibrium point B, the *IS* curve has shifted to the right due to real depreciation. Hence the money supply increase raises the equilibrium exchange rate from e_0^* to e_1^*. This moves the foreign exchange market equilibrium line in Figure 5.7, panel (b), to the right into FE_1, so that it passes through the point marked by the world interest rate and the new equilibrium exchange rate (B).

In Figure 5.8 the *LM* curve has shifted to LM_1. Output is stuck at Y_0 in the very short run. At this income level the money market only clears if the interest rate drops to i'. At this rate nobody wants domestic bonds. The exchange rate depreciates. As it rises above the new equilibrium exchange rate, prospects of future appreciation of the domestic currency emerge. As soon as the exchange rate has depreciated to e', appreciation expectations have grown large enough to compensate for the interest rate deficit. Investors are again indifferent between holding domestic or foreign bonds. The foreign exchange market is in equilibrium.

Depreciation has shifted *IS* to the right – even beyond IS_1, as at e' the exchange rate is higher than e_1^*, the new equilibrium rate which determines the

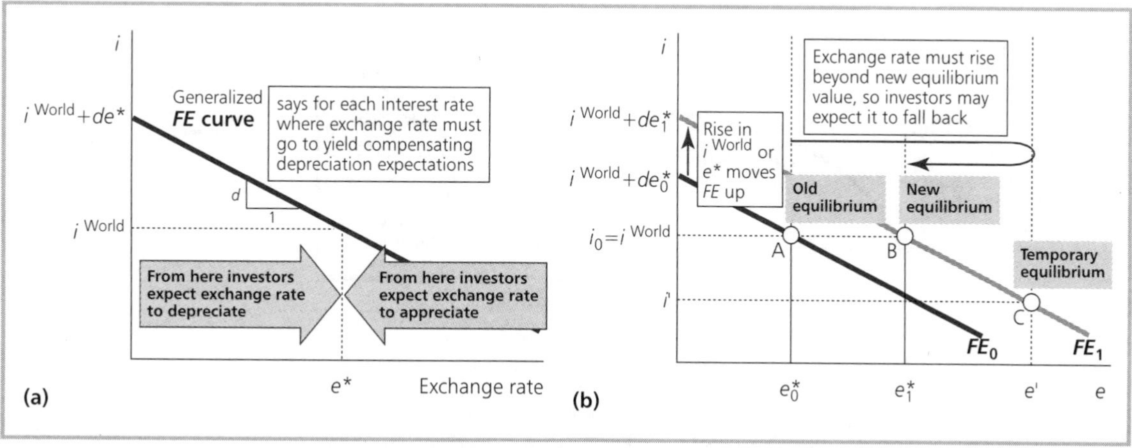

Figure 5.7 (Flexible exchange rates.) If investors expect the exchange rate to regress back towards equilibrium e*, foreign exchange market equilibrium may obtain at different interest rates, depending on where the exchange rate is relative to e* (panel (a)). If a money-supply increase rises *Y* under flexible exchange rates, the equilibrium exchange rate rises, shifting the generalized *FE* curve to the right (panel (b)).

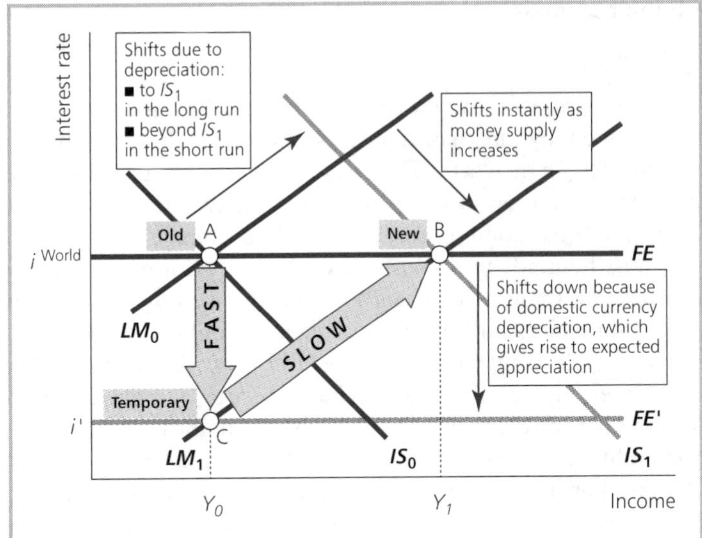

Figure 5.8 (Flexible exchange rates.) A money-supply increase shifts *LM* to the right. Only *i* and e can respond quickly. *Y* remains stuck at Y_0. Two things happen. The interest rate falls to *i'*, since only this equilibrates the money market. Since this drives investors out, the exchange rate depreciates. To restore open interest parity $i = i^{World} + d(e_1^* - e)$, *e* needs to rise above e_1^* (see also panel (b), Figure 5.9). This shifts *IS* right, even beyond IS_1. Gradually, as *Y* rises, the economy moves along LM_1 towards B while the exchange rate eases back towards e_1^*.

position of IS_1. This creates excess demand for goods and services, and income begins to rise. This raises the demand for money, the interest rate begins to rise, and the exchange rate inches back towards e_1^*. Appreciation expectations become smaller. The *FE* curve starts to move up. This process continues, and the point of intersection between the *FE* and the *LM* curves gradually moves up LM_1 until it reaches point B.

Exchange rate overshooting

Almost in passing we have hit upon a very important insight. Take a look at the adjustment dynamics triggered by a money-supply increase under flexible

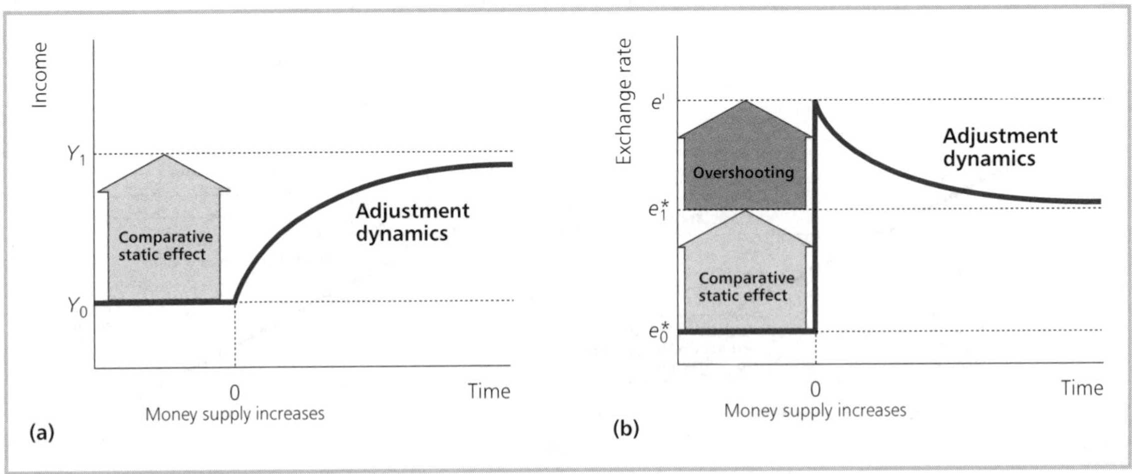

Figure 5.9 (Flexible exchange rates.) The Mundell–Fleming model suggests that the comparative static effects of a money-supply increase are higher income and a higher (depreciated) exchange rate. The exchange rate's response is quick and could bring about the required adjustment immediately. Output adjustment is slow. Output cannot respond immediately. In the short run, the exchange rate must also bear the output's burden of adjustment and overshoot its long-run response.

exchange rates (see Figure 5.9). Panel (a) plots output. Output dynamics is unexciting, the normal thing. Output must rise in the long run, but it needs time to achieve this.

Exchange rate overshooting occurs if the immediate response of the exchange rate to a disturbance (such as a money-supply increase) exceeds the response that is needed in the long run.

Panel (b) in Figure 5.9 shows the exchange rate, where something puzzling is happening. The exchange rate needs to depreciate in the long run (comparative static effect), from e_0^* to e_1^*. The immediate, short-run response of the exchange rate is to move beyond where it must go in the long run. After that the exchange rate gradually adjusts to its long-run level, apparently from the wrong side. This immediate, short-run overreaction of the exchange rate has become famous under the term **exchange rate overshooting**. It is considered a key characteristic of flexible exchange rates and will play an important role in later chapters.

5.6 WHEN PRICES MOVE

Remember our first encounter with money in the circular flow model in Chapter 1? By means of a numerical illustration we saw that endowing people with more money can lead to either more output (at given prices) or higher prices (for given output). The standard version of the Mundell–Fleming model considered so far focuses on the first option: at the current price level, firms are prepared to produce any volume of goods and services that aggregate demand desires. This assumption may be a useful approximation when there is slack in the economy. However, it is misleading when the economy operates at full capacity. This section gives a first flavour of this. A more general treatment of the interaction between aggregate supply and demand will be postponed until Chapters 7 and 8.

Consider an economy that operates at full capacity or potential income Y^*, employing all factors of production. It is reasonable to assume that if equilibrium income as determined by the fixed-price Mundell–Fleming model exceeds Y^*, firms raise prices. If aggregate demand falls short of Y^*, prices fall. We look at those policy measures that previously were found to affect equilibrium output: fiscal policy under fixed exchange rates, and monetary policy under flexible exchange rates.

Let the economy be at equilibrium point A in Figure 5.10. Let the government increase spending and the exchange rate be fixed. In a by-now familiar fashion, as G increases, IS shifts out to IS_1. The economy moves to B if output may temporarily be raised beyond Y^*. Income at B exceeds potential income. So prices move up. This affects the goods market, since it makes the real exchange rate EP^{World}/P appreciate, which shifts IS back to the left. But it also affects the real money supply. We pause here to see why.

Remember that the main purpose for holding money is to facilitate transactions. Transactions are purchases of real things, such as shoes, wine, bread or haircuts. To be able to buy the same basket of goods again and again the money balances held must have a constant buying power. In other words, the demand for money shown again in Figure 5.11 is a demand for real money balances. If the price level doubles, the nominal demand for money also doubles.

On the other hand, the central bank controls the *nominal* supply of money M. Previously we did not explicitly distinguish between the nominal money

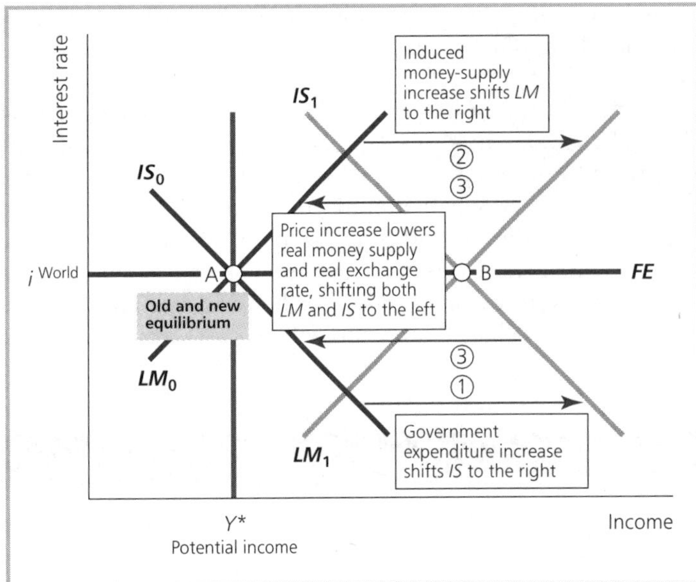

Figure 5.10 (Fixed exchange rates.) Raising government spending under fixed exchange rates leads from A to B. Since B is above potential income Y^*, firms start to raise prices. Rising prices make the real exchange rate EP^{World}/P appreciate, shifting *IS* back to the left. The real money supply M/P is also reduced, moving *LM* back to the left. The economy returns to A. Income and real money circulation are the same as before. Since government spending has fully crowded out net exports, the real exchange rate is now lower.

supply M and the real money supply M/P, since the price level was considered fixed. With the price level, which is an index anyway, being set to 1, which we may do without changing the argument, nominal and real money were even identical.

If the price level can change, it can affect the real money supply. If prices rise, the real money supply M/P obviously falls, even if the central bank keeps M unchanged. The vertical money supply line shifts to the left. Individuals are willing to make do with lower cash balances only at a higher interest rate. So the new money market equilibrium now obtains at the same level of income, but at a higher interest rate. Hence, if the price level rises with M remaining

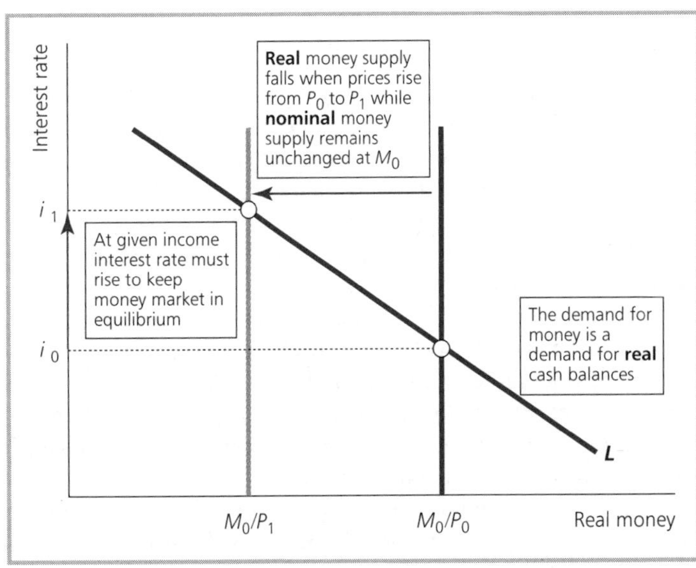

Figure 5.11 At any interest rate the private sector exercises a demand for real money L, as given by the negatively sloped line. The money supply M is nominal and fixed at M_0. A price increase from P_0 to P_1 shifts the vertical money-supply line to the left. The real money demand is only reduced to this lower level if the interest rate rises.

constant, the *LM* curve shifts to the left – just as it does when the nominal money supply is reduced at a constant price level.

So, returning to Figure 5.10, the price increase originating from the goods market shifts both the *IS* curve and the *LM* curve to the left. This process can only come to a halt when both curves are back in their original positions and the economy is back in the original equilibrium point A.

This has two interesting implications: since the position of the *LM* curve is determined by the real money supply, *LM* being back in its old position means that the real money supply is unchanged. Hence the nominal money supply and the price level must have increased by the same percentage. The position of the *IS* curve is determined by government expenditures and the real exchange rate. Since government expenditures have increased, net exports must be lower. Hence the real exchange rate must have appreciated. This was brought about by a price increase in the face of a constant exchange rate and foreign price level.

Consider next a money-supply increase under flexible exchange rates. The argument is very similar to the previous one (see Figure 5.12). The money-supply increase shifts *LM* to the right. As this tends to push the interest rate down, the home currency depreciates. This stimulates net exports, shifting the *IS* curve to the right. At point B output exceeds full capacity output Y^* and prices begin to rise. Rising prices reduce the real money supply, shifting *LM* to the left. Rising prices also make domestic goods more expensive compared with foreign goods. The real exchange rate falls (appreciates), which reduces net exports and shifts *IS* to the left. This process continues until both the money market and the goods market equilibrium curves are back in their original positions and the economy is at point A again. That means that the real money supply is the same as before the central bank increased the nominal money supply. So prices rose by just as much as the nominal money supply. It also means that the real exchange rate is unchanged. So the exchange rate depreciated by just as much as the price level rose.

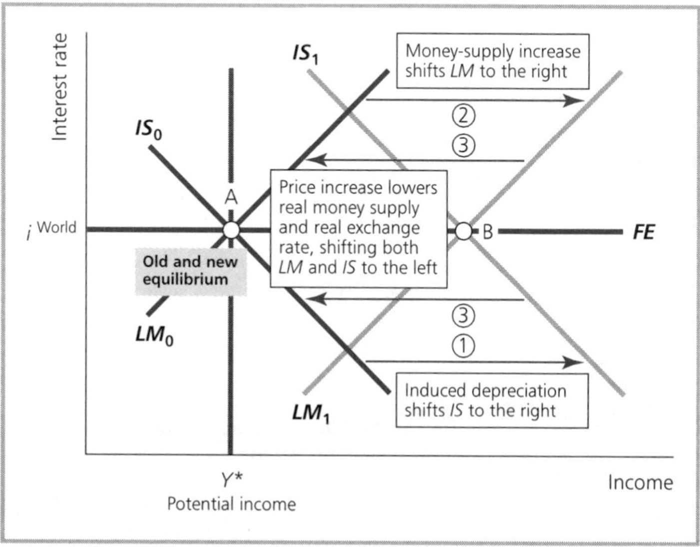

Figure 5.12 Under flexible exchange rates, a money-supply increase leads from A to B. Since B is above potential income Y^*, prices rise. This reduces the real money supply, shifting *LM* back to the left. The real exchange rate is also reduced, moving *IS* back to the left and the economy back to A. Income, real money circulation and the real exchange rate are the same as before.

5.7 TODAY'S EXCHANGE RATE AND THE FUTURE

Interesting insights into the behaviour of exchange rates are obtained by writing out full employment equilibria such as A in terms of algebraic equations.

Let us be more general than we were in Figure 5.12. There we assumed that financial investors do not expect the exchange rate to change, so that $i = i^{\text{World}}$ was the foreign exchange market equilibrium condition. In general, if for whatever reason the exchange rate is expected to depreciate, open interest parity in the general form given in equation (5.1) above holds. Introducing some shorthand, this foreign exchange market equilibrium condition can be written as

$$i = i^{\text{World}} + \varepsilon^{e}_{+1} \qquad \textbf{Open interest parity or } \textbf{\textit{FE}} \textbf{ curve} \qquad (5.4)$$

where $\varepsilon^{e}_{+1} \equiv (E^{e}_{+1} - E)/E$ is the expected rate of depreciation from today until next period. As long as expected depreciation remains the same, the economy's full employment equilibrium is at point C (Figure 5.13).

Point C, or other equilibria on the vertical line over Y^* that would result if the world interest rate or expected depreciation changed, may either be thought to obtain in the long run, after prices have had enough time to adjust, or even in the short run, if prices are very quick to adjust.

At equilibrium point C the interest rate and income remain unchanged. In order to keep the *IS* curve in the position that passes through C, the real exchange rate EP^{World}/P must remain unchanged. Suppose the real exchange rate required to make *IS* pass through C is 1, so that $EP^{\text{World}} = P$, or, taking logarithms (denoted by lower-case letters)

$$e + p^{\text{World}} = p \qquad \textbf{Long-run } \textbf{\textit{IS}} \textbf{ curve} \qquad (5.5)$$

At C the money market is also in equilibrium. Suppose the money demand function is semi-logarithmic (that means, the logarithm of real money demand depends on Y and i):

$$m - p = kY^* - hi \qquad \textbf{Semi-logarithmic } \textbf{\textit{LM}} \textbf{ curve} \qquad (5.6)$$

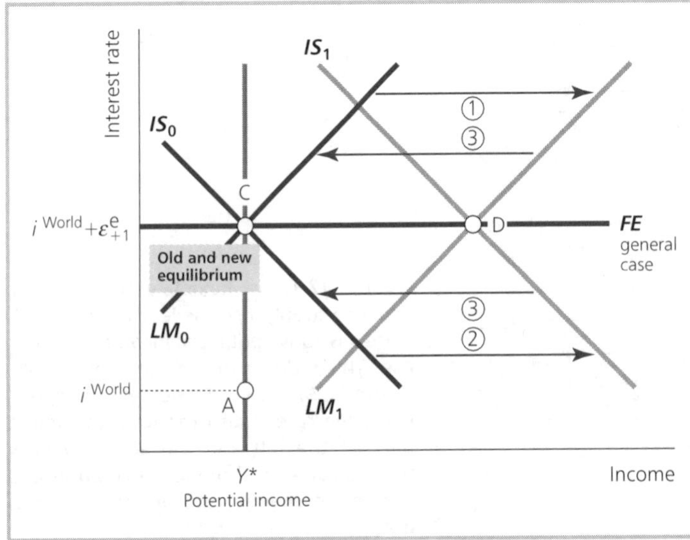

Figure 5.13 (Flexible exchange rates.) Expected depreciation drives a wedge between the domestic and the world interest rate. *FE* is in the blue position and the new long-run equilibrium is in C. Just as described in Figure 5.12 for the case of zero depreciation expectations, attempts to stimulate income by increasing the money supply are sooner or later nullified by price increases of equal magnitude.

Now let $Y^* = 0$, $p^{\text{World}} = 0$ and $i^{\text{World}} = 0$ (we can do this, since these exogenous variables may be at any arbitrary value anyway). Then substitute equation (5.5) into (5.6) for p and (5.4) into (5.6) for i to obtain $m - e = -h\varepsilon^{e}_{+1}$. Solving this equation for e gives

$$e = m + h\varepsilon^{e}_{+1} \tag{5.7}$$

The present exchange rate responds one-to-one to changes in the money supply, but it also reflects depreciation expected to occur tomorrow. This can be brought out in a slightly different form if we note that $\varepsilon^{e}_{+1} = e^{e}_{+1} - e$, which means that the expected rate of depreciation equals the difference between the logarithm of tomorrow's expected exchange rate and the logarithm of the current exchange rate. Substituting this into equation (5.7) and solving for e gives

$$e = \alpha m + (1 - \alpha)e^{e}_{+1} \tag{5.8}$$

where $\alpha = 1/(1 + h)$. The equation makes the important statement that today's exchange rate is a weighted average of today's money supply and the exchange rate expected to prevail tomorrow. So whatever the market expects to happen to the exchange rate in the future (an appreciation or a depreciation) in an almost self-fulfilling fashion already happens today.

Using this equation, the 2002 exchange rate depends on the concurrent money supply and on the exchange rate expected for 2003:

$$e_{2002} = \alpha m_{2002} + (1 - \alpha)e^{e}_{2003} \tag{5.9}$$

Does this mean that the investors' time horizon ends in 2003? No, for if we know that one year's exchange rate always depends on next year's exchange rate and the current money supply, we should anticipate that equation (5.8) also links the 2003 exchange rate to the exchange rate expected for 2004:

$$e^{e}_{2003} = \alpha m^{e}_{2003} + (1 - \alpha)e^{e}_{2004} \tag{5.10}$$

Taken together, equations (5.9) and (5.10) provide a link between 2004 and the exchange rate in 2002. This explains why it was to be expected that the prospects of EMU in 1999 would draw on exchange rates of earlier years.

This chapter's second look at booms and recessions leaves much of Chapter 2's and Chapter 3's **bottom lines** intact. Small changes in autonomous spending may cause large changes in income, and thus may be a cause of as well as a potential remedy for business cycle fluctuations. A refined picture has emerged, however. First, large income responses may not only be triggered by direct changes in autonomous spending. Indirect stimulation of spending via an expansion of the money supply may serve the same purpose. While we had already seen this result in Chapter 3, monetary policy works via the exchange rate in the open economy rather than directly via the interest rate. Second, which policy measures work and which do not crucially depends on the exchange rate system. The government spending multiplier of Chapter 2 only then reappears in the Mundell–Fleming model if exchange rates are fixed. Under flexible exchange rates government spending is completely crowded out by a fall in exports. Then monetary policy takes its place as an effective means of stimulating demand and income. Third, if the economy already operates at potential income, rising prices are likely to nullify efforts to stimulate income, no matter which instrument is being used.

CHAPTER SUMMARY

- The Mundell–Fleming model explains demand-side equilibria in the open economy as an interaction between the goods market, the money market and the foreign exchange market.
- Fiscal policy (that is, a change in government spending or a tax change) affects income when exchange rates are fixed. Under flexible exchange rates there is complete crowding out.
- Monetary policy affects output when exchange rates are flexible. When exchange rates are fixed, monetary policy is ineffective. The central bank is forced to sterilize (neutralize) any attempted money-supply increase immediately through foreign exchange market intervention.
- During the transition from one equilibrium to another, individuals may expect the exchange rate to change. Depreciation expectations affect the *FE* curve and, hence, the specifics of the adjustment process.
- Because after a disturbance the foreign exchange market and the money market adjust faster than the goods market, the exchange rate may be forced to overreact, that is, it overshoots its long-run equilibrium level.
- If the economy operates at potential output, there is full crowding out via price increases. In the case of a money-supply increase, the price increase drives the real money supply back to its original level. In the case of a government expenditure increase, the price increase makes the real exchange rate appreciate just enough to drive down net exports by as much as government expenditures increased.

KEY TERMS AND CONCEPTS

comparative static analysis
crowding out
dynamic analysis
exchange rate overshooting
fiscal policy
fixed exchange rates
flexible exchange rates
monetary policy
Mundell–Fleming model
stable

EXERCISES

5.1 Suppose the government raises the income tax rate. What are the effects on income, the interest rate and the exchange rate
(a) with a flexible exchange rate?
(b) with a fixed exchange rate?
(Derive your results graphically, assuming perfect international capital mobility.)

5.2 The central bank reduces the money supply. What are the consequences for income, the interest rate and the exchange rate
(a) with a flexible exchange rate?
(b) with a fixed exchange rate?
(Derive your results graphically, assuming perfect international capital mobility.)

5.3 Analyze the consequences of an increase of the world interest rate. Assume fixed exchange rates and perfect international capital mobility. What might be the reason for the increasing foreign interest rate? What does the result tell you about problems of international policy coordination?

5.4 How does a devaluation of the domestic currency in a system with fixed exchange rates and perfect capital mobility affect the domestic interest rate and output?

5.5 Your country is exposed to a positive demand shock (say, foreign demand for domestic goods increases) and you are in charge of monetary and fiscal policy. Formally, your country maintains a regime of flexible exchange rates with all trading partners, but for some reason you wish to keep the exchange rate where it was before the shock. What can you do? Use the graphical apparatus of the Mundell–Fleming model to explain your answer.

5.6 Exchange rates are flexible and capital is perfectly mobile. Depict the time paths of output, the interest rate and the exchange rate following an increase in government expenditure.

5.7 Suppose that investors suddenly lose confidence in the domestic currency and expect it to depreciate. Trace the consequences in the Mundell–Fleming model. What does the result tell you about 'self-fulfilling prophecies'? Will the induced changes in income and the exchange rate last?

5.8 Consider Figure 5.14, which depicts returns to US and German government bonds since 1960. What do these time series tell us about investors' expectations concerning the Deutschmark/dollar exchange rate?

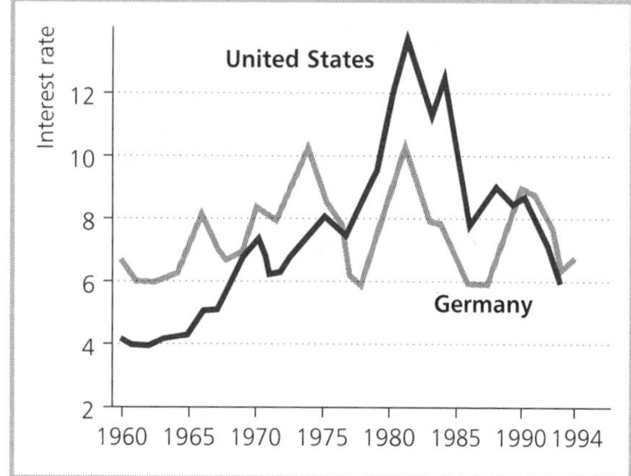

Figure 5.14

5.9 What does the *FE* curve look like if capital is perfectly immobile? What might be the reasons for such capital immobility? Analyze the effect of expansionary monetary and fiscal policy in a system of flexible exchange rates with perfect capital immobility.

RECOMMENDED READING

The original sources for the Mundell–Fleming model are the following:

- J. Marcus Fleming (1962) 'Domestic financial policies under fixed and floating exchange rates', *IMF Staff Papers* 9: 369–79.
- Robert A. Mundell (1962) 'Capital mobility and stabilization policy under fixed and flexible exchange rates', *Canadian Journal of Economic and Political Science* 29: 475–85.

A current view on the flexible vs fixed exchange rates controversy is offered by Stanley Fischer (2001) 'Exchange rate regimes: is the bipolar view correct', *Journal of Economic Perspectives* 15: 3–24.

APPLIED PROBLEMS

RECENT RESEARCH

Explaining exchange rates

If flexible prices keep the economy at potential income at all times, the exchange rate is determined by $e = m + h\varepsilon^e_{+1}$. The equation is this compact only because, in order to demonstrate the role of monetary policy in the clearest way possible, we held other variables, including foreign ones, constant and normalized them to zero. In reality other countries do not stand still. While we change our money supply, they change theirs. Taking this into account, the exchange rate measured against that of some other country is not only determined by our money supply, but, with a negative sign, by the other country's as well. Further, in reality potential income is not zero and even changes over time. So the difference between the two countries' income levels should also feature in the exchange rate equation. In this spirit Jeffrey Frankel (1979, 'On the mark: a theory of floating exchange rates based on real interest differences', *American Economic Review* 69: 610–22) estimates the following equation for the Deutschmark/dollar exchange rate (monthly data July 1974 to February 1978; standard errors in parentheses):

$$\begin{aligned} e = {} & \underset{(0.10)}{1.33} + \underset{(0.17)}{0.87}(m - m^*) - \underset{(0.22)}{0.72}(y - y^*) \\ & + \underset{(2.70)}{28.65}(\pi^e - \pi^{*e})_{+1} \qquad R^2 = 0.80 \end{aligned}$$

where *e*, *m* and *y* are the logarithms of the exchange rate, the money supply and real income, respectively; π^e denotes expected inflation. US variables carry an asterisk.

The first coefficient after the constant is not significantly different from 1 (the *t*-statistic for the null hypothesis that the coefficient is 1 is $(1 - 0.87)/0.17 = 0.73$). So if the German money supply rises by 1% relative to the US money supply, the Deutschmark depreciates by about 1%. The next coefficient states that if German income grows 1% over US income, the Deutschmark appreciates by 0.72%. The last coefficient measures the influence of the difference in inflation expectations. This difference is used as a proxy for expected depreciation: if the real exchange rate is to remain constant, then depreciation must reflect the inflation differential: $\varepsilon = \pi - \pi^*$. Then expected depreciation should equal the difference in expected inflation rates. The positive coefficient of 28.65 states that the more depreciation the market expects, the more the exchange rate depreciates today. The equation explains 80% of the variance of this exchange rate during the sample period.

Note: Frankel's equation also includes the difference in interest rates. Its coefficient is not significant and is not shown here.

WORKED PROBLEM

In and out of the United States

Net exports as a building block of the Mundell–Fleming model have been specified in equation (4.2) (Chapter 4) as (after rearranging)

$$NX = (x_2 + m_2)R + x_1 Y^{World} - m_1 Y \tag{5.4}$$

This type of equation should explain all net exports, the current account, or certain categories of net exports. Table 5.2 gives data for US net travel and transportation receipts (TRAVEL), the effective exchange rate of the currencies of major trading partners versus the dollar (R), US GDP (Y^{USA}) and OECD GDP (Y^{OECD}). Attempting to estimate equation (5.4) from these data gives

$$\underset{(0.36)}{\text{TRAVEL} = -6{,}102.1} - \underset{(2.68)}{273.80R} + \underset{(0.79)}{12.35Y^{USA}} - \underset{(0.24)}{205.71Y^{OECD}}$$

$R^2_{adj} = 0.56$; 22 annual observations 1973–1994

The equation does not perform quite as expected. While the real exchange rate index has the expected negative sign (since this index is the reciprocal of the dollar exchange rate versus other currencies), and with a *t*-value of 2.68 is also significant, income levels in the United States and in the OECD countries do not seem to exert the expected influence on net travel receipts. And even if the coefficients were significant, they would have the wrong sign. What may have caused this is that net travel expenditures cannot adjust immediately to changes in income levels or the real exchange rate. One way to check this is to assume that the above equation only models desired net exports NX^*. Actual net exports NX only adjust by a fraction of the change in desired travel expenditures each period:

$$NX - NX_{-1} = \alpha(NX^* - NX_{-1}) \tag{5.5}$$

Substituting equation (5.4) for NX^* into equation (5.5) and solving for NX gives

$$NX = (1-\alpha)NX_{-1} + \alpha(x_2 + m_2)R + \alpha x_1 Y^{World} - \alpha m_1 Y \tag{5.6}$$

So if adjustment is slow, net exports not only depend on the current real exchange rate and domestic and foreign incomes, but also on last year's net exports. Estimating this equation with our travel data yields

$$\underset{(0.57)}{\text{TRAVEL} = -3053.1} + \underset{(12.71)}{0.88\,\text{TRAVEL}_{-1}} - \underset{(3.38)}{117.36R} - \underset{(2.27)}{12.11Y^{USA}} + \underset{(2.79)}{782.32Y^{OECD}}$$

$R^2_{adj} = 0.96$; 22 annual observations 1973–1994

All coefficients are now as expected and, except for the constant term, significantly different from zero. Since the estimate for the autoregressive coefficient (in front of TRAVEL_{-1}) is $1 - a = 0.88$, we have $a = 0.12$. This means that, within a year, travel expenditures only adjust by a fraction of 0.12 to a change in desired travel expenditures, which makes for a very slow adjustment.

Table 5.2

	Travel in \$m	R (March 1973 = 100)	Y^{USA} in 1987 \$	Y^{OECD*}
1973	−3,158	98.9	3,268.6	69.4
1974	−3,184	99.4	3,248.1	69.1
1975	−2,812	94.0	3,221.7	63.6
1976	−2,558	97.6	3,380.8	68.8
1977	−3,565	93.4	3,533.3	72.0
1978	−3,573	84.4	3,703.5	74.9
1979	−2,935	83.2	3,796.8	78.5
1980	−997	84.9	3,776.3	78.9
1981	144	101.0	3,843.1	79.3
1982	−992	111.8	3,760.3	77.3
1983	−4,227	117.4	3,906.6	78.8
1984	−8,438	128.9	4,148.5	83.8
1985	−9,798	132.5	4,279.8	86.3
1986	−7,382	103.7	4,404.5	87.2
1987	−6,481	90.9	4,539.9	90.3
1988	−1,511	88.2	4,718.6	95.3
1989	5,071	94.4	4,838.0	98.4
1990	8,978	86.0	4,897.3	100.0
1991	17,957	86.5	4,867.6	99.7
1992	20,885	83.5	4,979.3	99.4
1993	20,840	90.0	5,134.5	99.1
1994	18,000	88.6	5,342.3	103.6

Note: * Index of industrial production (1990 = 100)

YOUR TURN

Business cycle links under different exchange rate regimes

A very important result from this chapter is that domestic income is affected by income developments abroad depending on whether exchange rates are flexible or fixed. Under flexible exchange rates there is no link between domestic and foreign income. If the rest of the world falls into a recession, the exchange rate works as a buffer, making sure domestic exports and income are not affected. Under fixed exchange rates no such buffer exists and domestic income will be dragged down by falling world income.

The income data for Austria, Germany and Norway given in Table 5.3 provide an opportunity to explore this implication of the Mundell–Fleming model. For both Austria and Norway, Germany is an important trading partner. The difference between the two countries relevant for our purposes is that Austria had a more or less fixed exchange rate versus the German mark during recent decades, while Norway's exchange rate was flexible. Hence, there should be a significant influence from German income on Austrian income, but not on Norwegian income. To test this, you may want to run a linear regression of the form $Y^A = c_0 + c_1 Y^D$ for Austria–Germany and a similar one for Norway–Germany.

As we noted in the your-turn section of Chapter 2 (see pp. 59–60), regressing two heavily trended variables on each other may give a statistically significant result even though the two have nothing to do with each other. This problem can be alleviated by taking first differences or growth rates of the variables involved. So you may want to run a regression of the form $\Delta Y^A/Y^A = c_0 + c_1 \Delta Y^D/Y^D$ and see whether the effect is there still for Austria but not for Norway.

Table 5.3

Year	Y^A	Y^D	Y^N
1975	54.3	52.6	44.6
1976	56.8	55.1	47.6
1977	59.4	56.8	49.4
1978	59.4	58.5	51.7
1979	62.3	61.0	53.9
1980	64.1	61.7	56.6
1981	64.0	61.8	57.2
1982	65.2	61.1	57.3
1983	67.1	62.1	59.3
1984	67.3	63.9	62.8
1985	68.8	65.3	66.0
1986	70.4	66.9	68.4
1987	71.6	67.8	69.8
1988	73.9	70.2	69.7
1989	77.0	72.8	70.4
1990	80.5	77.0	71.8
1992	84.4	89.1	76.4
1993	84.8	88.1	78.5
1994	86.8	90.2	82.8
1995	88.3	91.8	86.0
1996	90.1	92.5	90.7
1997	91.3	93.8	93.8
1998	94.2	95.8	95.7
1999	96.9	97.0	96.6
2000	100.0	100.0	100.0

To further explore this chapter's key messages you are encouraged to use the interactive online module found at

www.fgn.unisg.ch/eurmacro/tutor/MundellFleming.html

and many other features hosted at **www.fgn.unisg.ch/eurmacro**

CHAPTER 6

ENTER AGGREGATE SUPPLY

WHAT TO EXPECT After working through this chapter, you will understand:

1 In more detail the meaning of **potential income** or output.

2 How wages and employment are determined in the **labour market**.

3 How regulations, trade unions, and other labour market characteristics, or demographic features, may give rise to **involuntary unemployment** which persists in the long run.

4 Why **aggregate output** produced by firms may temporarily exceed or fall short of the level of potential output produced in equilibrium (or the long run).

By now we have a good understanding of aggregate demand, that is, of what happens on the economy's demand side. This contrasts with our understanding of aggregate supply, the treatment of which so far has been, well, rather simplistic. The only time we have explicitly touched upon the issue of firms' level of output was when we discussed money in the circular flow model in Chapter 1. There we considered two extreme cases of the **aggregate supply (*AS*) curve**, the line that indicates how much output firms produce at different price levels. For easy reference, Figure 6.1 replicates these two versions. The **horizontal aggregate supply curve** shown in panel (a) is the one we employed in Chapters 2–5 in the context of the Keynesian cross, the *IS-LM* model and the Mundell–Fleming model. It is usually referred to as the **extreme Keynesian aggregate supply curve**. It assumes there is slack and the presence of one or more production factors in abundance. Then how much firms produce depends only on demand. At the given price level, firms supply any level of output that is demanded. But then the price level never changes! How does this correspond with the real world where continuous price changes in the form of inflation are the rule rather than an exception? Quite obviously, a horizontal aggregate supply curve cannot be the whole story.

The **aggregate supply curve** shows the total quantity of goods and services supplied by all firms in the economy at different price levels.

The **extreme Keynesian aggregate supply curve** is horizontal, stating that, at the current price, firms are ready to produce any output that is demanded. A refined Keynesian aggregate supply curve will be introduced later.

Panel (b) in Figure 6.1 shows a **vertical aggregate supply curve**. Firms supply potential output Y^* no matter what the price level is. This curve is generally referred to as the **classical aggregate supply curve**, for reasons that will become evident in a moment. The drawback here is that, unless we assume that the *AS* curve shifts backwards and forwards all the time, only prices change, but never income. This is clearly at odds with real-world observations of business cycles, evidence of which was presented in Chapter 2. Again, a vertical aggregate supply curve cannot be the whole story either.

The **classical aggregate supply curve** is vertical, stating that firms produce only one output Y^*, no matter how high prices are.

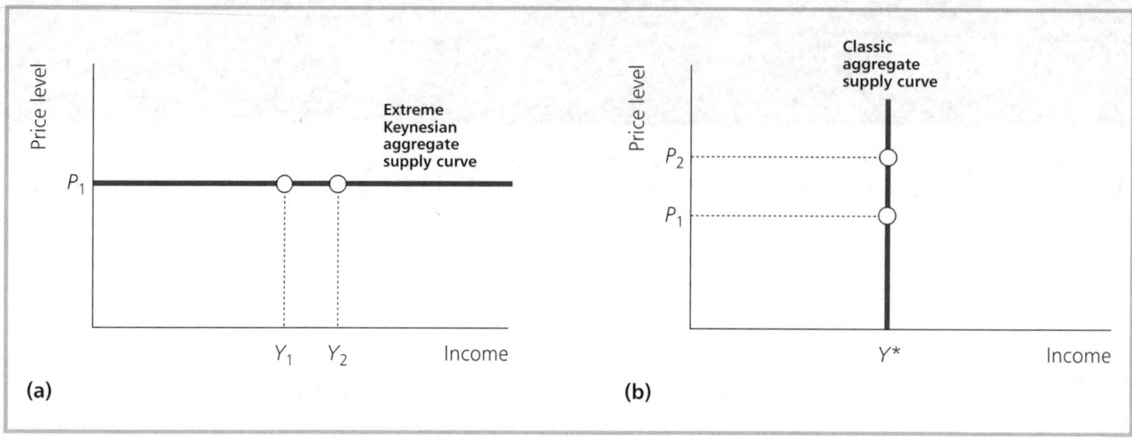

Figure 6.1 The panels repeat two extreme views of an aggregate supply curve employed so far. In panel (a), firms supply any volume of goods which the market demands at the given price level. In panel (b), firms supply one specific volume of output only, no matter what the price level is.

It is time to take a closer look at the economy's supply side. This chapter will do so by addressing three questions:

1 What exactly is potential output? How is this mysterious variable Y^* really determined?
2 How is it possible that in macroeconomic equilibrium, when income and output are at the potential level Y^*, involuntary unemployment exists and persists?
3 What can induce firms to supply output levels that deviate from potential output?

6.1 POTENTIAL INCOME AND THE LABOUR MARKET

Potential or equilibrium output is what an economy produces if it leaves no available factors of production idle. What are these factors? It is easy to draw up a long list of what contributes to the production potential of a country: the number of factories, the number of workers, their qualifications, the area and quality of land, the climate, natural resources, property rights, the political and legal system, and so on. These factors can be grouped into two main categories: capital K and labour L. So output Y at any point in time is a function F of these two factors:

$$Y = F(K, L) \qquad \textbf{Production function} \qquad (6.1)$$

Maths note. Formally, we assume for first and second derivatives $F_K, F_L > 0$ and $F_{KK}, F_{LL} < 0$.

The **production function** is the key to the economy's supply side. Figure 6.2 illustrates a production function and highlights two assumptions which economists usually make about its shape:

- Output increases as either factor increases.
- If one factor remains fixed, increases of the other factor yield smaller and smaller output gains.

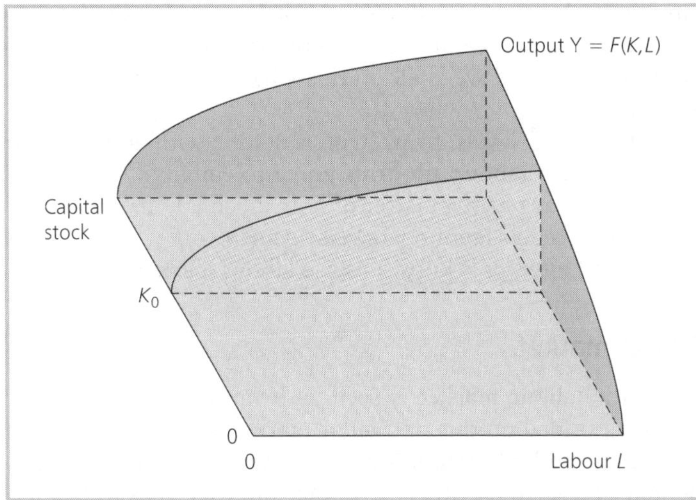

Figure 6.2 The full-scale **3D production function** shows how, for a given production technology, output rises as greater and greater quantities of capital and/or labour are being employed.

This second assumption refers to partial production functions, obtained by placing a vertical cut through the production function parallel to the axis measuring the factor that varies. Figure 6.3 shows such a partial production function, obtained in this case by fixing the capital stock at K_0.

Note. Strictly, the marginal product of labour is output gained by an infinitesimally small increase in labour. Our text and graph magnifies this by looking at a one-unit increase in labour.

The **partial production function** is drawn for given technology and stock of capital. The function itself tells us how much output is produced with a given labour input. For example, according to the partial production function drawn for a capital stock of K_0 in Figure 6.3, L_1 units of labour produce Y_1 units of output. The slope of the production function indicates (as an approximation) by how much output increases if we add one unit of labour. The output gain accomplished relative to a small increase in L – which is called the **marginal product of labour** – is measured by the slope of the production function. As the given capital stock is being combined with more and more labour, each additional unit of labour has to make do with less and less capital. Therefore, one-unit increases of L yield smaller and smaller output increases. The two tangent

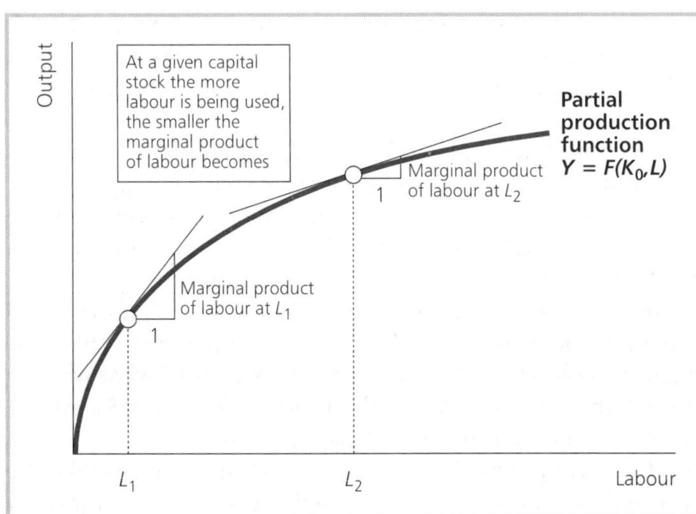

Figure 6.3 This partial production function shows how output increases as more labour is employed, while the capital stock remains fixed at K_0. The slope of $F(K_0, L)$ measures how much output is gained by a small increase of labour. The two tangent lines measure this marginal product of labour at L_1 and L_2 and indicate that it decreases as L rises.

lines measure this diminishing marginal product of labour. By similar reasoning, the marginal product of capital is also decreasing. It can be dealt with in the same kind of diagram, and we shall do this when discussing economic growth in Chapter 9.

So, knowing what income levels firms will generate with a particular amount of labour, **how much labour are firms going to employ?** As we shall see straightaway, this is just as much a matter of how much labour firms *want to employ* as it is of how much labour workers *want to offer*. The market where supply and demand interact is known as the labour market.

The classical labour market

In the classical view the **labour market** is seen as being just like any other market. The good being traded on this particular market is labour (measured in work hours). It is supplied by (potential) workers, and demanded by firms. The price for one unit of this good, the hourly wage, adjusts so as to balance supply and demand.

Let us look at the **demand for labour** first. Firms demand another unit of labour whenever they think it will raise more revenue than it costs. We know that how much (real) revenue another unit of labour produces (or how much more output it produces) can be directly read off the partial production function. This point is repeated in the upper panel of Figure 6.4.

If we measure the slope of the partial production function at all labour input levels and transfer all these marginal products onto a separate graph in the lower panel, the result is the downward-sloping **marginal product of labour schedule**. The nice thing about this schedule is that at the same time it is a **labour-demand curve.**

The **marginal product of labour schedule** indicates the additional output produced by one more unit of labour that obtains at various levels of employment.

The (aggregate) **labour demand curve** shows the (aggregate) quantity of labour that firms demand at different real wage rates.

To see this, let the real wage, $w \equiv (W/P)$, which can be measured along the ordinate in units of real output, be w_1. Then as long as employment falls short of L_1 the marginal product of labour always exceeds w_1, the marginal cost of labour, and it raises profits to increase employment. At employment levels above L_1 the marginal cost of labour exceeds its marginal product. Hence, given w_1, firms maximize profits by demanding exactly L_1 units of labour. This exercise leads to similar results for different market real wage rates. It turns out that the marginal product of labour curve indicates the employment that firms demand at different real wages, and thus is also the labour-demand curve.

Next we need to identify the supply of labour. To avoid confusion in this chapter and further down the road, let's lay down some terminology first.

The basic element to start with when thinking about employment is the **population**. The labour market diagram in Figure 6.5 marks this with a vertical grey line. Part of the population is inactive from an employment perspective. According to OECD definitions (also used by the EU) these are all persons younger than 15 or older than 64. Subtracting the number of those that are too young or too old from the total population gives us what we may call the **active population** N. However, not all of those who could potentially be active may choose to work. Subtracting those who voluntarily stay out of employment from the active population gives us the **labour force**. Unlike the population and the active population, which simply reflect demographics at

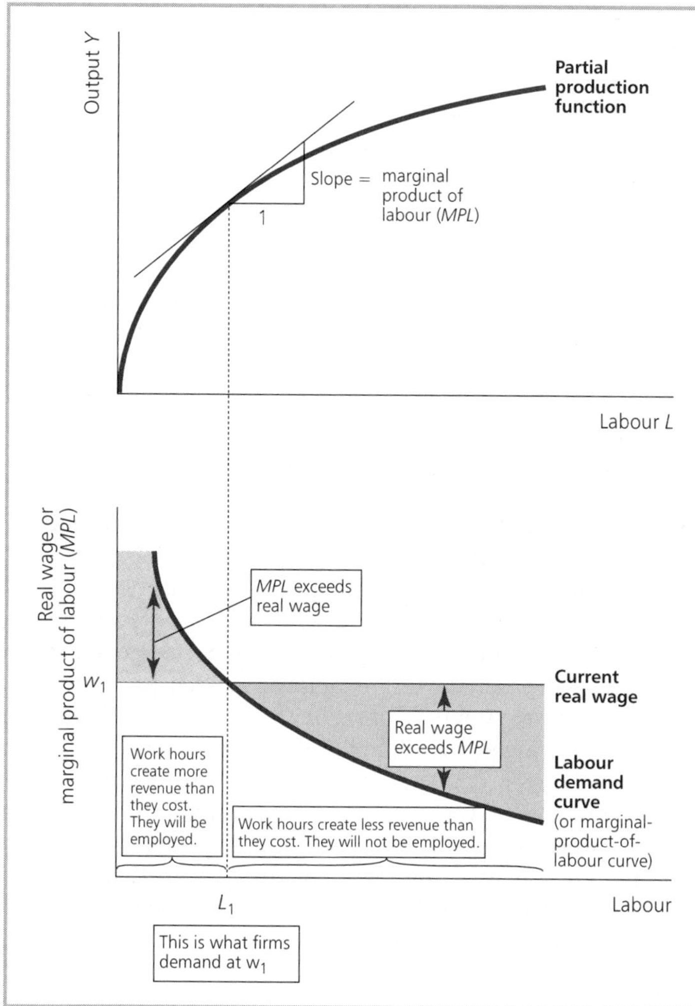

Figure 6.4 The upper panel repeats a partial production function. With a fixed capital stock, output increases as labour input increases. The lower panel depicts the marginal product of labour (MPL) as a function of labour. This marginal product of labour becomes smaller as the amount of labour already used increases. The **marginal product of labour** measures how much one more unit of labour is worth to the firm. Hence, at a real wage such as w_1 the firm keeps demanding more and more labour until the marginal product of labour falls below the real wage. This happens when labour input exceeds L_1.

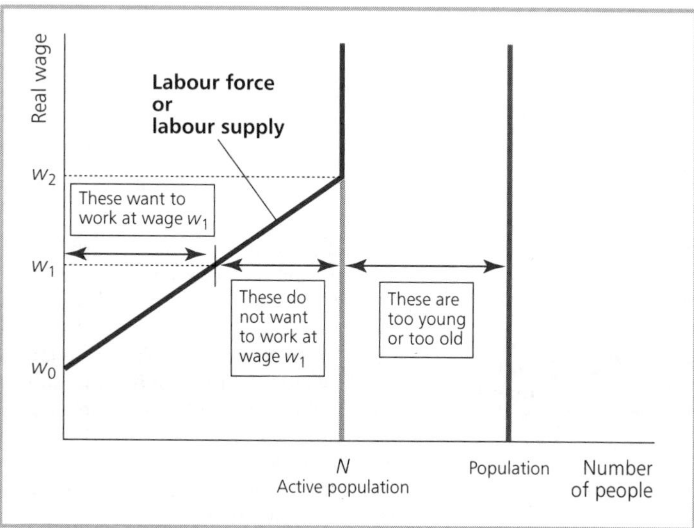

Figure 6.5 The **labour force** is obtained by subtracting from the total **population** those who are too young or too old to work, and those who do not want to work. Since the labour force thus counts all those who offer their labour, successfully or not, we may also call it the **labour supply**.

Empirical note. In 1994 the EU population was 371.5 (millions). The active population (age 15 to 64 according to OECD definitions) was 245.6, while the labour force was 165.9. Out of those, 147.3 were working and 18.6 were looking for work.

any point in time, the labour force is not a fixed number. As Figure 6.5 illustrates, it is a curve that reflects how the willingness of people to work depends on how much it pays to work. The sketch assumes that if the real wage exceeds w_2 everybody who is eligible for work also wants to work. Thus in this segment the active population and the labour force are the same. As the real wage moves below w_2, however, more and more people withdraw from the labour force, giving the labour-force curve a positive slope in this segment. At the lower end nobody is prepared to work for less than w_0. So here the labour force is zero.

The aggregate **labour supply curve** shows the (aggregate) quantity of labour supplied by workers at different real wage rates.

Put another way, the labour force is that part of the population that can and wants to offer themselves for work. Therefore, we may also refer to the labour force as the **labour supply**. The upward-sloping **labour supply curve** reflects the assumption that more labour is being supplied as working becomes more attractive through higher pay. Figure 6.6 combines a labour supply curve with a labour demand schedule, both in linear form. Under perfect conditions the market clears at employment L^* and the real wage w^*.

Note that employers' demand for and workers' supply of labour depends on the real wage $w \equiv W/P$, which is the money wage divided by the price level. Under the ideal conditions assumed here, changes in the price level do not impact on the labour market equilibrium. For example, if workers initially supplied the market-clearing amount of labour L^* at a money wage of €20 per hour, with the price level being at €10, $(W/P)^*$ equalled 2. After prices doubled to €20 workers only continue to supply L^* if money wages rise to €40 in order to keep the real wage, the buying power of labour income, unchanged at 2. For similar reasons, firms only keep demanding L^* if money wages respond to price changes so as to hold the real wage at 2. The crux of this argument is that with perfectly flexible money wages, the price level does not affect the market-clearing real wage and employment. But then, neither can it affect output. Therefore, the classical labour market discussed here implies a vertical aggregate supply curve as depicted in Figure 6.1, panel (b).

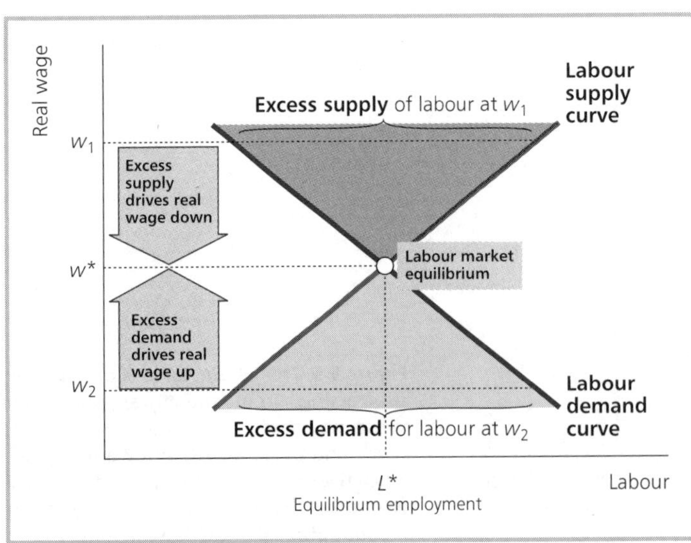

Figure 6.6 At a real wage such as w_1 workers supply more labour than firms want. Those who cannot find work bid down the wage until it is at w^*. If the wage is at w_2 firms want to employ more labour than workers are ready to supply. Competition among firms for scarce labour bids up the real wage until it is at w^*. Only at the real wage w^* does demand equal supply at L^*, and the labour market comes to rest in equilibrium.

Figure 6.7 shows the steps that lead from a labour market equilibrium that is independent of the price level to a vertical aggregate supply curve. In the lower left-hand panel equilibrium employment L^* is determined. The partial production function in the panel above shows the equilibrium output that results from this employment. The 45° line brings this potential output around to the diagram in the lower right-hand panel. Here, no matter where the price level is, the economy's output is always at Y^*. We call the level of output that results when the labour market is in equilibrium **potential output.**

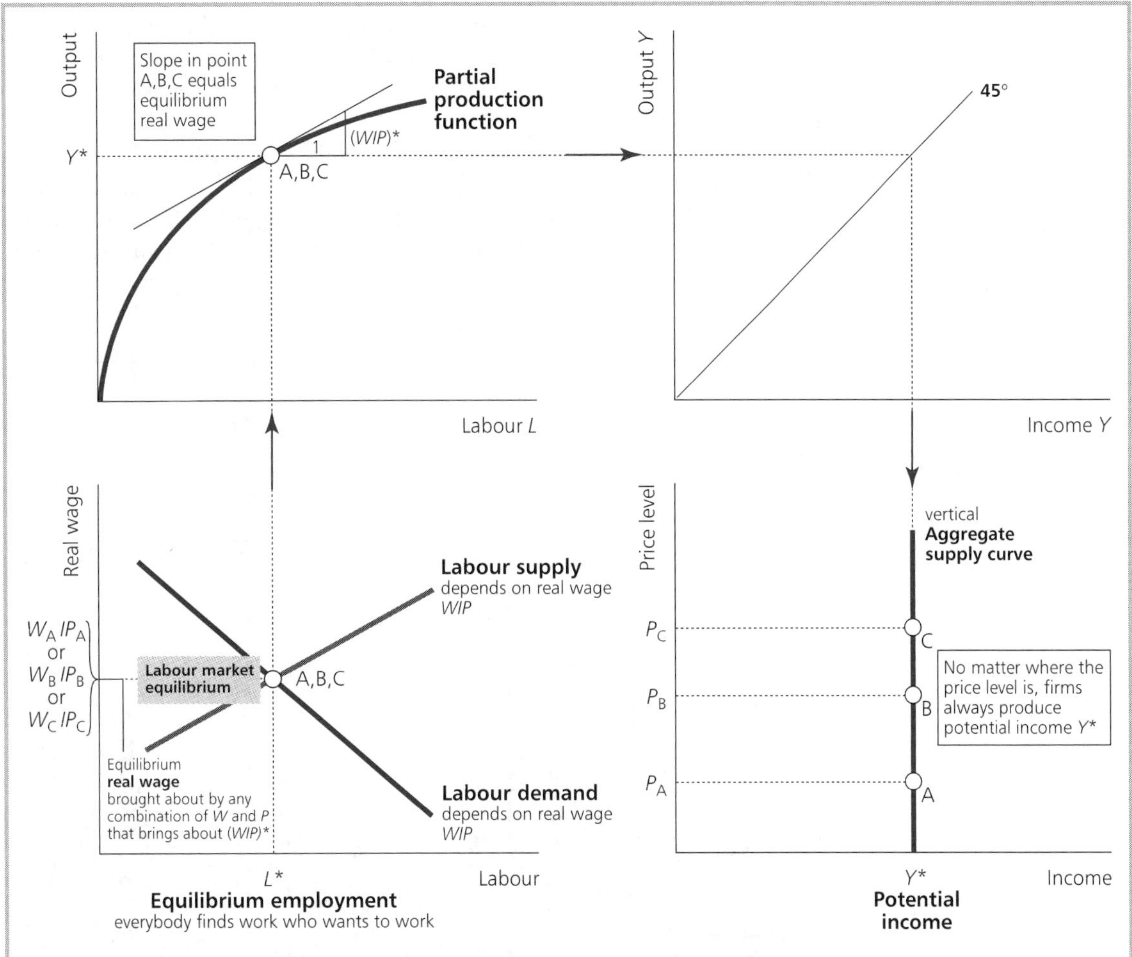

Figure 6.7 Proceeding clockwise from the labour market in the bottom left-hand diagram, it is shown that the classical view of the labour market implies a vertical aggregate supply curve. The reason is that the labour market clears only at one real wage $(W/P)^*$ and at one level of employment L^*. $(W/P)^*$ may be brought about by an infinite number of combinations of W and P. If P rises, W only needs to rise by the same percentage. So no matter how high prices are, as long as the real wage clears the market, employment is L^* and output is Y^*.

6.2 WHY IS THERE UNEMPLOYMENT IN EQUILIBRIUM?

In the classical view the real wage adjusts instantly so as to clear the labour market at all times. Everyone who wants to sell labour at that real wage can do so. Everyone who wants to buy labour can do so too. In this benchmark scenario not all people work. But those who want to work at the current wage do find a job. Involuntary unemployment does not exist.

This conclusion conflicts with the reality of very high unemployment rates which most European countries suffer. As Figure 6.8 documents, European unemployment is not a phenomenon that could be caused by a short-lived, temporary displacement of the labour market from equilibrium. However, such displacements do occur and we will look at them in section 6.3. European unemployment appears to be a long-term problem that seems unlikely to disappear of its own accord.

Having developed a benchmark view of the labour market in the preceding section, we now ask how reality differs from this ideal, or *classical view*. Conditions in the real world are not perfect, as suggested by last section's model. Many factors may keep the labour market from reaching an equilibrium

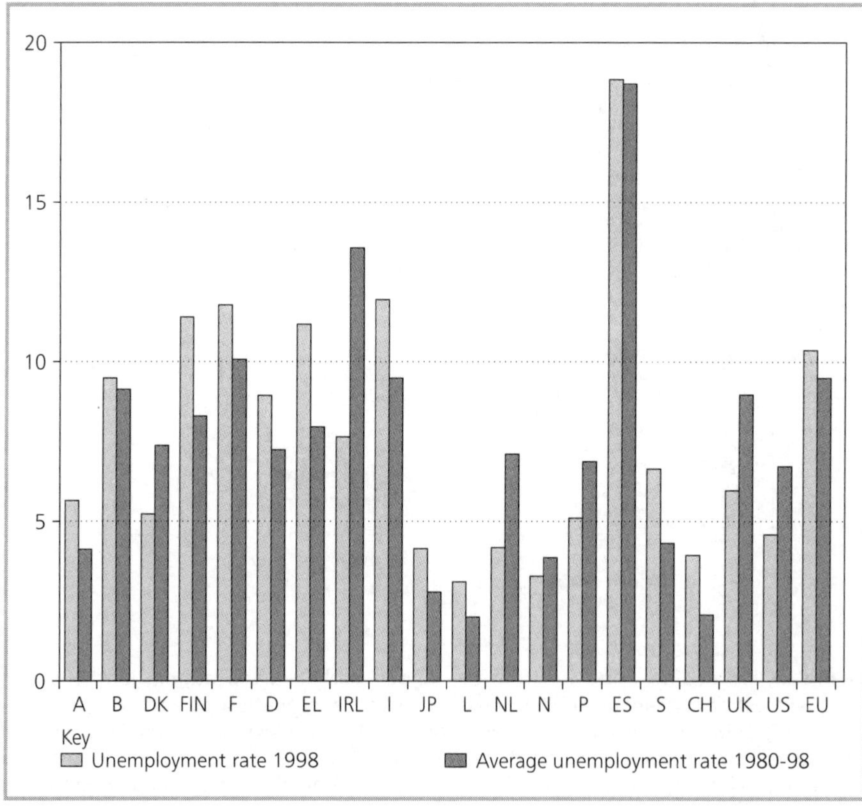

Figure 6.8 Unemployment rates in Europe average close to 10% over the past twenty years. Rates in 1998 were above average in some countries, and below in others, possibly reflecting different phases of the business cycle.
Source: OECD, *Economic Outlook*, December 1999.

such as at A, B, C in Figure 6.7, in which no involuntary unemployment exists. The introduction of real-world features into the labour market will give us a number of clues as to the possible causes of today's unemployment problem. We now discuss some of these features.

Minimum wages

In most industrial countries governments feel compelled to restrict or guide market forces in the labour market by implementing some sort of minimum wage legislation. The noble intentions of such legislation are undisputed. But a look at our labour market diagram reveals unintended side effects (Figure 6.9). Of course, as long as law-makers fix the minimum wage below w^*, it remains ineffective. Employers will voluntarily raise wages to w^* and expand employment to L^*, as in the classical case. As legal minimum wage rates are raised beyond w^*, say to w_{min}, two things happen. First, employers, facing higher **unit labour costs**, *reduce* their demand for labour to L_D. Second, workers *expand* their supply of labour to L_S. With the wage being prevented by law from falling, in order to equalize supply and demand, labour in the amount of $L_S - L_D$ remains involuntarily unemployed.

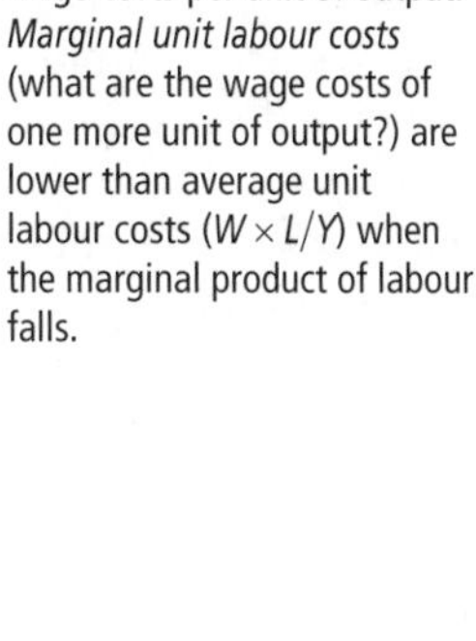

Unit labour costs are the wage costs per unit of output. *Marginal unit labour costs* (what are the wage costs of one more unit of output?) are lower than average unit labour costs ($W \times L/Y$) when the marginal product of labour falls.

Involuntary unemployment needs to be distinguished from **voluntary unemployment.** If N is the total labour force, unemployment statistics typically include both involuntary unemployment $L_S - L_D$ and voluntary unemployment, which may be as large as $N - L_S$. These people do not really want to work at the wage w_{min}, but may be tempted to take advantage of unemployment benefits nevertheless.

Minimum wages come in many forms: as an economy-wide wage floor enacted and periodically adjusted by the government; in the form of industry-wide wages negotiated periodically by trade unions and employers, declared binding by the government. Even legal action primarily motivated by concerns for justice and equality, such as outlawing wage discrimination for reasons of sex, religion, age, and so on, may have an impact on the segment of the labour

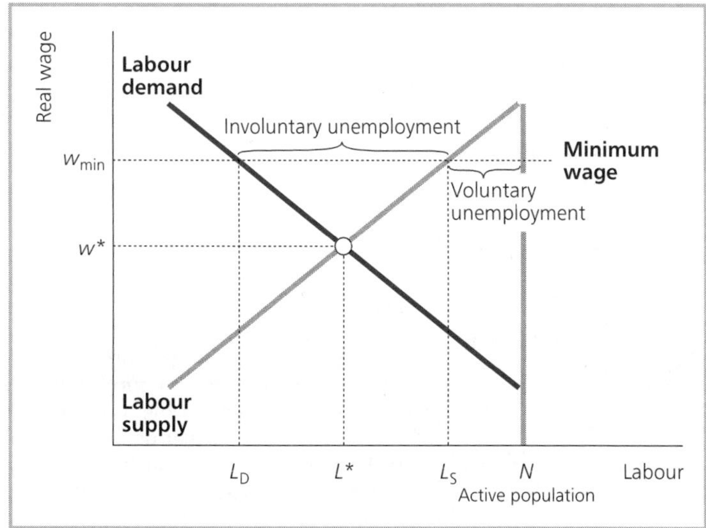

Figure 6.9 If regulations prevent the wage from falling below w_{min} the labour market cannot clear. At w_{min} L_S units of labour are offered and L_D units are demanded. This produces involuntary unemployment at the magnitude $L_S - L_D$.

force involved in a similar way to that resulting from direct minimum wage legislation.

The **tax wedge** is the difference between the labour costs of firms and the wage that workers take home.

A second possible cause of unemployment, also under the government's control, is the **tax wedge**. This is where taxes (and similar things, such as social security contributions) drive a wedge between the labour costs of firms and the pay that workers actually take home. Figure 6.10 illustrates how the tax wedge affects employment.

Suppose there is no tax initially, so that negotiated wages reflect the labour costs of firms and the net pay of workers. The market clears at the wage rate w_0^* (not shown) and employment is L_0^*. Now the government introduces two kinds of tax. First, a tax is levied on workers' incomes. This drives the take-home wage below the negotiated wage, making workers less eager to work at each negotiated wage rate. The labour supply curve shifts left and employment falls. Second, firms are subjected to a payroll tax. This raises employers' labour costs above the negotiated wage rate and reduces the number of workers that can be profitably employed at each negotiated wage. The labour demand curve shifts left and employment moves further down to L_1^*.

To sum this up, higher taxes and social security contributions drive employment down. Thus, the number of those who cannot be employed rises. Note, however, that all who drop out of employment do so *voluntarily*. Therefore, **involuntary unemployment is not caused by the tax wedge**. But some of those who voluntarily drop out may exploit the unemployment insurance system and drive up official unemployment statistics.

Monopolistic trade unions

Another institutional feature which causes labour markets in many industrial countries – and particularly in a host of European economies – to deviate from the ideal classical scenario, is the prominent role of **trade unions** in the wage negotiating process. Wages are set in a collective negotiating process between

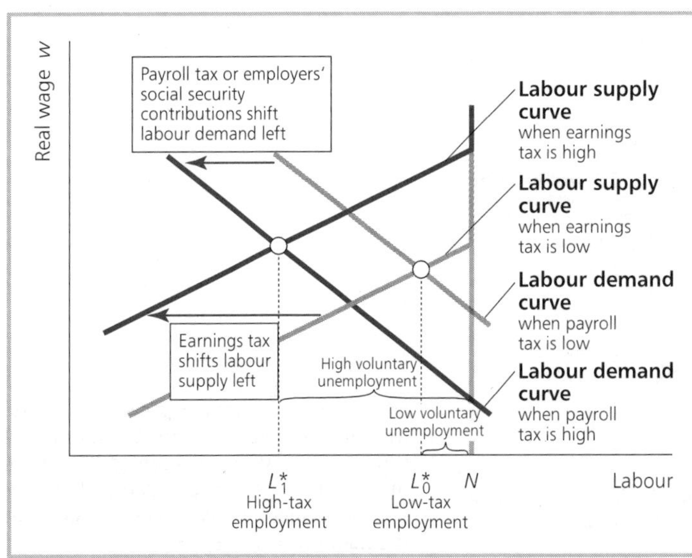

Figure 6.10 An earnings tax shifts the labour supply curve left and drives down employment. A tax on the firms' payroll shifts the labour demand curve left and also drives down employment. Both taxes drive employment further below available employment and may raise the voluntary unemployment included in official unemployment rates.

a trade union and one large employer or an association of employers. These negotiated wage rates then serve as minimum wages for individual shops or industries throughout regions or entire countries. In many economies, such as Germany's, negotiated wages represent minimum wages and are also binding for workers who are not members of the trade union.

Like any monopolist in a traditional goods market, trade unions do not possess the power to set both wages *and* employment levels. What they can do is set wages at their discretion. After that, employers are free to decide on how much labour to demand at the given wage rate. This choice, as has been shown above, is always the respective point on the labour demand curve. Trade unions anticipate that they will eventually end up on the labour demand curve. So they will choose a wage rate that predetermines that point from all the options offered by the labour demand curve which best serves trade union interests.

What are the interests of the trade union? One simple but reasonable assumption is that trade unions care about both employment L and high wages by maximizing the *wage sum* S:

$$S = L \times w \qquad \text{Wage sum} \qquad (6.2)$$

Maths note. If you are unfamiliar with hyperbolas, suppose $w = 5/L$. Use a pocket calculator to compute the real wages for all L from 1 to 10. Plot these values in a w-L diagram and you have a **hyperbola**.

Trade union **indifference curves**, which depict those combinations of L and w that produce some given wage sum S' (that is why the union is indifferent between them) are given by

$$w = \frac{S'}{L} \qquad \text{Union indifference curve} \qquad (6.3)$$

The indifference curves have the shape of hyperbolas, as Figure 6.11 shows. The wage sum increases as we move northeast. So, given that possibilities are restricted by the menu offered by the labour-demand schedule, the trade union maximizes the wage sum at the point of tangency between the labour demand schedule and an indifference curve.

This tangent point might lie on that part of the labour-demand curve south-

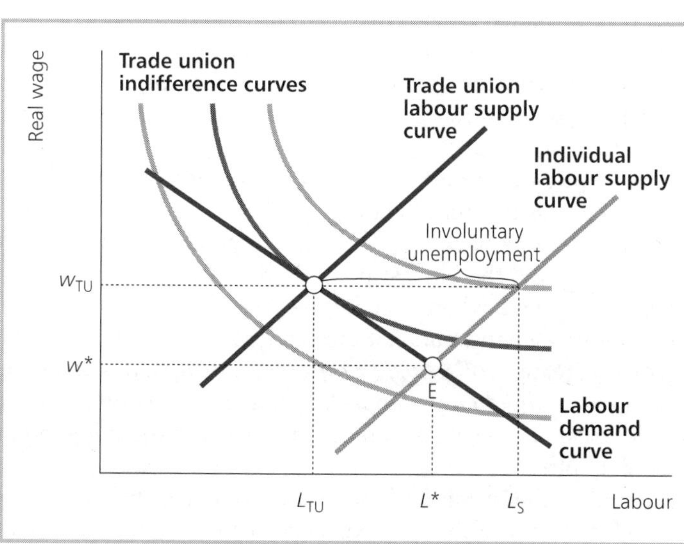

Figure 6.11 Monopolistic trade unions who care about wages and employment bargain for real wages determined by the point of tangency between one of their grey indifference curves with the labour demand curve. The resulting wage w_{TU} typically exceeds the wage w^* obtained in a competitive labour market. As a result, involuntary unemployment is at $L_S - L_{TU}$.

east of E. This point would not be a feasible outcome, however, since in this situation individuals would not be willing to supply the amount of labour demanded by firms. The best that trade unions could do in this situation would be to settle for w^* and the concomitant employment level L^*. It is not particularly logical that trade union preferences would lead them to go for exactly the same bargaining result that the market generates without them. If trade unions are to make any difference and thus justify their role in the collective bargaining process, they will go for a wage rate that is higher than the wage rate that would clear a perfect market.

If the real wage does not fall despite the existence of involuntary unemployment, we speak of a **real wage rigidity**. We now turn to other explanations of why real wages may be rigid.

A **real wage rigidity** exists if the real wage does not fall despite the existence of unemployment.

Insiders and outsiders

As before, let workers be represented by a monopolistic trade union. Let the economy be in the same equilibrium that we identified in the preceding section. Now, however, assume that the trade union only cares about employed members, the **insiders**. Union members who are out of employment, be it voluntarily or not, are **outsiders**. In many countries, only employed trade union members can exercise active membership rights, such as voting about whether to accept a bargaining settlement between union leaders and employers.

Insiders are all currently employed workers. **Outsiders** are those currently out of employment who are seeking employment.

If the interests of outsiders are being ignored in collective bargaining, this means that whether these people find employment or not is irrelevant. So the indifference curves of the trade union must have a kink at the current employment level. Here the indifference curves all turn horizontal, since employment gains beyond the current level accrue to outsiders and therefore do not yield utility to the union. Thus, additional employment of outsiders could not possibly compensate the trade union (members) for wage concessions.

Next, let the economy be hit by an adverse supply shock which shifts the labour demand curve to the left. The two oil price explosions of the 1970s are usually considered to have had such an effect. Wages and employment after the shock are determined by the point of tangency between an unkinked union indifference curve and the new labour demand curve. Once employment has been reduced to L_1 all union indifference curves become horizontal at this level (see Figure 6.12).

This alone does not create new or additional unemployment. But it may do so if the shock is reversed. Assume that the oil price shock was temporary and the labour demand curve moves back into the original position. Now unions maximize utility by negotiating the highest possible real wage for the current insiders, L_1, which is obtained where one of the new kinked indifference curves touches the labour demand curve. Employment stays at L_1, but the wage rises to w_2. This creates *collectively voluntary unemployment* in the amount $L_2^s - L_1$ and raises *individually involuntary unemployment* way above the level that would exist at the trade union monopoly bargaining point without insider–outsider effects.

In addition to the trade union version of the insider–outsider theory there is a second version which does not rely on the existence of a union. It argues that,

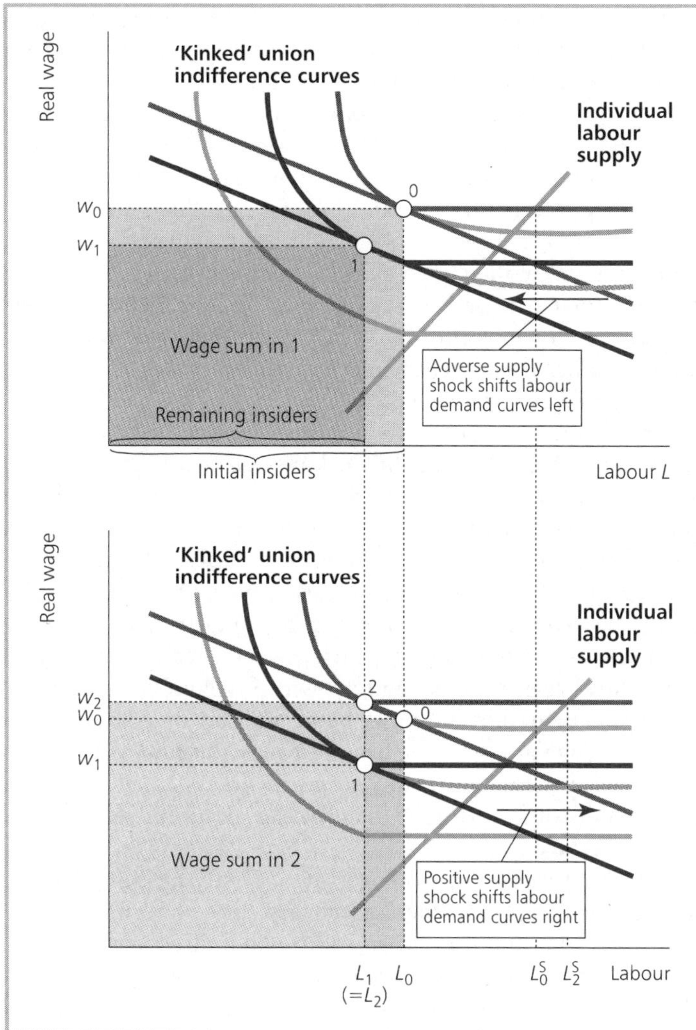

Figure 6.12 Initially collective wage bargaining brings the labour market to point 0, where the highest possible union indifference curve just touches the grey labour demand curve. Union indifference curves are horizontal to the right of L_0 since the union is not concerned with the employment of these outsiders. Next, an adverse supply shock shifts labour demand down to the blue position, moving the economy to point 1. After the supply shock is reversed in period 2, only L_1 insiders are kept employed. Real wages rise to w_2 and unemployment is higher at $L_2^s - L_1$ than it was before the shock.

because of specific knowhow that can only be acquired within the firm and because of turnover (hiring and firing) costs, insiders can extract a premium over the wage for which outsiders are willing to work. Again, the result is involuntary unemployment.

Efficiency wages

Efficiency wage theory argues that raising the real wage may lower costs per unit of output by raising labour productivity.

So far we have assumed that labour productivity depends only on the amount of capital with which labour is combined, but not on the received wage. **Efficiency wage theory** questions this assumption. Various arguments are advanced as to why the work *effort*, or efficiency, as it is called in the context of these theories, and hence (given a specific amount of capital) labour productivity may increase with the real wage. These are as follows:

- *Nutrition.* This basic idea has played a major role in development theory. It is argued that as farmers raise wages above the subsistence level, farm workers become stronger and healthier and, consequently, more productive. While there are, sadly enough, still too many countries in the world for which such arguments are highly relevant, the relationship between nutrition and efficiency does not describe a feature of today's industrialized countries.

- *Adverse selection.* Here the basic idea is that workers are heterogeneous, being equipped with different individual skills and productivities. When hiring workers, firms find it difficult to sort out those workers with high productivity. Workers know their own skill levels much better. Since they expect firms to learn their true productivity sooner or later, better workers are more likely to apply for jobs endowed with a high salary or wage than bad ones. Thus, the higher the wage, the more qualified and productive the firm's workforce must be expected to be.
- *Shirking.* Firms may find it difficult to monitor continuously the work efforts of their workers. A worker caught shirking during a spot check will be fired, however. As long as the firm pays the market wage only, this is not really a punishment, since a worker can always get an equivalent job with the same pay elsewhere. To provide an incentive to reduce shirking, the firm must raise the wage rate above the market clearing wage. Will that do any good, since it must be expected that all firms in the industry pay efficiency wages (wages that are above the market clearing wage)? Yes, because if all firms pay an 'excessive' real wage we end up with involuntary unemployment. If a worker is caught shirking now, he or she can indeed expect to receive the same real wage at any other firm, but may not find a job. So as long as unemployment benefits are below wages, workers caught shirking must expect their real income to drop. This provides an incentive to reduce shirking and increase efficiency.
- *Turnover costs.* Labour turnover is costly to firms. Costly hiring and firing activities include advertising and other search activities, screening candidates, contract negotiations and legal fees. Additional indirect costs may be related to on-the-job training for new workers and the time it takes for them to find their best place in the firm's structure. If a worker's probability to quit is negatively related to the real wage, a firm may profit from paying higher wages than other firms by enjoying lower turnover costs.
- *Fairness.* This explanation augments the economic view of the labour market with sociological elements. It focuses on the simple observation that there is a distinctively positive relationship between the morale of people and their perception of whether they are being fairly treated. While this notion is intuitively appealing, it has also been substantiated by empirical research, such as laboratory experiments, to show that subjectively perceived fairness affects work quality or productivity.

Before we look at how efficiency–wage considerations impact on the labour market, Figure 6.13 illustrates the classical case with which we have worked so far. Panel (a) shows that labour productivity or efficiency is at x' for all wage levels. Unit labour costs, the real wage costs of one unit of output produced, w/x', are simply marked by the slope of a ray through the origin which intersects the vertical efficiency line at a given real wage. Since efficiency is constant, unit labour costs obviously double as wages rise from 1 to 2. Panel

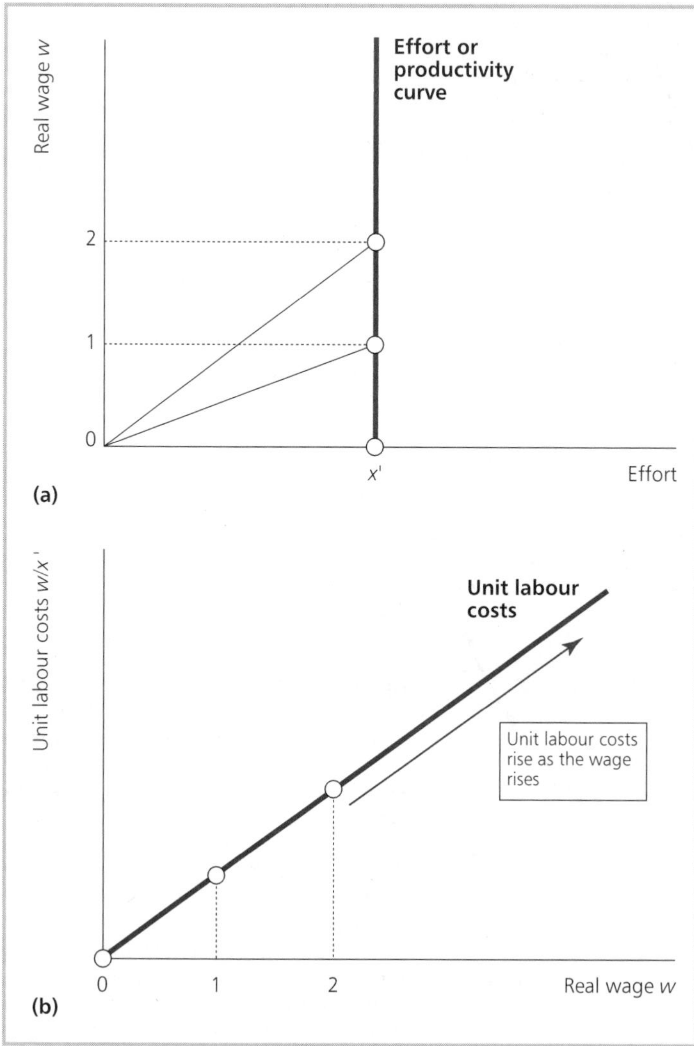

Figure 6.13 Panel (a) illustrates the assumption employed so far, that work effort is at x', independent of pay. Unit labour costs are w/x', and thus vary with the wage. They are represented by the slope of a ray from the origin to the point of intersection between the vertical line over x' and the horizontal line at the current wage. Panel (b) illustrates that unit labour costs increase linearly with the real wage w.

(b) shows the general relationship between unit labour costs and the wage rate to be a positively sloped straight line through the origin. Employers who want to minimize unit labour costs thus will try to pay the lowest wage they can.

Next, Figure 6.14 contrasts this orthodox view with the efficiency–wage argument. The innovation in panel (a) is highlighted by comparing it with panel (a) of Figure 6.13: work effort is positively related to the wage rate. It is zero if the wage is zero. As long as pay is low, effort rises faster than the wage rate. Beyond some threshold w_x saturation sets in, and additional wage increases yield smaller and smaller efficiency gains. The consequence of this relationship between effort and wage rates for unit labour costs can be traced again by following the slope of a ray from the origin to the effort curve (see Figure 6.14, panel (a)). Initially, since for low pay levels effort rises faster than the wage rate, the slope of this ray becomes smaller as firms raise wages. Beyond the wage rate w_x, however, unit labour costs rise. Panel (b) illustrates how this translates into a U-shaped relationship between unit labour costs and

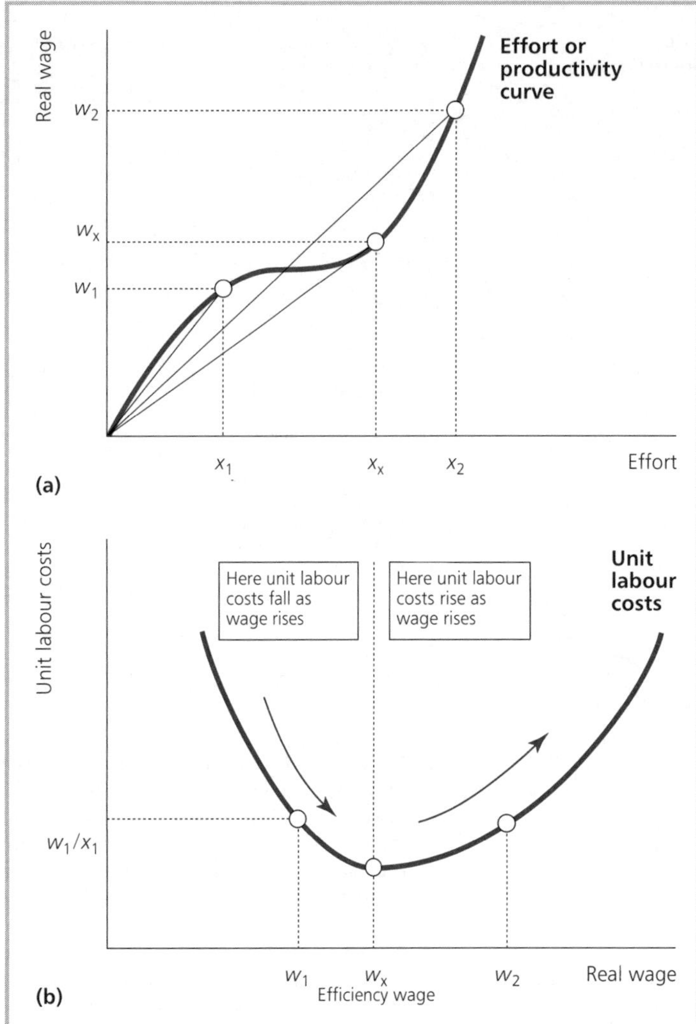

Figure 6.14 Panel (a) proposes that work effort (that is, productivity) may be related to the real wage. As the wage increases, productivity first increases at an accelerating and then at a decelerating pace. Unit labour costs, w/x, vary with the wage. They are represented by the slope of a ray from the origin to the point of intersection between the horizontal line at the current wage and the effort curve. Panel (b) illustrates that unit labour costs initially fall as firms raise wages, but increase again as wages move beyond w_x, yielding a U-shaped unit labour costs curve.

the wage rate. The wage rate w_x that minimizes unit labour costs is called the **efficiency wage**.

The **efficiency wage** is the wage that minimizes unit labour costs.

A simple model

A simple model may illustrate how the efficiency wage considerations introduced above fit into our previously developed picture of the labour market, and how they account for the existence of involuntary unemployment in equilibrium.

Let output Y depend on physical labour input L and on labour effort or efficiency x (which depends on the real wage w):

$$Y = Y[x(w)L] \qquad \textbf{Partial production function} \qquad (6.4)$$

Then the firms' profits Π are given by the difference between output (which equals the firms' revenue) and wage costs.

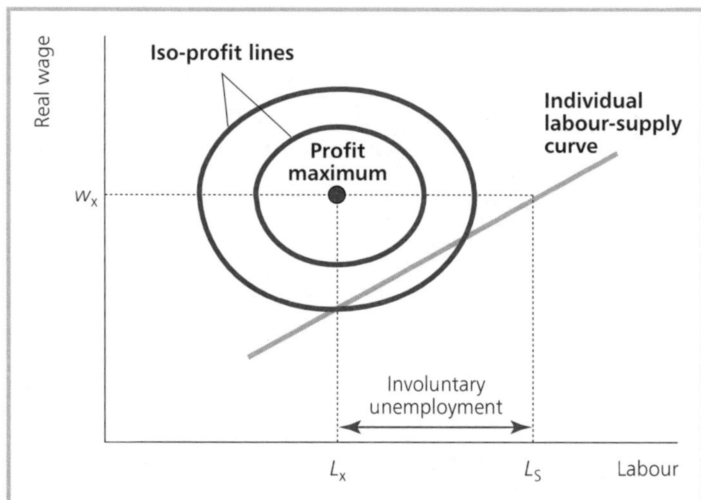

Figure 6.15 If work effort increases with the real wage, unit labour costs are minimized (and profits are maximized) by paying w_x and employing L_x. Moving away from w_x or L_x in either direction reduces profits. Hence iso-profit lines are concentric around the profit maximum. Workers who do not find employment at w_x cannot bid down wages since firms voluntarily pay w_x in order to minimize costs. As a result, involuntary unemployment in the amount $L_S - L_x$ persists.

$$\Pi = Y[x(w)L] - wL \qquad \text{Profits} \qquad (6.5)$$
$$\text{Profits} = \text{Output} - \text{Wage costs}$$

If efficiency initially increases faster than the real wage, and then slower, as sketched in Figure 6.14, iso-profit lines look like circles, with a clearly defined maximum in the centre (Figure 6.15). Firms maximize profits by voluntarily paying the efficiency wage w_x and setting the employment to L_x. Firms do not want to employ more labour, since at the level of labour productivity determined by w_x additional labour would cost more than it produces. Also, while firms could obtain L_x labour input at a lower wage rate, they refrain from doing so. The reason is that if wages drop below w_x, productivity falls faster than the wage.

CASE STUDY 6.1 Ford's focus: an experiment in efficiency wages

Something bizarre happened at the world's first car plant in Dearborn, Michigan, in 1913. Henry Ford really caught his workers off guard by telling them that from 14 January 1914, they would not only have to work less but would earn more as well. What qualifies this step as one of the best known experiments in efficiency wages is its magnitude. As shown in columns 2 and 3 of Table 1, the length of a workday was reduced by more than 10% from 9 to 8 hours. A day's pay more than doubled from $2.34 to $5. Both changes combined made the hourly wage rise by 138% from 26 cents to 62 cents.

Table 1 Wages, work hours and turnover costs at Ford's Dearborn plant

Year	Daily wage $	Daily work hours	Implied hourly wage $	Fluctuation rate %	Firing rate %	Absence rate %
1913	2.34	9	0.26	370	62	10
1914	5.00	8	0.62	54	7	2.5
1915	5.00	8	0.62	16	0.1	

Source: D. Raff and L. Summers (1987) 'Did Henry Ford pay efficiency wages?', *Journal of Labor Economics*, October.

Case study 6.1 continued

Did this dramatic increase in labour costs really pay off? Not directly so, it appears. While productivity did increase from 1913 to 1914 by some estimated 30% to 50%, as efficiency wage theory proposes, this gain falls way short of the increase in labour costs.

Changes in unit labour costs may be too narrow a measure, however. Some other side effects of the huge wage increase may provide a broader, more complete picture. As column 5 shows, in 1913 production at Ford suffered from a very high fluctuation rate. This rate standing at 370% means that Ford on average had to replace each worker it started with at the beginning of the year 3.7 times! This must have caused enormous costs in areas such as training, administration including bookkeeping, recruitment and so on. As the numbers for 1914 and 1915 show, Henry Ford's wage increase brought down fluctuation rates substantially.

Other measures show similar trends. The firing rate, for example, came down from 62% in 1913 to 0.1% in 1915. Further, while in 1913 some 10% of Ford's workforce was absent on an average workday, this rate was brought down to 2.5% within one year. All these factors must have contributed to the fact that Ford enjoyed a sizeable increase in profits between 1913 and 1914, despite higher unit labour costs.

The numbers presented here cannot possibly give a complete account of why Ford's profits rose. We also cannot be sure what motivated Ford's exceptional step. Nor is it clear whether the implemented wage increase was of optimal size from the perspective of efficiency wage theory, or perhaps too large. What the numbers do demonstrate, however, is that wages may have quite sizeable effects on productivity and turnover costs, as emphasized by efficiency wage theory.

The unintended side effect of the firms' profit-maximizing behaviour is that we end up with involuntary unemployment in the amount $L_S - L_x$.

Mismatch

The concept of the classical labour market rests on various simplifying assumptions. The more important ones are as follows:

- All transactions are done in one place. There is **no geographic dimension**.
- **Labour is homogeneous.** There are no particular skills, experiences or talents needed to fill a specific job opening. Hence, any unemployed worker can be hired by any firm with a job vacancy.
- All participants in the labour market possess **perfect information.** Firms know where to find unemployed workers, and workers are always aware of job openings.

Figure 6.16 shows how the labour market is affected if we give up these assumptions. The two light blue lines give the gross employment supplied and demanded at various wage levels. As the real wage differs from w^* supply and demand are not equal. Employment is now determined by whichever of the two is smaller. For $w > w^*$ this is demand, for $w < w^*$ it is supply.

Now assume that because of geographical or vocational mismatch, or because of imperfect information, at any wage level a certain fraction of supply and demand remains ineffective. Then effective supply and demand curves are given by the dark blue lines. These are obtained by subtracting that part from gross demand (supply) which is not seen by employers (workers), or which is of no use because of geographical mismatch or misfit skills.

As a consequence, labour market 'equilibrium' obtains at lower employment L^*. Equilibrium carries unfilled vacancies and involuntary unemployment. The latter is measured by the horizontal distance between the effective and the

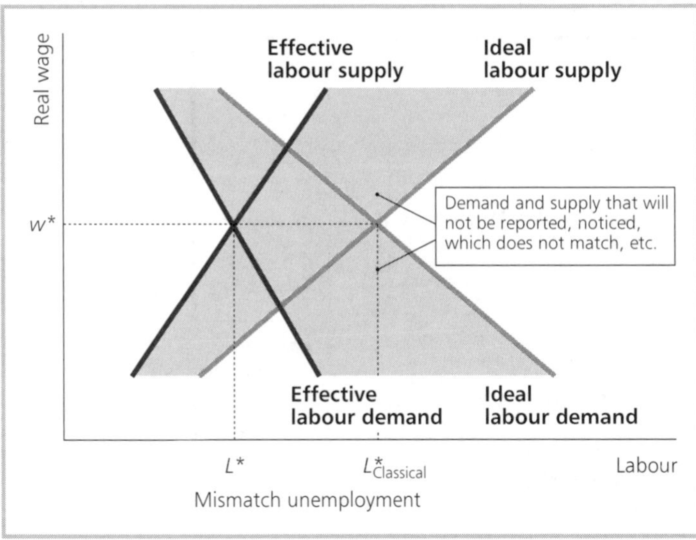

Figure 6.16 In a labour market with mismatch and information problems, labour demand and supply are not given by their respective ideal curves (light blue lines), but by their respective effective schedules indicated by the dark blue lines. As a result, involuntary unemployment results and coexists with unfilled vacancies.

gross labour supply curve at the equilibrium wage w^*. It is generally referred to as *mismatch unemployment*. Other terms that refer to unemployment (or components thereof) in equilibrium are **structural unemployment** and **frictional unemployment**.

Structural unemployment is unemployment that does not go away in equilibrium, due to institutions or habits.

Frictional unemployment exists because it takes time to find existing jobs, to relocate or to retrain.

A flow perspective of the labour market

The theories outlined above provide static pictures of the labour market and the causes of involuntary unemployment. This section offers a different perspective by shifting the attention to the flows in the labour market, and is intended to augment the ideas laid out above, not to replace them.

Consider Figure 6.17. At all times the **labour force** is made up of people who are employed and those who are unemployed. However, unlike what we assumed for the sake of simplicity in previous models, the labour force never remains constant. New entrants, made up of school leavers, graduates, immigrants or people who re-enter the labour market after a temporary exit, increase the labour force. Exits because of death, retirement, or the pursuit other interests cause it to shrink.

Whether the labour force grows or shrinks, and whether and how its composition changes, depend on the net flows into the respective segments:

- If entrants exceed exits, such as when the baby boomers entered the labour market, the labour force grows.
- If entrants into unemployment exceed exits, unemployment rises. Entrants and exits may be in and out of the labour force, or from and into employment through hiring and firing.
- If entrants into employment exceed exits, employment rises. Entrants and exits may be in and out of the labour force, or from and into unemployment.

As simple as it is, the flow diagram of the labour force in Figure 6.17 helps to make the crucial point that all structural changes or policy measures that affect any of the flows eventually have an impact on the observed level of unemployment.

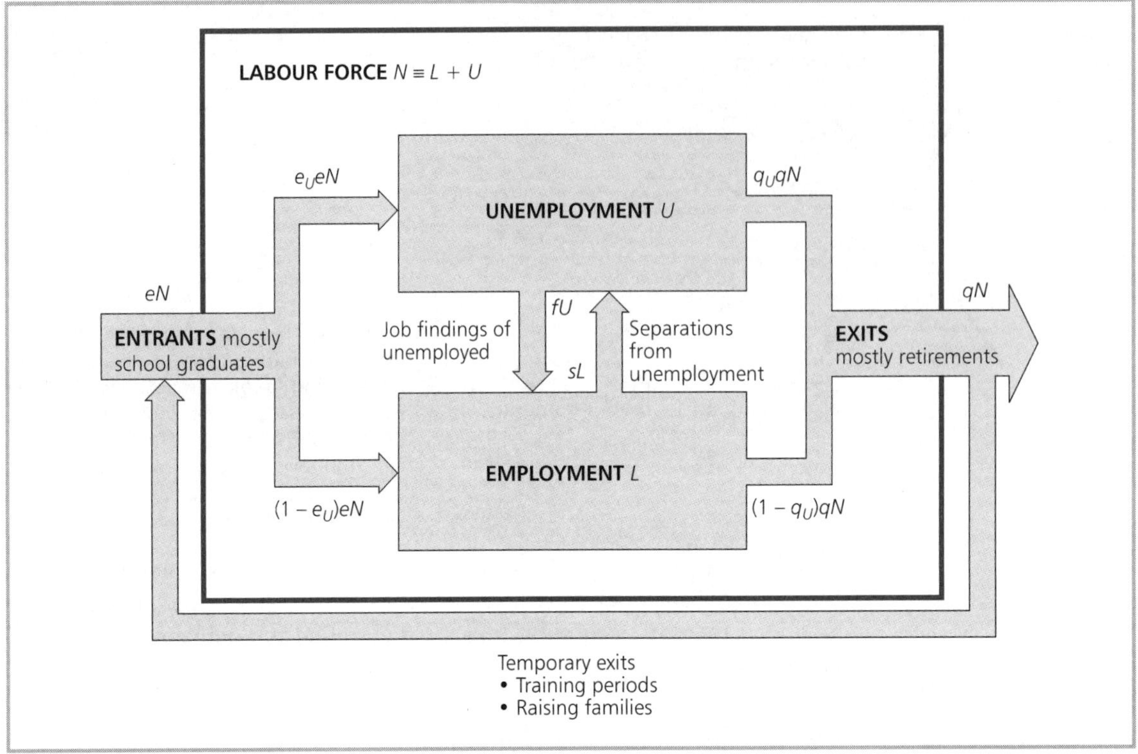

Figure 6.17 The labour market is not static. It reflects the continuous flows into and out of the labour force and between unemployment and employment. Demographic changes, institutional reforms and policy measures which affect any of these flows also affect the rate of unemployment observed in equilibrium.

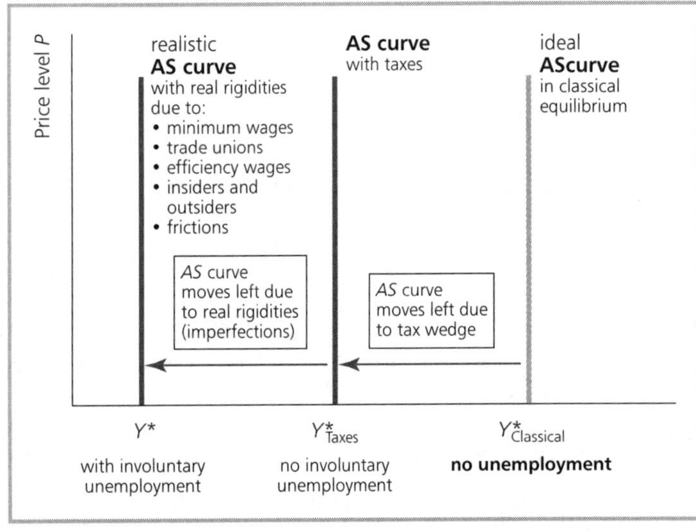

Figure 6.18 When nominal wages are fully flexible, as we assumed throughout the first part of this chapter, the *AS* curve is vertical. If the labour market is classical, all who are willing to work do work and produce output $Y^*_{Classical}$. Taxes move *AS* to the left due to a voluntary reduction of employment. If real rigidities exist, however, output is still lower at Y^*, and some workers remain involuntarily unemployed.

BOX 6.1 A flow model of the labour market

We start by noting that the labour force (which we suppose to equal the active population) N comprises employment L and unemployment U:

$$N = L + U$$

Changes in unemployment must equal the net changes of the labour force and of employment:

$$\Delta U = \Delta N - \Delta L$$

Unemployment can change during a given period of time because:

- some fraction s of employed people lose their job
- a fraction f of unemployed workers finds a job
- a fraction q quits the labour force, say because of retirement, out of which the fraction q_u was previously unemployed
- a fraction e enters the labour force, say upon graduating from school, out of which the fraction e_u becomes unemployed immediately:

$$\Delta U = sL - fU - q_u qN + e_u eN$$

The equilibrium level of unemployment U^*, which obtains if U does not change any more, is obtained by letting $\Delta U = 0$ and solving for U:

$$U^* = [sL + (e_u e - q_u q)N]/f$$

The equilibrium rate of unemployment u^* results after dividing both sides by N:

$$U^*/N \equiv u^* = sL/fN + (e_u e - q_u q)/f$$

After noting $L/N \equiv 1 - u^*$ and collecting terms, we obtain an equation that shows how the rate of unemployment depends on a few structural coefficients which characterize flows in the labour market.

$$u^* = s/(s + f) + (e_u e - q_u q)/(s + f)$$

The numerator in the second term of the equation focuses on demographic characteristics. The effect of those characteristics on the equilibrium unemployment rate is straightforward and can be read off the equation without recourse to calculus: the more people enter the labour force each period, and the more of those who become unemployed, the higher is the unemployment rate. This would predict that unemployment rises when baby boomers enter the labour market, or also that increasing participation ratios of women temporarily, until quit ratios are also affected, raises equilibrium unemployment. Similarly, unemployment is affected in the opposite direction by rising quit rates and quits out of unemployment. This explains why early retirement programmes for workers are such a popular policy tool among politicians.

The effects of finding and separation rates are a bit more complicated:

$$\frac{\partial u^*}{\partial f} = -\frac{s + (e_u e - q_u q)}{(s + f)^2} = \frac{-u^*}{s + f} < 0$$

$$\frac{\partial u^*}{\partial s} = \frac{f - (e_u e - q_u q)}{(s + f)^2} = \frac{1 + u^*}{s + f} > 0$$

The formal results do conform with intuition: a higher finding rate reduces equilibrium unemployment and a higher separation rate raises it. The magnitudes of each of these effects do depend on the current size of the other variable, however.

For example, the quantitative effect that a given increase of the finding rate has on the unemployment rate depends on the separation rate: the higher the separation rate, the smaller will be the accomplished reduction of the unemployment rate. The obvious reason is that if jobs are lost easily, an increase in job findings does not do all that much to unemployment.

Similarly, the quantitative effect of a given reduction in the separation rate on the unemployment rate depends on the current separation rate. So the two rates do not affect unemployment additively, but interactively. Policies geared towards reducing unemployment are thus well advised to go for improvements in both the separation and the findings rate rather than emphasizing only one of them.

Real rigidities and the aggregate supply curve

When discussing the classical view of the labour market we noted that both firms and workers base decisions on the real wage, that is on the buying power of wages. Price movements would not change that real wage which equated labour demand with supply, and, hence, would not change employment and output. This makes the aggregate supply curve a vertical line over potential output or income denoted by $Y^*_{\text{Classical}}$ in Figure 6.18.

Most imperfections discussed in this section make the real wage rise above the market clearing real wage. This reduces actual employment below market clearing employment, and, via the production function, output below the level of output produced in the classical scenario. Since trade union monopoly wages or unit labour cost reducing efficiency wages are also cast in real terms, a changing price level does not affect the established unemployment equilibria. Hence, all that an imperfection such as a monopolistic trade union does is to move the vertical aggregate supply curve to the left towards a lower output level Y^* and create individual involuntary unemployment.

6.3 WHY MAY ACTUAL OUTPUT DEVIATE FROM POTENTIAL OUTPUT?

The final question to be addressed in this chapter is what induces firms to supply output levels that differ from potential output. By drawing an *AS* curve for the short and medium run which is horizontal or positively sloped, we imply that the adjustment of wages and/or prices, which makes the long-run *AS* curve vertical, takes time. This needs explanation and, as trivial as it may seem to laypeople, is giving economists a very hard time!

Rather than giving a superficial summary of the many pertinent approaches that economists have discussed in recent years, we focus on one approach which economists are employing frequently in applied work. This **New Keynesian theory of aggregate supply** exploits the institutional feature that wages are not negotiated day by day, as the classical model of the labour market implies, but are laid down in contracts for a fixed period of time.

Sticky wages due to long-term contracts

About 80% of wage contracts negotiated by trade unions in the United States are three years in length! This is extreme by European standards. But even in Europe typical contracts last a minimum of one year. Figure 6.19 shows how this institutional characteristic influences wages, employment and, by the same token, aggregate supply.

We assume a simple but reasonably realistic structure.

- Negotiations fix the nominal wage for the length of the contract. This rate is binding, no matter what happens later on to the price level and, hence, to the real wage.
- Firms can then employ any number of available workers at the negotiated nominal wage.

The familiar-looking bottom left-hand diagram in Figure 6.19 permits us to trace the wage setting and employment decisions. First we consider *wage setting*. When the wage contract is signed, neither employers nor workers know the price level that will apply during the time for which the wage is set. Hence, bargaining is based on expectations of real wages and the outcome is where the expected labour supply curve cuts the expected labour demand curve. This yields an expected real wage that, given price level expectations P^e, fixes the nominal wage W_0 to be written into the contract.

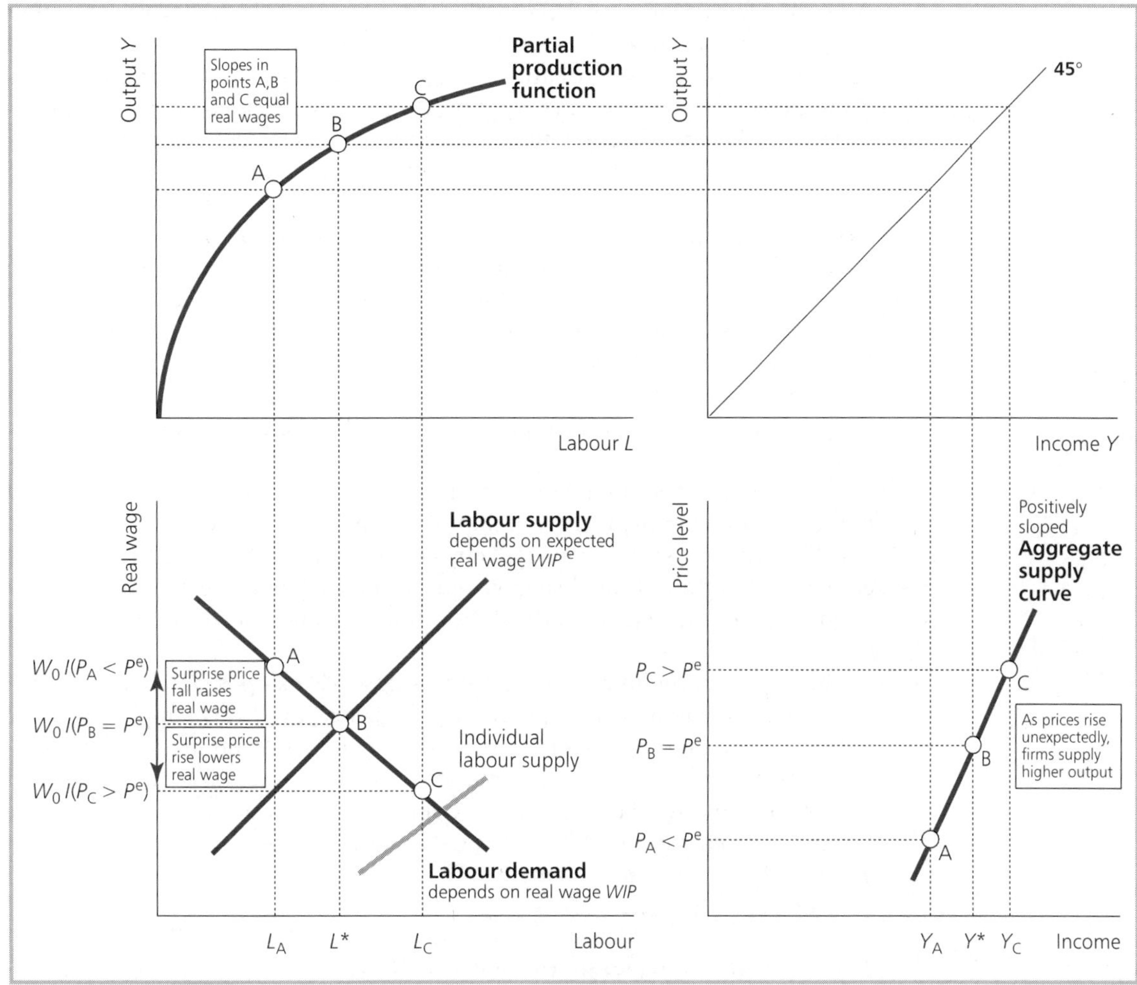

Figure 6.19 Labour market participants commit themselves to a long-term nominal wage contract at which they expect the market to clear. Employment is L^* and output equals potential output Y^*. If prices are then lower than expected, the real wage is higher than planned. Employment falls below L^* to L_A. Output falls below potential output to Y_A. The opposite occurs if the price level is higher than expected. The firms' higher demand for labour leads then to higher employment if enough involuntary unemployment is available.

Second, we consider *employment*. The negotiated nominal wage W_0 will clear the labour market if prices are as expected. Then the real wage is as expected and employment is L^*. Frequently, however, prices will not be as expected. Consider the case $P_A < P^e$, where prices turn out to be lower than anticipated. Then the real wage is higher than anticipated. Labour is more expensive than expected during negotiations. According to their demand schedule, firms reduce employment to L_A. Since, in addition, the higher wage increases the labour supply, a substantial amount of unemployment occurs.

Next, consider the opposite case $P_C > P^e$. Now, the opposite reaction is observed. Labour is cheaper than anticipated, and firms increase demand to L_C. Here the similarity to the previous case breaks down, however. Firms cannot generally find the desired number of workers at such a low real wage.

And nobody can force workers to work at a wage at which they would rather not. So does that mean that employment falls if prices rise unexpectedly and drive down real wages? Probably not, as firms will only then not find workers if the expected labour market equilibrium L^* was a full-employment equilibrium without individual involuntary unemployment, as derived from the classical labour market. In the presence of certain real rigidities, as discussed in the previous section, firms searching for workers may still be successful.

Suppose contracts were negotiated by a monopolistic trade union. Then nominal wages and expected equilibrium employment reflect the collective trade union labour supply curve derived previously, which lies northwest of the individual labour supply curve, shown as a grey line in Figure 6.19. Even though the real wage falls below the real wage targeted by the trade union, firms can (up to a certain threshold) obtain additional workers out of the pool of involuntarily unemployed workers. In the graph employment rises to L_C.

The result of this discussion is that, in the presence of contractually fixed money wages, employment moves up or down with the price level (relative to P^e). The production function (top left-hand diagram in Figure 6.19) translates employment into output. Bringing output levels down into the lower right-hand diagram in Figure 6.19 shows that income increases when prices increase.

The important point to note about this positively sloped *AS* curve is that if prices are as expected, no matter how high or low, firms supply potential output Y^*. So it is obviously not the absolute price level that matters for aggregate supply. Only unexpected increases of the price level raise output beyond Y^*, and unexpected falls of the price level drive output below Y^*. A linear formal approximation of this positively sloped aggregate supply curve is $Y = Y^* + 1/\lambda(P - P^e)$, or, solving for P

$$P = P^e + \lambda(Y - Y^*) \qquad \textbf{Aggregate supply curve} \qquad (6.6)$$

This equation also reveals the link to the vertical aggregate supply curve derived in section 6.1. If the price level is as expected, no matter how high or low, actual supply is at potential output. This follows from letting $P = P^e$ in equation (6.6) which yields $Y = Y^*$.

In concluding this chapter, Figure 6.20 shows the two aggregate supply curves we have derived. In an economy with long-run wage contracts, the vertical aggregate supply curve (which is likely to be to the left of the classical *AS* curve) is where we are if the price expectations held during wage negotiations turn out to be correct afterwards. If prices move up or down unexpectedly, the positively sloped *AS* curve indicates how aggregate supply responds.

Before we can determine on which one of the two *AS* curves and where on that curve the economy is at a particular point in time, we need to answer two questions: where is the price level, and what price level did the market expect? The price level is obviously determined by supply and demand. To answer the question, therefore, we need to look at the interaction between aggregate demand and aggregate supply. To know which price level people expect, we must look at how expectations are being formed. Both these issues will be addressed in the next chapter.

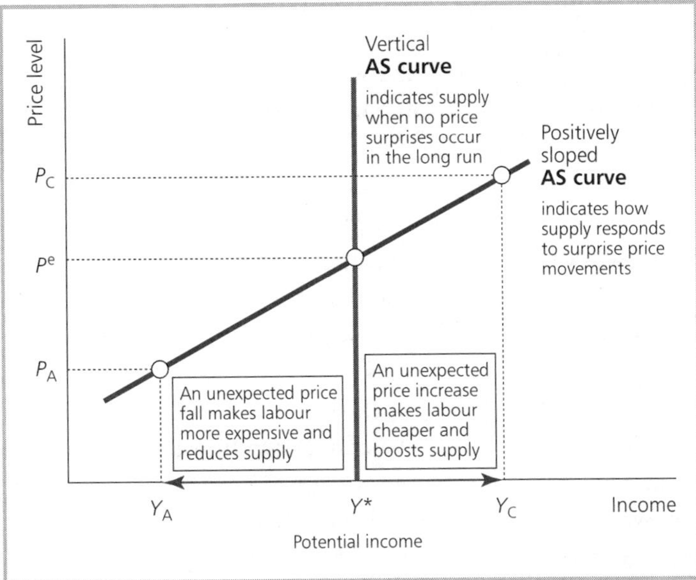

Figure 6.20 In the long run, or if prices move as expected, the *AS* curve is vertical. Firms produce Y^* independently of prices. Unexpected movements of the price level push supply above or below Y^*.

CHAPTER SUMMARY

- Potential output is produced with all employment that the labour market yields in equilibrium.
- In the *classical view* perfectly flexible real wages keep the labour market in permanent equilibrium. No involuntary unemployment occurs.
- Taxes reduce the equilibrium level of employment. They do not cause involuntary unemployment.
- New Keynesian theories challenge this classical result on two grounds. First, it is argued, real rigidities may give rise to labour market equilibria with involuntary unemployment. Second, nominal wage rigidities may permit temporary displacements from equilibrium.
- Real rigidities prevent the real wage from moving down until the market clears. Sources of real rigidities are minimum wage legislation, monopolistic trade unions, efficiency wages and insider–outsider effects.
- Nominal rigidities in the labour market prevent the nominal wage from bringing about the real wage adjustment required after a price change. One important institutional feature making nominal wages rigid (or sticky) is the existence of long-term wage contracts. Nominal rigidities give rise to a positively sloped *AS* curve, at least in the short run.

KEY TERMS AND CONCEPTS

aggregate supply curve
classical aggregate supply curve
classical labour market
efficiency wage theory
efficiency wage
extreme Keynesian aggregate supply curve
frictional unemployment
insiders
involuntary unemployment
Keynesian labour market
labour demand curve
labour supply curve
long-term wage contracts
marginal product of labour
minimum wages
mismatch unemployment
nominal wage rigidity
outsiders
potential output
real rigidity
real wage rigidity
sticky wages
stock-flow model of labour market
structural unemployment
tax wedge
trade unions and employment
unit labour costs

EXERCISES

6.1 Suppose that, due to a technological innovation, labour productivity increases by 50%. How does this affect the partial production function? How does it affect the labour demand curve?

6.2 Suppose that the nominal wage rate rises from £11 to £13.22, while the index of the price level increases from 241 to 296. Does this increase or decrease the real wage rate?

6.3 Explain intuitively why both labour demand and labour supply depend on the real wage rate instead of the nominal wage rate.

6.4 What happens to potential output if workers attribute a higher value to leisure than before, which makes them supply less labour at any given real wage rate? Trace the consequences step by step, using the diagram of Figure 6.6.

6.5 Suppose that the government levies a proportional tax on labour income.

(a) The government uses the tax revenue for government consumption. What are the effects on potential output?

(b) Suppose that the government uses the tax revenue for public investment, improving the infrastructure and thus labour's productivity. What happens to the result you derived in (a)?

6.6 Measuring unemployment is trickier than it may seem at first glance. Find out how it is measured in

(a) the United States
(b) Germany
(c) the United Kingdom.

Which procedure comes closest to measuring the concept of 'involuntary unemployment' suggested by the theory? If you are not living in one of these countries, how does the definition employed in your country fit in?

6.7 The argument in this chapter (illustrated in Figure 6.9) seems to make a compelling case against minimum wages. Can you think of arguments in favour of minimum wages?

6.8 Figure 6.21 depicts average rates of unionization and unemployment from 1985 to 1995 for thirteen European countries.

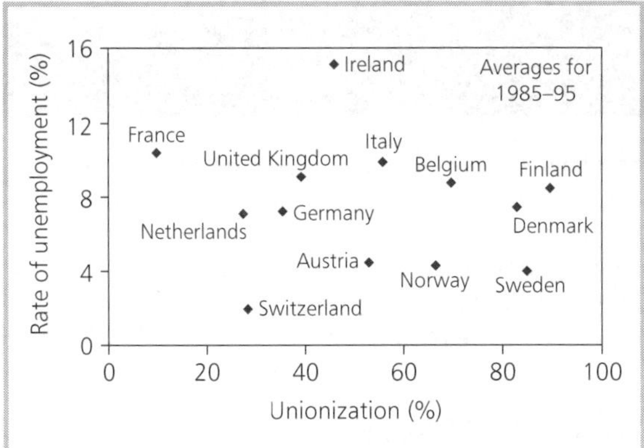

Figure 6.21

(a) Do these data support the link between monopoly power of trade unions and the rate of unemployment suggested by the theory?
(b) Is the rate of unionization a good measure to reflect the degree of monopoly power on the supply side of the labour market?

6.9 In past decades one of the dominant ideas was that there was a fairly constant 'natural rate' of unemployment in equilibrium, not affected by transititory business cycle fluctuations. Use the insider–outsider model to explain why reality seems to contradict this idea.

6.10 Use the logic of the efficiency-wage model to determine the effects of rising unemployment benefits on the optimal real wage rate. (Hint: How do unemployment benefits influence the effort curve in Figure 6.14?)

6.11 What happens to the *AS* curve
(a) if the government improves the flow of information between enterprises with vacant positions and potential employees?
(b) if administrative prescriptions prevent workers from moving across regions?
(c) if programmes to change professional qualifications are increasingly supported by the government?
Explicitly use the theoretical concepts presented in the chapter.

6.12 Your American friend boasts of the US economy's 'higher ability to adjust' due to a large number of 'extremely mobile workers who build cars in Detroit today and sell shoes in Miami tomorrow'. What concept does your friend have in mind? Does the advantage come at a cost?

6.13 Suppose that the labour market is dominated by binding long-term contracts, giving rise to an *AS* curve that is positively sloped in the short run. How does an increase in the productivity of labour affect this *AS* curve?

RECOMMENDED READING

An overview of the state of macroeconomics at the beginning of the 1990s is given in N. Gregory Mankiw (1990) 'A quick refresher course in macroeconomics', *Journal of Economic Literature* 28: 1645–60.

An excellent account of how macroeconomics has shaped (or failed to shape) US economic policy is given in Paul Krugman (1994) *Peddling Prosperity: Economic Sense and Nonsense in the Age of Diminished Expectations*, New York and London: Norton. There you will find many of the concepts that have been introduced here, put to work in an attractive and entertaining real-world setting. More recent developments are discussed in a similar fashion in Paul Krugman (1999) *The Return of Depression Economics*, New York and London: Norton.

APPLIED PROBLEMS

RECENT RESEARCH

Why do unemployment rates differ between countries?

To explain the differences in unemployment between twenty countries, Richard Layard, Stephen Nickell and Richard Jackman (*Unemployment: Macroeconomic Performance and the Labour Market*, Oxford: Oxford University Press, 1991) estimate the following cross-sectional equation (absolute *t*-statistics in brackets):

Unemployment rate (%, average 1983–88)
= 0.24 (0.1)
+0.92 (2.9) benefit duration (years)
+0.17 (7.1) replacement ratio (%)
−0.13 (2.3) active labour market spending (%)
+2.45 (2.4) coverage of collective bargaining
−1.42 (2.0) union coordination
−4.28 (2.9) employer coordination
−0.35 (2.8) change in inflation (% points)
$R^2_{adj} = 0.91$

The equation accounts for over 90% of the differences in unemployment rates. The first six variables measure institutional characteristics of the labour market. The first two refer to how well workers are protected in case of unemployment. Both the duration of benefits and, even more so, their level are important. If the replacement ratio (the percentage of unemployment benefits as a share of the last wage income received) rises from, say, 50% to 60%, unemployment moves up by 1.7 percentage points. Active labour market spending (on things like placement, counselling, training, recruitment subsidies) appears to succeed in reducing unemployment. The more people who are covered by collective bargaining agreements, the higher the unemployment rate. It helps, however, if union or employers coordinate wage bargaining. The final coefficient on the change of inflation shows how monetary policy can influence unemployment. A country that raised inflation by 10 percentage points between 1983 and 1988 would have ended up with an unemployment rate 3.5 percentage points lower.

WORKED PROBLEM

Unemployment and the black economy

By definition, unofficial economic activity in what is called the black economy escapes being recorded in a country's GDP. While no official data on the size of the unofficial economy exist, informed estimates range from around 5% up to some 25% of GDP (see Table 6.1).

It is conceivable that official and unofficial employment are substitutes: if one goes up, the other goes down. Then the size of the black economy should go up if unemployment rises. To check this, we estimate (*t*-values in parentheses)

$$\text{BLACK} = \underset{(0.12)}{0.28} + \underset{(4.97)}{1.09}u \qquad R^2_{adj} = 0.70$$

The result suggests a very strong correlation between the two. The insignificant constant term implies that as unemployment vanishes, the black economy vanishes as well. Also, unemployment and the black economy move one-on-one. As unemployment rises by 1%, the unofficial economy grows by 1% of GDP. So, within this small sample of data, it looks as though unemployment does not affect total economic activity (official plus unofficial) very much. Its effect is to shift activity into the shadow, out of reach of the taxman, with grim consequences for the government budget.

Table 6.1

	B	CH	D	E	F	I	J	NL	S	UK	US
BLACK unofficial economy as % of GDP	13	4	9	25	8	20	4	7	13	7	7
u unemployment rate	10	5	9	23	12	11.5	3	7	8	9.5	6.5

YOUR TURN

The Phillips curve

This chapter developed the *SAS* curve that links inflation to income. A mirror image of the *SAS* curve is the Phillips curve (to be discussed in Chapter 15). Assuming that income and unemployment are negatively related, the Phillips curve proposes that inflation and unemployment are negatively related: $\pi = \pi^e + a(u - u^*)$. Thus the Phillips curve combines the combinations of unemployment rates and inflation available for short-run policy choices. Table 6.2 gives unemployment and inflation rates in Switzerland between 1981 and 1996. Use these data to estimate a Phillips curve and evaluate the result.

(Hints: Treat u^* as a constant to be estimated. You may want to experiment with different functional forms, supposing that inflation depends on u, or on $1/u$, or on $\ln u$. For lack of data on inflation expectations we need to resort to adaptive expectations formation such as $\pi^e = \pi_{-1}$. Recall that the constant term in the Phillips curve includes the natural rate of unemployment. You may want to take into account the effect of the improvement of Swiss unemployment insurance in 1984 on equilibrium unemployment by allowing the constant term to be different after 1984. This can be done by including a so-called dummy variable which is zero before 1984 and 1 in 1984 and after.)

Table 6.2

Year	u	π
1980	0.2	4.0
1981	0.2	6.6
1982	0.4	5.7
1983	0.9	2.9
1984	1.1	2.9
1985	1.0	3.4
1986	0.8	0.8
1987	0.8	1.4
1988	0.7	1.9
1989	0.6	3.2
1990	0.5	5.4
1991	1.1	5.9
1992	2.5	4.0
1993	4.5	3.3
1994	4.7	0.9
1995	4.2	1.8
1996	4.2	1.8

To further explore this chapter's key messages you are encouraged to use the interactive online module found at

www.fgn.unisg.ch/eurmacro/tutor/labourmarket.html

and many other features hosted at **www.fgn.unisg.ch/eurmacro**

CHAPTER 7

BOOMS AND RECESSIONS (III)
AGGREGATE SUPPLY AND DEMAND

WHAT TO EXPECT After working through this chapter, you will understand:

1. How to draw the **aggregate supply curve in price–income space.**
2. How to derive the **aggregate demand curve** and draw it **in price–income space.**
3. The concept of **adaptive expectations.**
4. How to use the ***AD-AS* model** to trace how an economy moves **in price–income space.**
5. That the **policy options** offered by the model **depend on whether we have fixed or flexible exchange rates.**

This chapter brings together what we have learned so far and consolidates it into a coherent explanation of macroeconomic fluctuations around potential income. The two isolated results that we want to merge are what we learned about aggregate supply (the firms' production decisions) in the last chapter, and what we learned about aggregate demand (the spending decisions) in Chapters 2–5.

The Mundell–Fleming model focused on aggregate demand. Aggregate supply only enters this model hypothetically, by asking what equilibrium income would be if, at the current price level, firms were ready to produce all goods and services that are demanded. This assumption is only reasonable when the economy operates well below capacity, with a substantial share of production facilities being idle.

Chapter 6 made a point of demonstrating that under normal conditions firms are only willing to supply one specific level of output at a given price level, namely the level indicated by the *AS* curve. If the Mundell–Fleming model's demand-side equilibrium differs from aggregate supply, we end up with excess demand or excess supply in the goods market. In such situations prices are likely to change and to restore equilibrium.

This chapter follows the lead given in Chapter 5, where we briefly touched upon this issue of the confrontation of aggregate demand with aggregate supply that is fixed at potential income Y^*. Now, however, we use the more realistic positively sloped aggregate supply curve derived in section 6.3 of Chapter 6.

7.1 THE SHORT-RUN AGGREGATE SUPPLY CURVE

In Chapter 6, section 6.3, we acquired a qualitative understanding of the aggregate supply (*AS*) curve. When prices rise unexpectedly, firms extend production beyond its normal level, causing the AS curve to feature as a positively sloped line in a price–income diagram. The economic reasoning behind it is that once nominal wages are fixed by collective contracts, higher prices mean lower real wages W/P. And the lower the real wage, the more workers will firms seek to employ and the more output will be produced. This relationship was summed up in the equation

$$P = P^e + \lambda(Y - Y^*) \tag{7.1}$$

We already noted during its introduction in Chapter 6 that this linear relationship between prices and income was only an *approximation* of the *AS* curve in the neighbourhood of its current level of prices. The further we move away from this level, the more imprecise this approximation becomes. You may see that by noting that according to equation (7.1) an increase in prices from 1 to 2 raises aggregate output just as much as an increase from 100 to 101. This does not make sense economically, because in the first case real wages (with nominal wages fixed) are cut in half, and in the second case they fall by a meagre 1%. To make economic sense, the same percentage drop in the real wage should always trigger the same output response, no matter whether the price level is 1, 100 or 1,000,000. But this means that at a higher price level you need a larger price increase to prompt the same change in output. This calls for a *non-linear AS* curve as drawn in Figure 7.1, panel (a).

A drawback of this refined perspective of the *AS* curve is that non-linear curves are a bit more cumbersome to handle graphically and very awkward to

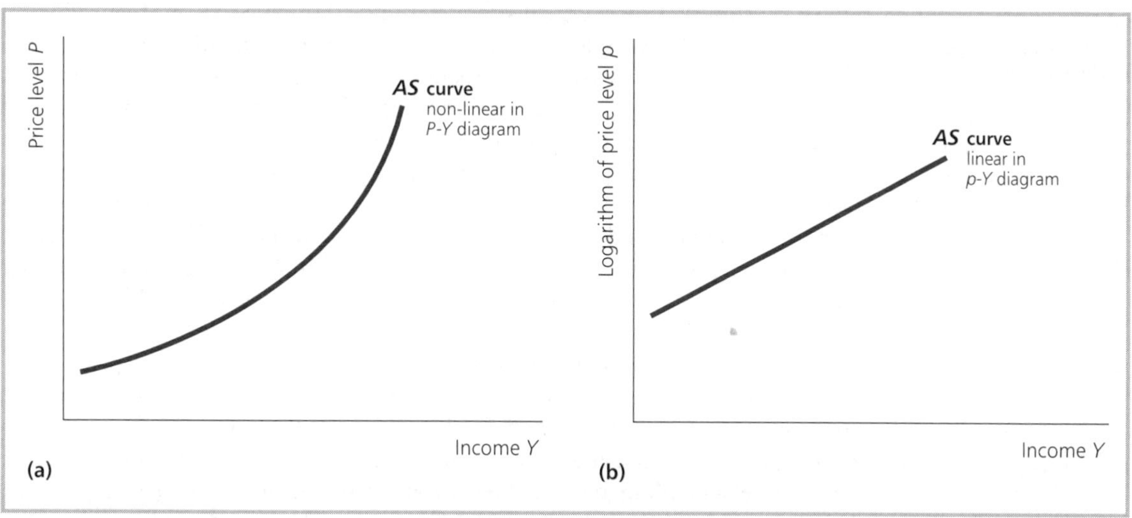

Figure 7.1 The linear *AS* curve derived in Chapter 6 is only an approximation. By developing the argument more accurately, we find the *AS* curve to be a curved line in a price–income diagram as shown in panel (a). Conveniently, when this precise *AS* curve is redrawn in a diagram that uses a logarithmic scale, or that measures the logarithm of the price level on the vertical axis, it turns out to be a straight line as depicted in panel (b).

manipulate mathematically. Fortunately, the kind of non-linearity encountered here is a specific one we can take care of by assuming that the natural logarithm of the price level $\ln P$ is linearly related to income, that is $\ln P = \ln P^e + \lambda(Y - Y^*)$ or, after defining $\ln P \equiv p$,

$$p = p^e + \lambda(Y - Y^*) \qquad \textit{AS} \textbf{ curve} \qquad (7.2)$$

As you may remember if you worked through the appendix on logarithms in Chapter 1, a given change in p (the logarithm of P) always indicates the same percentage change in P, no matter how high p and P are. So a linear relationship between p and Y, as given in equation (7.2) and shown in Figure 7.1, panel (b), reflects the economic mechanisms of the labour market correctly and is in substance equivalent to displaying the *AS* curve as in panel (a). The bonus is that we may continue to work with a linear equation.

The positively sloped *AS* curve shows what firms are willing to produce at different price levels. They will do so only if sufficient demand is there. Therefore, the supply-side decisions reflected in the *AS* curve must be augmented by information about the economy's demand side.

7.2 THE AGGREGATE DEMAND CURVE

The natural counterpart to the labour market, which stands behind the *AS* curve, is the Mundell–Fleming model. The labour market and *AS* curves show output supplied, assuming that all output produced will also be demanded. The Mundell–Fleming model focuses on the demand side of the economy. It assumes that whatever is demanded will eventually, in equilibrium, be supplied. So if we arrive at an equilibrium of $Y^* = 100$, this means that 100 units will be demanded, provided firms produce them. The Mundell–Fleming model *assumes* that they are being produced. Our previous discussion of aggregate supply, however, says they may not. For this reason, from now on we will refer to the Mundell–Fleming equilibrium as **demand-side equilibrium**. The issue to be addressed in this section is how demand-side equilibrium is affected by the price level. The reason we need to know this is that we found aggregate supply to depend on the price level according to equation $Y = Y^* + \frac{1}{\lambda}(p - p^e)$. For given price expectations this aggregate supply curve is a positively sloped line in a p-Y diagram. If we want to represent the economy's demand side, as represented by the Mundell–Fleming model, in the same diagram and analyze its interaction with aggregate supply, we first need to find out how demand-side equilibrium income is affected by the price level.

The term **demand-side equilibrium** refers to the income level at which the economy would be in equilibrium, provided that firms supply all goods and services that are being demanded.

We noted earlier that the assumption of a permanently fixed price level, which underlies the standard Mundell–Fleming model, is acceptable only in situations of severe capacity underutilization or in the very short run. We also showed, however, that the effect of price increases on output can be traced in the Mundell–Fleming model. The usual presentation is awkward to work with. First, neither the price level nor inflation can be read directly off the axes. Second, it is difficult to analyze the interaction between the Mundell–Fleming model and the supply side of the economy, which was shown to depend on inflation and inflation surprises.

What we would like to have is a graphical representation of supply decisions and of demand-side equilibria in a common diagram, with inflation on one axis and income on the other. This will prove useful in analyzing today's foremost macroeconomic problems – inflation and unemployment – in graphical terms.

Equilibrium income and the price level: the *AD* curve

How does an increase in the price level affect equilibrium in the Mundell–Fleming model? Since the argument focuses on different transmission channels under different exchange rate regimes, we must answer this question separately for flexible and fixed exchange rates.

The first step is to derive the aggregate demand (*AD*) curve in a price–income diagram. In a second step, to be taken in Chapter 8, we move on to a representation in an inflation–income diagram by means of dynamic aggregate demand (*DAD*) curves. The algebra of *AD* and *DAD* curves is not difficult, but it is cumbersome. Therefore, it is relegated to appendices. The main text develops the *AD* curve by means of graphs and discussion.

Flexible exchange rates

Figure 7.2 shows the economy initially in equilibrium at Y_0 with a price level of P_0. Recall that under flexible exchange rates income is determined by the equilibrium conditions in the money market, the *LM* curve, and in the foreign exchange market, the *FE* curve, alone. This was shown in Chapter 5. The real exchange rate changes endogenously so as to make *IS* go through the point where *LM* and *FE* intersect. If we leave all other exogenous variables that affect *LM* and *FE* (including the nominal money supply) unchanged, an increase in the price level reduces the real money supply and thus shifts *LM* up. This moves the point of intersection between *FE* and *LM* to the left, thus lowering equilibrium income to Y_1. An accompanying real appreciation drives down net exports, moving *IS* to the left as well.

The lower graph in Figure 7.2 projects the result onto a *P*-*Y* surface. When prices were low at P_0, income was high at Y_0. This fixes one demand-side equilibrium point. When prices rose to P_1, income fell to Y_1: a second equilibrium point. This generalizes into a negative relationship between income and prices. We may approximate this relationship linearly by writing

$$P = a - bY + \text{other factors} \qquad \textbf{\textit{AD} curve} \qquad (7.3)$$

What are the 'other factors' that determine the position of the *AD* curve? These must definitely be all those factors that were previously found to affect equilibrium income in the Mundell–Fleming model at a given price level. Since, under flexible exchange rates, income is determined by the point of intersection between the *FE* curve and the *LM* curve, the *IS* curve is redundant. The real exchange rate simply adjusts to make *IS* pass through the point where *FE* and *LM* cross. Hence, under flexible exchange rates, *the 'other factors' are those that affect the positions of* FE *and* LM.

The *LM* curve only shifts due to changes in the real money supply *M*/*P*. Changes of *P* have already been discussed. They move the economy along the *AD* curve. Increases in *M* shift *LM* to the right, raising income at any given price level. Hence if *M* rises, the *AD* curve shifts to the right.

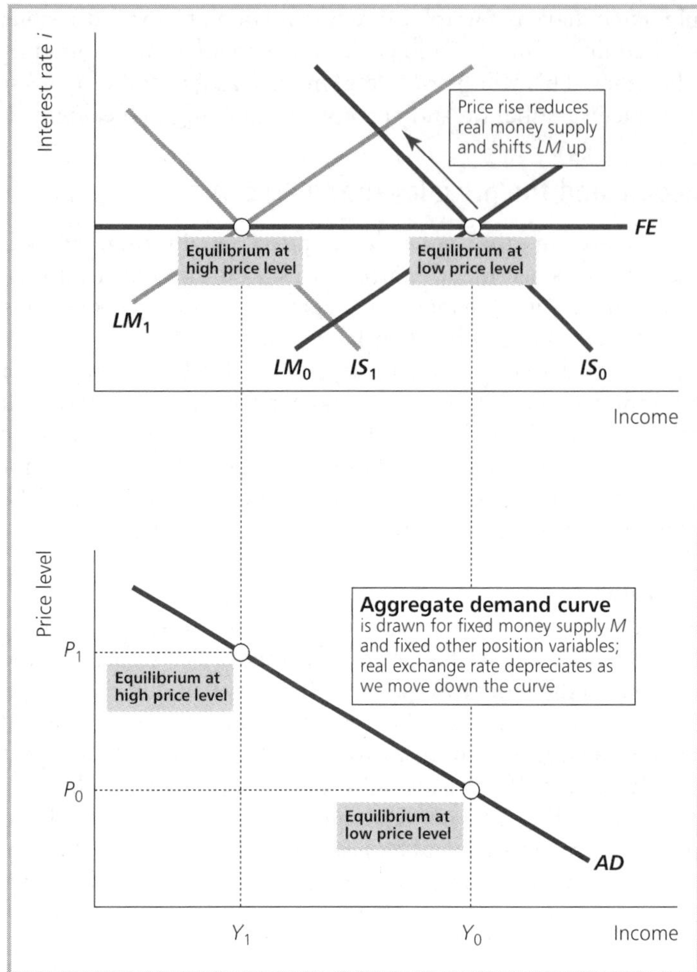

Figure 7.2 (Flexible exchange rates.) Prices are low at P_0, LM is at LM_0 and output at Y_0. Now a price rise to P_1 reduces the real money supply M/P, moving LM up to LM_1. The new equilibrium at the price level P_1 obtains where LM_1 and FE intersect. Output has dropped to Y_1. Since IS shifts into IS_1 endogenously, the real exchange rate appreciates The line in the lower graph generalizes this negative relationship between P and Y. It is called the aggregate demand curve (AD).

The position of the FE curve is determined by two factors: the world interest rate, now given as i^W, and expected depreciation ε^e. Both shift the foreign exchange market equilibrium line up. Figure 7.3 shows that this moves macroeconomic equilibrium up and to the right along the LM curve, raising income. As this leaves the price level unchanged, the lower panel shows the implied shift of the AD curve to the right.

With these arguments a preliminary way to write the complete AD curve under flexible exchange rates is

$$P = a - bY + \text{other factors } [M(+), i^W(+), \varepsilon^e(+)] \qquad \textbf{AD curve} \text{ flexible exchange rates} \qquad (7.4)$$

Fixed exchange rates

Under fixed exchange rates the IS curve and the LM curve switch roles. Income is determined by the intersection between the FE curve and the IS curve. Now the LM curve becomes technically redundant because the money supply must adjust so as to make LM pass through the point where FE and IS cross.

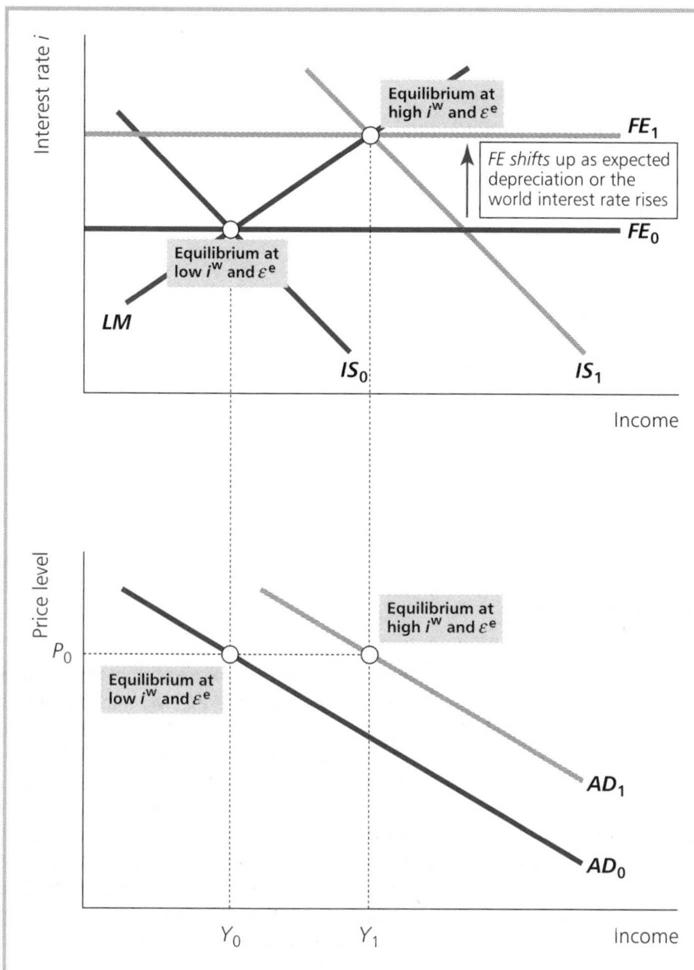

Figure 7.3 (Flexible exchange rates.) Initially prices are at P_0 and income is Y_0. Now the world interest rate or depreciation expectations rise, shifting *FE* up into FE_1. If the money supply and prices are unchanged the *LM* curve stays put. The new equilibrium obtains where *LM* and FE_1 intersect. (*IS* moves endogenously into IS_1 via a real depreciation.) The lower graph notes that, with unchanged prices, a rise in i^W or ε^e raises income. Since this would apply at any initial price level, the whole *AD* curve shifts to the right.

Following the above line of argument, Figure 7.4 starts from an initial demand-side equilibrium in the Mundell–Fleming model at a low price level. As the price rises, the real exchange rate $R = EP^W/P$ appreciates (i.e. *falls*), depressing net exports and shifting *IS* to the left. Equilibrium income falls from Y_0 to Y_1. Again, the lower panel shows that this implies a negatively sloped aggregate demand curve in the *P*-*Y* plane.

Evidently, the *AD* curve looks the same under flexible and under fixed exchange rates. Again, we may tentatively write

$$P = a - bY + \text{other factors} \qquad \textit{AD} \textbf{ curve} \qquad (7.5)$$

What differs is the transmission channel from price changes to income changes. (Note also that the slope parameter b is different under the two exchange rate systems. See the appendix on pp. 190–1.) Under flexible exchange rates the starting point is the exogenous reduction in the real money supply caused by the price increase. This makes the real exchange rate appreciate endogenously. Under fixed exchange rates the starting point

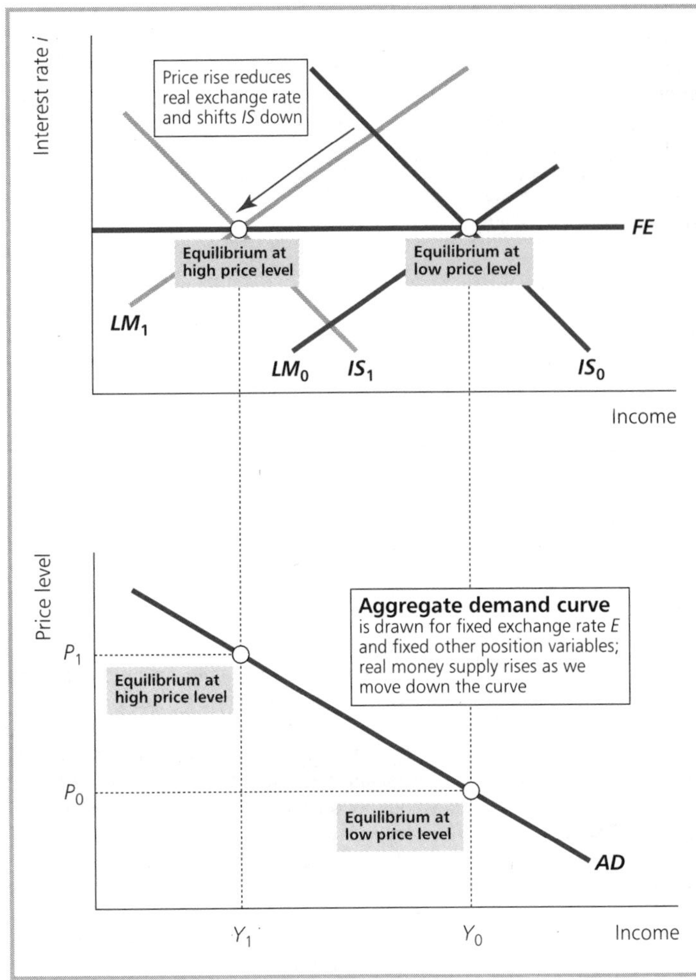

Figure 7.4 (Fixed exchange rates.) Prices are low at P_0, LM is at LM_0 and output at Y_0. Now a price rise to P_1 reduces the real exchange rate EP^W/P, moving IS to IS_1. The new equilibrium obtains where IS_1 and FE intersect. Income has dropped to Y_1. LM shifts into LM_1 endogenously due to a reduction of the real money supply. The line in the lower graph generalizes this negative relationship between P and Y. It is the aggregate demand curve (AD) under fixed exchange rates.

is an exogenous reduction in the real exchange rate caused by the price increase. This obliges the real money supply to decline endogenously.

This has one important implication when we draw *AD*. Under flexible exchange rates *AD* is drawn for a given nominal money supply *M*. As we move along the curve, the real exchange rate changes. Under fixed exchange rates *AD* is drawn for a given nominal exchange rate. As we move along the curve, the real money supply changes. Common to both exchange rate systems is that the real money supply and the real interest rate rise as we move down *AD*.

When exchange rates are fixed the 'other factors' are those that affect *FE* or *IS*. The *IS* curve only shifts due to changes in all factors that affect the demand for goods and services: government expenditures or tax policy, world income, the exchange rate and the world price level. As any of these variables rise, the *IS* curve shifts to the right, raising income. Since this happens at a given price level, the *AD* curve shifts to the right.

As mentioned above, the position of the *FE* curve is determined by the world interest rate i^W and expected depreciation ε^e. Both shift the foreign exchange market equilibrium line up. Since under fixed exchange rates the equilibrium moves along the *IS* curve, income falls. Figure 7.5 shows this and the resulting shift of the *AD* curve to the left.

With these arguments the complete *AD* curve under fixed exchange rates now reads

$$P = a - bY + \text{other factors } [E(+), P^W(+), G(+), Y^W(+), i^W(-), \varepsilon^e(-)] \quad (7.6)$$

AD curve
fixed exchange rates

We now have a good qualitative understanding of the aggregate demand curves under flexible and fixed exchange rates. Both are negatively sloped lines in a *P*-*Y* diagram. The point to note here, again, is that the *linear* relationships between *P* and *Y* proposed in equations (7.3)–(7.6) are only *approximations* of the *AD* curve in the neighbourhood of its current price level. As we move away from this level, this approximation becomes less and less precise. The reason for this echoes the discussion of the functional form of the *AS* curve we had in section 7.1.

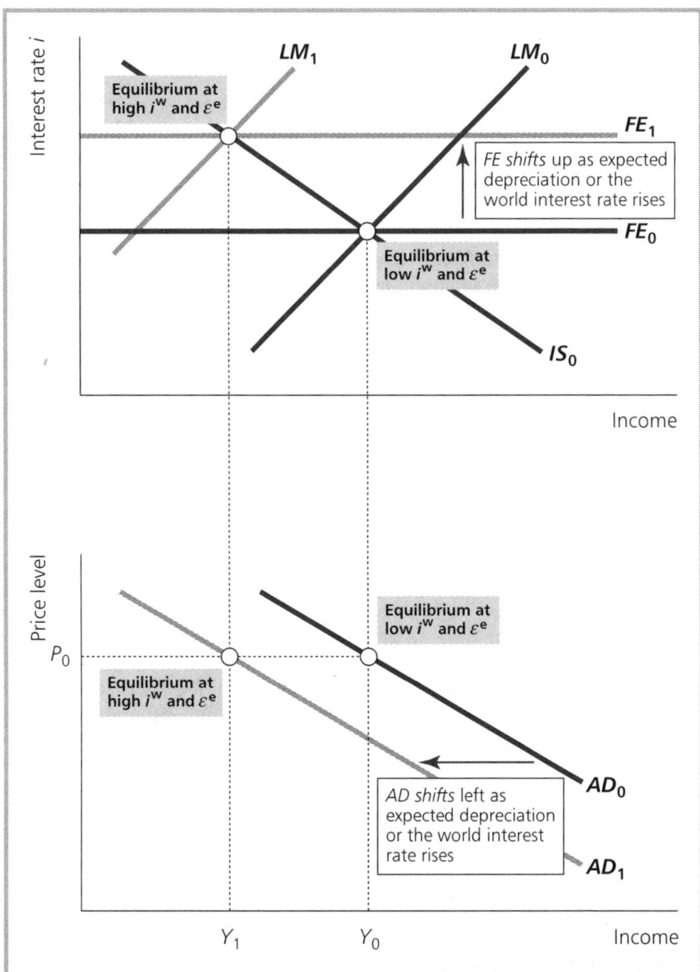

Figure 7.5 Initially prices are at P_0 and income is Y_0. Now the world interest rate or devaluation expectations rise, shifting *FE* up into FE_1. If the nominal exchange rate and prices are unchanged the *IS* curve stays put. The new equilibrium obtains where *IS* and FE_1 intersect. (*LM* moves endogenously into LM_1 via a forced reduction of the money supply.) The lower graph notes that, with unchanged prices, a rise in i^W or ε^e reduces income. Since this would apply at any initial price level, the whole *AD* curve shifts to the left.

Consider flexible exchange rates. According to equation (7.4) an increase of the price level from 1 to 2 lowers aggregate demand just as much as an increase from 100 to 101. This does not fit the economic reasoning behind the Mundell–Fleming model and the *AD* curve. Note that under flexible exchange rates prices affect aggregate demand because they affect the *real* money supply M/P. Now a price rise from 1 to 2 cuts the real money supply in half while a price rise from 100 to 101 cuts the real money supply by only 1%. In order to suit our economic line of reasoning, the same percentage change in the real money supply should always trigger the same output response, no matter what the initial price level is. This means that at a higher initial price level you need a higher price increase to prompt the same change in aggregate demand. This calls for a non-linear *AD* curve as drawn in Figure 7.6, panel (a). Again, the unwelcome mathematical side effect that arises from this can be avoided if we repeat what we did with the *AS* curve in section 7.1, that is postulate a linear relationship between the logarithm of *P* and income (and the other variables). Ignoring the constant term, the tentative *AD* curve under flexible exchange rates can now be spelled out explicitly as

$$p = m - bY + h(i^W + \varepsilon^e) \qquad (7.7)$$

***AD* curve** flexible exchange rates

So the position of the *AD* curve in p-Y space depends on the (logarithm of the) money supply, the world interest rate and expected depreciation. Note that it is crucial to include $m \equiv \ln M$ on the right-hand side and not M. Only by writing the logarithm of the money supply in this equation can we ensure that a change in the real money supply is required in order to move the curve.

Similar arguments apply under fixed exchange rates. Equation (7.6) states that a price increase from 1 to 2 reduces aggregate demand just as much as an increase from 100 to 101. This does not fit well with the economic reasoning

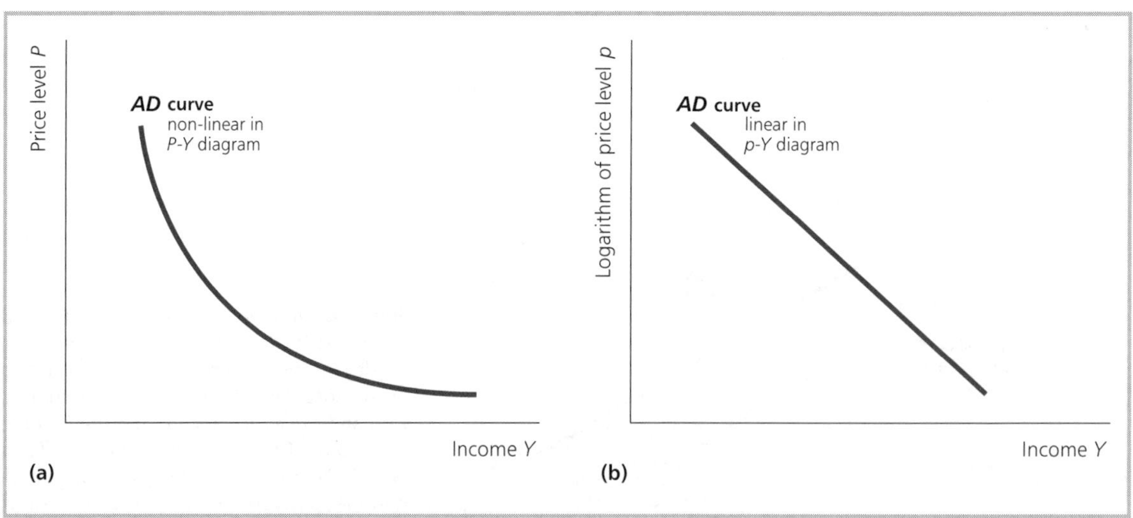

Figure 7.6 The straight *AD* curve derived and shown in Figures 7.2–7.5 is only an approximation. By developing the argument more accurately, we find the *AD* curve to be non-linear in a price–income diagram as shown in panel (a). Conveniently, when this precise *AD* curve is redrawn in a diagram that uses a logarithmic scale, or that measures the logarithm of the price level on the vertical axis, it turns out to be a straight line as shown in panel (b).

behind the Mundell–Fleming model and the *AD* curve. When exchange rates are fixed, prices affect aggregate demand because they affect the *real* exchange rate $R \equiv EP^W/P$. Now an increase of P from 1 to 2 cuts the real exchange rate in half. An increase from 100 to 101 reduces it by only 1%. To mend this inaccuracy of equation (7.6), the same percentage change in the real exchange rate should always trigger the same response in aggregate demand, independently of the initial price level. This calls for a non-linear *AD* curve as it was depicted in panel (a) of Figure 7.6. This non-linear relationship between P and Y is equivalent in content to a linear relationship between p and Y as shown in panel (b) and as expressed by the equation

$$p = e + p^W - bY + \gamma Y^W + \delta G - f(i^W + \varepsilon^e) \qquad \textbf{AD curve} \text{ (fixed exchange rates)} \qquad (7.8)$$

So the position of the *AD* curve in *p*-*Y* depends (under fixed exchange rates) on the (logarithm of the) exchange rate, (the logarithm of) world prices, world income, government spending, the world interest rate and expected depreciation. The exchange rate and world prices need to be entered as logarithms, because this ensures that the same percentage change of the real exchange rate always has the same effect on aggregate demand.

Time to pause – we have come a long way

The *AD* curve, the graphical image of demand-side macroeconomic equilibria, is an admittedly complex concept with a deep foundation that stretches over several chapters. Before we proceed to combine the *AD* curve with the *AS* curve to obtain the most sophisticated model of booms and recessions discussed in this book, let us pause, step back and recall what we achieved so far. Figure 7.7 reminds us of the main concepts and how they fit together.

We had chosen two kinds of perspectives. Initially, because it was the simpler perspective to start with, we considered the global (or closed) economy. It is composed of the goods market, which we analyzed in terms of the Keynesian cross and the *IS* curve in Chapters 2 and 3, and of the money market, which was also discussed in Chapter 3 in terms of the *LM* curve. Still in the same chapter, both markets were merged into the *IS-LM* or global-economy model that permitted the analysis of monetary and, in refined form, fiscal policy.

The second more demanding but more relevant perspective adopted was that of a national economy with international ties. The national-economy perspective embraces the *IS-LM* model as a starting block and adds trade in goods, services and international assets and the foreign exchange market. This is done in Chapter 4 and the completed model, the *IS-LM-FE* or Mundell–Fleming model is analyzed in Chapter 5.

Assuming fixed prices, the *IS-LM-FE* model is designed for the study of short-run effects. To explain why and how prices move in the medium and long run, we need to study the interaction between the economy's supply and demand sides. After aggregate supply had been given a somewhat shabby treatment in earlier chapters, Chapter 6 mends this by introducing the labour market. The labour market determines employment and, via the production function, output produced. The visual image of output supplied at different

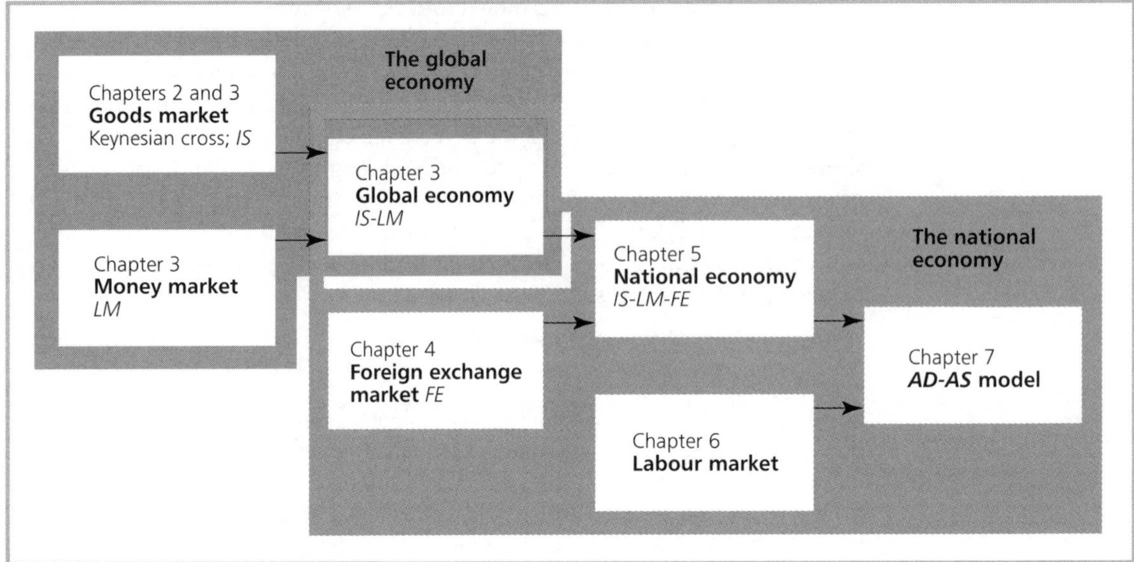

Figure 7.7 Note the building blocks assembled so far and how they fit together. The *IS-LM* model, our first model of the aggregate global economy, comprises the money market and the goods market (which is tantamount to the Keynesian cross). By adding the foreign exchange market to the *IS-LM* model (thereby introducing trade in goods and financial assets) we arrive at the basic model of the national economy. We call this the Mundell–Fleming or *IS-LM-FE* model. Chapter 6 refined this view of the national economy by adding the labour market, thus digging deeper on the supply side. Adding the labour market to the Mundell–Fleming model yields the aggregate-demand/aggregate-supply model, our workhorse for analyzing booms and recessions. (We might also go back and add the labour market to the *IS-LM* model to obtain a refined model of the global economy, but refrain from doing so.)

price levels is the *AS* curve. The visual image of demand-side equilibria as spelled out by the *IS-LM-FE* model is the *AD* curve. Merging both curves into one diagram permits us to analyze how aggregate supply and demand interact and drive income and prices. It is this *AD-AS* model, standing on the shoulders of the models discussed in earlier chapters, to which we now turn our attention.

7.3 THE *AD-AS* MODEL: BASICS

Before we put the *AD-AS* model to work by analyzing economic policy options, let us summarize what we know so far and identify the model's short-run and long-run equilibria. Keeping an eye on the time horizon is called for because the *AD-AS* model is our first model with an explicitly dynamic structure (that is, it has its roots in the labour market, the market behind the *AS* curve). Unlike previous, comparative static models that identify equilibria but say nothing about how we move from one equilibrium to another, the *AD-AS* describes such dynamic processes.

The *AD-AS* model is also our first macroeconomic model in which the demand side and the supply side show up as equals. The model is captured by two equations which vary somewhat depending on the exchange rate system.

Under flexible exchange rates the *AD-AS* model reads

$$p = m - bY + h(i^W + \varepsilon^e) \qquad \textbf{\textit{AD} curve, flexible exchange rates} \qquad (7.7)$$

$$p = p^e + \lambda(Y - Y^*) \qquad \textbf{\textit{AS} curve} \qquad (7.2)$$

Panel (a) in Figure 7.8 sums up what we know about the positively sloped *AS* curve. First, it moves up as the expected price level rises, because this would make trade unions demand higher money wages and induce firms to produce less output at any given price level. Second, as we move up on a given *AS* curve, drawn for given nominal wages and price expectations, the real wage declines. This makes labour cheaper and coaxes firms into hiring more labour and producing more output.

Panel (b) in Figure 7.8 enumerates our understanding of the negatively sloped *AD* curve. Under the system of flexible exchange rates assumed here, it moves up (or to the right) if either the money supply expands or if the domestic interest rate is driven up by rising world interest rates or an increase in expected depreciation. Both stimulate demand for domestic products. The first directly, because consumers buy more of our exports with their increased incomes. The second indirectly, by making our currency depreciate and our exports cheaper. Note that the identified shift variables are exactly those which affect income in the Mundell–Fleming model under flexible exchange rates. As we slide down a given *AD* curve, the real money supply increases and the exchange rate depreciates. The higher real exchange rate is needed to stimulate net exports and raise demand-side equilibrium income.

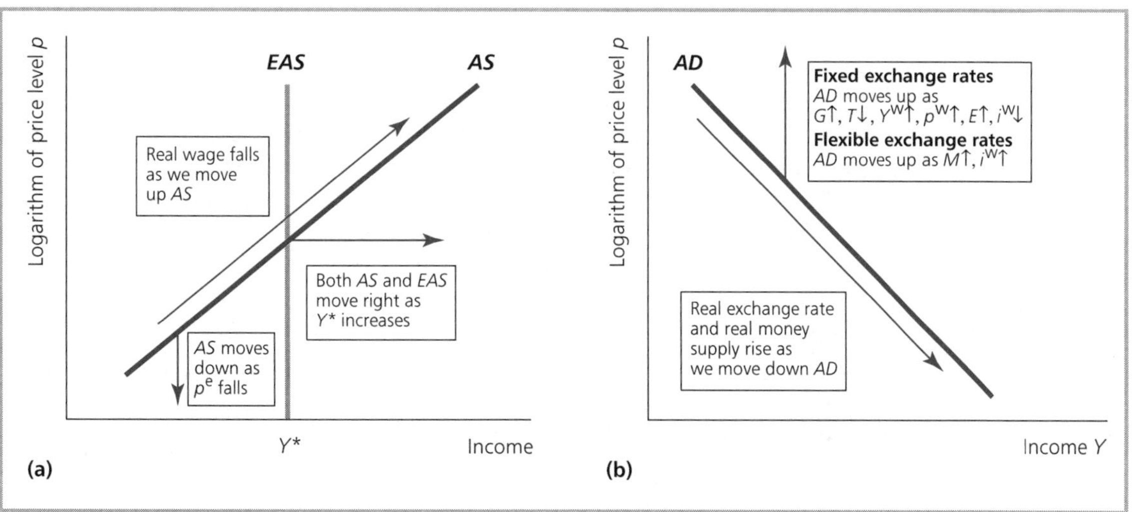

Figure 7.8 Panel (a) sums up what we know about the *AS* curves. Both *EAS* and *AS* move to the right if potential income increases, say due to technological improvements or a growing labour force. *AS* moves up if price expectations go up. Then unions request higher money wages which makes firms demand fewer work hours at any given price level. As we move up the *AS* curve the real wage declines. Only this can make firms hire more workers and generate more output. The *AD* curve shown for flexible exchange rates in panel (b) moves up if the money supply or world interest rates rise. These shift variables are those which affect income in the Mundell–Fleming model under flexible exchange rates. As we slide down the *AD* curve, falling prices increase the real money supply and make the real exchange rate depreciate.

Under fixed exchange rates the *AS* curve is unchanged, but the *AD* curve is different:

$$p = e + p^W - bY + \gamma Y^W + \delta G - f(i^W + \varepsilon^e) \qquad \textbf{AD curve (fixed exchange rates)} \qquad (7.8)$$

$$p = p^e + \lambda(Y - Y^*) \qquad \textbf{AS curve} \qquad (7.2)$$

While the *AD* curve has a negative slope under both exchange rate systems, this is where the similarity ends. First, the slope is not the same under fixed and flexible exchange rates, though we are using the same parameter $-b$ (see also the appendix to this chapter). Second, the position of the *AD* curve is affected by a different set of variables, or if by the same variables, then in different directions. The *AD* curve moves up if the exchange rate, world prices, world income or government spending increases, or if interest rates are driven down by falling world interest rates or a reduction in expected depreciation. Again, the link to the Mundell–Fleming model is that these are the very variables that affect income under fixed exchange rates. The real money supply and the real exchange rate both rise as we slide down the *AD* curve.

Short-run and long-run *AS* curves

In Chapter 6 we realized that there were two kinds of aggregate supply curves. One that describes the short-run response of aggregate supply to an unexpected increase in prices. This is equation (7.2), which was repeated for convenience in the preceding sections. As we move up or down this curve, we take expected prices p^e (and, implicitly, the nominal wage) as given. This is a situation which cannot prevail in the long run, of course. Suppose prices and expected prices equal 1, initially. Now prices rise by 50% to 1.5. If prices stay at that level for good, an expected price level of 1 underestimates actual prices by 1/3 period after period. This is costly and will obviously not go on for ever. Eventually actors will learn and raise expected prices closer towards actual prices. But this moves the *AS* curve up and thus affects income.

We will take a closer look at how people form expectations in the next chapter. It is sufficient for now to contend that in the long run, if individuals are capable of some rudimentary learning, expected and actual prices must be the same. Setting $p = p^e$ in equation (7.2) and solving for Y yields the long-run *AS* curve

$$Y = Y^* \qquad \textbf{Long-run AS curve}$$

which is a vertical line in p-Y space. Figure 7.9 combines the long-run *AS* curve (*LAS*) with the arbitrarily drawn *AD* and short-run *AS* curves.

The equilibrium price level

The *AD* curve identifies the level of aggregate demand obtaining at different price levels. Yet if we do not know prices, we cannot determine the level of aggregate demand. The *AS* curve identifies aggregate supply at different price levels. Again: we cannot identify aggregate supply until we know the price level. What helps here is that in equilibrium aggregate demand must equal aggregate supply. Graphically, therefore, the equilibrium price level is where the *AD*

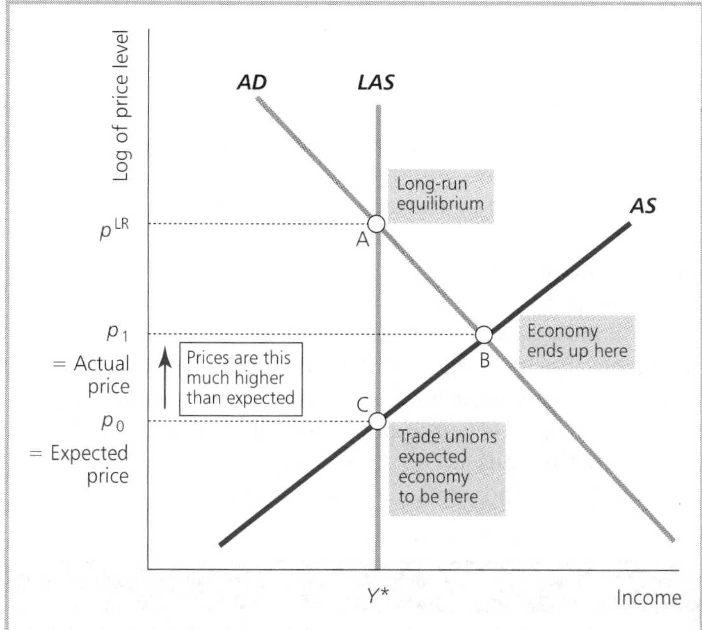

Figure 7.9 This graph emphasizes key points in the *AD-AS* diagram. C is the point trade unions have been aiming for. They must do so on the basis of expectations, since money wages cannot be renegotiated for a while after they are fixed in a contract. Obviously unions expected *AD* to pass through C and prices to equal p_0. Actually, the *AD* curve turned out to be positioned much further up, rendering prices unexpectedly high and real wages lower than planned. Firms employ an unusually large number of workers and the economy ends up in B. B cannot last, because it resulted from unions committing expectational errors. Once these are corrected the economy will settle into its long-run equilibrium in A.

curve and the *AS* curve intersect. But which *AS* curve? Didn't we just state that we have two – a short-run *AS* curve and a long-run *AS* curve? And these two *AS* curves do not necessarily intersect the *AD* curve at the same point. Do we then have two equilibrium price levels? Exactly so: one that applies in the long run and one that applies in the short run, just as we have one *AS* curve for each time horizon.

Point A, where the *AD* and the long-run *AS* curves intersect, identifies the *long-run equilibrium* price level p^{LR}. Remember: each point on the *AD* curve corresponds to a simultaneous equilibrium in the goods market, the money market and the foreign exchange market. Each point on the long-run AS curve corresponds to a long-run equilibrium in the labour market in the sense that the plans and expectations of both employers and trade unions have worked out. Neither party wants to revise wages and thus move away from this point as long as there is no change in monetary, fiscal or exchange rate policy, or in the economic conditions in the rest of the world. Thus point A qualifies as a long-run equilibrium in which all four markets clear and prices are as expected at $p = p^e = p^{LR}$ and income is at its potential level Y*.

B, the point of intersection between the *AD* curve and the short-run *AS* curve, is a *short-run equilibrium*. Since B is also on the *AD* curve, all three markets on the demand side of our model economy are in equilibrium. With B being *on* the short-run *AS* curve but *off* the long-run *AS* curve, it corresponds to a short-run, temporary equilibrium in the labour market only. In this equilibrium the employers' plans work out, because they employ all the labour they want at the current real wage, but not the trade unions' plans. Here B is to the right of the long-run *AS* curve. So real wages are lower than what trade unions had aimed for (because prices are higher than expected). Unions are stuck with this (in their view less than ideal) situation as long as current wage contracts last. When these expire, unions will renegotiate the money wage rate, which changes the current equilibrium.

C is the point the trade unions had been aiming for. By basing their wage negotiations on an expected price level of $p0$ they made the *AS* curve pass through C. Had prices turned out as expected, income would have equalled potential income and trade unions' utility would have been at a maximum (subject to the restriction provided by the labour demand curve).

The link between the temporary, short-run equilibrium at B and the long-run equilibrium at A is provided by the ability of trade unions to learn from and correct expectational errors. Since prices at B are higher than expected, for whatever reason, a rational response by trade unions will be to expect higher prices when entering next year's wage negotiations than they expected last time. But higher expected prices position the *AS* curve further up, moving the point of intersection with the *AD* curve northwest. This process continues until the economy eventually ends up at A. We will look at such dynamic processes in more detail below and particularly in Chapter 8.

7.4 POLICY AND SHOCKS IN THE *AD-AS* MODEL

Let us now put the *AD-AS* model to work. First, by looking at the effects of fiscal and monetary policy, then by analyzing how the national economy is affected by economic changes in the world around us.

Fiscal policy

Fiscal policy, that is, the use of government spending or taxes as a means of influencing the course of the economy, has already been analyzed in the context of the Mundell–Fleming model in Chapter 5. There we learned that fiscal policy is only effective when exchange rates are fixed. Under flexible exchange rates an increase in government spending only crowds out net exports by making the exchange rate appreciate. In the context of the *AD-AS* model this means that under flexible exchange rates an increase in government spending cannot shift the *AD* curve. So there is no change in aggregate income or the price level. What a look at the *AD-AS* diagram conceals, however, are the changes going on underneath the highest level of aggregation. As already indicated, even though Y does not change when G increases, the *composition* of aggregate demand changes. This is easily revealed by considering the circular flow identity introduced in this book's introductory chapters. From the requirement that leaks out of and injections into the circular flow of income must balance we obtained the useful identity

$$\underbrace{(S - I)}_{\substack{0\ \ 0 \\ 0}} + \underbrace{(T - G)}_{\substack{0\ \ + \\ -}} + \underbrace{(IM - EX)}_{\substack{+\ \ - \\ +}} = 0$$

The row beneath the variables indicates in which direction each variable changes after the increase in G. S and T do not change because they depend on income, and income does not change, so we have zeros there. I is also unchanged because the interest rate, on which investment depends, does not change. Drawing these insights together, we note that $S - I$ remains unchanged, but the government budget surplus deteriorates. With $T - G$ going down and $S - I$ unchanged, $IM - EX$ must rise in order to keep the identity. Since income is unchanged, net imports can only rise if the exchange rate appreciates. This raises imports and reduces exports, permitting us to fill in the + and − sign beneath *IM* and *EX*. This small exercise is an illustration of the potential of the circular flow identity (while not being a real model in its own right) to provide useful information when combined with insights from models like the *AD-AS* model.

Let us turn next to fixed exchange rates, the scenario in which fiscal policy can affect aggregate income. Figure 7.10 assumes that the economy is in a long-run equilibrium in A_0 and shows the corresponding AD_0 and AS_0 curves. Income is $Y_0 = Y^*$ and prices are p_0. Since the economy has been in this situation for a while, expected prices equal actual prices. Now suppose in period 1 the government decides to increase spending, which had not been anticipated when the currently binding wage contracts were negotiated at the end of period 0. Thus the *AS* curve, the position of which reflects the current money wage W_1, stays put while the rise in *G* moves AD up into position AD_1. Let us first focus on what happens in period 1 and compare the effects with those derived in previous, simpler models.

The increase in government spending has increased aggregate demand at all price levels. If the price level was fixed at p_0, aggregate demand would rise to Y'_1. This is identical to the income response that would result in the Keynesian cross and in the Mundell–Fleming model. There we assumed that the aggregate supply curve was of an extreme Keynesian nature, namely horizontal, meaning that firms were prepared to meet any level of demand at the current price level. AD_1 would indeed intersect such a horizontal *AS* curve in point A'_1.

Our refined *AS* curve indicates a different story. At the current price level firms would not profit from producing more than Y^*. Hence, they will not do so. This means that demand exceeds supply at the price level p_0. In the face of

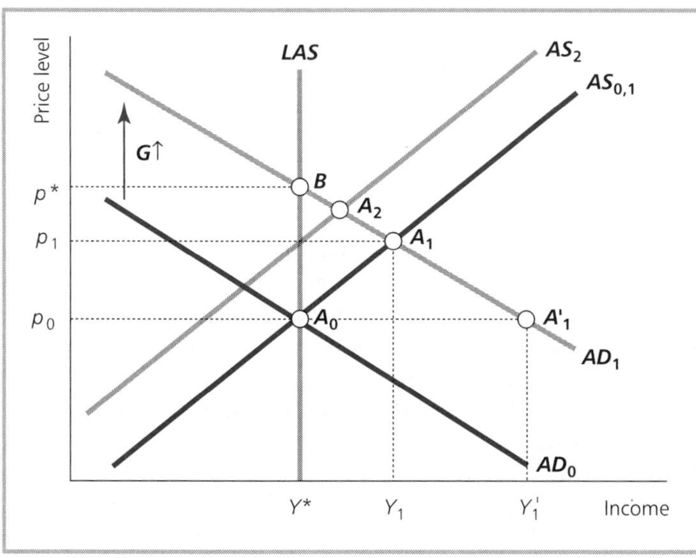

Figure 7.10 When the government raises spending, aggregate demand goes up at all price levels. Consequently, the *AD* curve shifts to the right. If the *AS* curve was horizontal, as implicitly assumed in the Keynesian cross, the *IS-LM* and the Mundell–Fleming model, income would rise to Y'_1. When *AS* is positively sloped, however, firms increase production only if prices go up and lower the real wage. Rising prices at the same time reduce aggregate demand. With supply sliding up the *AS* curve and demand up *AD*, supply finally equals demand when prices reach p_1 and income is Y_1. A_1 is only a temporary equilibrium based on faulty expectations, however. After expectational errors have been corrected, the economy settles into B.

Note. While demand exceeds supply at p_0, excess demand is not $Y_1' - Y^*$. Y_1' is demand-side equilibrium income. Demand would only be this high if income was this high. Since income is smaller, at Y^*, demand is smaller than Y_1' but larger than Y^*.

excess demand for goods, prices will begin to rise. This has consequences both on the supply side of the economy and on the demand side. On the supply side, where the nominal wage is fixed, real wages fall and firms begin to hire more workers who produce more output. As we start to move northeast along $AS_{0,1}$ aggregate supply increases. On the demand side, where the exchange rate is fixed, rising prices reduce the real exchange rate. Domestically produced goods become more expensive compared to foreign goods. Demand for our products falls as we move up on AD_1 in a northwesterly direction. With rising prices causing the supply of goods to increase and the demand for goods to fall, excess demand will eventually be eliminated after prices have risen to p_1 and the economy has settled into a new, temporary equilibrium at A_1.

Point A_1 only represents a temporary equilibrium, as explained above. Prices have moved higher than trade unions had anticipated, eroding real wages. When at the end of period 1 new wages will be negotiated for period 2, unions will do so on the basis of expected higher prices. To make matters simple, suppose trade unions always expect prices to remain for the next period where they are now. This is a special case of **adaptive expectations** (to be discussed in more detail in Chapter 8) and reads

Adaptive expectations are formed on the basis of the recent history of the variable under consideration alone. Expectations adapt to what the variable did in the past. Adaptive expectations are driven by the general equation

$$p^e = p^e_{-1} + a(p_{-1} - p^e_{-1})$$

How quickly expected prices adapt to actual prices is measured by the coefficient a.

$$p_t^e = p_{t-1}$$

Applied to the current situation this means that prices expected for period 2 equal prices observed in period 1: $p_2^e = p_1$. This moves AS_2 into a position where it passes through the point where a horizontal line through A_1 intersects the long-run AS curve. Since this shows that supply is reduced at all price levels, there is now excess demand at p_1. Using the same arguments advanced above, this will cause prices to rise again until we find a new, temporary equilibrium in A_2. Since period 2 prices were again higher than expected by trade unions, expectations will be revised upwards again, shifting the AS curve up in period 3. The entire process continues until the economy finally settles into its new long-run equilibrium at point B. This new long-run equilibrium is characterized by the same level of income generated at A, before government spending was increased, and by higher prices. So if an economy operates at near full capacity (which we call potential income) an expansionary fiscal policy only has a temporary effect on income. Temporary may well mean a number of years, however. Beyond that, in the long run only prices are affected.

Monetary policy

Let us now look at the effects of monetary policy in the *AD-AS* model. Since we learned in Chapter 5 that the central bank has no control over the money supply when exchange rates are fixed, we only look at flexible exchange rates. Figure 7.11 does more than trace the consequences of a money supply on income and prices, however, paying tribute to our claim that the six frames assembled piled upon each other trace the events observed in the *AD-AS* model back to what happens in the Keynesian cross, the Mundell–Fleming model and the labour market. The Keynesian cross and the Mundell–Fleming model are shown in frames 1 and 2 from the top. Frame 3 features the *AD* curve. The bottom frame depicts the labour market, though slightly modified

CASE STUDY 7.1 International evidence on the quantity equation and the *AD* curve

You may have wondered how the quantity equation $PY = VM$ introduced in Chapter 1 relates to the *AD* curve discussed in this chapter. Well, you simply solve this equation for P to obtain $P = VM/Y$, which is a negatively sloped line in a price–income diagram. So the quantity equation can be seen as some rudimentary *AD* curve. It also moves up when the money supply increases. But it is rudimentary in the sense that it does not rest on any detailed study of demand-side markets. For example, it does not explain when V, the velocity of circulation changes, and what factors might ignite such changes. The *AD* curve is more explicit in this respect, attributing this role to the interest rate, and identifying the factors that might influence the interest rate.

The quantity equation and the *AD* curve have in common that they are incomplete explanations of income and prices without an aggregate supply curve. Without an *AS* curve both curves only offer a menu of possibilities: when the money supply increases, either prices go up, or income goes up, or both grow a little bit.

The quantity equation is usually used to make long-run statements about the behaviour of prices. In this and the last chapter we argued that the long-run *AS* curve is vertical, meaning that income is constant at Y^*. Then there is a one-to-one

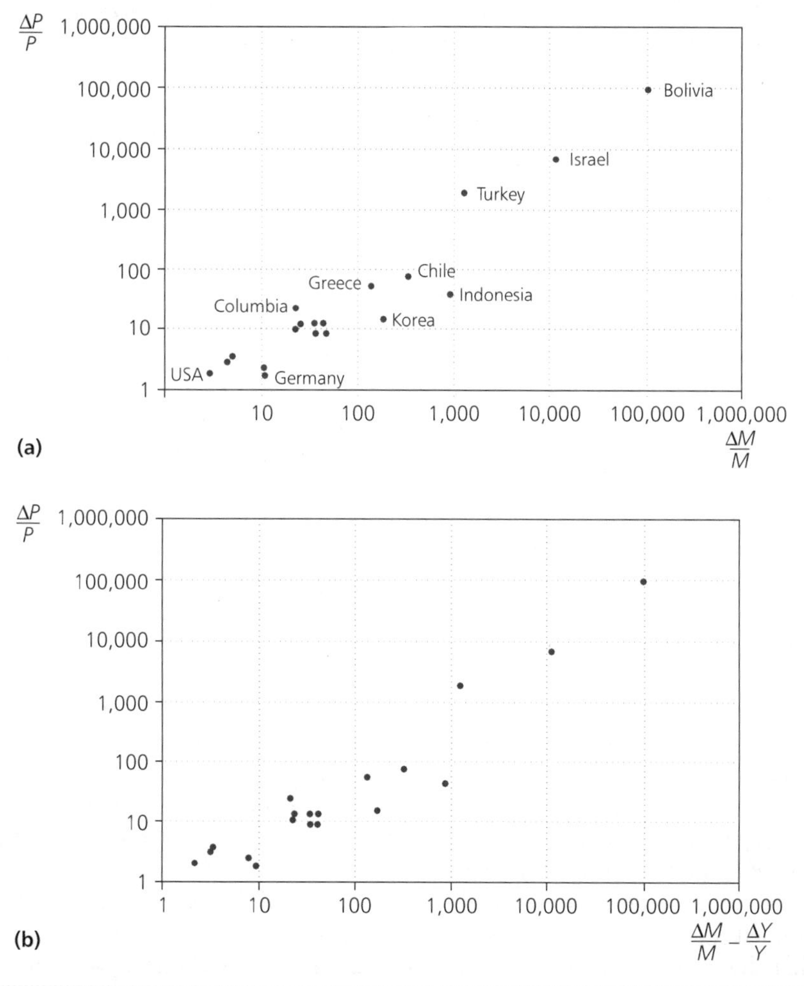

Figure 1

Case study 7.1 continued

relationship between P and M for any given year. For the year 2000 we have $P_{2000} = VM_{2000}/Y^*$. For 1969 we have $P_{1969} = VM_{1969}/Y^*$. Subtracting the second equation from the first and dividing the obtained difference by the second equation we obtain

$$\frac{P_{2000} - P_{1969}}{P_{1969}} = \frac{M_{2000} - M_{1969}}{M_{1969}} \qquad (1)$$

which proposes that the price increases can be traced back to money supply increases to their full extent. Panel (a) in Figure 1 shows that this implication of the quantity equation (and of the *AD* curve) receives some empirical support from the displayed group of countries, since all countries are roughly positioned along a straight line through the origin with slope 1.

Equation (1) is not precise in the sense that potential output Y^* is not really constant. We assume so for convenience when analyzing business cycles, but as Figure 2.2 underscored, such short-run fluctuations occur against the background of long-run income growth due to population growth and technological progress. Since money supply increases administered to accommodate higher income levels need not lead to higher prices, a more general (approximate) version of equation (1) is

$$\frac{P_{2000} - P_{1969}}{P_{1969}} = \frac{M_{2000} - M_{1969}}{M_{1969}} - \frac{Y_{2000} - Y_{1969}}{Y_{1969}} \qquad (2)$$

The right-hand part shows the evidence based on this refined equation. There are minor, though barely visible improvements in the closeness of data points to the 45° line. Remaining deviations must be attributed to changes in the velocity of circulation over time.

compared with Chapter 5. In order to be able to use the same measurement on the horizontal axis as the other five frames, the demand for labour exercised by firms is translated into output units using the production function. The same is done for the labour supply. Frame 2 from the bottom shows the *AS* curve, and the third frame from below finally features the *AD-AS* model.

Initially, in period 0, the economy is in the long-run equilibrium identified by the dark blue lines and dots in all six frames. In period 1 the central bank expands the money supply, shifting the *LM* curve in the Mundell–Fleming frame to the right into the light blue position. Nothing has happened yet to the *AD* curve, in the Keynesian cross, and on the economy's supply side. Only after the incipient downward pressure on the interest rate in the Mundell–Fleming diagram makes the exchange rate depreciate does the aggregate expenditure line in the Keynesian cross move up and the *AD* line shift to the right into their respective light blue positions. So these curves are not directly affected by the money supply, but indirectly via the money supply's effect on the exchange rate. The *AE* line sums up all planned spending, including exports. So as the exchange rate depreciates and exports rise, the *AE* line moves up, causing income to rise via the multiplier effect. Regarding the *AD* curve we see that if it moves to the right after a money supply increase it is because the exchange rate depreciates and demand-side equilibrium income is higher at any given price level. Note that the rightward shift of the *AD* curve is equal to the increase in income observed in the Keynesian cross and the Mundell–Fleming model, because the price level is assumed constant in these models.

The light blue dots identify the new equilibrium obtained in the Mundell–Fleming model and show where this equilibrium is positioned in the other diagrams. Since prices and real wages have not changed yet, this new demand-side equilibrium sits horizontally to the right of the initial dark blue

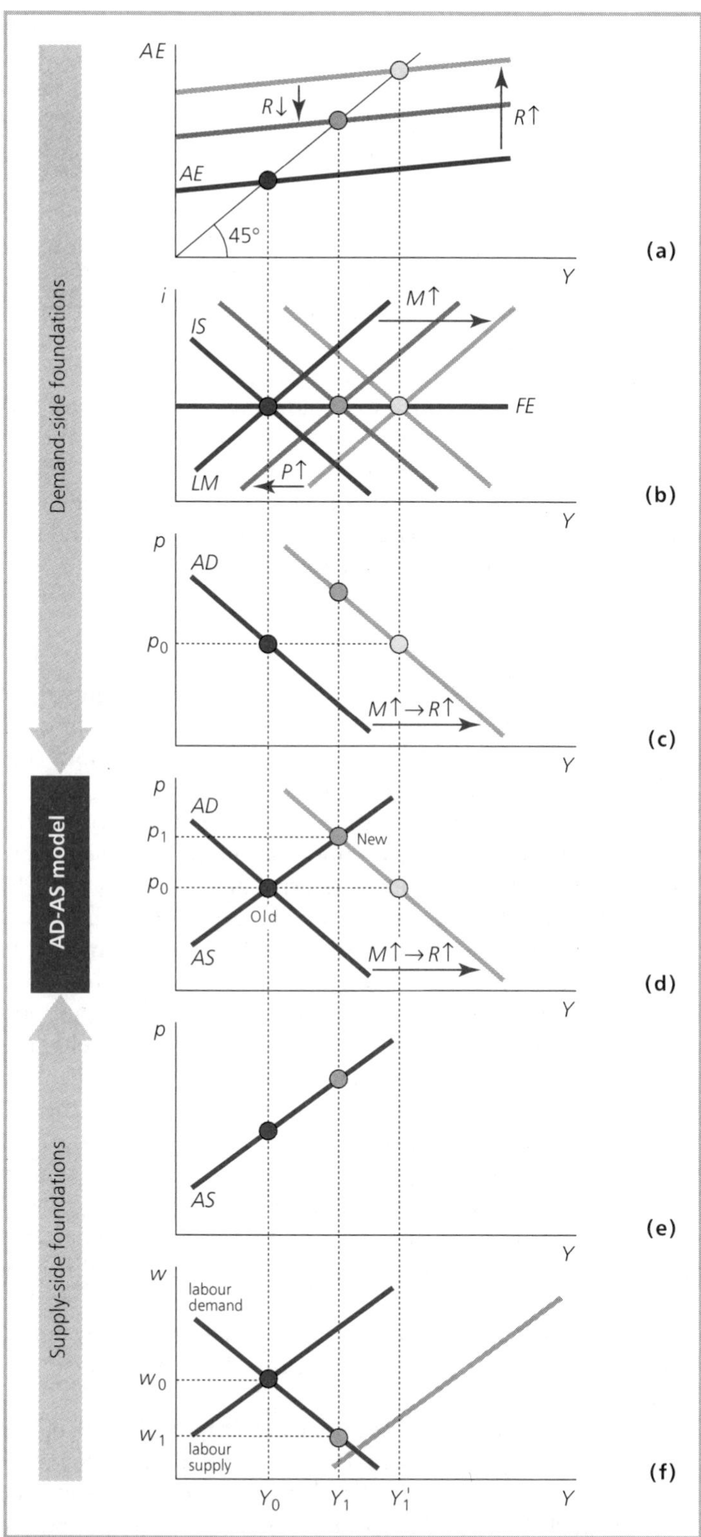

Figure 7.11 This figure emphasizes the foundations of the *AD-AS* model. When the money supply increases, the *LM* curve moves right in the Mundell–Fleming diagram (panel (b)). This drives up the exchange rate and shifts *IS* to the right too. The impact of exchange rate depreciation on aggregate expenditure can also be seen in the Keynesian cross (panel (a)) where equilibrium income rises to Y_1' as in the Mundell–Fleming model. Since this happens at unchanged prices, it means a shift of *AD* to the right (panels (c) and (d)). Since supply has remained at Y_0 so far, demand exceeds supply. Excess demand drives prices up. On the supply side, as documented in panels (d), (e) and (f), this drives down the real wage, raising employment and output. On the demand side, rising prices lower the real money supply and the exchange rate, shifting the aggregate expenditure line down in the Keynesian cross and demand-side equilibrium income left in the Mundell–Fleming panel (b). In panels (c) and (d) we witness an upward move along *AD*. Prices rise to make supply increase and demand fall until at p_1 excess demand in the goods market is eliminated and income is Y_1.

dots in frames 3–4 from the top. The important point to note is that the money supply increase has driven a wedge between supply and demand. The exchange rate depreciation induced by the money supply increase has raised aggregate demand but not aggregate supply (see *AD-AS* frame). This excess demand at the current level of prices triggers price increases that affect both aggregate demand and aggregate supply.

On the demand side, because rising prices reduce the real money supply and therefore the real exchange rate, exports fall. This moves the *AE* line down in the Keynesian cross and the *IS* curve (along with the *LM* curve) left in the Mundell–Fleming frame. On the *AD* curve this fall in income shows a movement up in a northwesterly direction.

On the supply side, rising prices reduce real wages. This increases the demand for labour and employment (since we assume involuntary unemployment to exist at potential income), resulting in an upward move on the *AS* curve. The goods market only clears after prices have increased to p_1. This is when the dampening effect of price increases on demand and the stimulating effect on supply combined are large enough to remove the excess demand that the money supply increase had generated at the initial price level p_0.

Bottom line

This chapter has merged our, by now, quite sophisticated understanding of the economy's demand side, developed in Chapters 1–5, with the insights into the supply side obtained in Chapter 6. The interaction between supply and demand explains the macroeconomic role of prices. Comparing this chapter's analyses of fiscal and monetary policy with pertinent analyses within the Mundell–Fleming model (see Chapter 5), we note that both instruments lose some of their potency. In the *AD-AS* model the price increases generated by expansionary policies dampen their effects on income even in the short run. They turn out to be smaller than they were in the Mundell–Fleming model. In the long run, prices even rise so much that no effect on income remains.

The *AD-AS* model is a very powerful tool for understanding the temporary ups and downs in modern economies. However, as presented in this chapter, it has one severe practical disadvantage that becomes obvious when we consider the history of price movements documented for 15 countries in Figure 7.12. None of these countries experienced a period of stable prices between 1960 and 2000. The *AD-AS* model in p-Y space assumes that in long-run equilibrium prices are stable. Prices only move temporarily, during phases of excess demand. This does not seem to fit the empirical picture where there appears to be permanent inflation, even in equilibrium. Inflationary equilibria can occur in the *AD-AS* model, but it is impractical to display and analyze them in a price–income diagram. The reason is simply that such an equilibrium would move up the long-run *AS* curve and, sooner or later, out of view.

Because of this practical limitation we consider the graphical form of the aggregate demand–aggregate supply model introduced in this chapter as only a stepping stone on the way to a more refined presentation that suits the discussion of inflation much better. This form of the *AD-AS* model will be derived and discussed in more detail in the next chapter.

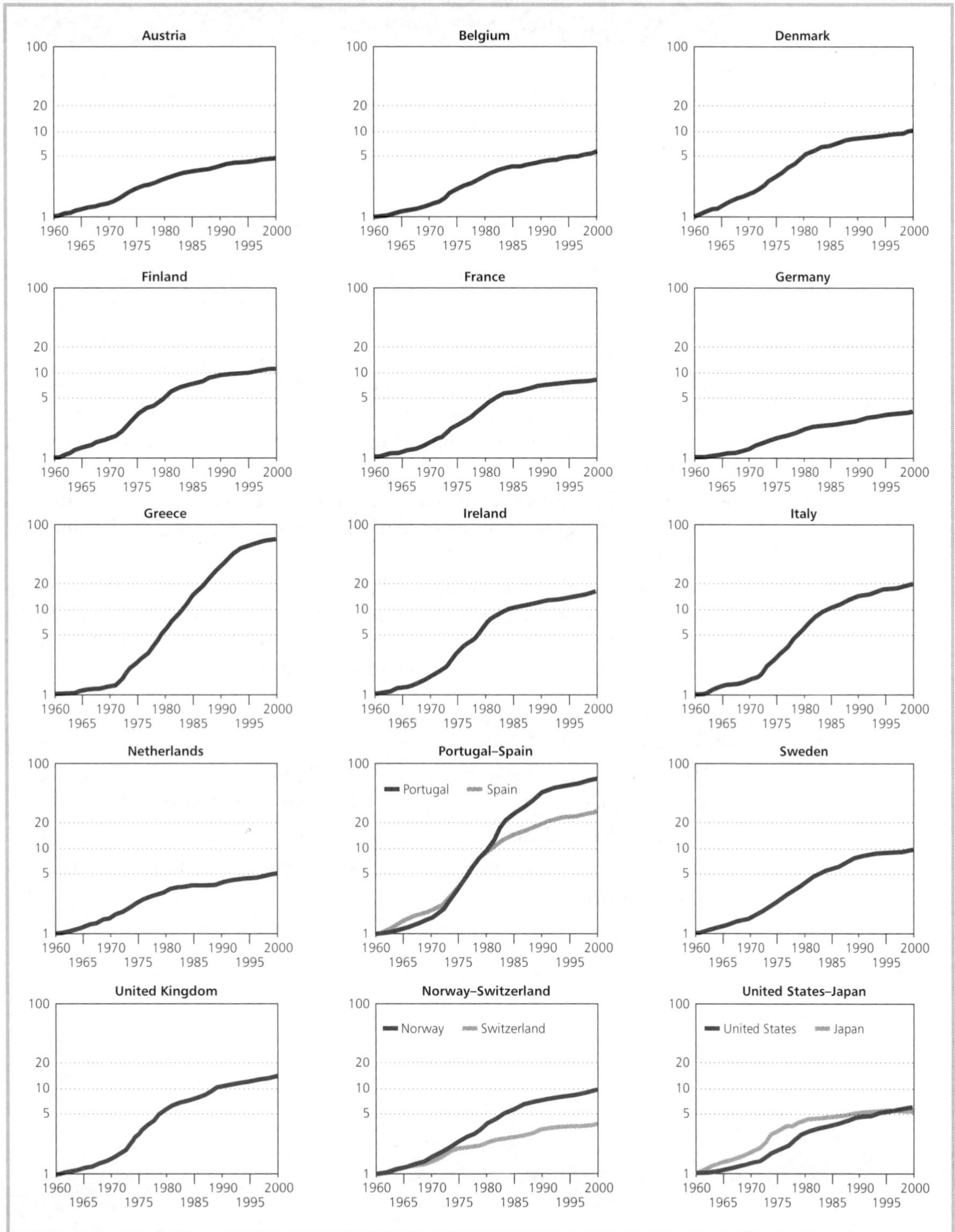

Figure 7.12 Price levels in Europe and the world, 1960–2002

CHAPTER SUMMARY

- An economy's supply side can be represented in price–income space by means of a vertical long-run aggregate supply curve (*LAS*) and a positively sloped short-run aggregate supply curve (*AS*).
- The demand side can be represented in price–income space by means of a negatively sloped aggregate demand curve (*AD*).
- Under flexible exchange rates the aggregate demand curve has a negative slope for the following reason. A price increase reduces the real money supply. Since the domestic interest rate cannot deviate from the world interest rate, the demand for money must be reduced by a decline in income.
- Under fixed exchange rates the aggregate demand curve has a negative slope for the following reason. A price increase reduces the real exchange rate. This appreciation creates an excess supply of domestic goods at the old level of income. Since the interest rate is fixed to the world interest rate, the supply of goods can only equal the demand for goods at a lower level of income.
- All policy measures and changes in the economic environment that affected demand-side equilibrium income in the Mundell–Fleming model, shift the *AD* curve.
- All income responses identified in the Mundell–Fleming model also show up in the *AD-AS* model. However, these effects disappear in the long run. In the short-run the effects are smaller than they were in the Mundell–Fleming model because there is some crowding-out via price increases.

KEY TERMS AND CONCEPTS

_AD_ curve
_AD-AS_ model
aggregate demand curve
demand-side equilibrium
expected price level
fiscal policy
long-run equilibrium
monetary policy
short-run equilibrium

EXERCISES

7.1 When deriving the *AS* curve in Chapter 6 we assumed that real rigidities (say, in the form of monopolistic trade unions) cause involuntary unemployment at normal employment levels. Now consider an economy in which no such real rigidities exist. Normal employment is determined by the point of intersection between the individual labour supply and the labour demand curves. What does the *AS* curve look like in this case? Does it make a difference whether individuals enter longer-term wage contracts or whether wages can be renegotiated any time?

7.2 This chapter derives the *AD* curve for the national economy from the *IS-LM-FE* or Mundell–Fleming model. Derive the global-economy *AD* curve graphically from the *IS-LM* model.

7.3 Figures 7.2 and 7.4 derive the *AD* curve for the national economy under flexible and fixed exchange rates. Find out by means of graphical analysis, under which exchange rate system the *AD* curve is steeper.

7.4 Suppose world interest rates go up, driving the rest of the world into a recession (that is, world income falls). Use the *AD-AS* model to analyze how this affects prices and income in our national economy. Do your results depend on whether exchange rates are fixed or flexible?

7.5 What happens to the *AD* curve with flexible exchange rates and perfect international capital mobility if
(a) the money supply increases?
(b) the world interest rate decreases?
(c) a major trading partner dips into a recession?

7.6 Why does an increase in the world interest rate shift the *AD* curve *up* under flexible exchange rates, but *down* under fixed exchange rates?

7.7 Why does a change in world income shift the *AD* curve under fixed exchange rates but not when exchange rates are flexible? Start with the Mundell–Fleming model to determine which curves shift (and which do not) as foreign income increases. Does that mean that changes in foreign income do not change anything if exchange rates are flexible?

7.8 Suppose a country's potential income Y^* increases because lawmakers reduce trade union monopoly power. What will be the short-, medium- and long-run effects on prices and income?

7.9 Suppose the economy's demand side can be described by the Keynesian cross with the equilibrium condition

$$Y = AE = 0.4Y + 1000$$

(a) What is the level of income?
(b) Suppose government spending rises by 100. What is the new demand-side equilibrium income?
(c) If the income level computed under (a) was equal to potential income and the short-run AS curve was positively sloped, what is the excess demand generated by the increase of government spending by 100 at the initial price level?

7.10 Box 5.1 demonstrated that the *FE* curve is vertical when a country controls cross-border capital flows. Derive the *AD* curve graphically for this case of controlled capital flows.
(a) Consider flexible exchange rates first. Which policy variables and exogenous variables shift the *AD* curve?
(b) Now derive the *AD* curve for fixed exchange rates. Which variables determine the position of the *AD* curve?

RECOMMENDED READING

For an alternative to the *IS-LM-FE* model that replaces the money market (*LM* curve) with the assumption that the cental bank follows a simple interest rate rule, see David Romer (2000) 'Keynesian macroeconomics without the *LM* curve', *Journal of Economic Perspectives* 14: 149–69.

An accessible general perspective on the future of macroeconomics by a Nobel prize winner is given in Robert M. Solow (2000) 'Toward a macroeconomics of the medium run', *Journal of Economic Perspective* 14: 151–8.

APPENDIX THE ALGEBRA OF THE *AD* CURVE

The algebra of the *AD* curve is straightforward, though tedious. Two assumptions make it easier on us, without affecting the substance of the results:

1 In two behavioural functions we propose a linear relationship between a variable and the *logarithm* of some variable. The economic justification for this has been given in the text.

2 We let investment be exogenous, independent of the interest rate (which makes *IS* vertical). We thus focus on one transmission channel between the monetary sector (money market plus foreign exchange market) and the goods market only. Again, as the main text illustrates, this does not affect the qualitative results.

The goods market equilibrium condition serves as a point of departure:

$$Y = C + I + G + NX \tag{A7.1}$$

Letting $C = cY$, $I = 0$ and $NX = x_1 Y^{W} + x_2(e + p^{W} - p) - m_1 Y + m_2(e + p^{W} - p)$ and solving for Y yields

$$Y = \frac{x_2 + m_2}{1 - c + m_1}(e + p^{W} - p) + \frac{x_1}{1 - c + m_1} Y^{W} + \frac{1}{1 - c + m_1} G \tag{A7.2}$$

The *logarithm* of the real money demand $m - p$ (which equals supply at all times) depends on income and the interest rate

$$m - p = Y - hi \tag{A7.3}$$

Postulating semi-logarithmic relationships in equations (A7.2) and (A7.3) renders the benefit of keeping all equations encountered below additive.

Flexible exchange rates

Under flexible exchange rates the foreign exchange market equilibrium condition reads

$$i = i^{W} + \theta(\bar{e} - e) + \bar{\varepsilon}^{e} \tag{A7.4}$$

The last two terms describe expected depreciation. These comprise two terms. First, the exchange rate is expected to regress towards its equilibrium value (indicated here by a bar) according to $\theta(\bar{e} - e)$, as we had assumed previously. In an inflationary equilibrium we need to add a second term $\bar{\varepsilon}^{e}$. This ensures that even if the exchange rate is in equilibrium, investors expect the exchange rate to change if they expect the equilibrium exchange rate to depreciate.

Under flexible exchange rates, aggregate demand is determined by the intersection between *LM* and *FE*. Substituting equation (A7.4) into (A7.3) yields

$$m - p = Y - hi^{W} - h\theta\bar{e} + h\theta e - h\bar{\varepsilon}^{e} \tag{A7.5}$$

This equation still contains two endogenous variables, e and $\bar{e}$. To eliminate e, we solve equation (A7.2) for e to obtain

$$e = p - p^W + \frac{1 - c + m_1}{x_2 + m_2} Y - \frac{1}{x_2 + m_2} G - \frac{x_1}{x_2 + m_2} Y^W \tag{A7.6}$$

To obtain $\bar{e}$ we write the goods market equilibrium (A7.2) and the monetary sector equilibrium (*LM* plus *FE*), equation (A7.5), in terms of equilibrium values:

$$\bar{Y} = \frac{x_2 + m_2}{1 - c + m_1} (\bar{e} + p^W - \bar{p}) + \frac{x_1}{1 - c + m_1} Y^W + \frac{1}{1 - c + m_1} G \tag{A7.7}$$

$$m - \bar{p} = \bar{Y} - h(i^W + \bar{\varepsilon}^e) \tag{A7.8}$$

Substituting equation (A7.8) for $\bar{p}$ in (A7.7) and solving for $\bar{e}$ gives

$$\bar{e} = m - p^W - \left(1 - \frac{1 - c + m_1}{x_2 + m_2}\right)\bar{Y} + h(i^W + \bar{\varepsilon}^e) - \frac{x_1}{x_2 + m_2} Y^W - \frac{1}{x_2 + m_2} G \tag{A7.9}$$

Now substitute equations (A7.6) and (A7.9) for e and $\bar{e}$ in (A7.5) and solve for p to obtain the ***AD* curve under flexible exchange rates**

$$p = m - \frac{x_2 + m_2 + h\theta(1 - c + m_1)}{(1 + h\theta)(x_2 + m_2)} Y + h(i^W + \bar{\varepsilon}^e) + \frac{(1 - c - x_2 + m_1 - m_2)}{(1 + h\theta)(x_2 + m_2)} \bar{Y} \tag{A7.10}$$

Compare equation (A7.10) with (7.7). The influence of m, Y, and i^W is the same in both equations, denoting the first fraction in equation (A7.10) by b. The role of depreciation expectations differs slightly since ε^e is considered exogenous in the text, but endogenous in this appendix.

Fixed exchange rates

Under fixed exchange rates the demand-side equilibrium obtains directly from the goods market. The monetary sector simply follows what happens in the goods market.

Solving equation (A7.2) for prices yields the ***AD* curve under fixed exchange rates**

$$p = e + p^W - \frac{1 - c + m_1}{x_2 + m_2} Y + \frac{x_1}{x_2 + m_2} Y^W + \frac{1}{x_2 + m_2} G \tag{A7.11}$$

Compare equation (A7.11) to (7.8). The influence of e, p^W, Y, Y^W and b is the same, denoting the three fractions by b, γ and δ. The position variables of *FE*, i^W and ε^e do not show up here because we let *IS* be vertical.

To further explore this chapter's key messages you are encouraged to use the interactive online module found at

www.fgn.unisg.ch/eurmacro/tutor/ADAS.html

and many other features hosted at **www.fgn.unisg.ch/eurmacro**

CHAPTER 8

BOOMS AND RECESSIONS (IV)
DYNAMIC AGGREGATE SUPPLY AND DEMAND

WHAT TO EXPECT After working through this chapter, you will understand:

1 How to draw the **aggregate supply curve in inflation–income space.**

2 How to draw the **aggregate demand curve in inflation–income space.**

3 The concepts of **adaptive and rational expectations**, and how individuals choose to form expectations.

4 How to use the *DAD-SAS* **model** to trace how an economy moves in inflation–income space.

5 That the **policy options** offered by the *DAD-SAS* (and the *AD-AS*) model **depend on whether we have fixed or flexible exchange rates.**

6 That the economy's **responses** to monetary and fiscal policy **depend on how individuals form expectations.**

In Chapter 7 we assembled a complete macroeconomic model of the business cycle in which four markets interact and prices are endogenous. This is the model we were driving at from the beginning of this text. The form in which the aggregate demand–aggregate supply model is presented and handled graphically and algebraically has one major drawback, however: it does not permit a direct analysis of inflation. Of course, inflation is nothing but a steady increase in prices. So when we analyze prices we implicitly analyze inflation as well. From a practical viewpoint, however, it would be desirable to make inflation more explicit. After all, real-world economies rarely feature full price stability, as the long-run equilibrium in the *AD-AS* diagram would imply. In fact, only a minority of economists would even recommend striving for complete price stability. Monetary policy discussions these days centre on whether central banks should aim at an inflation target, not at a price level target, and if they should, whether the inflation target should be 2, 3 or 4%. When monetary policy becomes restrictive, the inflation rate falls, but rarely the level of prices. Disinflation, a reduction of the inflation rate, is something completely different from deflation, a reduction of the price level.

For the reasons stated, this chapter recasts the *AD-AS* model in a form that permits its graphical analysis in an inflation–income diagram. We will call this the *DAD-SAS* model, though it should be emphasized, however, that the *DAD-SAS* model is not really a new model, but simply the *AD-AS* model in new, more practical clothing.

A second main theme of this chapter is the formation of expectations. While expected prices already played a role in Chapter 7's *AD-AS* model, we were content with a rather elementary treatment. In this chapter we look at expectations formation in much more detail, discussing the whole spectrum of possibilities from adaptive via rational expectations to perfect foresight.

Equipped with a refined understanding of expectations we take a second look at fiscal and monetary policy. The key insight will be that what policy-makers can achieve depends crucially on the way the public forms expectations.

8.1 THE AGGREGATE-SUPPLY CURVE IN AN INFLATION–INCOME DIAGRAM

In Chapter 7 we drew the *AS* curve in a diagram with the (logarithm of the) price level on the vertical axis, as a straight line. The underlying formula is

$$p = p^e + \lambda(Y - Y^*) \qquad \textit{AS}\ \textbf{curve} \qquad (8.1)$$

To obtain a formulation that can be drawn in an inflation-income diagram is no magic. Simply subtract (the logarithm of) last period's price level p_{-1} from both sides of (8.1) to obtain $p - p_{-1} = p^e - p_{-1} + \lambda(Y - Y^*)$. The difference $p - p_{-1}$ is the change in the logarithm of the price level. This approximates the percentage rate of change of the price level (see appendix to Chapter 1), which is the rate of *inflation* π. The other difference $p^e - p_{-1}$ is expected inflation π^e. So we may rewrite equation (8.1) as

$$\pi = \pi^e + \lambda(Y - Y^*) \qquad \textit{SAS}\ \textbf{curve} \qquad (8.2)$$

This is simply a new way of writing the aggregate supply curve. Written like this, it states that the level of output firms are willing to supply depends on normal output Y^* and on unexpected or surprise inflation. We call this curve the *SAS* curve, where the first *S* stands for *surprise*.

The **SAS curve** indicates the aggregate output that firms are willing to produce at different inflation rates.

Of course, equations (8.1) and (8.2) state the same thing. Equation (8.2) is more convenient to work with in an inflationary environment and yields a

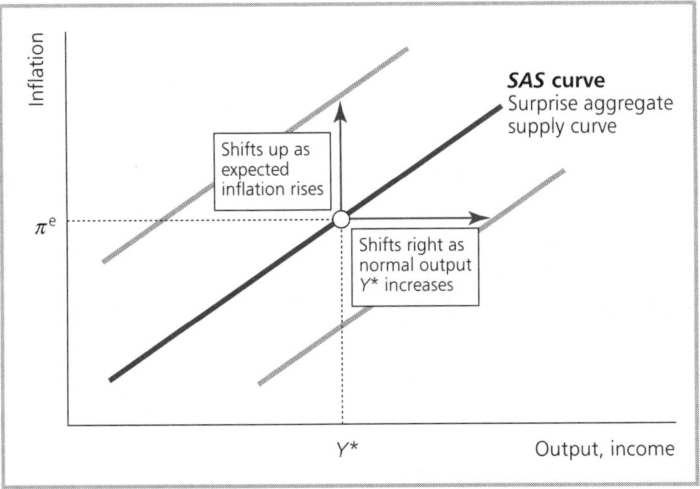

Figure 8.1 The *SAS* curve has a positive slope. If inflation is as expected, potential output Y^* is produced. If inflation is higher than expected, real wages are too low and firms hire more labour and produce more than normal. The *SAS* curve shifts up as π^e rises and moves to the right as Y^* increases.

basis for viewing aggregate supply in an inflation–income diagram (see Figure 8.1). This positively sloped *SAS* curve shows what firms are willing to produce at different inflation rates. They will do so only if demand is there. Therefore, as in the context of last chapter's *AD-AS* model, the supply side represented by the *SAS* curve must be augmented by information about the demand side.

8.2 EQUILIBRIUM INCOME AND INFLATION: THE *DAD* CURVE

It would be nice to have the aggregate demand curve in a form that permits us to draw demand-side equilibria in the same diagram as the *SAS* curve. To obtain such a representation in inflation–income space, recall that in Chapter 7 we found the *AD* curve to read

$$p = m - bY + h(i^W + \varepsilon^e) \qquad \textbf{\textit{AD} curve, flexible exchange rates} \qquad (8.3)$$

under flexible exchange rates and

$$p = e + p^W - bY + \gamma Y^W + \delta G - f(i^W + \varepsilon^e) \qquad \textbf{\textit{AD} curve, fixed exchange rates} \qquad (8.4)$$

in a system of fixed exchange rates.

Looking at flexible exchange rates first, we can derive a dynamic representation of the aggregate-demand curve for inflation–income space, a ***DAD* curve**, by manipulating equation (8.3). Copying what we did in section 8.1 when we rewrote the *AS* curve, take first differences on both sides of equation (8.3) (which means that we deduct last period's values), remembering $\pi = p - p_{-1}$ and defining the money growth rate $\mu = m - m_{-1}$, to obtain:

$$\pi = \mu - bY + bY_{-1} + h(\Delta i^W + \Delta\varepsilon^e) \qquad \textbf{\textit{DAD} curve, flexible exchange rates} \qquad (8.5)$$

Note. The appendix p. 216 derives very much the same *DAD* curve with more plausible *endogenous* depreciation expectations. Considering $\Delta\varepsilon^e$ exogenous in the main text's graphical discussion provides a handle for analyzing the role of **market psychology**, that is, what happens if investors lose confidence in a currency for no obvious reason.

Among the last two factors in this equation, the presence of Δi^W takes care of the dependence on the world economy. The presence of $\Delta\varepsilon^e$, which we treat as an exogenous variable here, may reflect the impact of **market psychology**.

Why does money growth μ enter with a coefficient of exactly 1? Recall from previous discussions of the Mundell–Fleming model that when all factors affecting equilibrium remain constant, income does not change. One factor that needs to remain constant under flexible exchange rates is the real money supply. So if all other factors remain unchanged as well ($\Delta i^W = \Delta\varepsilon^e = 0$), nominal money needs to grow at the rate of inflation in order to keep real money constant and to keep income where it was one period ago ($Y = Y_{-1}$).

Under fixed exchange rates with occasional realignments the **expected devaluation** is the probability of a realignment times the expected size of the realignment. Example: $\varepsilon^e = 0.2 \times 10 = 2$. If the probability of a 10% realignment rises from 0.2 to 0.5, the expected devaluation becomes 5 (%). Hence devaluation expectations have changed by $\Delta\varepsilon^e = 5 - 2 = 3$.

Under fixed exchange rates with possible devaluations the *DAD* curve is derived by taking first differences on both sides of equation (8.4):

$$\pi = \varepsilon + \pi^W - bY + bY_{-1} + \gamma\Delta Y^W + \delta\Delta G - f(\Delta i^W + \Delta\varepsilon^e) \qquad \textbf{\textit{DAD} curve, fixed exchange rates} \qquad (8.6)$$

Here the rates of devaluation and world inflation enter with a coefficient of 1.

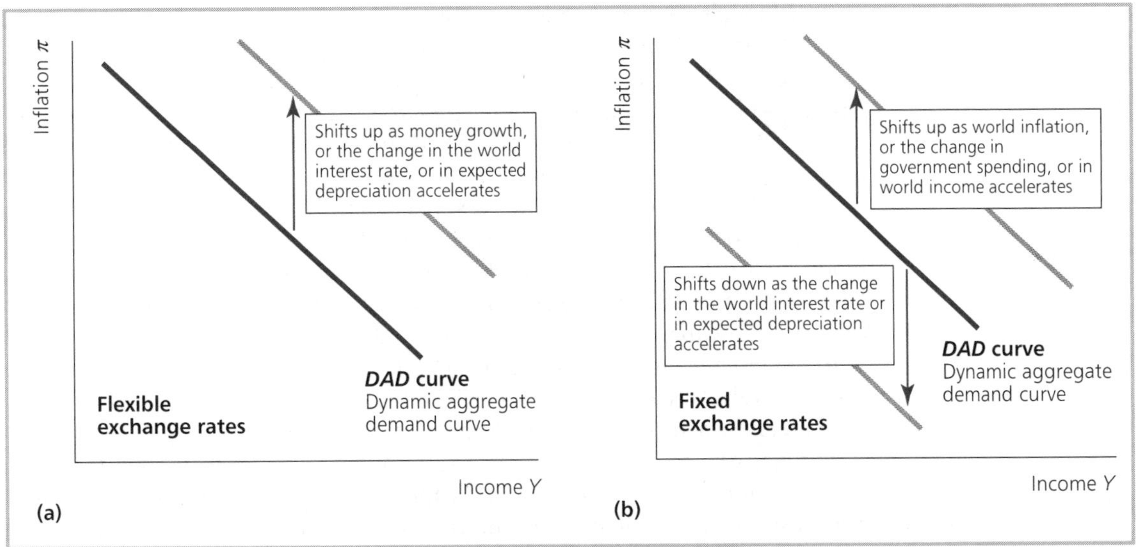

Figure 8.2 The *DAD* curve has a negative slope. As we move down *DAD* the real exchange rate rises, and so does aggregate demand. Panel (a) demonstrates that under flexible exchange rates the position of *DAD* is mainly determined by money growth, μ, but also by changes in the world interest rate and changes in expected depreciation. The curve moves up as any of those factors increases. Panel (b) shows that under fixed exchange rates the position of *DAD* is mainly determined by world inflation π^W, but also by changes in world income, government spending, the world interest rate, and expected devaluation. As any of those factors increases, *DAD* moves. It moves up with the first three factors and down with the last two.

The reason is that for unchanged other factors (that is $\Delta Y^W = \Delta G = \Delta i^W = \Delta\varepsilon^e = 0$) the real exchange rate must remain constant to keep (demand-side) equilibrium income where it was last period. The real exchange rate EP^W/P remains unchanged if domestic inflation equals the sum of devaluation and world inflation. Our knowledge of the *DAD* curve is summarized in Figure 8.2.

8.3 THE *DAD-SAS* MODEL

Our macroeconomic model is now complete. It boils down to two equations, or curves, which can be analyzed in a simple π-Y diagram. The equations comprising the *DAD-SAS* model under flexible exchange rates read

$$\pi = \mu - bY + bY_{-1} + h(\Delta i^w + \Delta\varepsilon^e) \qquad \textit{DAD}\text{ curve, flexible exchange rates}$$

$$\pi = \pi^e + \lambda(Y - Y^*) \qquad \textit{SAS}\text{ curve}$$

The *DAD-SAS* model under fully fixed exchange rates ($\varepsilon = \Delta\varepsilon^e = 0$) reads

$$\pi = \pi^W - bY + bY_{-1} + \delta\Delta G + \gamma\Delta Y^W - f\Delta i^W \qquad \textit{DAD}\text{ curve, fixed exchange rates}$$

$$\pi = \pi^e + \lambda(Y - Y^*) \qquad \textit{SAS}\text{ curve}$$

Do not let the unpretentious elegance of this model deceive you. The *DAD* curve is nothing but a new way of stating the insights obtained during our discussions of the Mundell–Fleming model. If we want to know what is going on behind the curve, say in the money market or the balance of payments, we must go back to the Mundell–Fleming model and its constituent markets. But note again: the Mundell–Fleming model and the *DAD* curve are merely two different ways of stating the same thing. Therefore, the Mundell–Fleming model and the *DAD* curve (taken alone) cannot give different answers to the same question.

The *SAS* curve combines, and to some extent hides, all the insights already gained or to be gained in our discussions of the economy's supply side: the labour market (in Chapter 6), the capital stock and economic growth (in Chapters 9 and 10). The curve says that firms are ready to supply output in excess of full-capacity or potential output only if inflation turns out to be higher than anticipated. In the absence of unanticipated inflation, output rests at its normal level Y^*. We treat Y^* as a fixed number during graphical discussions of the model. In reality, as will be discussed in Chapter 9, potential output grows over time, due to improvements in technology, a growing labour force and accumulation of human and physical capital. Potential output also goes hand in hand with unemployment, a substantial part of which may be involuntary.

With these important reminders we now proceed to analyze how the economy's supply and demand sides interact.

Equilibrium in the *DAD-SAS* model

The *DAD-SAS* model is dynamic. It describes the development of income, inflation and (behind a veil) the interest rate, the exchange rate and the composition of aggregate demand over time. Two factors make the model inherently dynamic. First, the *DAD* curve moves over time as income changes, since its position is endogenously determined by last period's income. Second, the position of *SAS* depends on expected inflation. Inflation expectations may be wrong, may change over time in response to actual inflation, and hence shift the position of the *SAS* curve. Before we trace the dynamic interaction between the economy's demand and supply sides in subsequent sections, we pause here to identify long-run results – the equilibrium.

Note. In Chapter 7 we called the vertical line denoted by $Y = Y^*$ the long-run aggregate supply curve (*LAS*), because under adaptive inflation expectations adjustment towards it takes time. We now switch terminology, calling $Y = Y^*$ the equilibrium aggregate supply curve (*EAS*). This is more general and accomodates the situation when under other inflation expectations schemes, analyzed below, adjustment is immediate.

In the **long run**, or **in equilibrium** if you like, all adjustment processes have petered out and individuals make no more mistakes. In the context of our model, this means that individuals anticipate the rate of inflation correctly. If this is the case, we may substitute $\pi = \pi^e$ into the *SAS* curve equation to obtain the equilibrium aggregate supply (*EAS*) curve

$$Y = Y^* \qquad \textit{EAS} \text{ curve}$$

Thus, in equilibrium, the aggregate supply curve is simply a vertical line through normal output Y^* (just as the vertical classical *AS* curve) (see Figure 8.3), a fact we already know and that applies independently of the current exchange rate regime.

This has a straightforward implication for the equilibrium aggregate demand curve. Since, in equilibrium, aggregate supply cannot change, we may let $Y - Y_{-1} = 0$ in the *DAD* curve. Under *flexible exchange rates* we thus obtain the equilibrium aggregate demand (*EAD*) curve (letting $\Delta i^W = \Delta \varepsilon^e = 0$)

$$\pi = \mu \qquad \textit{EAD} \text{ curve, flexible exchange rates}$$

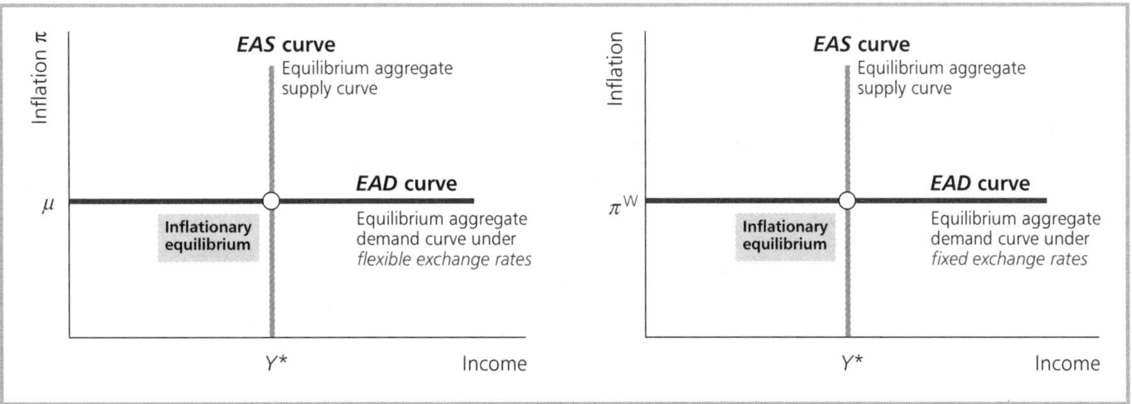

Figure 8.3 In equilibrium the labour market clears and income remains at Y^*, no matter where inflation is. So *EAS* is vertical. For the demand-side equilibrium (as given by the *AD* curve) to remain unchanged, the real money supply must stay constant under flexible exchange rates (hence $\pi = \mu$ in panel (a)), or the real exchange rate must remain the same under fixed exchange rates (hence $\pi = \pi^W$ in panel (b)).

This *EAD* is a horizontal line where inflation equals the money supply growth rate. The intersection between *EAD* and *EAS* determines the inflationary equilibrium in which money growth determines inflation and output is at Y^*.

Under *fixed exchange rates* (letting $\Delta G = \Delta Y^W = \Delta i^W = 0$) the *EAD* curve turns out to be

$$\pi = \pi^W$$

EAD **curve**
fixed exchange rates

Thus, equilibrium inflation is given by world inflation. Next we would like to learn how to analyze the consequences of *permanent shocks*, which define a new equilibrium, and *transitory shocks*, which displace the economy from equilibrium. Let us begin by going through the mechanics of how to determine the positions of *DAD* and *SAS* curves at specific points in time.

How to draw and trace *DAD* and *SAS* curves

To position the *SAS* or *DAD* curve, all we need to do is identify one point on the curve and then draw the curve with a positive or negative slope, respectively, right through it.

- *Positioning SAS*. We know from equation (8.2) that if inflation were exactly as expected ($\pi = \pi^e$), output would be at its normal level ($Y = Y^*$). Therefore *mark expected inflation on the vertical axis. Then go horizontally to the right until you hit the vertical line over* Y^*. This is a point on the current *SAS* curve! Now simply draw the curve with positive slope through this point.
- *Positioning DAD*. Under flexible exchange rates, if income remained where it was last period, inflation would equal the growth rate of the money supply (since $\pi - \mu = -b(Y - Y_{-1})$). Under fixed exchange rates, if income remained where it was last period, inflation would equal world inflation (since $\pi - \pi^W = -b(Y - Y_{-1})$, holding the other factors constant). Therefore *mark last period's income on the horizontal axis. Move vertically up until you hit either the horizontal line (*EAD *curve) at the money growth rate*

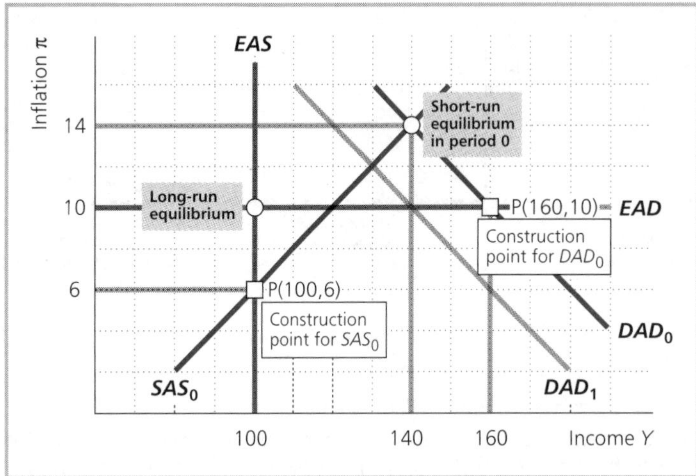

Figure 8.4 To position SAS_0: inflation expectations are 6; if inflation was also 6 (hypothetically!), income would be equal to potential income, which is 100. To position DAD_0: last period's income is 160; for income to remain there, inflation would have to equal money growth, which is 10. Actual inflation and income are obtained where DAD_0 and SAS_0 intersect.

when exchange rates are flexible, or the horizontal line at world inflation plus devaluation when exchange rates are fixed. This gives you a point on the current *DAD* curve! Draw the curve through this point.

Since this may sound a bit abstract, consider the following numerical flexible exchange rates example (see Figure 8.4). Let $Y^* = 100$, $\mu = 10\%$, $\pi^e = 6\%$, $Y_{-1} = 160$, and suppose $\lambda = b = 0.2$. To determine *SAS*, move up to a value of 6 on the vertical axis. Then move horizontally to the right to the vertical line at $Y^* = 100$. The point P(100, 6) pins down the current-period *SAS* curve at SAS_0. To determine *DAD*, start at 160 on the horizontal axis. Move straight up to the horizontal line at $\mu = 10$. The point P(160, 10) pins down the current-period *DAD* curve at DAD_0.

Note that P(100, 6) and P(160, 10) are just easily determined points that help locate DAD_0 and SAS_0. The actual macroeconomic outcome is determined by the point of intersection of the two curves. It turns out to be at P(140, 14).

It is this outcome that triggers the dynamics to move both curves into new positions next period. The position of DAD_1 is now determined by the fact that income during the preceding period had fallen to 140. Thus, the *DAD* curve moves down to the left. The position of SAS_1 is determined by new inflation expectations. Since period 0's inflation stood at 14% while only 6% had been expected, it is likely that inflation expectations will have been revised upwards. This moves the *SAS* curve up. But how far? There is no way of telling unless we know precisely how inflation expectations are being formed and revised. It is time to address this topic.

8.4 INFLATION EXPECTATIONS

Expectations play a pivotal role in economics. Besides our current concern with inflation expectations, recall previous discussions of whether consumers and investors expect income to change permanently or not. This issue crucially affected the multiplier derived in the Keynesian cross in Chapter 2, and continues to determine by how much the *DAD* curve shifts. Also recall the discussion of expected depreciation in the context of transition dynamics in the

Mundell–Fleming model in Chapter 5 and, of course, the role of expected prices in Chapters 6 and 7.

In stark contrast to the fact that almost everything in economics depends on expectations, no simple, easy-to-use hypothesis is accepted of how individuals form expectations. We will discuss why, and show what the consequences are in the *DAD-SAS* model.

Adaptive expectations are being formed on the basis of what the variable actually did in the past. Adaptive inflation expectations are driven by the equation $\pi^e = \pi^e_{-1} + a(\pi_{-1} - \pi^e_{-1})$. How quickly expectations adapt to actual inflation is measured by the adjustment coefficient a.

A seasoned workhorse in economics is the assumption of **adaptive expectations**. The general idea is that if previous expectations were wrong, individuals move them closer to what actually happened.

Adaptive expectations have one big advantage: they are simple and easy to compute. Their simplest form (letting $a = 1$ in the margin note) is

$$\pi^e = \pi_{-1}$$

which, in many situations will give you a reasonable first shot. What will be tomorrow's weather? The same as today's. Who will be the world's best golfer one year from now? The same guy who holds this title now. What will be Europe's best-selling car next year? The same as this year. Panel (a) in Figure 8.5 generalizes these examples. It illustrates that whenever we are dealing with a variable that changes infrequently, adaptive expectations do a reasonable job and lead to low average forecast errors. As well as being simple, adaptive expectations can also be quite accurate if the variable to be forecast does not change very often or only in small steps. Panel (b) shows a variable that changes more often, i.e. every period. In this case adaptive expectations constantly lag behind and forecast errors are sizeable on average.

The stylized patterns given in Figure 8.5 are also encountered in real-world macroeconomic time series. Figure 8.6 shows inflation rates in Germany between 1959 and 1968 (panel a) and in the United Kingdom between 1966 and 1975 (panel b). Adaptive expectations would have performed quite satisfactorily during the time span picked for Germany, with an average absolute forecast error of only 0.7 percentage points. Performance during the UK episode would have been comparatively poor, with an average forecast error of more than 3 percentage points.

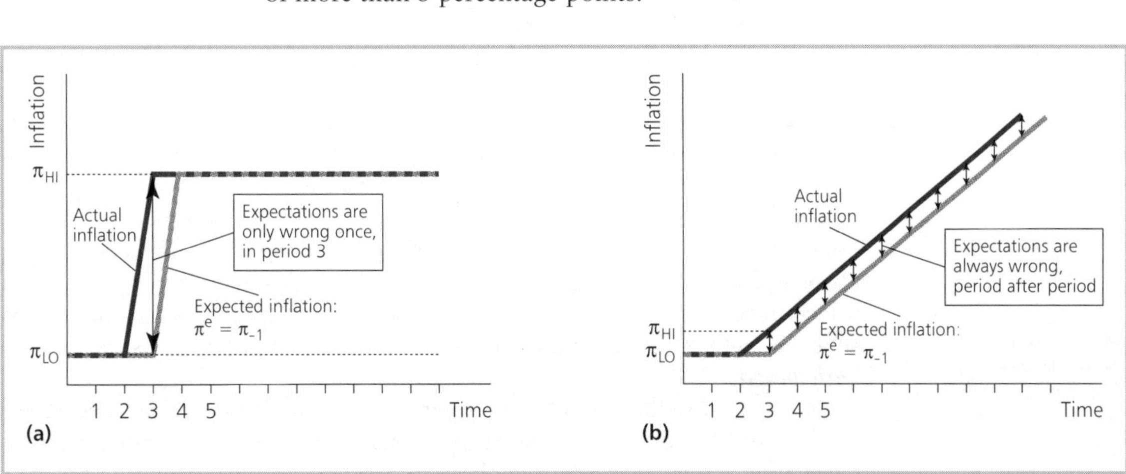

Figure 8.5 Adaptive expectations (here $\pi^e = \pi_{-1}$) perform well if inflation changes infrequently (panel (a)). If inflation changes constantly, such expectations would prove erroneous period after period (panel (b)).

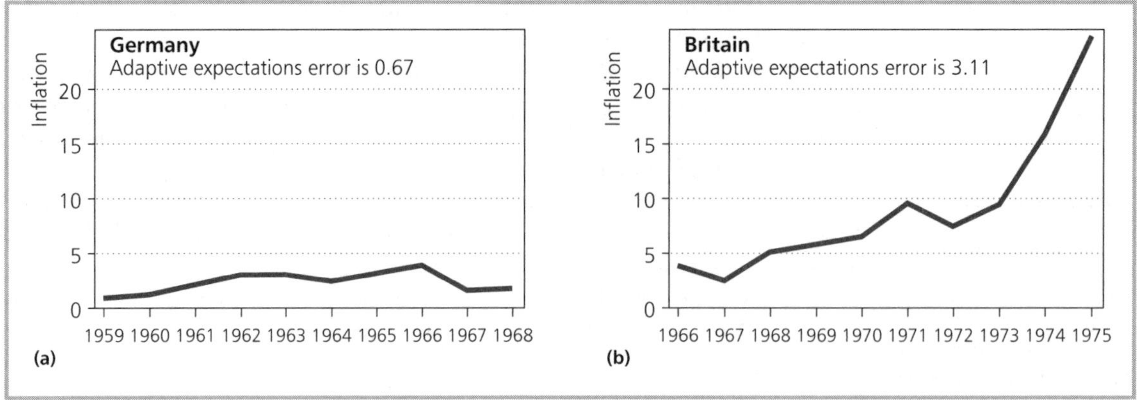

Figure 8.6 Large changes in German inflation were infrequent between 1959 and 1968. Adaptive expectations ($\pi^e = \pi_{-1}$) worked well, missing actual inflation by only 0.67 percentage points on average. Britain experienced constantly changing inflation rates from 1966 to 1975. Adaptive expectations would have been wrong by more than three percentage points on average.
Source: IMF, *IFS*.

Rational expectations draw on all available information. This may include a wide set of other variables, or even knowledge of a macroeconomic model such as *DAD-SAS*.

If adaptive expectations perform poorly *and* if errors are costly, individuals will look for ways to improve forecasts. In this attempt they process all information that is available to them. Such expectations have been coined **rational expectations**.

The crucial question in the context of rational expectations is: what information is available? An established benchmark case in macroeconomics is to assume that individuals know just as much as the economists who built the model, namely the model itself. For instance, if we want to determine rational inflation expectations in the context of the *DAD-SAS* model, as we shall do shortly, we must assume that individuals *know* how this model relates inflation to other endogenous and exogenous variables.

To give a simpler example, assume that our model stated that inflation always equals last period's money growth rate, $\pi = \mu_{-1}$. Rational expectations make use of this knowledge and expect inflation to follow money growth with a one-period lag: $\pi^e = \mu_{-1}$. All that individuals need to do is observe money growth and transform it into a perfect forecast.

This recipe does not work, however, if the variable to be forecast is related to other variables that are also not yet known, say $\pi = \mu$. Then the task of forecasting inflation simply becomes the task of forecasting money growth. But conventional macroeconomic models do not explain policy changes. Policy changes usually come as surprises even for individuals who form rational expectations. If even policy changes are foreseen, we will speak of **perfect foresight**, implying that there is no uncertainty left, no surprises possible. Perfect forsight permits us to trace the effects of policy measures that are *anticipated*.

Perfect foresight is never wrong. It assumes that individuals know and foresee everything, taking the concept of rational expectations to the extreme.

Rational expectations are an important benchmark case. But the label's implication that all other expectations formation schemes are not rational is misleading. As has been stressed above, other expectations formation schemes, such as adaptive expectations, have the advantage of being simpler and cheaper – cheaper in terms of the time and attention that we need to pay to the issue, and in terms of other resources. A rational individual weighs the costs that she needs to incur in order to improve expectations performance against the benefits expected to accrue. The result is **economically rational expectations**. What these are may vary over time and space, from market to market. In some cases economically rational expectations may indeed be *rational* or *perfect foresight* in the above narrow sense, but often they may be adaptive in a rather crude way. To cover the entire spectrum we shall analyze policy measures under all three expectations formation schemes introduced here.

Economically rational expectations suppose that individuals collect information and increase the sophistication of their forecasts only to the point where the costs begin to exceed the expected benefits.

8.5 THE *DAD-SAS* MODEL AT WORK

We are finally in a position to put the *DAD-SAS* model to work. This section looks at monetary policy to show the effects of a permanent change in the context of the model, and at fiscal policy, which is used to represent a transitory change.

Monetary policy

Since we want to focus on the role of money growth, all other exogenous factors previously found to affect the position of the *DAD* curve are assumed to remain constant. This is tantamount to letting their first differences be zero, and yields a compact representation of the *DAD-SAS* model:

$$\pi = \mu - bY + bY_{-1} \qquad \textit{DAD}\text{ curve (flexible exchange rates)}$$

$$\pi = \pi^e + \lambda(Y - Y^*) \qquad \textit{SAS}\text{ curve}$$

The permanent policy change considered here is an increase of the money growth rate from μ_{LO} to μ_{HI}. The economy's response to this change depends critically on how individuals form inflation expectations.

Adaptive expectations

In Figure 8.7, let the economy be in the inflationary equilibrium point at μ_{LO} and Y^*. In period 1 the central bank raises the growth rate of the nominal money supply to μ_{HI}. As money grows faster than prices, the real money supply increases, shifting the original *DAD* curve to the right into DAD_1. To pin down the position of DAD_1, follow the method given above: hypothetically, if inflation rose to μ_{HI} simultaneously with money growth, the real money supply would not change, and demand-side equilibrium income could remain at Y^*. Hence the *DAD* curve shifts up by $\Delta\mu = \mu_{HI} - \mu_{LO}$.

Inflation does not follow money growth instantaneously. Nominal wages for period 1 were set before we entered period 1, based on adaptively formed inflation expectations $\pi_1^e = \pi_0$. SAS_0 tells how firms respond to a perceived increase in demand, given the current nominal wage. Any perceived demand increase makes firms move up SAS_0, raising both prices and output. Equilibrium in period 1 is given at π_1 and Y_1, the point of intersection between DAD_1 and SAS_0 (which also happens to be SAS_1).

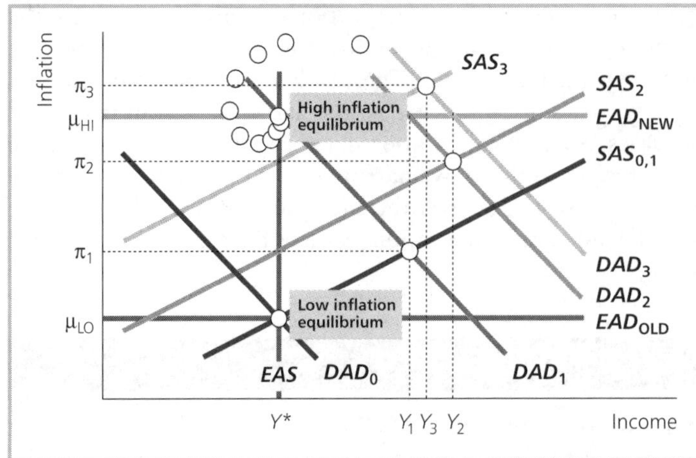

Figure 8.7 The economy is in a low inflation equilibrium with DAD_0 and SAS_0. An unexpected increase in money growth to μ_{HI} shifts *DAD* into DAD_1, raising income along SAS_1 to Y_1 and inflation to π_1. This process continues along a path sketched by white circles until the economy settles into the high inflation equilibrium at $\pi = \mu_{HI}$ and $Y = Y^*$.

Now labour market participants revise plans. They expect inflation to be at π_1 in period 2, raising the nominal wage by that rate. This moves the aggregate supply curve to SAS_2. The *DAD* curve does not remain in its period-1 position either. If the real money supply remained unchanged, income could remain at Y_1. This moves the curve into position DAD_2. Equilibrium in period 2 is at inflation π_2 and income Y_2.

The development in periods 3, 4, 5 and so on, can be tracked in a similar fashion. Figure 8.7 doesn't show demand and supply curves beyond period 3 as the graph is crowded enough already. The details of the later phase of the adjustment process should not be overemphasized. They are sensitive to specific parameter constellations and are quantitatively unimportant. There is a general lesson, however, that we should keep in mind: if inflation expectations adjust slowly, a permanent increase in money growth raises income for some time above its normal level. As inflation catches up with money growth, and temporarily exceeds it, income eases back towards its normal level.

This result also applies if reasons other than the adaptive formation of inflation expectations prevent nominal wages or prices from adjusting quickly. These may be adjustment costs or uncertainty about the nature of an observed increase in demand.

DAD-SAS and Mundell–Fleming: a look behind the scene

Let us pause to look at what is going on beneath the surface of the *DAD-SAS* model as displayed in the π-Y diagram. The purpose of this interlude is to emphasize that whatever happens in the *DAD-SAS* model can be traced back to the Mundell–Fleming model, and vice versa. We look at the immediate response to an increase in money growth first, which moves the economy up along SAS_1.

The short-run response in *DAD-SAS* and *IS-LM-FE* representation In Figure 8.8 the economy is in equilibrium at point A. The upper panel shows this in the *DAD-SAS* model. The lower panel depicts it in the Mundell–Fleming model.

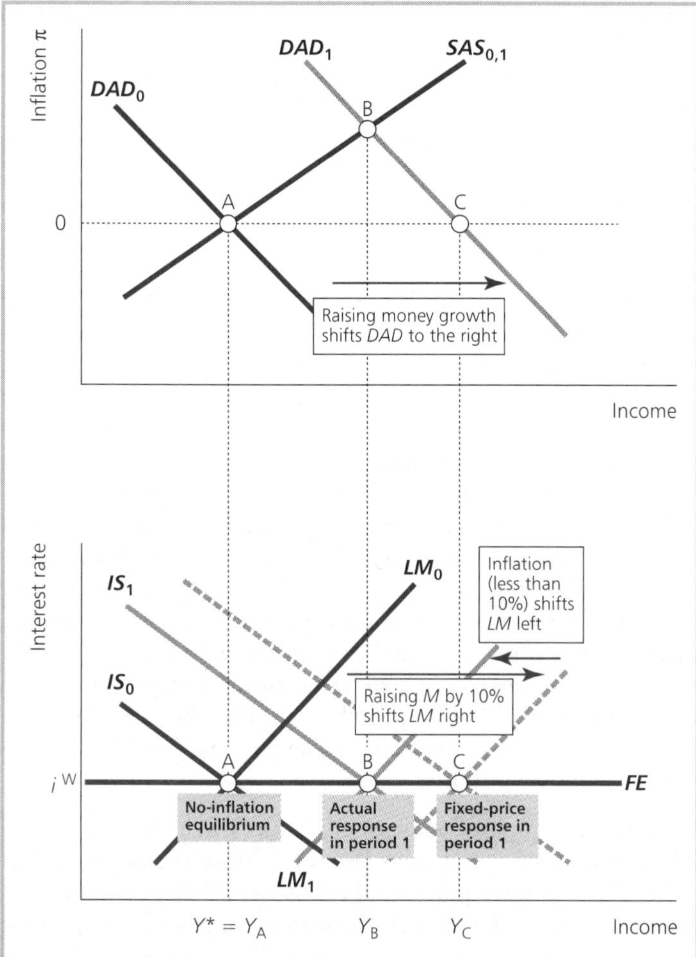

Figure 8.8 (Flexible exchange rates.) An acceleration of money growth shifts *DAD* to the right. In the Mundell–Fleming model this shifts *LM* and, through endogenous depreciation, *IS* to the right into the blue broken positions. Since insufficient supply at the old price level triggers inflation, the economy moves from C to B along DAD_1 in the upper panel. In the lower panel the rising price level reduces the real money supply and the real exchange rate. *LM* and *IS* move back into the solid light blue position. Income has increased from Y^* to Y_B, and not to Y_C as it would have if the *SAS* curve was horizontal.

For convenience, suppose the initial equilibrium is non-inflationary, that is $\pi_0 = \mu_0 = 0$. In period 1 the money supply growth rate increases from 0 to 10%, so that the *nominal* money supply rises by 10%. In the Mundell–Fleming model, where prices are considered fixed, the *real* money supply also increases by 10%. This shifts *LM* to the right into the broken blue position. If the price level really did not respond, the exchange rate would depreciate just enough to shift *IS* right into the broken blue position, raising income to Y_C. In the upper panel, income would also have risen to Y_C if inflation had stayed at 0. However, this would have required the *SAS* curve to be horizontal.

Now *SAS* is not horizontal, but positively sloped. This means that the labour market is not prepared to supply output Y_C at unchanged prices. Only as prices rise (or inflation goes up) and real wages fall, will output increase along SAS_1. Given DAD_1, period 1 equilibrium in the upper panel is at B. How does this translate into the lower panel? Well, the increase of inflation from 0 to π_1 nibbles away at the real money supply increase. As a result, *LM* shifts back left into the light blue position, bringing the economy to point B. At the same time, inflation reduces the real exchange rate, shifting *IS* back left into the light blue position.

So, after taking into account the price changes required to bring aggregate supply up to meet aggregate demand, the Mundell–Fleming model gives the same income response to the money supply increase as the *DAD-SAS* model. The drawback of the Mundell–Fleming model is that it does not tell us what price changes do indeed occur as we move from one equilibrium to another.

The long-run response in *DAD-SAS* and *IS-LM-FE* representation Let us now look at how the *long-run adjustment* from A to A′ is reflected in the Mundell–Fleming diagram. First, note some properties of A′. In the new equilibrium, the movements of *LM* and *IS* that occurred during the transition from A to A′ have ended. So the real money supply, which determines the position of *LM*, remains constant, meaning that money and prices grow at the same rates: $\pi = \mu$. The real exchange rate, which determines the position of *IS*, must be constant as well, meaning that depreciation equals inflation (supposing world inflation is 0): $\varepsilon = \pi$. So π, μ and ε are all 10%. If our currency depreciates by 10% period after period, the market sooner or later expects this. Financial investors are then only prepared to hold domestic bonds if these carry interest rates 10% higher than the world interest rate – as compensation for the anticipated loss in value through depreciation. So the new position of *FE* is at $i^{W} + 10$, which identifies the new long-run equilibrium A′ in the lower panel of Figure 8.9. The fact that both *LM* and *IS* pass through A′ offers two new insights:

1 Since *LM* has shifted up compared with where it was when the equilibrium was A, the real money supply has fallen. Do not confuse this with the fact that once we are at A′, inflation equals money growth and M/P remains constant. During the *transition* from A to A′ the sum of all price changes must have been larger than the sum of all changes in the money supply. The resulting reduction of the real money supply is needed, since individuals want to hold less (real) money when interest rates are at 10% (as at A′) than at interest rates of 0% (that applied at A).

2 It is tempting, but wrong, to think that for similar reasons the real exchange rate must have depreciated to shift *IS* out and make it go through A′. To see why this is wrong, we now need to stress the distinction between the nominal interest rate i and the real interest rate $r \equiv i - \pi$ that results after we deduct inflation from the nominal interest rate. This distinction was not important in earlier chapters in which the price level was considered fixed. There i was both the nominal and the real interest rate. Now, with inflation brought into the picture, we need to recognize that the interest rate that determines investment decisions of firms is the real interest rate.

The **real interest rate** is the nominal interest rate (as observed in the market) minus the inflation rate. It deducts from nominal interest payments the purchasing power lost due to price increases.

Suppose a bank lends £100 for one year to a firm that wants to invest. At a 5% interest rate the bank will have £105 at the end of the year. If prices have remained the same, the purchasing power of the £100 lent out has increased by 5%. Therefore, the real return, or the **real interest rate**, is 5%. Now assume that same scenario, except that prices rose by 5%. Then the £105 which the bank has at the end of the year only buys what the £100 would have bought

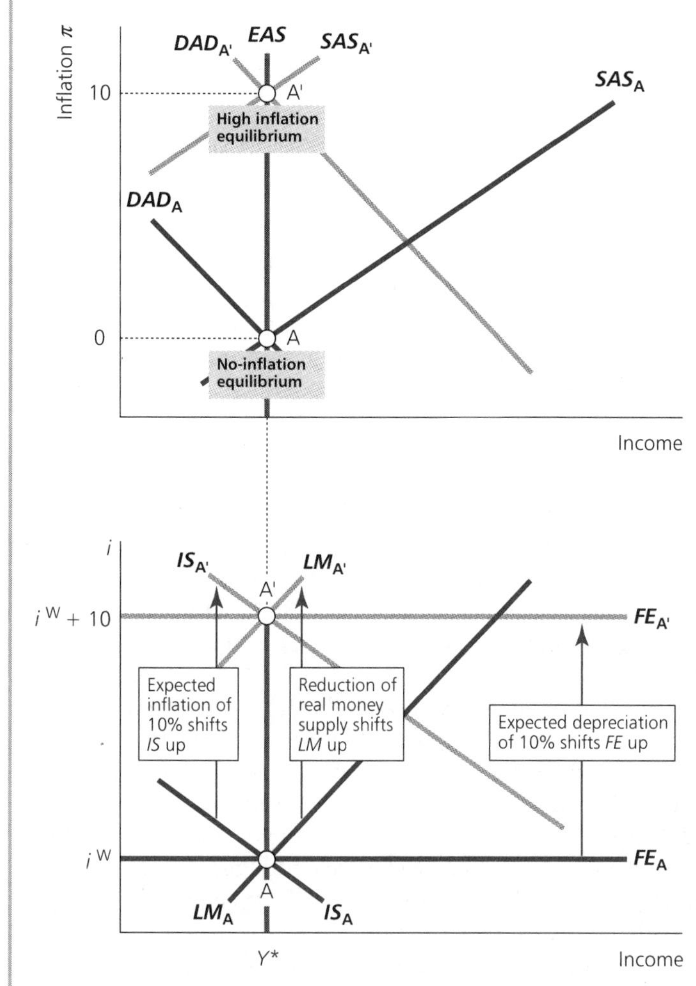

Figure 8.9 (Flexible exchange rates.) After inflation has adjusted, *DAD* and *SAS* are in the light blue positions and the economy has moved from A to A' (upper panel). Inflation is at 10% permanently, and ε also is 10%. In equilibrium this depreciation must be expected. This shifts the *FE* curve up by ten percentage points in the lower panel. The intersection between this new *FE* line and the vertical line over potential income marks A'. To shift *LM* up to pass through A', the real money supply must have fallen. *IS* shifts up because it must go up by ten percentage points to keep the real interest rate unchanged.

Maths note. Repeating the derivation of the *IS* curve in Chapter 5 with the new investment function $I = \bar{I} - b(i - \pi)$ gives the new *IS* curve for an inflationary environment

$$i = \pi - \frac{1 - c + m_1}{b}Y + \frac{x_2 + m_2}{b}R + \frac{\bar{I} + G + x_1 Y^W}{b}.$$

Since $di/d\pi = 1$, a one percentage point rise in π shifts *IS* up by 1 percentage point.

at the beginning of the year. Everything costs 5% more. The bank has not received any real compensation for lending the money. The real interest rate is 0. To receive the same real compensation that the bank received when there was no inflation, the nominal interest rate would have to be 10%. Then the real interest rate would be $r = 10\% - 5\% = 5\%$. With the same argument, the firm that borrows the money also knows that, in the face of inflation, the pounds it gives back to repay the loan will be worth less than the pounds it received. Thus, what is relevant for firms deciding how much to borrow and which investment projects to undertake is the real interest rate which takes account of inflation.

Rewriting the investment schedules as $I = \bar{I} - b(i - \pi)$, the *IS* curve shifts up one by one if inflation goes up. The increase of inflation from 0 to 10% shifts the *IS* curve up into A′, since the nominal interest rate needs to be 10 percentage points higher to make firms undertake the same level of investment as at A. No change in the real exchange rate is needed.

The **Fisher equation** (named after the American economist Irving Fisher, 1867–1947) says that interest rates change if either the real interest rate or inflation changes. The implication that a one percentage point increase in inflation raises the nominal interest rate by one percentage point is called the **Fisher effect**.

The decomposition of the nominal interest rate into the real interest rate and inflation is known as the **Fisher equation**. Augmented with the assumption of an approximately constant normal real interest rate $\bar{r}$, it constitutes a theory of the behaviour of nominal interest rates:

$$i = \bar{r} + \pi \qquad \textbf{Fisher equation} \qquad (8.7)$$

Keep in mind, however, that this version of the Fisher equation only holds in equilibrium, on *EAS*. During booms the interest rate falls below what equation (8.7) says; during recessions it rises above what equation (8.7) says. The key reason for this is that firms and banks do not know inflation when they agree on the interest rate for a loan, but need to base decisions on inflation *expectations*. Equation (8.7) does not qualify as a short-run relationship because inflation may differ from expected inflation, and because income may be above or below normal levels for a while.

Rational expectations

Under rational expectations individuals look beyond the history of the variable they want to forecast. Assume here that they know just as much as we know by now. Once they observe a shock or policy change, they use the *SAS-DAD* model to compute its effect on next period's inflation. They cannot foresee, however, when monetary policy changes its course. This comes as a surprise.

The starting point is the inflationary equilibrium A_0 in Figure 8.10. In period 1 monetary policy switches from the old money growth rate μ_{LO} to μ_{HI}. Since this had not been anticipated in period 0, wage contracts for period 1 are based on inflation expectations π_0. Thus the aggregate supply curve remains in $SAS_1 = SAS_0$. For the same reason as under adaptive expectations, equilibrium in period 1 obtains at point A_1, at higher income and higher inflation.

Events in and after period 2 differ from what happened under adaptive expectations. Individuals realize that the rate of money growth has changed. So no more surprises occur in the future. Individuals can employ their knowledge of the *DAD-SAS* model to compute correct inflation forecasts. What is

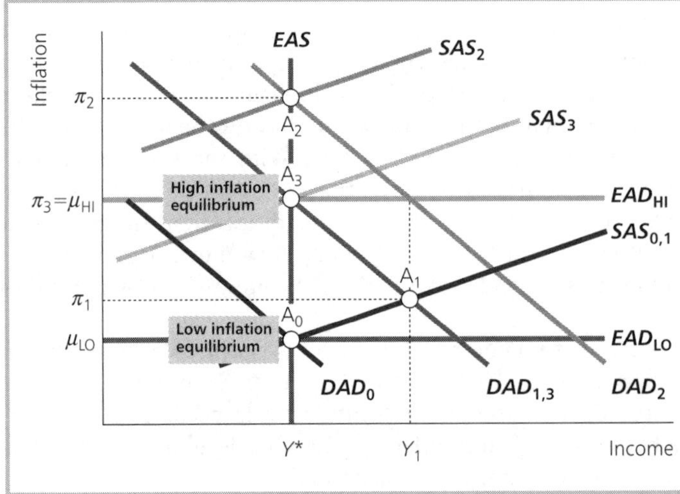

Figure 8.10 Starting from A_0, an unexpected acceleration of money growth moves the economy to A_1. If money growth remains high, DAD_2 obtains in period 2. Since high money growth and its consequence for inflation is anticipated, *SAS* is at SAS_2, and the economy is in A_2. In period 3 and after, A_3 obtains.

Note. This statement is an approximation. As the algebraic treatment in the appendix (pp. 216) reveals, raising money growth raises the expected equilibrium rate of depreciation. Thus DAD_1 rises slightly higher than shown here, and the real money supply falls. For small or modest changes in money growth this effect is not important. We ignore it to keep things simple.

the correct, or rational inflation forecast for period 2? Two points must be noted here:

1 SAS_2 intersects *EAS* at the *expected* inflation rate.
2 *Actual* inflation is determined by the intersection between SAS_2 and DAD_2.

Combining points 1 and 2, actual and expected inflation can only be the same if SAS_2 and DAD_2 intersect on *EAS*. This holds in general:

> The rational expectation of next period's inflation is given by the point of intersection between the *EAS* curve and the *DAD* curve anticipated for next period.

So inflation is correctly anticipated to rise to $\pi_2 > \mu_{HI}$, bringing output back to its normal level, where it remains. This moves the *SAS* curve into SAS_3, and actual and expected inflation is at μ_{HI} in period 3 and ever after.

To sum up: under rational expectations an unexpected, permanent increase in the rate of money growth stimulates output temporarily via surprise inflation. This effect evaporates one period later, leaving the economy with a permanently higher rate of inflation.

Perfect foresight

Individuals have perfect foresight if there are no surprises. They foresee everything: changes of endogenous variables, changes in the international environment and policy changes too.

In the current context this means that individuals foresee in period 0 that monetary policy will change in period 1. This could be either due to the central bank credibly *announcing* the policy change, or because individuals have learned to understand what makes central bankers tick. If the shift of the demand curve to DAD_1 is anticipated, rational expectations of next period's inflation rate are given by the point of intersection between DAD_1 and *EAS*. Incidentally, rational inflation expectations coincide with the new money growth rate. Hence, the real money supply remains unchanged and income remains at its equilibrium level (see Figure 8.11).

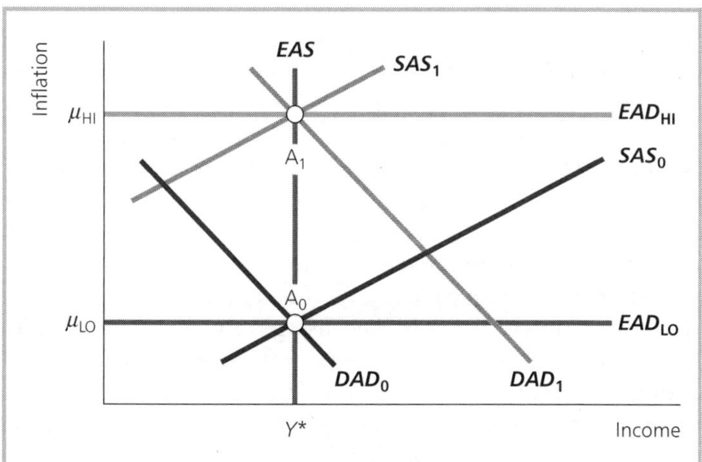

Figure 8.11 If the rise of the money growth rate is anticipated, the shift of *DAD* to DAD_1 is foreseen by the labour market. Anticipation of the correct inflation rate puts *SAS* into SAS_1 and the economy directly moves from A_0 into A_1, where it remains.

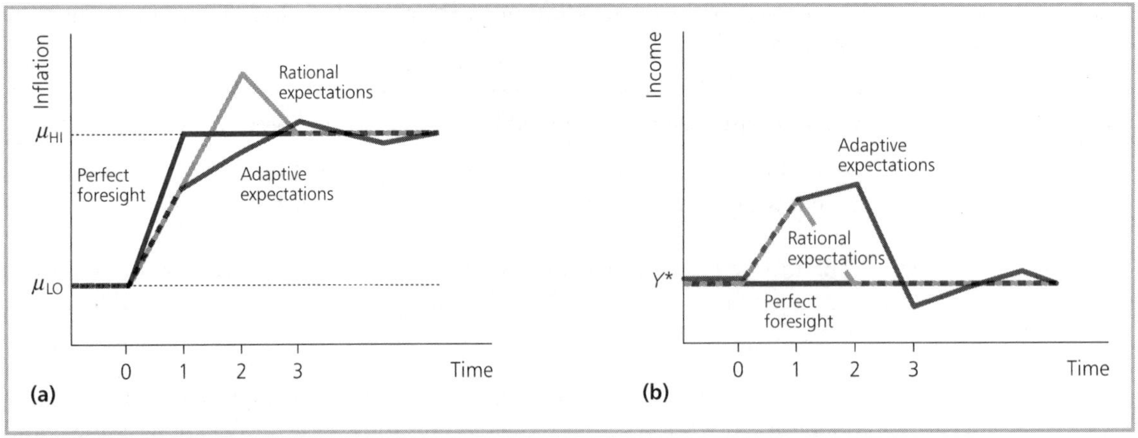

Figure 8.12 Panel (a) shows the response of inflation; panel (b) shows the response of income to a permanent increase of money growth. The responses are affected by how people form expectations.

Figure 8.12 compares the time profiles of inflation and income, respectively, under the three expectations formation schemes. They restate and sum up what we already encountered in Figures 8.9–8.11.

Fiscal policy

We now turn to an analysis of fiscal policy. Chapter 5 showed that governments may use tax and expenditure changes to affect income under an international arrangement of fixed exchange rates. For easy reference, a stripped-down version of the *DAD-SAS* model under fixed exchange rates is

$$\pi = \pi^{W} - bY + bY_{-1} + \delta\Delta G \qquad \textit{DAD} \text{ curve, fixed exchange rates}$$

$$\pi = \pi^{e} + \lambda(Y - Y^{*}) \qquad \textit{SAS} \text{ curve}$$

This compact version of the *DAD* curve assumes that world income remains constant, and that there are no realignments of the exchange rate.

Adaptive expectations

In Figure 8.13 the economy is in an initial equilibrium in which inflation is determined by the world inflation rate. This is because the commitment to a fixed exchange rate forces the central bank to let the home money supply grow at the rate of world inflation. Raising government expenditures by $\Delta G_1 = G_1 - G_0$ shifts the *DAD* curve to the right. Since this comes unexpectedly, the economy moves up an unchanged *SAS* curve, experiencing an income boost and some inflation.

The experienced inflation π_1 is expected to prevail next period, $\pi_2^e = \pi_1$. This shifts the aggregate supply curve up to SAS_2. At the same time, the aggregate demand curve shifts back down to DAD_2 because government expenditures do not rise any further and, hence, $\Delta G_2 = G_2 - G_1 = 0$. Here the joint effect is that inflation continues to rise while income falls. In period 3 inflation begins to recede and income falls further, below its normal level. In time, inflation eases back to its original level, and so does income.

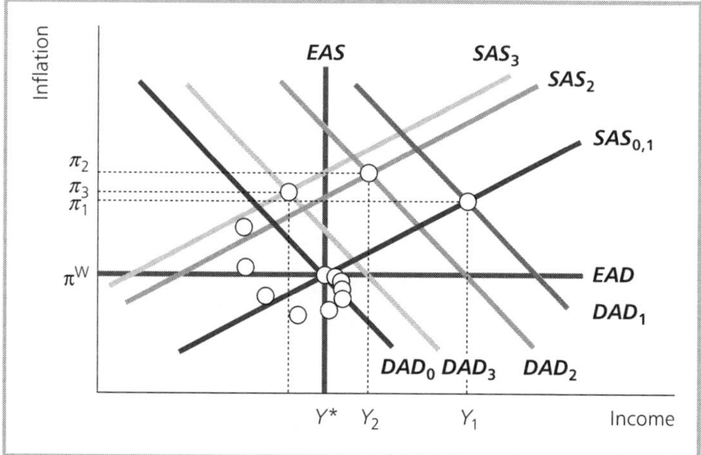

Figure 8.13 The exchange rate is fixed and the economy is in equilibrium with DAD_0 and SAS_0. A one-time increase in government spending shifts *DAD* into DAD_1, raising income along SAS_1 to Y_1 and inflation to π_1. Higher inflation expectations shift *SAS* into SAS_2 next period. *DAD* shifts down, however, since *G* does not rise any further. This process continues as sketched by the white circles until the economy is back in the initial equilibrium at $\pi = \pi^W$ and $Y = Y^*$.

Again, the details of the adjustment process depend on specific parameter constellations. For instance, if the *DAD* curve is very flat, inflation may already fall in period 2, driving income below Y^* earlier. The big picture, however, is not sensitive to parameter specifics. A one-time expenditure increase stimulates income and kindles inflation. Both these effects are short-lived, however, and are followed by falling inflation and even a temporary recession.

Rational expectations

If the income rise comes as a surprise but subsequent implications for inflation are correctly foreseen, the economy responds as shown in Figure 8.14. First-period results are the same as in the adaptive expectations scenario. The unexpected increase in government expenditures raises income to Y_1 and inflation to π_1. In period 2 *DAD* shifts down to DAD_2. Since this is expected, inflation expectations are rationally set to π_2, positioning *SAS* at SAS_2. Thus income is back to its normal level and remains there. In period 3 inflation is back to the level of world inflation as well.

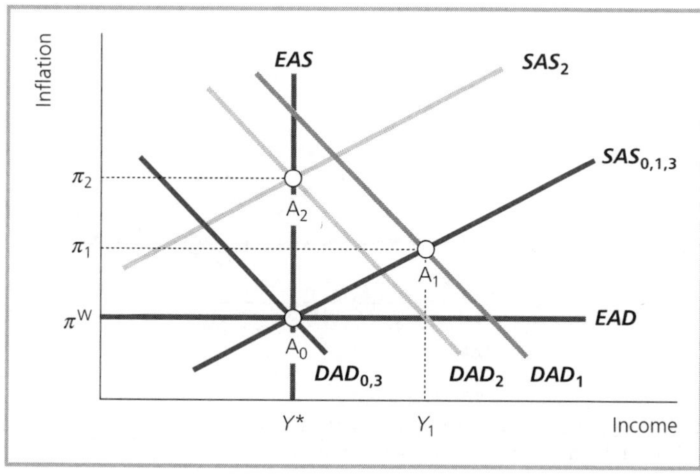

Figure 8.14 Starting from A_0, an unexpected increase in government purchases moves the economy to A_1. Since *G* does not rise any further, DAD_2 obtains in period 2. Since inflation expectations are formed rationally, *SAS* is at SAS_2, and the economy is at A_2. Finally, in period 3 and after, A_0 obtains.

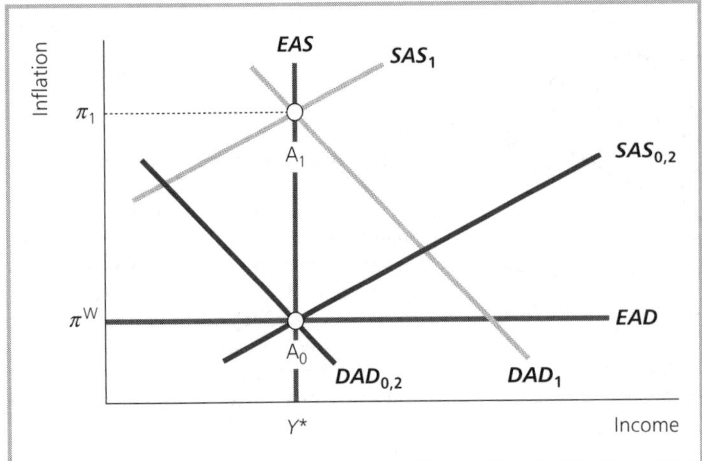

Figure 8.15 When the increase in government purchases is anticipated, the shift of DAD to DAD_1 is foreseen by the labour market. Anticipation of the correct inflation rate puts SAS into SAS_1 and the economy moves from A_0 into A_1. Similarly, the position of DAD_2 is anticipated by the labour market, which puts SAS into SAS_2 and the economy back into A_0. Here the economy remains.

Perfect foresight

Fully informed individuals already anticipate the first-period shift of aggregate demand to DAD_1. Hence, rational expectations move the aggregate supply curve up to SAS_1 (see Figure 8.15). The attempt to stimulate output evaporates, leaving only inflation at π_1. In period 2 things are back to what they were before the expenditure rise.

Again, Figure 8.16, panels (a) and (b), compares inflation and output, respectively, under the three expectations scenarios. The crucial point is that output effects become shorter as we move from adaptive via rational expectations to perfect foresight.

Policy effectiveness in the *DAD-SAS* model

Our look at monetary and fiscal policy has brought out one point quite clearly: the extent to which policy may influence income and output crucially hinges upon how individuals form inflation expectations. Only if there is a strong

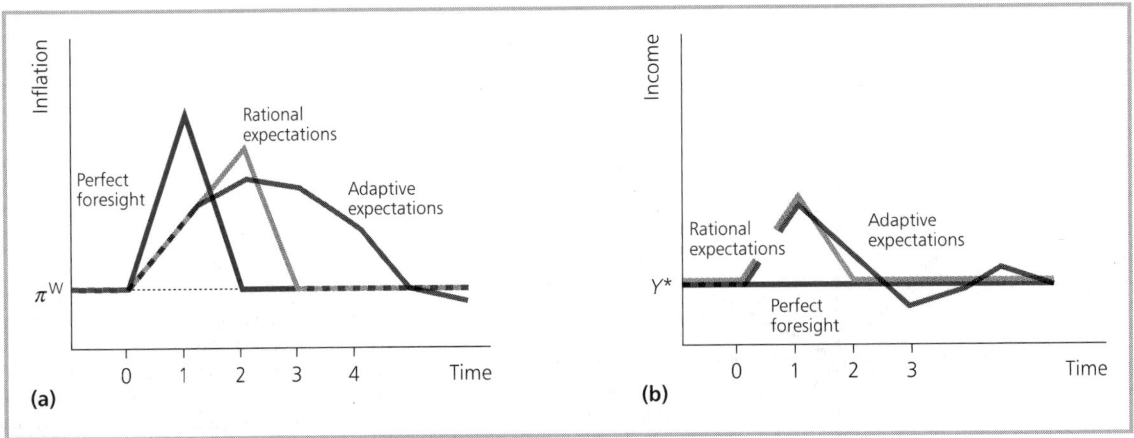

Figure 8.16 Panel (a) shows the response of inflation; panel (b) shows the response of income to a one-time increase in government purchases. The responses are affected by how people form expectations.

CASE STUDY 8.1 Quantity equation, Fisher equation and purchasing power parity: international evidence

Focusing on business cycles, Chapter 8 and the preceding chapters focused on the short-run relationships between monetary aggregates. While these relationships can be complicated in the short and medium run, long-run (or equilibrium) relationships are quite simple and serve as useful anchors from which variables may only deviate temporarily.

One way of identifying the key long-run relationships is by considering the Mundell–Fleming model (Figure 1), with an added long-run *AS* curve at Y^* (which we presume constant for convenience). The point of intersection marks the long-run equilibrium in which all markets clear. For the economy to remain in this equilibrium, the *LM* curve, the *IS* curve and the *FE* curve must stay put in the indicated positions. What does this imply?

LM curve

The position of the *LM* curve is determined by the real money supply M/P. If *LM* must not shift, the real money supply must not change. Hence *M* and *P* must grow at the same rates. Inflation π must equal money growth μ, so the empirical implication is that in the long run

$$\pi = \mu \qquad \text{from \textbf{quantity equation}} \qquad (1)$$

Inflation equals money growth, not necessarily from year to year, but in the long run, over a span of decades.

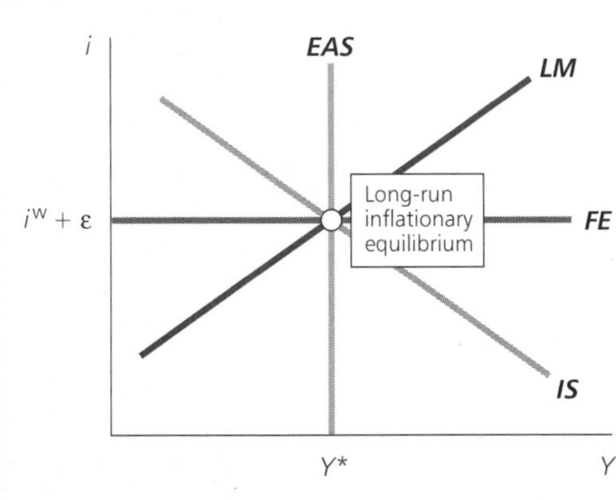

Figure 1

IS curve

The position of the *IS* curve depends on the real exchange rate, government spending and world income. Keeping world income constant in line with domestic income, and noting that government spending cannot continuously change (relative to income) in the long run, then the real exchange rate must not change if *IS* must not shift. Thus $EP^W/P =$ constant. Thus foreign prices in domestic currency, EP^W must grow at the same rate as domestic prices *P*. Since the growth rate of foreign prices in domestic currency is approximated by the rate of depreciation ε plus world inflation π^W, this condition reads $\varepsilon + \pi^W = \pi$. Solving for ε yields

$$\varepsilon = \pi - \pi^W \qquad \text{from \textbf{purchasing power parity}} \qquad (2)$$

which says that in the long run the rate of depreciation equals the interest differential between our country and the rest of the world.

FE curve

The position of the *FE* curve depends on the foreign interest rate and expected depreciation. Since expected and actual depreciation should be the same in equilibrium, the equilibrium *FE* curve reads $i = i^W + \varepsilon$. Substituting equation (2) for ε and noting that $i^W - \pi^W$ is the world real interest rate r^W, we obtain the so called Fisher equation which states that the nominal interest rate is the sum of a constant (representing the real world interest rate) and inflation:

$$i = r^W + \pi \qquad \textbf{Fisher equation} \qquad (3)$$

The three long-run relationships behind equations (1)–(3) – the quantity equation, purchasing power parity, and the Fisher equation – are confronted with data from a sample of countries in Figure 2. Panel (a) looks at the *quantity equation* and shows that in the long run inflation always goes hand in hand with money growth. This relationship becomes particularly strong when inflation is very high, as during hyperinflations. Panel (a), of course, is only a slightly modified version of Figure 1 in Case study 7.1.

Case study 8.1 continued

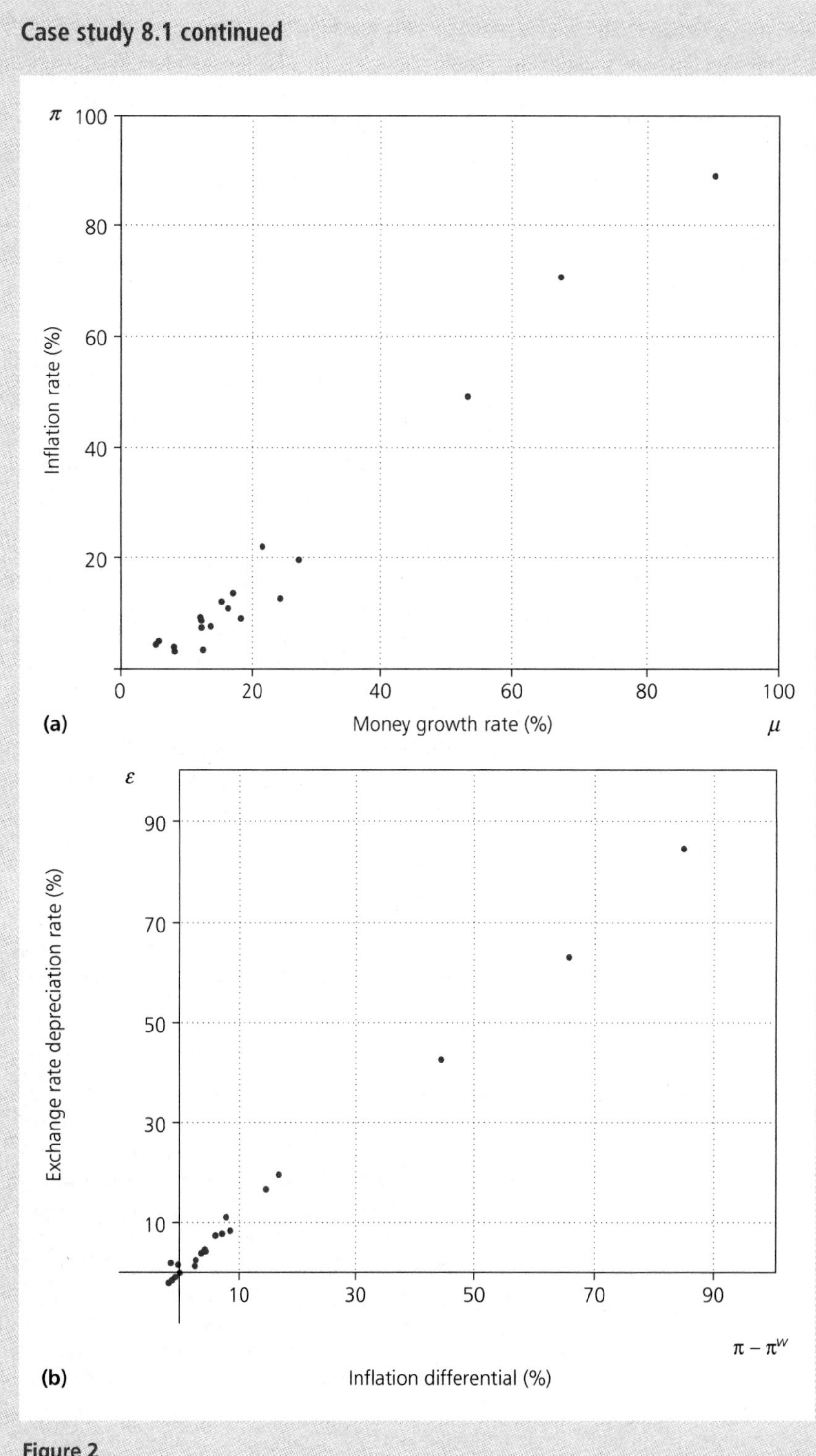

Figure 2

Case study 8.1 continued

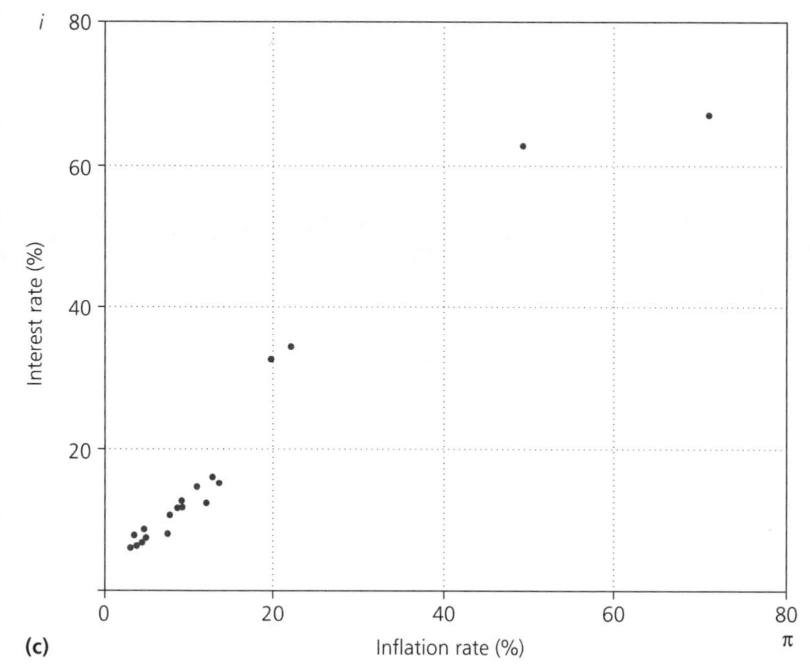

Figure 2 *(continued)*

Purchasing power parity is being tested in panel (b). Being averages over some three decades, the data are well in line with equation (2). The more we inflate relative to the rest of the world, the faster the exchange rate depreciates.

Finally, panel (c) supports the Fisher equation which proposes a one-to-one relationship between the nominal interest rate and inflation.

Food for thought

Does the validity of these equilibrium relationships depend on the exchange rate regime? Why or why not?

To be more realistic, suppose potential income (at home and abroad) grows at a constant rate. Which of the equilibrium conditions is affected by this, and how?

adaptive element in expectations formation will output gains last for some time. If expectations are rational, only the initial policy surprise may create a short-lived income rise. Finally if the policy stimulus is anticipated, as is assumed under the hypothesis of perfect foresight, income does not respond at all.

Note. Recent empirical research found that even anticipated policy affected output. The underlying transmission channel is not well understood yet. The implication is that the kind of temporary output effect derived above may also obtain if inflation expectations are not adaptive.

The length of the output response to unexpected policy intervention depends on the structural characteristics of the economy. In particular, the longer wage contracts are, the longer output responses will last. This is because observation of the policy shock can only lead to renegotiated wage contracts after the old contracts expire.

The general lesson for policy-makers is ambiguous. It is in their power to influence output, but they can do so only via surprise implementation of monetary and fiscal policy. Surprises work at the cost of expectations errors of labour market participants, however. So the more often the government or the central bank resorts to surprises, the more frequent and the larger the committed expectations errors are, and the more likely individuals will feel compelled to sharpen their forecasting technique. Somewhere down the road they will be able to identify the situations in which policy-makers normally respond and anticipate (and thus nullify) all policy interventions. The lesson would be to use policy sparingly to retain its potency.

CHAPTER SUMMARY

- An economy's supply side can be represented in inflation–income space by means of a vertical long-run or equilibrium aggregate supply curve (*EAS*), and a positively sloped surprise aggregate supply curve (*SAS*).
- The demand side can be represented in inflation–income space by means of a negatively sloped dynamic aggregate demand curve (*DAD*).
- Under flexible exchange rates the aggregate demand curve has a negative slope for the following reason. A price increase reduces the real money supply. Since the domestic interest rate is fixed to the world interest rate, the demand for money must be reduced by a decline in income.
- Under fixed exchange rates the aggregate demand curve has a negative slope for the following reason. A price increase reduces the real exchange rate. This appreciation creates an excess supply of domestic goods at the old level of income. Since the interest rate is fixed to the world interest rate, supply can only equal demand at a lower level of income.
- The simplest version of adaptive expectations lets individuals expect last period's inflation to occur again next period. Forming expectations this way is simple and cheap. If inflation changes only infrequently, it may also be quite accurate.
- If simple expectations formation results in large and frequent errors, and if errors are costly, individuals are likely to move on to a more elaborate expectations formation. One such elaborate scheme is rational expectations.
- If individuals form rational expectations, we expect them to know as much as we do. That means, they are assumed to know our model.
- Under fixed exchange rates fiscal policy (that is, a government expenditure change or a tax change) may temporarily affect output and income if it comes as a surprise.
- Monetary policy affects output when exchange rates are flexible, if it comes as a surprise.
- Anticipated fiscal or monetary policy does not affect output. All it does is have an impact on inflation.

KEY TERMS AND CONCEPTS

adaptive expectations
DAD curve
DAD–SAS model
EAS curve
economically rational expectations
fiscal policy
inflation expectations
monetary policy
perfect foresight
policy effectiveness
rational expectations
SAS curve
surprises

EXERCISES

8.1 In this chapter the *SAS* curve was written as $\pi = \pi^e + \lambda(Y - Y^*)$. Derive aggregate supply in the long run, that is, when inflation expectations equal actual inflation.

8.2 Under flexible exchange rates, domestic inflation is determined by the growth rate of domestic money supply, whereas inflation is determined by the foreign inflation rate if the exchange rate is fixed.
(a) Explain why.
(b) Suppose you govern a country whose economy is linked to other economies by fixed exchange rates. A reduction of inflation is overdue. Are you inclined to switch to a regime of flexible exchange rates?

8.3 Consider an economy with flexible exchange rates, which can be described by the following *DAD* and *SAS* curves:

$\pi = \mu - 0.025(Y - Y_{-1})$ *DAD* curve
$\pi = \pi^e + 0.075(Y - Y^*)$ *SAS* curve

Assume that output in the preceding period was 150 units, which is 50 units below full employment output Y^*. The growth rate of money supply is 10% and agents expect an inflation rate of 5%.
(a) Draw the *DAD* and the *SAS* curves and compute output and inflation in equilibrium.
(b) The central bank considers reducing the money growth rate from 10% to 5%. Assume that the inflation expectations of the agents remain unchanged and draw the new *DAD* and *SAS* curves to analyze the effect on inflation and output of such a policy.

8.4 It is often claimed that the government can permanently keep output above potential output, but at an ever 'accelerating' inflation rate. Explain this statement using the *DAD-SAS* model.

8.5 Trace the short-run and long-run effects of a surprising once-and-for-all increase in the foreign inflation rate for an economy with adaptive inflation expectations and
(a) a flexible exchange rate
(b) a fixed exchange rate.

8.6 Trace the short-run and long-run effect of an unexpected reduction of foreign inflation for an economy with a fixed exchange rate for the case of
(a) adaptive inflation expectations
(b) rational inflation expectations.

8.7 Consider an economy with a flexible exchange rate. Inflation expectations are formed rationally, but contracts extend over two periods. Every period, 50% of the contracts expire and are rewritten for the following two periods. Analyze the effect of a once-and-for-all increase in the money growth rate if
(a) the policy change comes as a surprise
(b) the policy change is announced one period ahead.

RECOMMENDED READING

A closed-economy version of the *DAD-SAS* model is developed in Rudiger Dornbusch and Stanley Fischer (1994), *Macroeconomics*, 6th edn, McGraw-Hill: New York. Unfortunately, this feature has been dropped from later editions of this text.

A critical discussion of the aggregate-supply/aggregate-demand apparatus as a teaching device is given in David Colander (1995) 'The stories we tell: A reconsideration of AS/AD analysis', *Journal of Economic Perspectives* 9: 169–88. I hesitate to recommend reading it at this stage, however, as it may throw you off balance. While a number of the issues raised are worth thinking about, much of the criticism advanced there lacks substance. It attacks presumed blunders in the presentation of *AS* and *AD* which we avoid, as do most other textbooks I know.

APPENDIX THE ALGEBRA OF THE *DAD* CURVE

The *DAD* curves under flexible and fixed exchange rates can easily be derived from the *AD* curves assembled in the appendix to Chapter 7.

Flexible exchange rates

Equation (A7.10) is the *AD* curve under flexible exchange rates. Taking first differences, denoting inflation by $\pi \equiv p - p_{-1}$ and money growth by $\mu \equiv m - m_{-1}$, letting the first fraction be b, and noting that potential income is fixed, so that $\Delta Y^* = \Delta\bar{Y} = 0$ gives the **DAD curve under flexible exchange rates** as

$$\pi = \mu - b(Y - Y_{-1}) + h(\Delta i^{W} + \Delta\bar{\varepsilon}^{e})$$

Fixed exchange rates

Equation (A7.11) is the *AD* curve under fixed exchange rates. Taking first differences yields the **DAD curve under fixed exchange rates.**

$$\pi = \varepsilon + \pi^{W} - \frac{1 - c + m_1}{x_2 + m_2}(Y - Y_{-1}) + \frac{x_1}{x_2 + m_2}\Delta Y^{W} + \frac{1}{x_2 + m_2}\Delta G$$

Again, the position variables of the *FE* curve, i^{W} and ε^{e} do not show here because we assumed the *IS* curve to be vertical, that is, investment is independent of the interest rate.

APPENDIX THE GENESIS OF THE *DAD-SAS* MODEL

A common phrase cautions that you may not see the wood for the trees. Perhaps you feel a bit like this having worked through all this material. If so, the schematic representation of the genesis of the *DAD-SAS* model in Figure 8.17 asks you to step back and put each of the concepts introduced in place.

We started by looking at the economy's demand side, assuming that supply did not require special attention, since firms would supply whatever was demanded anyway. The first stepping stone was the **Keynesian cross.** There all

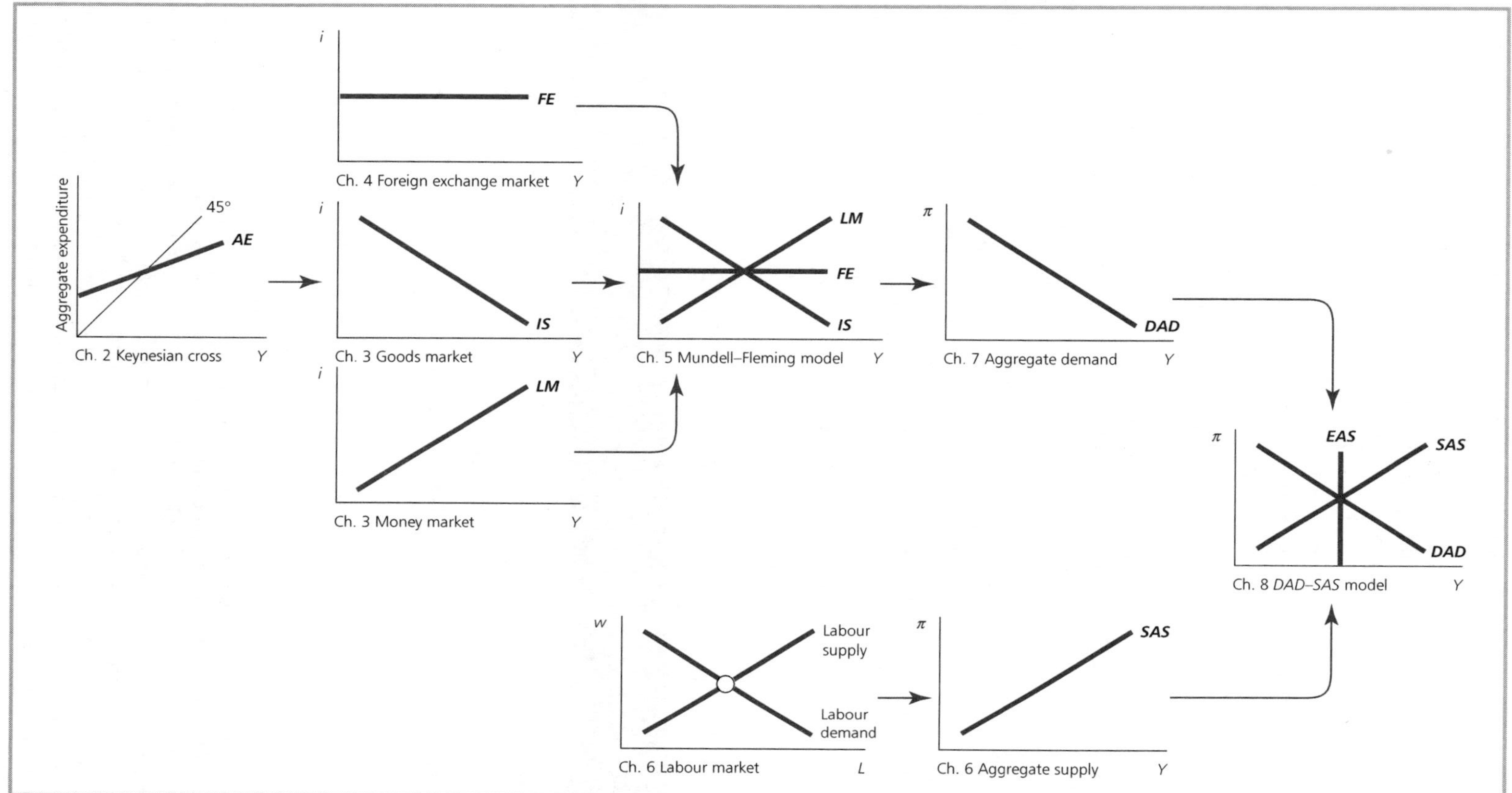

Figure 8.17 The genesis of the *DAD-SAS* model.

categories of demand except consumption were exogenous or depended on variables like the interest rate or the exchange rate that were exogenous. In a second stage we refined the goods market, representing all possible equilibria by the ***IS* curve.** Since treating interest rates and exchange rates as exogenous variables was not satisfactory, we introduced the money market, which clears on the ***LM* curve**, and the foreign exchange market, which clears on the ***FE* curve.** Putting these three markets together yields the **Mundell–Fleming model.** This model simultaneously determines the interest rate, the exchange rate and aggregate income, and permits a first analysis of how fiscal and monetary policy or shocks from the rest of the world affect our economy. A weakness of the Mundell–Fleming model is the assumption of a fixed price level. Dropping this assumption, different current equilibrium income levels obtain at different inflation rates. These are summarized in the *AD* curve or, which is the same concept in different clothing, in the ***DAD* curve** shown here.

The analysis of aggregate supply started in the **labour market.** In an ideal setting, labour supply and demand would interact so as to produce a real wage at which nobody would be out of work involuntarily. Institutional features or imperfections may prevent the labour market from reaching this ideal. When inflation changes, in particular if it does so unexpectedly, employment moves away from its normal level, and so does output supplied. The levels supplied in aggregate at different inflation rates are combined in the ***SAS* curve.**

The ***DAD-SAS* model** or, alternatively, the *AD-AS* model we chose not to show here, draws the demand side (*DAD*) and the supply side (*SAS*) together. It permits the analysis of the effects of policy measures and external shocks on inflation and the deviation of income from potential income.

APPLIED PROBLEMS

RECENT RESEARCH

How does monetary policy affect output?

Under flexible exchange rates the *DAD-SAS* model discussed in this chapter reads

$$\pi = -bY + bY_{-1} + \mu \qquad (1)$$

$$Y = Y^* + \frac{1}{\lambda}\pi - \frac{1}{\lambda}\pi_{-1} \qquad (2)$$

We had managed to keep its dynamic structure simple and transparent by assuming that most adjustments take place immediately and that inflation expectations are simply $\pi^e = \pi_{-1}$. Reality may be more complicated: consumption may not respond to income changes immediately; exports are likely to react to a new exchange rate only with a lag; and so on. Because of this, and particularly when they work with higher frequency data such as observed quarterly, economists often prefer not to restrict the model's dynamics by a priori assumptions, but *let the data speak*. For this purpose the above model is generalized to something like

$$\pi = a_0 + a_1\pi_{-1} + a_2\pi_{-2} + a_3Y_{-1} + a_4Y_{-2} + \text{SHOCK1} \qquad (1')$$

$$Y = b_0 + b_1Y_{-1} + b_2Y_{-2} + b_3\pi_{-1} + b_4\pi_{-2} + \text{SHOCK2} \qquad (2')$$

where SHOCK1 and SHOCK2 stands for all the exogenous influence on the two equations revealed by our analysis, such as monetary and fiscal policy, world variables or supply-side shocks. Economists call such a system of equations a *vector autogression* (VAR), because a vector of endogenous variables (here π and Y) is regressed on past values of this vector.

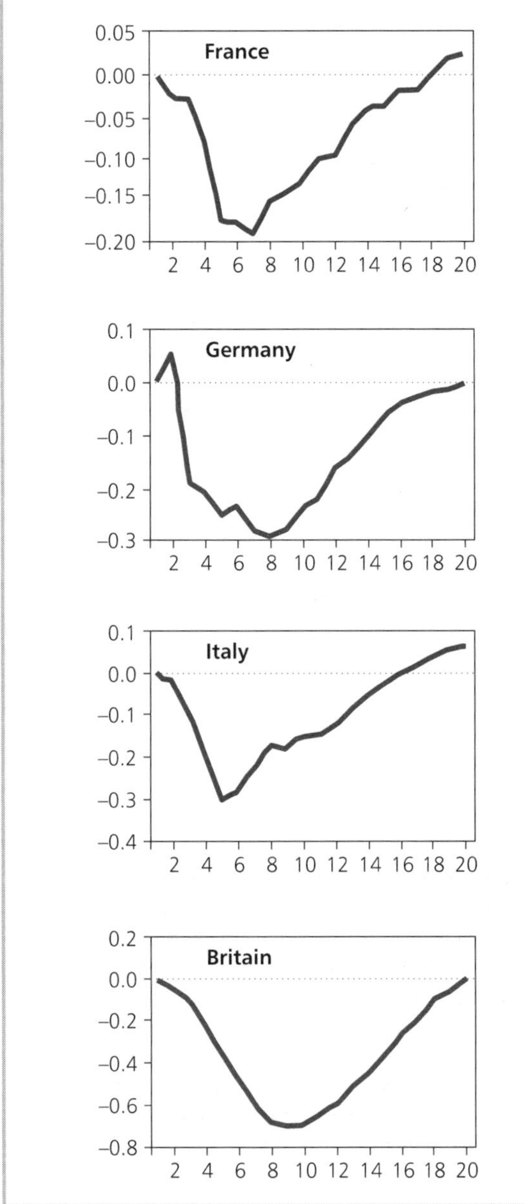

Figure 8.18

OLS estimation of the two equations yields numerical values for the *a*s and *b*s. We may then simulate, that is compute from period to period, how a shock of type 1 (in the first equation) or of type 2 (in the second equation) translates into a response of income and inflation over time.

In the above spirit, Stefan Gerlach and Frank Smets ('The monetary transmission mechanism: Evidence from the G-7 countries', Bank for International Settlements, Basle, Working Paper No. 26, April 1995) estimate a VAR model with three endogenous variables, inflation, output and the interest rate, allowing for a maximum lag of five periods (measured in quarters). After employing an advanced procedure (that is beyond our scope) to identify monetary shocks from other demand shocks and from supply shocks, their estimated model generates the following output responses to a standardized one-unit contraction of the money supply (see Figure 8.18).

The interesting aspect about this result is that the behaviour of output after a one-time reduction of the money supply is so similar in the four countries and matches quite well what the simple *DAD-SAS* model proposes. After the reduction of the money supply, output begins to fall (except for a small upwards blip in Germany), reaching its lowest point in the second year. Thereafter output rises again. It takes four to five years, however, until the shock has been absorbed and output is back to normal.

WORKED PROBLEM

Inflation forecasts for Italy

Forming an inflation expectation is like a forecast of next period's inflation. In this sense the OECD forecasts of macroeconomic variables are this organization's expectations of what these variables will be. (There is one fundamental difference between the OECD's expectations and mine. OECD forecasts may and probably do influence the market's expectations, and thus may feature a self-fullfilling element. We ignore this complication here.) Table 8.1 gives the OECD's annual inflation forecasts for Italy along with subsequent actual inflation rates. One question of interest is how the OECD computes forecasts. Are OECD inflation expectations formed adaptively, as proposed in most parts of the text, or by much more complicated and elaborate methods? One way to check this is by trying to explain OECD forecasts by the general form of adaptive expectations introduced in the margin note on p. 199, which reads $\pi^e = \pi^e_{-1} + a(\pi_{-1} - \pi^e_{-1})$. Rearranging gives $\pi^e = (1 - a)\pi^e_{-1} + a\pi_{-1}$. Estimating this equation with the above data gives

$$\pi^e = \underset{(1.67)}{1.15} + \underset{(2.20)}{1.05}\pi_{-1} - \underset{(0.65)}{0.29}\pi^e_{-1} \qquad R^2_{adj} = 0.87$$

Annual data 1984–95

Table 8.1

	1983	1984	1985	1986	1987	1988	1989	1990	1991	1992	1993	1994	1995
OECD inflation forecasts (in %)	15.5	13	9	7.5	5.5	5.8	5.2	7.2	6.9	5.7	5.6	4.5	3.3
Actual inflation rates (in %)	14.9	12	9	6.3	5.3	5.7	6.3	6.2	6.8	5.4	4.8	4.7	4.9

This first result to note is that this simple equation explains 87% of the variation in OECD forecasts, which appears to be quite a lot. The constant term is 1.15 but not significantly different from zero. Last period's inflation goes almost one-to-one into the forecast, and the t-value of 2.20 meets our rule of thumb for significance. By contrast, with an absolute t-statistic of 0.65 the coefficient of −0.29 for last period's forecast is not significant. Summing this up, the hypothesis $\pi^e = \pi_{-1}$ employed to facilitate the graphical presentation in the text appears to describe OECD forecasts for Italy between 1984 and 1995 quite well.

YOUR TURN

The Economist and the law of one price

Purchasing power parity suggests that one unit of currency should have the same buying power in different countries (in terms of this chapter's variables: $EP^W = P$). When applied to a specific good, purchasing power parity turns into the law of one price: expressed in a common currency, a given good should have the same price in all countries.

Table 8.2 gives prices for *The Economist* as cited on the title page of 17 June 1996 and the same day's sterling/local currency exchange rates for seventeen European countries plus the United States.

Table 8.2

Country	Price in local currency	Exchange rate
A	60	0.061
B	160	0.021
CH	7.7	0.517
D	7.9	0.426
FIN	24	0.139
F	27	0.126
DK	34	0.111
GR	1000	0.003
HU	600	0.004
IRE	2.3	1.027
I	8000	0.0004
NL	8.9	0.380
N	35	0.099
P	680	0.004
E	590	0.005
S	35	0.097
GB	2.2	1
US	3.5	0.648

Check whether prices set by *The Economist* obey the law of one price. You may want to start from the equation $P_i = R_i P_{UK}/E_i$, where P_i is the local currency price in country i, E is the sterling rate per currency unit of country i, and R_i measures how the price in country i relates to the price charged in Britain, $P_{UK} = 2.20$, transformed into local currency. If $R = 1$ the law of one price holds. To check this, take logarithms to obtain $\log P_i = \ln R_i + \ln 2.20 - \ln E_i$. Testing whether the data support the law of one price is done against the null hypotheses that the coefficient of $\ln E$ is 1 and that the constant term is $\ln 2.20$ (or $\ln R = 0$).

To further explore this chapter's key messages you are encouraged to use the interactive online module found at

www.fgn.unisg.ch/eurmacro/tutor/DADSAS.html

and many other features hosted at **www.fgn.unisg.ch/eurmacro**

CHAPTER 9

ECONOMIC GROWTH (I)
BASICS

WHAT TO EXPECT After working through this chapter, you will understand:

1 What determines the levels of **income and consumption in the long run**.
2 What **growth accounting** is and how it is used to measure **technological progress**.
3 Why and how a country ends up with the **capital stock** it has.
4 Why having a **larger stock of capital may** open more consumption possibilities, but may also **require people to consume less**.
5 Why **some countries are rich and some are poor**.
6 **What makes income per head grow** over time.

We now possess a model that permits us to understand what makes *actual* income fluctuate around *potential* income. This *DAD-SAS* model explains why the circular stream of income oscillates – that is, becomes wider and thinner within its natural bed. We have not yet discussed what shapes the bed of the stream, since we assumed that this shaping would proceed slowly and thus has different causes to the more short-run fluctuations of the stream. It is these longer-run trends in income to which we now turn.

9.1 STYLIZED FACTS OF INCOME AND GROWTH

The empirical motivation for turning our attention to the determinants of potential income and steady-state income derives most forcefully from international income comparisons. As we saw in Chapter 2, a person in the world's richest economies on average earns 50 times as much as a person in the poorest countries. Such differences, documented again for a different set of countries and data in Figure 9.1, can hardly be attributed to an asynchronous business cycle with one country being in a recession and the other enjoying a boom, though business cycles *are* important. In the course of a recession income may recede by 3–5%; by up to 10% if the recession is bad; or even more if it is a deep recession like the Great Depression of the 1930s. But this happens very seldom, and not even this would come close to accounting for income differences observed within Europe, let alone the rest of the world.

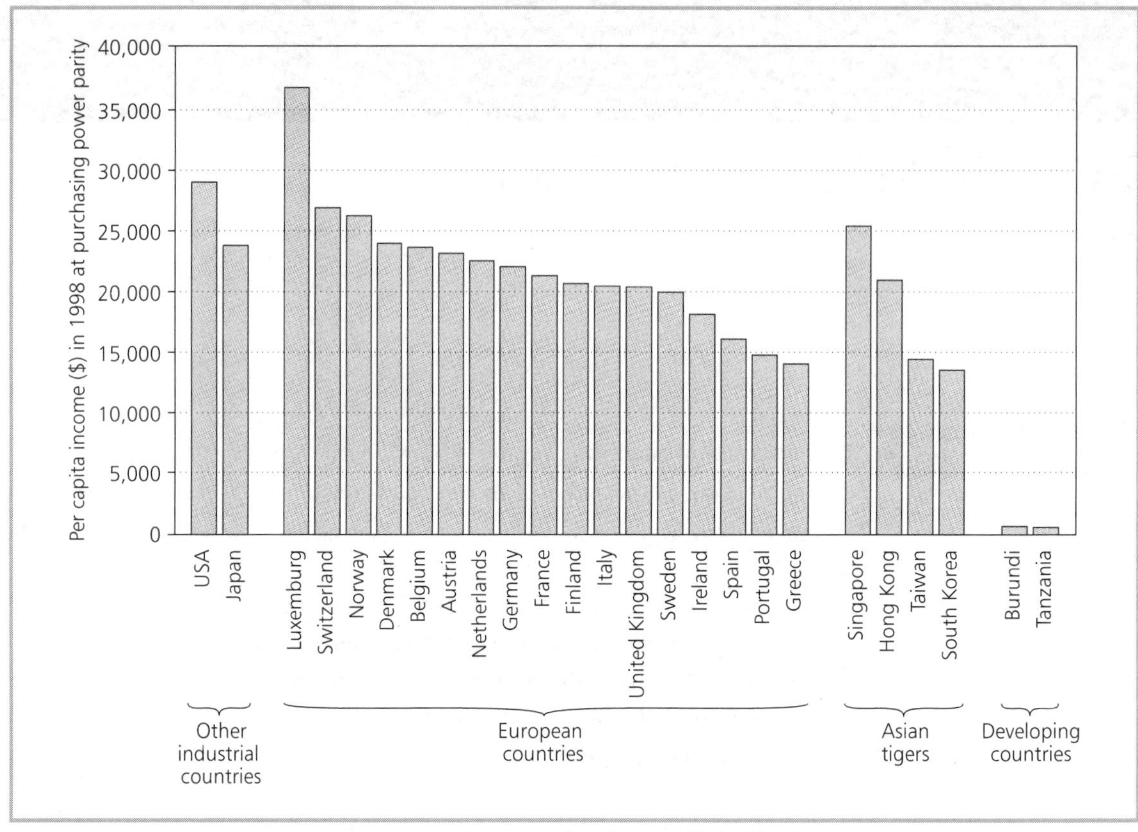

Figure 9.1 In Europe per capita incomes (adjusted for differences in purchasing power) in the richest countries remain about twice as high as in the poorest countries. Worldwide, however, per capita incomes in the industrialized countries are some 50 times higher than in the poorest countries. For example, per capita incomes in Burundi and Tanzania are $561 and $483, respectively, compared with $23,622 in Belgium and $36,703 in Luxemburg.
Source: *World Bank Atlas* 2000, The World Bank (own estimate for Taiwan).

The bottom line is that while the models we added to our tool box in the first eight chapters of this text are important and useful vehicles for understanding and dealing with business cycles, they do not help us to understand international differences in income. The reason for such huge income gaps can only be discrepancies in equilibrium income, that is, potential income.

The ultimate goal of this analysis is to develop an understanding of international patterns in income and income growth as depicted in Figures 9.1 and 9.2. Figure 9.2 focuses on income growth rates instead of income levels. To prevent the business cycle effects of a given year from blurring the picture, average growth rates for the longer period 1960–92 are given. The first thing to note is that just as incomes differ substantially between countries, so does income growth. The Asian tigers grew almost three times as fast as some European countries and the US, and even within Europe some countries grew twice as fast as others.

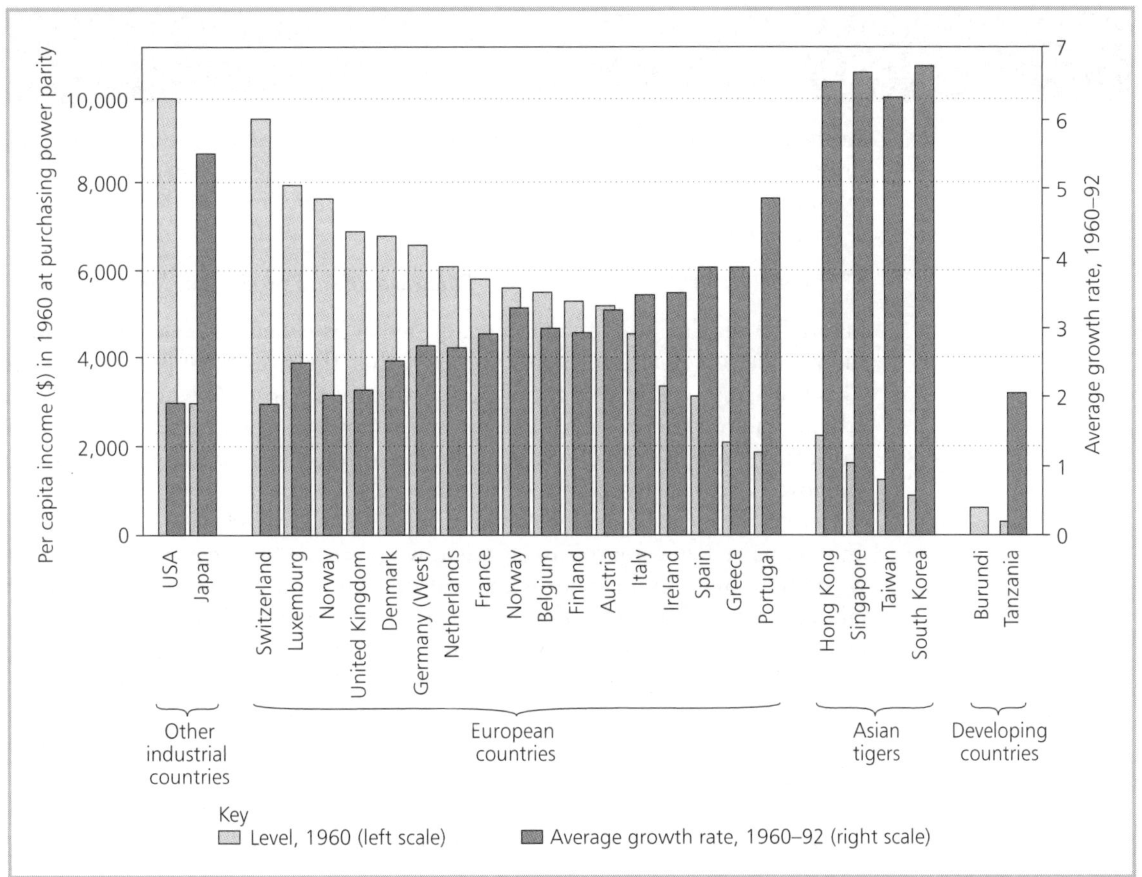

Figure 9.2 The graph compares average income growth between 1960 and 1992 with per capita incomes in 1960. There is a negative correlation for the European countries. Those with low incomes in 1960 enjoyed high growth after that date. Japan, the USA and the Asian tigers also fit this pattern. Burundi and Tanzania do not fit in. With their low 1960 income levels they should have experienced much higher income growth since then.
Source: Penn World Tables 5.6.

Figure 9.2 also shows income levels. This time it is those observed in 1960, at the start of the recorded growth period. The group of European countries reveals a negative relationship between the initial level of income and income growth. Countries starting at lower income levels tend to grow faster. Thus incomes converge: lower incomes gain ground on higher incomes.

It appears, though, that this convergence property is not robust across continents and cultures. Many Asian economies, Japan and the tigers are examples, grew much faster than European counterparts with similar incomes in 1960. Other countries, unfortunately (Burundi and Tanzania are the examples shown here), do not seem to catch up at all and appear trapped in poverty. These are some of the more important observations we will set out to understand in this and the next chapter.

9.2 THE PRODUCTION FUNCTION AND GROWTH ACCOUNTING

At the core of any analysis of economic growth is the production function. We draw again on the production function we made use of when studying the labour market in Chapter 6. Real output Y is a function F of the capital stock K (in real terms) and employment L:

$$Y = F(K, L) \qquad \textbf{Extensive form of production function} \qquad (9.1)$$

Figure 9.3 displays this function again, which is called the **extensive form** of the production function. Note, however, that the axes have been relabelled. This is because we now shift our perspective. In Chapter 6, when deriving the labour demand curve, we asked how at any point in time, with a given capital stock that could not be changed in the short run, different amounts of labour employed by firms would affect output produced.

Here we want to know why a country has the capital stock it has. To obtain an unimpaired view on this issue, we now ignore the business cycle. For a start we assume that employment is fixed at normal employment L_0, at which the labour market clears. In order not to have to differentiate all the time between magnitudes per capita or per worker, we even suppose that all people work. So the number of workers equals the population. All our arguments go through, however, if workers are a fixed share of the population. If this share changes, the effects are analogous to what results from a changing population as will be discussed in section 9.6.

The assumptions that economists make about the production function shown in Figure 9.3 are (adding a third one) as follows:

- Output increases as either factor or both factors increase.
- If one factor remains fixed, increases of the other factor yield smaller and smaller output gains.
- If both factors rise by the same percentage, output also rises by this percentage.

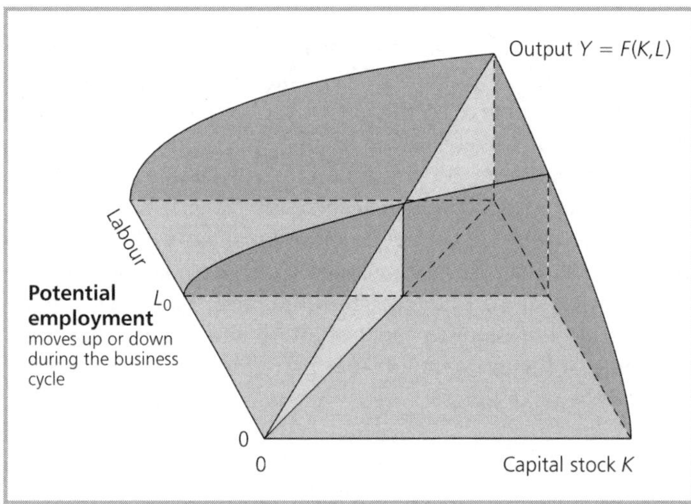

Figure 9.3 The 3D production function shows how, for a given production technology, output rises as greater and greater quantities of capital and/or labour are being employed. As a reminder, for first and second derivatives we assume $F_K, F_L > 0$ and $F_{KK}, F_{LL} < 0$.

As we know from Chapter 6, the second assumption refers to partial production functions. For our current purposes we place a vertical cut through the production function parallel to the axis measuring the capital stock. Figure 9.4 shows the obtained partial production function that fixes labour at L_0.

What we said about the partial production function employed in Chapter 6 applies in a similar way to the one displayed in Figure 9.4. The output gain accomplished by a small increase in K (which is called the **marginal product of capital**) is measured by the slope of the production function. As the given labour input is being combined with more and more capital, one-unit increases of K yield smaller and smaller output increases. As the two tangents exemplify, there is decreasing marginal productivity of capital.

The **marginal product of capital** is the output added by adding one unit of capital.

An important point to note is the following: this chapter's discussion of economic growth ignores the short-lived ups and downs of the business cycle by keeping employment at potential employment L^* at all times. Hence the partial production function given in Figure 9.4 measures how **potential output** Y^* varies with the capital stock. Consequently, throughout this chapter, whenever we talk about output or income, we really mean potential output or income! Having said this, we will refrain from characterizing potential employment and output by an asterisk in the remainder of this and the next chapter. Actual output in 1997, with the capital stock given at K_{1997}, may be above potential output Y_{1997} if there is a boom, or below Y_{1997} in a recession. Such deviations, due to temporary over- or underemployment of labour, are ignored here, but are exactly what the *DAD-SAS* model explained.

Note. Equation (9.1) really should have been written $Y^* = F(K, L^*)$ to explain how potential output relates to the capital stock at potential employment. We drop the asterisk with the understanding that ***Y* and *L* denote potential output income and potential employment in this and the next chapter!**

The third assumption refers to the level at which the economy operates. If we double all factor inputs, the volume of output produced also doubles (see Figure 9.5). This is assumed to hold generally, for all percentages by which we might increase inputs. The production function is then said to have **constant returns to scale**. Diminishing returns to scale can be ruled out on the grounds that it should always be possible to build a second production site next to the old factory and employ the same technology, number of workers and capital to produce the same output.

A production function has **constant returns to scale** if raising all inputs by a given factor raises output by that same factor.

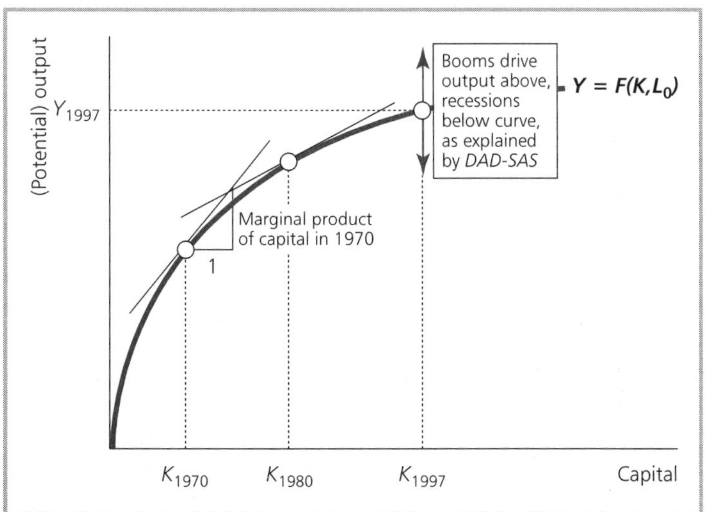

Figure 9.4 This partial production function shows how output increases as more capital is being used, while labour input remains fixed at L_0. The slope of $F(K, L_0)$ measures how much output is gained by a small increase of capital. The two tangent lines measure this marginal product of capital at K_{1970} and K_{1980} and indicate that it decreases as K rises.

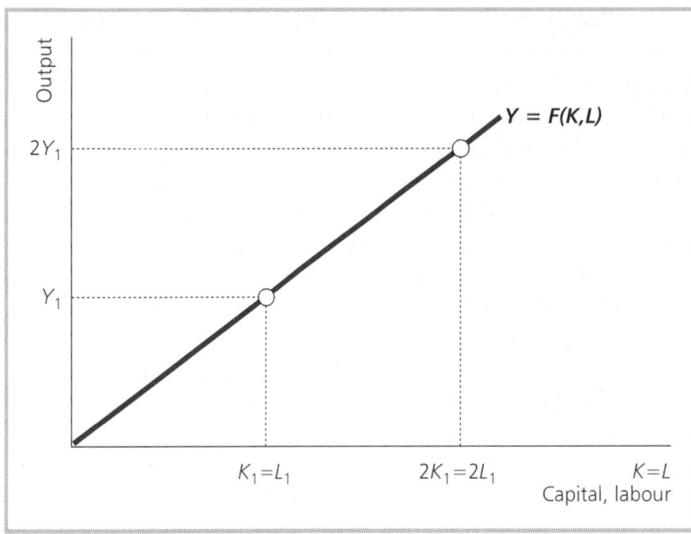

Figure 9.5 This production function shows how output increases as capital and labour rise in proportion. $F(K,L=K)$ is a straight line, indicating that we assume *constant returns to scale*: if capital and labour increase by a given percentage, output increases by the same percentage.

Growth accounting is similar to national income accounting. The latter provides a numerical account of the factors that contribute to national income, without having the ambition to explain, say, why investment is as high as it is. Similarly, **growth accounting** tries to link observed income growth to the factors that enter the production function, without asking why those factors developed the way they did. This question is left to growth theory, to which we will turn below.

Note. The formulation of this particular functional form as a basis for empirical estimates is due to US economist turned politician Paul Douglas and mathematician Charles Cobb.

As the word 'accounting' implies, growth accounting wants to arrive at some hard numbers. A general function like equation 9.1 is not useful for this purpose. Economists therefore use more specific functional forms when turning to empirical work. The most frequently employed form is the **Cobb–Douglas production function:**

$$Y = AK^{\alpha}L^{1-\alpha} \quad \textbf{Cobb–Douglas production function} \quad (9.2)$$

As Box 9.1 shows, this function has the same properties assumed to hold for the general production function discussed above, plus a few other properties that come in handy during mathematical operations and appear to fit the data quite well.

Equation 9.2 states that income is related to the factor inputs K and L and to the production technology as measured by the leading variable A. This leaves two ways for economic growth to occur, as Figure 9.6 illustrates. In panel (a) we keep technology constant between 1950 and the year 2000. Income grows only because of an expanding capital stock and a growing labour force. In panel (b) technology has improved, tilting the production function upwards. As a consequence GDP rises at any given combination of capital and labour employed.

The two motors of economic growth featured in the two panels of Figure 9.6 operate simultaneously. Growth accounting tries to identify their qualitative contributions. This is tricky, since the three factors comprising the multiplicative term on the right-hand side of equation 9.2 interact, affecting each other's contribution. A first step towards disentangling this is to take

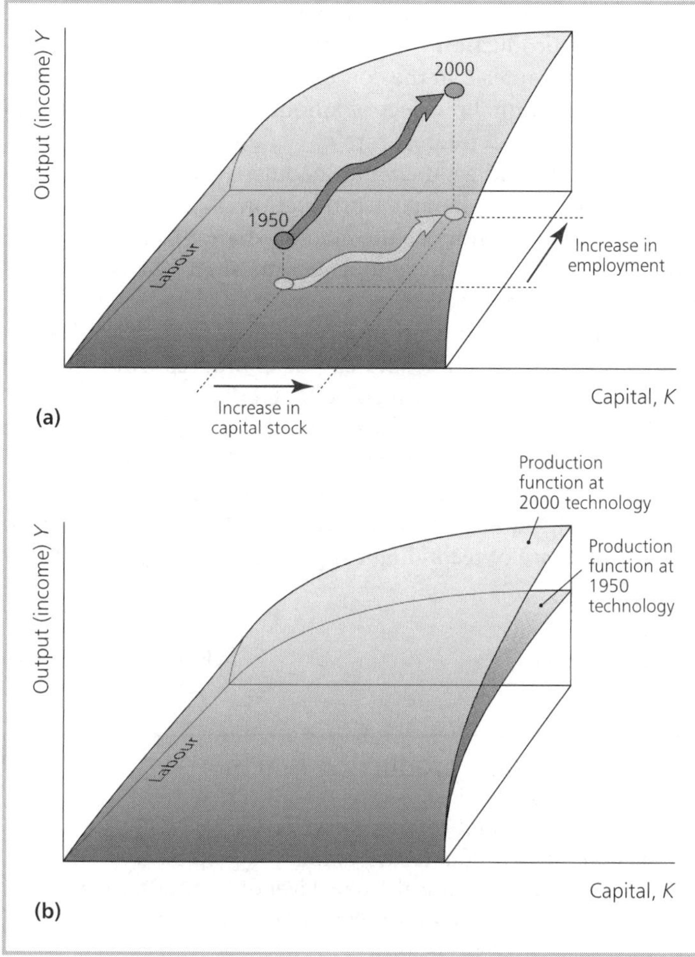

Figure 9.6 The two panels give a production function interpretation of income growth. Panel (a) assumes constant production technology. Then the production function graph does not change in this diagram. Income has nevertheless grown from 1950 to 2000 because the capital stock has risen and employment has gone up. Panel (b) illustrates the effect of technological progress on the production function graph. The upwards tilt of the production function would raise income even if input factors did not change. In reality all three indicated causes of income growth play a role: capital accumulation, labour force growth and technological progress..

Source: Case, Fair, Gärtner and Heather, *Economics*, Harlow: Prentice Hall Europe, 1999.

natural logarithms. This yields

$$\ln Y = \ln A + \alpha \ln K + (1 - \alpha)\ln L \tag{9.3}$$

meaning that the logarithm of income is a weighted sum of the logarithms of technology, capital and labour. Now take first differences on both sides (meaning that we deduct last period's values) to obtain $\ln Y - \ln Y_{-1} = \ln A - \ln A_{-1} + \alpha(\ln K - \ln K_{-1}) + (1 - \alpha)(\ln L - \ln L_{-1})$. Finally, making use of the property (mentioned previously and derived in the appendix on logarithms in Chapter 1) that the first difference in the logarithm of a variable is a good approximation for this variable's growth rate, we arrive at

Maths note. An alternative way to derive the growth-accounting equation starts by taking the total differential of the production function $Y = AK^{\alpha}L^{1-\alpha}$ which is $dY = \alpha AK^{\alpha-1}L^{1-\alpha}dK + (1-\alpha)AK^{\alpha}L^{-\alpha}dL$. Now divide by Y on the left-hand side and by $AK^{\alpha}L^{1-\alpha}$ on the right-hand side to obtain (after cancelling terms)

$$\frac{dY}{Y} = \alpha\frac{dK}{K} + (1-\alpha)\frac{dL}{L}$$

which is the continuous-time analogue to equation (9.4).

$$\frac{\Delta Y}{Y} = \frac{\Delta A}{A} + \alpha\frac{\Delta K}{K} + (1-\alpha)\frac{\Delta L}{L} \qquad \textbf{Growth accounting equation} \tag{9.4}$$

stating that a country's income growth is a weighted sum of the rate of technological progress $\Delta A/A$, capital growth and employment growth. All we need to know now before we can do some calculations with this equation is the magnitude of α. This is not as hard as it may seem, at least not if we assume that our economy operates under perfect competition. Perfect competition ensures that each factor of production is paid the marginal product it generates. As we already saw in Chapter 6 in the context of the labour market, then the real wage w equals the marginal product of labour. Similarly, the marginal product of capital equals the (real) interest rate r.

Empirical note. Between 1991 and 1998, the European Union had a labour income share $wL/Y = 1 - \alpha$ of 70.1%. The Netherlands had the lowest value at 65.6%, and Britain the highest at 73.4%.

Total labour income is wL, and total capital income rK. A very useful and convenient property of the Cobb–Douglas production function is that the exponents on the right-hand side indicate the income share this factor gets of total income. Hence $1 - \alpha = wL/Y$ is the labour income share and $\alpha = rK/Y$ is the capital income share (for a proof see Box 9.1 on the Cobb–Douglas function). The labour income share $1 - \alpha$ is around two-thirds for most industrial countries. It is relatively stable over time and can be computed from national income accounts by dividing total labour income by GDP.

Once we have a number for α, equation (9.3) can be used to sketch the graph of the contributions of technology, capital and labour to the development of (the logarithm of) income. Does it matter that technology cannot really be measured? Actually not; in fact, equation (9.4) is usually used to compute an estimate of the rate of technological progress. Solving it for $\Delta A/A$ yields

$$\frac{\Delta A}{A} = \frac{\Delta Y}{Y} - \alpha\frac{\Delta K}{K} - (1-\alpha)\frac{\Delta L}{L} \qquad \textbf{Solow residual}$$

BOX 9.1 The mathematics of the Cobb–Douglas production function

Instead of the general equation $Y = AF(K, L)$, economists often use the **Cobb–Douglas production function**

$$Y = AK^{\alpha}L^{1-\alpha} \qquad (1)$$

with α being a number between zero and one. It has the same properties given for equation (1), but can be used for substituting in numbers and is easier to manipulate mathematically.

Diminishing marginal products

We obtain the marginal product of labour by differentiating (1) with respect to L:

$$\frac{dY}{dL} = (1-\alpha)AK^{\alpha}L^{1-\alpha-1} = (1-\alpha)A\left(\frac{K}{L}\right)^{\alpha} \qquad (2)$$

This expression becomes smaller as we employ more labour L. Thus the marginal product of labour decreases. Similarly,

$$\frac{dY}{dK} = \alpha AK^{\alpha-1}L^{1-\alpha} = \alpha A\left(\frac{L}{K}\right)^{1-\alpha} \qquad (3)$$

reveals that the marginal product of capital also falls as K rises.

Constant returns to scale

If we double the amount of capital and labour used, what is the new level of income Y'? *On substituting* $2K$ for K and $2L$ for L into the production function, we obtain

$$Y' = A(2K)^{\alpha}(2L)^{1-\alpha} = A2^{\alpha+1-\alpha}K^{\alpha}L^{1-\alpha} = 2AK^{\alpha}L^{1-\alpha} = 2Y$$

Hence, income doubles as well. Generally, raising both inputs by a factor x raises output by that same factor x. Thus returns to scale are constant.

Constant income shares

If labour is paid its marginal product, say in a perfectly competitive labour market, then the wage rate equals (2), and total labour income wL as a share of income is written as

$$\frac{wL}{Y} = \frac{(1-\alpha)AK^{\alpha}L^{-\alpha}L}{AK^{\alpha}L^{1-\alpha}} = 1-\alpha \qquad \textbf{Labour income share}$$

If $1 - \alpha$ is the labour income share, the remainder, α, must go to capital owners. To verify this, determine rK/Y, letting the interest rate r equal the marginal product of capital given in (3).

CASE STUDY 9.1 Growth accounting in Italy

As Figure 1 shows, Italian GDP rose by almost 30% between 1981 and 1996. If we plug Italy's average labour income share of 71% during that period into a logarithmic Cobb–Douglas function we obtain

$$\ln Y = \ln A + 0.29 \ln K + 0.71 \ln L$$

To display the percentages that each of the right-hand side factors contributed to income growth since 1981, we may normalize Y, K and L to one for this year, so that their respective logarithms become zero.

The upper curve in Figure 1 shows the logarithm of income, which is the variable we set out to account for. The lowest curve depicts $0.71 \ln L$, the contribution of employment growth. It shows that if income growth had relied on employment growth alone, it would have been even lower in 1996 than it had been in 1981. The second curve adds the contribution of capital stock growth to employment growth. This combined effect is clearly positive. The remaining vertical distance to the $\ln Y$ line must be due to technological progress. It is obvious that improvements in production technology constitute the major factor behind Italy's income growth.

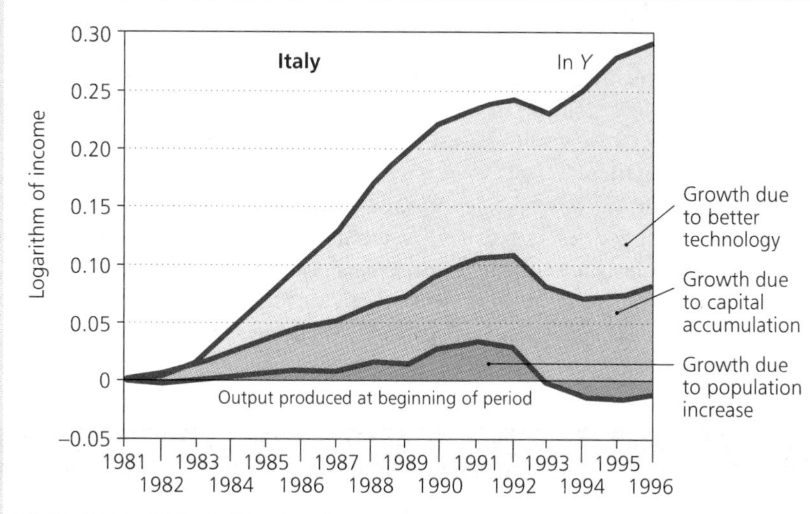

Figure 1

To plug in numbers, suppose income grew by 4.5%, the capital stock by 6%, employment by 1.5%, and $\alpha = 1/3$. Then

$$\frac{\Delta A}{A} = 0.045 - \tfrac{1}{3}0.06 - \tfrac{2}{3}0.015 = 0.015$$

The equation says that of the 4.5% observed growth in income 2 percentage points may be attributed to the growth in the capital stock and another 1 percentage point to employment growth. This leaves 1.5 percentage points of income growth unexplained. Since these cannot be attributed to input factor growth, they must represent improved technology. This number fills the gap in the growth accounting equation (9.4), the residual, and is generally referred to as the **Solow residual.** The Solow residual serves as an estimate of technological progress. Table 9.1 shows empirical results obtained in the fashion described above.

One interesting result is that the four included European economies had very similar growth experiences from the 1960s through the 1980s.

Table 9.1 Sources of economic growth in six OECD countries

	Percentage of income growth attributable to each source		
	Technological progress	Growth of capital stock	Employment growth
Britain	61	38	0
Germany	55	45	0
France	63	33	4
Italy	65	32	2
Japan	45	44	11
USA	20	37	42

Source: S. A. Englander and A. Gurney, (1994) 'Medium-term determinants of OECD productivity growth', OECD Economic Studies, 22.

Employment growth played no role at all. About one-third of the achieved increase in output is due to an increase of the capital stock. Almost two-thirds, however, resulted from improved production technology.

The experience of Japan and the United States was somewhat different. In both countries, technological progress played a much smaller role than in Europe. This is most striking in the United States, where improved technology only contributed 20%, while 42% of achieved output growth came from an increase in employment.

Growth accounting describes economic growth, but it does not explain it. Growth accounting does not ask why technology improved so much faster during one decade than during another, or why some countries employ a larger stock of capital than others. But it provides the basis for such important questions to be asked. We now begin to ask these questions by turning to **growth theory.**

9.3 GROWTH THEORY: THE SOLOW MODEL

The Solow growth model, sometimes called the neoclassical growth model, is the workhorse of research on economic growth, and often the basis of more recent refinements. We begin by considering its building blocks and how they interact.

We know from the circular flow model (or from the Keynesian cross) that, in equilibrium, planned spending equals income. Another way to state this is to say that leakages equal injections: $S - I + T - G + IM - EX = 0$. To retain the simplest possible framework for this chapter's introduction to the basics of economic growth, let us reactivate the global economy model with no trade and no government ($IM = EX = T = G = 0$). (Growth in the open economy and the role of the government will be discussed in the next chapter.) Then net leakages are zero if

$$I = S \tag{9.5}$$

(Planned) investment must make up for the amount of income funnelled out of the income circle by savings. If people consume the fraction c out of current income, as captured by the consumption function $C = cY$, they obviously save the rest. Thus the fraction they save (and invest) is $s = 1 - c$. Total savings are

$$S = sY \tag{9.6}$$

Combining (9.5) and (9.6) gives

$$I = sY$$

Substitution of (9.1) for Y yields

$$I = sF(K, L) \tag{9.7}$$

There is a second side to investment, however. It does not only constitute demand needed to compensate for savings trickling out of the income circle, but it also adds to the stock of capital: by definition it constitutes that part of demand which buys capital goods. Note, however, that in order to obtain the net change in the stock of capital, ΔK, we must subtract depreciation from current gross investment I. If capital depreciates at the rate δ, we obtain

$$\Delta K = I - \delta K \tag{9.8}$$

Substitution of (9.7) into (9.8) gives

$$\Delta K = sF(K, L) - \delta K \tag{9.9}$$

Maths note. Equation (9.9) is a difference equation in K. Standard solution recipes fail because the equation is non-linear due to the F function. Therefore economists usually resort to qualitative graphical solution methods.

Equation (9.9) tells us that the capital stock grows when the first term on the right-hand side, private savings or gross investment, exceeds the amount of capital we lose through depreciation. A graph sheds light on when this is the case.

The first term on the right-hand side is the production function already shown above, multiplied with the savings rate. Figure 9.7 shows both the production function and the savings-and-investment function.

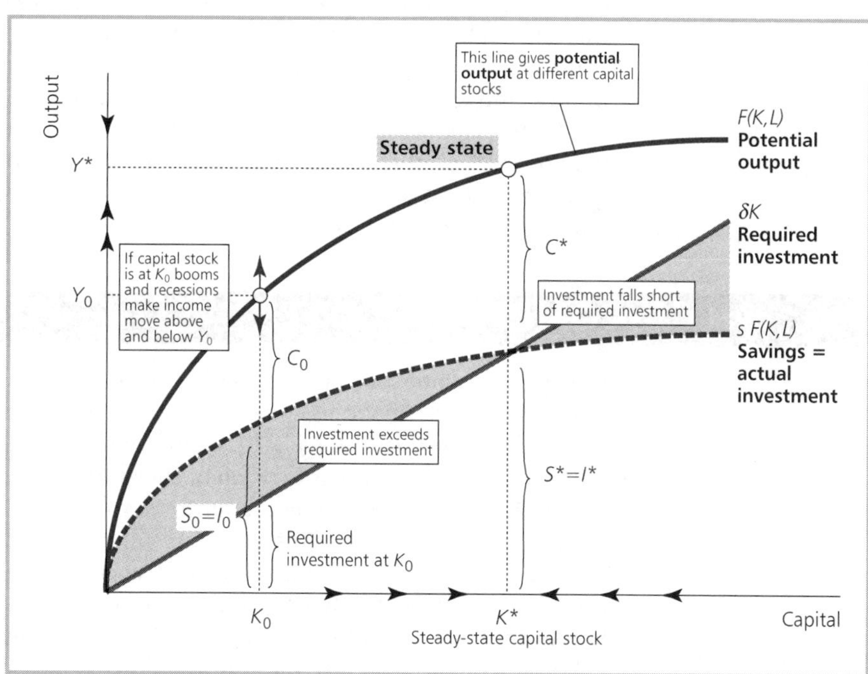

Figure 9.7 The solid curved blue line shows how much is being produced with different capital stocks. The broken blue line measures the fixed share of output being saved and invested. The difference between the curved lines is what is left for consumption. The grey straight line shows investment required to replace exactly capital lost through depreciation. If actual investment equals required investment, the capital stock and output do not change. The economy is in a *steady state*. If actual investment exceeds required investment, the capital stock and output grow. If actual investment falls short of required investment, the capital stock and output fall.

Note. The **requirement line** shows the amount of investment required to keep the capital stock at the indicated level.

The second term on the right-hand side is a straight line with slope δ. Let us call this the **requirement line**, because it states the investment required to keep the capital stock at its current level. If the savings function is initially steeper than δ, there is one capital endowment K^* at which both lines intersect. It is only at this capital stock that required and actual investment are equal.

The reason that K^* stands out among all other possible values for K is because it marks some sort of gravity point. This is the level to which the capital stock tends to converge from any other initial value. To see this, assume that the capital stock falls short of K^*. Then actual investment as given by the savings function obviously exceeds required investment. So in the entire segment left of K^* net investment is positive and the capital stock grows. This process only comes to a halt as K reaches K^*.

If K initially exceeds K^*, actual investment falls short of the investment level required to replace capital lost through depreciation. So to the right of K^* the capital stock must be falling, and it continues to do so until it eventually reaches K^*. Once we know K^*, the equilibrium or **steady-state** level of the capital stock, it is easy to read the steady-state level of income Y^* off the production function.

To avoid confusion, it is important to distinguish the two equilibrium concepts that we now have for income. **Potential income** is a short- or medium-run concept. It is the level around which the business cycle analyzed in the first eight chapters of this book fluctuates within a few years. During that time the capital stock cannot change much and may well be taken as given. In Figure 9.7 this capital stock may be at K^* or at any other point such as K_0. Booms and recessions occur as vertical fluctuations around the potential output level marked by the partial production function. **Steady-state income** is the one level of potential income that obtains once the capital stock has been built up to the desired level. Returning to this level after a displacement, say, during a war, may take decades.

9.4 WHY INCOMES MAY DIFFER

(Potential) income levels may differ between countries if the parameters of our model differ. For one thing, the labour force (which we simply set equal to the population) can differ hugely between countries. Remember that by postulating a fixed labour force L_0 we had sliced the neoclassical production function at this value. For a larger labour force we would simply have to place that vertical cut further out. This would result in a partial production function (with labour fixed at $L_1 > L_0$) which is steeper and higher for all capital stocks (see Figure 9.8). So an increase of the labour force (say, due to a higher population) turns the partial production function upwards.

For a given savings rate the upward shift of the production function pulls the savings function upwards too. If more is being produced at each level of the capital stock, more is being saved and invested. Since, on the other hand, depreciation remains unaffected by population levels, the new investment curve intersects the requirement line at a higher level of the capital stock. Not surprisingly, therefore, high population countries should also have high capital stocks and high aggregate output. Note that this result says nothing about

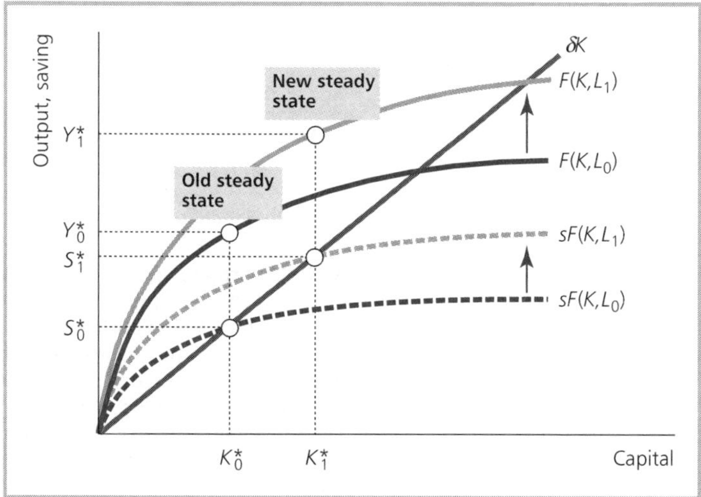

Figure 9.8 An increase of the workforce from L_0 to L_1 turns the partial production function upwards, while keeping it locked at the origin. The curve is higher and steeper for all capital stocks. The savings function moves upwards too. It now intersects the unchanged requirement line at higher levels of output and capital.

per capita levels of capital and income, which may be the variables we are ultimately interested in.

An important catchphrase in discussions of international competitiveness and comparative growth is *productivity gains*. While in our model marginal and average factor productivity change during transition episodes, this is due to changing factor inputs. These effects are important and may be long-lasting. But they do peter out as we settle into the steady state. When we talk about productivity gains in the context of growth, however, we really mean the more efficient use of inputs. Such *technological progress* implies that given quantities of labour and capital now yield higher output levels.

Figure 9.9 illustrates the effects of a once-only improvement of the production technology. Any quantity of capital, combined with a given labour input, now yields more output than with the old technology. The production function turns upwards, just as it did when population increased. The investment function turns upwards too. With the requirement line remaining in place,

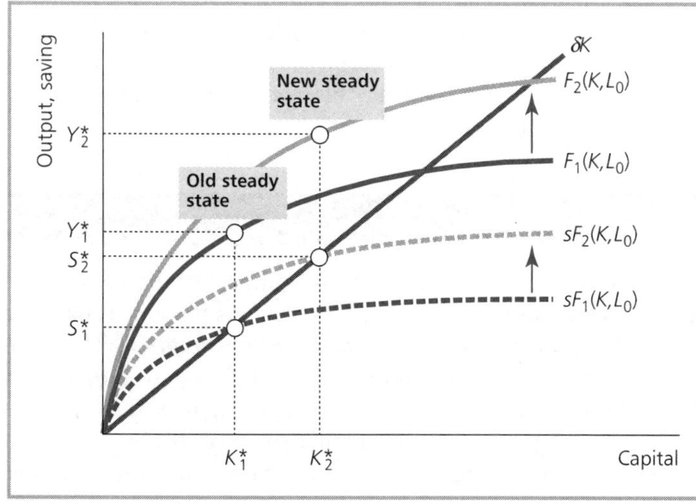

Figure 9.9 An improvement in production technology, which changes the production function from F_1 to F_2, turns the partial production function upwards, while keeping it locked at the origin. The curve is higher and steeper for all capital stocks. The savings function moves upwards too. It now intersects the unchanged requirement line at higher levels of output and capital.

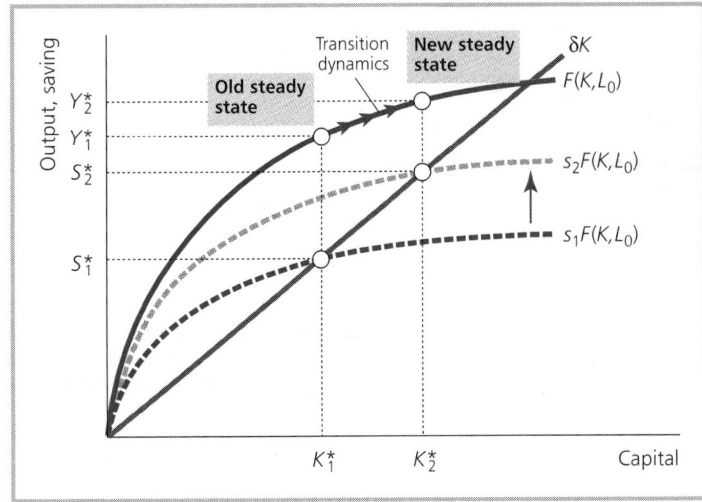

Figure 9.10 An increase of the savings rate from s_1 to s_2 turns the savings function upwards, while leaving the partial production function in place. The savings function now intersects the requirement line at higher levels of output and the capital stock. The movement from the old to the new steady state is called *transition dynamics*.

both the equilibrium capital stock and equilibrium output rise. Despite the striking similarity between Figures 9.8 and 9.9 there is an important difference: although income rises in both cases, technological progress raises *income per capita* while population growth does not.

A third parameter that may differ substantially between countries is the savings rate. The effect of raising the savings rate is also easily read off the graph (Figure 9.10). While in this case the production function stays put in its original position, the higher share of output being saved and invested is now turning the savings function upwards. With depreciation being independent of the savings rate, the point of intersection between the new investment function and the new (= old) requirement line lies northeast of the old one. This result is important. It shows that for a given population and given technology, the steady-state level of income can be raised by saving more.

A **steady state** is an equilibrium in which variables do not change any more. The movement from one steady state to another is called **transition dynamics**.

Figure 9.10 may also sharpen our understanding of the terms **steady state** as opposed to **transition dynamics** along the potential income curve: if the savings rate rises, a new steady state or long-run equilibrium obtains in which the income is higher. Once the new steady state is reached, however, income does not grow any further. Income growth is zero in both steady states. To move from the old to the new steady state takes time, however, as higher savings only gradually build up the capital stock. During this period of transition we do observe a continuous growth of income.

9.5 WHAT ABOUT CONSUMPTION?

Before getting too excited about the detected positive impact of the savings rate on income, remember that to work and produce as much as possible is hardly a goal in itself. Rather, the ultimate goal is to *maximize consumption*. The complication with this is that it is not clear at all what a higher savings rate does to consumption. While we have seen above that a higher savings rate leads to higher income, a higher savings rate leaves a smaller share of this income available for consumption. Without closer scrutiny the net effect remains ambiguous.

To clarify things, put the savings rate at its maximum, $s = 1$. Then the savings-and-investment function turns all the way up into a position that is identical to the production function. Whatever is being produced is being saved and invested. The good news is that this drives the capital stock up to its *maximal* steady-state level K^*_{max}, and also provides maximum steady-state income Y^*_{max}. The bad news is that not a penny of this income is left for consumption. Consumption is zero (see Figure 9.11).

At the other extreme, with a savings rate of zero, the investment function becomes a horizontal line on the abscissa. People consume all their income and save and invest nothing. Depreciation exceeds investment at all positive levels of the capital stock. So the capital stock shrinks and continues to do so until all capital is gone and no more output is produced and no more income can be generated. Thus, again, consumption is zero (see Figure 9.12).

With these two corner results, and after having shown in Figure 9.7 above that positive consumption is possible for an interior value of the savings rate, a savings rate must exist somewhere between the two boundary values of zero and one, checked above, which maximizes consumption. To identify this savings rate, remember that *in the steady state savings equals required investment*. Therefore consumption possibilities that can be maintained in the steady state are always given by the vertical distance between the production function and the requirement line. Initially, as long as the production function is steeper than the requirement line, this distance widens as the capital stock grows. The reason is that additional capital yields more output than it sucks up savings needed to maintain this increased capital stock. At higher levels of the capital stock we observe the opposite effect. The switch occurs at a threshold where the slopes of the production function and the requirement line are equal. The **golden rule of capital accumulation** says that the savings rate should be set to s_{gold}, just so as to yield the capital stock K^*_{gold}, the output level Y^*_{gold} and the consumption level C^*_{gold}.

The **golden rule of capital accumulation** defines the savings rate that maximizes consumption. At the resulting capital stock additional capital exactly generates enough output gains to cover the incurred additional depreciation.

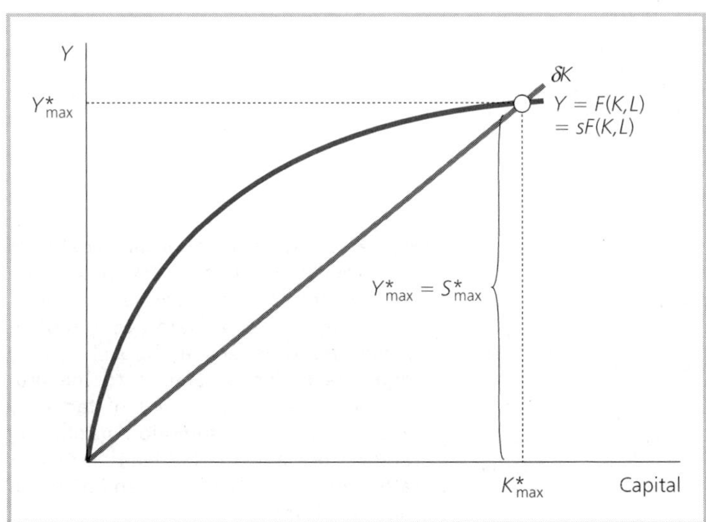

Figure 9.11 If individuals save all their income ($s = 1$), the savings-and-investment function coincides with the production function. Capital and income grow to their maximum levels. But since all of that maximum income must be saved to replace depreciating capital, nothing is left for consumption.

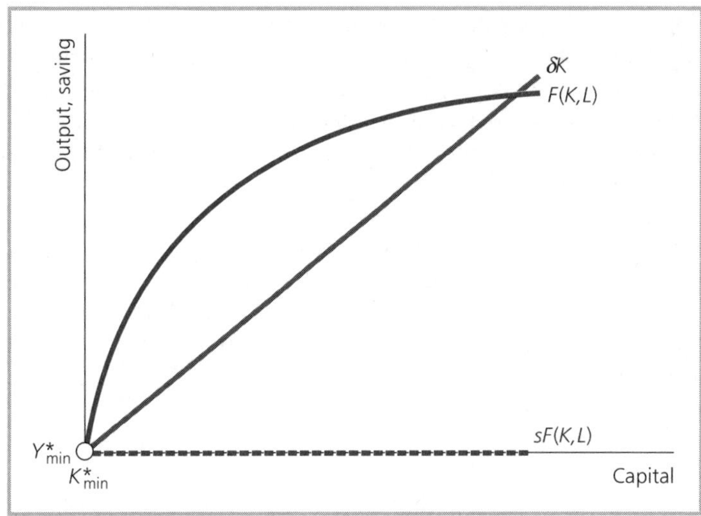

Figure 9.12 If individuals do not save at all ($s = 0$) the savings-and-investment function coincides with the abscissa. Capital and income fall to zero. Therefore, even though individuals are ready to spend everything they earn, no income leaves nothing for consumption.

To pick out the *golden steady state* from all available steady states, proceed as follows (see Figure 9.13):

1 Draw in the production function. Ignore the savings function for now, as we do not know the golden savings rate yet.
2 Draw in the requirement line. In a steady state actual investment equals required investment. So the requirement line defines all possible steady states available at various savings rates.
3 Note that the vertical distance between the production function and the requirement line measures consumption available at different steady states.
4 Consumption is maximized where a line parallel to the requirement line just touches the production function. This point defines golden-rule output and the golden-rule capital stock.
5 Since the actual savings curve must intersect the requirement line at the golden-rule capital stock, this identifies the golden-rule savings rate.

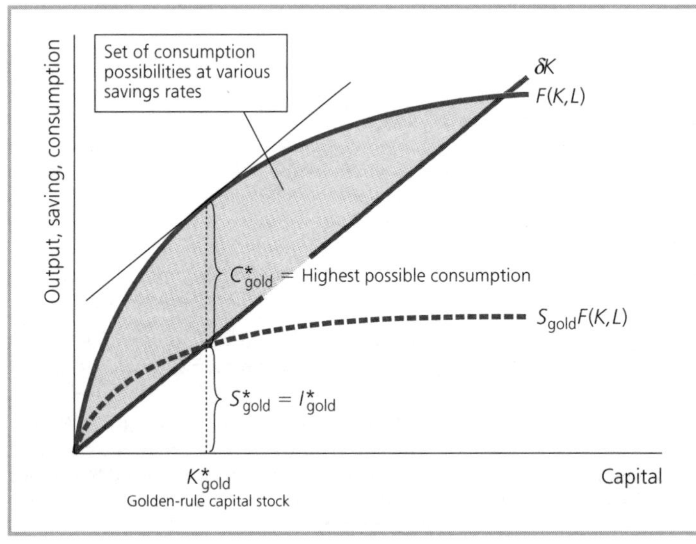

Figure 9.13 The vertical distance between the production function $F(K, L)$ and the requirement line δK measures consumption at various steady states. Consumption is maximized where a parallel to the requirement line is tangent to the production function. This point of tangency determines the consumption-maximizing capital stock and the golden-rule savings rate required to accumulate and maintain this capital stock.

If the actual savings rate does not correspond with the savings rate recommended by the golden rule, should the government try to move it towards s_{gold}, say by offering tax incentives? Well, that depends.

Assume first that the savings rate is too high. Then a lower savings rate raises consumption immediately, at the given capital stock, but also in the long run, as the golden rule indicates. So lowering the savings rate is unequivocally a good thing to do. Not to do it would be foolish or, as economists say, *dynamically inefficient*.

Now assume that the savings rate is too low. Raising it would provide for higher consumption in the long run. The immediate effect, however, is to lower consumption at the given stock of capital! So the question boils down to how much weight we want to put on today's (or *this* generation's) consumption as compared to tomorrow's (or *future* generations') consumption. This is not for the economist to decide. His or her proper task is to set out the options.

Empirical note. Most countries save less and, hence, accumulate less capital than the golden rule suggests. Thus, they do face the dilemma of whether to reduce today's consumption in order to raise tomorrow's.

Figure 9.14 illustrates the inferior steady-state paths (see the two lower straight lines) generated by savings rates which deviate from s_{gold}. The graph makes the point that choices for policy-makers are simple when the savings rate is too high (blue line). Then a reduction to s_{gold} generates immediate and long-run rewards in the form of permanently higher consumption. The lower grey path illustrates the dilemma that policy-makers are facing when s is initially too low. Then the path of permanently higher consumption can only be obtained at the cost of temporarily lower consumption.

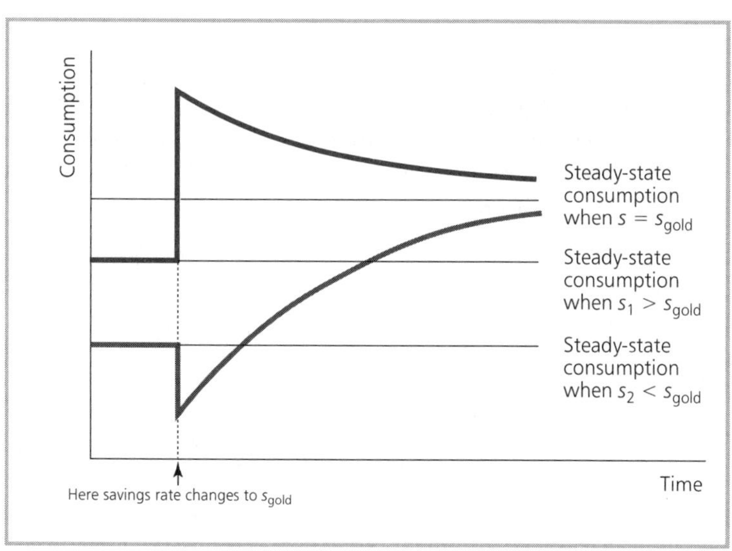

Figure 9.14 Savings rates smaller or larger than the one given by the golden rule restrict the country to lower consumption paths. Choices differ in the two cases. If $s > s_{gold}$, reducing the savings rate improves consumption now and forever. Not to do so is dynamically inefficient. If $s < s_{gold}$, the country faces a dilemma. To raise s to s_{gold} only pays off later. Before consumption improves the country goes through a period of reduced consumption.

9.6 POPULATION GROWTH AND TECHNOLOGICAL PROGRESS

Populations grow continuously. So the partial production function shifts upwards all the time, making the capital stock and income rise and rise. Even after the economy has settled into a steady state, we are still required to draw new production and savings functions for each new period, but this is awkward. Also, the representation used so far puts countries like Germany and Luxembourg on quite different slices cut off our three-dimensional production function shown as Figure 9.3. That means that we have to use a different partial production function for each country.

To get around such problems, we now recast the Solow growth model into a form that is better suited for comparing economies of different sizes and for analyzing countries with growing populations. This version should measure *output per worker* on the ordinate and *capital per worker* on the abscissa. To obtain such a *new representation of the same model*, we first need to know what determines output per worker. This is not difficult. Recall our assumption that the production function $Y = F(K, L)$ has constant returns to scale. Then, say, doubling both inputs simply doubles output: $2Y = F(2K, 2L)$. Or multiplying all inputs by the fraction $1/L$ multiplies output by $1/L$ as well:

Maths note. The properties $f'(k) > 0$ and $f'' < 0$ can be shown to follow from what we assumed for $F(K, L)$.

$$(1/L)Y = F[(1/L)K, (1/L)L]$$

Cancelling out, this is written as

$$Y/L = F(K/L, 1)$$

Now represent per capita (or, since we let employment equal the population, per worker) variables by their respective lower-case counterparts (that is $k \equiv K/L$ and $y \equiv Y/L$). Denote the resulting function $F(k,1)$ more concisely as $f(k)$, without the redundant parameter of 1, and we have the desired simple function, called the **intensive form**,

$$y = f(k) \qquad \textbf{Intensive form of production function} \qquad (9.10)$$

Per capita income is a positive function of capital per worker only. As Figure 9.15 shows, y increases as k increases, but at a decreasing rate.

Next we need to know what makes k rise or fall. Capital per worker changes for three reasons:

1 Any investment per capita, i, directly adds to capital per worker.
2 Depreciation eats away a constant fraction of capital per worker.

These are the two factors influencing capital formation already considered above, although here we cast the argument in per capita terms. There is a third and new factor:

3 New entrants into the workforce require capital to be spread over more workers. Hence, capital per worker falls in proportion to the population growth rate n.

Maths note. The total differential of $k \equiv K/L$ is $d(K/L) = (1/L)dK - (K/L^2)dL$ or $d(K/L) = dK/L - (K/L)(dL/L)$. Substituting the variables defined in the text gives $dk = i - nk$. The expression given in the text follows if depreciation of capital per worker, δk, is subtracted, and we take discrete changes of k (Δk instead of dk).

Combining these three effects yields

$$\Delta k = i - \delta k - nk \qquad (9.11)$$

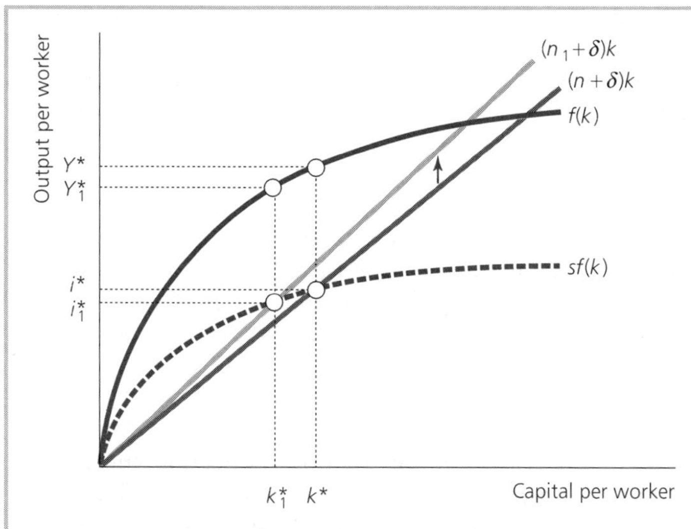

Figure 9.15 The solid curved line shows per capita output as a function of the per capita capital stock. Per capita savings and investment are a fraction of this output. The steady state obtains where per capita savings equal required investment per capita. If population growth increases, the requirement line becomes steeper. The new steady state features less capital and lower output per worker.

The first term on the right-hand side states that investment per worker i directly adds to capital per worker. The second term states that depreciation eats away a fraction δ of existing capital per worker. The third term states that an n% addition to the labour force makes the capital stock available for each worker fall by $n \times k$.

Investment per worker i equals savings per worker sy. So replacing i in equation (9.11) by sy and making use of equation (9.10), we obtain

$$\Delta k = sf(k) - (n + \delta)k$$

In the steady state the capital stock per worker does not change any more ($\Delta k = 0$). Hence, the two terms given on the right-hand side must be equal. To achieve this, investment not only needs to replace capital lost through depreciation, but must also endow new entrants into the workforce with capital. This is why the slope of the requirement line is now given by the sum of the depreciation rate and of population growth.

With the relabelling of the axes in per capita terms and the augmented requirement line, the graphical representation and analysis of the model proceeds along familiar lines.

The steady state obtains where the investment function and the requirement line intersect. If the capital stock per worker is smaller than its steady-state value k^*, actual investment exceeds required investment and income and capital per worker grow. In the region $k > k^*$ the opposite obtains and both k and y fall.

What happens if two countries are identical except for population growth? The only effect that higher population growth has is to turn the requirement line $(n + \delta)k$ upwards. Now each period a higher percentage of workers must be equipped with capital if the capital stock per worker is to stay at its current level. At the old steady state k^*, investment is too low and k begins to fall towards the lower steady-state level k_1^*. So the model yields the testable empirical implication that *countries with higher population growth tend to have lower capital stocks per worker and also lower per capita incomes.*

Another unrealistic assumption employed so far is that the economy in question operates with the same production technology all the time. In reality technology appears to improve continuously. One way to incorporate technology into the production function is by assuming that it determines the efficiency E of labour. The production function then reads

$$Y = F(K, E \times L)$$

where the product $E \times L$ is labour measured in efficiency units. Representing technology in this fashion is particularly convenient for our purposes. All we have to do is divide both sides of the production function not by L, as we had done above, but by $E \times L$. This yields a new production function

$$\hat{y} = f(\hat{k})$$

with $\hat{y} \equiv Y/(EL)$ and $\hat{k} \equiv K/(EL)$.

Maths note. The total differential of $\hat{k} \equiv K/(EL)$ is $d(K/(EL)) = (1/(EL))dK - (K/(EL^2))dL - (K/(E^2L))dE$ or $d(KE/L) = dK/(EL) - (K/(EL))(dL/L) - (K/(EL))(dE/E)$. Substituting the variables defined in the text gives

$$dk = \hat{i} - (n + \varepsilon)\hat{k}.$$

The expression given in the text follows after depreciation of capital per worker, $\delta\hat{k}$, is subtracted, and we take discrete changes of $\hat{k}$.

For a familiar graphical representation of this production function we simply write output *per efficiency unit of labour* $\hat{y}$ instead of output *per worker* on the ordinate. The abscissa now measures capital per efficiency unit $\hat{k}$. The production function shows how output per efficiency unit of labour depends on capital per efficiency unit (see Figure 9.16).

The requirement line now tells us how much investment per efficiency unit of labour we need to keep the capital stock per efficiency unit at the current level. In order to achieve this, investment must now

- replace capital lost through depreciation (as above),
- cater to new workers (as above), and
- equip new efficiency units of labour created by technological progress, which we assume to proceed at the rate ε (this is new):

$$\Delta\hat{k} = \hat{i} - (\delta + n + \varepsilon)\hat{k}$$

The steady-state and transition dynamics are obtained along reasoning analogous to the one employed above. In equilibrium, income per efficiency unit

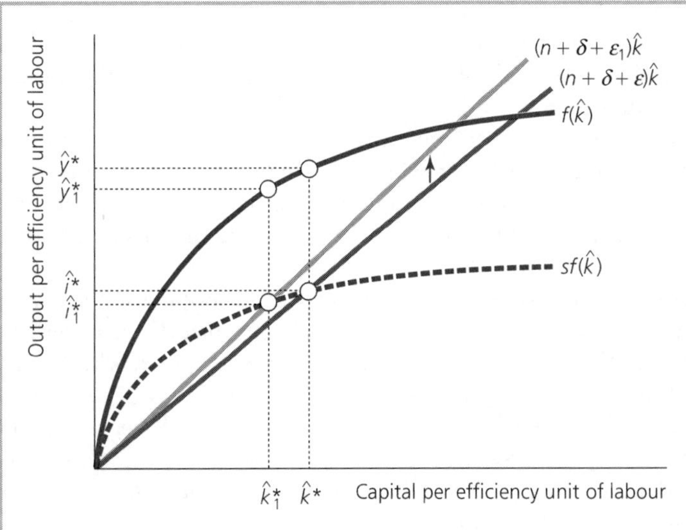

Figure 9.16 The axes measure output and capital per efficiency unit of labour. With this qualification the production function, the savings function and the requirement line look as they did in previous diagrams. The steady-state and transition dynamics are determined along by-now familiar lines. If technology improves, making labour more efficient, the requirement line becomes steeper. The new steady state features less capital and lower output per efficiency unit, but more capital and higher output per worker.

remains constant. Since *efficiency units* of labour grow faster than labour, due to technological progress, output (and capital) per worker must be growing. So we finally have a model that explains *income growth* in the conventional meaning of the term.

As regards comparative statics, a faster rate of technological progress turns the requirement curve upwards, thus lowering capital and income *per efficiency unit*. Does this mean that faster technological progress is bad? With regard to per capita income, the answer is no. Remember that the one-off technology improvement analyzed in section 9.4 raised capital and output *per worker*. The same result must apply here, where the one-off technological improvement simply occurs period after period. Therefore, *faster technological progress raises the level and the growth rate of output per worker.*

CASE STUDY 9.2 Income and leisure choices in the OECD countries

When microeconomists analyze individual behaviour they usually assume that two things enhance a person's utility: first, consumption (which is limited by income); second, leisure time (the time we have to enjoy the things we consume). This makes it obvious that judging the well-being of a country's citizens by looking at income would be just as one-sided as judging their well-being by looking at leisure time.

Using data for the year 1996, Figures 1 and 2 show that a country's per capita income and its leisure time need not necessarily go hand in hand. Figure 1 shows per capita incomes relative to the OECD average normalized to 100. The richest country in the sample is the USA, with per capita income 35% above average. The poorest country is Portugal, whose income falls short of the OECD average by 33%. Figure 2 ranks countries according to leisure time per inhabitant. As we may have expected, there appears to be some trade-off: many countries with the world's highest per capita incomes are at the end of the leisure timescale. They appear to achieve their high incomes mostly by working a lot, and having much less time left for

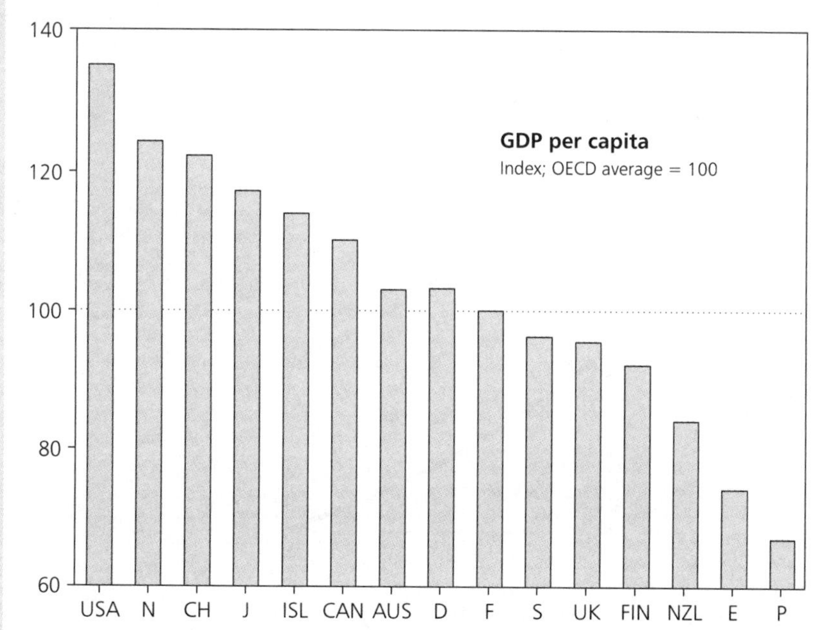

Figure 1

Case study 9.2 continued

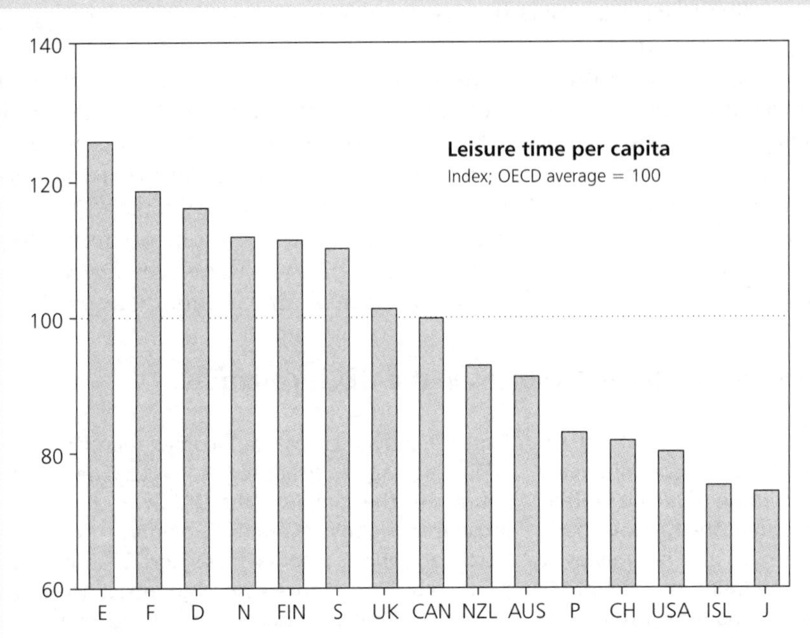

Figure 2

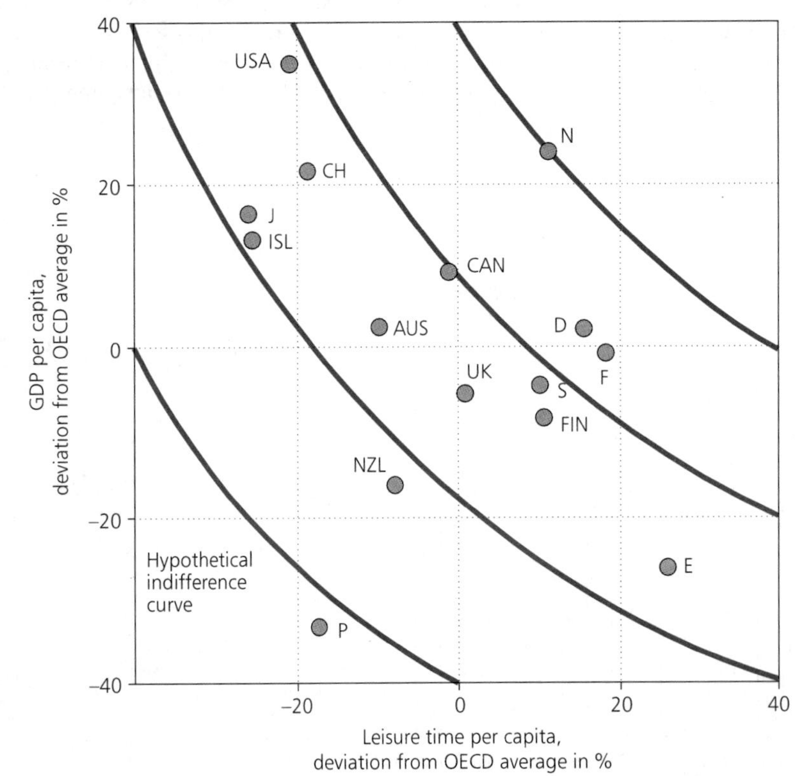

Figure 3

Case study 9.2 continued

off-work activities than others. On the other hand some countries with very low per capita incomes are doing very well in the leisure time ranking. Spain is one such example.

Exceptions from this general trade-off appear to be Portugal, which fares poorly both in terms of income and leisure time, and Norway which (probably helped by North Sea oil revenues) generates one of the highest per capita incomes while at the same time enjoying above average leisure time.

Figure 3 merges the data shown separately in Figures 1 and 2 into a scatter plot. This diagram illustrates the apparent trade-off situation from a somewhat different angle. Most countries that clearly perform above average in one category pay for this by dropping below average in the other category. As just mentioned, though, clear exceptions from this general rule are Norway and Portugal (and, to some extent, New Zealand).

So which country's citizens are better off? This is difficult to say. Strictly speaking, one country's citizens are only unequivocally better off than others, if they have both more income and more leisure time. For example, Norwegians are certainly better off than Canadians. Britons are better off than New Zealanders, and the Swiss are better off than the Japanese. However, whenever one country is better off in one category, but worse off in the other, we cannot really tell. This applies when comparing France with the USA, or Spain with Australia. Without a way of weighing 1% more leisure time against 1% less income, no judgment is possible.

As a crude attempt, however, note that in the OECD area a day contains about eight hours of work time and eight hours of leisure time. In equilibrium, one hour of leisure time may be worth about as much as we can produce in one hour of work time. If not, individuals would (try to) either work more and enjoy fewer hours of leisure, or work less to have more time off. So 1% more income is worth about the same as 1% more leisure time.

This means that indifference curves in leisure/income space would have a slope of about −1 when income and leisure time are at the OECD average, or exceed or fall short of it by the same percentage. This would be the case on a 45° line connecting the lower left and upper right corners of the diagram. If both income and leisure time yield decreasing marginal utility, indifference curves might look like those sketched in the diagram. A country's citizens' utility level would then be the higher the further to the right is the indifference curve reached by that country.

One might argue that countries need not all have the same preferences. So each country may optimize choices in the context of its own set of indifference curves, and its location in Figure 3 may simply be the best it can do. Then, of course, we have no generally accepted basis for making comparisons between countries.

Data source and further reading: J.-C. Lambelet and A. Mihailov (1999) 'A note on the Swiss economy: Did the Swiss economy really stagnate in the 1990s, and is Switzerland really all that rich?' *Analyses et prévisions*.

9.7 EMPIRICAL MERITS AND DEFICIENCIES OF THE SOLOW MODEL

Empirical work based on the Solow growth model usually proceeds from the assumption that, in principle, the same production technologies are available to all countries. Thus all countries should operate on the same partial production function and experience the same rate of technological progress. This leaves only two factors that may account for differences in steady-state per capita incomes.

The first is the savings or investment rate. The higher a country's rate of investment, the larger the capital stock per worker, and the higher is per capita income. Figure 9.17 looks at whether this hypothesis stands up to the data by

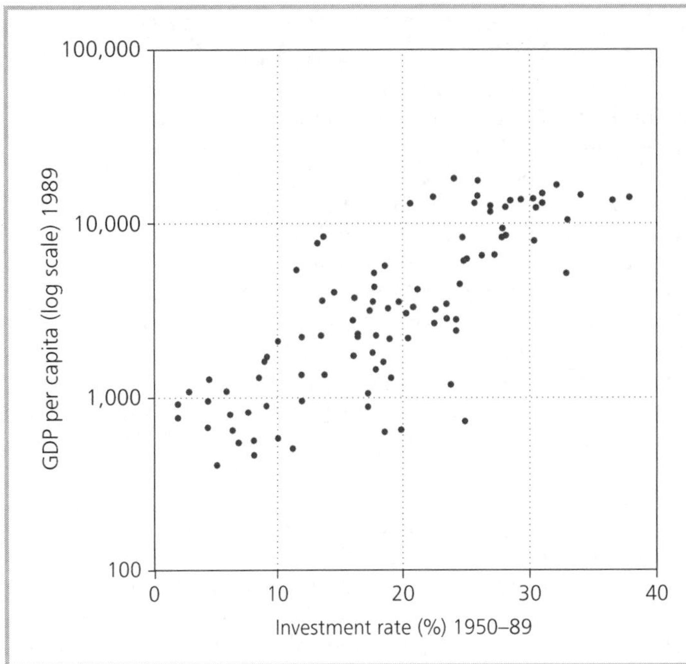

Figure 9.17 According to the Solow model, the higher a country's savings or investment rate (and, hence, capital accumulation), the higher its income (per capita). The graph underscores this prediction for a large number of the world's economies.
Source: R. Barro and J. Lee: http://www.nuff.ox.ac.uk/economics/growth/barlee.htm.

plotting per capita income at the vertical and the investment rate at the horizontal axis for a sample of 98 countries.

By and large, the data support this aspect of the Solow model, but not perfectly so, since the data points are not lined up like pearls on a string, but instead form a cloud. However, we should only have expected a perfect alignment if there were no other factors that influence per capita income. If two countries with the same investment rate differ in these other factors, they will have different per capita incomes.

This chapter's basic version of the Solow model singles out one such factor: the population growth rate. The faster the population grows, the smaller is per capita income. The reason is that if the population grows fast, a lot of new workers enter employment every year. They arrive with no capital. Hence, a large part of what those who work save is needed to equip new entrants with capital. Only a relatively small part of saving can be used to replace depreciated capital. As a consequence, this country cannot afford a high capital stock per worker and must be content with a comparatively low per capita income.

Figure 9.18 checks whether this second hypothesis is supported by the data, and the answer is yes. Again, the relationship is not strict. In fact, the cloud of data points is fairly wide. But again, this does not come as a surprise, since different savings rates would give countries that have the same rate of population growth different per capita incomes.

Empirical note. Worldwide some 60% of the differences in national per capita incomes can be attributed to differences in the investment rate and in population growth.

When researchers use statistical methods to study the combined influence of investment rates and population on per capita incomes, they usually find that 60% of the income differences can be traced back to differences in investment rates and population growth. So the basic Solow model appears to be carrying us a long way towards explaining why some countries are rich and why some are poor. But it also leaves a sizeable chunk of income differences unexplained.

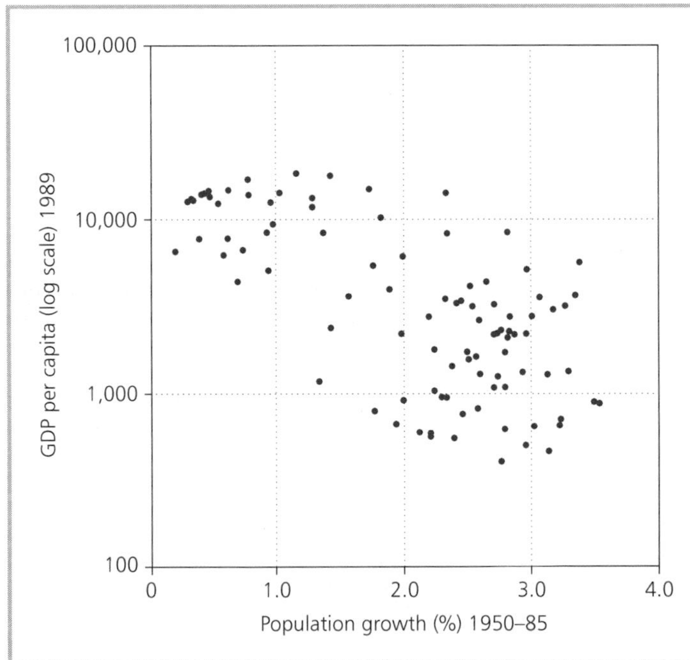

Figure 9.18 According to the Solow model, the higher a country's rate of population growth, the lower its income (per capita). This prediction also seems to hold for a large number of the world's economies, though less clearly so than the prediction checked in Figure 9.17.

Source: R. Barro and J. Lee: http://www.nuff.ox.ac.uk/economics/growth/barlee.htm.

While the above argument implicitly assumes that all countries have already settled into their respective steady states, other work explicitly acknowledges that adjustment may be slow and that most countries are on a transition path. Then incomes would differ, even if all countries had the same steady state. In this case, the Solow model yields an interesting proposition regarding the relationship between the level of income and income growth.

Per capita incomes in countries that are in the steady state only grow at the rate of technological progress. If a country's capital stock is below its steady-state value, income growth is higher than the rate of technological progress, because the capital endowment per worker rises. If the capital stock exceeded its steady-state value, per capita income could not grow at the rate of technological progress because capital endowment per worker falls. All this can be generalized into the so-called **absolute convergence hypothesis**, which states that there is a negative relationship between a country's initial level of income and subsequent income growth. Figure 9.19 checks whether empirical data feature income convergence.

Empirical note. In homogeneous groups of countries, lower income levels are typically related to higher growth rates. In more diverse samples this does not apply.

There are two messages in this data plot. First, there is no worldwide convergence of incomes. Many poor countries grow more slowly than the rich countries, thus widening the income gap. Second, within relatively homogeneous groups of countries (the Western European countries have been singled out in blue), convergence does indeed occur.

Do these two observations and the Solow model match? Well, at least they do not contradict it. The Solow model only proposes absolute convergence for countries with the same steady states, that is, for countries with similar investment rates and population growth. This holds reasonably well for Western Europe, and it is why incomes there do seem to converge. On the

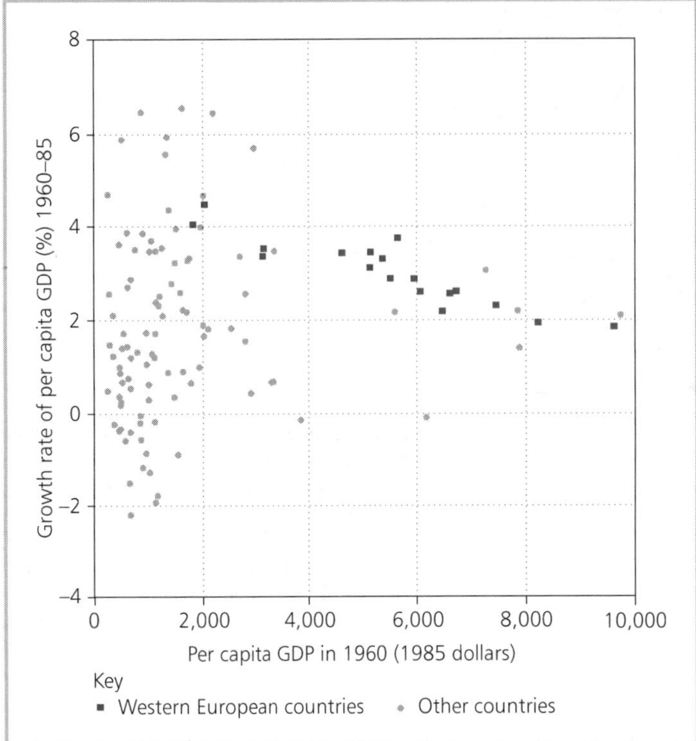

Figure 9.19 The data for 122 countries visualize a key finding of empirical growth research: worldwide, there is no absolute convergence of incomes. While many low-income countries (say, in the \$0–2000 bracket) experienced faster income growth than high-income countries (say, in the \$6000–10000 bracket), just as many experienced much slower growth. This picture changes if we focus on western European countries only (highlighted in blue): there, basically all countries with low incomes in 1960 grew faster than those countries that had high incomes at that time. This finding generalizes as: within groups of homogeneous countries (with similar history, culture, political system, etc.) absolute incomes appear to converge.

Source: R. Barro and J. Lee: http://www.nuff.ox.ac.uk/economics/growth/barlee.htm.

Empirical note. Between 1900 and 1998 Burundi's population grew at an average of 2.6% per year and the average investment rate was 9%. By comparison Germany's population growth was 0.5% and the investment rate was 21%.

other hand, population growth and savings and investment rates differ dramatically between different regions of the world. Thus across continents, religions and cultures sizeable differences in the steady states exist and the Solow model would only postulate convergence to those specific steady states. This is the **relative convergence hypothesis**.

While the empirical evidence assembled above underscores why the Solow model is a useful first pass at long-run issues of income determination and growth, it also hints at some important questions that remain open, such as the following:

- Some 40% of international differences in per capita incomes cannot be attributed to differences in population growth and investment rates, as our workhorse model indicated. This suggests that not all countries operate on the same partial production function. A possible reason for this might be that we have overlooked an important production factor.
- From a global perspective there seems to be no convergence of income levels. While part of this can be attributed to differences in population growth and investment rates alone, this does not suffice. Again, does that mean that our view of the production function was too simple?
- A more fundamental, conceptual defect of the Solow model is that it does not really explain economic *growth*. Rather, per capita income growth occurs driven by exogenous technological progress, as a residual which the model does not even attempt to understand.

These main points are illustrative of some of the deficits of the basic Solow model which have motivated refinements and a new wave of research efforts on issues of economic growth. The next chapter looks at some of these refinements and discusses some of the more recent achievements.

CHAPTER SUMMARY

- The level of output produced in a country is determined by the stock of capital, the labour force and the state of production technology.
- The rate of saving determines the capital stock and, hence, output. A rise in the savings rate increases output permanently, but has no permanent effect on the growth rate. It raises the growth rate during a (very long) transition period, however. If the marginal productivity of capital does not decrease, as in the *AK* model, higher savings may give rise to higher growth permanently.
- Higher savings always raise income, but may reduce consumption. The golden rule of capital accumulation determines the savings rate that maximizes consumption (per capita). At the capital stock resulting from this rule the addition of more capital would not generate the additional income needed to replace obsolete or worn-out capital that needs to be written off.
- The only factor that, in the presence of constant returns to scale, can make living standards grow in the long run is technological progress.

KEY TERMS AND CONCEPTS

convergence hypothesis
factor income shares
growth accounting
golden rule of capital accumulation
neoclassical growth model
potential income
requirement line
Solow model
Solow residual
steady-state income
technology
transition dynamics

EXERCISES

9.1 Consider the following production technology. There are two factors of production – capital and labour. To produce one unit of output you need at least two units of capital and three units of labour. Assume that arbitrarily small amounts of output can be produced.

(a) Draw the partial production function in Y–K space, assuming employment to stand at nine units.

(b) Does the marginal productivity of capital diminish?

(c) Does the function exhibit constant returns to scale?

9.2 A country's production function is given by $Y = AK^{0.5}L^{0.5}$. In the year 2001 we observed $K = 10{,}000$, $L = 100$ and $Y = 10{,}000$. Suppose that during the following year income grew by 2.5%, the capital stock by 3% and employment by 1%. What was the rate of technological progress?

(a) Address this question first by computing the Solow residual from the growth accounting equation.

(b) The text stated that the growth accounting formula is only an approximation. To quantify the involved imprecision, answer the above question next by proceeding directly from the production function. This yields the precise number. Compare the results obtained under (a) and (b).

9.3 Consider the Cobb–Douglas production function: $Y = K^{\alpha}L^{\beta}$.

(a) Under what conditions do marginal returns to capital diminish if labour stays constant?

(b) Under what conditions does the function display constant returns to scale?

(c) Suppose marginal returns to capital do not diminish. Is it still possible for the function to exhibit constant returns to scale?

9.4 Suppose two countries have the same steady-state capital stock, but in country A this is due to a larger population, whereas in country B it is due to a more advanced technology and thus higher productivity. How does the steady-state income of country A differ from the steady-state income of country B? Does it make sense to say that country B is richer than country A?

9.5 Consider two countries (C and D) that are identical except for the savings rate, which is higher in country C than in country D. Which country is richer? Does this necessarily mean that welfare is higher in the richer country?

9.6 Suppose two countries, Hedonia and Austeria, are characterized by the following production function: $Y = K^{0.3}L^{0.7}$. In both countries the labour supply is constant at 1, there is no technological progress, and the depreciation rate is 30% (an unrealistically high portion, compared with empirical estimates).

(a) Compute the golden-rule level of the capital stock.

(b) What is the savings rate that leads to the golden-rule capital stock?

(c) Suppose you are in charge of the economy of Hedonia where the savings rate is 10%. Your goal is to lead Hedonia to eternal happiness by implementing the golden-rule steady state. To this end you impose the golden-rule savings rate. Compute the levels of income and consumption for the first five periods after the change of the savings rate, starting at the initial steady state. Draw the development of output and consumption and explain why you might run into trouble as a politician.

(d) Being kicked out of Hedonia, you are elected president of Austeria where people save 50% of their income. Do the same experiment as before and explain why, in the not too distant future, Austerians will build a monument in your honour.

9.7 Judge the prosperity of an economy where the growth rate of income is 8% due to a constant rate of population growth of 8%. Is this economy better or worse off than an economy with 4% growth and a population growth rate of 3%?

9.8 How does a change in the savings rate affect the steady-state growth rate of output and consumption? Does this result also hold for the transition period (i.e. until the new steady state is reached)?

9.9 Consider an economy where population growth amounts to 2% and the exogenous rate of technological progress to 4%. What are the steady state growth rates of
  (a) $\hat{k}, \hat{y}, \hat{c}$ (where the hats denote 'per efficiency unit of labour')?
  (b) k, y, c (that is, per capita capital, income and consumption)?
  (c) K, Y, C?

9.10 The economy is in a steady state. The efficiency of labour grows at a rate of 0.025 (2.5%), population growth is 0.01, and depreciation is 0.05 annually.
  (a) At what rate does K grow?
  (b) How large is $I/(EL)$ if $\hat{k}^* = 100$?
  (c) At what rate does per capita income grow? If the production function is $\hat{y} = 10\hat{k}^{0.5}$, what is the steady-state output per efficiency unit of labour?
  (d) What is the country's savings rate?
  (e) What should the country save according to the golden rule?

RECOMMENDED READING

Robert M. Solow (1970) *Growth Theory: An Exposition*, Oxford: Oxford University Press. An extension, including human capital (to be addressed in Chapter 10) and empirical tests, is put forward in N. Gregory Mankiw, David Romer and David Weil (1992) 'A contribution to the empirics of economic growth', *Quarterly Journal of Economics* 107: 407–37.

A discussion of how the political setting matters for economic growth is given in 'Democracy and growth: Why voting is good for you', *The Economist*, 27 August 1994, pp. 15–17.

APPLIED PROBLEMS

RECENT RESEARCH

Does the distribution of income affect economic growth?

The Solow model proposes that, under certain conditions, countries converge to a common income level. Starting from this proposition, Torsten Persson and Guido Tabellini (1994, 'Is inequality harmful for growth?', *American Economic Review* 84: 600–21) study the question of whether economic growth, in addition to the initial level of income as proposed by the convergence hypothesis, is also affected by how income is distributed in a society. They measure the convergence potential of a country by GDPGAP, which is the ratio between the country's GDP and the highest current GDP of any country in the sample. The higher that ratio is, the smaller growth is expected to be. Income inequality is measured by INCSH, i.e. the share in personal income of the top 20% of the population. So the higher INCSH is, the more unevenly income is distributed. To eliminate short-run (business cycle) fluctuations, observations (data points) are measured as averages over subperiods of 20 years each, starting as far back as 1830. Including 9 countries in the sample gives 38 such subperiods (or observations). The following regression obtains:

$$\underset{}{\text{GROWTH}} = \underset{(5.72)}{7.206} - \underset{(2.70)}{2.695}\ \text{GDPGAP} - \underset{(3.07)}{6.911}\ \text{INCSH}$$

$$R^2_{\text{adj}} = 0.30$$

The result suggests, first, that growth features convergence. The lower a country's income is relative to the leading country, that is the smaller GDPGAP, the faster income grows. Second, a more uneven distribution of income depresses growth. The coefficient of –6.911 (which is significantly different from zero, as the *t*-statistic of 3.07 indicates) suggests that if the income share of the top 20% of the population increases from, say, 0.50 to 0.65, income growth falls by a full percentage point ($-6.911 \times 0.15 = -1.03665$). The coefficient of determination of 0.298 reveals, however, that the two variables included in the regression explain only

30% of the variation of growth between countries and across time.

WORKED PROBLEM

Do European incomes converge?

Table 9.2 gives real per capita incomes in 1960 (in \$1,000, purchasing-power adjusted) and average income growth between 1960 and 1994 in 18 western European countries. Do these numbers support the convergence hypothesis of the Solow model? To obtain an answer to this question we may regress average income growth $\Delta Y/Y$ (in %) on 1960 income Y_{1960} (in \$1,000). The estimation equation is

$$\Delta Y/Y = 4.35 - 0.273 Y_{1960} \quad R^2 = 0.85$$
$$(26.09)\ (9.61)$$

Table 9.2

	GDP/capita in \$1,000 1960	Average growth 1960–94
Austria	5.152	2.9
Belgium	5.554	2.7
Denmark	6.748	2.4
Finland	5.384	2.7
France	5.981	2.7
Germany	6.660	2.6
Greece	2.066	3.6
Iceland	5.191	3.0
Ireland	3.147	3.9
Italy	4.660	3.0
Luxembourg	8.269	2.4
Netherlands	6.104	2.6
Norway	5.656	3.4
Portugal	1.864	3.8
Spain	3.165	3.4
Sweden	7.505	2.0
Switzerland	9.637	1.7
United Kingdom	6.509	2.3

The obtained coefficient of −0.273 is in line with the convergence hypothesis. \$1,000 less income in 1960 gave rise to an additional 0.273 percentage points of annual income growth during the following 34 years. The *t*-statistic of 9.61 for this coefficient permits us to refute the null hypothesis of no convergence ($c_1 = 0$). The coefficient of determination of 0.85 tells us that 85% of the differences in average income growth between the 18 countries included in our sample may be attributed to income differences that existed back in 1960.

The constant term 4.35 indicates how fast a country would have grown, had its income in 1960 been zero, which does not make a lot of economic sense. Alternatively, we may measure 1960 income as deviation from the average income of all countries in that year. The regression equation then becomes

$$\Delta Y/Y = 2.90 - 0.273(Y_{1960} - Y_{average}) \quad R^2 = 0.85$$
$$(51.23)\ (9.61)$$

Nothing has changed, except for the constant term. Its value of 2.90 says that a country that started with average income in 1960 grew at a rate of 2.9%.

YOUR TURN

Convergence plus distribution

Data on income inequality are provided by a number of sources. Try to find a measure of and data on the distribution of income in the countries included in the sample studies in the worked problem above. (In case you do not succeed, try 'Measuring income inequality: a new database', *World Bank Economic Review*, September 1996.) Now check whether you can replicate the Persson–Tabellini result, which says that a more uneven distribution of income depresses GDP growth. Do so by augmenting the growth equation used in the worked problem with your measure of income inequality.

To further explore this chapter's key messages you are encouraged to use the interactive online module found at

www.fgn.unisg.ch/eurmacro/tutor/Solow.html

and many other features hosted at **www.fgn.unisg.ch/eurmacro**

CHAPTER 10

ECONOMIC GROWTH (II)
ADVANCED ISSUES

WHAT TO EXPECT After working through this chapter, you will understand:

1. How **government spending and taxes** fit into the Solow growth model.
2. How the **globalization of capital markets** affects a country's income and growth prospects.
3. What the **difference is between physical capital and human capital**, and how these affect income and growth.
4. What **poverty traps** are and what measures can get a country out of them.
5. The nature of and processes behind **endogenous growth**.

So far we employed a global-economy model without government to explain and understand national growth experiences. We saw that even such a deliberately simple model carries us a long way towards understanding international income and growth patterns. But we also saw that it leaves us with a number of loose ends. Also, this baseline model does not permit us to analyze the recent pronounced moves towards globalization in the form of more international trade and integrated, worldwide capital markets. And the model is rather subdued in the sense that things are the way they are and there was no discussion of what governments or other institutional bodies could do to improve a country's material fate.

This chapter tries to mend this by first asking how the government fits into the Solow model and how public spending and taxation decisions affect a country's long-run macroeconomic performance. It also looks at the emerging trend to not necessarily place our savings in a local bank's savings account, but to go farther afield and invest our money in Turkish government bonds, US blue chip stocks, or some start up company in the Philippines. Another topic we have on our agenda since the beginning of the last chapter is what keeps some countries trapped in poverty, and what can be done about it. And finally, moving close to the frontier of current research on economic growth, we discuss the role of education and the quality of the workforce, and what other mechanisms beside technological improvements may make per capita incomes improve – endogenously.

10.1 THE GOVERNMENT IN THE SOLOW MODEL

In Chapter 1 we summed up the leakages from and the injections into the circular flow of income in the equation $S - I + T - G + IM - EX = 0$. Rearranging this into

Arranged this way, the **circular flow identity** reveals that national saving is either invested at home or abroad.

$$\underbrace{\underset{\text{Domestic investment}}{I} + \underset{\text{Foreign investment}}{(EX - IM)}}_{\text{Total private investment}} = \underbrace{\underset{\text{Private saving}}{S} + \underset{\text{Public saving}}{(T - G)}}_{\text{National saving}}$$

reveals a more general correspondence than the simple $I = S$ equation used in the basic Solow model. The complete circular flow identity implies that *all national saving, both private and public, equals total private investment, at home and abroad*. When discussing economic growth in Chapter 9 we ignored the government sector and international trade (setting $T = G = IM = EX = 0$), thus ending up with the equality between private saving and investment $S = I$. Let us now keep the government in the equation while still leaving out the foreign sector (the role of foreign investment will be discussed in the next section). Investment is then determined by

$$I = S + T - G$$

So investment may be financed by private and public saving, since $T - G$ is the government budget surplus, or government saving. Assuming that individuals save a constant fraction s of disposable income, $S = s(Y - T)$, where $s = 1 - c$, we obtain

$$I = s(Y - T) + T - G \tag{10.1}$$

Now recall from last chapter that the capital stock K changes if investment exceeds depreciation, $\Delta K = I - \delta K$. Substituting (10.1) into this equation, making use of the production function $Y = F(K, L)$, and rearranging terms gives

$$\Delta K = sF(K, L) + (1 - s)T - G - \delta K$$

The first three terms on the right-hand side represent national savings (which equals investment). The last term is depreciation. Following the line of argument employed in Chapter 9, we may determine the steady state (in which $\Delta K = 0$) graphically (see Figure 10.1). δK is a straight line through the origin. National savings is composed of $sF(K, L)$, the broken dark blue curve that is proportional to the production function, and the terms $(1 - s)T - G$, which bear on the vertical position of the national savings line.

Figure 10.1 reveals why high government spending is considered so harmful for the longer-run prospects of the economy. A rise in government spending shifts the savings line down, reducing national savings and investment at any level of K, reducing the steady-state capital stock and steady-state income.

The obvious reverse side of this is that taxes do exactly the opposite. As they rise, national savings and investment increases and steady-state income moves higher. But then why do economists not fervently recommend tax increases?

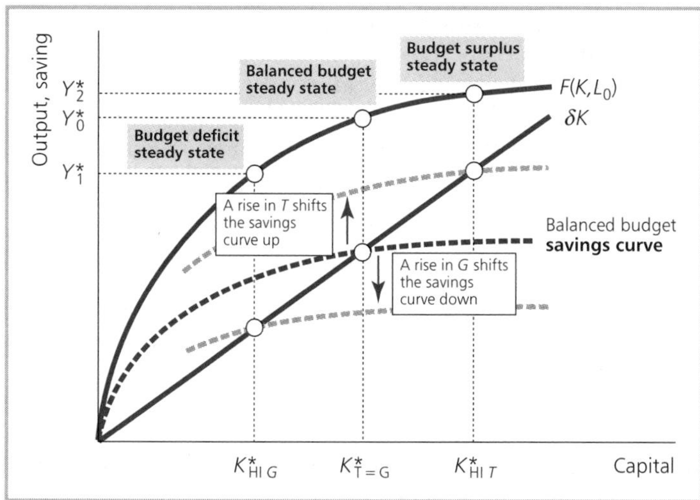

Figure 10.1 The no-government ($G = T = 0$) steady state features the capital stock $K^*_{T=G}$ and income Y^*_0. Raising government spending shifts the savings line down, lowering the steady-state levels of K and Y. Taxes operate as involuntary savings. As they rise the savings line shifts up and the steady-state levels of both K and Y rise.

There are a number of reasons – some more of an economic nature, and some more political:

- Remember that the variable we would ultimately like to maximize is consumption. Just as the Golden Rule gave us an optimal private savings rate in last chapter's basic Solow model, similar reasoning yields an optimal, golden national savings rate in the current extended model with government. If national savings is already at the level suggested by the Golden Rule, tax rises would be detrimental to steady-state consumption.
- Even if conditions are such that a tax rise would raise steady-state consumption, its effect on *current* consumption is negative. This is because the current capital stock and current income are given, and higher taxes leave us with less income at our disposal. Consumption then develops according to the lower adjustment path outlined in Figure 9.15. A decision to raise taxes in order to spur national savings then involves a weighing of current consumption sacrifices against future gains. If we place less weight on future consumption compared with current consumption, it may well be rational not to raise taxes.
- A tax increase does not only lower current potential consumption at given current potential income, as proposed by the Solow model. As we learned from our discussion of business cycles in Chapters 2–8, raising taxes will also drive the economy into a recession, driving income and consumption temporarily below their respective potential levels. This aggravates the argument advanced in the previous paragraph.
- Governments exhibit a tendency to spend all their receipts, thus raising G whenever T rises. Raising G and T by the same amount, however, reduces investment and steady-state income. This is because a €10 billion increase in G shifts the savings line *down* by exactly €10 billion, while the matching €10 billion increase in T shifts the savings line *up* by only €8 billion (supposing $s = 1 - c = 0.2$). The attempt of the government to save by raising taxes leaves the private sector with less disposable income (€10 billion less). So individuals save €2 billion less. A rise in taxes, that is an increase in public savings, *crowds out* some private savings.

- It is very important to note, and often overlooked, that for the above results to hold we must assume that the government only consumes and never invests. This is obviously not true as a certain share of public investment goes into roads, railways, the legal system, and education. How does this affect our argument? Suppose, government spending is composed of government consumption G_C and government investment G_I, so that $G \equiv G_C + G_I$. Then the capital stock changes according to

  $$\Delta K = I + G_I - \delta K \tag{10.2}$$

  The circular flow equation $I = S + T - G_C - G_I$ can be solved for total investment, private and public, $I + G_I = S + T - G_C$. Substituting this into equation (10.2) gives

  $$\Delta K = S + T - G_C - \delta K$$

  Suppose, further, that the government routinely invests a fraction α of all government spending, so that $G_I = \alpha G$ and $G_C = (1 - \alpha)G$. Substituting $G_C = (1 - \alpha)G$ and $S = s[F(K, L) - T]$ into equation (10.2) gives

  $$\Delta K = sF(K, L) + (1 - s)T - (1 - \alpha)G - \delta K$$

Empirical note. Governments typically spend a rather small share of outlays on investment projects. In Germany, for example, the government invests less than 4% of its spending. This falls way short of private savings rates, which run around 25%.

The question of whether an increase in government spending that is being financed by a tax rise of equal size boosts steady-state income or not, does not have a clear-cut answer. It obviously does boost income if $\alpha > s$, that is if the government invests a larger share of its spending than the private sector is prepared to save and invest out of disposable income. Then total investment, the steady-state capital stock and steady-state income all rise. A rise in G that was fully used for public investment would certainly push up steady-state income, even if accompanied by a tax increase of equal size. Note, however, that during the transition to this new, better steady state, individuals have to make do with lower disposable income and lower consumption. By contrast, matching reductions of G and T always bear short-run gains in consumption, even though the long-run, far-away options are worse.

The **Ricardian equivalence theorem** is named after British economist David Ricardo (1772–1823) who first advanced the underlying argument.

Some economists advocate an extreme view of the crowding out of private savings by taxes that we encountered above. The **Ricardian equivalence theorem** maintains that government deficit spending does not affect national savings at all. In terms of Figure 10.1, no matter whether G rises, or T rises, or both rise, the savings line does not change; the government does not do anything to the steady state. The reason, according to this view, is that households realize that running a deficit and adding to the public debt today will lead to higher interest payments and eventual repayment in the future. To provide for the higher taxes that will then be needed (to provide for interest payments or repayment), individuals start saving more today. They save exactly the same amount the government overspent. The essence of this argument is that it is irrelevant whether higher government spending is financed by higher taxes or by incurring debt. In no case will it reduce national savings, but only private consumption.

The main argument advanced against Ricardian equivalence is that lives are finite. Then people have no reason to save more if they expect future generations to repay the debt. The counter argument here is that since people typically leave bequests, they obviously care about the welfare of their offspring. This

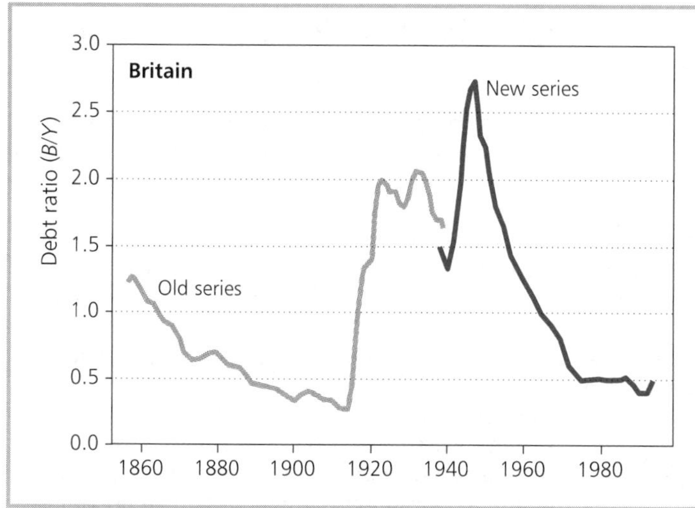

Figure 10.2 Debt ratios in the United Kingdom rose dramatically during each of the two world wars. Hardly anyone would argue that these public 'investments' yielded insufficient returns to society. Judging government spending in terms of social returns is also the proper approach under less dramatic circumstances.
Source: B. R. Mitchell (1988) *British Historical Statistics*, Cambridge University Press.

should make them act as if lives would never end. If a smaller weight is placed on the utility of our children, grandchildren and so on as compared to our own utility, this weakens the Ricardian equivalence argument. Private savings may then be expected to respond to budget deficits in a Ricardian fashion, but not to the full extent of keeping national savings unchanged. This is also very much what the mixed empirical evidence on the issue seems to suggest.

But then if continuing deficit spending and growing debt is crowding out some private savings and investment, isn't this justification enough to oppose deficits and debt? Not generally – the point to emphasize is that deficit spending crowds out *private* investment. As we have already argued above, total investment, public and private, is only then guaranteed to fall if the deficit is caused by government consumption. If the government is running up the public debt by investing in education, infrastructure, basic research, national security, and so on, the call can be made only after comparing the returns of the government's projects with the returns of the private projects that are crowded out. Returns on the first category can be extremely high. Frequently cited examples are wars that typically make the national debt explode. Figure 10.2 illustrates this for the United Kingdom. Not even the most passionate proponents of balanced budgets would argue that the British victory in the Second World War was not worth the budgetary efforts, to generations alive then and to subsequent generations.

10.2 ECONOMIC GROWTH AND CAPITAL MARKETS

So far economic growth has been discussed from the viewpoint of an isolated individual country. Economists call such an economy a **closed economy**. We had not even bothered to make use of this term since closed economies are on the verge of extinction. A few remaining examples that come to mind are Libya and North Korea. As a rule though, modern economies are **open economies**. Since the closed economy model is nevertheless useful in helping us understand what happens globally, in a world that does not do business with

CASE STUDY 10.1 National incomes during the Second World War, east and west of the Atlantic

Wars have dramatic impacts and leave scars on society and personal lives. Also, effects on macroeconomic aggregates, such as income and prices, are often drastic. Without implying, of course, that wars are properly considered a macroeconomic event, nevertheless they often provide a 'laboratory experiment' that reveals important macroeconomic insights.

Figure 1 shows real GNP in France and the USA between 1938 and 1949. What strikes the eye is the contrasting experience:

- French income took a deep dive just after the beginning of the Second World War and did not recover fully until long after the war had ended.
- In the United States income rose sharply after the country was drawn into the war in December 1941. It dropped back towards the country's long-run growth path after the war had ended.

Do the tools and models of macroeconomics at our disposal explain these differences?

GNP in France

Consider GNP: France's direct involvement in the war, with large parts of the country being invaded and occupied by German troops, led to a destruction of a substantial part of the capital stock – factories, roads, bridges, ports and so on. It is estimated that by the end of the war about a third of France's capital stock (cars, trucks, railway stations, factories, etc.) had been destroyed. Demand-side considerations were dwarfed by these enormous adverse supply-side effects.

The macroeconomic consequences of changes in a country's production factors are best traced in the Solow growth model. A stylized account of France's experience is given in Figure 2. The point of intersection between the investment function and the investment requirement line identifies France's pre-war steady state. War-time losses of productive capital drove the capital stock to the left and income down the production function accordingly. This is where France started at the end of the war. The data suggest that while the initial recovery was quick, it still took France decades to fully rebuild its capital stock to the level desired.

GNP in the USA

US involvement in the Second World War was very different from that of France. The US mainland was

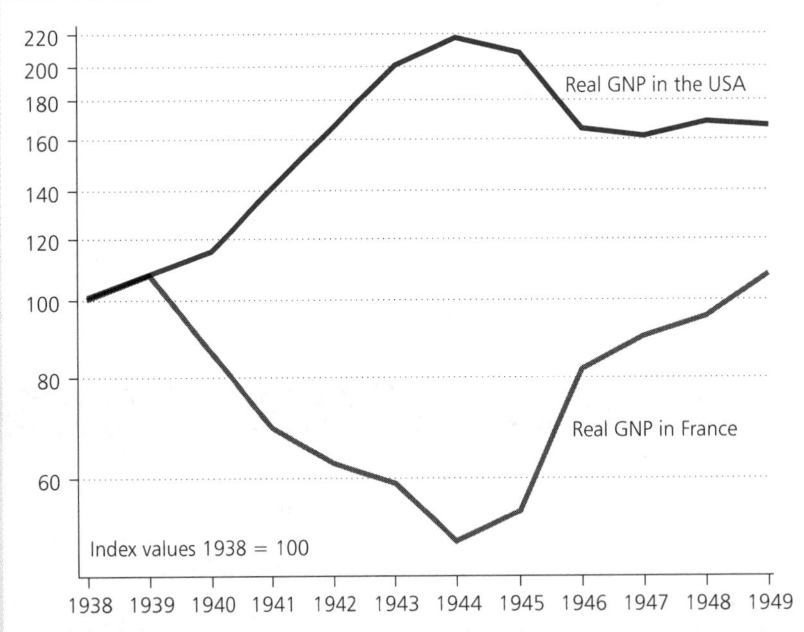

Figure 1

Case study 10.1 continued

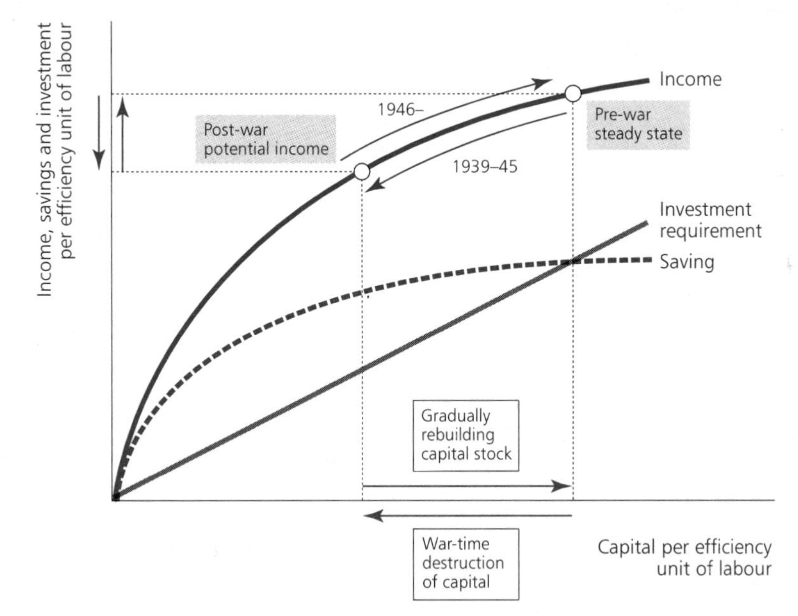

Figure 2

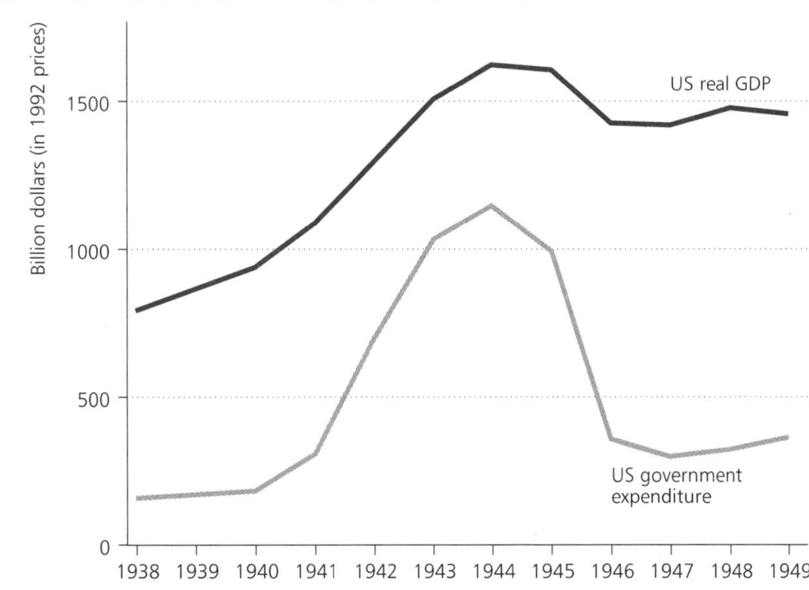

Figure 3

never a direct target for German or Japanese attacks, not to mention invasions. Thus the US capital stock stayed at or near its steady-state level throughout those years. What changed dramatically when the US government prepared for and fought the war, however, was the level of government spending and, thus, of aggregate demand. Figure 3 shows how the level of total government expenditure, expressed in 1992 prices, rose from $158 billion in 1938 to a peak level of $1,158 billion

Case study 10.1 continued

in 1944. In 1947 government spending was back down to \$290 billion.

A proper model to analyze such huge changes of aggregate demand on aggregate income is the aggregate-supply/aggregate-demand model. Figure 4 depicts America's pre-war situation as at 1940 and traces the stylized macroeconomic responses as they should have happened according to the *DAD-SAS* model. The position of the *DAD* curve (the locus of demand-side equilibria) is determined by a number of factors. Ignoring all other influences in order to focus on the overwhelming surge of government spending, the *DAD* curve under fixed exchange rates (or for a large open economy) is written as $\pi = \pi^w - b(Y - Y_{-1}) + \beta\Delta G$. We complete this model by writing the *SAS* curve $\pi = \pi_{-1} - \lambda(Y - Y^*)$ and then use real numbers for ΔG to simulate the development of inflation and income.

Table 1 shows actual data for ΔG. Substituting these values into the above equation, the *DAD-SAS* model predicts movements of income and inflation as shown by the dots in Figure 4.

The model's response is an increase in income in 1941 and 1942. Income remains well above potential income in 1943, but drops back below its potential level in 1944. Comparing this with Figure 3, the difference between theory and reality is that actual US income did not come down as quickly as the *DAD-SAS* model suggested. Factors that may have contributed to this are:

- Inflation expectations may not have increased as quickly as we assumed.
- Wage and price movements may have been restricted during the war, if only in some sectors of the economy.
- Other exogenous or policy variables, such as taxes, are likely to have changed as well.
- Behavioural parameters may have changed. For example, wars caution people to save higher shares of their incomes, which affects the dynamics of the model.

But while the graphs and our focus on government spending alone does not trace all details in

Table 1 Change in US government spending (in 1992 dollars, billions)

Year	1940	1941	1942	1943	1944	1945	1946
ΔG	2.5	114	404	340	126	−146	−650

Source: *Survey of current business*, May 1997.

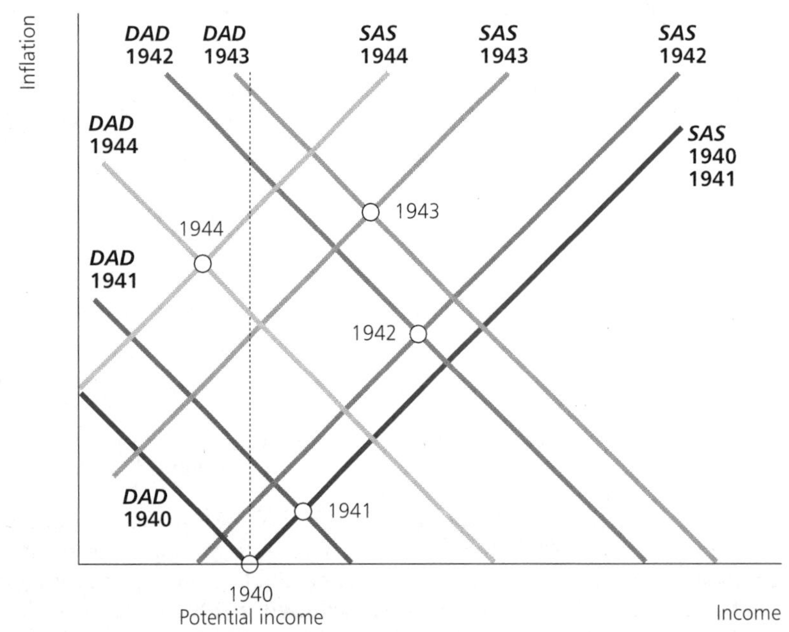

Figure 4

Case study 10.1 continued

US income movements during the Second World War, the big pattern is certainly there.

Bottom line

The main message of this case study is that the contrasting experiences of France and the United States during the Second World War are accounted for by France being subject to a destruction of its capital stock that dominated everything else, while the United States economy benefited from a surge in aggregate demand due to a dramatic increase in government spending. Two standard workhorses of macroeconomics, the aggregate-supply/aggregate-demand model and the Solow growth model permit us to trace the macroeconomic consequences of these influences. In essence, the bilateral comparison shown in Figure 1 emphasizes that the development of income may at times be driven by demand-side factors and at other times by supply-side factors.

Food for thought

While G and Y did move closely together in the USA during the Second World War, the government spending multiplier turns out to be only 0.4, which is unusually small. What factors may be responsible for such a small multiplier?

any outside partners, we call it the **global economy** model. The alternative model that describes an individual nation which interacts with other countries is, therefore, called the **national economy** model.

What, then, is the justification for having spent more than one full chapter on the global economy model of economic growth when it is so unrealistic? There are three reasons:

- It permitted us to introduce the idiosyncratic perspective of growth theory and its building blocks in the simplest possible, yet nevertheless demanding, framework.
- The obtained baseline results are of interest from the perspective of worldwide development.
- Many of the obtained results also apply to the national economy, though in a muffled form.

It is time now to move on and refine what we have learned by looking at how the obtained baseline results for the global economy are affected by international capital flows in the search for the highest yield. This new issue is discussed in terms of the standard graphical formulation of the Solow model. Figure 10.3 shows the familiar picture, only now we consider two countries instead of one. The two countries are linked by an integrated capital market like the one we considered to be the norm in the Mundell–Fleming and the *DAD-SAS* models. Let the two countries be 'The Netherlands' and 'Ireland'. The Netherlands is shown in the upper segment of the graph, Ireland in the lower one.

Both countries operate on the same production functions because they have access to the same technology. Also, capital depreciation proceeds at the same pace in both countries, so that the straight requirement lines are the same. The only difference between the two countries that matters at this level of aggregation is that the Irish savings rate is, and has been, much lower than the Dutch one. Thus, as we know from Chapter 9, the Dutch capital stock in the autonomous or closed-economy steady state is higher, making sure that Dutch steady-state income exceeds that of Ireland (all in per capita terms).

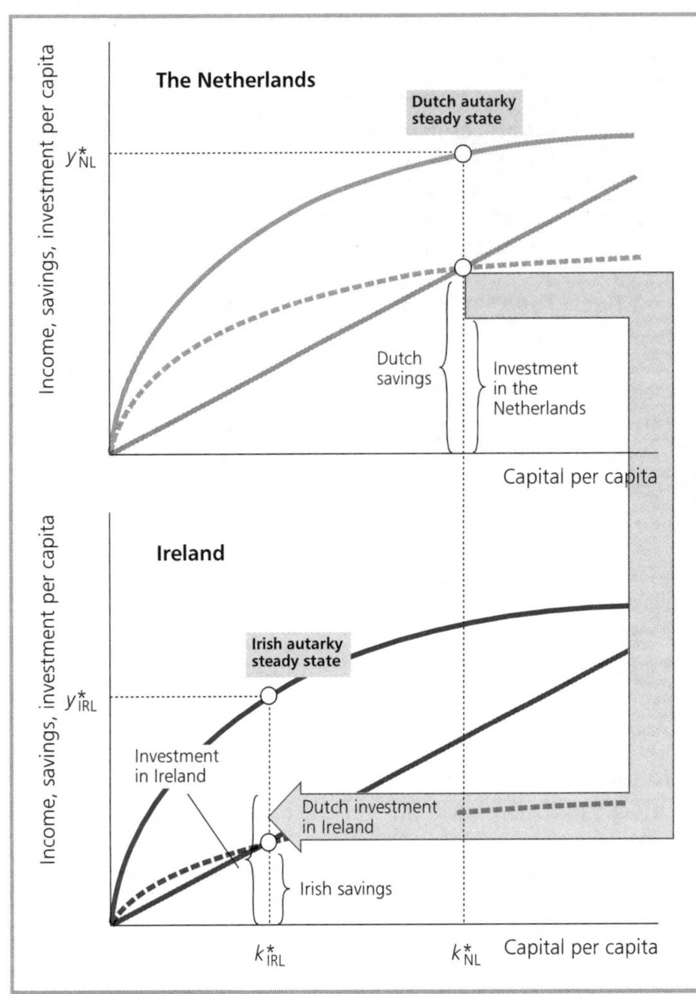

Figure 10.3 Here 'Ireland' and 'The Netherlands' have the same production functions and replacement lines. The Dutch save much more, however, so that capital and income per capita in the autarky steady state (with no capital flows across borders) is much higher. Due to the abundance of capital the marginal product of capital is much lower here than in Ireland. As soon as permitted, therefore, Dutch savings are invested in Ireland. The Dutch capital stock falls and the Irish capital stock grows. If the two countries were the same in all other aspects, the capital stock per capita would eventually be the same in both countries.

Maths note. The slope of the production function measures the marginal product of capital, independently of whether we use the *extensive form* $Y = K^{\alpha}L^{1-\alpha}$, holding L constant, or the *intensive form* $y = k^{\alpha}$. Differentiation yields $dY/dK = \alpha(L/K)^{1-\alpha} = \alpha k^{\alpha-1} = dy/dk$.

Enter cross-border capital flows. Remember that the slope of the partial production function measures the marginal product of capital. Under perfect competition this is the return investors can expect. Now, if both countries are initially in their respective 'autarky' steady states, which obtains when capital flows are controlled (as has been the case for many nations, including EU members, throughout the 1980s), abolishing controls opens new opportunities for investors. Due to a relative shortage of capital, investing in Ireland carries the promise of higher returns. This guides banks and portfolio managers to funnel Dutch savings out of the country and into Irish firms. Investment in the Netherlands is driven below savings. Investment in Ireland is driven above Irish savings. The Irish capital stock begins to grow. The Dutch one starts to fall. Both economies converge towards a new steady state in which the capital stock and investment are the same in both countries. Dutch capital exports equal Irish capital imports. What are the consequences of capital market integration?

Since the marginal product of capital is higher at Ireland's autarky point than at that of the Netherlands, the combined incomes of the two countries rise. The reason is that savings are taken out of the Netherlands, where capital is affluent and relatively unproductive at the margin, and funnelled into Ireland, where more income is generated than is lost in the Netherlands.

At a higher level of total income in both countries total savings and investment must be higher. This assertion may not be quite as obvious as this statement makes one believe, for reasons hidden in the following paragraph. Note, however, that since total income is higher, the combined capital stock must be higher. Since depreciation is the same in both countries, investment (and savings) must be higher in the free-capital-flows steady state than in the old capital-controls steady state.

Who benefits? Do the Netherlands suffer from abolishing capital controls? You may be inclined to think so, given that both the capital stock and income in this country fall. Note, however, that we are dealing here with one rare instance when a careful distinction between gross domestic product (GDP) and gross national product (GNP) as measures of income is crucial. Recall that GDP measures economic activity (or income) generated within the geographical boundaries of a country. GNP measures the incomes accruing to the inhabitants of a country independently of where these are generated. The partial production function given in the upper part of Figure 10.3 measures income generated within the boundaries of the Netherlands, that is Dutch GDP. This part of Dutch income does indeed fall, as is illustrated in the upper panel of Figure 10.3. But by investing part of their savings in Ireland, Dutch people can claim part of the income generated in Ireland. Again, since investments in Ireland outperform former investments in the Netherlands, the income gains accruing in Ireland more than make up for the drop in GDP experienced in the Netherlands. Thus Dutch GNP rises, as does Irish GNP.

So does the globalization of capital markets benefit everybody? In the aggregate, the answer is yes. All participating countries are likely to move up to higher (GNP) income levels. But beyond the aggregate, unfortunately the answer is no. Since the capital stock in the Netherlands falls (or grows at a slower pace than it would have otherwise), labour productivity falls (or lags behind). This exerts downward pressure on wages and total labour income in the Netherlands. The strain this puts on society is magnified by the fact that capital incomes rise even more than labour incomes fall. This is not only a problem that the rich countries of Europe face with regard to the poorer ones, but also a problem that Europe and other industrialized countries face with regard to the developing part of the world. (See Box 10.1 for a numerical look at this issue.)

Are there signs that in the real world capital does flow as proposed by the Solow growth model? An important caveat to the role of international capital flows central to the above arguments is the **Feldstein–Horioka puzzle**. It is posed by the empirical finding that gross domestic savings rates (comprising private and public savings) and domestic investment are highly correlated, very much as we would expect in a closed economy. This holds over time for individual countries, and across countries, as Figure 10.4 shows.

The **Feldstein–Horioka puzzle** refers to a contradiction between real-world experience and theoretical reasoning. The data show that countries with higher savings rates have higher investment rates, while theory suggests that under perfect mobility of international capital this should not be the case.

In **open economies** with perfectly free capital flows all countries' investment rates should be the same, independent of national savings rates. Data points should be positioned unsystematically around a horizontal line, but this is obviously not the case. In a **closed economy** investment and savings are

BOX 10.1 An illustration of the income and distribution effects of globalization

Countries A and B are identical in size, $L_A = L_B = 100$, depreciation rates, $\delta = 0.1$, and production functions, $Y = K^{0.5}L^{0.5}$. Savings rates differ at $s_A = 0.2$ and $s_B = 0$. Each country's *autonomous steady state* results from the equality between saving and depreciation, $sK^{0.5}L^{0.5} = \delta K$ (see Table 1).

Table 1

Country A	Country B
$0.2 \cdot K_A^{0.5} \cdot 10 = 0.1\,K_A$	$0 \cdot K_B^{0.5} \cdot 10 = 0.1\,K_B$
$20 = K_A^{0.5}$	$0 = K_B^{0.5}$
$K_A^* = 400$	$K_B^* = 0$
$Y_A^* = 200 = GDP_A$	$Y_B^* = 0 = GDP_B$

Autonomous steady states

Substituting numbers for s and δ we find that if country A operates autonomously, its steady-state capital stock is $K_A^* = 400$ and income is $Y_A^* = 200$. B does not save at all. It thus operates at the subsistence level with no income and capital (see table). Note that the incomes computed here are GDPs.

Steady states with a global capital market

Since country B does not save and will never own any capital, all global saving must be done by country A. Since interest rates must be the same in this steady state, capital stocks must be the same: $K_A = K_B = K$. K_B belongs to country A and yields interest income. A alone must save enough to maintain the world capital stock:

$$\underbrace{\underbrace{0.2(\underbrace{10\,K^{0.5}}_{GDP_A} + \underbrace{0.5 \cdot 10\,K^{0.5}}_{\substack{\text{Capital income}\\\text{inhabitants of A}\\\text{receive from B}}})}_{GNP_A}}_{\text{Country A's and world saving}} = \underbrace{0.1(\underbrace{K + K}_{\substack{\text{World}\\\text{capital stock}}})}_{\text{World depreciation}}$$

Solving this for the world capital stock yields $2K = 450$, of which half is in each country. Hence $K_A = 225$, $K_B = 225$, and $Y_A = Y_B = 150$.

Income distribution

Country A's GDP falls from 200 to 150 because its capital stock shrank from 400 to 225. But: GNP = GDP + factor incomes from abroad. Hence, since A owns B's capital stock, it gets all capital income generated in B. In the production function $Y = K^{0.5}L^{0.5}$ the capital income share is 50%. Hence A gets half of B's GDP, that is, $150/2 = 75$. This gives the gross national products:

$$GNP_A = \underbrace{150}_{\substack{75 + 75\\\text{Labour income}\quad\text{Capital income at home}}} + \underbrace{75}_{\substack{\text{Capital}\\\text{income from}\\\text{abroad}}} = 225$$

and

$$GNP_B = \underbrace{150 - 75}_{\substack{\text{Capital income}\\\text{generated in B}\\\text{to be paid to A}}} = 75$$

In this numerical exercise the workers of the rich country A are the losers of globalization. Their income drops from 100 to 75, while capital incomes rise from 100 to 150.

identical, lined up on a line with slope one (with deviations caused by measurement errors). However, this is not the case either. Instead the data are scattered around a positively sloped line that is flatter than the 45° line, having a slope of 0.58. This means that if a country's savings rate increases, more than 40% of added savings are invested abroad. Despite some variance in the data points that suggest the influence of other factors, there is an evident pattern: countries with savings rates of 24% or above are net investors in other countries. Countries with savings rates below 22% are capital importers. Only in the narrow (grey) band between 22 and 24% do we find a few countries that do not fit the general pattern.

So the mechanisms proposed by the Solow growth model seem to be at work, though not with the intensity the model suggests. Note that the data are for the 1980s, however, when more capital controls were still operational than

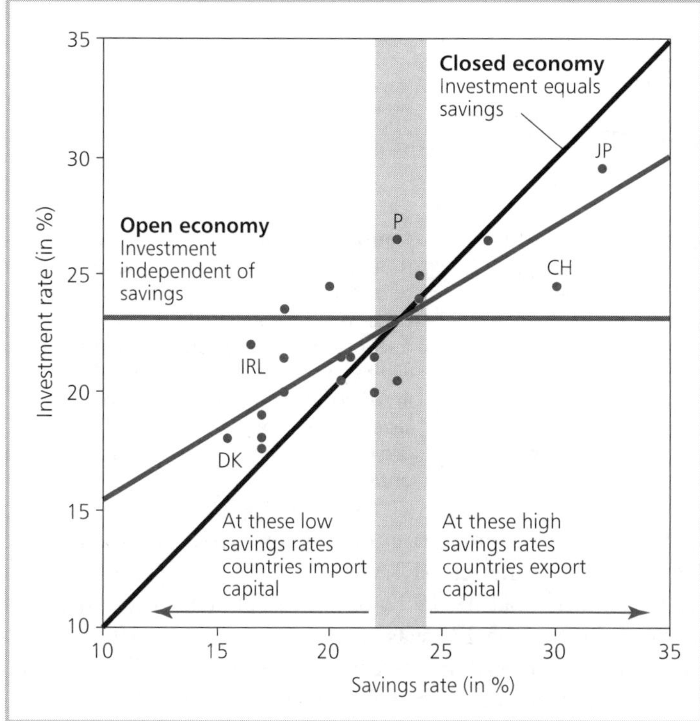

Figure 10.4 Open economies with free movement of capital should have investment rates that are independent of domestic savings rates (the horizontal line). In closed economies the correlation between the two should be 1 (the 45° line). Reality lies between these extremes. Investment goes up with savings, but high savers export capital while low savers import it. Data are averages for 1980–9.
Source: OECD, *Economic Outlook*.

nowadays. The liberalization of capital markets in Europe and other parts of the world should continue to intensify capital migration and further weaken the correlation between national savings and investment.

Empirical note. In 1992 only 1.4% of people *living* in the EU were *citizens* of other EU countries. By contrast, the share of foreign employment including workers from *outside* the EU was 4.2%.

To summarize then, the first major bonus that comes with integrated markets is that they provide for more flexibility to employ production factors where they are most productive. This section has elaborated on the effects that result from removing obstructions to free movement of capital. In terms of an aggregate EU (or world) production function these efficiency gains turn the partial production function upwards, raising the EU capital stock and income per capita. Similar effects could result, in principle, from free movement of labour. In practical terms, however, labour mobility is not likely to be a quantitatively relevant source for efficiency gains.

Integrated goods markets

Efficiency gains that result from the integration of capital markets are likely to be reinforced by removing barriers to trade in the product markets. Many economies are not large enough to support many suppliers to operate at an efficient level. Therefore, monopolies, monopolistic and other imperfect competition are frequent phenomena. Examples are banks, chemical industries, car manufacturers, airlines, and so on. Providing free access to all national markets for all firms (as initiated in the Single Markets Act of the European Union) will increase competition, which puts firms under pressure to use factors of production more efficiently than before. This again must be expected to turn the EU production function upwards. Figure 10.5 shows this

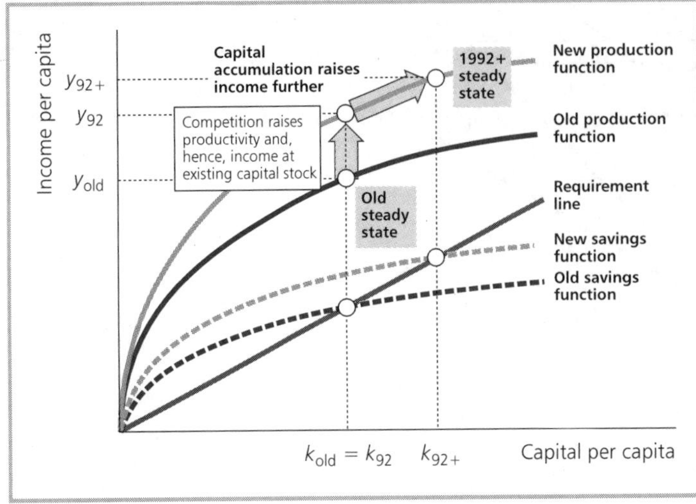

Figure 10.5 The single European market is thought to raise steady-state income in two stages. In a first stage, more competition raises productivity, turning the production function up. So even with the old capital stock more income will be generated. At this higher income people will save more. Thus the capital stock will grow, permitting income to grow further until y_{92+}.

effect that other, less advanced integration efforts also strive at, such as the Free Trade Agreement of the Americas (FTAA).

Empirical note. The Cecchini Report estimated that 'one market' would lead to efficiency gains between 4.25 and 6.5% of GDP. Other studies argued that these numbers were too low: they ignored that the capital stock would rise and overlooked the possibility of permanently higher growth (as in the *AK* model to be discussed below). Taking this into account, the present value of EU income could eventually rise between 11 and 35% of 1992 GDP.

Let EU output possibilities before 1992 be represented by the dark blue production function. Suppose the EU was in the indicated pre-1992 steady state, determined by the intersection between the requirement line and the dark blue dashed savings schedule. After the unification of EU markets in 1992 the more efficient use of production factors and competitive pressures (and opportunities) in the goods markets turn the production function up into the light blue position. At the old capital endowment per worker, income per worker would rise from y_{old} to y_{92}. This is not the end of the story, however. At higher income people save more. So savings exceed required investment, and the capital stock begins to rise. In a slow and long process income per worker grows to its new steady state level y_{92+}.

The factors discussed here suggest that the single-market project of the European Union should ultimately lead to higher incomes in the union, and trigger several decades of higher growth while economies make the transition from the old to the new steady state.

10.3 EXTENDING THE SOLOW MODEL AND MOVING BEYOND

Last section's extension of the Solow model to a scenario of national economies linked by global capital markets has severe consequences for the international convergence of incomes. Remember that the global (or closed-economy) version of the Solow model proposes *conditional convergence* only: income convergence towards a country's specific steady state as determined by its own national savings and population growth rates. By contrast, the open-economy version of the Solow model tells us that in a globalized world a nation's savings and population growth rates do not really matter. International capital flows in search of the highest yields make all countries end up with the same capital stock per worker and, hence, more or less the same per capita income. To the extent that international investment not only comes out of current income, but may also reflect the movement of existing capital (machines or entire production facilities) across borders, the speed of income convergence may be much more rapid than before the current wave of globalization.

Another look at income convergence data

We already saw in Chapter 9, Figure 9.19, that there is no worldwide convergence of incomes. When we take a closer look at groups of countries (say, as defined by income levels, or geographic regions) convergence is often found. Figure 10.6 illustrates this.

Plotting per capita income data from the second half of the 20th century on a logarithmic scale, panel (a) reveals income convergence among three of the

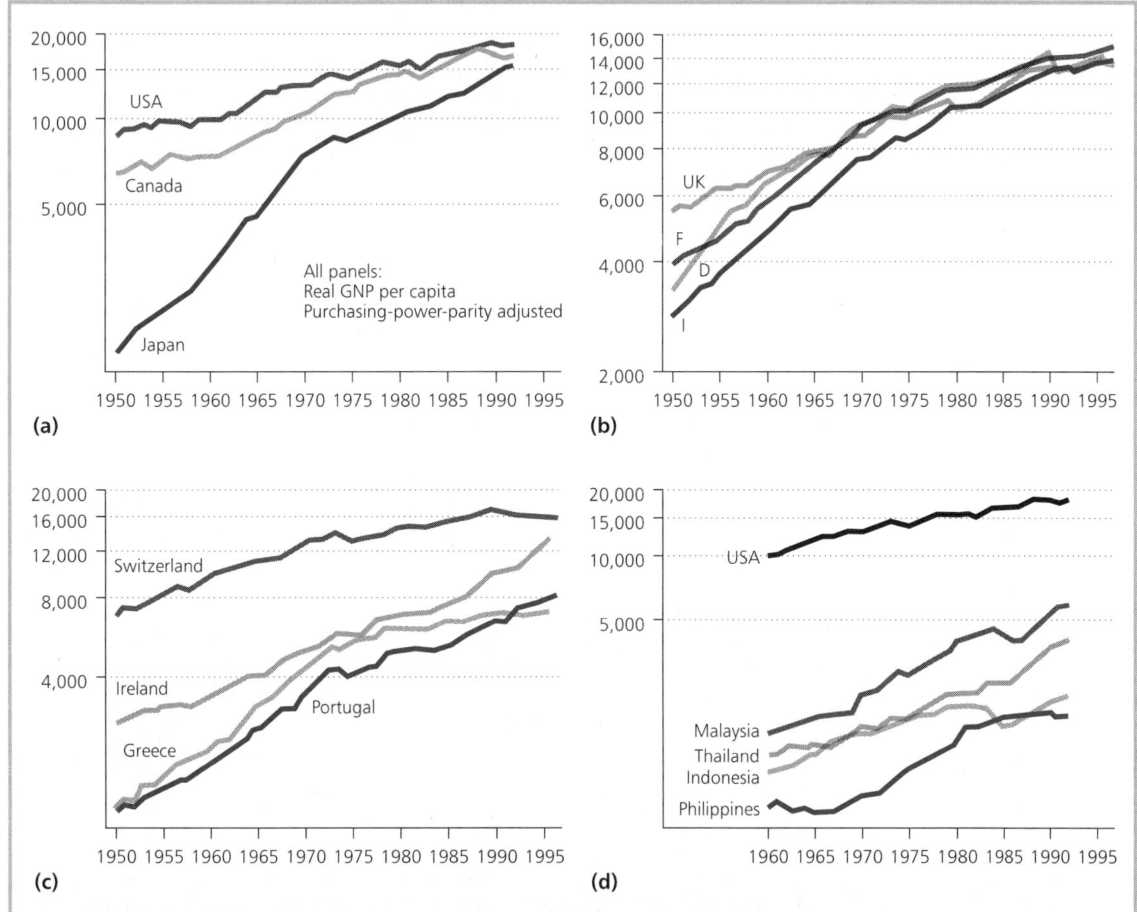

Figure 10.6 This figure presents evidence of income convergence within many of the world's regions and income brackets. Convergence appears particularly strong in panel (a) showing Canada, Japan and the USA, but also among the major European countries shown in panel (b). Convergence with Greece as an exception from the rule is documented in panel (c). Finally, panel (d) indicates hardly any convergence in south-east Asia, but, at least the region as a whole converged towards US income.

Sources: Penn World Tables; World Bank, *World Development Indicators*; A. Maddison, *Monitoring the World Economy 1820–1992*, OECD.

world's richest countries, and panel (b) shows the same for the four largest EU member states. Incomes also converge among smaller European countries (panel (c)), though convergence may sometimes pause, as it did in Greece. And finally, as shown in panel (d), even when income convergence within a region may not have occurred, as in this group of South-east Asian countries, the region as a whole has generally moved closer towards the world's highest per capita incomes.

But if all these partial observations are reasonably well in line with the general message of the Solow model regarding convergence, what is it then that spoils the global picture? The answer to this question has a lot to do with the African experience which departs drastically from the general trend in the rest of the world that we exemplified in Figure 10.6. Figure 10.7 shows per capita incomes in Gabon, the Ivory Coast, Senegal and Zambia as typical examples for the large group of Sub-Saharan African countries. In these countries per capita incomes not only did not converge towards those of the richer countries, but they stagnated or even fell, either as a general trend, or after some respectable growth had been achieved during the first one or two decades following independence. Overall, income growth in many countries in this region, but in others as well, appears disconnected from the global trend. It seems as if these countries were trapped in poverty. Is there a way to

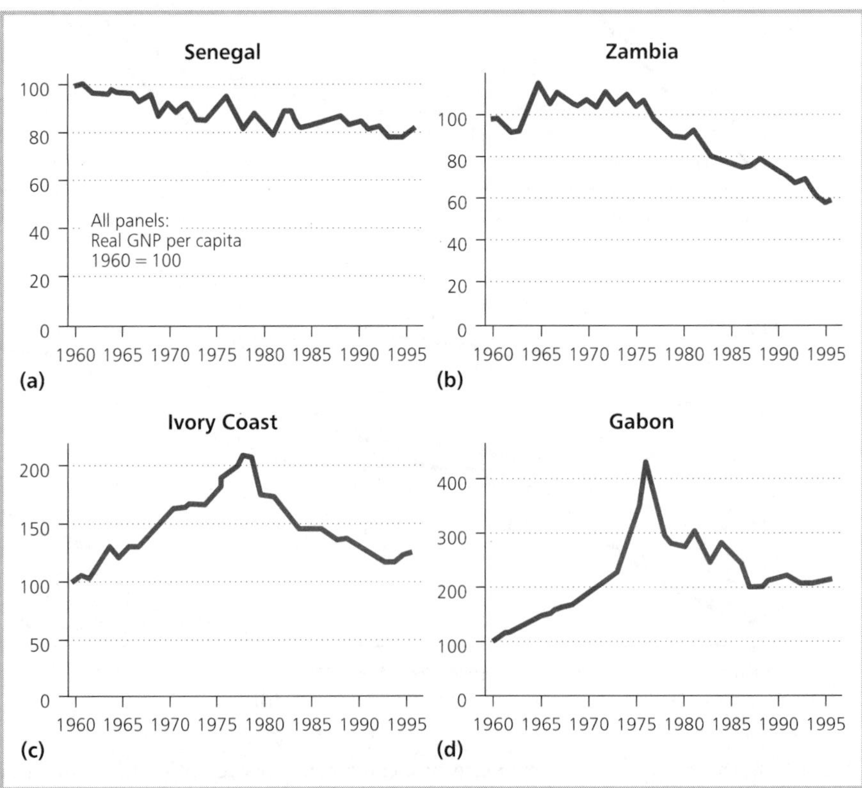

Figure 10.7 Given the worldwide trend towards ever higher per capita incomes, Africa is evidently a drastic exception. Many African countries, very often those among the world's poorest, have suffered falling per capita income for the past two decades or longer.
Sources: Penn World Tables; World Bank, *World Development Indicators*.

reconcile this sobering observation with the general approach of the Solow model?

One may be tempted to argue that the Solow model already provides for the possibility of some countries being poor and others rich, focusing on savings and population growth. While this is true, the model offers no plausible explanation of the huge size of observed income differences. A simple *numerical exercise* may illustrate this.

As we know from the discussion following equation (9.11), the steady-state condition in the per-capita Solow model is $\Delta k = 0 = sy - (n + \delta)k$. Let the per capita production function be $y = \sqrt{k}$. Substituting this into the steady-state condition for y and solving the resulting equation for $\sqrt{k} = y$ gives

$$y = \frac{s}{n + \delta}$$

Substituting some real numbers for s and n and a plausible magnitude of 0.1 for δ into this equation, we obtain $y = 0.08/(0.028 + 0.1) = 0.63$ for a hypothetical economy with the parameters of Sierra Leone and $y = 0.21/(0.004 + 0.1) = 2.02$ if we use the savings and population growth rates of Denmark. So, given the differences in s and n, Denmark's per capita income should be about three times as high as Sierra Leone's. In 1998, however, Denmark's per capita income was more than 50 times as large as Sierra Leone's. So, realistically, while the Solow model may explain modest differences in incomes, it is not capable of providing a realistic account of the magnitudes of actual income gaps observed in today's world. We must, therefore, look for modifications and refinements of the Solow model that may provide such an account. The concepts we will encounter during this expedition are *poverty traps*, *human capital*, and *endogenous growth*.

10.4 POVERTY TRAPS IN THE SOLOW MODEL

When a model has more than one stable steady state, the low-income steady state is often called a **poverty trap**. Once trapped in this steady state, the economy cannot escape without massive outside injections of capital.

A production function features **economies of scale** if output more than doubles when all inputs double.

Poverty traps may occur if one or more of the assumptions employed in the Solow model are violated. We look at the three building blocks of the model's graphical form to give examples of what may go wrong.

Poverty trap, type 1 The Solow model proposes a production function with constant returns to scale which implies decreasing marginal returns of the involved production factors. Now suppose that this does not hold over the entire range of feasible capital stocks. Instead, let there be **economies of scale** when the capital stock is very small. If these economies of scale are strong enough, the partial production function could feature increasing marginal products of capital in this segment. Over the entire range the partial production function might look as shown in Figure 10.8.

If households still save a constant fraction of income, the saving and investment line mimics the production function, featuring an increasing slope at low values of K and a decreasing slope as we move further to the right. So what? The shape of the investment curve has changed slightly. Does this matter? As a result we now have three points of intersection between the investment curve

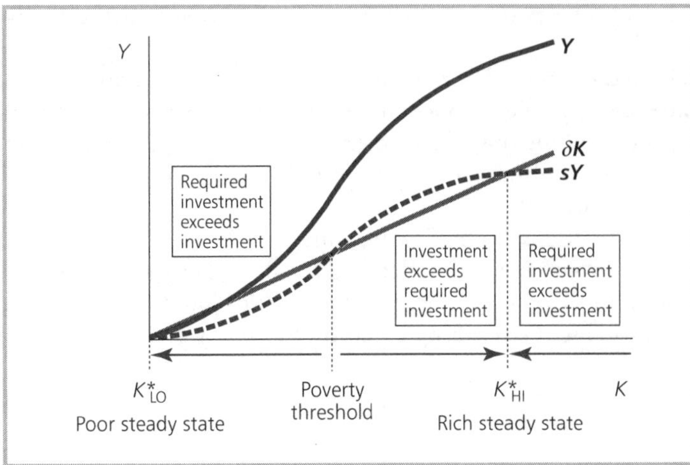

Figure 10.8 One type of poverty trap may occur when there are economies of scale at low levels of the capital stock. Then a second (positive) level of the capital stock exists at which the savings and required investment lines intersect. Since here the savings line cuts through the required investment line from below, it constitutes an unstable equilibrium which marks a threshold separating capital stocks that shrink towards the poor steady state from capital stocks that grow towards the rich steady state.

and the requirement line – one more than before. We always had two points of intersection and, hence, two steady states. But we never even mentioned the one positioned in the origin. We will see in a minute, why the current scenario makes this one more important.

Let us consider the stability properties of our three steady states. We learned previously, that K grows when savings and investment exceeds required investment, and that K falls in the opposite case. Applying this in the neighbourhood of the 'rich' steady state all the way on the right, we are led to conclude that it is stable. If the capital stock exceeds K^*_{HI}, it falls. If it is below K^*_{HI}, it rises. Or does it?

In the region below K^*_{HI} savings only exceeds depreciation as long as the capital stock exceeds the marked poverty threshold. Once the capital stock falls below this threshold, it will fall further and further until all capital is gone. This has dramatic policy implications. Suppose a country is in the poor steady state and receives international aid to build up its capital stock and move out of poverty. Such aid may generate results in the form of rising income. But if aid is not sufficient to push the capital stock beyond the poverty threshold, the country descends back into poverty once aid flows less generously or even subsides. The lesson this seems to teach is that aid which comes in as a trickle is a waste. What is needed is a **big push**, an investment injection big enough to drive the capital stock beyond the poverty threshold. After that the country may be left to stand on its own feet and continue to grow into the rich steady state.

Poverty traps may also derive from other causes. Figure 10.9 shows two more possibilities.

Poverty trap, type 2 Panel (a) in Figure 10.9 shows a scenario almost identical to the one discussed above. Only this time the anomalous savings function is not due to economies of scale, but to a more sophisticated savings behaviour. Households (can) save only a small fraction of income when incomes are low (and the capital stock is small). The savings rate rises to some finite positive fraction s when income rises. Since the savings line is similar to the one we had in Figure 10.8, and its intersection with the requirement line determines

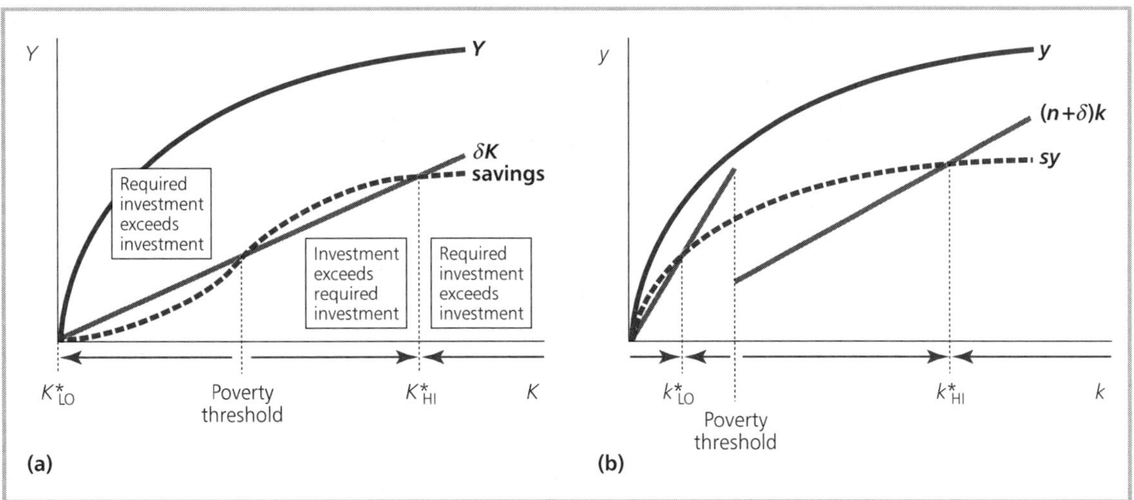

Figure 10.9 Two other kinds of poverty traps are shown here. Panel (a) depicts one similar to type 1 discussed in Figure 10.8. The only difference is that the cause is not economies of scale in the production function but non-linear savings behaviour. Panel (b) shows that non-linear population growth may also be the cause of a poverty trap.

steady states, we again have three steady states: two stable ones – a poor one at the subsistence level and a rich one; and an unstable one in between that functions as a poverty threshold. Only after this mark is crossed does endogenous capital accumulation make the country rich.

Poverty trap, type 3 Panel (b) of Figure 10.9 lets the requirement line be different from the way it looked in the usual scenario. Remember that required investment per capita is $(\delta+n)k$. So far we had assumed that for any given country the population growth rate n was just a constant number, 1 or 2.6%, that had to be added to the depreciation rate to obtain the slope of the requirement line. Suppose now that population growth is at n_{LO} up to a given capital stock, but drops to $n_{HI} < n_{LO}$ once it reaches this threshold. The result is a segmented requirement line that is steeper at low capital stocks.

While the assumption employed here is definitely artificial and oversimplifying, it serves to make the point that once the requirement line is non-linear, there is more than one stable steady state. The low-income steady state is the gravity point for all capital stocks at which population growth is still high. The per capita capital stock at which the population growth rate drops defines the poverty threshold. Only after the capital stock has moved beyond this critical value can the country accumulate enough capital per worker on its own to move towards the high-income steady state.

You may wonder whether we wasted space by detailing different versions of poverty traps, when it seems that the lesson to be learned is always the same: if rich countries' governments, or better still, pertinent international organizations such as the **International Monetary Fund** (IMF) or the **World Bank,** want to use money earmarked for development aid efficiently and achieve outcomes that are long lived, they should go for a *big push*. Doing this at least offers the promise of generating lasting results. Spreading the same amount over a longer period of time is not likely to achieve anything but transitory effects on income that soon vanish.

This policy prescription is not undisputed. Critics insist that the globalization of capital markets renders development aid by governments and international organizations obsolete. As we learned in section 10.2, global capital markets cut the old link between a country's (per capita) capital stock and its propensity to save and population growth. So all that the world's poor economies need to do is open up for foreign investors. Then international capital in search of high yields will flow in, and will continue to do so until the country's capital stock has reached world standards.

Is this argument sound? Well, as so often, the answer depends. It depends on the kind of poverty trap a country is stuck in. In poverty traps of type 2 and 3 it is not the production function that causes the problem. Throughout, the marginal product of capital falls. Hence, poor countries will indeed attract international capital. If allowed in, this will guide the country out of poverty, across the poverty threshold, towards the rich steady state.

However, this does not work if the country is caught in a type 1 trap. In Figure 10.8 capital remains unproductive at low levels. Only as we move towards the poverty threshold does the marginal productivity improve significantly, enough to attract foreign investment. So the initial policy recommendation remains very much valid: a big push in the form of development aid is initially needed to make the country attractive to global capital markets. Only then will private investment take over and finish the job.

There are other possible explanations as to why incomes may differ much more than the basic Solow model implies. As is often the case, a specific empirical deficiency of the basic model led researchers to reconsider and rethink. Consider the following observation.

Independent of whether a country is on a transition path or in a steady state, if all countries share a common production function, differences in per capita incomes should be perfectly explained by differences in the capital stock per worker. How does this hypothesis fare against real world data? Consider the 1988 data for per capita incomes and capital stocks in Japan, Korea and the USA, marked by the shaded squares in Figure 10.10. Income per capita is highest in the USA. Per capita income in Japan is only 2/3 of that value, that of Korea only 2/7. On the other hand, the capital stock per capita in Japan is estimated to be 50% higher than in the USA, and even Korean levels are already half as high as American ones. This seems to imply that the three countries are on *different* production functions after all.

A valid caveat might be that estimating the capital stock is very tricky and results are necessarily crude and unreliable. So perhaps actual capital stocks in Japan and Korea, which cannot be observed, are much lower than estimated and, in effect, do put them on a common production function with the United States? There is a problem with this interpretation, however. Remember that the slope of the production function measures the marginal productivity of capital, and, hence, also the returns of capital investments. Now if Japan and Korea are not really in the shaded positions indicated by the data, but in their respective white positions on the US production function, capital should be much more productive and pay much higher returns than in the US. In fact, compared with returns in the US, returns in Japan should be twice as high and

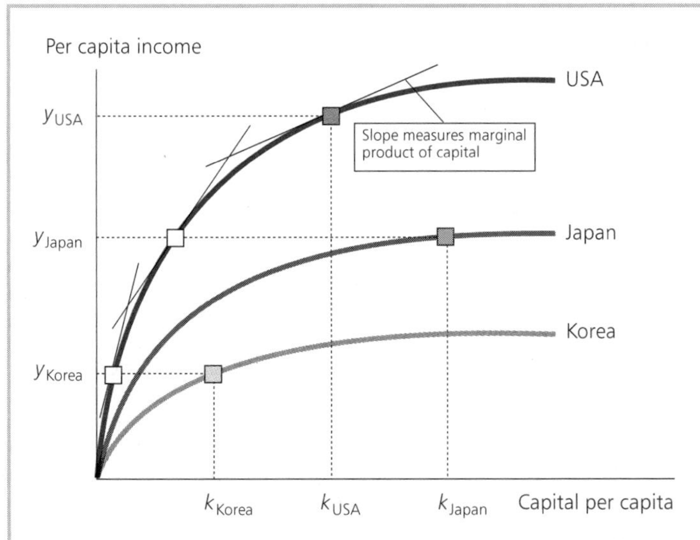

Figure 10.10 Data on the capital stock and income per capita (indicated by shaded squares) do not seem to put Japan, Korea and the United States on a common partial production function.
Source: Erich Gundlach (1993) 'Determinanten des Wirtschaftswachstums: Hypothesen und empirische Evidenz', *Die Weltwirtschaft*: 466–98.

in Korea even twelve times as high. This should attract foreign investment and make these countries capital *importers*. In reality, though, both Japan and Korea have *exported* net capital on a huge scale while the United States is the world's biggest importer of capital.

So while the Solow growth model seems to be a reasonable first look at the issues of economic growth, one more big issue remains open: *not all countries seem to operate on the same production function.*

This raises the question of whether we might have overlooked an important production factor. In trying to find an answer, one promising avenue of research starts by rethinking the definition of capital.

10.5 HUMAN CAPITAL

Traditionally, capital was thought to comprise objects such as machines, buildings, roads, cars, software – items that can be bought and used in the production process in combination with labour. Recent research recognizes that capital can also have a non-material dimension – knowledge, experience, skills. Since all these elements are implanted in the production factor labour, they are collected under the term **human capital**. Output then is a function of capital K, human capital H and labour L:

The abilities, experience and skills which determine the production capacity of the labour force are called **human capital**.

$$Y = F(K, H, L) \tag{10.3}$$

Proceeding as we did when we rewrote the narrower production function used above in per capita terms, we divide both sides of equation (10.3) by L to obtain

$$y = f(k, h) \tag{10.4}$$

Holding h, human capital per worker, constant, we may draw (10.4) in a y-k diagram. An increase in h turns this partial production function up. As illustrated in Figure 10.11, the comparative performance of Japan, Korea, and the

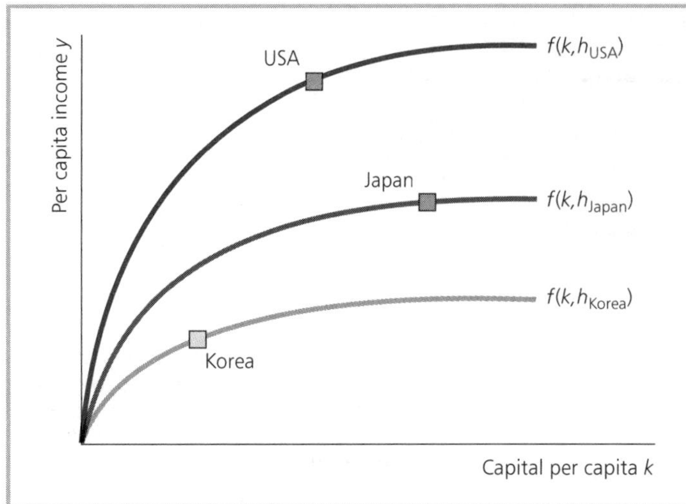

Figure 10.11 Korea, Japan and the United States are considered to be on the same human-capital augmented production function as given by equation (10.4) if Japanese human capital was higher than Korean, but lower than American. Then different partial production functions would apply for the three countries as shown here.

US in 1988 would fit our human-capital-augmented version of the Solow model if human capital in Japan were lower than in the US but higher than in Korea.

Empirical work has shown that incorporating human capital into the Solow model significantly improves the model's potential to explain international differences in income and growth. One problem with such studies is that human capital is very difficult to measure and empirical proxies are necessarily very crude. There are a few options, though, that let us cross-check whether the human capital rationalization proposed in Figure 10.11 makes sense.

Consider the United States and Japan. Here we still need to explain why the Japanese stock of capital (per capita) exceeds the American one. If we assume that both countries have roughly the same investment requirement line, the Japanese savings rate obviously needs to be much higher than the American one (see Figure 10.12). Looking at the data, this is indeed the case. Between

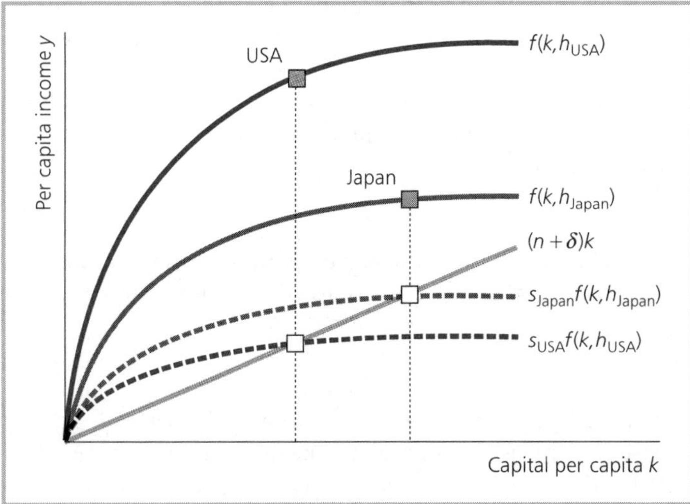

Figure 10.12 If Japan operates on a lower production function (say, due to lower human capital), the Japanese savings rate must be much higher in order to explain that the capital stock in Japan is higher.

1980 and 1990 savings in Japan amounted to 32% of income, while in the US they were as low as 18%.

It should be obvious that the inclusion of human capital does not change the basic philosophy of our growth model. If we assume that both technological progress and human-capital-augmented labour in the form $E \times H \times L$, then again everything remains the same if we look at capital per human-capital-augmented efficiency units:

$$\Delta\tilde{k} = \tilde{i} - (\delta + n + \varepsilon + \eta)\tilde{k}$$

where η is the human capital growth rate. With the appropriate relabelling of the axes we can now draw another version of the familiar diagram to determine steady states and transition paths (see Figure 10.13). The difference from earlier versions is that now the investment curve $\tilde{i} = f(\tilde{k})$ interacts with the requirement line $(\delta + n + \varepsilon + \eta)\tilde{k}$. To keep $\tilde{k}$ unchanged, investment must not only replace capital lost due to depreciation, but also accommodate population, efficiency and human capital growth.

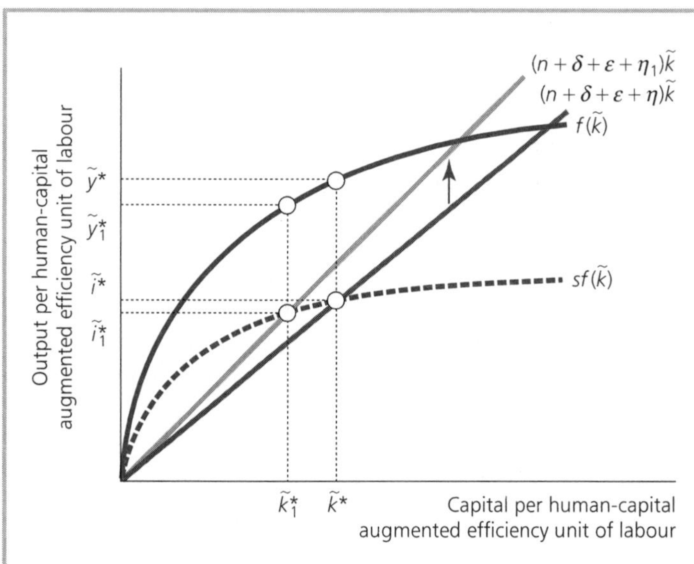

Figure 10.13 The axes measure output and capital per human-capital augmented efficiency unit of labour. Apart from this, the production function, the savings function and the requirement line look as they did in previous diagrams. Steady-state and transition dynamics are determined along familiar lines. If human capital growth rises, the requirement line becomes steeper. The new steady state features less capital, lower output per human-capital augmented efficiency unit, but more capital and higher output per worker.

Expanding the production function to include human capital has three noteworthy effects:

- There is another, testable empirical implication: the higher a country's human capital stock (per person), the higher is per capita income. Figure 10.14 checks this, using the average years of schooling as a measure of a person's human capital stock. Based on this measure, the positive effect of human capital on income is clearly brought out by the global sample of data.
- The generalized Solow model, which attributes income differences to differences in investment rates, in population growth and human capital, explains about 80% of the income differences observed between countries.
- The identified role of human capital in the production process gives expanded leverage for governments to influence a country's income. New emphasis is given to investment into education and training.

Empirical note. Some 80% of the differences in per capita incomes between countries can be attributed to differences in the investment rate, in population growth and in human capital.

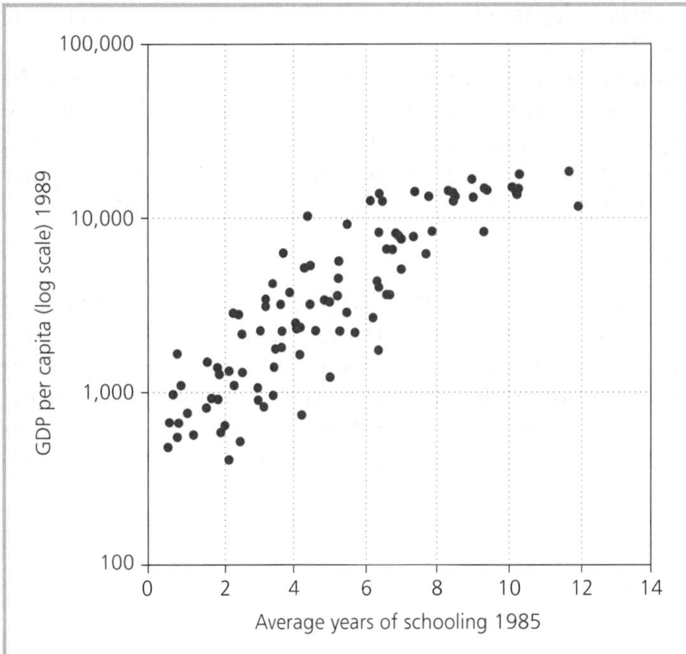

Figure 10.14 According to the extended Solow model that includes human capital in the production function, the higher a country's human capital per worker, the higher its per capita income. Using average years of schooling as a measure for human capital, the graph underscores this prediction for a large number of the world's economies.
Source: R. Barro and J. Lee: http://www.nuff.ox.ac.uk/economics/growth/barlee.htm

Maths recap. The logarithm of a variable which grows at a constant rate is a straight line. The rate of growth determines the slope of this line.

In a way, the version with human capital is the most general version of the Solow growth model. Since many previous, simpler versions may be considered special cases of this section's model, we will pause here to review the main results. As Figure 10.15 shows, the labour force grows at a slower rate than do output, capital and consumption, implying that output, consumption and the capital stock all grow on a per-capita basis. The differences in the slopes of the logarithmic growth paths reflect technological progress plus human capital accumulation.

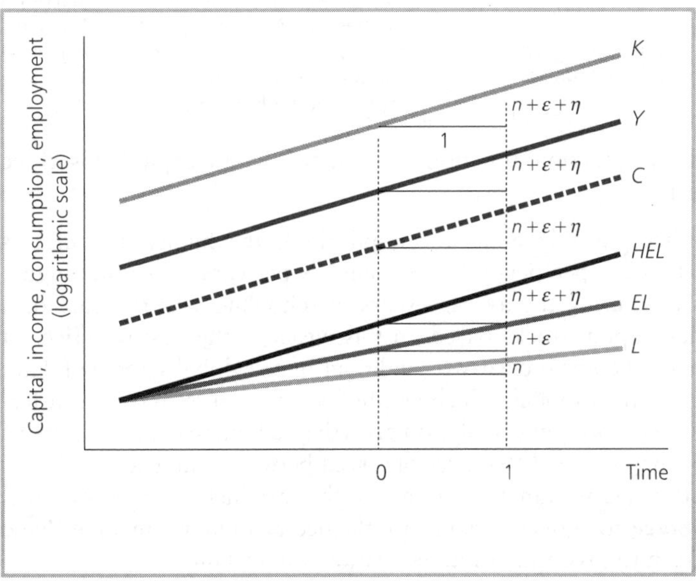

Figure 10.15 In the steady state, capital, output and consumption grow at the same rate. This rate exceeds population growth by the rate of technological progress plus the rate of human capital accumulation.

BOX 10.2 Labour efficiency vs human capital: an example

The general Cobb–Douglas production function $Y = AK^{\alpha}(HEL)^{1-\alpha}$ includes both labour efficiency E and human capital H. An example may demonstrate the necessity for drawing such a distinction:

- **Labour efficiency** E represents a form of technological progress. An example is the invention of the typewriter. Equipped with it, any secretary becomes more productive, independent of his or her typing skills.
- **Human capital** H is always attached to a specific person. In the context of our example, human capital could be the skill of 10-finger touch typing. While a typewriter even makes a person constrained to 2-finger look-and-peck typing more productive, 10-finger touch typing boosts productivity to yet another level.

The important difference between labour efficiency and human capital is that, in principle, the first is technological and, thus, available to everybody – worldwide. A country with the required financial means can always buy this technology on the world markets and equip its workers with it. Human capital, on the other hand, cannot be detached from the physical worker who acquired it. The human capital stock of a country is necessarily the result of a lengthy process of formal learning and training on the job. If countries feature significant differences in the human capital of their workers, then even global capital markets could not make their incomes converge quickly. The speed of income convergence would be restricted by how quickly human capital converges.

We may ask whether there are any merits to distinguishing between labour-augmenting technological progress and human capital accumulation. Indeed there are, though formally both variables play identical roles in the model. The difference is that technology, while making labour more efficient, is not tied to labour. It can easily be transferred across borders and make labour more efficient in any country. By contrast, human capital cannot be separated from a particular workforce. It must be accumulated in this workforce over time. This distinction is of great importance when we think about possible policies designed to influence economic growth.

10.6 ENDOGENOUS GROWTH

Endogenous growth occurs when forces within the model, such as capital accumulation, make income grow, rather than outside influences such as unexplained technological progress.

Despite its new merits, the human-capital-augmented Solow growth model still only explains income *levels*, and not why incomes *grow*. Growth in equilibrium is still due to exogenous improvements in production technology or human capital accumulation. Recently proposed new theories make a point of explaining how technological progress or human capital may be generated endogenously. We will look at one particularly simple example of such a model of **endogenous growth.**

The *AK* model

Suppose the production function includes human capital and has the form

$$Y = AK^{\alpha}(HL)^{1-\alpha} \tag{10.5}$$

where A reflects the production technology. Assume that human capital is positively related to the capital endowment per worker, say

$$H = K/L \tag{10.6}$$

because workers who have the opportunity to work with advanced computers and sophisticated software can sharpen skills and accumulate useful experience faster than others. Substitution of (10.6) into (10.5) gives the production function $Y = AK$, or, after dividing both sides by L, in per capita terms

$$y = Ak \tag{10.7}$$

Models of this type are referred to as *AK* models. What separates this production function from previous ones is that *the marginal productivity of capital* $\Delta Y/\Delta K = \Delta y/\Delta k = A$ *does not decrease as the capital stock rises*. Since capital not only aids in production directly, through its role as an input, it also has the side effect of raising human capital, and so output (per capita) increases linearly with the capital stock (per capita). Figure 10.16 illustrates why this *can* explain endogenous growth.

The partial production function $y = Ak$ is now a straight line, and so is the savings-investment line sAk. There is a single steady state, positioned at the origin. Whether this is stable or not depends on whether the requirement line $(n + \delta)k$ is steeper than the investment line. Panel (a) depicts the second case. Here the investment line is steeper than the requirement line, $sA > n + \delta$. Hence, for positive capital stocks and incomes, investment is always higher than the investment required to keep the capital stock where it is currently. Hence, once the capital stock is greater than zero, the capital stock grows, and grows, and never stops. And with it income grows and grows, and never stops growing. We have endogenous income growth fuelled by permanent capital accumulation.

Panel (b) shows that the *AK* model scenario is no guarantee of eternal growth. If the savings rate is too low relative to depreciation and population

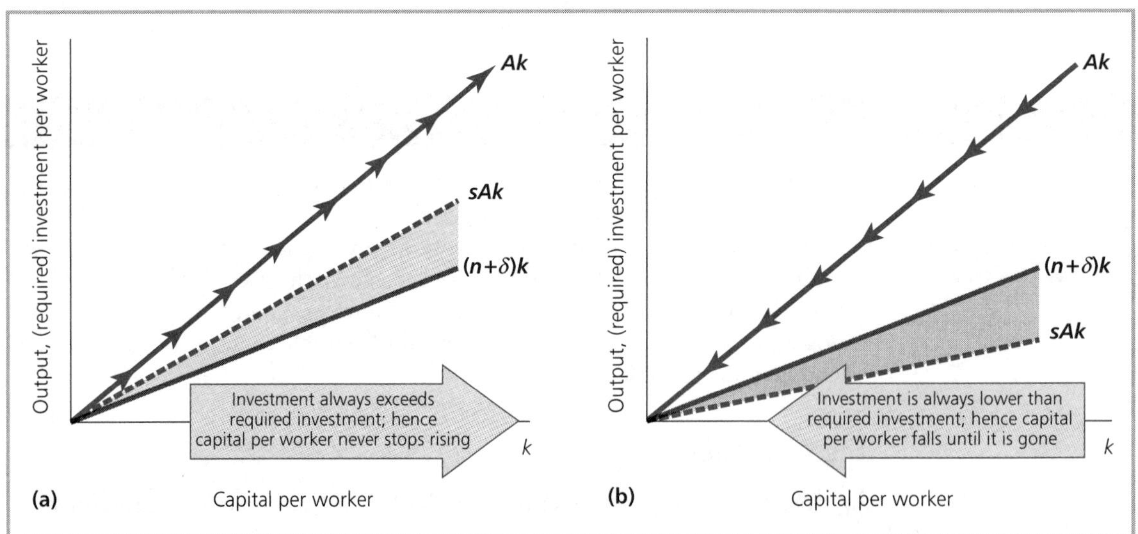

Figure 10.16 (a) When the marginal productivity of capital does not decrease, it is possible that actual investment always exceeds required investment. Then capital always continues to grow, making labour productivity grow, and causing permanent growth of output and consumption per capita. (b) In the *AK* model it is also possible that actual investment always falls short of required investment. Then the capital stock always continues to fall, and so do output and consumption per capita.

growth rates, $sA < n + \delta$, the capital stock is destined to shrink and income will drop all the way back to the subsistence level. So the poverty trap is also looming in the AK model.

Globalization

Does globalization help? Will investment flows rescue a low-saving country from the poverty trap? One would not think so, since the marginal product of capital that marks the payoff to investors is constant in a linear production function of the form $Y = AK$. It is the same in both panels (or countries) of Figure 10.16, and the same at all capital stocks. Put formally, the marginal product of capital, which equals the slope of the production function, is equal to

$$\frac{\Delta Y}{\Delta K} = A \tag{10.8}$$

Upon closer scrutiny, however, matters are a little more complicated. Remember that the production function for the individual firm is $Y = AK^{\alpha}(HL)^{1-\alpha}$. Under perfect competition, when each firm is small relative to the size of the economy, the individual firm will ignore the consequences its own investments have on human capital – because this effect takes time and a fluctuating workforce will spread it over the entire economy. With H considered given, the marginal product of capital from the firms' perspective is

$$\frac{\Delta Y}{\Delta K} = \alpha A\left(\frac{HL}{K}\right)^{1-\alpha}$$

On the AK line, where $H = K/L$, this reduces to

$$\frac{\Delta Y}{\Delta K} = \alpha A \tag{10.9}$$

This has two interesting implications:

- The marginal product of capital as seen by individual firms is also the same for all countries, and it is independent of the savings rate. This means that poor countries will not attract the foreign investment needed to reverse the downward drift of their incomes. Globalized capital markets are of no help.
- The marginal product of capital is higher from the perspective of society than it is in the calculation of an individual firm, since $A > \alpha A$. Because the creation of human capital is a public good, firms may not invest enough. This may justify subsidization of investment or savings by the government.

Empirical implications

The AK model has empirical implications that differ from those of the Solow model. Proceeding from the per capita version of the model, which allows for the fact that in reality populations do grow, this production function reads $y = Ak$. It implies the growth-accounting equation

$$\frac{\Delta y}{y} = \frac{\Delta A}{A} + \frac{\Delta k}{k} \tag{10.10}$$

meaning that per capita income growth is the direct sum of the rate of technological progress and per capita capital growth. The capital stock per worker changes according to $\Delta k = sAk - (\delta + n)k$. Dividing both sides by k we obtain the growth rate of k:

$$\frac{\Delta k}{k} = sA - (\delta + n) \tag{10.11}$$

Substituting (10.11) into (10.10) we finally obtain

$$\frac{\Delta y}{y} = \frac{\Delta A}{A} + sA - \delta - n \tag{10.12}$$

This equation has *two empirical implications*:

- A country's per capita income growth is higher, the higher its savings rate s.
- A country's per capita income growth is lower, the higher its population growth rate n.

Both hypotheses resemble implications of the Solow model. But now, in the *AK* model, s and n affect income *growth*, while in the Solow model they affected income *levels*.

Figure 10.17 looks at the first implication by plotting per capita income growth against the investment rate. The data are in line with the implications of the *AK* model, revealing that higher investment rates accompany or cause higher income growth.

The second implication is scrutinized in Figure 10.18. The support for the *AK* model is much weaker here. If there is a negative correlation between per capita income growth and population growth, a trace of visual support comes

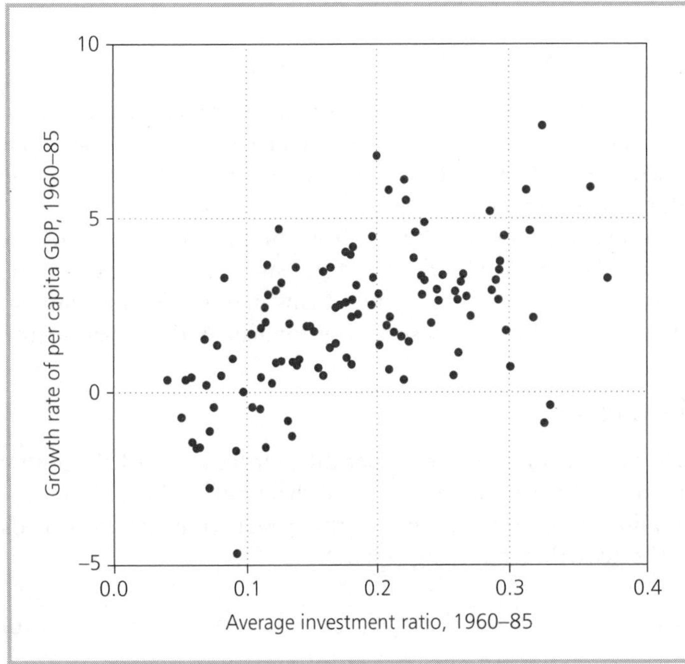

Figure 10.17 The *AK* model predicts that countries with higher savings or investment rates experience higher income growth per capita. The graph shows that this prediction is well in line with actual investment and per capita income growth rates in this global sample.
Source: R. Barro and J. Lee: http://www.nuff.ox.ac.uk/economics/growth/barlee.htm

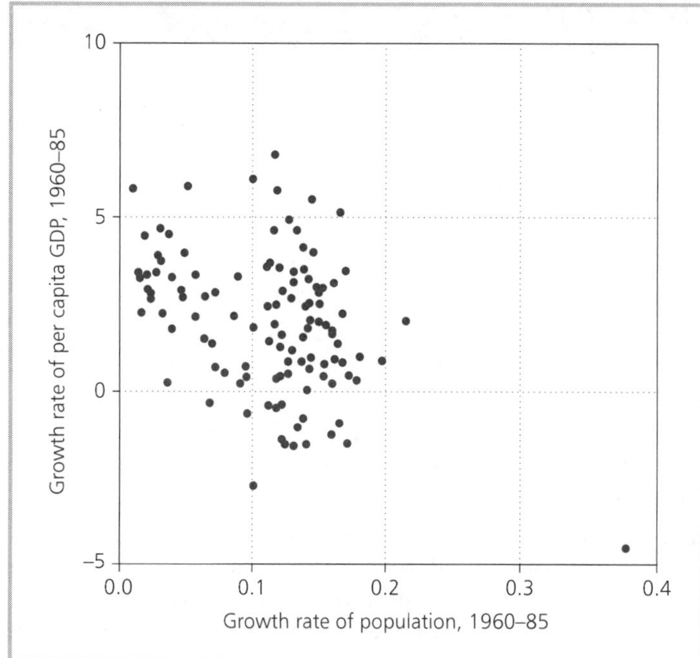

Figure 10.18 The *AK* model implies that those countries with higher population growth rates experience lower income growth per capita. The graph shows that there is some support for this prediction in the data for this global sample.
Source: R. Barro and J. Lee: http://www.nuff.ox.ac.uk/economics/growth/barlee.htm

mostly from a single country (Kuwait on the lower right). However, a small negative correlation is not enough, since equation (10.12) claims that the correlation coefficient should be −1. This is clearly not the magnitude conveyed by the data.

Solow growth model vs endogenous growth models

The Solow model, and its offspring, focused on the role of savings and capital accumulation as determinants of income. Growth of income per worker can occur either endogenously during some period of transition to a higher-income steady state, or for technological progress which falls from the sky. Recently advanced endogenous growth models attempt to remedy or overcome these and other perceived weaknesses of the Solow model by looking at the processes which generate technological advancements, at human-based skills and how these are acquired and enter the production process, and at public investment into infrastructure. Much of this work is important and exciting, but it is too early to pass judgement on the ideas advanced.

For practical purposes the difference between the Solow model and certain endogenous growth models like the *AK* model may be less dramatic than their fundamentally different philosophies suggest. In the *AK* model an increase of the savings rate may raise output growth permanently. In the Solow model it would lead to higher growth during some period of transition to the new steady state only. Empirical work based on the Solow model suggests that this transition period may last anything between 20 and 40 years.

CHAPTER SUMMARY

- The only factors that, in the presence of constant returns to scale, can make living standards grow in the long run are technological progress or human capital accumulation.
- The globalization of capital markets should raise GNP in all participating countries. GDP and wage incomes may well fall (relative to trend) in those countries that until now had higher savings rates and income levels.
- The globalization of capital markets raises capital incomes relative to wage incomes in the initially rich countries. It may thus make the functional distribution of income (between capital and labour) more uneven.
- The integration of labour and product markets is well under way in Europe, and projected in other regions. This should raise income levels by raising productivity and boost growth rates for a number of decades through capital accumulation.
- There is nothing inherently wrong with public deficits and debt. Deficit spending and debt accumulation needs to be justified, however, either by the higher total investment that results from it, or by rates of return on public investments that exceed potential rates of return on private projects that are crowded out.
- If the production function, savings behaviour or other features differ from what is assumed in the standard Solow model, there may be more than one stable steady-state income. The low-income steady state may work like a poverty trap, and efforts to raise income above this level often fail.
- Ways out of poverty traps depend on the specific nature of the trap at hand. In some cases an opening of capital markets to international investors will do. In other cases a big push of development aid may be needed.
- A higher capital stock may boost the accumulation of human capital. This may cause capital productivity to fall more slowly than expected or not at all, as illustrated by the *AK* model. The result is endogenous growth through capital accumulation.

KEY TERMS AND CONCEPTS

_AK_ model
endogenous growth
Feldstein–Horioka puzzle
foreign investment
globalization
human capital
income distribution
national savings
poverty trap
public saving
Ricardian equivalence

EXERCISES

10.1 Let the production function be $Y = K^{\alpha}L^{\beta}$. Under what conditions does this function generate increasing returns to scale? Do increasing returns to scale suffice to generate an increasing marginal product of capital?

10.2 Suppose we are looking at the global economy with a standard constant return to scale production function. Let us now introduce the public sector, where $T - G$ is public saving.

(a) What happens to steady-state income if the government raises T (without increasing public spending)? What happens to per capita consumption in the long and in the short run? (Can you make a definite/unconditional statement?)

(b) Suppose the government is not able to save the increase in tax revenue, but spends all of the surplus immediately for government consumption: What happens now to steady-state income?

(c) Finally, suppose that not all the government spending is used for consumption goods, but a part of it is used for public investment. What share of the additional tax revenue must the government invest if steady-state income should increase in response to the policy action, and the private savings rate is 20%?

10.3 Consider an economy with the following production function: $Y = K^{0.5}L^{0.5}$. The labour force L is 100, the savings rate is 0.3, and the rate of depreciation is 0.1.

(a) Determine the steady-state levels of per capita income and consumption.

Now suppose that the government wants to increase national savings by levying an income tax of 20%.

(b) Compute the new level of steady-state per capita consumption. Does it increase or decrease compared with the result obtained in (a)? What happens to per capita consumption in the short run?

(c) Consider the steady state where $t = 0.5$. Is it dynamically inefficient? Proceed as in (b).

10.4 Consider two separate economies that are identical in the size of their labour force ($L_A = L_B = 100$) and the production function including technology, but differ in their savings rates. The production function for both economies is $Y = K^{0.5}L^{0.5}$. Let the rate of depreciation be 10%. Suppose, the savings rate in country A is 25%, whereas people in country B do not save at all.

(a) Determine the autonomous steady-state incomes and capital stocks in both countries. What is the level of per capita consumption in each country?

Now suppose that a global capital market is introduced such that capital can be transferred from one country to another costlessly.

(b) Determine the steady state incomes and capital stocks in both countries in this new environment. What happens to income (GNP) and thus consumption, both in the long and in the short run?

10.5 Consider a world with two economies and a global capital market. Again, the two countries are alike except for their savings rate (the savings rate in country B is smaller). Thus, in the initial steady state: $K_A = K_B$, $Y_A = Y_B$, but $GNP_A > GNP_B$ and, thus, $C_A > C_B$.

(a) What will happen to investment flows (and thus Y, K, GNP and C) if technology in country B improves? What happens, if the technology boost occurs in country A?

(b) Suppose next that the depreciation rate of capital in country A increases (because of ecological reasons, e.g. in country A there are more floods, thunderstorms or fires). Does this have any impact on the steady-state variables of Y, K, GNP or C?

(c) Finally, imagine that the population in country B doubles (say, because of reunification). What implications does this have on the two economies? (Consider again Y, K, GNP and C, but also per capita consumption.)

10.6 Start from the basic scenario supplied in Box 10.1. In a situation with a global capital market, how are GDP, GNP and factor income shares affected if
(a) the savings rate in country A falls to $s_A = 0.1$?
(b) country B's population is four times as large as country A's ($L_B = 4L_A$)?

10.7 Consider an economy with the Cobb–Douglas production function $Y = K^{0.5}L^{0.5}$. The savings rate is 0.3, the rate of depreciation 0.05 and the rate of population growth n depends on per capita income: if per capita income is low, population grows at a rate of 0.1, if per capita income is high, the population growth rate reduces to 0.05.
(a) Determine per capita output and consumption in both steady states.
Next suppose that the economy is initially in the steady state with $n = 0.1$. The population growth rate declines as soon as per capita income has reached 2.5 units. Now the World Bank decides on a development programme for this country.
(b) How big does the help package from the World Bank need to be in order to be effective in the long run? (Determine the required per capita capital transfer.)
(c) What happens if the per capita capital transfer is smaller than required? (Explain why the steady state income cannot rise in this case.)

10.8 Consider an economy with the following production function: $Y = K^{0.5}(HL)^{0.5}$, where H is human capital which grows at the constant rate $\eta = 5\%$ and the population growth rate is $n = 1\%$.
(a) Determine the steady-state levels of $\tilde{y}$ and $\tilde{c}$ for $s = 0.2$ and $\delta = 0.1$.
(Hint: Start by determining the steady-state condition for capital per human-capital-augmented efficiency unit of labour.)
(b) What are the growth rates of income, consumption and capital in the steady state?
(c) What happens to per capita consumption, and why?
Suppose now that the government wants to raise welfare and, therefore, starts an education reform, which raises η from 5% to 10% at zero costs.
(d) What are the short- and the long-run effects on per capita production, $\tilde{c}$ and per capita consumption? What do you conclude about the success of the education reform (does it unambiguously increase welfare)?

10.9 Recall our numerical exercise with data for Denmark and Sierra Leone in section 10.3. This time suppose the production function reads $Y = \sqrt{K}\sqrt{HL}$ which, after dividing both sides by L, rewrites $Y/L \equiv y = \sqrt{k}\sqrt{H}$. Given the data for n, s and $\delta = 0.1$, how many times higher would human capital have to be in Denmark in order to account for a 50 times higher level of per capita income?

10.10 Consider an economy with the per capita production function $y = Ak$.
(a) How does the per capita capital stock evolve over time?
(b) What happens to this economy, if $sA > n + \delta$?
(c) What happens if $sA < n + \delta$?

10.11 Again, let the production function be $y = Ak$. Suppose now that $A = 0.5$, $s = 0.2$, $n = 0.03$ and $\delta = 0.05$.
(a) Determine the per capita consumption growth rate in this economy.
(b) Where does growth in this model come from?
(c) What would happen if the depreciation rate changed from 0.05 to 0.1?

RECOMMENDED READING

The issues touched on in this chapter are the focus of much recent and current research. Examples of the many recent papers worth reading are:

- Paul Collier and Jan W. Gunning (1999) 'Why has Africa grown slowly?', *Journal of Economic Perspectives* 13: 3–22, who distinguish between 'policy' and 'destiny' factors that caused slow growth in Africa over the past three decades.
- Alan B. Krueger and Mikael Lindahl (2001) 'Education for growth: Why and for whom?', *Journal of Economic Literature* 39: 1101–36. This paper provides a discussion of and empirical evidence on the effects of schooling on individual income, on the one hand, and on GDP growth on the other hand.

A survey of recent empirical literature on growth and convergence is provided by Jonathan Temple (1999) 'The new growth evidence', *Journal of Economic Literature* 37: 112–56.

APPENDIX A SYNTHESIS OF THE *DAD-SAS* AND THE SOLOW MODEL

The tool-box assembled in the first ten chapters contains two major models:

- The ***AD-AS*** or ***DAD-SAS*** **model**, which serves to explain the short-run fluctuations of income; and
- The **Solow model** (plus extensions), our workhorse for understanding the long-run trends in income.

Figure 8.17 in the Chapter 8 appendix, 'The genesis of the *DAD-SAS* model' had already reviewed the building blocks of the *DAD-SAS* model and indicated how they fit together. Figure 10.19 picks up this information and shows where the Solow model and its foundations fit into this road map of macroeconomics.

The road map distinguishes between the economy's **demand and supply side**. The *DAD-SAS* model focused on the demand side, augmented by the short- and medium-run aspects of the supply side as represented by the labour market. Broadening our view of the supply side, the lower part of the graph starts from the **production function** in the lower left. The production function implies two partial production functions, one holding K fixed and one holding L fixed. The first leads to the firms' labour demand curve and, matched with the labour supply curve, determines the employment level at the current capital stock. The second partial production function is an integral part of the Solow growth model and helps determine the capital stock in the long run. The capital stock, in turn, impacts on how much income can be produced with a given level of employment and, hence, codetermines the position of the long-run aggregate supply curve (*EAS*) at potential income. Hence, by explaining slow movements of income occurring in the long run, the Solow model provides an anchor for the *DAD-SAS* model.

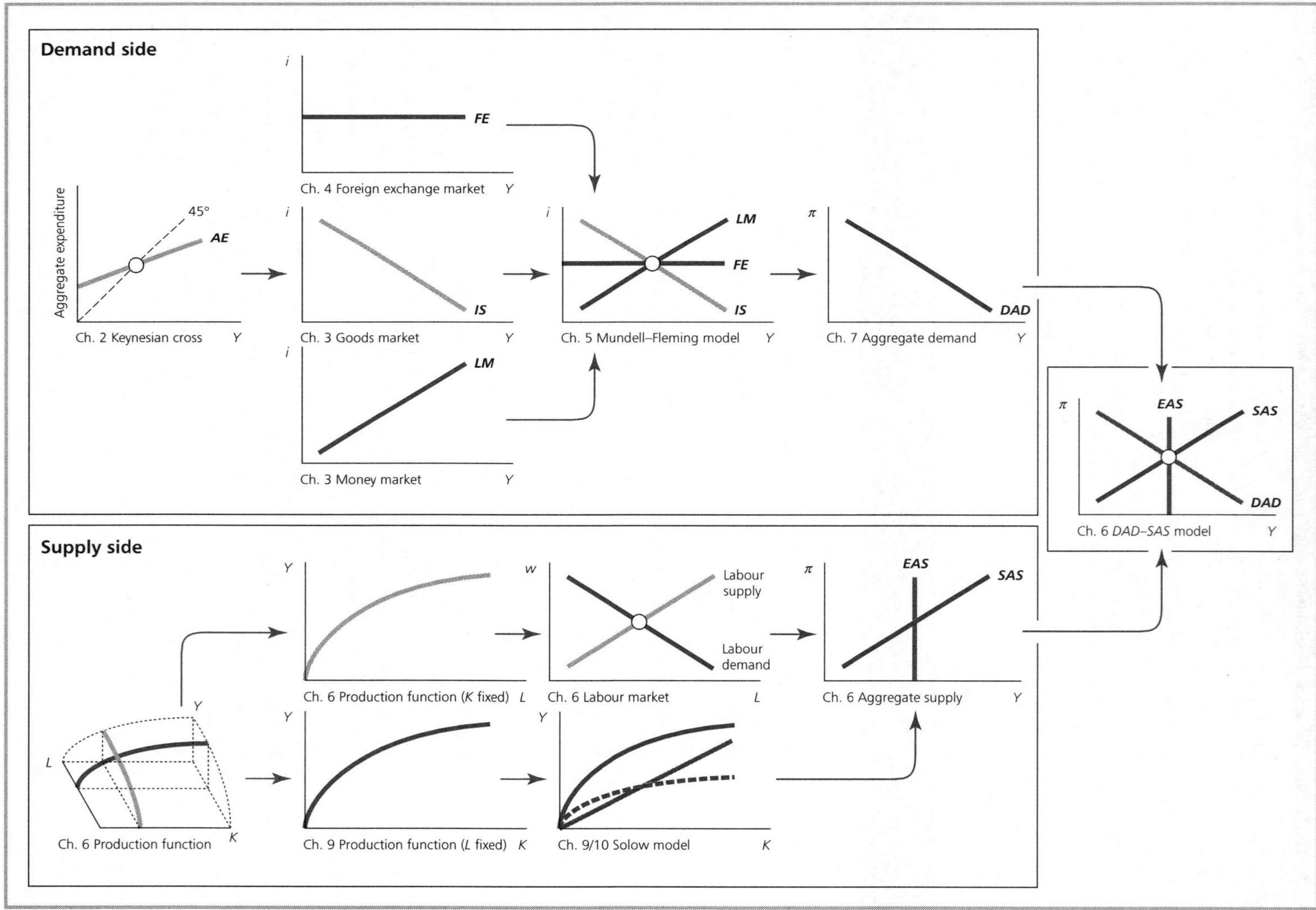

Figure 10.19 A synthesis of the *DAD-SAS* and Solow model.

APPLIED PROBLEMS

RECENT RESEARCH

Human capital and income growth

This chapter augmented the Solow model with human capital. In this model an increase in human capital generates higher GDP growth for years, if not decades, until the new, higher steady-state income level is finally reached. What complicates the empirical testing of this model is that human capital is a complex variable for which no simple measure exists. Researchers very often use the level of education as a proxy for human capital. In this spirit, Robert Barro ('Human capital and growth' (2000), *American Economic Review Papers and Proceedings* 91: 12–17) regresses GDP growth on years of secondary and higher schooling of females and males, and on various other variables. Selected results drawn from different regressions are shown in Table 10.1.

A striking result is that better schooling (and, hence, human capital) of men seems to spur income growth while better schooling of women does not. According to the estimated coefficient of 0.0044, which due to the *t*-statistic of 2.44 is significantly different from 0, an additional year of male secondary or higher schooling raises income growth by almost half a percentage point. The coefficient for female years of schooling is even negative, though insignificant statistically. How can female education not matter for growth when our model says it should? Barro suggests that this may be due to ongoing discrimination of women in many countries which prevents an efficient use of well-educated females in the labour market.

Does this mean that while discrimination lasts it does not pay to invest in female education? Not at all. Note that Barro's regressions also signal a negative effect of the fertility rate. Now the fertility rate and female education are not independent of each other, but move together, in opposite directions (there is a negative correlation in the data). Females with more school years have fewer children. So when a country invests in female education, discrimination may prevent direct effects on income growth. But since this drives down fertility and, hence, population growth, income growth is spurred nevertheless. If Barro's presumption is correct, this effect is strengthened if female discrimination in the labour market is reduced.

Table 10.1 Effects on income growth

Independent variable	Coefficient	*t*-statistic
Male secondary and higher schooling	0.00440	2.44
Female secondary and higher schooling	−0.00110	−0.275
Fertility rate (logarithm)	−0.00275	5.50

WORKED PROBLEM

Testing the *AK* model

This chapter showed that, according to the *AK* model, the *growth rate* of per capita income varies negatively with population growth and positively with the investment (or savings) ratio. We now want to check if these relationships as summarized in equation (10.12) hold for a group of 22 countries (representative of the larger sample of 135 countries shown in Figures 10.17 and 10.18) for which data are given in Table 10.2.

Table 10.2

	Per-capita-income growth $\Delta y/y$ (in %)	Investment ratio I/Y (in %)	Population growth rate n (in %)
Algeria	2.01	24.04	2.85
Congo	3.52	29.19	2.73
Ethiopia	0.34	5.40	2.34
Ivory Coast	0.86	12.72	3.92
Kenya	0.97	17.64	3.58
Zimbabwe	1.75	21.28	3.16
Guatemala	0.95	8.93	2.83
Haiti	0.17	6.94	1.76
Honduras	0.79	13.89	3.32
Mexico	2.49	19.65	2.99
Nicaragua	0.90	14.10	3.19
Panama	3.42	26.62	2.60
Peru	0.83	12.29	2.72
India	1.38	16.83	2.24
Israel	3.22	28.96	2.82
Nepal	0.38	5.77	2.38
Austria	3.36	23.45	0.28
Belgium	3.24	23.66	0.30
Cyprus	4.68	31.47	0.60
Norway	3.77	29.35	0.59
Switzerland	1.79	29.80	0.75
Australia	2.16	31.67	1.71

All variables are averages for 1960–1985.

Regressing per-capita income growth on the investment ratio gives us the following empirical relationship (absolute *t*-statistics in parentheses):

$$\underset{}{\frac{\Delta y}{y}} = \underset{(1.61)}{-0.60} + \underset{(7.52)}{0.13}\frac{I}{Y} \qquad R^2_{\text{adj}} = 0.73$$

Hence, investing 1% more of output increases the income growth rate by 0.13%. This result fits well with the visual impression that we get from looking at Figure 10.17 and is in line with what we expect from the *AK* model. The estimated coefficient is also highly significant due to its *t*-statistic of 7.52). Finally, in this sample 73% of the differences in income growth rates between countries can be attributed to differences in investment ratios.

The regression of income growth on population growth gives:

$$\frac{\Delta y}{y} = \underset{(6.03)}{3.40} - \underset{(2.84)}{0.64}n \qquad R^2_{\text{adj}} = 0.25$$

So, a 1% increase in the population growth rate decreases the income growth rate by about two-thirds of a percentage point. Again, this result is as expected from both the model and Figure 10.18. At 0.25 the coefficient of determination is much lower than it was in the preceding equation, however.

YOUR TURN

More on the *AK* model

This chapter's worked problem used statistical methods to gauge whether real world data support the *AK* model. One may argue, though, that the obtained results did not tell us much beyond what we already had learned from inspecting Figures 10.17 and 10.18. (This is not quite true, however, since econometric analysis provides information on the reliability or significance of results, something that 'eyeball econometrics', visual inspection of graphs, cannot provide.) An obvious disadvantage of graphs is that they can only display the relationship between two variables. This does not do complete justice to equation (10.12) which says that both the investment ratio and population growth affect income growth at the same time. Econometrics can handle much more complicated relationships by performing *multiple regressions.*

Regress income growth on both the investment ratio and population growth at the same time. Compare the coefficients obtained from this multiple regression with those obtained from the simple regressions reported in the worked-problem section. Why might they differ?

Which aspects of your results support the *AK* model? Which aspects do not?

To further explore this chapter's key messages you are encouraged to use the interactive online module found at

www.fgn.unisg.ch/eurmacro/tutor/Solow2country.html

and many other features hosted at **www.fgn.unisg.ch/eurmacro**

CHAPTER 11

ENDOGENOUS ECONOMIC POLICY

WHAT TO EXPECT After working through this chapter, you will know:

1. **What makes governments tick.**
2. Why **government policies may *create* booms and recessions** rather than fixing them.
3. What a **political business cycle** is, and what it looks like.
4. What **time inconsistency** means, and why it may lead democracies astray into equilibria with undesirably high inflation rates.
5. How to view monetary (and fiscal policy) in the context of a **game between the government and the labour market**, in which the labour market makes the first move.
6. That **ways out of the time inconsistency trap** include tying the hands of policy-makers, making them more susceptible to reputational considerations, and making them act more conservatively in terms of concern for price stability.

Policy-making is the control of macroeconomic instruments, say, the decision to raise taxes next year or to intervene in the foreign exchanges today. **Institutions** provide guidelines or restrictions for policy-makers. The European Monetary Union is an institution, as is the WTO, or the European Central Bank with its underlying laws.

The first ten chapters completed the tool-box for understanding how economies work on the aggregate level. And this is where conventional textbooks stop. But it falls short of what we need in order to understand many current macroeconomic events, including the experience of, the issues of, and further plans and prospects for European economic integration. The reason is that, yes, by now we appreciate how particular institutions or specific policy measures affect the economy. Therefore, it should also be clear that the European economies are where they are and face the problems they do *because* of the policies that were conducted and *because* of the institutions that were constructed or inherited. But since neither policy choices nor the design of institutions do regularly follow the recommendations of economists, we must next ask what determines the choices of **policy-makers** and the design of **institutions**. Conventional macroeconomics is not equipped to answer such questions. It is these questions and related issues that will be addressed in this chapter.

11.1 WHAT DO POLITICIANS WANT?

A **constraint** lists what people can get, given a budget or other limiting factors. **Preferences** indicate what people want.

When economists set about explaining the decisions of consumers, firms, investors, households, workers and any other players in the economic arena, they follow an established standard procedure. Step 1 identifies the available options. For a household, these are given by the budget **constraint**, which reduces purchasing options to those that the household can afford. Step 2 picks the best option out of affordable options. This requires the specification of **preferences**, that is, what consumers like and how they rank their options.

Steps 1 and 2 are standard fare in *microeconomics*. The building blocks of *macroeconomic* models are also thought to reflect the optimal choices of individual decision-makers, sometimes in an explicit, non-compromising fashion, and sometimes in an indirect, simplifying, pragmatic way. One example in this book which followed standard microeconomic procedure was the discussion of monopolistic trade unions as a potential cause of unemployment in Chapter 6. We assumed that the options available to the trade union were restricted to points on the demand-for-labour curve of firms (step 1). Next we defined trade union preferences in terms of the wage sum (step 2). This permitted us to postulate that trade unions' wage bargaining will aim for that point on the labour demand curve that maximizes the wage sum. It never crossed our minds that by simply telling the trade union to reduce the real wage in order to eliminate unemployment would actually make them do it. We were well aware that if our recommendation would lead to a reduction of the wage sum, the union would not follow.

Curiously, when economists talked about monetary and fiscal policy issues in the not too distant past, they naively assumed that all they had to do was confront the policy-maker with their recommendations, and he or she would implement them. Such a view of policy-making is obviously not consistent with how economists analyze the behaviour of other actors – and this is changing.

In order to understand why policy-makers conduct the policies they do, sometimes adopting, but frequently ignoring advice from economists, and why they shape institutions the way they do, we must also follow standard procedure.

Step 1: the constraint

The options of the government are restricted by the economy, by the interplay of goods prices, interest rates, wages, exchange rates, income and so on, as it results from the interaction of various markets. In the context of our current discussion the economy is condensed into the *DAD-SAS* model. In the very short run, that is, within the current period, demand-side (monetary and fiscal) policies geared towards shifting *DAD* are restricted in what they may achieve by the short-run *SAS* curve.

Step 2: the preferences

Like everybody else, politicians maximize utility. However, this assertion is trivial – in fact, useless. You cannot put it to use or prove it wrong unless you become more specific about the things that yield utility to politicians.

Economists do that in other fields too: utility maximization of firms is often narrowed down to profit maximization. Trade union utility was represented by the wage sum. Individuals are often thought to maximize income.

Now what do politicians maximize? Things that they appear to be interested in include changing the course of their country according to what they think is good – such as, a proper place in the history books, power, prestige, and much more. This makes for a rather complicated utility function, and it is hard to see how it fits into our *DAD-SAS* model. Fortunately, two arguments make politicians' preferences more transparent and more useful for our purposes. First, many of the above and other things that politicians are presumably interested in can only be pursued properly when in office. So politicians who need to be elected must pay close attention to *public support*. Second, public support for governments very much reflects how the economy is doing (a case in point is former US President Bill Clinton's 1992 War Room slogan, 'It's the economy, stupid!'). When making that judgement, the public measures the state of the economy by a digestible number of key indicators. The chief variables emerging from decades of empirical research are inflation and unemployment, both of which the public likes to be low. Since unemployment is low when income is high, and vice versa, we may also postulate that *the public likes low inflation and high income*. This way the public's preferences are expressed in terms of exactly those two macroeconomic variables measured along the axes in Chapter 8's graphical treatment of the *DAD–SAS* model. This will come in handy below.

Let public support for the government depend on inflation π and income Y according to

$$s = \bar{s} - 0.5\pi^2 + \beta Y \qquad \textbf{Public support function} \qquad (11.1)$$

where s stands for the public support of the incumbent party or government, say, as measured by the vote share received at an election or in an opinion poll. We will give an alternative interpretation to this equation below. As displayed in Figure 11.1, public support or government utility, if public support is

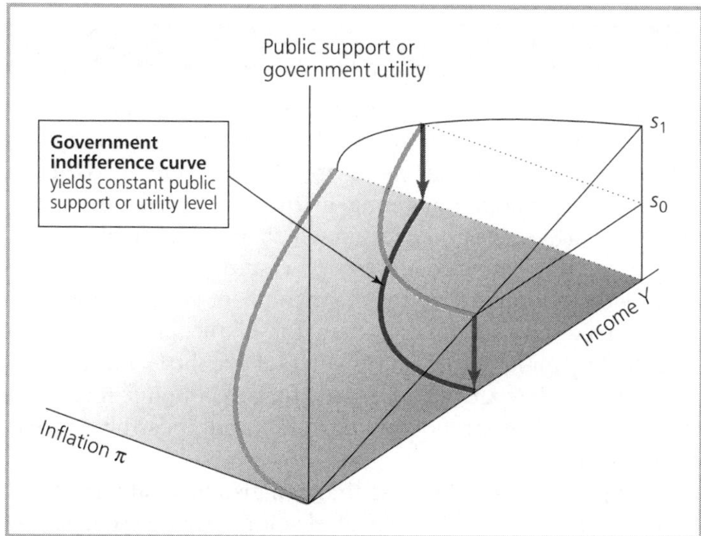

Figure 11.1 Public support for the government rises linearly as income rises. It falls faster and faster as inflation increases. A given level of support, s_0, determined by placing a horizontal cut at the appropriate height, can result from different combinations of inflation and income. The cut determines this curved line, which can be projected down onto the inflation–income surface. Placing the cut higher up at s_1 gives an indifference curve further to the right.

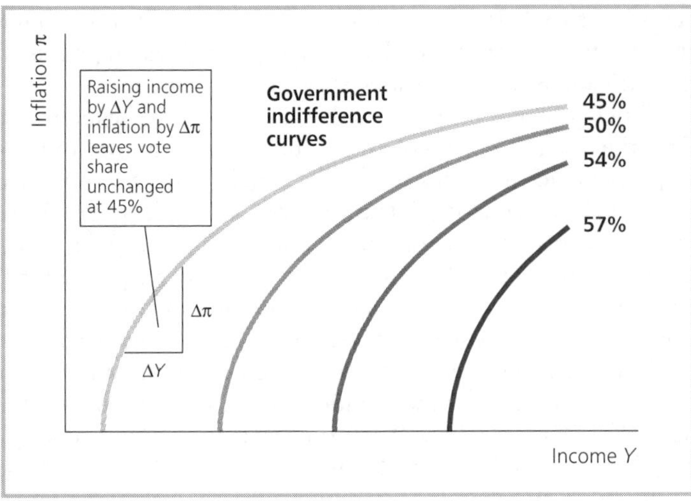

Figure 11.2 Government indifference curves or iso-support curves represent greater support by voters or the public if they are located further to the right.

what the government is interested in, rises as income rises, and falls, at an accelerating pace, as inflation goes up.

A **government indifference curve** (which we also call an **iso-support curve**) in π-Y space lists all combinations of π and Y between which the government is indifferent (or that yield the same public support).

To represent government preferences in 2D on the inflation–income plane we may resort to the concept of indifference curves. **Government indifference curves** combine all macroeconomic outcomes that yield a given level of public support, say s_0. In order to obtain this indifference curve (which, in fact, is an **iso-support curve**), slice horizontally through the 3D vote function at a height s_0 indicating the vote share you want to maintain. The curved edge of this slice aligns all pairs of inflation and income that guarantee the government the support s_0. This curve can be projected down onto the π-Y surface. To identify macroeconomic situations that yield a higher support level s_1, just place the horizontal cut higher at s_1. Projected down onto the π-Y surface, this indifference curve (not shown here) is to the right of the previous one, reflecting, of course, that as we move right towards higher income levels, the government draws more votes. Figure 11.2 shows a set of government indifference curves.

11.2 POLITICAL BUSINESS CYCLES

Support levels in Figure 11.2 are measured and ranked in terms of government vote shares achieved at (hypothetical) elections. Actual elections are not being held every period, however, but only at more or less regular intervals. If the government primarily cares about remaining in office, it need only worry about public support during years or quarters in which an election takes place. How does public support translate into an election result?

Being rational individuals, voters vote for the incumbent government if it is *expected* to produce a better performance than the challenging opposition parties during the forthcoming term. Since voters have little incentive to become very well informed, they are likely to settle for an economic forecast of this performance that simply extrapolates current (and, possibly, recent) achievements into the future.

To construct the simplest conceivable case that can also be easily dealt with in a graph, let voters cast votes on the basis of election-year macroeconomic performance only. Anything that happened prior to the election year is completely ignored (or forgotten). Then the indifference curves depicted in Figure 11.2 may also be considered **iso-vote curves**. They directly translate election-year inflation and income into a government vote share. Assume, to keep things simple still, that election periods (two years long) and non-election periods (two years long) alternate. The interests (and behaviour) of the government in these two periods is quite different. During election periods the government tries to produce a state of the economy that yields the highest vote share according to equation (11.1). By contrast, states of the economy during non-election periods are not being judged by the government on the basis of the public support they spawn immediately, but on the basis of their effect on the public support that can be generated when the next election comes up.

What does all this mean for our understanding of economic policy? For a start, let the economy be in the no-inflation equilibrium given by point A in Figure 11.3. Assume that we are in an election year and the aggregate supply curve is in position SAS_E. The government knows that votes will be cast on the basis of this year's economic performance. Iso-vote curves indicate how the state of the economy translates into votes. The government's vote share rises as we move onto indifference curves positioned further to the right. What are the government's options?

One option is to keep inflation at zero. The economy stays put in the current non-inflationary equilibrium – and the government is voted out of office with a vote share of 45%. A second option is to switch to expansionary policy. This shifts *DAD* to the right, and, for given inflation expectations, the economy moves up SAS_E. As we move up *SAS*, election prospects look brighter and brighter. The reason is that, at very low inflation rates, voters rate the gain from an income increase achieved by moving up SAS_E higher than the loss resulting from the accompanying increase in inflation. But this does not go on for ever. At point E, where SAS_E just touches one of the indifference curves, these two effects balance exactly. If we moved beyond this crucial point, election prospects would begin to deteriorate. So the best thing a government with an eye on getting re-elected can do is to stimulate the economy just enough to

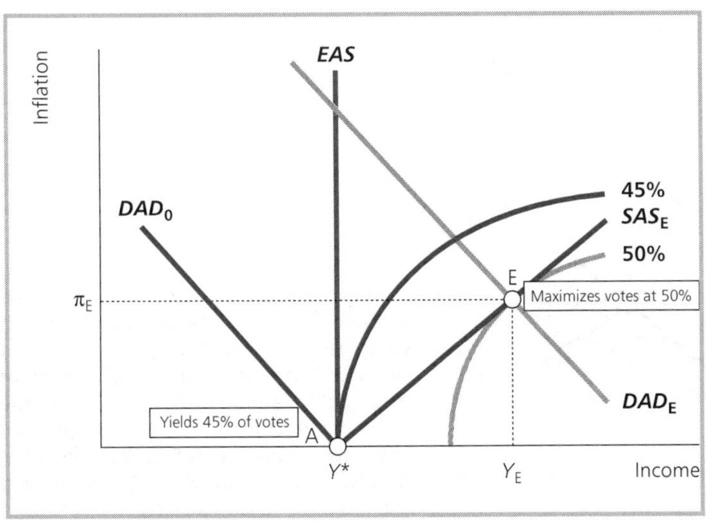

Figure 11.3 Let SAS_E be the aggregate supply curve during the election year. Then SAS_E describes all combinations of inflation and income that the government can generate by manipulating the *DAD* curve. The maximum vote share obtainable here is 50%. It results if *DAD* is moved into DAD_E, where SAS_E is tangent to an iso-vote curve.

bring it to point E. This situation maximizes the government's vote share. In the graph it just secures re-election with a vote share of 50%.

The policy instrument to be used depends on the exchange rate system. Increasing money growth shifts *DAD* up under flexible exchange rates. Under fixed exchange rates tax cuts or government expenditure increases will do the job.

A lesson we learned from Chapter 8 is that a situation as given by E cannot be sustained. If the government raises inflation to π_E in the election year in order to raise income and win the election, inflation expectations will be higher in the year *after* the election. In the simple case $\pi^e = \pi_{-1}$ this shifts *SAS* up to SAS_N for the non-election period, making for a much less favourable trade-off when the next election comes up (see Figure 11.4). How is the government going to respond to this? Is it going to regret that it started to meddle with the economy for re-election purposes in the first place?

That depends. Under two conditions it need not really have any regrets. Remember that public support during non-election periods does not matter to the government. If inflation expectations are formed adaptively and if voters forget or discount past states of the economy, the government can bring down inflation in the non-election period without costs in terms of future votes. Assume that it wants inflation expectations to be back to 0 for the next election period, so that *SAS* will be at SAS_E again. Then all the government has to do in the non-election period is shift down the *DAD* curve to DAD_N, thereby creating a recession and squeezing inflation out of the system. By the time the election arrives next period, this recession will already be forgotten. The government may again stimulate the economy, move up SAS_E to E, and win the election.

In contrast to *normal* business cycles, **political business cycles** have their roots in the political system, usually in the motivation of politicians or parties.

Note the blaspheme in this result: the government, the principal addressee of economists' advice, the very institution that we expect to draw on our improved understanding of how the economy works to *smooth* the course of the economy, uses just this understanding to generate booms and recessions that would not be there otherwise. Since this business cycle is generated by politicians, for political reasons, it is called a **political business cycle**.

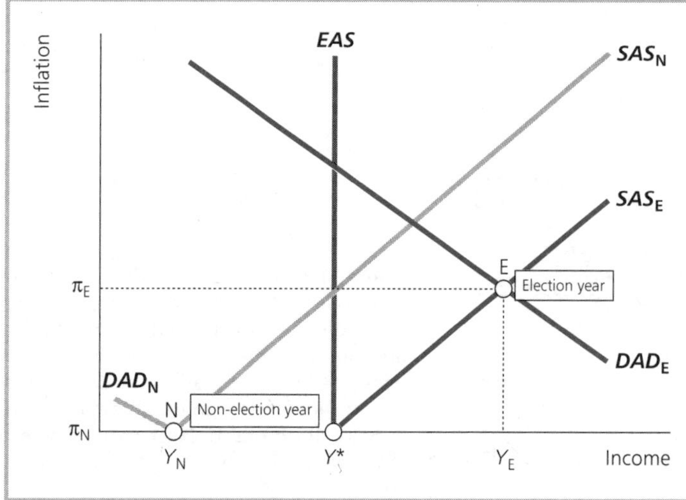

Figure 11.4 Instead of keeping the economy steady at the best point on *EAS*, which is $\pi = 0$ and $Y = Y^*$, a government that maximizes votes at periodic elections may deliberately want to make the economy fluctuate. Monetary expansion moves the economy to E in election years. Restrictive policy moves *DAD* down and the economy to N in non-election years.

11.3 RATIONAL EXPECTATIONS

As has just been indicated, the possibility of a political business cycle derives from the assumption that inflation expectations are being formed adaptively. Adaptive expectations are an economical forecasting scheme wherever they perform well, or if it is not easy to improve upon them. How well do adaptive expectations perform and how difficult is it to improve upon them in the context of the political business cycle?

Expectations are never correct during the political business cycle. The election year boom is created by inflating unexpectedly. The non-election year recession is due to a surprise disinflation. Hence, formation of adaptive inflation expectations commits systematic errors that follow the simple time pattern given in Figure 11.5. If the government were to exploit adaptive expectations formation repeatedly, individuals would soon see through the emerging pattern. Is it difficult to improve inflation forecasting? Not really – all that individuals need to realize is that demand expands during election periods and contracts when there is no election.

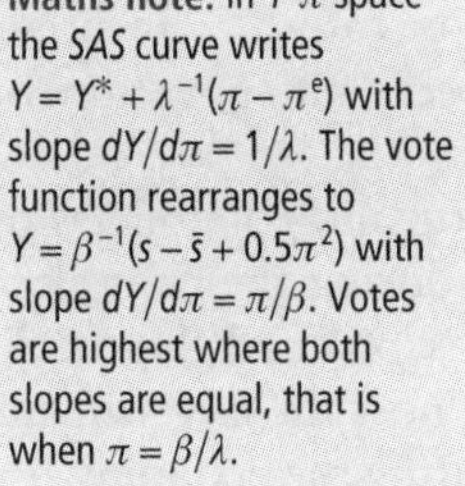
Maths note. In Y-π space the *SAS* curve writes $Y = Y^* + \lambda^{-1}(\pi - \pi^e)$ with slope $dY/d\pi = 1/\lambda$. The vote function rearranges to $Y = \beta^{-1}(s - \bar{s} + 0.5\pi^2)$ with slope $dY/d\pi = \pi/\beta$. Votes are highest where both slopes are equal, that is when $\pi = \beta/\lambda$.

What complicates rational expectations formation in the context of the political business cycle is that where the government puts the *DAD* curve is not independent of the expected inflation rate. On the other hand, rational expectations formation is facilitated by the fact that, even though the position of the *DAD* curve that maximizes votes depends on π^e, the government always generates the same election period inflation rate. Given the vote function (11.1) above, this vote-maximizing inflation rate is β/λ. If this sounds a bit abstract, consider Figure 11.6.

Figure 11.6 contains a set of aggregate supply curves, each reflecting a different expected inflation rate. Once inflation expectations have been formed and wages have been negotiated, the *SAS* is fixed to a unique position. Given this position, and no matter where it is, the government stimulates demand so as to move up along *SAS* to the point where it is tangent to an indifference curve. In the diagram we end up at E_1 if expected inflation is π_1, at E_2 if

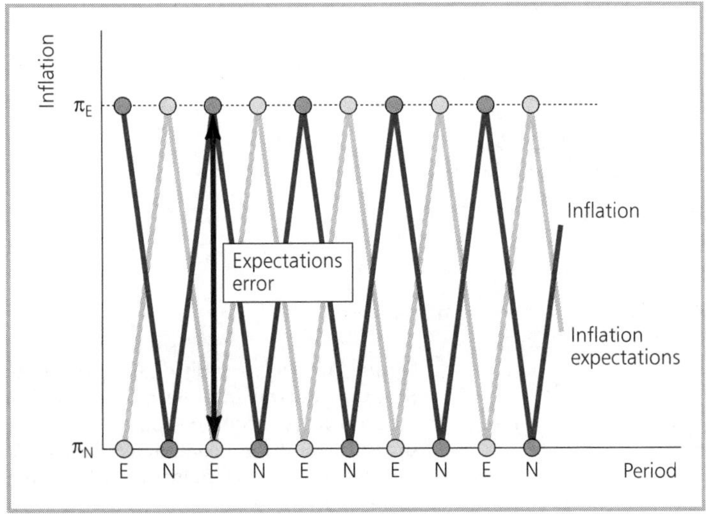

Figure 11.5 In the two-period example of a political business cycle, inflation is always π_E in election years and π_N in non-election years. Inflation expectations lag behind by one period, thus following just the opposite pattern. Expectations errors also follow a very easy-to-recognize two-period pattern.

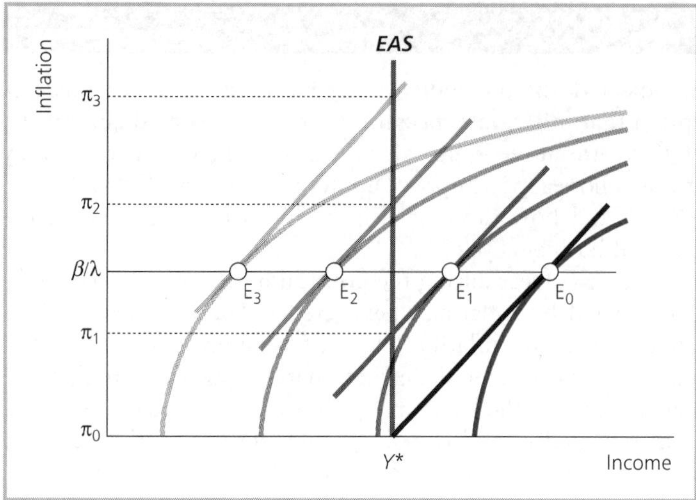

Figure 11.6 The public support function employed here has a special property. No matter what inflation rate is expected, i.e. no matter where the *SAS* curve is positioned, public support is always maximized by generating the same inflation rate $\pi = \beta/\lambda$. This may require different rates of money growth, however, depending on which inflation rate is expected.

expected inflation is π_2, and so on. With the particular vote function employed here, it turns out that all Es obtain at the same inflation rate β/λ. In other words, no matter what inflation the labour market expects, the government always spawns the same inflation rate β/λ.

So an economy that anticipated the election-related 'stop and go' policies of the government rationally expects inflation to be at β/λ during the next election period. The economy does not then end up at E as planned, but at E′ instead (Figure 11.7). The irony is that, in terms of votes, now the government is worse off than if it had never even considered manipulating the economy for election purposes and had stayed at A. Vote shares related to A are 45%, E yields 50%, and E′ yields 42% only.

The inflation bias derived here for the election period also obtains for non-election periods if income and inflation experienced then is still remembered by voters on election day. To see this, just assume that states of the economy during election and non-election periods influence voters' decisions with equal

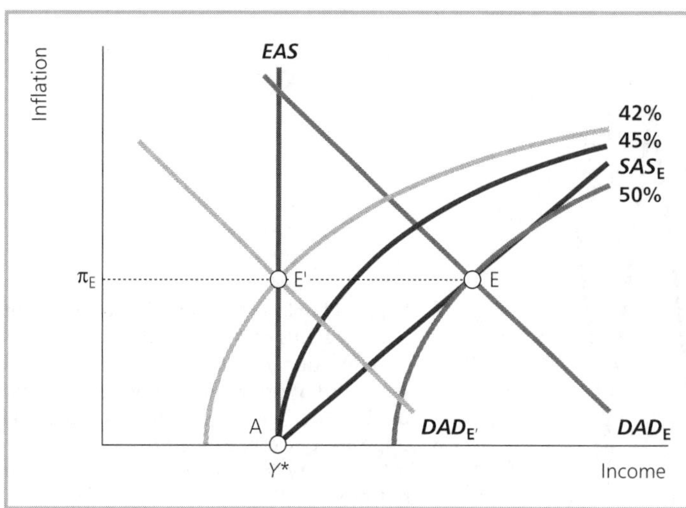

Figure 11.7 Once individuals anticipate that the government inflates to β/λ during election years, inflation expectations move up to β/λ and the economy ends up in E′ instead of E, the point at which the government was aiming.

weight. Then the period length behind equation (11.1) is a full election term. But then elections are implicitly being held in every such period, and the rational expectations bias results in every period.

An alternative way of arriving at the results that the inflation bias obtains in every period, election or not, is by adopting a view entertained in a very influential line of research. It simply states that *politicians are also voters*, and thus have the same preferences as voters. They too like inflation to be low and income to be high, independent of re-election considerations. So they try to maximize a utility function such as equation (11.1) at all points in time.

Is there any way out of the rather unpleasant position in which the government has been put by people forming expectations rationally? Couldn't the government simply pledge that it will never again resort to election-period stimulations? If individuals buy that, wouldn't it bring the economy at least back to point A? The big question is whether the government can succeed in persuading the economy that it will stick to the pledged new course.

11.4 POLICY GAMES

From a stylized perspective, the government has two options (to stimulate or not to stimulate), and so has the economy (to expect stimulation or not to expect stimulation). Given this, four stylized outcomes may result every time this *game* is played (see Figure 11.8):

1 The labour market does not expect an expansion and the government does not expand (point A).
2 The labour market does not expect an expansion but the government expands anyway (point E).
3 The labour market expects an expansion and the government really expands (point E′).
4 The labour market expects an expansion but the government refrains from expanding (point N).

Ranking these points in terms of the vote shares they deliver gives E > A > E′ > N. You may substantiate this claim by adding the four relevant government indifference curves to Figure 11.8. Decision problems in which the ultimate outcome depends on the moves taken by more than one player are called **games**.

Economists speak of a **game** if individual A's best choice depends on what individual B does, and B's best choice depends on what A does.

Let's make the current game a bit more specific. The two **players** are the government and a monopolistic trade union. The union represents labour in collective wage negotiations so as to maximize the wage sum. Assume that the vote-maximizing inflation rate stands at 10%. The options of the government are either to expand ($\pi = 10$) or not to expand ($\pi = 0$). The trade union can base wage claims either on an expected expansion ($\pi^e = 10$) or on the belief that the government will not expand ($\pi^e = 0$). Table 11.1 presents this game and the possible outcomes in the form of a matrix.

One feature that we have not mentioned yet is that the game is *sequential*. The trade union must move first. It cannot wait to observe what the government does, but has to form an inflation expectation and commit to a nominal wage for the length of the contract, typically a year. In a second step, after

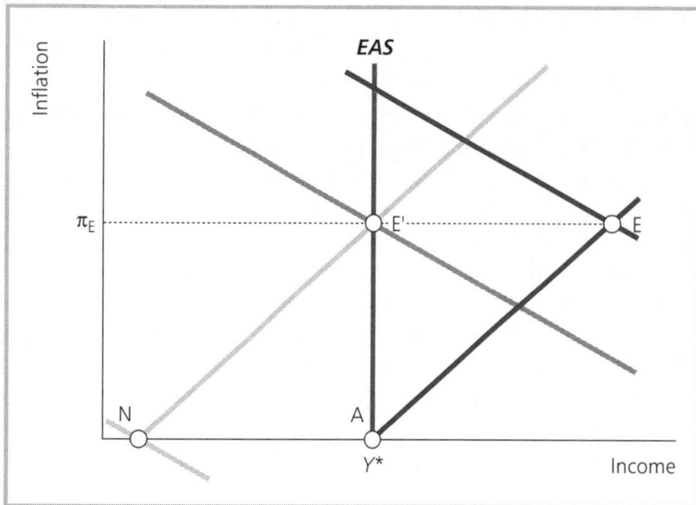

Figure 11.8 Inflation is determined in a 'game' between the labour market and the government. First the labour market fixes wages based on an expectation of whether the government will inflate or not, which results in the light or dark blue *SAS* curve, respectively. Then the government inflates to π_E or does not inflate. To inflate always yields higher support than the option not to inflate. Hence, inflation is expected and we end up in E′.

nominal wages are fixed, the government may decide to inflate or not, as it pleases.

The best thing that the trade union can do is anticipate the government's reaction. By making its first step the union effectively narrows the government's choices down to either the top row or the bottom row in the matrix. So the first question to be asked is: if we, the trade union, decide for the top row by not expecting inflation, what will the government do subsequently? The government can choose between inflation (which yields 50% of votes) and non-inflation (which yields 45% of votes). So it will certainly opt for inflation. The second question is: what will the government do if we expect it to inflate? This puts us in the second row. Again, the government's choices are to inflate (which gives 42% of votes) or not to inflate (which gives 38% of votes). And

Table 11.1 The policy game between the trade union and the government. Here the inflation game is cast in terms of specific numbers and a labour market dominated by a monopolistic trade union which maximizes the wage sum. The trade union tries to anticipate inflation correctly, for if it errs, the wage sum falls. No matter what the union expects, votes for the government are always highest if it inflates. Hence $\pi = 10$ is the dominant strategy, and is expected. The economy ends up at E′.

		Government (maximizes votes; moves second)	
		Does not expand $\pi = 0$	Expands $\pi = 10$
Trade union (maximizes wage sum; moves first)	Expects no expansion $\pi^e = 0 \rightarrow w = 0$	A $Y = Y^*$; $\pi = 0$ Vote share: 45% Wage sum unchanged	E $Y > Y^*$; $\pi = 10$ Vote share: 50% Wage sum falls
	Expects expansion $\pi^e = 10 \rightarrow w = 10$	N $Y < Y^*$; $\pi = 0$ Vote share: 38% Wage sum falls	E′ $Y = Y^*$; $\pi = 10$ Vote share: 42% Wage sum unchanged

again, the obvious choice is to inflate. Since the government's optimal choice is always to inflate, no matter what the trade union expects, this is called a **dominant strategy**. But then this is also the action that the trade union must rationally expect. So under rational expectations the union expects the government to inflate, the government does inflate, and the economy ends up at point *E′*.

The importance of this result derives from the fact that the country is stuck in a suboptimal situation. Voters and the government, who share the same utility function, could both be made better off, without making anybody else worse off, by reducing inflation, moving down from E′ to A. But within the scenario postulated here, this does not seem to be feasible. As long as the short-run *temptation to inflate* exists, a pledge not to inflate is not credible. We may say that democracies, as institutions, have a built-in **inflation bias**.

An **inflation bias** exists if the inflation rate in equilibrium is higher than the optimal long-run inflation rate of zero.

When **time inconsistency** is at work, a policy that seems optimal from today's view is no longer considered optimal when it is time to act.

What gives rise to this inflation bias is a general problem called **time inconsistency**. It does not only plague monetary policy, as discussed here. It is at work whenever a policy that initially seemed ideal for today and the future is no longer considered to be so by the decision-maker when the time comes to act upon it. Generations of parents have experienced this problem, without knowing its name. Efforts to influence their offspring's behaviour often turn into a game in which parents vow stern consequences, but find it preferable not to follow through when it is time to act. And policy-making in other areas, from taxing imports to paying subsidies, are haunted by the apparent impossibility to follow through on a plan which, at the outset, looked perfectly reasonable.

Wait, though. Perhaps we only came up with such a worrisome result because we overlooked the fact that the government and the trade union play this type of game not only once, as we assume above, but again and again? Let's look at this by assuming that the government and the trade union play this game twice. Couldn't the government's pledge to low inflation during the first round of play become credible because keeping it might carry the added benefit of low inflation expectations (and, hence, a more favourable trade-off) when the game is played the second time? To understand this, let's get more specific again.

The government may consider that if it announced and implemented low inflation this period, it could coax trade unions into also believing a low inflation announcement next period. This would put next period's *SAS* curve into SAS_E and permit the government to renege on its announcement and maximize utility at E. So the added benefit from playing the low inflation card this period, to be reaped next period, is to achieve E instead of E′. The gain in terms of votes (or utility) is 8 percentage points. Next, look at how this affects the game played in the first round.

The 8 percentage points vote bonus next period accrues whenever the government does not expand this period. So the effect on next period's votes must be added to the direct benefits of the low inflation strategy, measured in current-period votes. Adding 8 percentage points to all entries in the left-hand column pushes the total benefit from this strategy to 53% and 46%, respectively (see Table 11.2).

No matter what the trade union does, the best response for the government now appears to be not to inflate. Doesn't this turn 'do not inflate' into the dominant strategy and remove the inflation bias? Unfortunately not – because

Table 11.2 The policy game with two-period horizon. If the government not only cares about votes this period, but also about next period's votes, it may consider that playing the no-inflation card this period may make the no-inflation strategy credible next period, offering better options then. The value of this, if it did accrue, would be eight percentage points. Adding this to the 'does-not-expand' column appears to make no-inflation the dominant strategy.

		Government	
		Does not expand	Expands
Trade union	Expects no expansion	A Vote share: 45 + 8 = 53% Wage sum: 100	E Vote share: 50% Wage sum: 95
	Expects expansion	N Vote share: 38 + 8 = 46% Wage sum: 93	E′ Vote share: 42% Wage sum: 100

our line of reasoning does not pass the test of rationality. The flaw is that the government *mistakenly* believes that its policy stance today influences next period's inflation expectations. When the game is played the second time, it is the *final play*. So the government need not worry about losing its reputation any more. It would not do any good one period later. Trade unions realize this and rationally expect high inflation in period 2, the final period, and the government does deliver. But when second-round behaviour and outcomes are already determined, efforts to influence second-round expectations are futile. The eight percentage points of added benefits written into the low-inflation column in Table 11.2 are not real. So the government will play the high inflation strategy in period 1. Since this is rationally expected, both period 1 and period 2 outcomes are E′, the inflation bias position.

This line of reasoning can be generalized. Playing this game repeatedly, five times or fifty times, does not help to get rid of or reduce the inflation bias while there is a recognized final round of play. By backward induction we can always demonstrate that if the outcome in the final round must be E′, E′ also results in the second last round. But then E′ must also result in the third last round, and so on.

The only scenarios that may partly fix or alleviate the inflation bias problem are, first, if the game is being played an infinite number of times, or second, if the final round is determined stochastically, say, by throwing a dice. In both cases there is no previously identifiable final round from which to trace back the inflation bias to the present. Reputational considerations may play a role in such a context, and may help to reduce the time inconsistency problem.

This innocent-looking result is not trivial. Popular thought holds that politicians can be prevented from drifting away from the preferences of their constituencies by limiting the number of terms they may serve in office. The foremost example of this is the US presidency. The results derived here point to the opposite effect. The only way to keep politicians in line with what is good for voters is by *avoiding* fixing a final term in office.

11.5 WAYS OUT OF THE TIME INCONSISTENCY TRAP

Having identified the apparent inflationary bias in democracies, are there ways out of it? Any such remedy must tackle the very causes of the inflation bias. As Figure 11.9 highlights once again, the inflationary bias, or time inconsistency dilemma, if you wish, is made up of three ingredients:

1 The **constraint**, as represented by the *SAS* curve. Anything that would make the short-run or surprise aggregate supply curve steeper would reduce the inflation bias.
2 The **preferences**, as represented by iso-vote or indifference curves. Anything that makes monetary policy care less about income gains (or other gains from surprise inflation) makes indifference curves flatter. The result is a smaller inflation bias.
3 **Instrument potency**. This refers to the ability of the policy-maker to manipulate the money supply so as to maximize utility. If monetary policy was taken out of the control of the policy-maker, the *DAD* curve could not be shifted into the position shown in Figure 11.9. To the extent that *DAD* has to remain lower, reduced inflation expectations would keep *SAS* lower as well, removing or reducing the inflation bias.

Modifying the constraint

There is little established knowledge about how the government should make the *constraint* more favourable. More than anything else, making the *SAS* curve steeper would call for more flexible money wages – say, due to shorter wage contracts and automatic inflation adjustment clauses. Under most countries' laws, such things fall under the autonomy of employers and trade unions.

Changing preferences

A number of things can be done here. Most straightforwardly, if preferences play such a decisive role, why not simply appoint a person to the position of

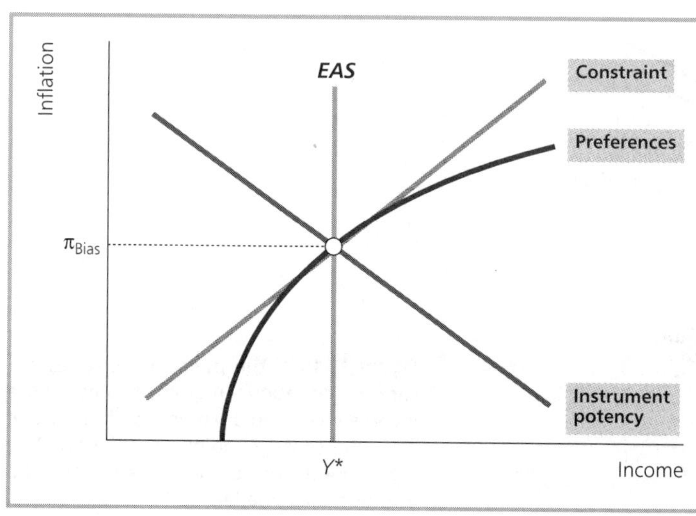

Figure 11.9 The inflationary bias results from the interplay of three factors: the **constraint** (as represented by *SAS*), restricting available states of the economy; the **preferences** of the government, implying a short-run temptation to stimulate; **instrument potency**, which refers to the power of the policy-maker to employ demand management discretionarily.

central bank governor who is known for his or her relentless commitment to price stability? Such people would have a rather flat, if not horizontal, set of indifference curves and could successfully maintain a high level of price stability. Figure 11.10 illustrates this effect.

Two problems are related to this remedy. First, its implementation may be painful in terms of income losses. Any new central bank governor may have to prove his or her commitment to price stability and build up such a reputation over time. During this time, monetary policy must be more restrictive than expected, which carries recessionary side effects. Second, other disturbances, supply shocks in particular, may hit the economy. In such situations a certain concern for income on behalf of the central bank may be desirable for society as a whole.

A second way to affect the preferences driving monetary policy is by making the central bank independent of the government. This only helps, of course, if the central bank has less to gain from surprise inflation than the government. This is quite likely to be the case. If the indifference curves represent public support or re-election prospects, a central bank (which does not have to seek re-election) is less likely to care than a government. If indifference curves represent politicians' utility, government officials have interests in surprise inflation that go beyond the temporary income gains discussed above, which central bank officials do not have. Most important among those effects, surprise inflation reduces the real value of government debt. This makes surprise inflation very tempting for the *government* of a country with large public debt, but much less so for the central bank.

Eliminating instrument potency

As mentioned before, if monetary policy cannot be employed for surprise-stimulations of aggregate demand, the labour market need not anticipate related inflationary consequences, and the inflationary bias is reduced or disappears altogether. Two options stand out in this context.

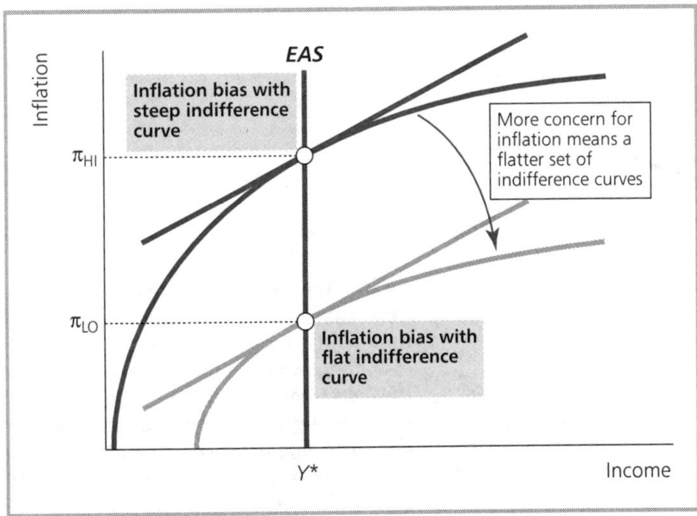

Figure 11.10 If the policy-maker does not care much about higher income, more income is needed as compensation for one more percentage point of inflation. This makes indifference curves flatter and the inflation bias smaller.

The **Friedman rule**, after US Nobel prize winner Milton Friedman, calls for the money supply to grow at a constant rate approximating long-run income growth.

The **Taylor rule**, proposed by US economist John Taylor, says the interest rate should deviate from its long-run target if inflation differs from its target and/or income departs from potential income.

1 **Adopting a money growth rule.** Specifying a money growth rule by explicit or implicit contract, by law, or even in the constitution, could be done in a number of ways: by specifying a fixed number, of which the **Friedman rule** would be an example; or by formulating an appropriate response to the general macroeconomic conditions, as stated in the **Taylor rule**. If this rule is properly designed to prevent the government or the central bank from using monetary policy to create surprise inflation, it can eliminate the inflationary bias (see Figure 11.11).

2 **Fixing the exchange rate.** A second way to take monetary policy out of the hands of domestic policy-makers is by fixing the exchange rate to some foreign currency or a basket of foreign currencies. Under such conditions money growth is taken out of domestic policy-makers' discretion. Instead, it must follow the path required to keep the exchange rate at the fixed level. While long-run inflation is a monetary phenomenon in the sense that it reflects the growth of our money supply, fixing exchange rates turns it into an *imported* monetary phenomenon. The pace of inflation is set by monetary policy in the country (or countries) to which our currency is pegged. This other country's inflation bias, which our model calls world inflation, becomes *our* inflation bias. An extreme case of fixing the exchange rate is a currency union. In the case of European Monetary Union (EMU), monetary policy is delegated to a supranational authority, the European Central Bank (ECB). It is the preferences of the ECB and its independence from member governments that eventually determines the inflation bias of EMU and its individual members.

Figure 11.12 illustrates how committing to a fixed exchange rate can be a way of reducing inflationary bias. Government and society may benefit from doing so if the inherent domestic inflation bias exceeds the world inflation rate. If the domestic bias is lower than world inflation, joining a fixed rate system would aggravate the problem of inflation.

Note, however, that price stability can only be imported in the described fashion if the exchange rate is permanently fixed, and credibly so. Periodic

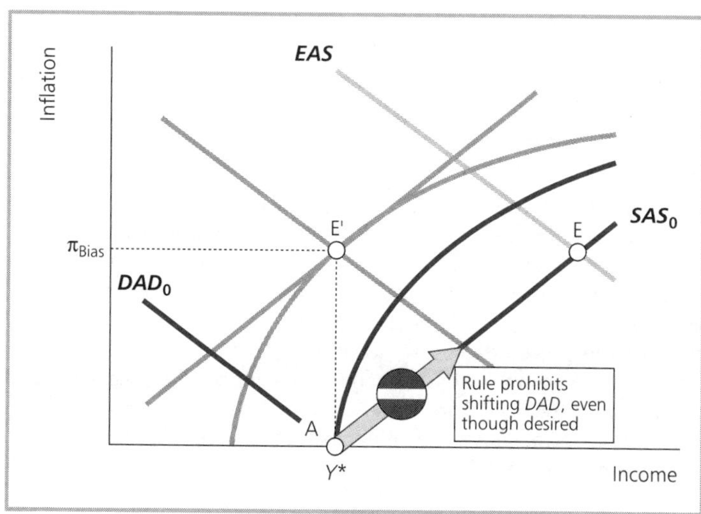

Figure 11.11 The policy-maker would *like* to move up along SAS_0 towards E. Under rational expectations this would lead into E′. The law ties the policy-maker's hands, freezing *DAD* in DAD_0. Aware of this, the labour market rationally expects zero inflation, which results in SAS_0. The economy stays at the superior point A with no inflation bias. A fixed exchange rate does the same trick. Then A reflects the inflation bias of the country to which we peg our currency.

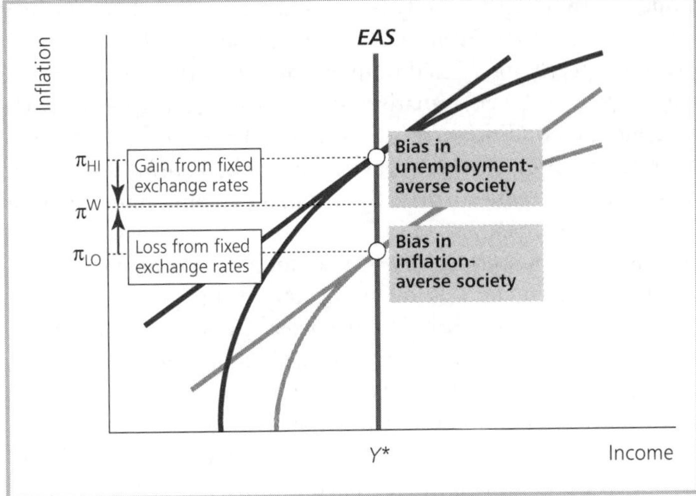

Figure 11.12 If a society or government is strongly averse to unemployment, thus valuing income gains highly, it has steep indifference curves and a high inflation bias. Such a country can reduce its inflation bias by fixing the exchange rate. An inflation-averse country has a low inflation bias. It may experience a deterioration of its inflation performance after fixing the exchange rate.

devaluations would drive a wedge between world inflation and domestic inflation, causing inflation performance to deteriorate. We shall return to these issues in the context of the European Monetary System in Chapters 12 and 14.

CASE STUDY 11.1 Who wanted the euro? The role of past inflations

In the second half of the 1990s, during the advent of the euro, a single European currency was not equally welcome in all 15 member states of the European Union. At the high end of the spectrum, 70% of Italy's public welcomed a single European currency while only 15% rejected it. At the low end only 25% of Danes wanted the euro while a hefty 60% said 'nej'. Why this difference? If a country's public decides rationally, opinions should reflect the benefits that the euro is expected to bring for the country.

A key accomplishment expected from the introduction of the euro is that it would discipline monetary policy by transferring responsibility for it from the often quite government-dependent national central banks (that generated a high inflation bias) to the very independent European Central Bank (expected to guarantee a very low inflation bias). Who would benefit most from this rearrangement? It must obviously be those countries that, without the disciplining effect of the Maastricht convergence criteria and the common currency, suffered from the highest inflation rates (revealing the lowest discipline in national monetary policy) in the past. Figure 1 illustrates the essence of this argument, using Austria, Germany, Spain and Italy as examples. The indicated dots represent past performance. The dot for the European Central Bank marks expected future performance should the country adopt the euro. So Spain and Italy can expect a relatively large drop in their inflation rates and, if all these countries' citizens have the same preferences as indicated by the indifference curves shown, should benefit the most. Thus we should expect: *The higher a country's inflation rate was in the past, the more its public should welcome the euro.*

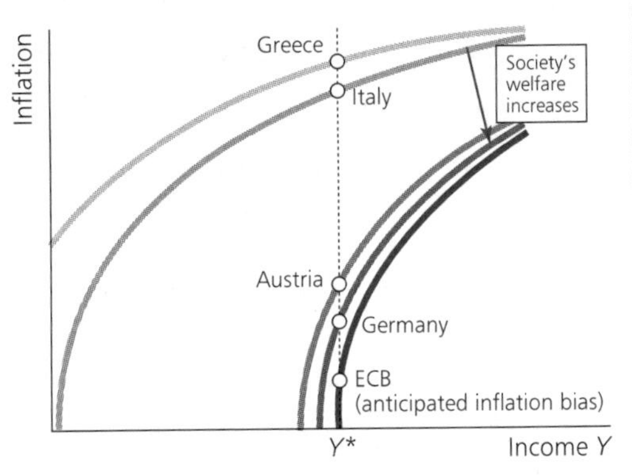

Figure 1

Case study 11.1 continued

Figure 2 permits a detailed examination of this hypothesis. The horizontal axis measures average inflation between 1980 and 1996 (measuring the monetary discipline produced by national central banks) for each of the 15 member states. The vertical axis measures the euro acceptance ratio (yes percentage divided by no percentage).

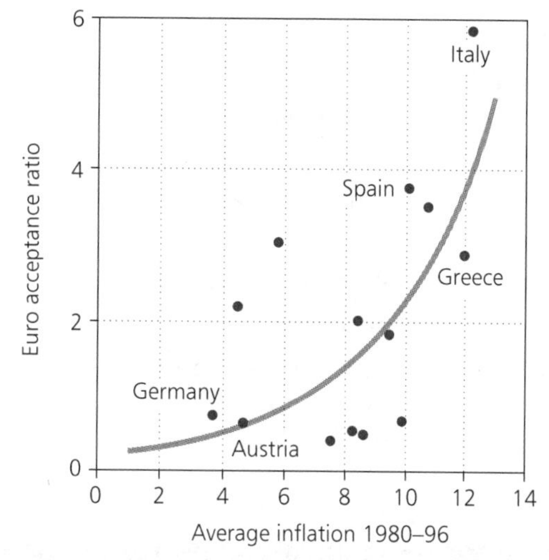

Figure 2

The data support the above hypothesis. Countries like Italy and Greece, who had experienced very high average inflation of some 12% between 1980 and 1996, welcomed the euro the most. Acceptance ratios were 7 and 5, respectively. Austria and Germany, on the other hand, whose central banks had been able to keep inflation in check quite well even without the euro, bluntly rejected the euro. Acceptance ratios were only 0.5 and 0.6, respectively.

In terms of this chapter's discussion of the inflation bias and how it depends on the conservativeness and independence of the central bank from the government, the public in the EU member states seems to know quite well why it wants the euro – or why it doesn't.

Source and further reading: Manfred Gärtner (1997) 'Who wants the euro – and why? Economic explanations of public attitudes towards a single European currency', *Public Choice* 93: 487–510.

CHAPTER SUMMARY

- Governments favour certain states of the economy over others. While they dislike inflation, they usually welcome inflation surprises. The main reason is that this may generate temporary gains in income, which the government may want itself or expect to draw applause from voters. Another reason that the government may feel tempted to generate surprise inflation is that this may reduce the real value of government debt.
- If inflation expectations feature an adaptive element and if voters' memories are not perfect, re-election motives may tempt governments to create a political business cycle.
- A political business cycle typically features booming output and income during the time leading up to an election, and a recession soon after the election.
- If inflation expectations look through the election pattern, becoming rational, the political business cycle disappears.
- A policy geared towards price stability often lacks credibility. Rational inflation expectations anticipate that governments may be willing to trade higher inflation for temporarily higher income. As a consequence, democracies seem to suffer from an inflationary bias.
- The inflationary bias may be characterized as the outcome of a game played between the trade union and the central bank. Playing this game repeatedly does not change the outcome, as long as there is a pre-fixed final round of play.

- When the final round of play is not foreseen, say because it is determined by chance, reputational considerations may reduce the inflationary bias.
- Ways out of the inflationary-bias/time-inconsistency dilemma are as follows:
  - Appointing conservative (i.e. inflation-averse) central bankers.
  - Making the central bank independent of the government.
  - Establishing fixed rules for monetary policy which the central bank must obey.
  - Pegging one's currency to that of a country with a proven low inflation record.

KEY TERMS AND CONCEPTS

central bank independence
constraint
Friedman rule
government indifference curve
inflation bias
institutions
instrument potency
iso-support curve
policy games
policy-makers
political business cycle
preferences
public support function
Taylor rule
time inconsistency dilemma
vote maximization

EXERCISES

11.1 Suppose that due to a shift in voters' preferences, fighting inflation yields less political support compared with increasing output. How is this reflected in the slopes of the government indifference curves? What do these indifference curves look like if the public is entirely indifferent towards inflation?

11.2 Let Germany's *SAS* curve be $Y = 1 + (\pi - \pi^e)$, that is it has slope 1 and normal output is 1. The public support or vote function is $s = 50 - 0.5\pi^2 + Y$.

(a) What is the vote-maximizing inflation rate? (Hint: votes are maximized when the slope of the indifference curve equals the slope of *SAS*. The mathematics is much simpler if the indifference curve is solved for Y (and not for π) and its slope $dY/d\pi$ is derived as a function of π.)

(b) Suppose inflation expectations are $\pi^e = 0.5$. Can the government win the election?

(c) What are the government vote shares in the cases $\pi^e = 0$ and $\pi^e = 1$?

11.3 Let Italy's *SAS* curve be the same as Germany's, while its vote function is $s = 50 - 0.5\pi^2 + 10Y$.

(a) By how much can Italy reduce its inflation bias by fixing the exchange rate between the lira and the Deutschmark?

(b) What may keep Italy from entering such an exchange rate arrangement?

11.4 We understand why a political business cycle (PBC) may occur if elections are to be held every two years.

(a) What happens to the PBC if a coin is tossed each year and an election is called only if we have 'tails'?

(b) What happens to the PBC if a dice is rolled and only a six results in an election?

11.5 Consider the evolution of inflation and income over time for the United Kingdom (see Figure 11.13). Find out the relevant election dates and decide whether the data support the theory of a PBC.

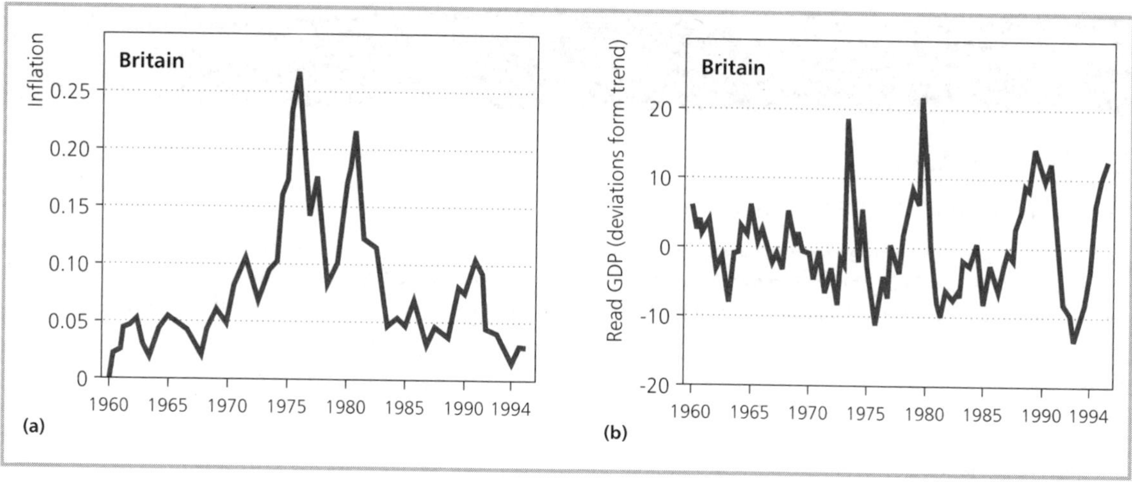

Figure 11.13

11.6 Suppose the popularity of the government in an economy with flexible exchange rates not only depends on inflation and income but also on the 'strength' of the domestic currency. How does this affect the government's inclination to trigger off politically motivated monetary expansions? Do you think that putting 'currency strength' into the government's utility function is a reasonable approach?

11.7 It was shown in this chapter that with a specific objective function of the government, the inflation bias amounts to β/λ. Thus, the inflation bias increases with β and decreases with λ. Explain intuitively the effect of these two parameters. (Hint: for the influence of λ you have to go back to the derivation of the aggregate supply curve.)

11.8 In this chapter it was assumed that unions move first, choosing their expectations on inflation, and that the monetary authority decides on monetary policy afterwards. Assume a particular institutional framework that makes the government choose monetary policy first and lets unions move second. Would such a reversal eliminate the inflationary bias?

11.9 Consider the development of inflation in the United States and Germany from 1960 to 1990. Until 1973 the Deutschmark was tied to the US dollar by fixed exchange rates. Remember that in a system of fixed exchange rates a small country's inflationary bias is dictated by the larger country to which its currency is tied. Does the graph you assembled support the hypothesis that Germany and the United States maintained such a relationship? Try to explain why the system of fixed exchange rates eventually broke down in 1973.

RECOMMENDED READING

Models of political business cycles are surveyed in Manfred Gärtner (1994) 'Democracy, elections, and macroeconomic policy: Two decades of progress', *European Journal of Political Economy* 10: 85–109.

The empirical evidence is reviewed in Bruno S. Frey and Friedrich Schneider (1988) 'Politico-economic models of macroeconomic policy: A review of the empirical evidence', in Thomas D. Willett (ed.) *Political Business Cycles: The Political Economy of Money, Inflation, and Unemployment*, Durham and London: Duke University Press, pp. 239–75.

Applications to US presidential elections are discussed in Ray C. Fair (1996) 'Econometrics and presidential elections', *Journal of Economic Perspectives* 10(3): 89–102.

APPLIED PROBLEMS

RECENT RESEARCH

The economy and US presidential elections

Ray C. Fair (1996, 'Econometrics and presidential elections', *Journal of Economic Perspectives* 10(3): 89–102) offers a non-technical update of earlier efforts to explain the Democratic Party's share by economic variables and what he calls incumbency variables. His new equation reads as follows:

Endogenous variables:
V Democratic Party's share of the two-party vote

Exogenous variables:

Variable	*Coefficient*	*t-value*	*Explanation*
cnst.	0.468	(90.62)	constant
I	−0.034	(1.26)	Democrats are in White House ($I = 1$); Republicans are in White House ($I = -1$)
$I{\cdot}d$	0.047	(2.09)	$d = 1$ if world war went on during last 15 quarters; else $d = 0$
$g3{\cdot}I$	0.0065	(8.03)	**income growth** during last 3 quarters ($g3$)
$p15{\cdot}I{\cdot}(1-d)$	−0.0083	(3.40)	**inflation** during last 15 quarters ($p15$)
$n{\cdot}I{\cdot}(1-d)$	0.0099	(4.46)	number of last 15 quarters with **good news** (meaning $g > 2.9$).
DPER	0.052	(4.58)	Democratic President is running ($DPER = 1$); Republican President is running ($DPER = -1$)
DUR	−0.024	(2.23)	number of consecutive terms in office by incumbent party (negative for Republicans)

$R^2 = 0.96$; 20 presidential elections 1916–92

The economic variables highlighted in the equation all have a significant influence on the incumbent's re-election prospects: if income growth speeds up by 1 percentage point, his vote share rises by 0.65 percentage points. If inflation moves up by 1 percentage point, his vote share falls by 0.83 percentage points. There is an added bonus to high income growth. For each quarter in which it exceeds 2.9%, which represents good news, the vote share rises by 0.99 percentage points. The equation explains 96% of the variation in the Democratic Party's vote share. It predicts the winner in 17 out of the 20 presidential elections since 1916 correctly. The use of the *I* dummy variable serves to turn effects on the Democratic vote share around when a Republican holds the presidency. The *d* dummy variable serves to sever the link between inflation and good news, and the vote during the world wars.

WORKED PROBLEM

Who wanted the euro? (part I)

Journalists and politicians closely monitored public attitudes towards the single European currency. Table 11.3 gives the result of one such opinion poll conducted in December 1995. Those in favour of the euro outnumber those opposing it 5 to 1 in Italy, but are in a 0.46 minority in Denmark.

These attitudes certainly reflect complex fears, hopes and historical experiences. Most of these have been ignored in this chapter's discussion. Instead, it was emphasized that from a macroeconomic perspective those countries that suffered from the highest inflation rates in the past may gain most from moving to a single currency. To look into how far this argument carries us, let us regress the

Table 11.3

	A	B	D	DK	E	F	FIN	GB	GR	I	IRL	NL	P	S
EMUYES	0.90	2.73	0.71	0.46	3.93	2.54	0.75	1.06	3.22	5.08	3.47	1.70	1.63	0.52
AVINFL	4.72	5.89	3.70	7.52	11.96	8.50	8.61	9.86	10.79	12.13	10.15	4.49	9.51	8.3

measure of acceptance of European Monetary Union, EMUYES, on each country's average inflation rate since when the European Monetary System was put on track in 1980, AVINFL. This yields

$$\text{EMUYES} = -0.77 + 0.34\ \text{AVINFL} \qquad R^2_{\text{adj}} = 0.35$$
$$(0.74)\ (2.85)$$

The equation says that in part the differences in euro acceptance in the EU countries can be attributed to different inflation experiences. Those who did well in the past see less necessity for the euro than those who did not. We may go further, pursuing the argument that inflation hurts people at an accelerating rate as inflation goes up. We may incorporate this by raising AVINFL to the power of 2. The result is

$$\text{EMUYES} = 0.27 + 0.024\ \text{AVINFL}^2 \qquad R^2_{\text{adj}} = 0.45$$
$$(0.45)\ (3.40)$$

A non-linear relationship seems to explain public attitudes to the euro even better. In fact, if we make the non-linearity even more extreme, say, by raising AVINFL the to power of 6, this seems to fit the data even better, raising the coefficient of determination to 0.63.

$$\text{EMUYES} = 1.09 + 0.000001\ \text{AVINFL}^6 \qquad R^2_{\text{adj}} = 0.63$$
$$(3.56)\ (4.85)$$

The implication is that the public does not seem to worry about inflation as long as it remains at low or moderate levels. But concern arises quickly and dramatically as inflation goes up further.

YOUR TURN

Inflation and central bank independence

This chapter suggests that central banks should be expected to have flatter indifference in inflation–income space than governments, making them less prone to resort to inflation. So the more independently of the government a central bank can pursue monetary policy, the lower inflation should be on average. Use the data in Table 11.4 on average inflation rates between 1980 and 1996 (AVINFL) and central bank independence (CBI) to investigate this hypothesis.

Table 11.4

Country	CBI index	AVINFL
A	9	4.72
AUS	9	8.91
B	7	5.89
CH	12	4.04
D	13	3.70
DK	8	7.52
E	5	11.96
F	7	8.50
GB	6	9.86
GR	4	10.79
I	5	12.13
IRL	7	10.15
JP	6	5.23
NL	10	4.49
NZ	3	10.87
P	3	9.51
USA	12	6.24

To further explore this chapter's key messages you are encouraged to use the interactive online module found at

www.fgn.unisg.ch/eurmacro/tutor/politicalbusinesscycle.html

and many other features hosted at **www.fgn.unisg.ch/eurmacro**

CHAPTER 12

THE EUROPEAN MONETARY SYSTEM AND EUROLAND AT WORK

WHAT TO EXPECT This chapter puts the tools acquired earlier to work on some key European experiences and projects. We will see:

1. How the *IS-LM* and Mundell–Fleming models can be used to understand international spillover effects of economic policy.
2. How a monetary system works and what caused the 1992 crisis in the European Monetary System (EMS).
3. How EMS member states where affected by the 1992 crisis, what choices they had, and why some chose different options than others.
4. That the EMS is an exchange rate target zone and how the exchange rate behaves within such a zone.
5. What is meant by the credibility of a target zone and how market psychology may affect this credibility in a self-fulfilling fashion.
6. How fiscal and monetary policy works in Euroland, and what the roles of the Stability Pact and no-bailout clauses are in this context.

It is harvest time – time to show that the tools acquired so far in this book are not merely nice, shiny gimmicks, but serve to improve our understanding of what goes on in the real world in a significant way. And there is much to understand and address: wild swings in exchange rates; speculative attacks and currency crises, and efforts to contain and prevent these by new institutional arrangements; inflation and hyperinflations that may erode a lifetime's nominal savings within months; government and private debt explosions threatening employment and growth.

This chapter looks at the issue of **international monetary arrangements,** of which the exchange rate system is a key building block. Regarding exchange rate systems, the models we have learned to work with have always been discussed under the polar cases of flexible and fixed exchange rates. As we have mentioned a number of times, however, while these extremes are useful theoretical benchmarks, they are rarely encountered in such purity in the real world, as the historical data on current and capital account balances given in Figure 4.4 underline. In practice, countries have invented and experimented with many shades in between and beyond these stylized benchmarks. Europe's history and immediate future is particularly rich and exciting in this respect, and there is much to be learned from past and ongoing issues and events.

In the current chapter we focus on two experiences and projects: one is the European Monetary System that has been instrumental in Europe's economic integration, with periods of success and episodes of crisis. The second is the introduction of Europe's single currency, the euro, completed on 1 January 2002, probably the boldest such effort in economic history. We will look at how this new arrangement affects policy-making and what risks it carries.

12.1 PRELIMINARIES

As a background for the discussion to follow we need to provide some institutional information and some smaller concepts.

The European Monetary System

The EMS came into operation in March 1979. It embraced twelve European countries that had pegged their exchange rates at an official parity between any pair of currencies. It was the final stepping stone on the way to full monetary union, as laid out in the treaty of Maastricht, to replace national currencies by the common currency **euro** on 1 January 2002. The EMS differed from an *ideal* system of fixed exchange rates in two respects:

1 Official parities are understood to be central rates around which exchange rates may fluctuate within a margin. For most of the existence of the EMS the upper limit of this band was 2.25% above parity, the lower limit 2.25% below. As an exception, wider bands of ±6% were temporarily entertained for some currencies. In an effort to end the EMS crisis of 1993 all bands except for the guilder/Deutschmark exchange rate were widened to ±15%.
2 Central parity rates are considered fixed but adjustments may be negotiated. Realignments were implemented frequently for some currencies (eight times in the case of the Italian lira between 1979 and 1987), but only as an exception for most.

With most of the countries that were members of the European Monetary System adopting the euro in 1998, a new system was put in place called **EMS II**. As of 2002 the only EMS II member is Sweden. While being marginalized at present, EMS II may gain importance during the EU's eastern enlargement, facilitating the monetary integration of new members and their eventual adoption of the euro.

Euroland

The majority of EU members have given up their national currencies in favour of a single European currency called the euro. This part of the EU is usually referred to as the euro zone, the euro area or Euroland. The transition process began in 1998, when exchange rates between national currencies and the euro were irrevocably fixed, the European Central Bank (ECB) was founded and participants were determined. It ended on 1 January 2002 when euro bills and coins entered circulation and national currencies were withdrawn. The current list of members comprises Austria, Belgium, France, Finland, Germany,

Greece, the Netherlands, Ireland, Italy, Luxemburg, Portugal and Spain. Britain, Denmark and Sweden have opted not to participate.

For a more comprehensive account of European economic and monetary integration you may want to consult Figure 12.1.

The national economy versus the global economy

When discussing business cycles we have taken either of two perspectives: that of the *global economy* that does not have an external sector; and that of the *national economy* which is too small to have a noticeable effect on the rest of the world and thus takes the world interest rate and world income as exogenous variables. This is often referred to as the *small open economy*.

Both models complement each other quite nicely. The global economy model can be used to represent the world around us – the world minus the national economy we are looking at. Since the national economy is too small

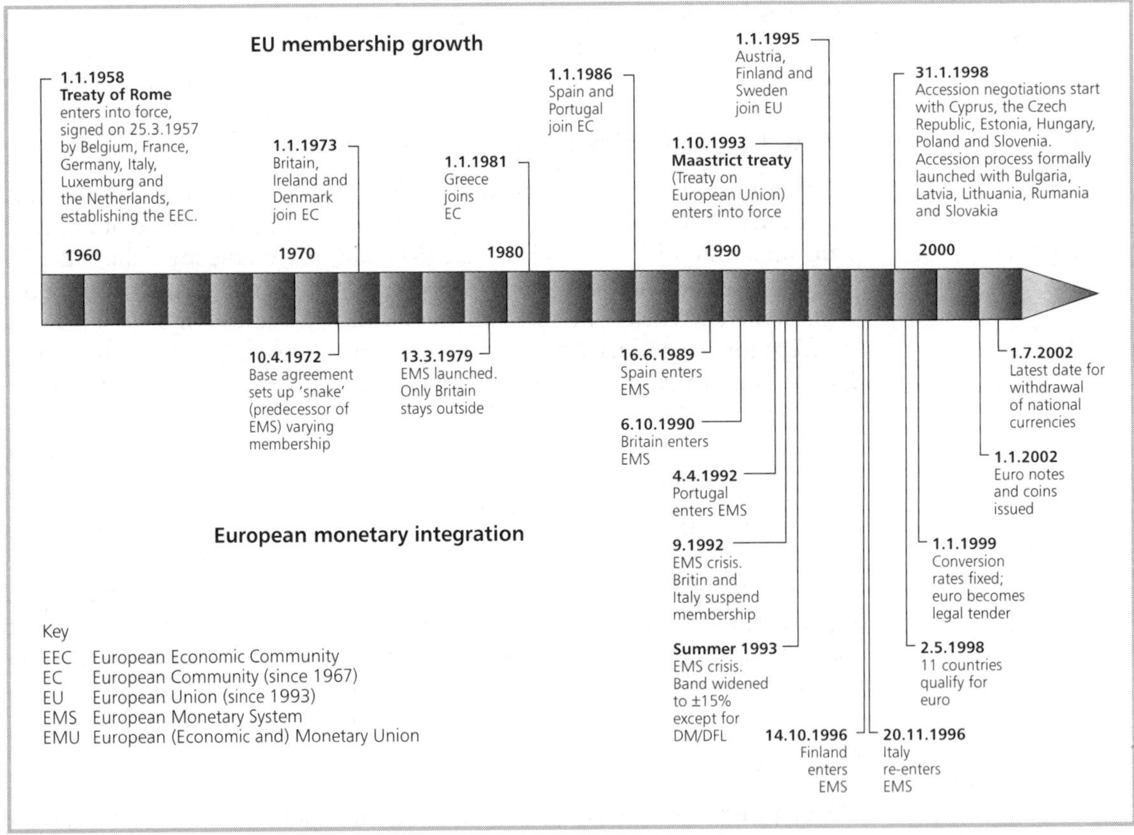

Figure 12.1 EU membership increased from the six countries that signed the Treaty of Rome on 25 March 1957 to 15 at the turn of the millennium. Membership may rise to around 25 within a few years. The current name EU was adopted in 1993 when the Treaty of Maastricht came into force. European monetary integration was spawned (or propelled) by the collapse of the Bretton Woods System of fixed exchange rates around 1971. Starting with the initiative of a handful of countries to stabilize their exchanges rates in the 1970s, monetary integration efforts peaked when 12 countries discarded their national currencies in favour of the euro on 1 January 2002. Under EMS II only Denmark is pegging its currency to the euro as of 2002. Britain and Sweden do not entertain such plans.
Source: Case, Fair, Gärtner and Heather, *Economics*, Harlow: Prentice Hall Europe, 1999.

to really affect the rest of the world, no great harm is done by ignoring the rest of the world's trade and financial relations with this national economy. So the global economy model (which we also call the *IS-LM* model, because it has no foreign exchange market) explains how world income and the world interest rates are being determined (see Figure 12.2).

World income and the world interest rate then set the stage on which the national economy performs: i^W positions the *FE* curve for the national economy; Y^W codetermines the national economy's *IS* curve (Figure 12.2).

This is a very specific kind of interaction, of course, in which effects run in one direction only. It is useful for analyzing a small country's economy in its global environment. Analyzing the interaction between two similar-sized countries or between large economic blocs requires some adjustments, however, as we will see later in this chapter.

The *n*th currency

We argued earlier that fixing the exchange rate takes monetary policy out of the hands of the central bank. While this is generally true, it does not apply to all countries in the system. Basically, an exchange rate is simply the price of one money currency in terms of another. In a way (and we have already looked at this in some detail) this price reflects the relative amounts of the two currencies in circulation. To keep this relative amount at a value that leaves the exchange rate unchanged, you do not need two central banks that cooperate and intervene. If two countries fix the exchange rate, one of the two central banks may move its money supply as it pleases, as long as the other one does exactly what is needed to keep the exchange rate at parity.

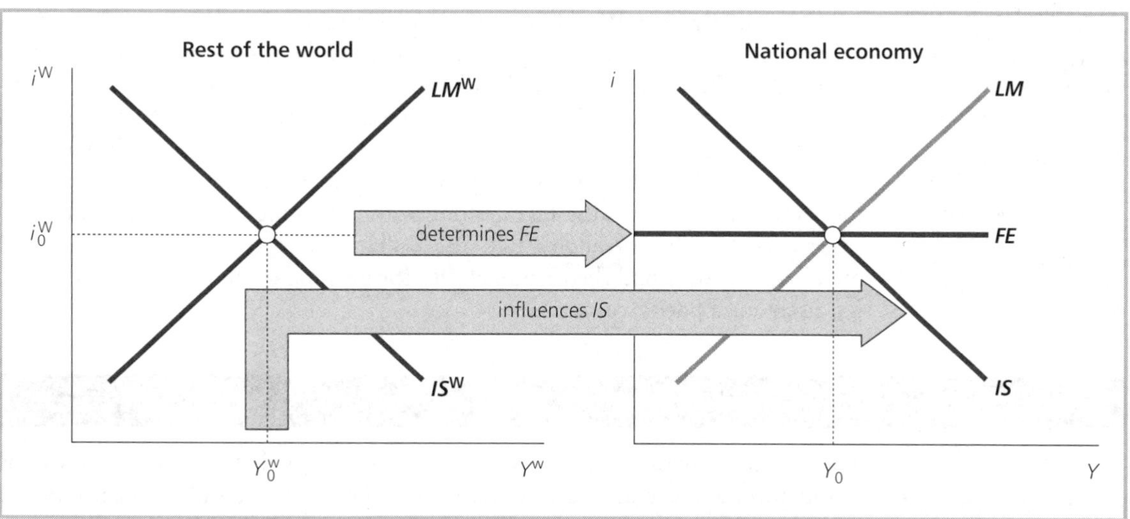

Figure 12.2 The *IS-LM* and the Mundell–Fleming model complement each other. The Mundell-Fleming model describes the working of the (small) national economy, which is affected by the (rest of the) world income and the (rest of the) world interest rate. The *IS-LM* model can be used to describe the rest of the world (the world minus our small national economy), and how income and the interest rate in this 'rest of the world' are determined. These then affect the national economy.

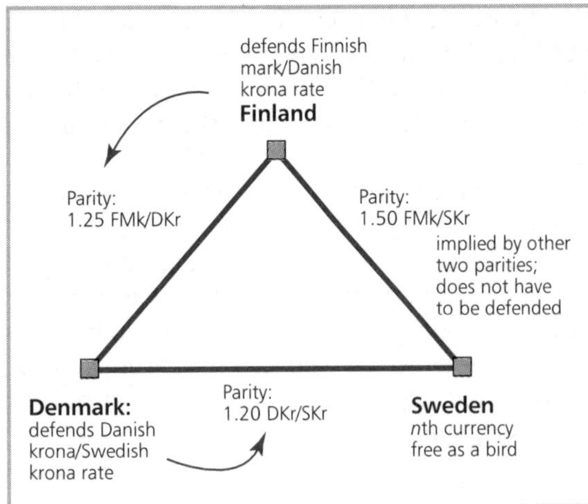

Figure 12.3 A Nordic Monetary System, with Sweden being the anchor. If three countries fix three bilateral exchange rates, one of them may conduct monetary policy as it pleases. If Denmark intervenes to keep the Danish krona/Swedish krona rate at parity, and Finland defends the Finnish mark/Danish krona rate, at the same time they defend the Finnish mark/Swedish krona rate. This frees Sweden from the obligation to intervene. In a system with n countries only $n - 1$ central banks must intervene. The nth country is free.

As Figure 12.3 illustrates, this also holds if three countries fix bilateral exchange rates. If, in a Nordic Monetary System, Denmark and Sweden were to set the rate of exchange between Danish and Swedish krona to 2, it suffices if Denmark intervenes to maintain that rate. If Finland and Denmark fix their mark/krona rate to 2, then Finland alone can maintain that rate by intervention. But then these two rates implicitly guarantee a Finnish mark/Swedish krona rate of 4, without Sweden doing anything. So Sweden controls the nth currency.

The term 'nth currency' derives from the general insight that in a system involving n currencies only $n - 1$ central banks must intervene. The last one, issuing the nth currency, is free to determine its own course of monetary policy.

The **Bretton Woods** system was a system of fixed exchange rates operational until 1971. It was designed at an international conference held in 1944 in Bretton Woods, New Hampshire. Under the accord one fine ounce of gold was worth US$35. Other countries then defined the values of their own currencies in terms of US dollars.

Under the **Bretton Woods** system, operational during the twenty-five years following the Second World War, the role of the nth currency was explicitly assigned to the US dollar. The EMS avoided formally appointing an nth currency. It even required all countries involved to share the burden of intervention. Most experts agree, however, that, in practice, the Deutschmark had adopted the role of the nth currency. So the Bundesbank (Buba) set the pace of monetary policy within the EMS, along with managing the exchange rate with regard to outside currencies like the dollar and the yen. The other $n - 1$ member countries had the responsibility for keeping exchange rates within the bands around parity values.

12.2 THE 1992 EMS CRISIS

There is an obvious analogy with the relationship between the rest of the world and the individual country studied in Figure 12.2, and with the country with the nth currency in an exchange rate system and the other member countries. In the first case, the rest of the world sets the interest rate with which the individual small open economy must live. In an exchange rate system, such as the EMS or the Bretton Woods system, the nth currency controls monetary policy and generates an interest rate the other member countries have to live

CASE STUDY 12.1 German unification as a tug of war

Planning and implementing German unification provided economists with a huge laboratory experiment. Here we look at this event for two purposes: first, because it provides an interesting application of the Mundell–Fleming model introduced in Chapter 5. Second, because many see it, or its mishandling, as the culprit responsible for derailing the EMS in 1992–3.

The issues

In the wake of *perestroika* it became clear in early 1990 that East and West Germany were moving towards full monetary, economic and political integration. From a macroeconomic perspective this entailed merging the two countries' goods and labour markets and introducing a common currency. This confronted West German authorities with the issues laid out in Figure 1(a) in the context of the Mundell–Fleming model.

The situation in West Germany prior to unification may be thought of as a long-run equilibrium. With the mark being the *n*th currency in the EMS, the Bundesbank (Buba) could conduct monetary policy at its discretion, determining German interest rates freely and thereby positioning the *FE* curve for the other EMS members.

Against this background, the question of immediate concern was how to merge the two economies without repercussions on the interest rate (which might strain the EMS) and without creating inflation (which would run counter to the legal responsibility and spoil the track record of the Buba). A plan to achieve this would have to contain three components:

- An estimate of **potential output in East Germany**. Given potential output in West Germany, this would yield an estimate of unified potential output.
- A plan to position the ***IS* curve for united Germany** so as to intersect the potential output line at the EMS interest rate.
- A plan to position the ***LM* curve for united Germany** so as to intersect the potential output line at the EMS interest rate.

Kohl's master plan

Estimating productivity and income levels of centrally planned economies has always been difficult, not least because their products are not valued by markets. With these caveats, East German per capita income was estimated to be around 80% of the western level, yielding an East German GNP estimate of DM 130 billion. Adding this to West German GNP of DM 700 billion gives an estimate of the united equilibrium aggregate supply curve at $Y^* = 830$.

A forecast of the position of the *IS* curve had to start with an assumption of investment and consumption behaviour and an estimate of additional government expenditures. The latter could not simply be obtained by extrapolating West German government spending levels, but needed to include what were thought to be sizeable transfers to the east, needed to lick the East German infrastructure into West German shape and cover social security and unemployment payments. The Kohl government claimed that **DM 50 billion of government transfers** annually would suffice. As this would require a substantial amount of deficit spending (public borrowing from the private sector) this would put the *IS* curve to the right of the ideal *IS* curve drawn into Figure 1(a).

Finally, the position of the *LM* curve would be crucially affected by the rate at which East German currency would be converted into West German Deutschmarks. A high conversion rate would mean that the Buba would have to supply little additional liquidity, shifting the *LM* curve moderately to the right, making the interest rate rise. A low conversion rate would force the Buba to pump a lot of liquidity into the new *Länder*. This would cause a large shift of *LM* to the right. Combined with the large shift of the *IS* curve to the right this would stimulate output way beyond full employment output, thus triggering inflation.

The Buba and the administration had conflicting preferences regarding the choice of a conversion rate. The Buba wanted to maintain or regain price stability. Consequently, it pleaded for a rather high conversion rate of 2 : 1, though this meant higher interest rates and lower income. The government, probably with an eye on the first general election in united Germany scheduled for late 1990 (and won by Kohl), wanted to avoid making any decisions that would depress income. Inflation could be expected to materialize with a lag long enough not to hurt re-election prospects. In a stunning revelation of the limitations of Buba independence, the government simply steamrolled the Buba and committed to a conversion rate of 1 : 1.

➤

Case study 12.1 continued

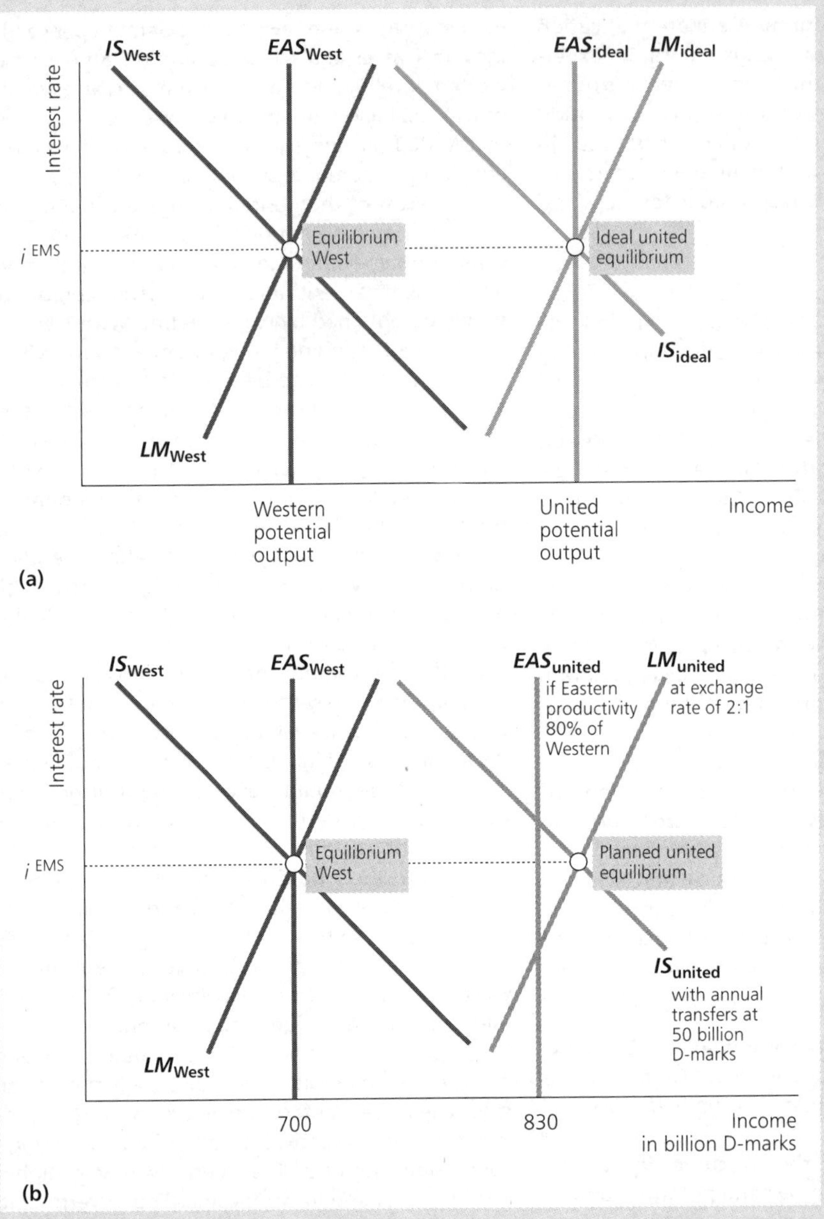

Figure 1

The light blue lines in Figure 1(b) sketch the macroeconomic constellation anticipated to result from the described decisions.

The Bundesbank strikes back

Instead of the ideal plan, the Buba found itself being pushed into an increasingly uncomfortable position with a very high inflation potential while the administration's unification plans took shape in 1990. Two developments aggravated existing fears of an inflation surge:

- As for many formerly communist countries, capital stocks, productivity and capacity levels

Case study 12.1 continued

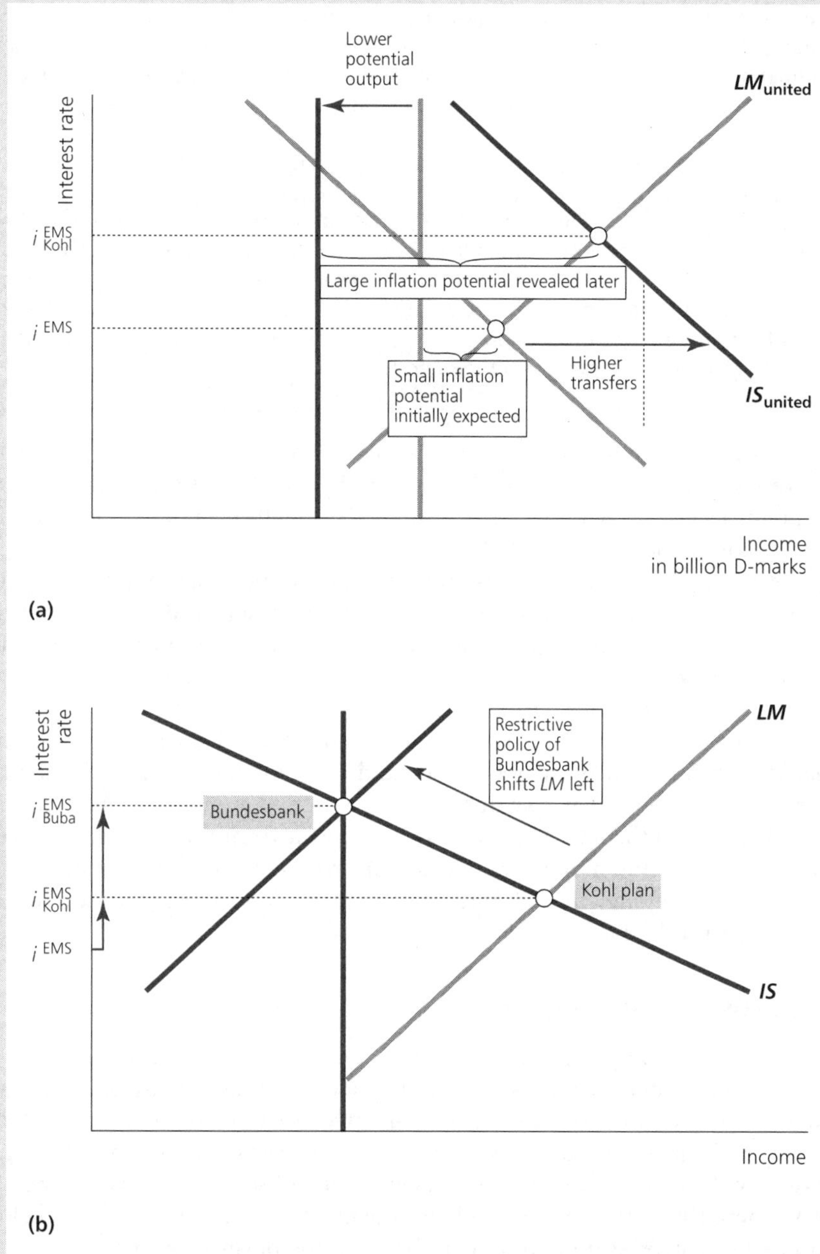

Figure 2

had been significantly overestimated for East Germany. New insights gained rapidly during 1990 and 1991 placed potential output much further to the left than our sketch of the Kohl plan had assumed in Figure 1.

- Partly due to the previous point, transfers to the east had to be revised upwards dramatically. Instead of the initially circulated numbers of DM 50 billion annually, transfer requirements soon turned out to be around DM 150 billion. As a

Case study 12.1 continued

consequence of the upward revision of transfers by DM 100 billion annually, the *IS* curve turned out to be located much further to the right than planned.

Figure 2(a) compares the actual situation which Germany found itself in following unification (dark blue lines) with the Kohl plan (light blue lines). The differences are due to the three developments listed above.

The Buba had already found the *Kohl plan* unacceptable. Unable to fend it off or strike a compromise, it had protested the 1 : 1 conversion rate, considering the inflation potential intolerable and incompatible with its legal obligations. Rather than staying put and waiting for inflation to reduce the real money supply and eliminate excess demand, the Buba decided to follow the relentless disinflation course on which it had already embarked prior to unification, in the face of 5%-plus inflation rates in 1989. The *LM* curve shifted up sharply into the full blue position (Figure 2(b)). The price to be paid for this was further increases in the already high interest rate, which peaked at 8.5% in July 1992 and set the stage for the 1992 EMS crisis discussed in the main text.

with in one way or another. The strains this can put on such a system made the Bretton Woods system collapse in 1971 and pushed the EMS to the brink of failure in 1992. We will use the *IS-LM* and Mundell–Fleming models to bring out the core issues of the 1992 EMS crisis.

The trigger of the crisis is usually seen as the peculiar mix of fiscal and monetary policy following German unification. A sharp increase in government spending was needed to start rebuilding the public infrastructure and provide financial incentives to attract private investment in the east of the country, and to cushion soaring unemployment. This would shift *IS* way to the right in an *IS-LM* diagram for the country with the *n*th currency. Concerned that this stimulation of aggregate demand may sooner or later trigger price increases, the Bundesbank switched to a restrictive monetary policy, shifting the *LM* curve to the left. The most striking result from this interplay between fiscal expansion and monetary contraction was a sharp rise in German interest rates, with the money market rate peaking at 9.4% in 1992 (for more details see Case study 12.1).

Repercussions and options

The high and rising interest rates in Germany were bound to have repercussions on other members of the European Monetary System of fixed exchange rates. Prior to the unification-related rise in German interest rates, a typical EMS member state's economy, say the Netherlands', may be represented by the lower of the three points in Figure 12.4. We can leave it open for now where this was relative to full employment, since, as we shall see below, different countries were in different phases of the business cycle.

The foremost effect of the development in Germany (described in Case study 12.1) for the Netherlands is an upward shift of the *FE* curve. This leaves the Netherlands with two stylized options:

- *Option #1*. Stay in the EMS. This amounts to defending the current exchange rate by buying guilders, thus reducing the money supply. The upward shift of the *LM* curve drives up Dutch interest rates as well, thus driving down output and income.

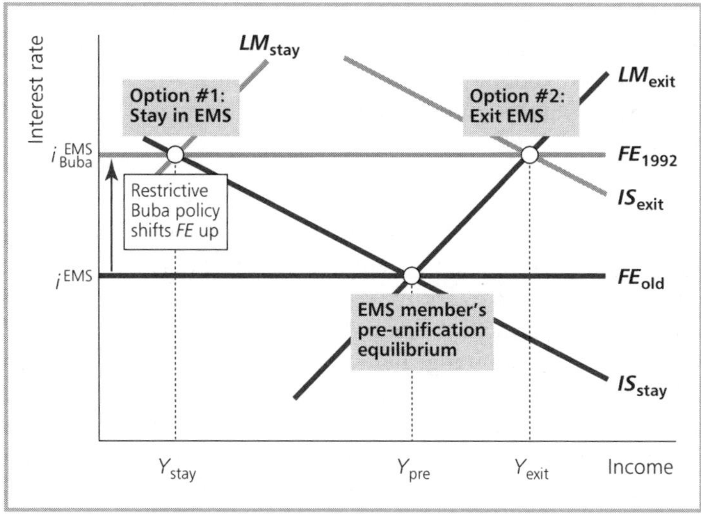

Figure 12.4 By driving up German interest rates, which determine interest rates in the EMS, the Bundesbank confronted other members with a difficult choice: remain in the EMS and suffer a fall in income, or leave the EMS and benefit from temporarily higher income.

- *Option* #2. Leave the EMS. This would return the money supply to Dutch control and fix *LM* in the old position. The adjustment to a new equilibrium takes place via a depreciation of the Dutch guilder, which stimulates exports and shifts the *IS* curve out into the light blue position. Again, Dutch interest rates are driven up, but this time income rises.

And equivalent to the second option, at least for the moment, the Netherlands could also realign the guilder versus the Deutschmark and keep membership in the EMS active.

Choices

Governments tend to make choices on the basis of cost–benefit comparisons. The major *drawback* of staying in the EMS (option #1) compared with leaving it (option #2) are the negative effects on income and employment. This added burden may be more difficult to bear if the country is already in a recession. As our discussion in Chapter 11 suggests, public support (or re-election prospects) by and large reflect the state of the economy. So a government of a country already in a recession may not survive the further deterioration to be expected from option #1. It is therefore likely to do almost anything that promises quick improvement, such as resorting to option #2.

The major *advantage* of option #1 over option #2 is clearly that it keeps the country's option alive to be part of European Economic and Monetary Union (EMU). Countries that wished to take part needed to meet a series of **convergence criteria** evaluated in 1997. One of these, the exchange rate convergence criterion, required that the currency of each member state must have remained within the normal fluctuation margins of the EMS for at least two years prior to the evaluation. This excluded both exiting the EMS and realigning parities on its own initiative. While exiting in late 1992 would not have ruled out being back on track in 1997, it would have put membership prospects in rather serious jeopardy. In the light of this, a country was more likely to remain in the EMS and fight it out if it were seriously interested in taking part in economic monetary union and if its failure to meet other convergence criteria was not likely to rule out EMU membership anyway.

To see whether this framework explains actual choices made in 1992, consider the three largest EMS members besides Germany. Table 12.1 summarizes the states of these nations' economies and ranks their interests in and their prospects for an eventual participation in economic and monetary union and a common currency.

France

France had committed itself fully to EMU. Plans to make the Banque de France more independent of the government, as required by the Maastricht Treaty, were being finalized. It was also working with determination on the other Maastricht criteria, of which it met all five in 1991 and four in 1992. In 1992 the French economy was not booming, but was not stalling either. Growth was down from the very high rates experienced in the second half of the 1980s, but still amounted to 4.5% over the 1990–2 period. So the high interest rates brought about by the Bundesbank were certainly not welcome, but did not hit the French economy with a recession already under way. In this situation, with a lot at stake regarding EMU and a modestly comfortable state of the economy, France decided to remain in the EMS and fight it out.

Italy

Italy's economy looked very much the same as that of France, with possibly slightly more of a downward trend. EMU prospects were completely different, however. While Italy was also interested in participating in the common European currency to come, it had not been able yet to meet a single one of the five criteria spelled out in Maastricht. Prospects to change that soon looked dim. Leaving EMS, therefore, could not do much additional harm. Not surprisingly, Italy was one of the countries that decided to leave EMS.

United Kingdom

The UK's position contrasted sharply with that of France. There was a very strong opposition to EMU, even within the government. Negotiations in

Table 12.1 EMU aspirations and the business cycle. In 1992, interest in being part of EMU was probably highest in France and lowest in the United Kingdom. Prospects to meet the convergence criteria were intact in France, but bleak in Italy. Having shrunk by 2.1% since 1990, Britain's economy was much less prepared to take further strain than the other two.

	Interest in and prospects for European Monetary Union	Income growth 1990–92	
France	Seriously interested in EMU; meets all five convergence criteria in 1991 and four in 1992.	Total:	4.5
		1990:	2.5
		1991:	0.8
		1992:	1.2
Italy	Interested in EMU; does not meet any convergence criterion in 1991 or 1992.	Total	4.1
		1990:	2.1
		1991:	1.2
		1992:	0.8
United Kingdom	Modestly interested in EMU; meets two convergence criteria in 1992; signed Maastricht Treaty only after given right to opt out.	Total:	−2.1
		1990:	0.4
		1991:	−2.0
		1992:	−0.5

Source: Swiss National Bank, *Monatsberichte*

BOX 12.1 Convergence criteria in the Maastricht Treaty

In 1988 European governments set up the Delors Committee to examine the issue of economic and monetary union and to develop a programme aimed at its implementation. The resulting Delors Report led to the Maastricht Treaty on European Union, which was negotiated in December 1991 and came into force in November 1993. While this treaty covers a wide range of integration issues, its most prominent feature is the formalization of how to bring about economic and monetary union and, in particular, a common currency (termed *euro* in 1995). In addition to other more general, softer criteria, the **Maastricht Treaty** spells out the following main **criteria for monetary and fiscal convergence** as a precondition for a country's participation in European Monetary Union:

- Government debt must not exceed 60% of GDP.
- The government budget deficit must not exceed 3% of GDP.
- Inflation must not exceed average inflation in the three EU countries with the lowest rates by more than 1.5 percentage points.
- Interest rates on government bonds must not exceed average rates in the three EU countries with lowest inflation by more than 2 percentage points.
- Membership in the EMS must have been maintained for no less than two years without having initiated a devaluation.

These criteria also have to be met by prospective future members of EMU.

Maastricht could only be kept from breaking down by granting Britain the right to opt out of monetary union. In this regard, therefore, little was to be lost by exiting EMS in 1992. More importantly, Britain was in an entirely different phase of the business cycle from France and Italy. Income had fallen by 2% in 1991 and was still falling in 1992. Additional restrictive effects from the high German interest rates appeared increasingly unbearable. Against this background, it is of little surprise that Britain was the first country to quit EMS during the crisis.

The Mundell–Fleming model and some arguments from political economy provide a good first grasp of the macroeconomic issues and choices surrounding the unification of the two Germanies and the EMS crisis of 1992. To obtain more detailed insights into the anatomy of currency crises, of which there were more before and after 1992, we need to take a closer look at how the EMS works. We begin by introducing the concept of exchange rate target zones and then proceed to discuss speculative attacks.

12.3 EXCHANGE RATE TARGET ZONES

As noted at the beginning of this chapter, what sets the EMS apart from an ideal system of fixed exchange rates is that it allows exchange rates to fluctuate within a band around parity. Figure 12.5 shows central rates of exchange for the Deutschmark against the Danish krona, the French franc, the guilder, the lira, the peseta, and the pound, and, when applicable, bands of intervention. While bands have normally been ±2.25% around the central rate, occasionally countries have been granted wider bands of ±6%. The 1993 EMS crisis even forced authorities to widen the band to ±15% for most currencies.

The graphs illustrate the evolution of EMS I until the irrevocable fixing of exchange rates for countries that adopted the euro on 1 January 1999, and

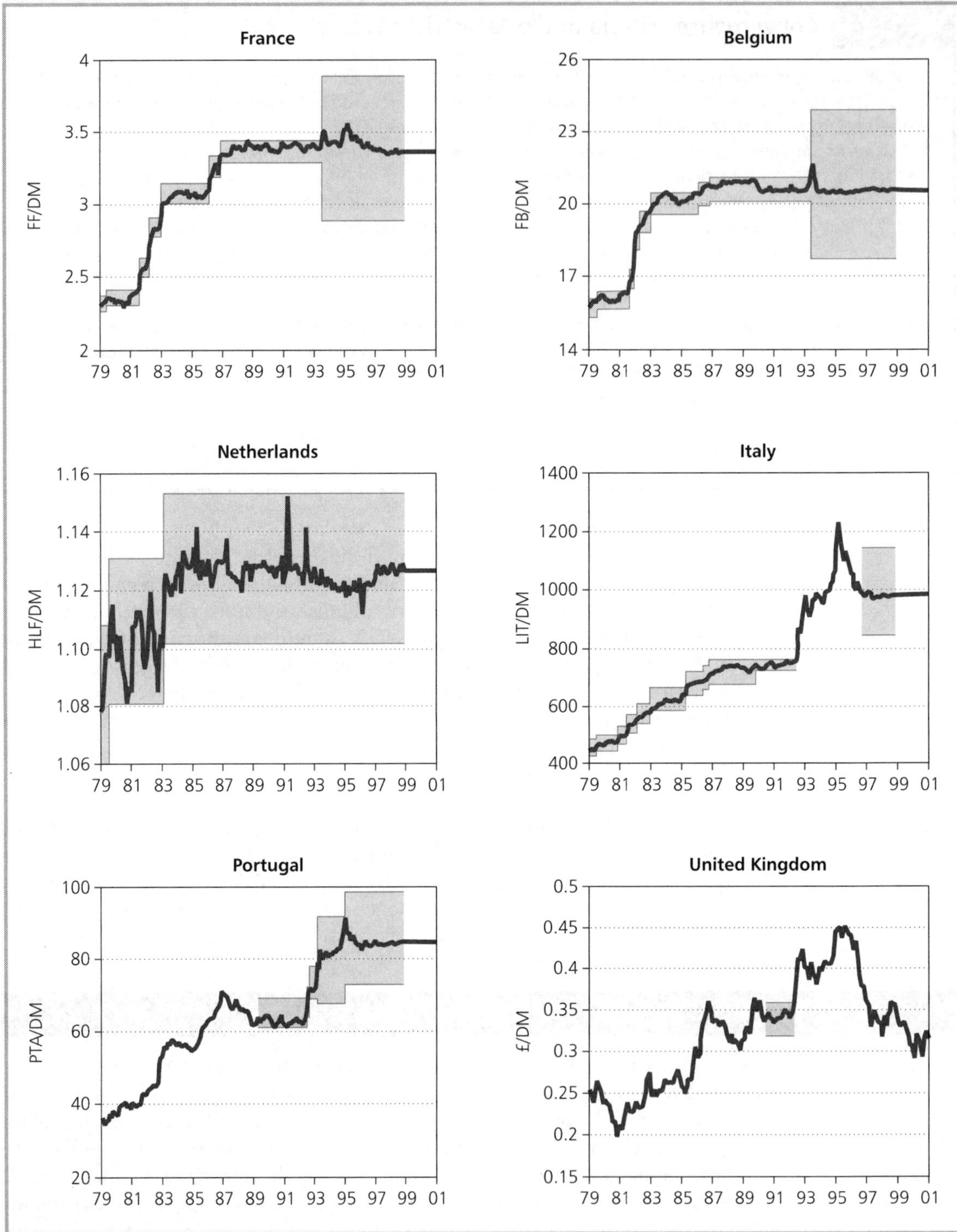

Figure 12.5 Exchange rates and EMS target zones for six countries.
Source: Eurostat.

offer samples of its diversity. After frequent realignments during its early stage the system settled into its most successful phase between 1987 and 1992, during which no realignments took place. It is interesting to note that wider bands, as in the case of Italy, may leave bands overlapping, so that the exchange rate may ease from one band into the next without dramatic jumps. This contrasts with the realignments of the French franc in the early years, which made the franc jump into the new band. Note also the dramatic and permanent depreciations of the pound and the lira after leaving the EMS, the undramatic effect of the widening of the bands to ±15% on exchange rates, and the near monetary union between the guilder and the Deutschmark.

As an exchange rate hits or threatens to hit one of the limits, the countries involved have the two options mentioned earlier. Normally, they are obliged to intervene by buying or selling foreign currency in order to keep the exchange rate in the band. Or, as an exception, the country may negotiate a realignment, a new central parity with the other member countries. At times this has been considered necessary rather frequently. Between 1987 and 1992 no such realignments were necessary. A third option, to which Italy and the United Kingdom resorted in October 1992, was to suspend membership of the Exchange Rate Mechanism (ERM), letting the exchange rate be determined by market forces only.

Foreign exchange market intervention is the purchase or sale of foreign currency by the central bank aimed at influencing the exchange rate.

Before we discuss how exchange rates behave within bands or target zones, as they are often called, we discuss the role of **foreign exchange market intervention**. Central banks, even in countries that are not part of some fixed exchange rate system, have been found to intervene in the foreign exchange market to reverse or stem movements of currency prices. What does that do?

To keep the argument simple, take an economy with perfectly flexible prices, so that potential output is produced all the time. As we have seen in Chapter 5, then the current exchange rate e is a weighted average of the exchange rate expected for tomorrow and the fundamental determinants of the exchange rate, such as the money supply. Consider only this one fundamental variable, m, and let the others be zero. Then the exchange rate equation is

$$e = \alpha m + (1 - \alpha)e^{e}_{+1} \tag{12.1}$$

This formulation again highlights the prime reason for the apparent volatility and instability of foreign exchange markets. Whatever the market believes, happens. If the exchange rate is expected to appreciate, it appreciates. We shall return to this below.

On a rational basis, if the market does not expect the fundamental determinants of the exchange rate, here represented by m, to change next period, then it will not expect the exchange rate to change. Then tomorrow's exchange rate is expected to be the same as today's. Inserting $e^{e}_{+1} = e$ into equation (12.1) and solving for e gives

$$e = m \tag{12.2}$$

Movements of the money supply, which we use as a stand-in for all fundamentals, translate one-to-one into movements of the exchange rate. The blue line, drawn with a slope of 1, in Figure 12.6 illustrates this.

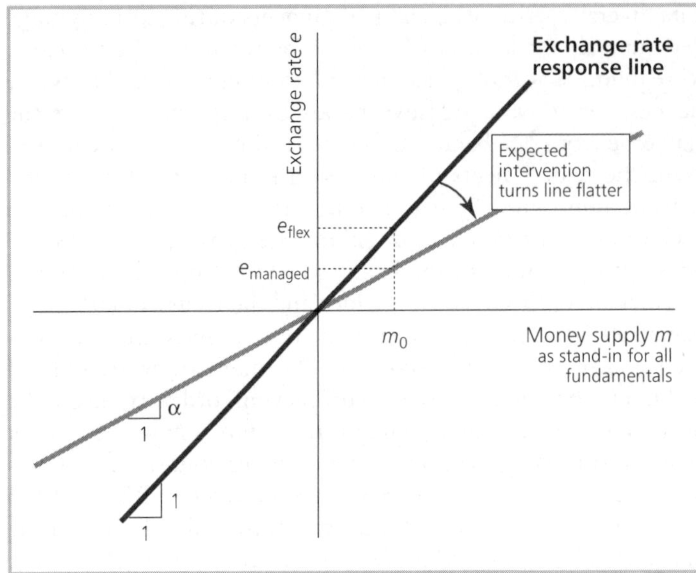

Figure 12.6 Under flexible exchange rates, if the money supply moves to m_0, and is expected to stay there, the exchange rate rises to e_{flex}. If central bank intervention is expected to reduce the money supply next period, the exchange rate rises to $e_{managed}$ only. As this argument applies for all current levels of m, foreign exchange market intervention turns the exchange rate response line into the flatter, light blue position.

Our assumption that the money supply is not expected to change next period does not mean that it cannot do so. Recall from Chapter 3 (Box 3.1 'What is money?') that the central bank only controls the monetary base M0. Broader monetary aggregates M are connected to the monetary base by means of a multiplier, $M = B \times \text{M0}$. Expressed in logarithms this is written as $m = b + \text{m0}$. The multiplier is affected by many different things, some of which are little understood. To reflect this, let changes in b be random, $b = b_{-1} + v$, where v is a random variable with an expected value of zero. Substituting this into the above definition of money, we obtain what is called a **random walk** for m:

A variable follows a **random walk** if it is just as likely to rise next period as to fall. The change of such a variable is not predictable. The expected change is zero.

$$m = m_{-1} + v \qquad (12.3)$$

According to equation (12.3) each period the likelihood that the money supply rises is just as high as the likelihood that it falls. Hence it is best to expect that it does not change at all, and we obtain equation (12.2) again.

The scenario discussed is reminiscent of flexible exchange rates. The path of monetary policy is completely unaffected by observed movements of the exchange rate. This is different under a so-called **managed float.** Assume that the central bank has a target level for the exchange rate of $\hat{e} = 0$. With that aim it always adjusts the monetary base m0 so as to reverse previous random effects on the money supply and bring the money supply back to a target level of zero. While the actual money supply next period is $m_{+1} = v_{+1}$, the expected money supply is $m^e_{+1} = 0$. This sets the expected exchange rate to $e^e_{+1} = 0$. Substituting this into equation (12.1) gives

Managed floating is a mixture between flexible and fixed exchange rates. Central banks intervene to influence the exchange rate (say, to keep it within some range), but do not defend a fixed rate.

$$e = \alpha m$$

The point to note here is that *foreign exchange market intervention makes the exchange rate response line flatter* (see the light blue line with slope α in Figure 12.6). Our specific example reveals that a given deviation of the money supply (or of a composite fundamental) from its target level leads to a smaller deviation of the exchange rate from its equilibrium level if the fundamental is expected to be driven back to its target level next period, than if this is not the case. From a more general perspective we have a continuum of slopes: the more vigorous the intervention response of the central bank is expected to be, the flatter the exchange rate response line will be. For example, if the central bank was known to reverse only half of an observed deviation of the fundamental from its target level next period, the slope of the exchange rate response line would be between that of the dark blue line and that of the light blue line in Figure 12.6.

Maths note. The target zone literature casts equation (12.1) in continuous time. This prevents the exchange rate from actually moving out of bounds before intervention strikes back. We stick with the discrete-time view entertained throughout this book and downplay the above possibility by assuming that the time unit is very small, say, a minute.

Target zones are a combination of flexible exchange rates (near the centre of the band) and one with mandatory interventions (at the margins). It should be clear from the above discussion that if central banks intervene as soon as the exchange rate moves away from the central rate, this will flatten the exchange rate response line. A more surprising insight into the workings of a target zone system is obtained if we employ the following two stylized assumptions:

1 The target zone is only defended by intervention at the margins. Within the band the exchange rate is left to be determined by market forces alone.
2 Market participants are fully convinced that there will be no realignment of the central rate. In other words, the target zone is perfectly credible.

It can be shown by means of some fairly complicated mathematics that the exchange rate response line in such a target zone is *S*-shaped, as shown in Figure 12.7. Here the following reasoning will suffice.

Let the exchange rate be at parity and the money supply at the corresponding value of $m = 0$. Since the money supply can only change randomly, with an expected value of zero, it is equally likely that it will hit or exceed m_{UP}, where a flexible exchange rate would break through the upper bound, or that it will fall below m_{LO}, where a flexible exchange rate would fall below the lower limit. In other words, the probability of a positive intervention is exactly the same as the probability of a negative intervention. Hence the expected

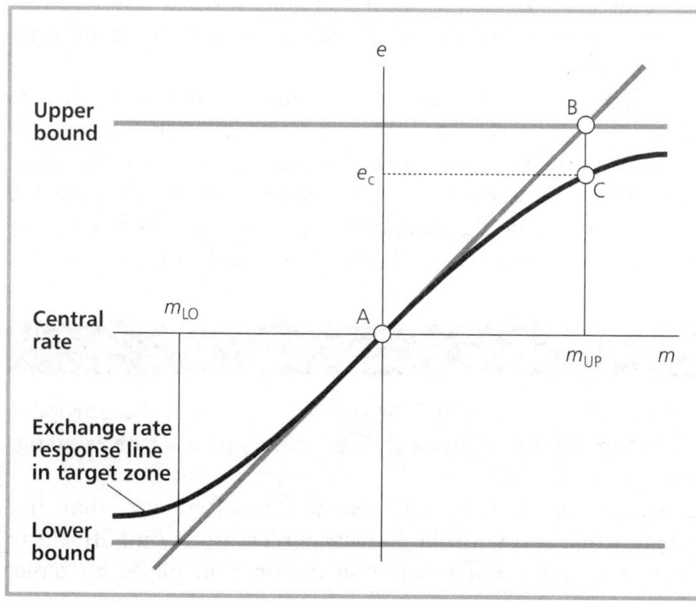

Figure 12.7 The straight line through A and B says which exchange rate obtains at a given money supply under flexible exchange rates; m_{UP} puts the exchange rate at the upper band. In a target zone this money supply moves the exchange rate only to e_C, since the central bank will probably be forced to reduce the money supply next period. Generally, the response line in a target zone is *S*-shaped.

intervention is zero. The money supply is expected to remain where it is. The exchange rate response line has the same slope of 1 as under flexible exchange rates.

Next, let the money supply be at m_{UP}, which would place a flexible exchange rate on the upper bound. The probability that the next random shock places the money supply at m_{UP} or above is 50%. In such cases the central bank would have to intervene and keep m from actually rising. There is another 50% probability that a negative shock makes m fall. Combining these two possibilities results in an expectation that m (and e) will fall next period. As a consequence, the exchange rate does not rise as high this period as it would have without the expectation of intervention next period.

Figure 12.7 contrasts the behaviour of the exchange rate under flexible rates with that within a target zone. While m_{UP} would drive a flexible exchange rate up to the upper limit, in a credible target zone it will only move to e_C. Since the likelihood of future central bank intervention increases as we move closer to the upper bound, the exchange rate response line becomes flatter and flatter. Similar reasoning near the lower bound bends the target zone exchange rate response line into the shape of an *S*.

The most important property of an exchange rate target zone is that it dampens the fluctuations of the exchange rate. Reactions along the *S* curve to given fluctuations of fundamentals are smaller than under flexible exchange rates. If fundamentals that are beyond the control of the domestic policy-maker move out of bounds, the exchange rate still remains within. And even way inside the band, exchange rate responses are smaller due to the fact that the *S* curve has a slope smaller than 1. The effect is strengthened if interventions are not only undertaken at the margins but intra-marginal as well, as permitted, though not required, in the EMS. It is also one argument against the widely held view that widening the band to ±15% in 1993 had the same effect as suspending the EMS altogether and rendering exchange rates flexible. Then the exchange rate responses to movements in m would be described by the 45° line. If the wider bands have yielded *credible* bounds, however, they should dampen exchange rate fluctuations inside the band, even if exchange rates never hit the widest bounds.

Empirically, the *S* shape of the exchange rate response line has been found to be only a first approximation for the EMS. More realistic, though not radically different, properties obtain if the model concedes that bounds may be imperfectly credible and that the central bank may begin to intervene inside the band. The second modification has little significance for the following look at speculative attacks. However, the first one, credibility of the band, plays a key role.

12.4 SPECULATIVE ATTACKS

We are now ready to take a second look at the 1992 crises in the European Monetary System. Figure 12.8 presents a stylized sketch of a set of exchange rates in the EMS as we enter 1992.

To keep things simple and transparent, assume that after more than five years without realignments, and with the Maastricht Treaty's commitment to economic and monetary union and a common currency in place, all target

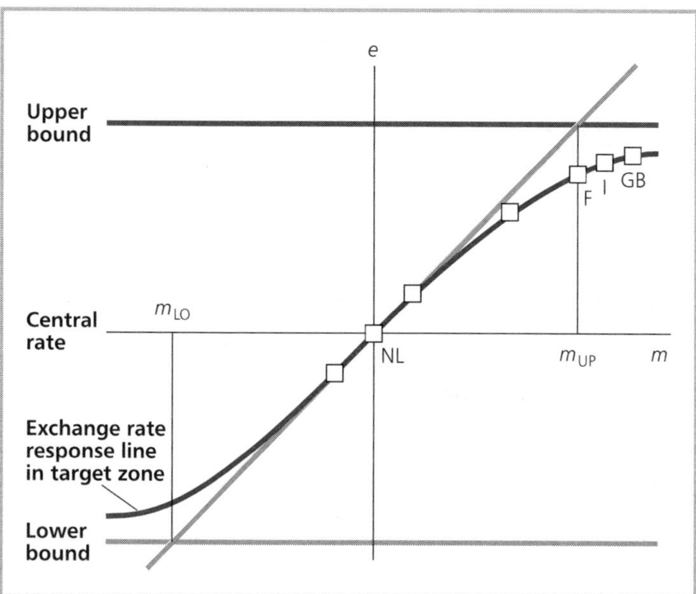

Figure 12.8 This shows a hypothetical line-up of EU members on the EMS exchange rate response line. Here the exchange rates of Britain and Italy only remain below the upper bound as long as the target zone is credible. If credibility deteriorates, the exchange rate response line begins to straighten and the exchange rates are pushed against the upper bound.

zones were perfectly credible. Then the same *S* curve applies for all member states, and we may line up countries according to how central rates compare with current fundamentals.

In the judgement of many observers, Britain had entered the EMS in 1990 with a substantially overvalued central rate for sterling. In other words, fundamentals would place its free-market exchange rate against, say, the Deutschmark, way above the central rate, possibly even outside the zone's upper band. So Britain would have to be located way to the right on the *S* curve. Next to Britain we may want to position Italy and France, and then the Iberian countries and Greece. The Dutch guilder had been comfortable near central parity for quite some time.

Consider now Figure 12.9, which expands the first quadrant of Figure 12.8 and focuses on Britain only. Sterling's pre-crisis position on the blue *S* curve was fine while the upper bound was credible. But, as the EMS began to lose credibility and EMU appeared doomed in the wake of the Maastricht Treaty's rejection by Danish voters, intensifying discussions in other countries, and of uncertain prospects for the French referendum, the *S* curve straightened somewhat to the slightly lighter blue position. Sterling hit the upper bound.

The trigger mechanism for the 1992 EMS crises, the credibility loss of the target zone, is also the one stressed by foreign-exchange dealers. When asked when they started to expect a realignment within the EMS, about two-thirds mentioned the Danish referendum (Table 12.2). Opinion polls indicating a close result for the French referendum and the crises surrounding the Finnish mark and the Swedish krona, neither being formal members of the EMS at the time (included in the category 'Other'), raised further doubts.

The EMS credibility crisis makes the British pound the first currency to hit the upper bound (step 1) and forced the Bank of England to intervene (step 2). To keep the pound within bounds, the money supply needed to be lowered from m_1 to m_2 by selling foreign exchange reserves. This loss of foreign

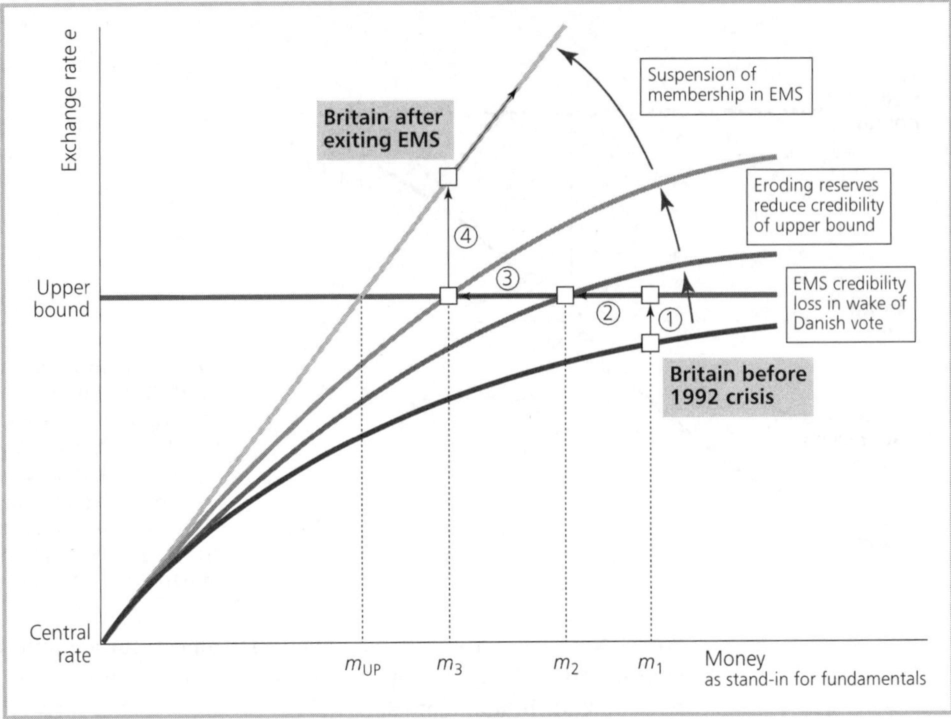

Figure 12.9 Before the 1992 crisis the British money supply was at m_1, and e was determined by the lowest, dark blue curve. When Denmark's 'no' undermined EMS credibility, the response line moved into the second, slightly lighter position, pressing e against the upper bound, forcing the Bank of England (BoE) to support the pound, reducing m to m_2. Eroding currency reserves reduced the target zone's credibility further, shifting the response line into the third position, forcing the BoE to reduce m to m_3. Leaving the EMS turned the response line straight, permitting sizeable depreciations of the pound out of previous bounds.

exchange reserves weakens the Bank of England's muscle for future defences of the upper bound. The market knows this quite well. Hence, the upper bound's credibility deteriorates further, straightening the *S* curve even more into the third position from bottom. Having started only weeks earlier, overwhelming foreign exchange market speculation forced Britain to suspend

Table 12.2 When did the market begin to expect a realignment? Questionnaires sent to foreign-exchange dealers indicate that realignment expectations within the EMS arose mainly after the Danish referendum on the Maastricht Treaty.

Question (in survey of foreign-exchange dealers):
When did you first begin to think that changes in the ERM exchange rates were imminent?

Answers:	%
Before the Danish referendum in June	21.8
Just after the Danish referendum	46.6
Upon hearing about public opinion polls in France during the run-up to the referendum	15.1
Other	22.7

Source: Barry Eichengreen and Charles Wyplosz (1993), 'The unstable EMS', *Brookings Papers on Economic Activity* 1: 51–124.

membership of the EMS on 16 September 1992. In line with the stylized path in Figure 12.9, sterling lost over 20% against the Deutschmark within days after leaving the EMS.

This graph should not imply that there is a set course of events once a speculative attack gets under way. Many such attacks have been fended off. Moving left, as characterized by steps 2 and 3, may eventually re-establish credibility, easing the exchange rate (and the S curve) back into the band.

Proof that the Bank of England did not accept defeat easily is given by a 5% jump of the interest rate within one day to fend off speculators (Figure 12.10). And Sweden, which was not a member of the EMS but had pegged the krona to the ECU in 1991, on 16 September raised its overnight lending rate to 500%!

The arguments given here augment the macroeconomic account of the 1992 crises given in the 'Choices' section (pp. 317–19). Here we looked at some details of currency crises which the previous story had not taken into account. There we focused on the cost–benefit ratios for some countries that were at the centre of speculation. In the context of the current target zone framework, these cost–benefit considerations suggest that, and explain why, the band for the British pound lost credibility sooner and faster than others, straightening the UK's S curve out sooner and faster. The earlier view thus easily augments and supports the current argument.

Self-fulfilling prophecies

Our view of speculative attacks during currency crises does not rest on the presumption of some sinister plot by speculators. Uncoordinated reactions by competitive markets suffice well.

On the other hand, it deserves to be emphasized that the process that we called a 'speculative attack' need not be triggered by a real reason. If *market psychology* alone and completely unfoundedly develops doubts about the credibility of the target zone, the S curve straightens and makes the exchange

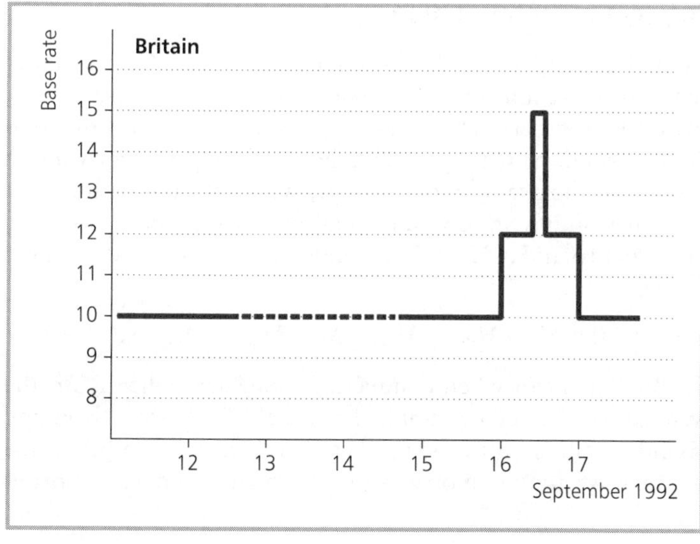

Figure 12.10 The final and fatal attack on the pound took place on 16 September 1992. To fend it off, the base rate, the Bank of England's instrument for controlling the money supply, was raised from 10% via 12% to 15%. When proved insufficient, the rate was led back to the old level and EMS membership was suspended. *Source*: *The Economist*.

rate actually move towards one of the bounds. This forces monetary authorities to intervene to reduce the foreign exchange reserves, thus reducing the credibility of the band further. The result will look like what we sketched for the 1992 crises of the EMS. So the initially unwarranted reservation about the viability of the current central rate and its surrounding band of fluctuation may indeed prove self-fulfilling.

This insight holds generally. Whatever the market expects in the foreign exchange market, happens in a self-fulfilling way. If such expectations lack a fundamental basis, however, these effects cannot last. In this light the data do not seem to support the view, at times widely held, that speculation drove the pound sterling out of the EMS, against fundamentals. Then the pound should have returned to previous EMS target zone levels once speculators had shifted attention to other currencies. As the UK panel in Figure 12.5 showed, this was not the case. Between September 1992 and September 1995 the pound on average remained 22% above its central parity rate versus the Deutschmark that applied while EMS membership was active. The same holds *a fortiori* for the lira.

12.5 MONETARY AND FISCAL POLICY IN EUROLAND

Our discussions have covered the global economy, the national economy, and the relationship between the two, that is, interdependence in a system of fixed exchange rates or a target zone. What we have not looked at yet is the case of a group of countries sharing a common currency, the experiment on which a large part of the European Union is embarking at the turn of the millennium. Such an arrangement is called a **currency union** or a **monetary union**. We will first look at how fiscal and monetary policy works in a monetary union and then check if our insights shed any light on why certain institutional arrangements and precautions were taken during the advent of the **European Monetary Union (EMU)**. Let us start by looking at monetary policy.

Monetary policy in a monetary union

Monetary policy in Euroland is conducted by the European Central Bank (ECB). True, technical operations are in the hands of national central banks, but these act only on ECB orders. Thus it is the ECB which controls the total supply of euros in Euroland. Note the wording, however. In a monetary union the central bank controls the overall money supply within the union. It has no control over the money supply in any individual member country. So if the total money supply in Euroland is M, and M_i denotes money supplied and held in country i, we have

$$M = M_A + M_B + M_D + M_E + M_F + M_{FIN} + M_{GR} + M_I + M_{IRE} + M_{LUX} + M_N + M_P$$

All that the ECB can control when conducting monetary policy is M, the aggregate. How much of it is being supplied and held in Austria, Belgium, Germany, Spain and so on, is up to the market. The ECB keeps a lid on the total, since the sum of national money supplies in all member countries equals M.

It does not matter which country's central bank actually conducts the expansion. To understand this, consider a stylized monetary union made up of two countries A and B only, Austria and Belgium. To make matters simple, suppose A and B do not trade in goods and services, though they do have integrated money and capital markets. Let us further ignore this monetary union's links with the rest of the world to focus on internal links only. The dark blue lines in Figure 12.11 depict an initial equilibrium (points C) in which both countries' interest rates are equal, of course.

Now suppose the ECB orders Austria's central bank to expand the money supply. The Österreichische Nationalbank complies, say, by purchasing Austrian government bonds from Austrian residents. This shifts LM_A to the right into the dashed position because this action injects liquidity into the Austrian economy. This added liquidity exerts downward pressure on the Austrian interest rates, moving the economy *towards* point D in the left-hand panel in Figure 12.11 (though not really *onto* D).

The downward pressure on interest rates makes Austrian bonds unattractive compared with Belgian bonds. So, Austrians will try to sell their bonds and purchase Belgian bonds. This moves euros across the border. The money supply falls in Austria but rises in Belgium. Technically, LM_B moves to the right from its original position, driving Belgian interest rates down, and LM_A moves left from its temporary dashed position, driving Austrian interest rates back up. This process cannot end before both countries' interest rates meet somewhere between their initial values and Austria's level associated with

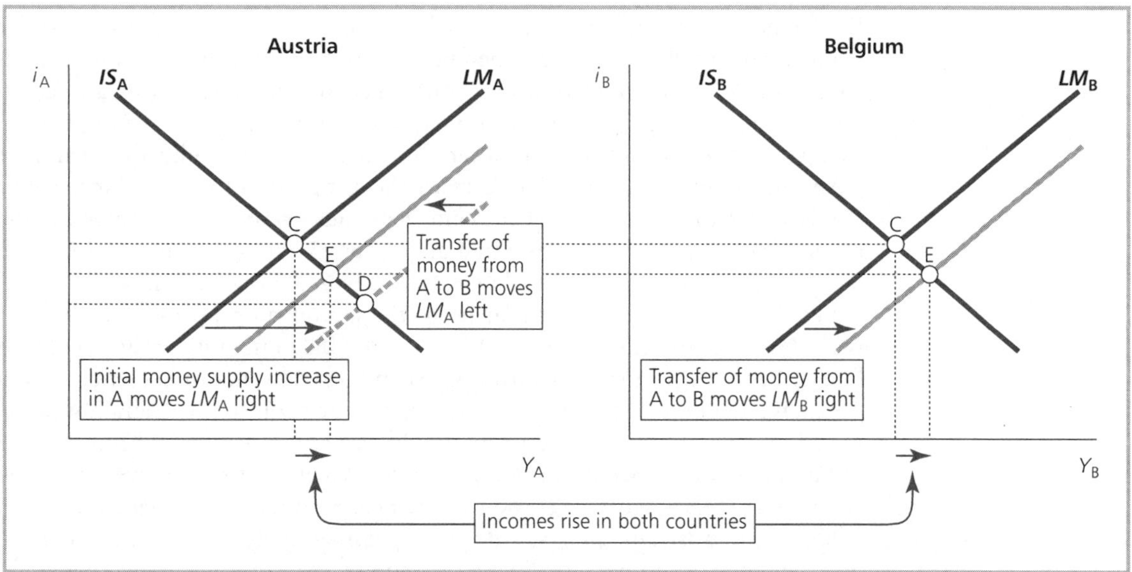

Figure 12.11 In a monetary union it does not matter in which country the money supply is actually increased, since it tends to spread evenly over all member states. One way to rationalize this is as follows: suppose the Austrian central bank increases the supply of euros, moving Austria's *LM* curve to the right. This tends to drive Austrian interest rates below Belgium's. This induces international investors to sell Austrian bonds and purchase Belgian bonds instead. This reduces the supply of euros in Austria and increases the supply of euros in Belgium. Thus, the Austrian *LM* curve moves to the left and Belgium's *LM* curve moves to the right. Movements come to a halt when both countries' *LM* curves intersect their respective *IS* curves at the same interest rate.

point D. In Figure 12.11 this is where the *LM* curves are at their light blue positions. In the end, the money supply has increased in both countries, independent of where the initial money supply increase took place. Interest rates in the monetary union have fallen and income has risen in all member countries.

To keep the argument reasonably transparent we assumed that Austria's central bank extended the money supply by purchasing Austrian bonds held in Austria. The same comparative static effect obtains, however, under more complicated assumptions. For example, if Austria's central bank extended the money supply by purchasing Austrian government bonds held in Belgium it would have increased Belgian money holdings with the same end result of the money supply increasing and interest rates falling in both countries. But the sequence of reactions would have been somewhat different. Reality is somewhere between these two extreme cases, though a bit closer to the first since individuals exhibit a clear home bias in their holding of financial assets: Austrians hold a much higher share of Austrian bonds (and stocks) in their portfolio than Belgians (or any other nationals) do.

How are the above results affected when Austria and Belgium trade? All variables still move in the same direction. There is a second stimulus to income, however. As Austria expands the money supply and its income increases, it raises its demand for Belgium's export goods, moving IS_B to the right. For the same reason, Austria's *IS* curve moves to the right as well. In equilibrium, both incomes are higher and interest rates lower.

Fiscal policy in a monetary union

Discipline in fiscal policy was, and will continue to be, an important test for countries wanting to qualify for membership in the European Monetary Union. And at the 1996 intergovernmental conference in Dublin heads of state agreed on a list of sanctions to come into operation if a member country resorted to excessive government spending after the start of EMU. Why this fear that governments might not be able to resist the temptation to spend excessively? While a full discussion of deficits and debt must wait until Chapter 14, the model employed here provides a first answer as to why governments dread the idea of other governments spending excessively in a monetary union.

Let Belgium and Austria again be in the equilibrium positions associated with the dark blue curves (Figure 12.12). Now Belgium unilaterally decides to boost income by raising government spending. The multiplier effect shifts Belgium's *IS* curve to the right into the light blue position. If Belgium was the world, income and the interest rate would rise and a new equilibrium would obtain at point D. Being in a monetary union with Austria, however, repercussions are felt in Austria as soon as the Belgian interest rate begins to rise.

Since the Austrian interest rate moves up with Belgium's, income falls, moving the economy northwest as shown in the left-hand panel in Figure 12.12. The result is an excess supply of money in Austria. In Belgium, while the interest rate is still below the value associated with point C, there is an excess demand for money. In this situation, as we have encountered before, excess liquidity flows out of Austria into Belgium. So the Belgian *LM* curve shifts to the right and Austria's *LM* curve moves to the left. The new equilibrium obtains on the light blue *LM* curves where interest rates are equal.

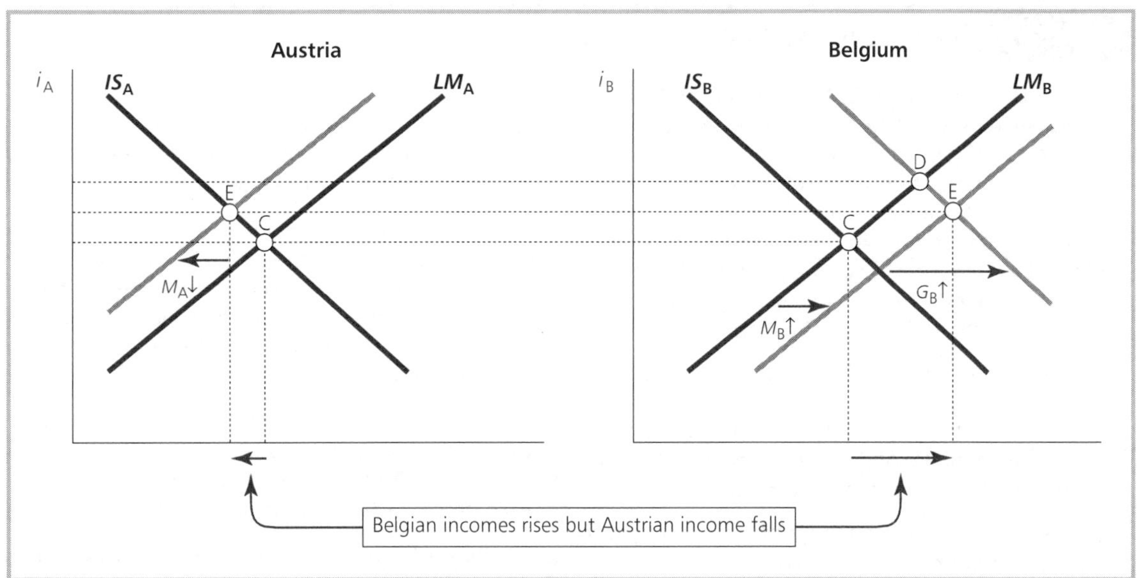

Figure 12.12 In a monetary union an expansionary fiscal policy move by one country can have negative repercussions on other countries' incomes. Suppose Belgium's government increases spending to stimulate Belgian incomes. While this succeeds, it drives up Belgian interest rates, attracting international investors. Since these sell their Austrian bonds, taking their euro proceeds out of Austria, the supply of euros in Austria falls. This shifts the Austrian *LM* curve left (and at the same time Belgium's to the right) and drives Austria's interest rate up (and at the same time Belgium's down) until both countries' interest rates match again. Since Austria ends up with a higher interest rate than before, it pays for Belgium's income gains by being driven into recession.

Constraints on fiscal policy: stability pact and no-bailout clauses

The result obtained in Figure 12.12 reveals why Austria has no sympathy whatsoever for Belgium's deficit spending: in a monetary union, one country can conduct expansionary fiscal policy to boost income at home. However, it will drive down incomes in the other member countries.

The prospect that in EMU individual countries may be tempted to discard fiscal discipline in pursuit of national income gains, for which the other members pay a price in the form of recessions, has motivated the member states to sign a 'Pact for Stability and Growth' (for details see Box 12.2). In a nutshell, this agreement permits Belgium (and other members) to resort to deficit spending in excess of 3% of GDP only if it slides into a severe recession of a 2% income contraction within 12 months. Deficit spending in less extreme times would give other members the right to levy a severe fine on Belgium.

The **no-bailout clause**: 'Overdraft facilities ... with the ECB ... in favour of ... governments ... of Member States shall be prohibited, as shall be the purchase directly from them by the ECB or national central banks of debt instruments.' (Maastricht Treaty, Article 104)

Another precaution contained in the Treaty on European Union, signed in Maastricht in 1992, is the **no-bailout clause** which strictly prohibits the ECB from bailing out national governments in the case of default. The idea here is that, as government debt rises relative to GDP as a consequence of extended deficit spending, financial markets will realize that this country's risk of defaulting on its debt or interest payments is increasing and, therefore, attach a risk premium *RP* for loans to this country. Similar to our discussion of the

BOX 12.2 The Pact for Stability and Growth

At the December 1996 Dublin summit and subsequent meetings, EU member states agreed on a Pact for Stability and Growth, aimed at ensuring a long-term orientation of fiscal policy. In essence, the pact is to prevent members from running excessive budget deficits. Extending the respective Maastricht criterion into phase 3 of European Monetary Union, the pact for stability and growth begins with the following judgement:

- Government budget deficit ratios smaller than 3% are not excessive.
- Government budget deficit ratios higher than 3% are normally considered excessive, unless the country suffered a serious economic setback.

Whether a serious economic setback has occurred is judged as follows:

- A decline in real GDP of at least 2% (in a year) is always a serious setback.
- A decline in real GDP of less than 0.75% is never a serious setback.
- A decline in real GDP of between 0.75 and 2% of GDP is evaluated for its seriousness on a case-by-case basis by the Council of Ministers (or ECOFIN, the supervisory body to be set up).

If a budget deficit is judged excessive, ECOFIN calls upon the member state to take effective measures within four months. Should the member fail to comply with the recommended measures, the Council of Ministers may apply sanctions with a two-thirds majority vote. These include:

- An interest-free deposit of 0.2% of GDP to be paid in the first year of excessive spending.
- In addition, 0.1% of GDP to be paid as a fine for each percentage point beyond the 3% limit.

The sum of both components is not to exceed 0.5% of GDP annually. If after two years the budget deficit is still excessive, the initial deposit of 0.2% of GDP becomes a fine.

Asia crisis in Case study 5.1, this modifies the equilibrium condition for the international capital market in our fictional two-country currency union to

$$i_B = i_A + RP_B$$

So, by provoking a higher default risk, rising Belgian government debt permits Austrian interest rates i_A to remain below Belgium's because of the Belgian risk premium RP_B. Therefore, the effect shown in Figure 12.12 will be muted. LM_B will not shift as much to the right and LM_A need not shift as much to the left. This is beneficial on two counts: Belgium's income gain remains smaller, making it less tempting to engage in deficit spending in the first place. And Austria's income loss also remains smaller, dampening the repercussions on this country. But while the theoretical implications of a no-bailout clause are undisputed, criticism has emerged on two issues. The first is whether the effect is strong enough to really keep government spending in check. If the government runs a large deficit of 5% of GDP in a given year, raising the ratio of the public debt relative to income from 90% to 95%, is that really going to have a noteworthy impact on the risk premium? The second criticism or caveat concerns the credibility of the no-bailout clause. When push comes to shove, will governments really permit a member to slide into bankruptcy? It is because of such doubts that EU governments considered it wise to augment the already installed no-bailout clause by the Growth and Stability Pact.

Bottom line

This chapter made the point that the Mundell–Fleming model is capable of sorting out the main policy issues and options in a variety of institutional environments. As an example of a major event that can be accessed by means of this model we looked at the merger of the two Germanies in 1990 and the ensuing crisis in the EMS. Augmented with the insight that policies are endogenous and that policy-makers have incentives of their own, observed policy decisions are easily rationalized. An even closer understanding of the 1992 climax is obtained by detailing the behaviour of exchange rates within target zones. The working of target zones gives credibility and speculation a prominent role and makes exchange rate systems such as the EMS vulnerable to warranted or unwarranted speculative attacks.

We further saw that the Mundell–Fleming model, extended into a two-country version, provides useful insights into the macroeconomics of a currency union such as EMU. In particular, it illustrates the risks of discretionary fiscal policy by individual countries and the necessity for restrictions.

CHAPTER SUMMARY

- The issues and policy decisions surrounding German unification are clearly identified by means of the Mundell–Fleming model.
- Enjoying the freedom of the *n*th currency in the EMS, the Bundesbank decided to fight potential inflation, confronting other EMS members with high interest rates.
- High interest rates meant lower aggregate demand for other EMS members. This was least acceptable for those countries already in deep recession. In 1992 this made Great Britain the candidate most likely to be the first to suspend membership.
- Exchange rates respond in a less volatile manner to observed changes in economic fundamentals if the central bank is expected to intervene in the foreign exchange market in a stabilizing fashion.
- A target zone like the EMS obliges central banks to intervene when the bounds are hit.
- A second major factor in igniting the EMS crisis of 1992 was the initial rejection of the Maastricht Treaty by Denmark and the intensifying discussion of the Maastricht Treaty in other countries. This undermined the credibility of the target zone and invited speculators to test the bounds for those currencies considered particularly vulnerable.
- 'Market psychology', in the sense that speculators spot weaknesses detached from fundamentals, affects exchange rates that are flexible or operate within a band. Therefore irrational speculation may well start an EMS crisis. However, the widely held view that speculation against the pound and the lira during the 1992 crisis was not warranted by fundamentals is not supported by how these two currencies fared after membership in the EMS had been suspended.
- Policy issues in a currency union can be analyzed within a two-country version of the Mundell–Fleming model.
- The European Central Bank controls the money supply in the euro area. It cannot control the money supply in individual member countries – very

much like the way the Bank of England cannot control the money supply in Essex, London or the Midlands. Therefore, monetary policy in a currency union affects all members in the same way.

- Expansionary fiscal policy by one member of a currency union has adverse effects on the other members. Rules as set out in the Pact for Stability and Growth, or no-bailout clauses may prevent such policies or dampen their negative effects on others.

KEY TERMS AND CONCEPTS

Bretton Woods
convergence criteria
currency union
currency crisis
default risk
EMS crisis
euro area
Euroland
European Monetary System (EMS)
European Monetary Union (EMU)
foreign exchange market intervention
*n*th currency
Maastricht Treaty
managed float
no-bailout clause
Pact for Stability and Growth
random walk
self-fulfilling prophecy
speculative attacks
target zone

EXERCISES

12.1 How would you check whether a country is in charge of the *n*th currency in a system of fixed exchange rates?

12.2 Suppose that a *small* open economy within the EMS went through a transformation similar to that following German unification. How would the course of events differ from that induced by German unification? (Hint: it is crucial to state at the outset what distinguishes a small from a large economy.)

12.3 Recast the policy issues surrounding German unification and the 1992 EMS crisis in the *DAD-SAS* model.

12.4 Consider the following EU members' exports to Germany as a share of GDP. In the context of the Mundell–Fleming model, why does this suggest that option #1, to stay in the EMS, was less painful for the Netherlands than it was for Italy, France or the United Kingdom?

	Exports to Germany as share of GDP
NL	0.16
I	0.04
F	0.04
GB	0.03

12.5 In this chapter you were introduced to the concept of a 'random walk' (equation (12.3)). To make this concept less abstract, generate your own random walk over 20 periods. This may be done as follows. Toss a coin and write a '1' if heads occur and '−1' if tails occur. Repeat this and add the result of the second round to the previous outcome (remember that the equation characterizing a random walk was $m = m_{-1} + \nu$, where ν is a random disturbance, i.e. the outcome of tossing a coin, in our case). Toss the coin a third time and add the result, and so on. What specific properties do you observe? (Repeating this exercise may give you an even better idea about the properties of a 'typical' random walk.)

12.6 Recall that in equation (12.1) the exchange rate was described as a weighted average of the money supply and expectations, i.e. $e = \alpha m + (1 - \alpha)e^e_{t+1}$. Suppose that $\alpha = 0.8$ and that the monetary authority's target level of money supply is $\hat{e} = 1$. Draw the exchange rate line for a non-intervening and an intervening monetary authority. Suppose that α decreases to the value of 0.4. How does this affect the exchange rate line? What reasons might lead to such a decrease?

12.7 Consider the stylized European Monetary Union comprising only two countries A and B. Suppose *LM* and *IS* are subject to occasional stochastic shocks (see our discussion in Box 3.5). Would you recommend the ECB to fix the money supply or to fix the interest rate? Discuss the issue under different assumptions about the nature of the shocks, which can either be synchronized (the same in both countries) or country-specific. This yields four constellations you need to discuss as listed in the following matrix:

	LM curve stochastic	*IS* curve stochastic
Synchronized shocks	(a)	(b)
Country-specific shocks	(c)	(d)

12.8 Suppose the two-country currency union discussed in the text is small compared with the rest of the world. How, then, does an increase in Belgium's government spending affect incomes in Belgium and Austria (assume A and B do not trade with each other, but do trade with the rest of the world)

(a) when the exchange rate versus the rest of the world is flexible?

(b) when the exchange rate versus the rest of the world is fixed?

RECOMMENDED READING

The authority on the early years of German unification is Gerlinde Sinn and Hans-Werner Sinn (1992) *Jumpstart: The Economic Unification of Germany*, Cambridge and London: MIT Press.

On European Monetary Union you may consult Charles Wyplosz (1997) 'EMU: why and how it might happen', *Journal of Economic Perspectives* 11: 3–22.

On target zones see Lars E. O. Svensson (1992) 'An interpretation of recent research on exchange rate target zones', *Journal of Economic Perspectives* 6: 119–44.

Finally, on currency crises and speculation, see Barry Eichengreen, Andrew K. Rose and Charles Wyplosz (1995) 'Exchange market mayhem: antecedents and aftermaths of speculative attacks', *Economic Policy: A European Forum* 21: 251–96.

APPENDIX THE TWO-COUNTRY MUNDELL–FLEMING MODEL

The usual perspective taken in this book when analyzing an individual country, the national economy, is that this economy is too small in economic size to have a measurable influence on the rest of the world. Such a small open economy can be analyzed by means of the Mundell–Fleming model, letting the 'world' variables be exogenous. Effects run in one direction only, from the rest of the world to the national economy, but not in reverse.

We took a similar perspective when discussing German unification effects on other EU members, neglecting that developments in France or Britain would feed back on the German economy. This helps simplify the analysis but, while results usually point in the right direction, is not completely accurate. The discussion of fiscal and monetary policy in a monetary union (section 12.3) for the first time explicitly looks at the interaction between two countries of similar size, using a separate Mundell–Fleming model for each country. This type of model is called the **two-country Mundell–Fleming model.**

Because the algebra of the two-country Mundell–Fleming model is cumbersome, the text settles for a graphical analysis. This appendix supplies selected algebraic results for the two-country Mundell–Fleming model that may be used to refine your understanding of how open economies interact under different institutional arrangements. No effort is made to be comprehensive, however. Also, results are only stated rather than derived.

Flexible exchange rates

Model:

$$Y_A = cY_A - bi_A + G_A + x_1 Y_B + x_2 E - m_1 Y_A + m_2 E \qquad Y_B = cY_B - bi_B + G_B + m_1 Y_A - m_2 E - x_1 Y_B - x_2 E$$

$$M_A = kY_A - hi_A \qquad M_B = kY_B - hi_B$$

$$i_A = i_B$$

Endogenous: Y_A, Y_B, i_A, i_B, E
Exogenous: M_A, M_B, G_A, G_B

Selected results:

$$Y_A = \frac{h}{2a}(G_A + G_B) + \frac{(1-c)h}{2ak}(M_A - M_B) + \frac{b}{a}M_A$$

$$i_A = i_B = \frac{k}{2a}(G_A + G_B) - \frac{1-c}{2a}(M_A + M_B)$$

with $a \equiv (1 - c)h + bk > 0$

Comments: What is new here, compared with the small-country Mundell–Fleming model, is that fiscal policy works: G_A affects Y_A. The reason is that A is now large enough to affect the two countries' common interest rate, so there is no complete crowding out. The effects here are symmetrical: it does not matter in which country government spending or the money supply changes.

Fixed exchange rates (*n*th currency supplied by country B)
Model: same as above
Endogenous: Y_A, Y_B, i_A, i_B, M_A
Exogenous: M_B, E, G_A, G_B

Selected results:

$$Y_A = \frac{bk + h(1 - c - x_1)}{a} G_A + \frac{hx_1 - bk}{a} G_B + \frac{b(1 - c + 2x_1)}{a} M_B + \frac{[h(1 - c) + 2bk](x_2 + m_2)}{a} E$$

$$i_A = i_B = \frac{k(1 - c + m_1)}{a} G_B + \frac{km_1}{a} G_A - \frac{(1 - c)(1 - c + m_1 + x_1)}{a} M_B - \frac{(1 - c)(x_2 m_2)k}{a} E$$

with $a \equiv (1 - c)(bk + 1 - c + m_1 + x_1) + 2m_1 bk > 0$

Comments: Results are very much in line with what we saw for the small open economy: government spending works, as does monetary policy conducted abroad. The interest rate is dependent on fiscal policy, the money supply in the *n*th-currency-country B, and the exchange rate.

Currency union
Model:

$$Y_A = cY_A - bi_A + G_A + x_1 Y_B - m_1 Y_A \qquad Y_B = cY_B - bi_B + G_B + m_1 Y_A - x_1 Y_B$$
$$M_A = kY_A - hi_A \qquad M_B = kY_B - hi_B$$
$$i_A = i_B$$
$$M = M_A + M_B$$

Endogenous: Y_A, Y_B, i_A, i_B, M_A, M_B
Exogenous: M, G_A, G_B

Selected results:

$$Y_A = \frac{bk + 2h(1 - c + x_1)}{a} G_A + \frac{2hx_1 - bk}{a} G_B + \frac{b(1 - c + 2x_1)}{a} M$$

with $a \equiv 2[bk + (1 - c)h](1 - c + m_1 + x_1) > 0$

$$i_A = i_B = \frac{k}{2[bk + (1 - c)h]}(G_A + G_B) - \frac{1 - c}{2[bk + (1 - c)h]} M$$

Comments: Results may be compared with what we discussed in Figure 12.12. There when Belgium raises government spending, interest rates go up. This also shows in the equation. We also found that while Belgian fiscal policy can stimulate Belgian income, this goes at the expense of Austria's income. In the above equation whether an increase in G_B raises or reduces Austrian income depends on the sign of the numerator $2hx_1 - bk$. Note that when we developed the graph we assumed the two countries did not trade, that is we let $x_1 = 0$. Then the effect of an increase of G_B on Y_A is unequivocally negative. If we make x_1 larger, Austrian exports become more dependent on income in Belgium. They thus benefit from a rise in Y_B. Once x_1 is large enough, an increase in Belgian government spending may increase income at home and abroad.

APPLIED PROBLEMS

RECENT RESEARCH

Intervention in the foreign exchange market

When central banks buy or sell foreign currency they intervene in the foreign exchange market. While they are obliged to do so under fixed exchange rates or within target zones, such as the EMS, they have been found to intervene voluntarily when exchange rates are officially flexible. The question of whether they intervene just to smooth the path of the exchange rate or in order to drive the exchange rate towards some perceived target exchange rate interested researchers in the 1980s. My paper 'Intervention policy under floating exchange rates: An analysis of the Swiss case' (*Economica* 54, 1987, pp. 439–53) reports the estimation equation

$$I_t = -9.92 - 0.10(e_t - e_{Target})$$
$$(7.74)\quad (2.38)$$

$R^2_{adj} = 0.75$ Monthly data 1974.01–1984.06

where I is intervention as measured by the change in foreign exchange reserves of the Swiss National Bank, e is the Swiss francs per dollar exchange rate and e_{Target} is a presumed exchange rate target assumed to be the average real exchange rate of 1973. The significant coefficient of −0.1 suggests that if the exchange rate was considered too low, the Swiss National Bank sold dollars.

The paper also reports the equation

$$I_t = -10.49 - 0.39\ \varepsilon_t \qquad R^2_{adj} = 0.75$$
$$(8.24)\quad (2.17)$$

Monthly data 1974.01–1984.06

where ε is the rate of depreciation. The significant negative coefficient of 0.39 (with a *t*-statistic of 2.17) suggests that whenever the Swiss franc depreciated (appreciated), the central bank sold (bought) dollars.

So it appears that the Swiss central bank's foreign exchange market interventions reflect two motives, 'exchange rate targeting', as suggested by the first equation, and what is called 'leaning against the wind', as suggested by the second equation.

WORKED PROBLEM

Interest rates and inflation

It is sometimes argued that of the two Maastricht criteria on inflation and interest rates, one is redundant. This is because, according to the Fisher equation, nominal interest rates simply contain an inflation premium over a (presumably constant) real interest rate:

$$\text{Interest rate} = \text{constant} + \text{inflation rate}$$

We may use the data in Table 12.3 on government bond yields and inflation to check the validity of the Fisher equation. The resulting regression equation is:

$$\text{INTEREST} = 5.32 + 1.32\ \text{INFLATION} \qquad R^2_{adj} = 0.83$$
$$(8.96)\quad (8.45)$$

83% of the differences in long-term nominal interest rates are explained by differences in inflation. The equation contains two interesting messages about real interest rates. First, they are currently very high. If a country had zero inflation, nominal (which then equals real) interest rates would stand at 5.32. Nominal interest rates do not vary with inflation with a factor of 1. The estimated coefficient of 1.32 suggests that nominal interest rates go up faster than inflation, which makes real interest rates higher at higher inflation. To test whether 1.32 is significantly larger than 1, we may test 1.32 against the null hypothesis that the true coefficient is 1. To obtain an appropriate *t*-statistic we compute 1.32 − 1 = 0.32 and divide this by the standard error, which is 1.32/8.45 = 0.17. So the *t*-statistic for 1.32 against the null of 1 is 0.32/0.17 = 2.1.

Table 12.3

Country	A	B	DK	SF	F	D	GR	IRL	I	LUX	NL	P	E	S	GB
Interest rate (in %)	7.3	7.9	8.6	9.4	7.8	7.1	18.4	8.5	12.3	6.2	7.2	11.7	11.5	10.7	8.4
Inflation rate (in %)	2.5	1.6	2.2	1.3	1.7	2.2	9.9	2.6	4.7	2.1	2.2	4.2	4.7	2.6	3.3

YOUR TURN

Are business cycles out of sync?

The Fisher equation is a long-run or equilibrium relationship between i and π. At potential income (on *EAS*), when the business cycle is in 'neutral', the real interest rate is constant. During a boom inflation rises more than nominal interest rates, and real interest rates fall. During recessions real interest rates rise. Use this information and the data given in the worked problem above to check whether in 1995 your country was in the same phase of the business cycle as the others. The general idea is to find out whether your country's interest rate was significantly higher or lower than the interest rate proposed by the estimated Fisher equation. (Hint: To find out whether Sweden's interest rate is exceptionally high or low, construct a dummy variable that is 1 for Sweden and 0 for all other countries. Then check whether this dummy variable's coefficient is significant.)

To further explore this chapter's key messages you are encouraged to use the interactive online module found at

www.fgn.unisg.ch/eurmacro/tutor/2countryMundellFleming.html

and many other features hosted at **www.fgn.unisg.ch/eurmacro**

CHAPTER 13

INFLATION AND CENTRAL BANK INDEPENDENCE

WHAT TO EXPECT After working through this chapter, you will understand:

1 What can be done in practical terms to reduce a country's inflation bias.
2 What role central bank independence plays (and the EMS played) in improving inflation performance.
3 Why having the most independent central bank, in a country or as the leader in a fixed rate system or currency union, may not be the best choice for a country that expects to be hit by occasional supply shocks.
4 Why Germany and Switzerland lost substantially more income during the 1974 oil price explosion than Britain and France.
5 That disinflation costs are measured by the sacrifice ratio, and how the latter is computed.
6 How much it typically costs to lower inflation by one percentage point, in euros, dollars, francs, pounds or other currencies.
7 What role the Maastricht criteria on interest rates and inflation played on the road to European Monetary Union.

Inflation is a political phenomenon, much less an economic one. From an economic perspective we know how to avoid inflation and how to reduce it. In the short run, outside influences on inflation that escape the control of the policymaker may interfere here. But beyond that, if inflation does not disappear in the medium and long run, it is not because we do not *know how* to get rid of it, but because we do not *want* to get rid of it. However, even the last statement is not quite accurate: we may want to get rid of it, but short-run incentives prevent us from following through.

Key building blocks of the political economy of inflation have already been discussed in Chapter 11. They feature prominently in academic discussions of **European monetary integration**. Both the blueprint for the European Central Bank and the merits of the EMS are mostly evaluated in terms of how they affect **inflation performance**. This chapter picks up the tools provided in Chapter 11 and examines how the institutional setting in which central banks operate affects inflation performance. The interrelationship between *central bank independence*, the *exchange rate system* and inflation will be discussed from a refined theoretical perspective. This perspective will be put to use in a number of case studies and more general attempts to understand real-world experience with inflation and how to fight it.

13.1 INFLATION, CENTRAL BANK INDEPENDENCE AND THE EMS

A major insight developed in Chapter 11 was that a country's average level of inflation may be much higher than the level that society (and the policy-maker) would like. The size of this **inflation bias**, which is caused by the **time inconsistency** of monetary policy, is determined by three factors:

1 The policy-maker's **preferences**, as represented by his or her indifference curves.
2 **Instrument potency**, the discretionary leeway that the policy-maker has in using monetary policy.
3 The **constraint** imposed by the macroeconomy on the policy-maker's choices, in the form of the slope of the *SAS* curve.

Chapter 11 has already discussed these factors. We now move on to look at them in more detail, one at a time, and then proceed to present some empirical implications and confront them with data.

Preferences

In Chapter 11, with regard to preferences, we noted that the *government* is likely to gain more from surprise inflation than the *central bank*. The reason is that, while both institutions may applaud the achieved income gains to the same extent, there are added bonuses that accrue only for the government. The most important one is that surprise inflation *reduces the government's real debt*. Since this reduces interest payments to service old debt, and provides an opening for incurring new debt, extra latitude is provided for government spending. Another bonus is that by making the central bank buy government bonds, thus creating money and inflation, the government can *finance part of its spending*. As a result, the government's indifference curve in inflation–income space is steeper than that of the central bank. Figure 13.1 illustrates this.

Whether actual monetary policy reflects the steep indifference curve of the government or the flat indifference curve of the central bank depends on how much independence the central bank enjoys from the government. This **central bank independence** does not only come in black and white: it is observed along a continuum between the extremes. This means that indifference curves also have many different slopes. They turn flatter as the central bank's independence gradually increases. Hand in hand with this comes a reduction of the inflation bias. The bottom line is that *countries with more independent central banks should feature lower average inflation rates*. Figure 13.2 presents some data on this issue and underlines that the reality conforms quite well with this implication of our model.

Central bank independence measures the extent to which the central bank may conduct monetary policy without having to respond to what the government wants.

It plots average inflation in eighteen countries against a measure of central bank independence. At one extreme, this measure assigns values of 13 and 12

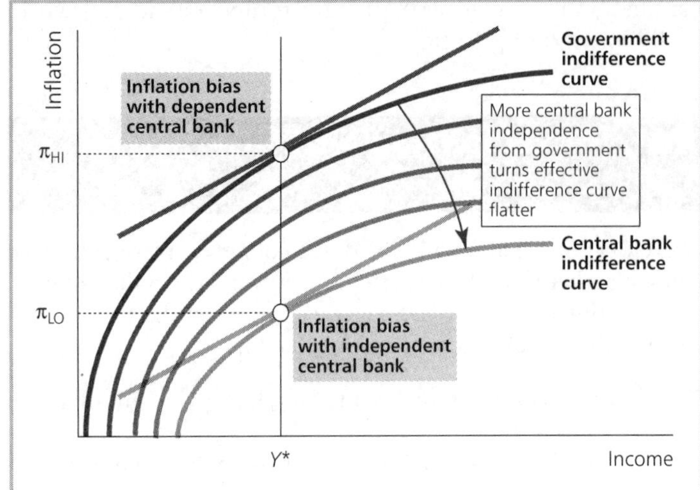

Figure 13.1 Governments benefit from surprise inflation not only because it boosts income, but also because it reduces real government debt. In addition, governments can raise income by creating inflation. This tends to make a government's indifference curve steeper than a central bank's, yielding a higher inflation bias. Making the central bank more independent flattens the effective indifference curve and lowers inflation.

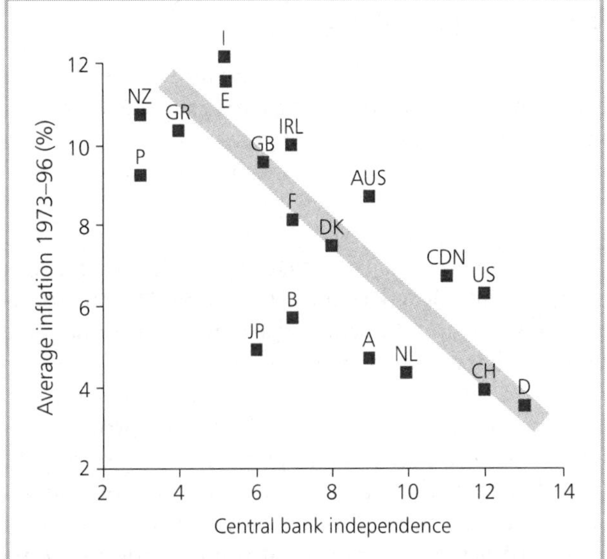

Figure 13.2 The figure shows average inflation between 1973 and 1996 to be negatively correlated with the independence of a country's central bank. *Sources*: IMF, *IFS* – for inflation; and for CBI – V. Grilli, D. Masciandaro and G. Tabellini (1991) 'Political and monetary institutions and public finance policies in the industrial countries', *Economic Policy* 13: 341 – 92.

Empirical note. Some 60% of the differences between the average inflation rates observed in industrial countries is explained by differences in the independence of their central banks.

to the highly independent central banks of Germany and Switzerland. On average these countries experienced inflation rates of about 4% between 1973 and the mid-1990s. At the other extreme, a value of 3 is assigned to the most government-dependent central bank of New Zealand (but see Case Study 13.1!). New Zealand's and other only slightly more independent central banks, like Italy's and Spain's, generated average inflation rates between 10% and 12%. All the other countries with central bank independence between these extreme values also feature inflation rates between the extremes.

In support of our theoretical arguments, the lesson taught by real-world experience appears to be a simple one: in order to permanently enjoy a substantially improved inflation performance, all a country needs to do is rewrite its central bank law. So why do not all countries simply do this? The answer to this question consists of three parts and will occupy us throughout this chapter.

First, a number of countries have indeed taken pertinent steps in recent years. One example comprises EU member states, which were required by the Maastricht Treaty to make their central banks more independent as a move towards EMU. Other countries like Canada, Great Britain and New Zealand have adopted *inflation targets*. As Case Study 13.1 illustrates, this also makes central bank indifference curves flatter at a defined threshold.

CASE STUDY 13.1 New Zealand's Reserve Bank Act: a case from down under

Being fed up with one of the worst inflation performances among industrial countries, in late 1984 New Zealand's incoming government directed the central bank to reduce inflation. After some success in the following years albeit at the cost of rising unemployment, this new objective was formalized in a new Reserve Bank Act in 1989. The Act directs the central bank to focus monetary policy exclusively on achieving and maintaining stability in the general level of prices. This goal is to be specified in a Policy Targets Agreement (PTA) to be negotiated between the minister of finance and the central bank governor who is to be appointed or reappointed.

The first PTA was signed on 2 March 1990. The agreement provided that an inflation rate between 0% and 2% was to be achieved by December 1992. Failure to achieve the goal formulated in the PTA could invoke the dismissal of the governor.

In terms of our standard graph this PTA made the central bank governor's indifference curves virtually horizontal at an inflation rate of 2%. As Figure 1 illustrates, an *SAS* curve now touches a kinked indifference curve on the *EAS* curve at $\pi = 2$. Assuming that control over inflation is not perfect, it is to be expected that the central bank will play it safe by keeping inflation well inside the target zone, around 1%.

Figure 2 illustrates the effect that the new Reserve Bank Act had on inflation. It shows that New Zealand had been on a disinflation path since the mid-1980s. The light blue zone indicates the inflation target range as laid down in the first PTA signed in 1990 and as confirmed or modified in subsequent PTAs agreed upon in the Decembers of 1990, 1992, 1996, 1997 and 1999. The initial target range for price stability of 0–2% was to be achieved by December 1992. When a new government was elected in October 1990, the PTA was renegotiated. And in the light of the Gulf crisis, the deadline for achievement of price stability was extended by twelve months until December 1993. The central bank achieved the target well ahead of this deadline – but missed it completely in 1994, 1995 and 1996. The answer to why Reserve Bank

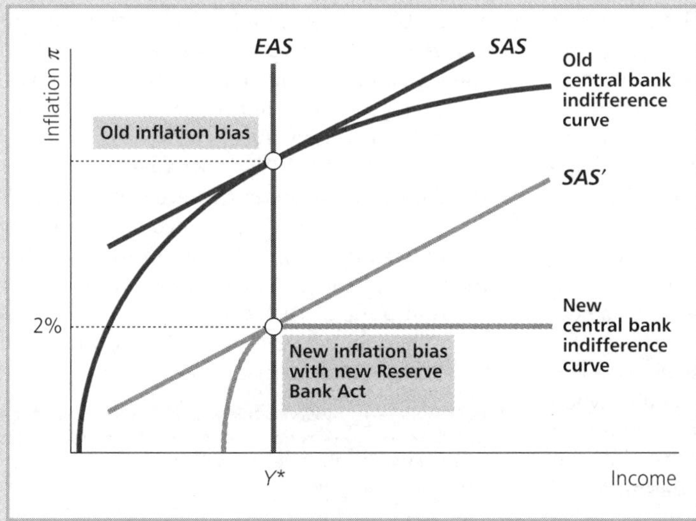

Figure 1

Case study 13.1 continued

Figure 2
Source: IMF, IFS

governor Donald T. Brash is still in office sheds some light on the practical problems with inflation targets, and reveals some rather amusing semantics.

From the beginning, the central bank questioned whether consumer price inflation (which is shown in Figure 2 and is called 'headline inflation') was really the appropriate measure of inflation performance. Instead, it eventually succeeded in having inflation performance gauged by a new rate called 'underlying inflation' which ignores inflation in certain sectors or categories and is typically lower than consumer price inflation. The Reserve Bank Act permits such loopholes. Others are that the price stability target may be renegotiated if indirect taxes change, if the terms of trade change significantly, or after a domestic crisis such as a natural disaster. What is more, the government may always order the central bank to change the inflation target, but must do so publicly and discuss reasons in parliament.

When even with this adjusted inflation rate the target was still missed in 1994, 1995 and 1996, the next PTA, signed in December 1996 featured a new definition of price stability including the 0–3% range of inflation. After some successful years this new target was missed again in 2000, when December prices were 4% higher than those in 1999. However, Dr Brash is still in office, and it remains to be seen what the next definition of price stability will be.

Another interesting aspect is how not only the definition of price stability evolved through successive PTAs, but also its weight and relation to other macroeconomic goals. In the 1990 and 1992 contracts, price stability was the only goal the Reserve Bank had to pursue. Nothing else existed. The PTA said that it should 'implement monetary policy with the intention of achieving/maintaining a stable general level of prices'.

The 1996 and 1997 contracts recognized that other macroeconomic goals existed by speaking of 'maintaining a stable general level of prices, so that monetary policy can make its maximum contribution to sustainable economic growth, employment and development opportunities within the New Zealand economy'. The implication is that, yes, these other goals exist, but we serve them best by maintaining price stability.

The December 1999 PTA goes one step further by stipulating: 'In pursuing its price stability objective, the Bank ... shall seek to avoid unnecessary instability in output, interest rates and the exchange rate.' This brings further macroeconomic variables into the picture and cautions the Reserve Bank to keep an active eye on the short-run side effects of monetary policy on these.

Further reading: The Reserve Bank of New Zealand homepage at www.rbnz.govt.nz provides much more information on this experience including the full-length PTAs.

Second, a perfect inflation performance brought about by a completely independent central bank comes with a price tag that scares some governments away. We will look at this in section 13.2, where we permit the economy to be hit by occasional *shocks to aggregate supply*.

Third, the transition from a high-inflation equilibrium to a low-inflation equilibrium may be accompanied by income losses and thus be quite painful. Section 13.3 looks into these *disinflation costs*.

Instrument potency

Instrument potency, the policy-maker's control over the money supply, may be removed in one of two ways.

Monetary policy may be required by law (or, as some have demanded, by the constitution) to follow a specific rule that simply leaves no room for discretion. This rule may come in the form of a **fixed rule** that specifies, say, 3% for annual money growth. We mentioned in Chapter 11 that Nobel laureate Milton Friedman had long advocated this type of rule. Alternatively, a **contingent rule** could make money growth dependent on the state of the economy. An example of such a contingent rule would be $\mu = Y^* - Y$, stating that if income Y falls short of equilibrium income Y^* by x units, money supply growth μ must equal x% also. While the optimal nature of such rules are discussed quite seriously in academic journals and empirical studies often find that the **Taylor rule** seems to predict monetary policy quite well, no country seems to have taken any pertinent steps yet to implement such a rule formally.

The **Taylor rule** reads $i = i^{\text{target}} + 0.5\,(\pi - \pi^{\text{target}}) + 0.5(y - y^*)$

A second way to deprive the domestic policy-maker of monetary instrument potency is by **pegging the currency** to some foreign currency, thus virtually handing monetary policy over to the foreign central bank. These days many countries endorse this option. It can, in fact, be done without the consent of the other country. According to the International Monetary Fund (IMF), in 2001 only 84 out of 184 countries covered had not pegged their currency in one form or other to one or more foreign currencies. And only 47 of those were committed to market-determined, flexible exchange rates. Out of those 47 countries (which include only Poland, Sweden, Switzerland, the UK and Turkey from Europe) many still intervened in the foreign exchanges on occasion in order to prevent undue fluctuations. The remaining 100 countries on which the IMF reports, seriously limited exchange rate movement by arrangements from a spectrum of possibilities that reach from the outright adoption of a foreign currency via a **currency board** to **crawling pegs**.

A **currency board** fixes a country's exchange rate and maintains total backing of its money supply with foreign exchange. Example: in Bosnia-Herzegovina 1 konvertibilna marka equals €0.51. Its central bank can only increase the money supply if the private sector is prepared to sell euros.

Under a **crawling peg** the exchange rate is adjusted periodically in small, preannounced steps.

A prominent European example of pegging the exchange rate is the European Monetary System. It played a major role from 1979 onwards as a forerunner to EMU, and its second version, EMS II, is designed to facilitate the monetary integration of new entrants into the European Union and EMU. To learn from this experience, we will now take a closer look at how inflation is determined in such a multi-currency system and then bring together the obtained insights with the involved countries' inflation performance.

Travelling back in time to the pre-euro era, suppose two economies, Germany and Italy, are evaluating plans to form a currency union. The motivation is that, instead of making its own central bank more independent, Italy may hand monetary policy over to the very independent Bundesbank, and thus be rewarded with the lower German inflation bias. Germany would keep the same inflation as before and does not seem to gain anything. It is therefore hard to see Germany's motivation for getting involved in such a currency union and assuming the role of the *n*th country. This becomes even more puzzling if we look at how the exchange rate system affects the constraint, the *SAS* curve.

The constraint

When a country moves from flexible to fixed exchange rates, its *SAS* curve becomes flatter when drawn onto a π-Y diagram. To acquire an intuitive understanding of this, we need to distinguish between consumer prices and producer prices.

The **consumer price index** measures the price of a fixed basket of consumption goods, part of which is produced domestically, and part of which is imported. The **producer price index** measures the average price of goods and services produced domestically.

The **consumer price index** measures how much a typical 'basket of consumption goods' costs in a particular country. This basket comprises goods produced at home and goods produced abroad. Consumer price inflation affects the buying power of nominal income. It is therefore the relevant inflation rate in the public support function. The **producer price index** measures how much producers receive for the goods and services produced at home. Only as producer prices inflate unexpectedly will output and income rise. Producer price inflation is the relevant inflation rate in the *SAS* curve.

As shown in Box 13.1, in a two-country world with Germany and Italy, consumer price inflation is a weighted average of the inflation of goods produced in Germany π_D and of goods produced in Italy π_I. The latter we must transfer into Deutschmarks, so we must add the rate of depreciation ε. This yields

$$\pi = \alpha\pi_D + (1-\alpha)\varepsilon + (1-\alpha)\pi_I \qquad \textbf{Index of consumer price inflation}$$

where α is the share of home-produced goods in the German consumption basket.

Under fixed exchange rates a surprise increase of German consumer price inflation π, say, from 0% to 10%, increases both the price of goods produced in Germany (which we assume to possess the *n*th currency) and of Italian goods by $\pi_D = \pi_I = 10\%$; $\varepsilon = 0$ by definition. If exchange rates are flexible, the same German consumer price inflation leads to a smaller change of German producer prices of, say, $\pi_D = 5\%$. The reason is the depreciation of the real exchange rate, which requires the nominal exchange rate to rise by 15%, if we suppose $\alpha = 0.5$. But since only the 5% increase of home-produced goods induces producers to raise output, the output increase will be smaller than under fixed exchange rates, when home goods prices rose by 10%. As a result, *the SAS curve is steeper under flexible exchange rates.* This effect is more pronounced if the economy is more open, that is if α is smaller. Then the share of foreign goods in the domestic price index becomes larger, and *exchange rate overshooting* drives an even larger wedge between π and π_D.

Figure 13.3 summarizes the effect of institutional factors on the slope of the *SAS* curve.

We are now equipped to discuss the stylized choices facing Germany and Italy. These are sketched in Figure 13.4.

If Germany and Italy fix the exchange rate and Italy provides the currency anchor (the *n*th currency), the system's inflation bias is π_{IEMS}. This would

BOX 13.1 The *SAS* curve under fixed and flexible exchange rates

Let the world consist of Germany and Italy only when both still had their national currencies. German consumers purchase a basket of goods containing a share α of goods produced in Germany and a share $1-\alpha$ of goods produced in Italy. If the prices of these goods are P_D and P_I respectively, the German price index is $P = P_D^{\alpha}(EP_I)^{1-\alpha}$. The lira prices of goods produced in Italy need to be multiplied by the DM/lira exchange rate to obtain their equivalent in marks. Taking logarithms of the price index equation and then taking first differences twice we obtain the following equation (in percentage rates of change):

$$\Delta\pi = \alpha\Delta\pi_D + (1-\alpha)\Delta\varepsilon + (1-\alpha)\Delta\pi_I$$

Fixed exchange rate

Fixing the exchange rate eliminates the middle term on the right-hand side ($\Delta\varepsilon = 0$). Any change in German consumer price inflation is now a weighted average of the domestic inflations of German and Italian goods:

$$\Delta\pi = \alpha\Delta\pi_D + (1-\alpha)\Delta\pi_I \qquad (1)$$

The control of the Bundesbank over both countries' money supplies makes both economies function (on the aggregate level) like one economy. But then $\Delta\pi_D = \Delta\pi_I$. Substituting this into equation (1) gives

$$\Delta\pi = \Delta\pi_D$$

An increase in consumer price inflation by 10 percentage points goes hand in hand with a 10 percentage points increase in producer price inflation. This raises output by 10% as well if *SAS* has slope 1.

Flexible exchange rate

Under flexible exchange rates the Banca d'Italia operates independently, isolating Italian producer prices from Bundesbank policy (for ease of exposition, suppose $\Delta\pi_I = 0$). Any change in German consumer price inflation is now a weighted average of changes in German producer price inflation and exchange rate depreciation:

$$\Delta\pi = \alpha\Delta\pi_D + (1-\alpha)\Delta\varepsilon \qquad (2)$$

Recall from Chapter 8 that when prices are sticky – which is what a positively sloped *SAS* curve indicates – the real exchange rate depreciates as we move up *SAS*. In other words, the initial exchange rate response is larger than the initial response in producer prices:

$$\Delta\varepsilon > \Delta\pi_D$$

Substituting this inequality into equation (10.2) gives

$$\Delta\pi > \Delta\pi_D$$

So when the Bundesbank generates surprise inflation, the initial effect on consumer prices is larger than the initial effect on producer prices. Raising π by 10% raises π_D by less than 10%. Hence output is raised by less than 10% as well. As a result, a steeper *SAS* curve obtains under flexible exchange rates.

Equation (2) suggests that flexible exchange rates make *SAS* steeper, the more open the economy (as measured by α) is.

make both countries worse off. If Germany provides the anchor, the systems bias is lower at π_{DEMS}. Now Italy gains in the form of a large reduction of its average rate of inflation. Germany's inflation performance deteriorates, though probably by much less than Italy's performance improves. In any case, Germany is probably only prepared to pay this price if Italy offers concessions in other areas.

Figure 13.4 displays only asymmetric solutions, in the sense that one country sets or dominates monetary policy in the system. Alternatively, and this is the vision that the founders of the EMS put on paper, a system could be symmetric. The member states were supposed to cooperate and share the burden of adjustment to a common policy. In terms of Figure 13.4, such a symmetric system would produce an inflation rate higher than that obtained

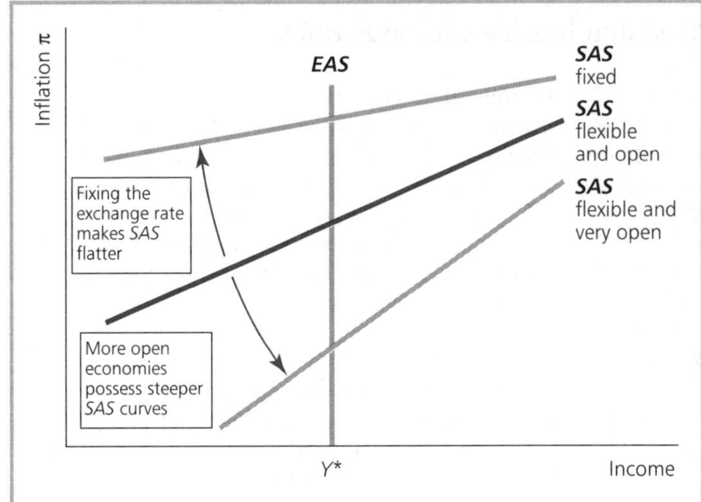

Figure 13.3 A country with flexible exchange rates has moderately sloped *SAS* surves, such as the dark blue one if it fixes the reexchange rate, and assumes the role of the *n*th currency. *SAS* curves become flatter. If exchange rates are flexible and the economy becomes more open, the *SAS* curves become steeper.

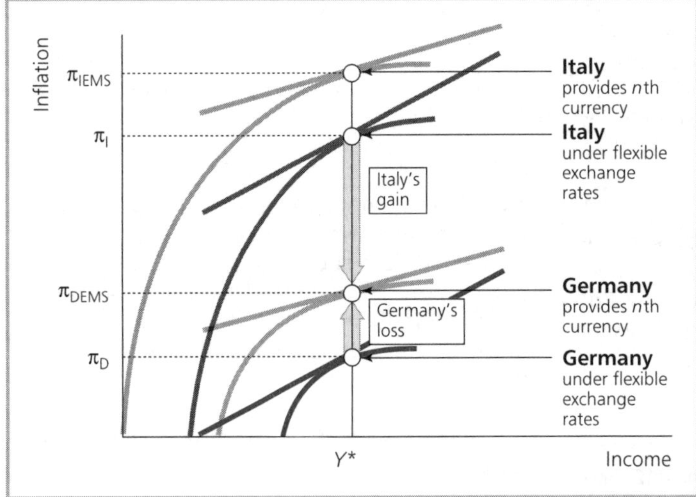

Figure 13.4 *SAS* curves are steeper under flexible exchange rates (dark lines) than under fixed ones (lighter lines). Germany's (Italy's) inflation bias is π_D (π_I) when rates are flexible and π_{DEMS} (π_{IEMS}) when rates are fixed. If the lira becomes the *n*th currency in the EMS, both countries' inflation performance deteriorates to π_{IEMS}. If the mark becomes the *n*th currency, Germany's performance deteriorates, but Italy's improves.

under German leadership. As measured by average inflation, this would make both Germany and Italy worse off. It does not come as a surprise, therefore, that the member states eventually put their own spin on the EMS blueprint, implicitly agreeing on an asymmetric solution that, at least at that time, was considered beneficial to all participants.

A currency union between two countries is obviously only feasible if the inflation bias of the high inflation country under flexible exchange rates is higher than the inflation bias that the low inflation country is likely to produce under fixed exchange rates. For this to be the case, preferences must differ substantially. This provides a simple explanation for the fact that Switzerland had much less interest in entering the EMS than, say, Ireland or Italy.

A quick transition from the high inflation equilibrium of the country that abandons monetary autonomy to the *n*th currency's low inflation equilibrium can only be expected in the ideal case of an irrevocably fixed exchange rate. Target zones, as the ±6% band operational for the lira until 1990, provided some temporary leeway. Resorting to occasional realignments even provided a permanent one. Figure 13.5 may help to judge the EMS's success in bringing down inflation. The light blue band area shows the spread in the inflation rates in the founding members of the EMS between 1980 and 1995. This spread has systematically narrowed and moved closer to a virtually unchanged lower limit. In addition to the spread, inflation in six countries is highlighted. One is Germany, which has formed or been near the lower limit throughout. Three others are Portugal, Spain and the United Kingdom, which joined the EMS at a later stage. Their inflation performance is shown beginning with the year in which they joined. Another is Italy, which was a founding member. Its inflation rate is shown from 1992, the year in which it suspended membership in the EMS. Finally, Greek inflation is shown for contrast, to exemplify inflation outside the EMS.

The graph conveys these messages, all of which are in line with the theoretical propositions discussed above:

1 Inflation in the countries that launched the EMS in 1979 had converged toward its lower end. The lower end has mostly been provided by German inflation. This suggests that the Deutschmark was the *n*th currency, a role carved out by mutual consent among the partners.
2 Countries that joined the EMS at a later date saw their inflation rates, if not within the band already, being sucked into or onto the narrowing band of the initial members.

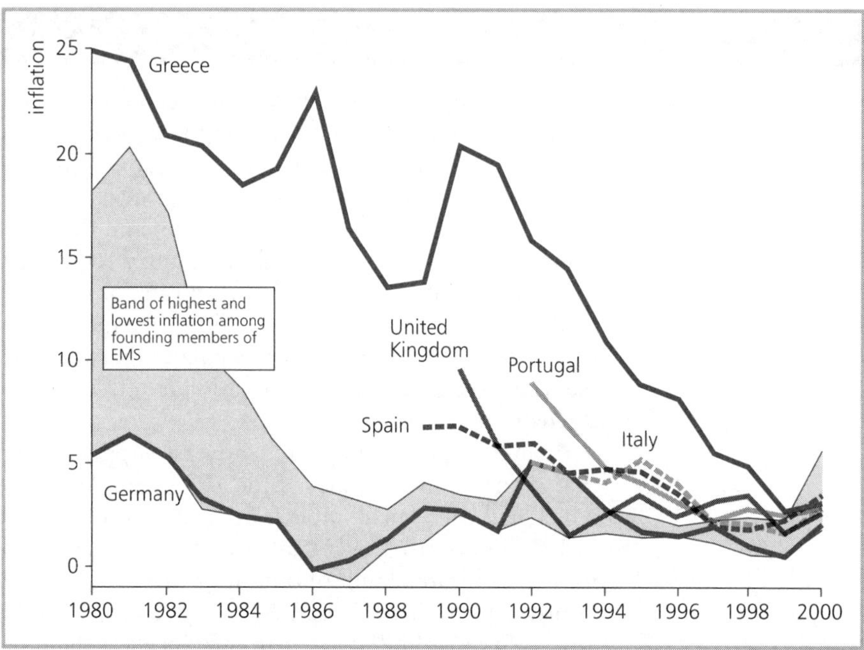

Figure 13.5 The graph shows that inflation rates of the founding members that remained in the EMS have converged (blue band). The inflation rates of Portugal, Spain and the United Kingdom were also drawn onto or into the band after they joined the EMS. This is not observed for Greece, which is the only EU member to not join the EMS before the turn of the millenium. Italy and the United Kingdom drifted out of the band for a while after 1992.
Source: IMF, *IFS*.

3 Countries that suspended membership in the EMS – Britain and Italy did so on 16 September 1992 – found their inflation rates drifting out of the EMS band, if only temporarily so.

A puzzling observation, though, is Ireland's inflation rate of 5.4% in 2000, quite visibly higher than those of other Euroland members. It will be interesting to see how this develops in the years to come. Our model certainly suggests that this cannot last.

Bottom line

From the perspective of price stability the best thing a country can do is one of the following:

1 bind its central bank by a zero inflation rule;
2 appoint the most conservative (that is, inflation-averse) central banker possible;
3 make its central banker as independent from the government as possible; or
4 peg the exchange rate to the currency of a country with one or more of the above features.

It appears that a central bank can never be too conservative, and is never independent enough. The next section puts this result in perspective. In a world in which unexpected things happen all the time, a central bank may indeed be too independent.

13.2 SUPPLY SHOCKS AND CENTRAL BANK INDEPENDENCE

So far we have discussed the political economy of inflation in an environment with no uncertainty. But what happens if outside events, beyond the direct control of the policy-maker, hit the economy unexpectedly? Due to their surprise nature, such events cannot be built into recent wage contracts. Thus they are bound to displace the labour market and the entire economy from equilibrium. In such a situation, might a country regret having a central bank committed (by a rule, by virtue of a fixed rate, or because of its preferences) to the goal of price stability only? Wouldn't it be nice, at least in such a situation, to have a central bank that strikes a balance between the income (and unemployment) consequences and the inflationary effects of such a shock? This section discusses these issues.

An archetypal example of an adverse supply shock is the oil price explosion that occurred in the wake of the 1973 Middle East crisis. By 1974 oil prices, which had been fairly stable for decades, were more than four times as high as in 1973. Since rising oil or other materials prices push up the production costs for each additional unit of output produced, firms will scale down production in order not to incur losses. At any given price level, and in a given period at any given rate of inflation, firms produce less than they did before the increase in oil prices. So the quadrupling of oil prices pushed the *SAS* curve to the left. (If the price increase is permanent it might also shift the *EAS* curve. We need not consider this here since we are are only looking at the short-run effects and choices.) The post-shock aggregate supply curve displays the central bank's options (see Figure 13.6).

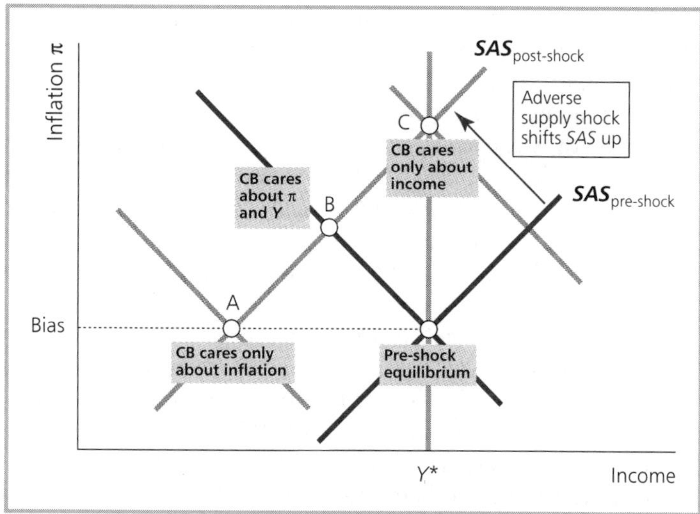

Figure 13.6 The economy starts from the indicated pre-shock equilibrium. An adverse shock to aggregate supply, such as an increase of oil prices, shifts the *SAS* curve left. If money growth remains unchanged, the economy moves to B. A central bank (CB) that only cares about inflation reduces money growth to obtain A. A central bank that does not want income to fall raises money growth to obtain C.

A neutral option is to keep money growth unchanged. This leaves *DAD* in its old position and moves the economy up *DAD* to point B, thus splitting the repercussions of the shock into an effect on income and an effect on inflation. Instead, a so-called *hard-nosed* central bank with extreme inflation aversion would permit no inflation. By topping the negative supply shock with a reduction of money growth *DAD* moves down, causing a large recession at point A. Finally, a so-called *wet* central bank would accept no decrease of income. It accommodates the negative supply shock with an acceleration of money growth. This moves *DAD* up, keeping income unchanged at the cost of substantial inflation at point C.

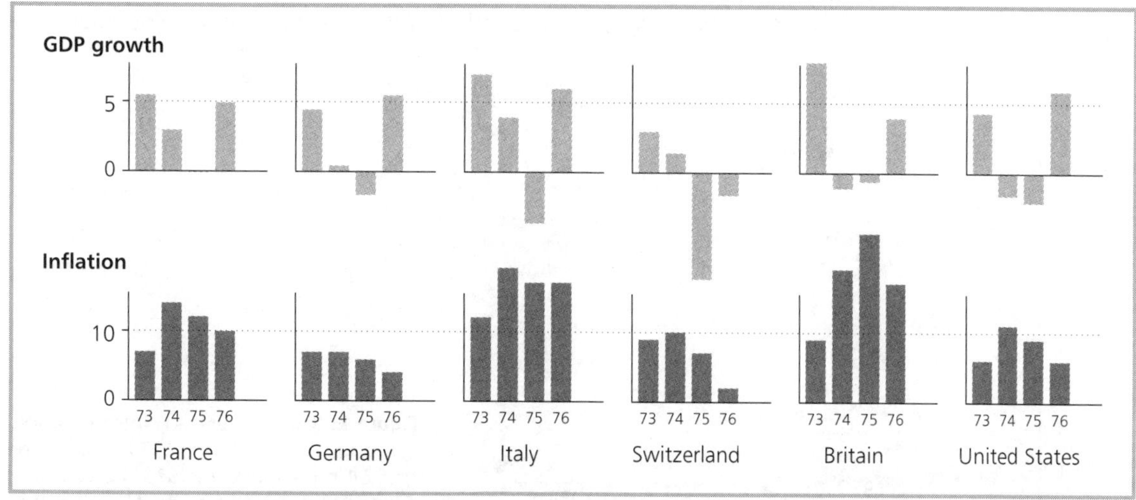

Figure 13.7 The figure shows income growth and inflation at the time of the 1974 oil price explosion in six countries. While France, Italy and Britain permitted inflation to rise substantially and permanently, the other three countries did not. (Germany and Switzerland even came out of the shock with lower inflation than they had before.) It appears as if the first three countries prevented growth from falling as much as it did in the other three.
Source: IMF, *IFS*.

Figure 13.7 shows the income and inflation responses to the 1974 shock in six industrial countries. Response patterns are similar in many respects. In 1974 and 1975 all income growth rates were substantially below previous experience. This is what happens in a growing economy if we move to the left of Y^*. In most cases growth was even negative. Finally, with the exception of Switzerland, growth was back to normal by 1976. Inflation experience is a bit more diverse. While most countries apparently accommodated the oil price shock by allowing inflation to increase dramatically, Germany and Switzerland kept a lid on inflation and even ended up with lower inflation after the shock.

Figure 13.8 combines the six countries' income and inflation experiences into a standardized π-Y diagram. For easier comparability, all countries are given a common point of departure for 1973. The vertical axis then measures by how much inflation *changed* in each country from 1973 to 1975. The horizontal axis measures the difference between actual and potential income in 1975.

The countries' positions relative to their situations in 1973 indicate a positively sloped line. In accord with the *DAD-SAS* model, those countries that permitted the smallest increase in inflation experienced the most severe income losses. Even more interestingly from the perspective of this chapter, the six countries' choices are readily explained by reference to the degree of independence of their central banks. The most independent central banks of Germany and Switzerland drove inflation even further down during the crisis, accepting the largest recessions. A small inflation rise was tolerated by the US Federal Reserve System, which is considered slightly less independent than the Bundesbank and the Swiss National Bank. Higher inflation was generated by the decidedly more government-dependent central banks of France, Italy and Britain, thus achieving a much smaller recession.

It is quite possible that the Germans and the Swiss would have benefited from having a less hard-nosed central bank in this extraordinary situation, one that would have permitted some inflation just this once. But if you have such

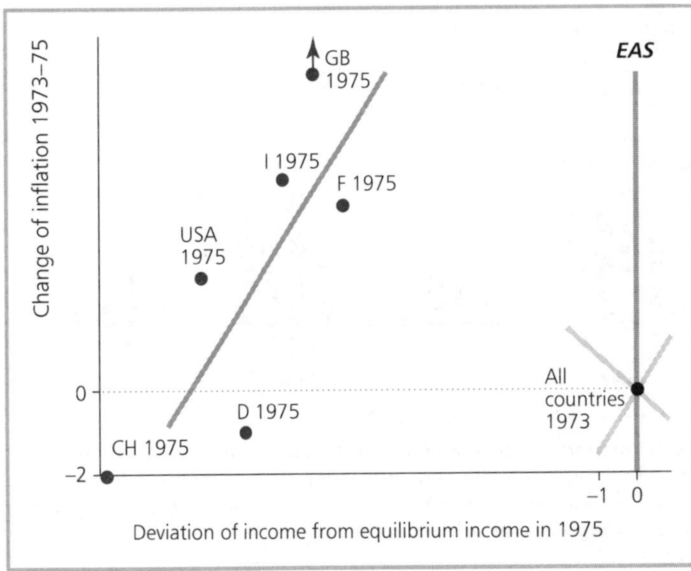

Figure 13.8 In a stylized interpretation, countries were on *EAS* in 1973, prior to the first oil price shock. In 1975 the countries were in the positions marked by blue dots. Shades of *SAS* and *DAD* curves insinuate an interpretation of the six countries' choices in the context of the theoretical framework given in Figure 13.6.
Source: IMF, *IFS*.

a government-dependent central bank when a shock hits, you also have it when there are no shocks. That means you also have a higher inflation bias generally. So one must balance these two effects. The choice is affected by how frequently shocks hit the economy. The more often they hit, the more we would like the central bank to take proper care of it. But if we expect shocks to hit frequently and the central bank to respond with inflation, this again affects the inflation bias and may render stimulation ineffective when a shock hits. So the choice is obviously a complicated one and we need to go back to the drawing board and work out the theoretical argument with proper care.

As a first step we need to consider the preferences of voters, governments and central banks. Until now we had assumed that higher income was *always* preferred to lower income. One might question the generality of this assertion for the following reason.

Let the economy be at full employment output $Y^*_{\text{classical}}$ as carved out by a perfect labour market. Then surprise inflation could make income rise still further along the *SAS* curve, but only by making people work at real wages at which they actually would have preferred not to work. This makes income increases beyond $Y^*_{\text{classical}}$ undesirable. So we may suppose the preference functions of the government, the public and the central bank to be of the general form (where Y^{d} stands for desirable income which is identical to $Y^*_{\text{classical}}$):

$$s = \bar{s} - \tfrac{1}{2}\pi^2 - \tfrac{1}{2}\beta(Y - Y^{\text{d}})^2$$

This new formulation stresses that public support for the government (or central bank utility) falls at an accelerating rate as either of two bads increases: inflation or the deviation of output from the desired full employment level. Indifference curves in this slightly more complex case are ellipse shaped around the most preferred point $\pi = 0$ and $Y = Y^{\text{d}}$ as shown in Figure 13.9. In the area to the left of desired income Y^{d} indifference curves look much the same as those employed in Chapter 11. Only as we move to the right of Y^{d} do things change. As long as the kind of real rigidities discussed in Chapter 6 keep potential income Y^* *below* desired income Y^{d}, all our insights obtained with the simpler preference function in Chapter 11 continue to apply.

Note a difference in the **government reaction function**, however. This function was horizontal in Chapter 11, meaning that the government would always respond with the same inflation rate once expectations had been formed. With our new refined preference function, the government reaction curve is negatively sloped, as Figure 13.9 illustrates. The economic rationale is that further income gains become successively less tempting as we move closer to desired income. Once desired income is reached, no further increases are desired, and no price in the form of inflation will be paid. As long as $Y^* < Y^{\text{d}}$, however, an inflation bias obtains in equilibrium (which is where the government reaction function intersects *EAS*).

Now suppose that the government's and the public's preferences are identical and may be represented by the ellipses in Figure 13.9. By handing monetary policy over to an *independent central banker with ultra-conservative preferences*, this country has eliminated inflation. Let the central banker's preferences be so flat that they permit no trade-off of inflation for more income. This central banker chooses zero inflation, which is the optimal equilibrium choice from society's viewpoint.

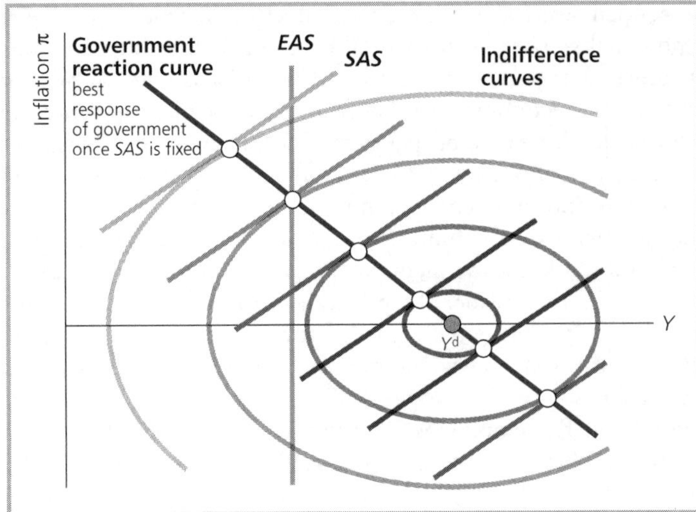

Figure 13.9 If the public prefers higher income only up to a point Y^d, iso-support curves are ellipse shaped, with $\pi = 0$ and $Y = Y^d$ at their centre. For any given *SAS* curve, optimal inflation is given by the point where *SAS* touches an indifference curve. Connecting these points gives a falling government reaction curve. Flatter ellipses, reflecting more concern for inflation, yield flatter reaction curves.

Now let the country be hit by a negative supply shock that shifts the *SAS* curve to the left (see Figure 13.10, which replicates the scenario of Figure 13.6). Since the central banker's overriding goal is to keep inflation at zero, his or her reaction is to reduce the money supply, shift down the aggregate demand curve, driving income down to point A. This is not society's preferred reaction, however. The public's preferences would have been served best by moving up along the *SAS* curve to B, the point of tangency with its own indifference curve. In this way the supply shock would have created a smaller recession at the cost of some inflation. So in this one instance the public would have been better off with a not-so-independent (or less conservative) central bank.

It would be premature to generalize from this example that central banks should not be too independent after all. If this kind of shock occurs frequently, the labour market would build the anticipated reaction of the not-so-

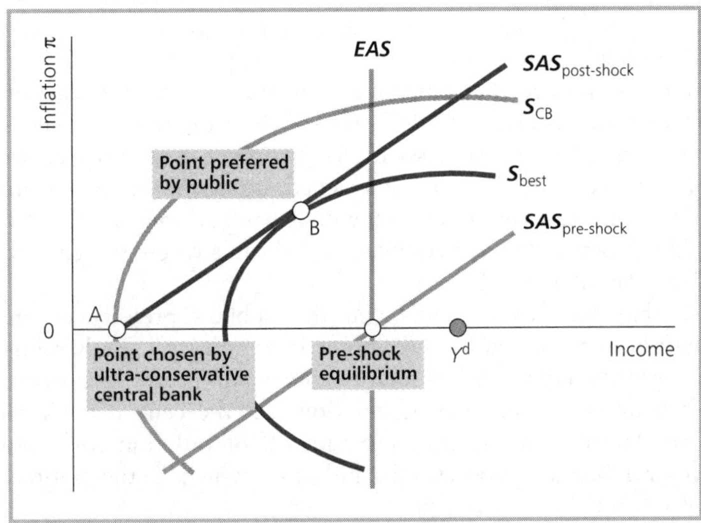

Figure 13.10 An adverse supply shock shifts *SAS* to the post-shock position. An ultra-conservative CB permits no inflation and steers the economy into point A. This gives the public the utility level S_{CB}. Less conservative choices further up on the post-shock *SAS* curve would have put society on higher utility levels. The best point would have been B.

independent central bank into inflation expectations, shifting the *SAS* curve upwards. The result would be a not-so-favourable trade-off.

To arrive at a more general result, we need to make some assumptions about how often supply shocks occur. Let the *SAS* curve have slope 1 and be affected by a shock σ:

$$\pi = \pi^e + Y - Y^* - \sigma \qquad \textbf{Stochastic } \textit{SAS} \textbf{ curve}$$

Suppose σ has a value of 1 in one-third of the cases, a value of -1 in one-third of the cases, or else a value of 0. As Figure 13.11 shows, shocks move the equilibrium aggregate supply curve with equal probability of 1/3 into one of three positions: EAS_+ at $Y^* + 1$, EAS_0 at Y^*, or EAS_- at $Y^* - 1$. An ultra-conservative central bank with very flat indifference curves that approximate horizontal lines does not permit inflation in each of the three cases and steers the economy into one of the three white points given in the graph. Obviously, no inflation bias results. Supply shocks transmit into income shocks to their fullest extent.

Now let the government hire a slightly less conservative central banker who has some concern for income fluctuations. Let her reaction function be given by the negatively sloped blue line. This line is steeper than the horizontal reaction function of the ultra-conservative central bank (that coincides with the abscissa), but less steep than the government's own (or society's) reaction function. Since shocks have an expected value of zero $((1 + 0 - 1)/3 = 0)$, it is rational to expect no shock to occur. Then the rational expectation is given by the intersection between the EAS_0 curve and the central bank's reaction line. This is also the inflation bias of the new moderately conservative central banker. But then the *SAS* curves in the case of a positive or a negative shock also reflect this bias. Instead of being moved into SAS_-, SAS_0 and SAS_+ by a negative shock, no shock and a positive shock, respectively, supply curves are higher at SAS'_-, SAS'_0 or SAS'_+. In the case of a negative shock, inflation is driven along SAS'_- above expected inflation to reduce the recession (point B′).

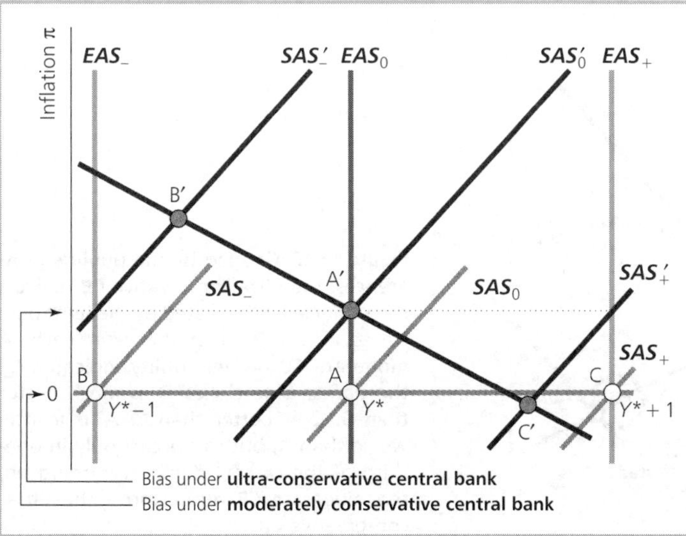

Figure 13.11 Shocks put potential income to Y^*, $Y^* + 1$ and $Y^* - 1$, each in one-third of all cases. The ultra-conservative CB never permits inflation, which puts the economy into points A, B or C. The moderately conservative CB's reaction function slopes down to the right (blue line). Its average inflation rate (or bias) puts *SAS* curves up (dark blue lines). Optimal responses in the three possible cases are A′, B′ and C′, respectively.

In the case of a positive shock, inflation is driven unexpectedly low along SAS'_{+}, to dampen the boom (point C′).

How does the performance of the moderately conservative central bank compare with the performance of the ultra-conservative central bank? To see this we repeat the choices of both banks in Figure 13.12. This time we add the (steeper!) indifference curves of the government (or the public), but move the underlying *SAS* curves into the background in order not to overcrowd the graph.

The following results obtain:

1 If no shock occurs, the ultra-conservative central bank chooses A, the less conservative one chooses A′. In terms of society's preferences, A is slightly better than A′ from the perception of the government and the public.
2 If a negative shock occurs, the two central banks choose B and B′. Here the not-so-conservative central bank's choice is clearly superior.
3 In the case of a positive shock the points to compare are C and C′. Again, the less conservative choice is clearly superior.

Since all three situations occur with equal probability, the combined results produced by the less independent central bank are preferred to the no-inflation results produced by the ultra-conservative central bank.

Pegging the exchange rate

The above arguments also apply to the choice of an anchor currency in an exchange rate system. There also, a central bank may be too conservative as the issuer of the *n*th currency to perform optimally in a world with uncertainty.

A further complication arises here if member states are not exposed to the same kinds of shocks. If the anchor country is hit by a shock while the other countries are not, and its central bank responds as seems appropriate from a domestic perspective, the other countries are unnecessarily displaced from

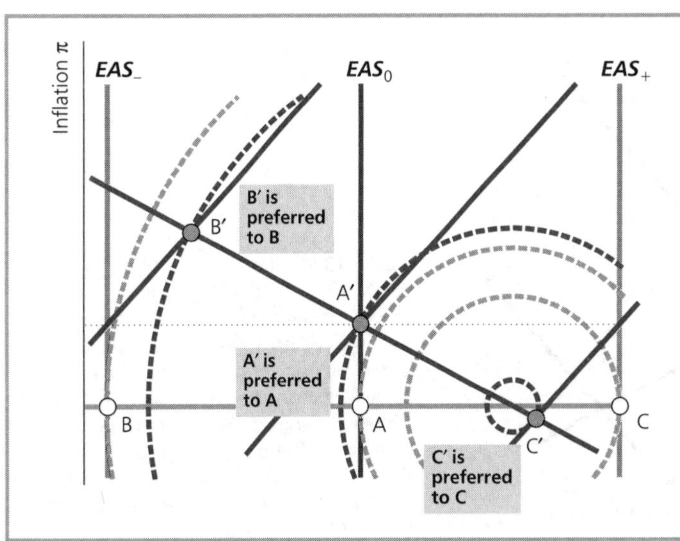

Figure 13.12 Gauged by the public's preferences, the ultra-conservative CB delivers the utility levels indicated by the light blue circles in one-third of the cases each. A moderate CB delivers utility indicated by the darker blue circles. B′ is much better than B. C′ is better than C. A′ is a little worse than A, but this occurs only in one-third of the cases. Adding everything up, the moderate CB outperforms the ultra-conservative CB.

their current equilibrium situations. The German unification shock and its repercussions on the other EMS members, discussed in Chapter 12, offers one such example on a rather grand scale. Another big one is the effect of the Vietnam war on fiscal and monetary policy in the United States, and the consequences transmitted by the Bretton Woods system onto many other countries.

Alternatively, one or more other members of the fixed exchange rate system may be subjected to a shock while the anchor country is not. In this case the concerned countries are unlikely to get the response they wish from the anchor country's central bank.

13.3 DISINFLATIONS AND THE SACRIFICE RATIO

So far we have been concerned with the average inflation performance of a country. This made us think about important issues. Now it is time to note that while average inflation rates can be readily understood in terms of the institutional factors discussed above, they are only one side of the coin. No country in the world has experienced an approximately steady level or path of inflation. Rather, inflation rates seem to exhibit systematic upward and downward movements that cannot be attributed to random shocks to the *DAD* and *SAS* curves of our model. Figure 13.13 shows a wide range of inflation experiences over the last forty years that support this interpretation.

If the occasional surges in inflation documented in the graphs are not to give rise to higher and higher inflation, they must be reversed by means of restrictive monetary policy. It is an important issue how such **disinflations** are to be engineered in order to minimize the accompanying **disinflation costs.** We will now look at disinflations and disinflation costs: first from a theoretical perspective, in the context of the *DAD-SAS* model; then from an empirical perspective that draws on real-world data and a case study.

Disinflation and its costs in the *DAD-SAS* model

What do we mean by disinflation costs? Consider a country that decides to cut money growth, and thus eventually inflation, in half. From what we learned in Chapter 8 about inflation and income dynamics in the *DAD-SAS* model, the income losses accompanying this disinflation depend on two factors: the *speed at which inflation expectations are reduced*, as indicated by the downward shift of the *SAS* curve; and the *flexibility of nominal wages*, as indicated by the slope of the *SAS* curve. Figure 13.14 looks at the first factor.

Starting from point A, suppose that the central bank *announces* in period 0 that it plans to halve money growth in period 1. What happens to income (and inflation) in period 1 depends on the responsiveness of inflation expectations to (or the credibility of) this announcement. Consider three stylized cases:

- If the labour market does not believe the disinflation announcement, *SAS* stays in SAS_{AE} and the economy moves to point B. Some inflation reduction is achieved, but there is also a large fall in income. The income loss per achieved reduction in inflation is high.

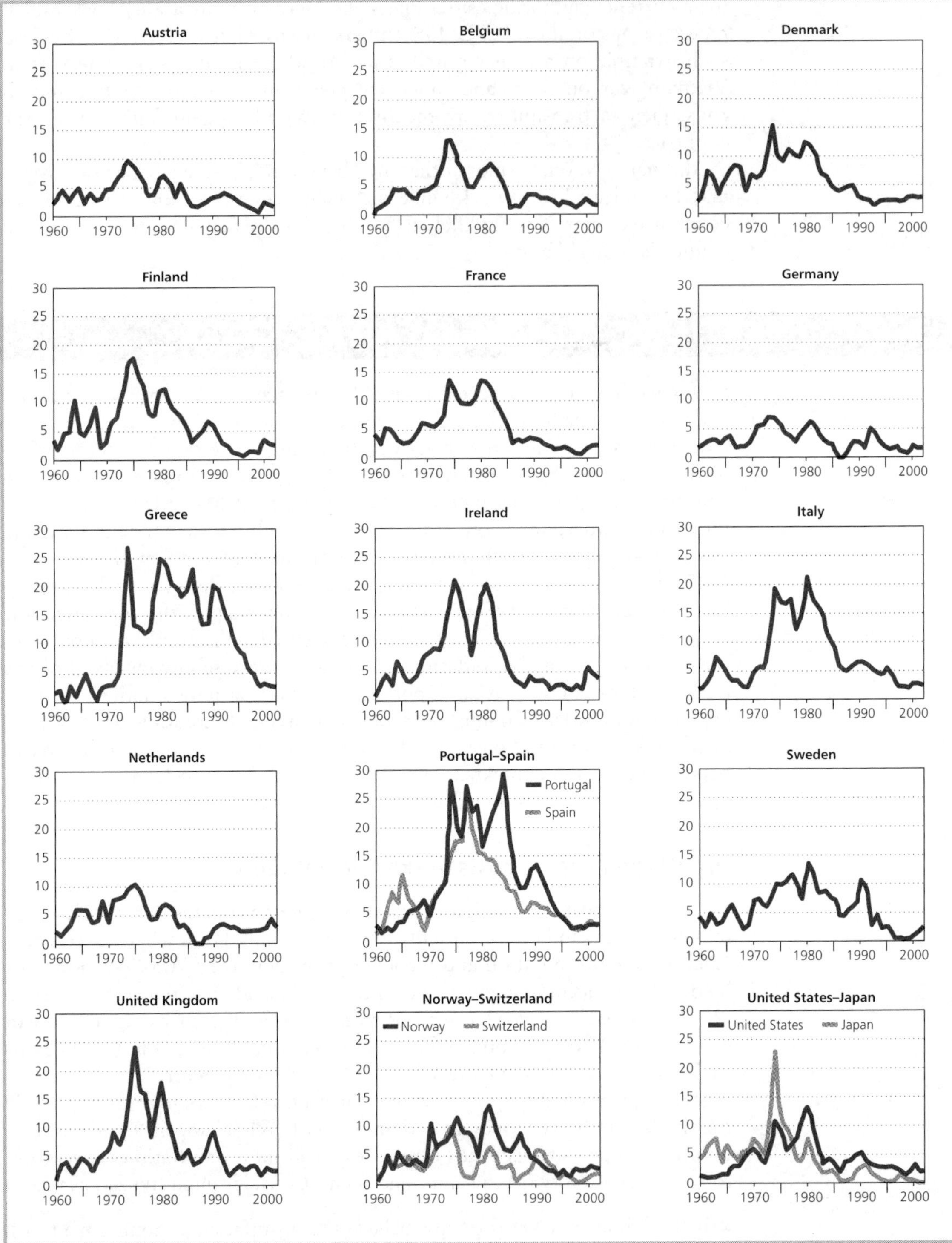

Figure 13.13 Inflation rates in Europe and the world, 1960–2002.
Source: IMF, OECD.

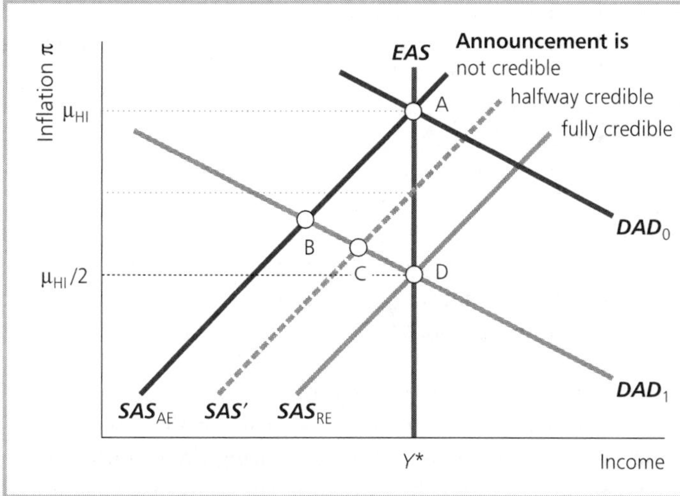

Figure 13.14 Being at A, the CB announces in period 0 that money growth will be reduced from μ_{HI} to $0.5\mu_{HI}$ next period. If this pledge is not credible, *SAS* stays in the dark blue position as under adaptive expectations. The economy ends up at B. If it is credible and its effects on inflation are foreseen, SAS_{RE} obtains and we move directly to D. If the announcement is half-heartedly believed, *SAS* moves to the dashed position and C obtains.

- The labour market believes the disinflation announcement. It adjusts inflation expectations rationally, shifting *SAS* down to SAS_{RE}. The inflation rate falls to the new target rate at no cost in terms of income losses. Inflation has been reduced without any cost.
- An intermediate case is that the labour market assigns some, but not full, credibility to the disinflation announcement. Attributing a probability of 50% for the policy change to happen puts *SAS* in the intermediate dashed position. Inflation is lower than in the first case and higher than in the second. The income loss is higher than in the second and lower than in the first case.

Figure 13.15 deals with the second influence on disinflation costs. To isolate this argument from the effect on expectations discussed above, consider the case in which the disinflation begins unexpectedly. Again the goal is to halve inflation by halving money growth. If nominal wage growth responds slowly to labour market disequilibria and, hence, the *SAS* curve is rather flat, only a

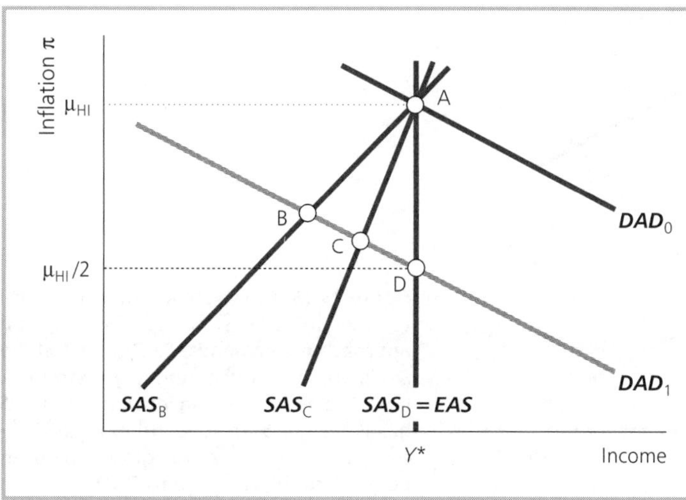

Figure 13.15 Beginning at A, money growth is cut in half unexpectedly in order to reduce inflation by 50%. If wages are very sticky, which makes *SAS* flat, inflation falls a little and income falls a lot. More flexible wages provide for a steeper *SAS* curve, giving more inflation reduction and lower income losses. Perfect wage flexibility makes *SAS* vertical. Inflation immediately falls to half its initial value at no sacrifice in income.

small part of the hoped-for reduction of inflation is achieved in period 1, at the cost of large income losses (point B). A more flexible labour market implies a steeper *SAS* curve and leads to point C. Finally, if wage growth is perfectly flexible, and hence the *SAS* curve is vertical, the inflation target is achieved immediately at no income-related cost.

The transition from a high inflation equilibrium to a low inflation equilibrium is costless in only two ideal scenarios: when the disinflation is announced prior to its implementation and this announcement is fully credible, or when the labour market is perfectly flexible, meaning that nominal wages move to balance supply and demand at all times. Whenever reality falls short of these ideal requirements, disinflations can only be engineered at the cost of income losses – and they take time.

The **sacrifice ratio** is the loss of income (usually measured in percentage of potential income) caused by reducing inflation by one percentage point.

To see how the incurred costs relate to the obtained benefits, economists use a *standardized measure of disinflation costs*: the **sacrifice ratio**. This is computed by first adding up all income losses incurred during the disinflation (as a percentage of potential income) and then dividing this sum by the achieved reduction of inflation (in percentage points):

$$\text{Sacrifice ratio} = \frac{\text{Total income losses}}{\text{Inflation reduction}}$$

So the sacrifice ratio is the price of one percentage point less inflation in terms of potential income forgone. For an illustration of how the sacrifice ratio is computed, suppose that a central bank decides to reduce inflation from 9% to 3%. Assume that an announcement is not credible. Instead, inflation expectations are formed adaptively according to $\pi^e = \pi_{-1}$. Figure 13.16 shows the big-leap approach to achieving the inflation target in period 1 immediately.

The **big-leap approach** attempts to produce a desired reduction of inflation in one giant step.

Figure 13.16, money growth must come to a halt ($\mu_1 = 0$) in order to shift DAD_1 far enough down to bring inflation down to its target level immediately ($\pi = 3$). This is at the expense of an income drop by 6%, however $[(Y^* - Y_1)/Y^* = 6\%]$. The current inflation rate of 3 is the rate expected for period 2. This shifts *SAS* into the light blue position. Appropriate demand

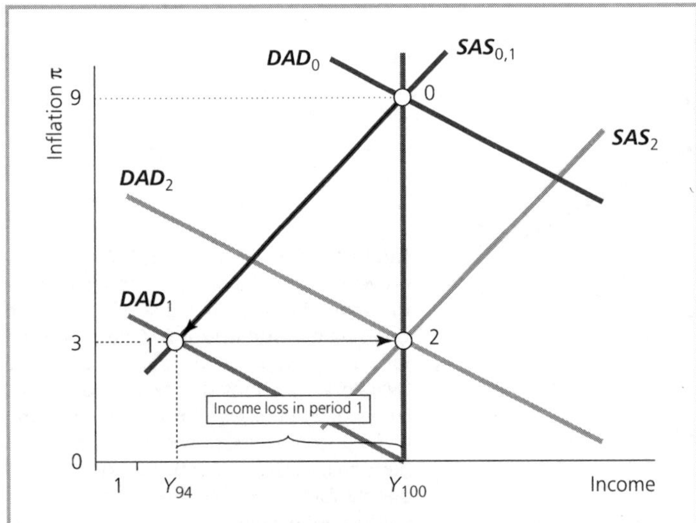

Figure 13.16 To reduce inflation from 9% to 3% in one step, as the big-leap approach recommends, *DAD* must shift to DAD_1. To this effect, money growth must be 0. The accompanying income loss, if *SAS* has slope 1, is 6. To keep inflation at 3% in period 2, money must grow again in period 2 to shift *DAD* up to DAD_2.

management holds inflation constant at $\pi_2 = 3$ and brings income back up to potential income Y^*.

Note two things. First, disinflation affects income only in period 1. Income is still in equilibrium in period 0, before the disinflation starts, and back in equilibrium in period 2, after the disinflation is over. So the sacrifice ratio is

$$SR = \frac{100(Y^* - Y_1)/Y^*}{\pi_0 - \pi_2} = \frac{100(100 - 94)/100}{9 - 3} = \frac{6}{9 - 3} = 1$$

Second, to achieve the inflation target quickly, money growth must follow a rather volatile pattern. (Recap: to identify this period's money growth in the graph, look for the point of intersection between this period's *DAD* curve and the vertical line over last period's income.) From a pre-disinflation rate of 9, money growth must fall to 0 in period 1, rise to 5 in period 2, and then fall back to 3 where it can stay. In particular, the acceleration in money growth from 0 to 5% in period 2, after the inflation target has already been reached, may create credibility problems for the central bank's new low inflation policy.

To avoid such wild swings in money growth, but particularly as a hedge against a severe recession, a **gradualist approach** to disinflation is often recommended. Figure 13.17 looks at such an example.

The **gradualist approach** attempts to achieve a desired reduction of inflation slowly, in a series of small steps.

Here the central bank reduces inflation from 9% to 3% in equal steps over a period of three years. In period 1 inflation is reduced to 7%. This surprise disinflation drives income down by two units to $Y_1 = 98$. Further disinflation steps, to 5% in period 2 and to 3% in period 3, keep income at 98, but do not drive it down any further. Once inflation is being kept stable at 3% in period 4, income rises back up into equilibrium and the disinflation is over.

Consider the sacrifice ratio for this gradual disinflation. Adding up the income losses for the disequilibrium periods 1, 2 and 3 we obtain

$$SR = \frac{100[(Y^* - Y_1) + (Y^* - Y_2) + (Y^* - Y_3)]/Y^*}{\pi_0 - \pi_4} = \frac{2 + 2 + 2}{9 - 3} = 1$$

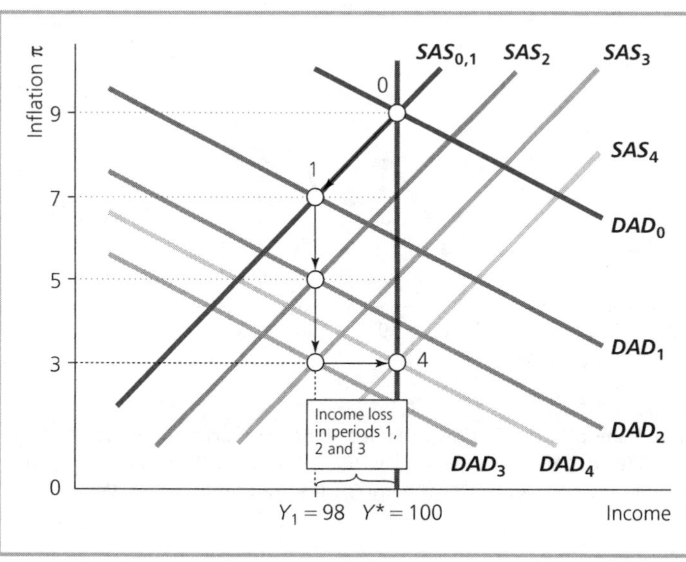

Figure 13.17 To bring inflation down from 9% to 3% in three steps, in line with the gradualist approach, *DAD* must first shift to DAD_1. Facing SAS_2, the next reduction to 5% in period 2 calls for another shift of *DAD* to DAD_2. When the inflation target of 3% is reached in period 3, income is still below Y^*. Only in period 3 is the new low inflation equilibrium reached.

Rather unexpectedly, the sacrifice ratio is exactly the same as with the big-leap approach. What is different, and what might be of concern, is the distribution of income losses over time. A deep recession (with an income drop of 6) in one year may not be the same as a minor recession (with an income deficit of 2) lasting three years.

The independence of the sacrifice ratio from the speed of the disinflation is a robust result as long as inflation expectations are being formed in a mechanical adaptive fashion. For markets that monitor monetary policy closely, it may be of interest in this context that the gradualist approach permits a more steady path of money growth. From periods 0 to 5, money growth rates are 9, 6, 5, 3, 4 and 3.

Disinflation and its costs in the real world – an alpine event

Computing the sacrifice ratio in a theoretical context is not difficult. But trying to do it in the real world poses problems. One major obstacle is how to identify disinflation episodes successfully. A disinflation episode is a time period during which the inflation rate is reduced deliberately, by purposeful policy action. This step is crucial, because we want to be sure that the change in inflation has caused the observed income response. A positive supply shock, for example, would shift *SAS* to the right, reduce inflation and raise output. It would obviously be a misinterpretation to conclude that the reduction in inflation has made income rise.

To eliminate such short-run or random fluctuations in inflation and focus on the bigger picture, we may smooth inflation data. Following a suggestion by Ball (1994), Figure 13.18 shows a moving average (over nine quarters, centred on the middle quarter) of Swiss inflation, in addition to the raw data. A fall of this smoothed inflation rate only qualifies as a disinflation if it

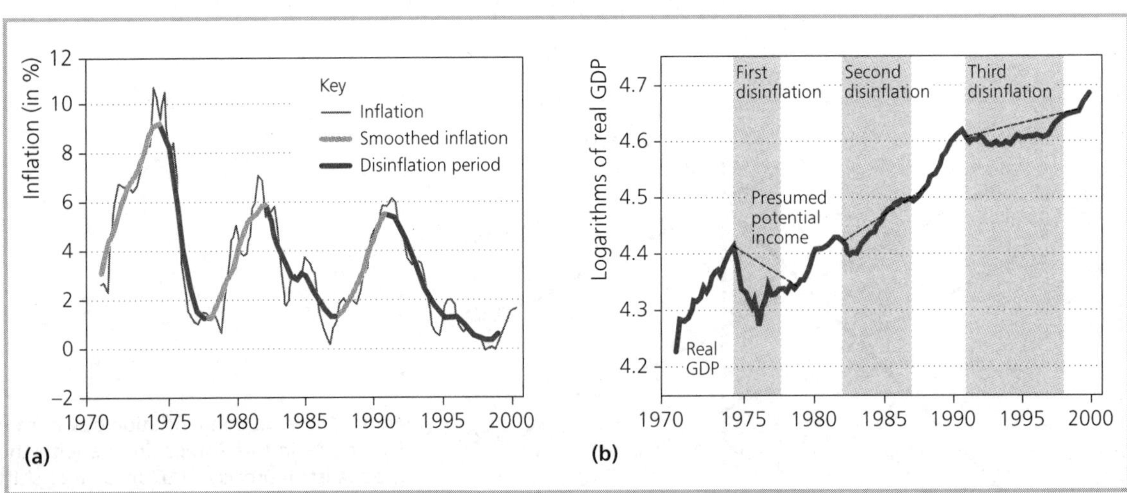

Figure 13.18 Panel (a) shows actual inflation and smoothed inflation in Switzerland. The bold segments highlight three disinflation episodes experienced since 1970. Panel (b) shows real GDP. Potential GDP is characterized by straight lines connecting incomes at the beginning and one year after the end of disinflation episodes. (Why? Check when Y is back at Y^* in Figure 13.16.)
Source: IMF, *IFS*.

exceeds a certain threshold, say, two percentage points. Application of this criterion to Switzerland identifies three disinflation episodes. Let us focus on the first one, which began in the second quarter of 1974 and ended in the fourth quarter of 1977. During this time the inflation rate was reduced from more than 9% to less than 2%.

Trying to compute the sacrifice ratio brings us to a second practical difficulty. In order to measure the effect of the disinflation on income, we need to guess what income would have done without the disinflation. In line with what we observed in Figure 13.16, it may be assumed that income is in equilibrium at peak inflation, just before the disinflation starts; that equilibrium obtains again one year (period) after the low inflation target is achieved; and that income would have moved linearly from the first to the second equilibrium level had there been no disinflation. Figure 13.18, panel (b), shows how this works for the first Swiss disinflation. Note that potential income is presumed to have fallen even without the disinflation (probably due to the first oil price explosion). The income loss during each quarter of the disinflation is now simply measured as the vertical distance between actual income and our guess of potential income.

Figure 13.19 displays this episode in a π-Y diagram, to bring out the similarity to the display of theoretical disinflations in Figures 13.16 and 13.17. For improved transparency, the episode is documented with annual data. The horizontal axis measures income as deviation from potential income (in %), since in the real world the latter changes over time.

Assuming that income was in equilibrium in 1974, when the disinflation began, and in 1978, the year after it ended, the disinflation affected income in the displayed fashion. In 1975 income fell short of equilibrium income by 6%. In 1976 it remained 6% below equilibrium income. In 1977 it began to catch up, but was still some 2% lower than potential income. Looking at annual averages, this accompanied an inflation reduction from 8% to 1%. This gives the sacrifice ratio

$$SR = \frac{6+6+2}{8-1} = \frac{14}{7} = 2$$

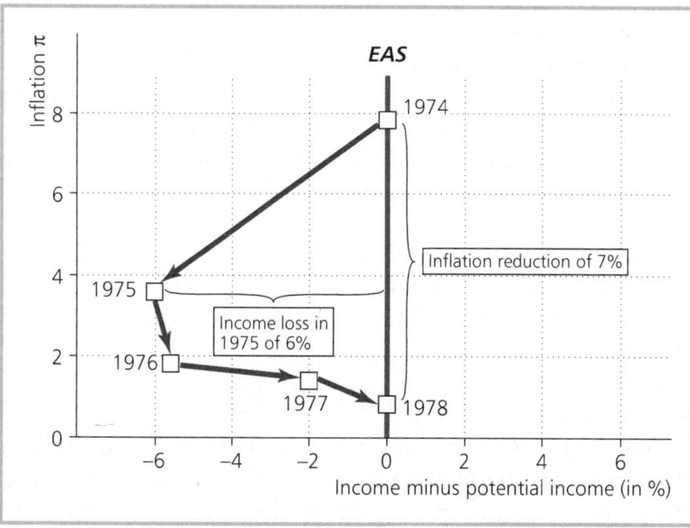

Figure 13.19 The graph traces the first Swiss disinflation in π-Y space. From about 8% in 1974 inflation is reduced via 4% in 1975, and 2% in 1976, to some 1% in 1977. Potential income is reached one year later. Income lost relative to falling potential income caused by quadrupling oil prices is 6% each in 1975 and 1976 and 2% in 1977. *Source*: IMF, *IFS*.

Empirical note. Average sacrifice ratios in European countries are estimated to range from 0.75 (France) to 2.92 (Germany).

The result is that one percentage point less inflation costs Switzerland 2% of a year's normal output during this disinflation. In 1995 prices this amounts to 7,000,000,000 Swiss francs. For each of Switzerland's 7 million inhabitants, one percentage point less inflation costs 500 francs. These numbers are corroborated by the other two disinflation episodes in Switzerland between 1982 and 1987, and between 1990 and 1996. The accumulated income losses from all three disinflations add up to about 70 billion Swiss francs.

The costs of inflation

According to what was said above, getting rid of a 10% inflation rate may well cost 20% of one year's income, or more. This is a high price, and the question is: why should we want to pay it? Because inflation is bad, of course. But why is 10% inflation worse than 5%, and 5% worse than 2%, and 2% worse than full price stability? This question must be kept apart from the question of why an increase of inflation, say from 5% to 10%, may be harmful.

The costs of increasing inflation

At first glance, this question appears to be ill-posed. Haven't we just seen that reducing inflation is costly? And don't we know that by symmetrical arguments an acceleration of inflation will spur temporary income *gains*? Yes, this is correct, even if such *gain ratios* (the income gain resulting from an increase in inflation by one percentage point) may not be exactly the same as the sacrifice ratios (say, if the *SAS* curves are curved rather than linear). But the fact that surprise inflation bears the promise of transitory income gains is exactly the reason that it is so tempting to inflate.

Then why should an acceleration of inflation be costly? To understand this, we must look behind income and see what happens to the distribution of wealth. Suppose an elderly man had saved during the earlier part of his life and now, via the banking system, lends his savings to young people (remember the lifetime consumption pattern discussed in Chapter 2?). Suppose he lends £10,000 to a young woman for one year. Both agree on a real interest rate of 3%. Since they expect 7% inflation, the nominal interest rate is 10%. So she expects to repay the loan plus interest after one year, which amounts to £11,000. Now assume that inflation turns out to be 10% instead of the expected 7%. If both had foreseen this, they would have agreed on a nominal interest rate of 13%, and on repayment of £11,300. So the elderly man receives less than he wanted and the young woman pays less than she was prepared to. The unexpected acceleration of inflation redistributed £300 from the man to the woman.

This result can be generalized: *the main cost of unanticipated inflation is that it redistributes wealth from creditors (those with savings) to debtors*. In reality this often means redistribution from the old to the young, or from the public to the government.

The costs of steady inflation

To return to our initial question: after the acceleration of inflation has been completed, why is a permanently higher rate of inflation of, say, 10% worse than a lower steady rate? A first answer, given by the *DAD-SAS* model, says that it is not. Since the long-run *EAS* curve is vertical at potential income, income is independent of the level of steady inflation. And neither does inflation seem to have an impact on any other real variables, such as, real wages, real interest rates, real exchange rates, consumption, taxes and so on. There is one real variable, however, that is affected. Remember that people determine their money holdings by comparing the return on money, which is zero, to the return on interest-bearing assets, which equals the nominal interest rate. Now if inflation is higher, the nominal interest rate must be higher to keep the real interest rate unchanged. Then people hold less money and spend more resources on replenishing their stock of money. What is the size of this effect? Empirical studies suggest that the real money supply falls by some 5% if nominal interest rates go up by one percentage point. So, as a rough guess, people would hold half the money at 10% inflation than what they would hold at 0%, meaning two instead of one or eight instead of four monthly trips to the cash machine. These so-called **shoe leather costs** are presumably not very high at moderate inflation rates, and are even partly offset by the fact that people now earn more interest since a larger part of wealth is kept in interest-bearing assets.

In a similar vein, higher inflation will use up the resources of firms that have to rewrite price lists and catalogues more frequently. We have already come across such **menu costs** in Chapter 8.

The image of presumably rather moderate costs of anticipated inflation derives from the assumption that institutions are designed to deal with an inflationary environment in a neutral way. However, an institution that hardly meets this ideal in the real world is the tax system. Taxes are usually levied on nominal wages, nominal wealth, nominal capital gains and nominal profits. If income taxes are not proportional, higher inflation gives rise to higher real taxes even though real income may not have changed. Similarly, real taxes on wealth and capital gains go up even if real wealth or real capital gains are unchanged. Such institutional deficiencies cause inflation to have distorting effects that are probably much higher than the shoe leather and menu costs discussed above.

The dependence of inflation costs on institutions adds a new dimension to the discussion of price stability. A country that does not want to live with 10% inflation may either lower inflation and make the accompanying sacrifices, or reform institutions so as to make the 10% inflation less painful. The latter option does not solve an apparent empirical problem, however, that remains little understood: high inflation rates seem to come with more variable inflation, which introduces uncertainty about future prices that may absorb substantial resources.

13.4 LESSONS FOR EUROPEAN MONETARY UNION

The discussions of this chapter pose three questions regarding the shape and future of European Monetary Union:

1 Does the European Central Bank possess an optimal degree of independence from government interference? 'Optimal' is used here in the sense that it combines a high degree of price level stability with a reasonable concern for income stabilization in times of exogenous shocks.

2 Are the current or prospective second-wave member states similar enough to be hit by the same kinds of shocks in a similar fashion? Similarly, are their business cycles synchronized enough?
3 Had inflation converged sufficiently at an early stage to avoid costly and painful disinflation efforts during the politically sensitive final phase of transition to **EMU**?

EMU stands for European Economic and Monetary Union. However, it is often understood to refer to this union's more controversial second part, European Monetary Union.

Regarding the first question, the *blueprint* for the European Central Bank makes it one of the most independent central banks in the world. If there is any risk, it is that the European Central Bank may be too independent.

On the second question, a lot of structural diversity still exists. Much of this cannot be removed in the short run. For example, the EU will have to live with the fact that the United Kingdom is a net exporter of oil while the other members are net importers, and the particular conflict of interest this might generate should the UK decide to adopt the euro. The lesson is simply that it may be more risky for some countries to have a common currency than it is for others. Theories of **optimum currency areas** spell out criteria against which to judge whether adopting a common currency may be beneficial or not.

An **optimum currency area** is a region or group of countries for which it is beneficial to have a common currency.

The Maastricht criteria on inflation and interest rates address the third question and the last part of the second. The inflation criterion is supposed to ensure that the final convergence of inflation rates, demanded by the transition to the *euro*, is not accompanied by large employment sacrifices in certain countries. This would have given EMU a bad start and might even put EMU membership in jeopardy for some. Figure 13.20 shows that two-thirds of current EU members met the current inflation target of 2.4% in 1996. Note that most who did not were not current members of the EMS, or had major devaluations within the EMS since 1993.

Business cycle synchronization is achieved if two or more countries normally move into booms and recessions together.

The Maastricht criterion on interest rates may serve as an indicator of **business cycle synchronization.** Recall that nominal interest rates contain an inflation premium, at least in the long run. From the perspective of the Fisher equation the interest rate criterion is redundant, since what it does is secure

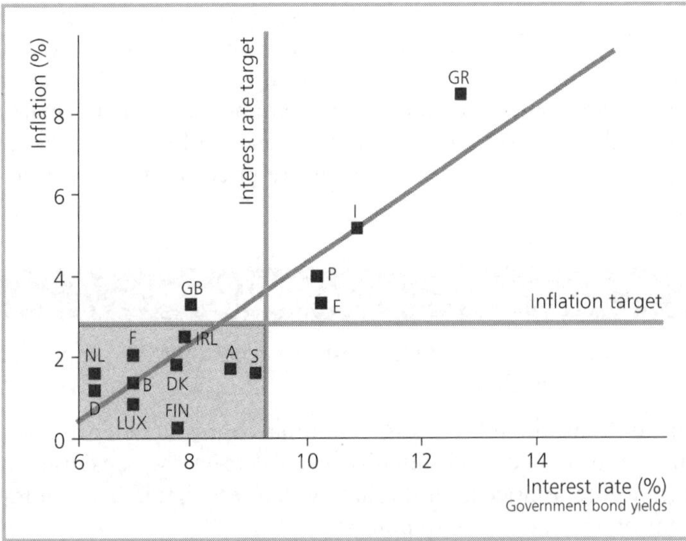

Figure 13.20 In equilibrium, on *EAS*, in the neutral phase of the business cycle, nominal interest rates are the sum of some fairly constant normal real interest rates and inflation.
Source: SBC, *Economic and Financial Prospects*.

inflation convergence. Figure 13.20 makes this point, showing that for only one out of the fifteen countries (Britain) does the interest rate criterion yield a different verdict than the inflation criterion. Note, however, that nominal interest rates are also subject to a liquidity effect. Due to sticky goods prices, nominal interest rates fall below normal levels during booms and rise during recessions. Therefore nominal interest rates may diverge even if two countries are on the same inflation trend, if business cycles are not synchronized. Deviation from a line with slope 1 through the data points in Figure 13.20 signals the extent to which a country's business cycle is out of sync compared with the others. This implies, however, that the interest rate criterion should be defined in terms of deviations from this line (above or below) instead of differences from the low inflation countries, and should use short-term interest rates instead of long-term rates as laid down in the Maastricht criterion.

CHAPTER SUMMARY

- A more independent central bank provides lower inflation. This proposition explains a large part of inflation differences between industrial countries.
- Countries that peg their exchange rate to some other currency see their inflation gradually converge with the other country's rate. Inflation experiences within the EMS support this proposition.
- Hard-nosed central banks are likely to respond to a negative supply shock with restrictive monetary policy to keep inflation from rising. Wet central banks, by contrast, are likely to respond with expansionary monetary policy to prevent a recession. The response of industrial countries to the oil price explosion of 1973/4 matches this pattern.
- If supply shocks are relatively frequent the best central bank for society may not be the most independent one, but one that has some concern for income stabilization.
- If supply shocks are relatively frequent it may not be optimal to peg the exchange rate to the country with the most independent central bank, but to one that has some concern for income stabilization.
- If two countries are being hit by supply shocks at different times or in opposing directions, pegging the exchange rate may not be beneficial.
- The sacrifice ratio measures the cost of reducing inflation by one percentage point in terms of lost income.
- The main cost of unanticipated inflation is that it redistributes wealth from creditors to debtors.
- Steady inflation causes shoe leather costs and menu costs. These costs are presumably small for moderate inflations. If institutions are not properly designed to deal with inflation, however, substantial distortions may add to these costs.

KEY TERMS AND CONCEPTS

big-leap approach
business cycle synchronization
central bank independence
consumer price index
crawling peg
currency board
disinflation
disinflation costs
European Monetary Union (EMU)
gradualist approach
inflation costs
inflation target
monetary policy rule
optimum currency area
producer price index
sacrifice ratio
supply shock
Taylor rule

EXERCISES

13.1 Cukierman has provided another index of central bank independence. His values for the countries shown in Figure 13.2 are, where available, given in Table 13.1.
Average inflation since 1973 is also given. Transfer the data onto a graph and judge visually whether the result obtained in the text also holds with this new index.

13.2 Let a country's stochastic *SAS* curve be given by $Y = Y^* + \pi - \pi^e + \sigma$, where σ equals 5 in 50% of the cases and −5 in the other 50%. The government's indifference curves are ellipse shaped, as postulated in the chapter. Whenever $\sigma = -5$, inflation is set to 10%; when $\sigma = 5$, inflation is 2%.

(a) What is the rationally expected inflation rate?

(b) Let $Y^* = 100$. What are the income levels in periods of positive supply shocks and in periods of negative supply shocks, respectively?

(c) What do the observed inflation rates tell you about where the government's desired output is, relative to potential output?

13.3 Let a country's supply side be represented by the *SAS* curve

$$Y = Y^* + (\pi - \pi^e)$$

Inflation expectations are being formed adaptively ($\pi^e = \pi_{-1}$). Suppose the country's central bank decides to bring inflation down from 8% to 1%. The disinflation process starts in period 1 and follows this pattern: 4% in period 1; 2% in period 2; 1% in period 3 and after.

(a) Compute the aggregate income losses and the sacrifice ratio.

(b) Display your results in a π-Y diagram. Compare your diagram with the Swiss disinflation engineered between 1974 and 1978 which is shown in the chapter.

13.4 One disinflation engineered by the Bank of England began in the second quarter of 1980 and ended in the third quarter of 1983. At the start of this period, trend inflation was at 16.6%; at the end it was 4.4%. Real GDP during this episode is given in Table 13.2.

Table 13.1

	A	AUS	B	DK	FIN	F	D	IRL	I	JP	NL	E	S	CH	GB	USA
CBI	0.31	0.58	0.19	0.47	0.27	0.28	0.66	0.39	0.22	0.16	0.42	0.21	0.27	0.68	0.31	0.51
Average inflation in %	8.91	4.72	5.89	7.52	8.61	8.5	3.7	10.15	12.13	5.23	4.49	11.96	8.3	4.04	9.86	6.24

Table 13.2

Quarter	80.2	80.3	80.4	81.1	81.2	81.3	81.4	82.1	82.2
UK real GDP	423.9	421.1	416.0	415.6	415.2	420.6	420.7	421.8	425.2
Quarter	82.3	82.4	83.1	83.2	83.3	83.4	84.1	84.2	84.3
UK real GDP[a]	425.8	428.2	436.7	438.0	442.2	446.7	451.6	449.4	449.2

Note: [a] In billions of British pounds (at 1990 prices).

(a) Compute the aggregate income losses that may be attributed to this disinflation. (Assume that GDP was at its potential level in the second quarter of 1980 and again in the third quarter of 1984. Assume that potential income would have moved linearly from the first value to the second, had the disinflation not been implemented.)

(b) Compute the sacrifice ratio for this disinflation episode.

13.5 Your country is stuck in an inflationary equilibrium with $\pi = 10\%$ and $Y^* = 100$. The economy is given by

$$\pi = \pi_{-1} + (Y - Y^*) + 0.1\pi_{OIL}$$

and

$$\pi = \mu - 0.5(Y - Y_{-1})$$

π_{OIL} denotes oil-price inflation. Although it would like to, your government does not dare to reduce inflation, since it does not want to bear the accompanying disinflation costs. Now in period 1, oil prices are cut in half permanently ($\pi_{OIL,1} = -50\%$).

(a) Assuming adaptive inflation expectations, $\pi^e = \pi_{-1}$, by how much can inflation be reduced in period 1 without affecting income?

(b) What is the appropriate monetary policy that keeps income at 100? (Compute μ_1, μ_2 and μ_3.)

(c) What happens if the government uses the opportunity to reduce inflation, immediately and permanently, to 0? (Trace μ and Y.)

(d) Answer questions (a) to (c) assuming that the fall in oil prices lasted only one year.

RECOMMENDED READING

The bible on issues of central bank independence is Alex Cukierman (1995) *Central Bank Strategy, Credibility, and Independence: Theory and Evidence*, Cambridge, MA and London: MIT Press.

The empirical evidence is gauged on a non-technical level in Alberto Alesina and Lawrence H. Summers (1992) 'Central bank independence and macroeconomic performance', *Journal of Money, Credit and Banking* 25: 151–62.

A survey of theoretical progress in political macroeconomics achieved in the 1990s is provided by Manfred Gärtner (2000) 'Political macroeconomics: a survey of recent developments', *Journal of Economic Surveys* 14: 527–61.

Regina Reinert (1996) 'The constitutional anatomy of the European Central Bank (ECB)', *Economic and Financial Prospects* No. 4, September, pp. 14–17, dissects the blueprint for the European Central Bank.

Sacrifice ratios are studied in Lawrence Ball (1994) 'What determines the sacrifice ratio?', in N. Gregory Mankiw (ed.) *Monetary Policy*, Chicago and London: University of Chicago Press.

A provoking view on inflation, central bank independence and monetary policy is offered in Paul Krugman (1996) 'Stable prices and fast growth: Just say no', *The Economist*, 31 August, pp. 17–20.

Laurence H. Meyer (2001) 'Inflation targets and inflation targeting', *Federal Reserve Bank of St Louis Review* 83: 1–13. This refines some of the issues discussed in this chapter by asking whether the US central bank, the Fed, should adopt the inflation-targeting rule or set an explicit numerical target for inflation within the context of its current dual mandate of promoting price stability and full employment.

APPLIED PROBLEMS

RECENT RESEARCH

What explains sacrifice ratios?

Lawrence Ball ('What determines the sacrifice ratio?', in N. G. Mankiw (ed.)(1994) *Monetary Policy*, Chicago and London: University of Chicago Press) computes a sample of sacrifice ratios for different disinflation episodes in different countries. One question that he analyzes is whether the obtained sacrifice ratios depend on the SIZE of the disinflation (by how many percentage points is inflation reduced from the beginning to the end of the episode?) and by the LENGTH (how many quarters did the disinflation last?). The obtained estimation equation for twenty-eight episodes is (standard errors in parentheses):

$$\text{SACRIFICE RATIO} = \underset{(0.325)}{1.045} - \underset{(0.061)}{0.198}\ \text{SIZE} + \underset{(0.034)}{0.120}\ \text{LENGTH}$$

$$R^2_{adj} = 00.30$$

Larger disinflations come at lower disinflation costs: the coefficient for SIZE is negative and significant (t-statistic = 0.198/0.061 = 3.25). On the other hand, spreading the disinflation over a longer time appears to make it more costly: the coefficient for LENGTH is positive, with a t-statistic of 0.120/0.034 = 3.53). The coefficient of determination is only 0.30, however, meaning that only 30% of the differences of sacrifice ratios between disinflation episodes may be traced back to the size and the length of the disinflation.

WORKED PROBLEM

Does central bank independence ease disinflation pains?

Inflation can be reduced by moving down along the *SAS* curve. Then the slope of *SAS* determines the incurred sacrifices. Or the *SAS* curve may be shifted down by reducing inflation expectations. If this is accomplished, inflation may be reduced at no or at low cost. According to what we learned in this chapter, an independent central bank (which desires lower inflation than a dependent one) should be expected to be more successful in reducing inflation expectations. Hence, more CBI should come hand in hand with lower sacrifice ratios. Table 13.3 gives average sacrifice ratios for nine countries and CBI data.

To see whether there is a relationship we run a regression to obtain (standard errors in parentheses):

$$\text{SACRIFICE RATIO} = \underset{(0.553)}{-0.441} + \underset{(0.058)}{0.206}\ \text{CBI} \qquad R^2_{adj} = 0.59$$

The puzzling and unexpected result is that countries with more independent central banks have experienced higher sacrifice ratios. CBI explains some 59% of the differences in sacrifice ratios and the coefficient on CBI is highly significant (absolute t-statistic: 0.206/0.058 = 3.55). Similarly puzzling results have been reported in a number of research papers. Convincing explanations have not been advanced yet.

Table 13.3

Country	AUS	CDN	F	D	I	J	CH	GB	USA
SACRIFICE RATIO	1.00	1.50	0.75	3.10	1.29	0.70	1.57	0.68	2.11
CBI	9	11	7	13	5	6	12	6	12

Table 13.4

Country	A	B	CH	D	DK	E	F	GB	GR	I	IRL	NL	P
Hourly wages in $	25.5	27	29	32.1	24.82	12	19	14	8	16.5	13	24	5.33
CBI	9	7	12	13	8	5	7	6	4	5	7	10	3
Overvaluation in %	1.23	1.12	1.52	1.29	1.35	0.95	1.18	1.01	0.68	1.04	0.94	1.22	0.76

YOUR TURN

Real wages and central bank independence

Wage costs are considered a key determinant of a country's international competitiveness. Table 13.4 gives hourly wages (converted into $) in thirteen European countries, ranging from $5.33 in Portugal to $32.1 in Germany. The second row gives the Grilli index of central bank independence. The last row gives the domestic currencies' overvaluation relative to the dollar as implied in the World Bank's *World Bank Atlas*. We had already used these data in Chapter 1.

If we compare wages in Britain with wages in Germany, we compare $WAGE_{\text{UK in £}}$ to $E_{\text{£/DM}} \times WAGE_{\text{D in DM}}$. Now German wages may exceed British wages for two reasons: because wages in Germany (expressed in DM) are pushed too high (by trade unions), or because the exchange rate is too high, that is, the mark is overvalued relative to the pound sterling. In the light of this, check whether international differences in wage costs may be attributed to currency overvaluation. Also look into the role played by CBI in this context.

To further explore this chapter's key messages you are encouraged to use the interactive online module found at

www.fgn.unisg.ch/eurmacro/tutor/centralbank.html

and many other features hosted at **www.fgn.unisg.ch/eurmacro**

CHAPTER 14

BUDGET DEFICITS AND PUBLIC DEBT

WHAT TO EXPECT After working through this chapter, you will understand:

1 How the budget deficit affects the public debt, and how the public debt affects the budget deficit.
2 What structural changes in the industrialized countries brought the issue of the public debt into the headlines.
3 What governments had to do in order to meet the Maastricht convergence criteria on deficits and the debt.
4 How the Maastricht criteria on deficits and debt relate to the other criteria, such as on inflation, and thus must be seen in context.
5 Why, when and for whom running a deficit and running up the public debt may be a burden.
6 For what reasons budget rules may be needed in a monetary union.

Until now the main thrust of the discussion has focused on monetary policy. Fiscal policy, the spending and revenue decisions of the government, have so far only made a brief appearance – as a means of influencing aggregate spending in the economy. It is time to take a closer look at the government budget – at spending and ways to finance spending, at budget surpluses and deficits and at the accumulation of such surpluses and deficits over time, which we call the public debt.

Understanding budget deficits and the public debt is particularly important in the context of current European developments. First, fixed exchange rates as offered by the European Monetary System (EMS I in the past and EMS II in the future), and even more so membership in the European Monetary Union, deprive countries of monetary policy as an instrument to influence the business cycle and to respond to shocks. This may make it tempting to use (or abuse) fiscal policy instead.

Second, but related to the first reason, the convergence criteria agreed upon in the Maastricht Treaty, which current participants had to and prospective future members will have to meet, comprise two on fiscal policy: one restricts budget deficits to less than 3% of one year's aggregate income; the other requires the public debt to be below 60% of income. To obtain a clearer understanding of the rationale behind these and other convergence criteria we need to take a closer look at fiscal policy and how it relates to monetary policy as discussed so far.

The chapter will conclude by discussing the argument that public deficits and debt place an unfair burden on future generations, and thus should be as low as possible, and that fiscal policy needs restrictions as spelled out in the Pact for Stability and Growth.

14.1 THE GOVERNMENT BUDGET

The government must balance expenditures and revenues, just as businesses and households do. It has some financing options, however, that are not available to private actors. Figure 14.1 displays the main sources of government revenues and uses of spending and defines some essential concepts.

On the expenditure side we have two categories. The first is regular government spending G, which we suppose here to comprise all public spending on consumption and investment, plus transfer payments. The second, being made explicit in Figure 14.1 for the first time, is the government's interest payment on public debt accumulated in the past, iB. Interest payments typically run at between 5% and 10% of government expenditures.

The prime source of revenue for the government are taxes T. We speak of a **budget deficit** if taxes fall short of expenditure:

$$\text{Deficit} = G + iB - T$$

A better structural measure of the current government's budget policies is the **primary deficit.** This ignores government interest spending on the public debt, since the current government has little control over this expenditure category:

$$\text{Primary deficit} = G - T$$

The government enjoys *two options to finance a deficit*. It can go into debt by *issuing government bonds* to the public, or it can simply *create money* and use it to pay for the goods and services it buys and the interest on old government debt. There is actually a third possibility which we ignore here. This is to

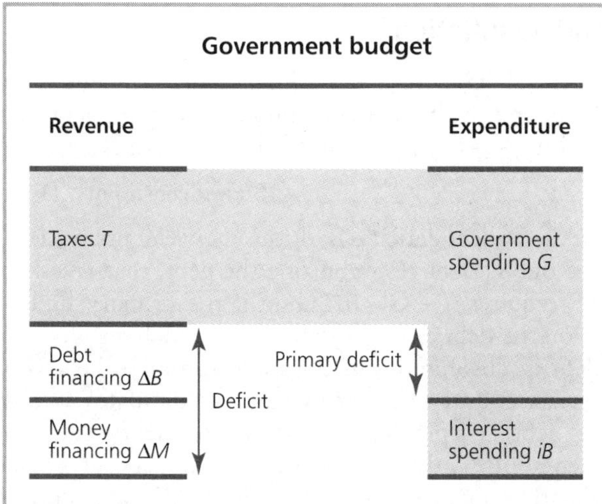

Figure 14.1 On the expenditure side there are government purchases G and interest payments on existing debt. Revenues comprise taxes and credit granted by the public (debt financing) or the central bank (money financing). If desired, G may be thought to include transfers. Then T must include items like social security contributions and unemployment insurance premiums. Unlike in previous chapters, G, T and B are nominal variables.

Empirical note. In 1994 European governments' privatization proceeds ran at \$33 billion, or 0.44% of GNP. Looking at the longer run, Britain, Europe's most dedicated privatizer, averaged some 0.07% of GNP each year during 1985–95 from 'selling the family silver'.

Empirical note. Bundesbank profits in 1995 were DM10.6 billion. Law provides that the lion's share of these profits, DM10.2 billion, had to be forwarded to the government.

sell public assets. In recent years in particular, European governments have been selling their telecoms, railroads, public utilities companies, airlines and more on a grand scale. This makes things easier for now, but it must remain a temporary phenomenon, and to the extent that these companies have been profitable, selling them may put pressure on rather than help the government budget further down the road. Since even during the current privatization euphoria and resizing of the public sector, this source of revenue barely amounted to a very small fraction of government revenue, we may safely ignore it here.

Note that not the entire deficit adds to the public debt, but only that part financed by issuing debt to the public. *Money financing does not add to the public debt.* This is most straightforward in countries where the government can simply decide to print money in order to finance the deficit, with its treasury issuing currency to pay for goods, services and interest. In countries where the government does not have that option, the central bank may help to finance deficits by open market purchases of government bonds. This results in claims of one government agency on another, and interest is paid by one government agency to another. Entertaining a consolidated perspective of the government, or because even the world's most independent central banks forward profits to the treasury, government bonds held by the central bank (or other government agencies) are not considered part of the public debt.

14.2 THE DYNAMICS OF BUDGET DEFICITS AND THE PUBLIC DEBT

The **public debt** is the net amount that the government owes to the private sector at home and to foreigners.

It is useful to consider the two ways of financing a budget deficit separately. We begin with the more important one and ignore money financing for now. Focusing on the financing of deficits by issuing new debt develops an understanding of the intrinsic dynamic interaction between **budget deficits** and the **public debt.** In a second step we then look into how the detected process links with monetary policy.

No money financing and no inflation

Suppose an independent central bank refuses to finance budget deficits by issuing money. Then $\Delta M = 0$, and the **budget constraint**, the requirement that revenues must equal expenditures, as displayed in Figure 14.1, reads

$$T + \Delta B = G + iB \qquad \textbf{Budget constraint} \qquad (14.1)$$

The equation indicates that the budget deficit ΔB, or the *change* in public debt, is related to the *level* of the public debt B. Stabilizing the debt, that is letting $\Delta B = 0$ in equation (14.1), requires $T - G = iB$. Only if the primary budget pays for interest payments on the debt does the debt remain unchanged.

Stabilizing the public debt in absolute terms does not appear to be a very reasonable goal to achieve. A country that grows and accumulates wealth may well find a growing debt acceptable, as long as the debt ratio, the ratio between debt and income, B/Y, does not grow. The Maastricht Treaty takes that view, specifying that in order to qualify for EMU a country's debt-to-income ratio must not exceed 60%. In addition, the deficit-to-income ratio, $\Delta B/Y$, must be below 3%, a criterion that continues to apply to EMU members according to the Pact for Stability and Growth.

As a basis for discussing these criteria, but also if we want to compare countries of different sizes, or a country with growing income at different points in time, we need to express the budget constraint in terms of income shares. Suppose the price level is constant at $P = 1$. Then Y is both nominal and real income. Dividing both sides of equation (14.1) by Y and expressing variables as income shares by their respective lower-case letters ($b \equiv B/Y$, $g \equiv G/Y$ and $t \equiv T/Y$) yields

$$\frac{\Delta B}{Y} + t = g + ib \tag{14.2}$$

Be sure to note that $\Delta B/Y \neq \Delta(B/Y) \equiv \Delta b$. To the left of the inequality sign is the **deficit ratio**, i.e. the *budget deficit as a share of income*, as referred to in one of the Maastricht criteria. It gives current excess spending of the government as a share of aggregate income. To the right of $\neq$ is the change of the **debt ratio**, i.e. the *change of the public debt as a fraction of income*. It measures the change in the burden of all accumulated past deficits as a fraction of income. To see the relationship between $\Delta B/Y$ and $\Delta(B/Y)$, proceed from the definition $b \equiv B/Y$ which rewrites $B \equiv bY$. For small changes of b and Y we can make use of the approximation

Maths note. This approximation mimics the product rule in differential calculus, according to which the total differential of $B = bY$ is $dB = dbY + dYb$.

$$\Delta B = \Delta bY + \Delta Yb$$

Dividing both sides by Y gives

$$\frac{\Delta B}{Y} = \Delta b + yb \tag{14.3}$$

where $y \equiv \Delta Y/Y$ denotes the growth rate of income. Substituting equation (14.3) into (14.2), noting that since inflation is 0 the nominal interest rate equals the real interest rate ($i = r$), and solving for Δb gives

$$\Delta b = g - t + (r - y)b \qquad \textbf{Debt ratio dynamics} \tag{14.4}$$

Mathematically minded people call equation (14.4) a *difference equation*. A difference equation reveals how the change of a variable over last period's value, here $\Delta b \equiv b_{+1} - b$, is related to the previous level of this variable. In the current context, equation (14.4) thus describes how b, the public debt as a share of income, evolves over time.

The debt ratio does not change any more if $\Delta b = 0$. Substituting this into equation (14.4) and solving for b yields the equilibrium or steady-state debt ratio

$$b^* = \frac{g - t}{y - r} \qquad \textbf{Equilibrium debt ratio} \tag{14.5}$$

The sign of b^* is undetermined. Whether a country is required to be in debt or to be a creditor for equilibrium to obtain, evidently depends on whether or not the differences given in the denominator and in the numerator in equation (14.5) are of the same sign. If they are of the same sign, as in cases A and D in

Figure 14.2, a constant debt ratio requires *debt*. In cases B and C the country needs to be a *creditor* in equilibrium. All this can be read off Figure 14.3. As the graphs also reveal, however, the sign of $r - y$ not only has an impact on the nature of the equilibrium but also on *stability*.

A **phase line** is the path along which a variable moves in a dynamic model.

Plotting the values of Δb against b, as in Figure 14.3, yields a **phase line**. It is a straight line with a slope equal to $r - y$ and a vertical intercept equal to the primary deficit $g - t$.

The movement of the economy along the phase line is easily determined: if $\Delta b > 0$, that is north of the horizontal axis, b grows and movement is to the right. If $\Delta b < 0$, that is south of the horizontal axis, b falls and movement is to the left. With these insights and the knowledge that we cannot move off the phase line, we may check the dynamic properties of the four cases.

- *Case A*. In case A the government runs a primary deficit, and real income growth exceeds the real interest rate. Equation (14.4) may then be represented by a negatively sloped line that has a positive intercept. The top left-hand panel in Figure 14.3 shows such a line. This macroeconomic scenario is stable. No matter at what debt ratio b we start, as long as the primary deficit is as given, we always end up with a debt ratio of b^* in the long run. The reasoning for this is as follows. The interest rate determines how fast the debt grows due to interest payments alone, if these are being financed by issuing new debt. The income growth rate, of course, determines how quickly income grows. So with a balanced primary budget and income growth that exceeds the interest rate, the debt ratio converges to zero. Convergence also obtains with a primary budget deficit. But then equilibrium obtains at a debt level at which the reduction of the debt ratio due to income growth exceeding the interest rate is exactly balanced by what the primary deficit adds to the debt ratio.
- *Case B*. Case B differs from case A with the countries now displaying a primary budget surplus. This makes the government a creditor in equilibrium. Due to $y > r$ this equilibrium is still stable.
- *Case C*. In this case the government runs a primary deficit as in case A. But now income growth falls short of the real interest rate. This has two important consequences. First, the government must be a creditor for the debt ratio to be in equilibrium. Second, this equilibrium is fragile. Any small

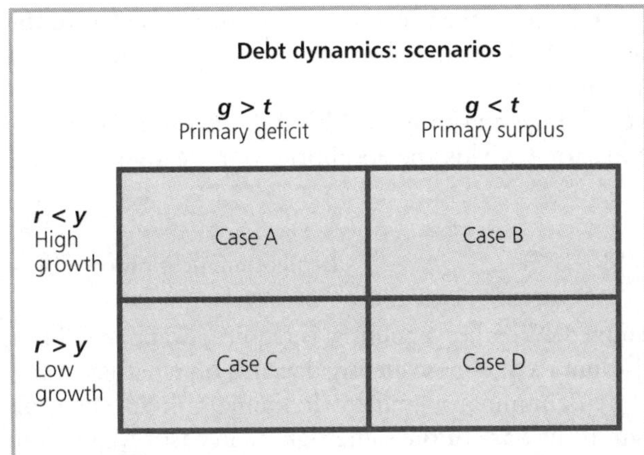

Figure 14.2 The dynamics of the public debt depend on whether the government runs a primary deficit or a surplus, and on whether growth exceeds or falls short of the real interest rate. This yields four different cases to be discussed separately.

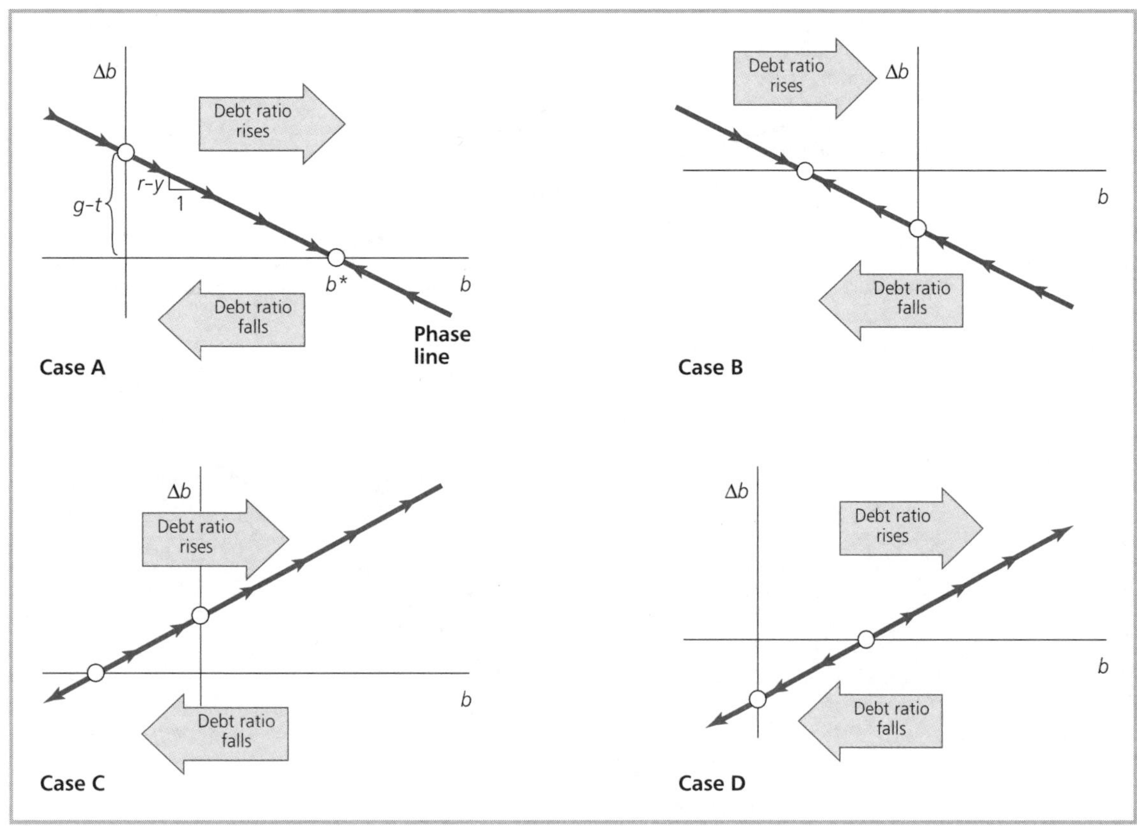

Figure 14.3 The four panels show the phase lines that describe the movement of the debt ratio b over time. If the slope of the phase line is negative (which is the case in A and B where $y > r$), the debt ratio converges to a steady state which is stable. If the slope is positive (as in cases C and D), a steady state exists, but it is unstable. After any small displacement the debt ratio moves away from it. Whether the steady-state debt ratio is positive or negative depends both on the sign of the primary deficit and on the slope of the phase line.

displacements trigger endogenous processes that make the debt ratio explode in either direction. Stabilization is only possible by appropriate adjustments of the primary deficit ratio.

- *Case D*. The dynamics of the debt ratio is characterized by instability as in case C. Due to the government running a primary surplus, equilibrium requires the government to be in debt.

To develop a better grasp of what happens as we move along a phase line, let us take a closer look at the dynamics of case A. Figure 14.4 shows this case again, with the phase line depicted in the upper panel being flatter than in Figure 14.3 for added realism, so that we may plausibly assume that the horizontal and the vertical axes are using the same units of measurement.

Now let the economy initially be at point 1 in the year 2001, running a primary deficit ($g_1 > t_1$), a budget deficit ($\Delta b_1 > 0$) and having a positive debt ratio ($b_1 > 0$). We know from our previous discussion that the economy does not remain at point 1. Because of the budget deficit in 2001, the public debt will increase and be higher in 2002 than it was in 2001. How high will it be? To find out, the 2001 deficit ratio needs to be added to the 2001 debt ratio to

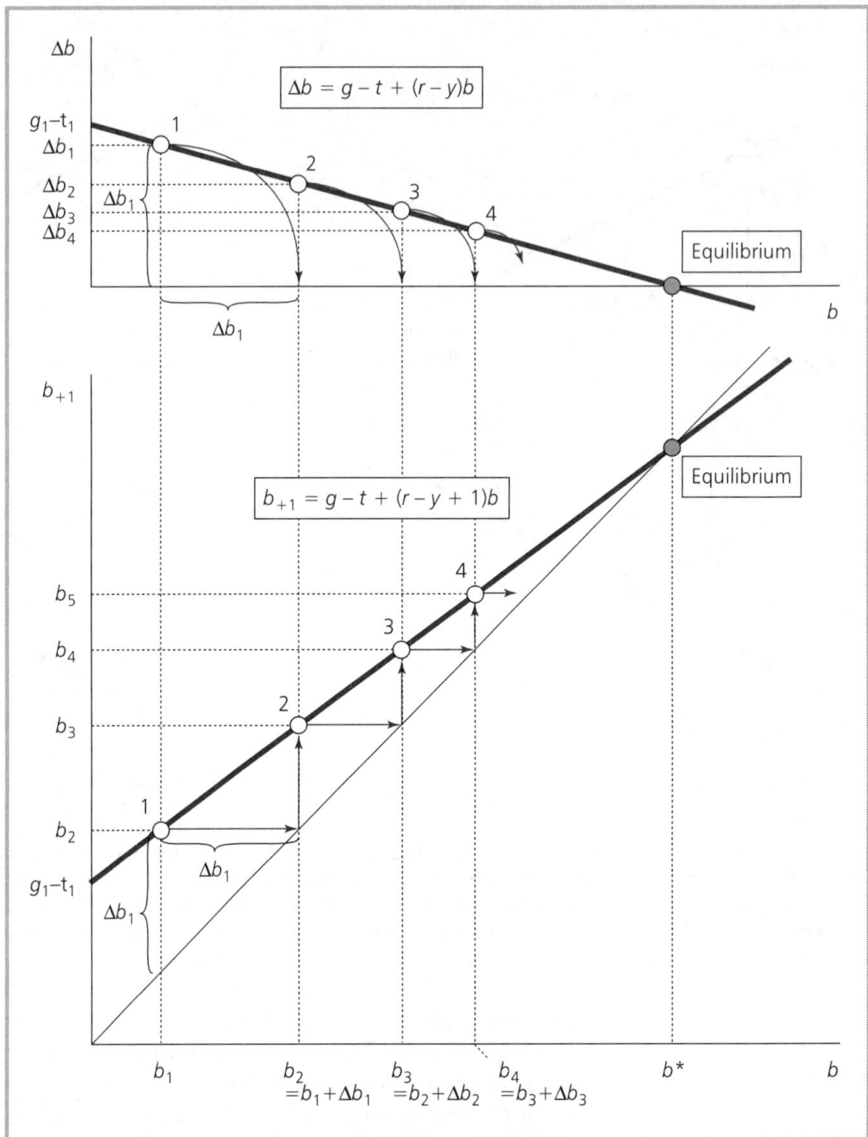

Figure 14.4 Path diagrams trace the development of dynamic models over time. They come in two forms. The upper panel measures the variable of interest, here *b*, on the horizontal axis and the change of the variable, Δb, on the vertical axis. Δb must be added to *b* to obtain next period's value of *b*. The path diagram in the lower panel also measures *b* on the horizontal axis, but next period's *b*, that is b_{+1}, on the vertical axis. When moving through time, next period's *b* must be transferred to the horizontal axis by means of the 45° line to become today's *b* as we enter the next period. This book uses the kind of phase diagram shown in the upper diagram. However, it may be useful to familiarize yourself with the type of diagram shown in the lower panel, as you will certainly encounter it in other courses, textbooks or journal articles.

yield the 2002 debt ratio ($b_2 = b_1 + \Delta b_1$). Graphically, therefore, the vertical distance of point 1 from the horizontal axis needs to be transferred to the horizontal axis and added to b_1. The rounded arrow depicts this transfer.

Having identified b_2, we can move up vertically until we hit the phase line in order to find out that the economy runs a deficit (ratio) of Δb_2 in 2002. This deficit again will add to the current debt next year, in 2003, and then we repeat the same procedure to find the 2004 debt ratio. Moving along the phase line step by step, driven by the described interaction between deficits and debt, this process continues under the parameter constellations presumed here until the debt ratio, with increments that get smaller and smaller, settles into its long-run equilibrium value of b^*.

There is another version of the phase diagram, which provides another way of depicting dynamic models in discrete time. Instead of writing debt-ratio dynamics as $\Delta b = g - t + (r - y)b$, which stands behind the phase line shown in the upper panel of Figure 14.4, we may substitute $\Delta b \equiv b_{+1} - b$ and solve for b_{+1} to obtain

$$b_{+1} = g - t + (r - y + 1)b$$

This alternative phase line can be displayed in a diagram that measures b_{+1} and b on its two axes (see bottom panel of Figure 14.4). Note this line's properties:

- It intersects the vertical line at $g - t$, just as the other phase line shown in the top panel.
- The difference $r - y$ determines whether the line is steeper or flatter than the 45° line.
- The line intersects the 45° line at b^*. Here $b_{+1} = b$, that is, the debt ratio does not change any more.

Now with the debt ratio being b_1 in the year 2001, the blue phase line tells us that the debt ratio increases to b_2 in 2002. Moving the dynamic equation one year ahead in time, we now use the 45° line to transfer b_2 from the vertical axis over to the horizontal axis. The phase line tells us that a debt ratio of b_2 in 2002 rises to b_3 in 2003. This continues under the current parameter constellations until the debt ratio, with increments that get smaller and smaller, eases into its long-run equilibrium at b^*.

The two approaches to phase-line analysis are shown in the two connected panels in Figure 14.4 in order to emphasize that they do lead to the same results. An advantage of displaying the models' dynamic behaviour as in the lower panel is that we can always read current and next period's values directly off the two axes. The advantage of using the version displayed in the upper panel, the version we prefer to use here, is that it shows budget deficits explicitly and thus facilitates the discussion of pertinent policy issues.

With such a rich menu of debt dynamics and equilibria available in theory, which is the relevant scenario in real life? The answer is that this depends on the country and on the year being considered. Table 14.1 shows how the primary surplus varies across countries and moves over time. There is no simple pattern in the data that hits the eye. At all points in time there were countries with a decidedly positive primary balance and countries that ran a

Table 14.1 Primary surpluses as a share of aggregate income: $t - g$. There is no clear pattern in the development of primary balances over time. At each point in time there are some countries that run a primary deficit and some that run a primary surplus. Note that since tax receipts are susceptible to the business cycle, so is the primary deficit.

	1975	1980	1985	1990	1995
Austria	−1.2	0.0	0.4	1.0	−2.2
Belgium	−1.8	−3.8	0.9	4.1	4.2
Denmark	−2.4	−2.8	4.1	1.8	1.7
Finland	1.9	1.9	2.1	3.6	−5.1
France	−1.7	0.8	−0.8	0.8	−1.8
Germany	−5.6	−1.6	1.1	−0.1	0.2
Greece	−2.1	−0.3	−6.7	−3.8	3.9
Italy	−8.1	−3.9	−5.2	−1.8	2.9
Ireland	−8.5	−8.5	−4.3	3.8	1.7
Netherlands	−1.2	−1.9	1.1	−0.7	1.6
Portugal	n.a.	8.4	0.9	3.2	0.4
Spain	0.1	−1.9	−4.2	−0.8	−1.0
Sweden	0.6	−4.4	−0.8	4.3	−4.7
United Kingdom	−1.2	−0.3	0.5	1.2	−2.1
Japan	−2.8	−3.4	0.9	3.6	−3.4
United States	−2.9	−0.1	−1.0	−0.4	0.5

Source: OECD, *Economic Outlook*

sizeable primary deficit. Some countries improved their primary balance over time, and some did not. In terms of the matrix given in Figure 14.2, countries were distributed fairly evenly in both columns and moved back and forth between them. If anything, more countries ran a primary surplus in 1995 than five, ten or fifteen years earlier. This 'trend' may not be quite realistic, however, since 1975 and 1980 were both recession years that followed major increases in oil prices. Recessions tend to make deficits larger than budgeted by depressing income and tax receipts.

Next, consider the difference between real income growth and the real interest rate, $y - r$ which determines the slope of the phase line. Table 14.2 reveals a clear pattern over time and easily explains why budget deficits and the public debt have moved to centre stage on the macroeconomic agenda. In the 1960s all countries for which data are available had real income growth rates that were much higher than real interest rates. Thus deficit spending would not cause public debt to run out of bounds, and substantial leeway was provided for fiscal policy. Denmark, for example, whose growth rate exceeded the real interest rate by three percentage points, could have afforded a primary deficit of 2% to meet today's Maastricht convergence criterion of a 60% debt ratio in the long run.

In the 1970s the picture started to change. With growth rates falling worldwide, the difference between income growth and the real interest rate became smaller and was even negative for Denmark. This process continued and intensified into the 1980s. Now there was just one remaining country in our sample that grew at a rate higher than the real interest rate. In terms of our case matrix in Figure 14.2, the industrialized countries, including the European countries, had moved from the first line, representative of the 1960s, to the second line, representative of the 1980s and 1990s. In terms of phase lines, a stylized

Table 14.2 Real income growth minus real interest rate: $y - r$. There is a clear pattern in the difference between growth and the real interest rate. In the 1960s and 1970s (with the exception of Denmark), real interest rates fell short of income growth in all countries. Since the 1980s the opposite applies. This puts all countries in the second row of the matrix in Figure 14.2 above.

	1960–9	1970–9	1980–9	1990–5
Austria	3.86*	1.69	−2.32	−2.01
Belgium	1.35	2.39	−3.71	−4.16
Denmark	3.01	−0.89	−4.95	−4.88
Finland	9.50	6.61	0.42	−9.10
France	4.07	3.79	−2.14	−4.62
Germany	0.13	0.13	−2.78	−1.42
Italy	3.62	5.46	−0.68	−5.25
Ireland	1.86	4.71	−0.12	−1.09
Luxembourg	6.30	2.35	−0.68	−1.72
Netherlands	4.59	2.20	−3.54	−2.89
Portugal	n.a.	11.16	3.66	−3.80
Spain	n.a.	6.20	−1.40	−4.76
Sweden	2.28	2.49	−2.00	−4.99
United Kingdom	0.07	3.09	−1.31	−3.79
Japan	10.16	6.03	−1.72	−3.71
United States	1.94	2.45	−2.57	−1.61

Note: From 1965.
Source: IMF, *IFS*; OECD, *Historical Statistics*.

representation and explanation of the big picture in international debt dynamics is as shown in Figure 14.5.

For a country with a constant primary deficit ratio the 1960s can be represented by the steep negatively sloped line. High income growth caused debt ratios to converge towards b^*_{1960s}. Whether this equilibrium was already attained, or the country was still on the way, growth weakened in the second half of the 1970s, turning the phase line upwards. For the country pictured here it remained negatively sloped, but became much flatter. As a result the debt ratio began to grow again (or to grow faster), moving towards a new equilibrium much further out to the right. While this process was probably still under way, the determinant of the slope of the phase line, $y - r$, weakened even

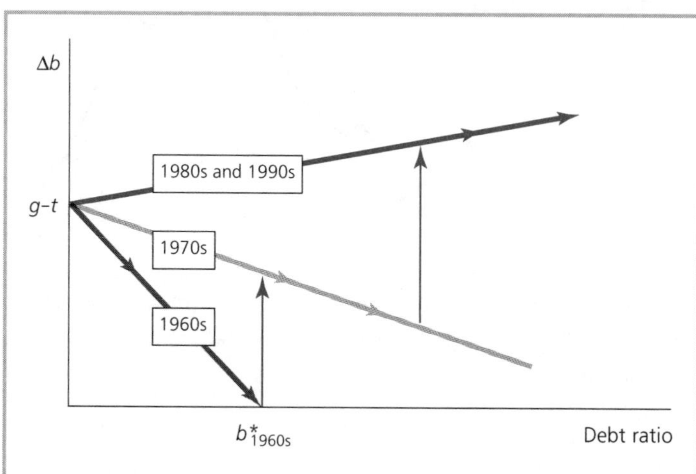

Figure 14.5 During the 1960s growth was much higher than the real interest rate, yielding a steep phase line and an equilibrium deficit ratio of b^*_{1960s}. In the 1970s the phase line becomes flatter, so that even with unchanged primary deficits the debt ratio would start to grow. Since the phase line became positively sloped in the 1980s, there is the danger of the debt ratio growing out of bounds.

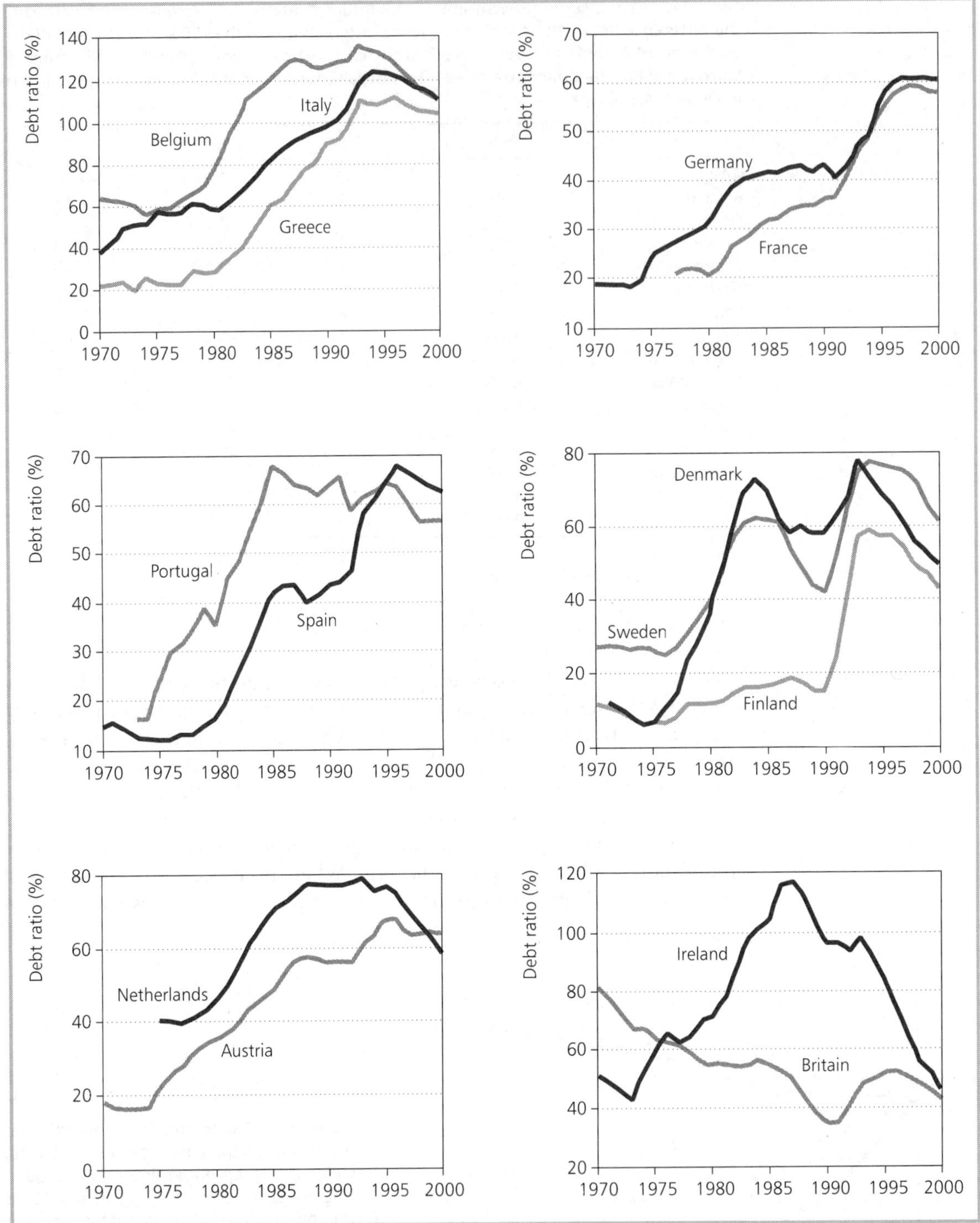

Figure 14.6 The history of debt ratios in EU member states.
Source: *Eurostat*.

further and turned negative. Not only did this speed up the growth of the debt ratio again, it also made the whole process inherently unstable. There were no longer any internal forces at work that would prevent the public debt ratio from growing out of bounds.

As Figure 14.6 shows, the development of debt ratios in current EU member states since 1970 reflects by and large the stylized interpretation proposed in Figure 14.5. With the exception of Great Britain (which entered the 1970s with the highest debt ratio of all), all countries saw their debt ratios rise dramatically from the mid- or late-1970s. Some stabilization efforts are visible in the mid- or late-1980s, with permanent success documented only in Ireland. In most countries there is a flattening of the path in the mid-1990s, often even a recent turnaround that is likely to reflect efforts to meet the Maastricht criterion on public debt.

The diagrams shown so far have focused on this *debt(-to-income) ratio*. Since there is another Maastricht criterion that restricts the *deficit(-to-income) ratio* to less than 3%, we now take a look at this variable. Equation (14.2) directly shows how the deficit ratio fits into our graphs. Solving the equation for $\Delta B/Y$ gives

Note. Since this section sets inflation to 0, we might also have written $(\Delta B/Y) = g - t + rb$ for the deficit ratio line. This would be misleading, however, as it is not correct when there is inflation. See equation (14.8) on p. 386.

$$\frac{\Delta B}{Y} = g - t + ib \qquad \textbf{Deficit ratio} \quad (14.6)$$

How the deficit ratio $\Delta B/Y$ relates to the debt ratio b is determined by a positively sloped line in a diagram with the deficit-to-income ratio on the vertical axis and the debt-to-income ratio on the horizontal axis. The intercept with the vertical axis is given by the primary deficit again. So the line intersects the phase line on the vertical axis. The slope of the line is always positive (since $i > 0$) and equal to the interest rate. It is steeper than the phase line (which has slope $r - y$), unless $y < 0$ or $i < r$. Panels (a) and (b) in Figure 14.7 add the newly developed deficit ratio line to the phase line diagrams shown in panels (a) and (d) of Figure 14.3.

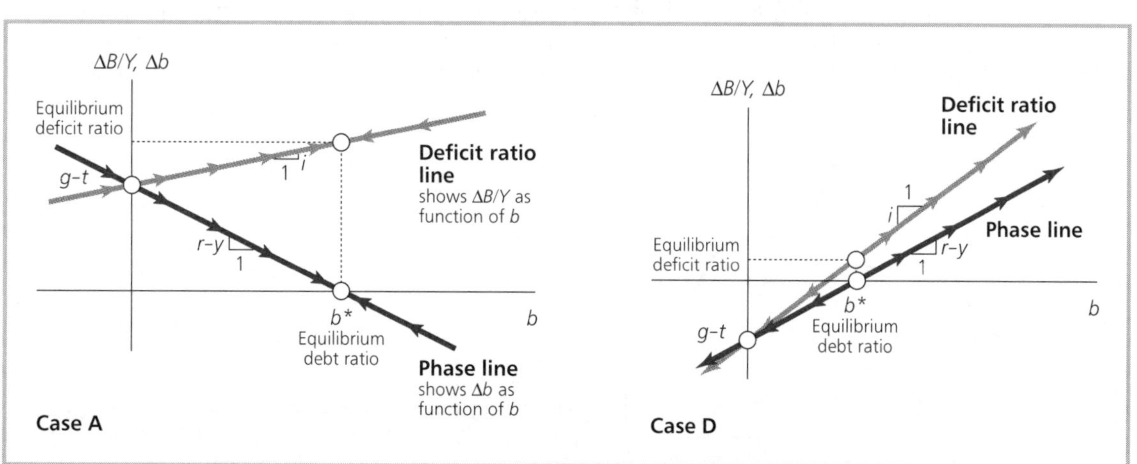

Figure 14.7 The dark blue *phase line* has slope $r - y$. It indicates the change of the debt ratio, Δb, that is associated with each level of the debt ratio b. The lighter *deficit ratio line* has slope i. It indicates the deficit ratio $\Delta B/Y$ that is associated with each level of the debt ratio.

CASE STUDY 14.1 The rise and fall of Ireland's public debt

While most European countries (the exception being Britain) had witnessed a steep increase of debt ratios since the start of the 1970s, it is noteworthy that one country, Ireland, had managed to reverse this trend well before it was forced to do so by the 1992 Maastricht Treaty. Figure 1 documents the rise and fall of Ireland's debt ratio, with the turnaround showing before the turn of the decade. To develop an understanding of Ireland's remarkable achievement, a useful place to start is the debt-ratio dynamics equation

$$\Delta b = g - t + (r - y)b \tag{1}$$

which states that two factors tend to make the debt ratio b grow: if the government runs a primary deficit, meaning that it spends more on goods and services, g, than it takes in as revenue, t; or if the real interest rate r exceeds real GDP growth y. Then an existing debt rises faster than GDP so that the debt ratio goes up even if the primary balance $g - t$ is zero. The graph of equation (1), the phase line, has a positive slope and describes an inherently unstable situation if $r > y$.

The lowest point in Figure 2 identifies Ireland's debt situation in 1980. The negatively sloped phase line passing trough this point indicates that the government ran a primary deficit of nearly 10% of GDP. Since GDP growth obviously exceeded the real interest rate on government debt, the situation nevertheless was inherently stable. Even if the Irish government's structural spending behaviour had never changed, while GDP growth and the real interest rate had remained the same, the debt ratio would never have exceeded 85% of GDP.

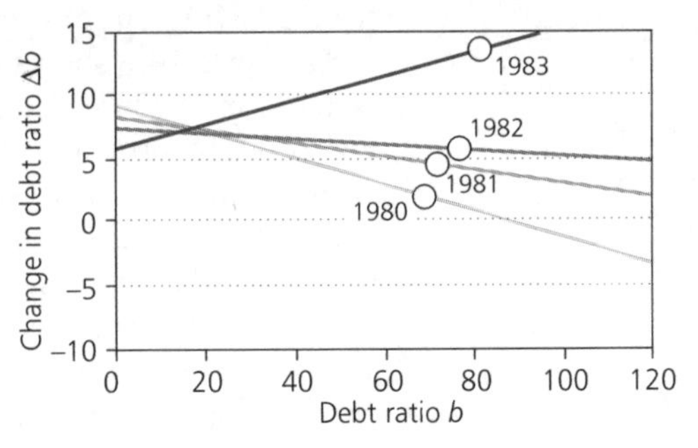

Figure 2

The other three points shown in Figure 2 trace the development between 1981 and 1983. Two trends are visible: first, the macroeconomic environment deteriorated step by step. The real interest rate rose compared with real income growth, rendering the situation inherently unstable as early as 1983. Second, the primary deficit was reduced in small steps to just over 5% of GDP in 1983. This did not do much good, however, in face of the unstable macroeconomic environment (meaning r exceeding y). Both factors together made the debt ratio rise at an accelerating pace.

The situation changed in two respects after 1983, as Figure 3 documents. First, the Irish government reduced the primary deficit ratio further. It was now driven below 5%. Also, the macroeconomic environment became more favourable again. With the exception of 1986, the phase lines

Figure 1

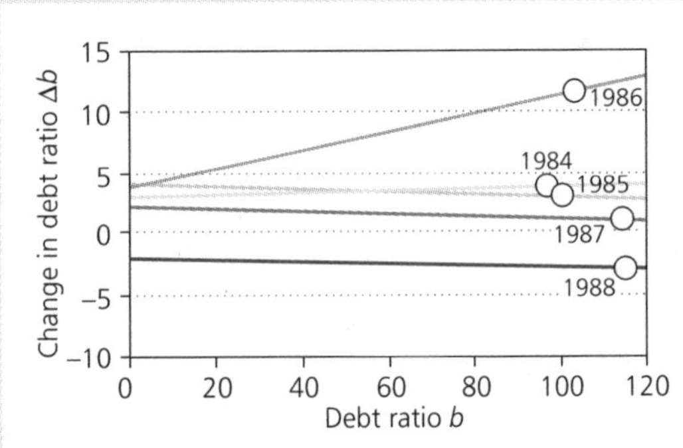

Figure 3

Case study 14.1 continued

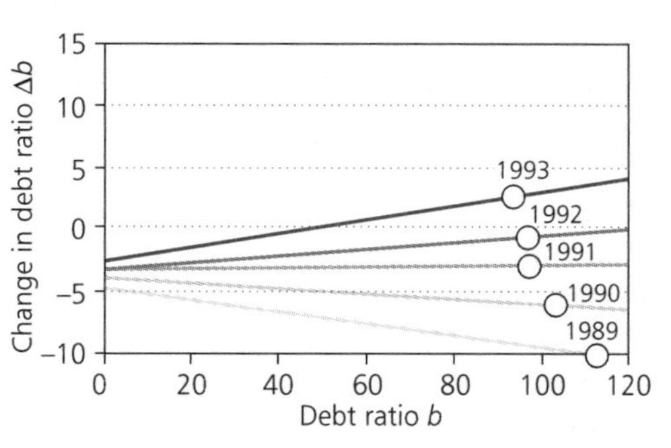

Figure 4

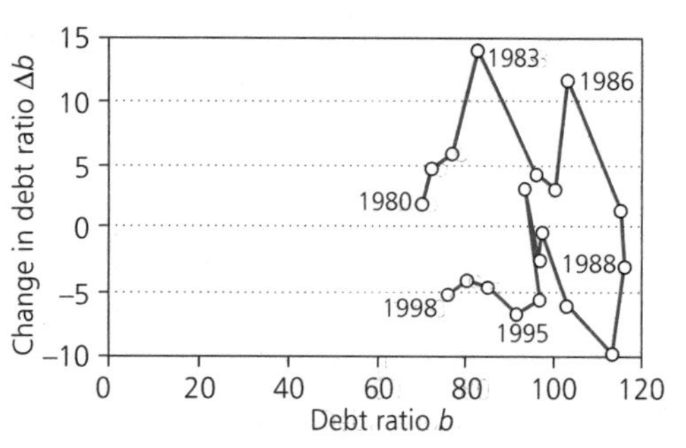

Figure 6

were now more or less horizontal, indicating that the real interest rate and real GDP growth were about the same. Whether the debt ratio rises or falls then crucially depends on the sign of the primary balance. As long as there was still a primary deficit, the debt ratio continued to rise, though now at a slower pace. The decisive and lasting change came in 1988, when the government budget moved into surplus for the first time (where it has remained since). For the first time in more than a decade this made the debt ratio fall.

Figure 4 shows the period between 1989 and 1993 when Ireland's government managed to keep the primary balance in surplus. Together with a mostly favourable macroeconomic environment, this permitted the debt ratio to fall quickly. This process was only briefly interrupted in 1993 when the interest rate was so much higher than the rate of growth that despite the primary surplus an increase in the debt ratio resulted in the year 1994.

The most recent period from 1994 to 1998, shown in Figure 5, is one with little change in policy or the macroeconomic environment. Stable primary surpluses and favourable macroeconomic conditions accomplished a steady fall of the debt ratio.

What is the **bottom line** of this case study? The Irish experience between 1980 and 1998 (summarized in an almost circular, clockwise movement in Figure 6) reflects both trends in fiscal policy and changes in the macroeconomic environment. The increase in the debt ratio between 1980 and 1988 basically occurred because the macroeconomic environment became unfavourable. An increase in government spending was not at the root of this development. By contrast, the primary deficit ratio even became smaller and smaller during these years. But only when the deficit turned into a surplus *and* the macroeconomic environment became more favourable did the debt ratio begin to come down. Had the primary deficit remained as high as it was at the beginning of the 1980s the debt ratio would obviously have continued to rise in the 1990s. Also, had the macroeconomic environment remained as it was at the beginning of the 1980s, Ireland's debt ratio would never have exploded the way it did.

Further reading: Brendan Walsh (1996) 'Stabilization and adjustment in a small open economy: Ireland, 1979–95', *Oxford Review of Economic Policy* 12: 74–86.

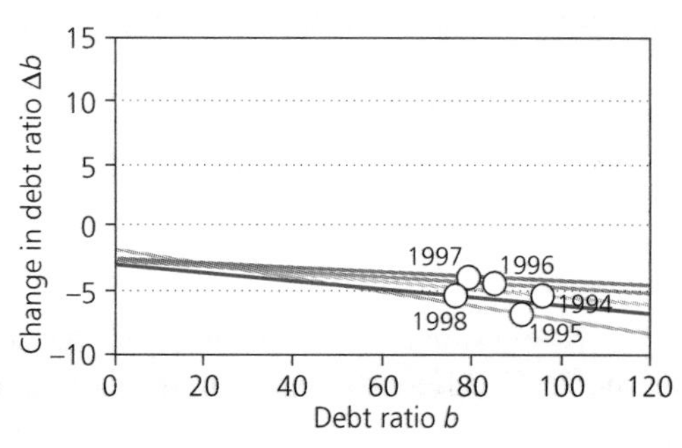

Figure 5

In case A, the debt ratio converges towards b^*. Movements along the phase line and into this equilibrium are being accompanied by synchronous movements along the deficit ratio line. Just vertically above b^* an equilibrium deficit ratio exists which happens to be stable in this scenario.

Case D represents the case in which the primary budget is in surplus and income growth falls short of the real interest rate. Here the equilibrium debt ratio is unstable. And so is the equilibrium deficit ratio, which is obtained by moving up vertically to intersect the deficit ratio line.

In the light of the severe political and economic obstacles surrounding budget cuts, **money financing** of deficits may loom as a highly tempting alternative. We have ignored this option so far, for good reasons. Some countries prohibit their central banks from financing government deficit spending beyond certain very tight limits. And even in countries where central banks and governments have that option, monetizing the debt has rarely been used to a substantial extent. This does not apply equally to all current EU members outside EMU and next-wave candidates, and the temptation to use the money press may rise as Euroland membership appears on the agenda and meeting the criteria by adjusting spending and taxes does not appear politically feasible.

With this motivation we next allow for money financing of deficits and for inflation, and then proceed to develop a wider perspective of fiscal and monetary policy.

Money financing and inflation

Drawing on Figure 14.1 once again, the budget constraint with money financing of the deficit is

$$T + \Delta B + \Delta M = G + iB \qquad \textbf{General budget constraint} \qquad (14.7)$$

Here M is central bank money or high-powered money, denoted $M0$ in Chapter 3. Transmission into other monetary aggregates appropriate in the macroeconomic models discussed throughout the book obtains via the applicable multiplier. Ignoring this here does not detract from the essence of the argument. Note further that central bank money also changes for motives other than financing the deficit, and through other channels such as buying and selling foreign exchange. So equation (14.7) is not meant to imply that monetization of the deficit is the sole source of central bank money creation, but to show the added contribution that may result from monetizing parts of the budget deficit.

To allow for price changes all variables are nominal and now need to be expressed relative to nominal income PY:

$$\frac{\Delta B}{PY} + \frac{\Delta M}{PY} + t = g + ib \qquad (14.8)$$

An approximation for $\Delta B/(PY)$ is obtained from solving the definition $b \equiv B/(PY)$ for B and forming the total differential (see maths note). After rearranging terms this yields

$$\frac{\Delta B}{PY} = \Delta b + (\pi + y)b \qquad (14.9)$$

Maths note. Rearranging $b = B/(PY)$ gives $B = bPY$. The total differential of a product of three variables is $dB = dbPY + dPbY + dYbP$, which can be proxied by $\Delta B = \Delta bPY + \Delta PbY + \Delta YbP$. Dividing by PY gives $\Delta B/(PY) = \Delta b + (\pi + y)b$, where $\pi = \Delta P/P$ and $y = \Delta Y/Y$.

The money financing ratio $\Delta M/(PY)$ may be expanded by M to yield

$$\frac{\Delta M}{PY} = \frac{\Delta M}{M}\frac{M}{PY} = \mu m \qquad (14.10)$$

where $m \equiv M/(PY)$ and, as a reminder, μ is the money growth rate. Substituting equations (14.9) and (14.10) into (14.8) and noting $r \equiv i - \pi$ yields our generalized description of debt ratio dynamics

$$\Delta b = g - t - \mu m - (y - r)b \qquad \textbf{General debt ratio dynamics} \qquad (14.11)$$

This generalization has provided two insights. First, the slope of the phase line, and hence the stability of the process, depends explicitly on the difference between income growth and the *real* interest rate. We had already presumed so above, by equating the nominal interest rate with the real interest rate at the absence of inflation. Now we have arrived at this result while explicitly allowing for inflation. Second, the position of the phase line not only depends

BOX 14.1 Seignorage vs inflation tax revenue

When the government (via the central bank) prints money, two things happen:

- The government endows itself with purchasing power, with a claim on the real output produced in the economy. This kind of government revenue is called **seignorage**.
- To the extent that the increase in the money supply leads to inflation, the public loses part of its income. Real income lost due to inflation is sometimes referred to as **inflation tax**.

In equilibrium seignorage and the inflation tax are mirror images of each other (the part of real income claimed by the government is not available any more for purchase by the public); but outside of equilibrium they are not.

Seignorage is defined as

$$\mu \frac{M}{P} \qquad \textbf{Seignorage}$$

The fraction measures the purchasing power of the nation's money supply which we have called the real money supply. If the government prints an additional 1% of the current money supply, its seignorage revenue equals 1% of the current money supply's purchasing power.

The inflation tax is defined as

$$\pi \frac{M}{P} \qquad \textbf{Inflation tax}$$

If inflation is 2%, the public's real money holdings shrink by 2%. To bring them back up to the desired level, individuals need to add a part of their nominal income to their money holdings. This part of income, 2% of real money holdings, is not available for consumption. It is as if individuals were paying a tax.

It is useful to compare seignorage and the inflation tax in terms of the *DAD-SAS* model. If money growth is accompanied by inflation of the same magnitude, income remains unchanged at $Y = Y^*$. Then the cake (real income) did not increase and seignorage must equal the inflation tax. Government revenue goes up at the expense of reduced purchases of the public. If $\mu > \pi$, say as we move up the *SAS* curve, the cake (real income) increases. Seignorage may now exceed the inflation tax because part of the government's additional claim on real output can come from the additional income generated by the money supply increase. In the extreme Keynesian scenario with fixed prices all seignorage revenue comes out of added output. Then the public pays no inflation tax in the short run.

There is a natural limit to how far seignorage may rise as inflation rises. The more inflation the government generates the higher interest rates rise. But higher nominal interest rates make holding money more costly and, therefore, reduce real money holdings M/P. After some threshold people are likely to reduce real money holdings faster than inflation eats away at the existing real money supply. Further increases in inflation then reduce rather than increase seignorage.

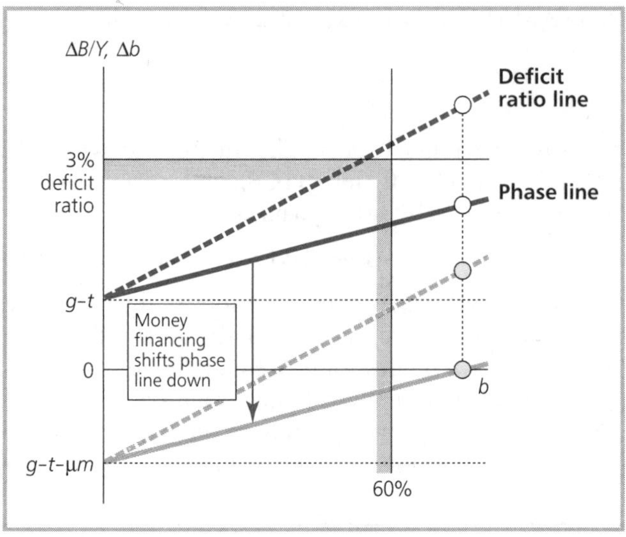

Figure 14.8 To stabilize the debt ratio of an economy (being in the white points) the phase line needs to be shifted down into the light blue position. This can also be achieved at an unchanged primary deficit by resorting to money financing of government spending.

on the primary deficit, but also on the amount of money financing relative to income. The government's revenue raised by money creation is known as **seignorage**, the flip side of which is the **inflation tax.**

Figure 14.8 illustrates that the required downward shift of the phase line into the lower, light blue position may be accomplished or ameliorated by printing money. If this appears as an easy loophole for governments that shy away from addressing structural budget problems, the time has come to put all five convergence criteria of the Maastricht Treaty into context.

14.3 MAASTRICHT, THE FISC AND THE CENTRAL BANK

We now proceed to provide a coherent view of how the Maastricht criteria on deficits and debt are related to the other three criteria. Consider Figure 14.9 in which the fiscal position of a country, say, France, is such that the Maastricht criterion on debt is not met. Echoing the above discussions, in order to stabilize the debt ratio (and initiate a movement back towards the Maastricht bounds) the phase line needs to be shifted down by the amount A indicated by the blue arrow. Since the vertical intercept is given by $g - t - \mu m$, this can be achieved either by reducing public spending, by raising taxes, by accelerating money growth or by an appropriate combination of these measures. Algebraically, we need $\Delta(g - t) - \Delta\mu m = A$.

The top right-hand diagram in Figure 14.9 maps this **budget adjustment requirement** A onto the horizontal axis by means of a 45° line. The bottom right-hand diagram shows the policy options. The vertical axis measures the change in money financing, $\Delta(\mu m)$ and the horizontal axis measures the change in the primary deficit ratio, $\Delta(g - t)$. The adjustment may be brought about by money financing, by changes in the primary budget or by an appropriate combination of the two. The primary budget alone would have to change by $\Delta(g - t) = A$. The money growth rate alone would have to change approximately by $\Delta\mu = A/m$. The negatively sloped line shows all options that

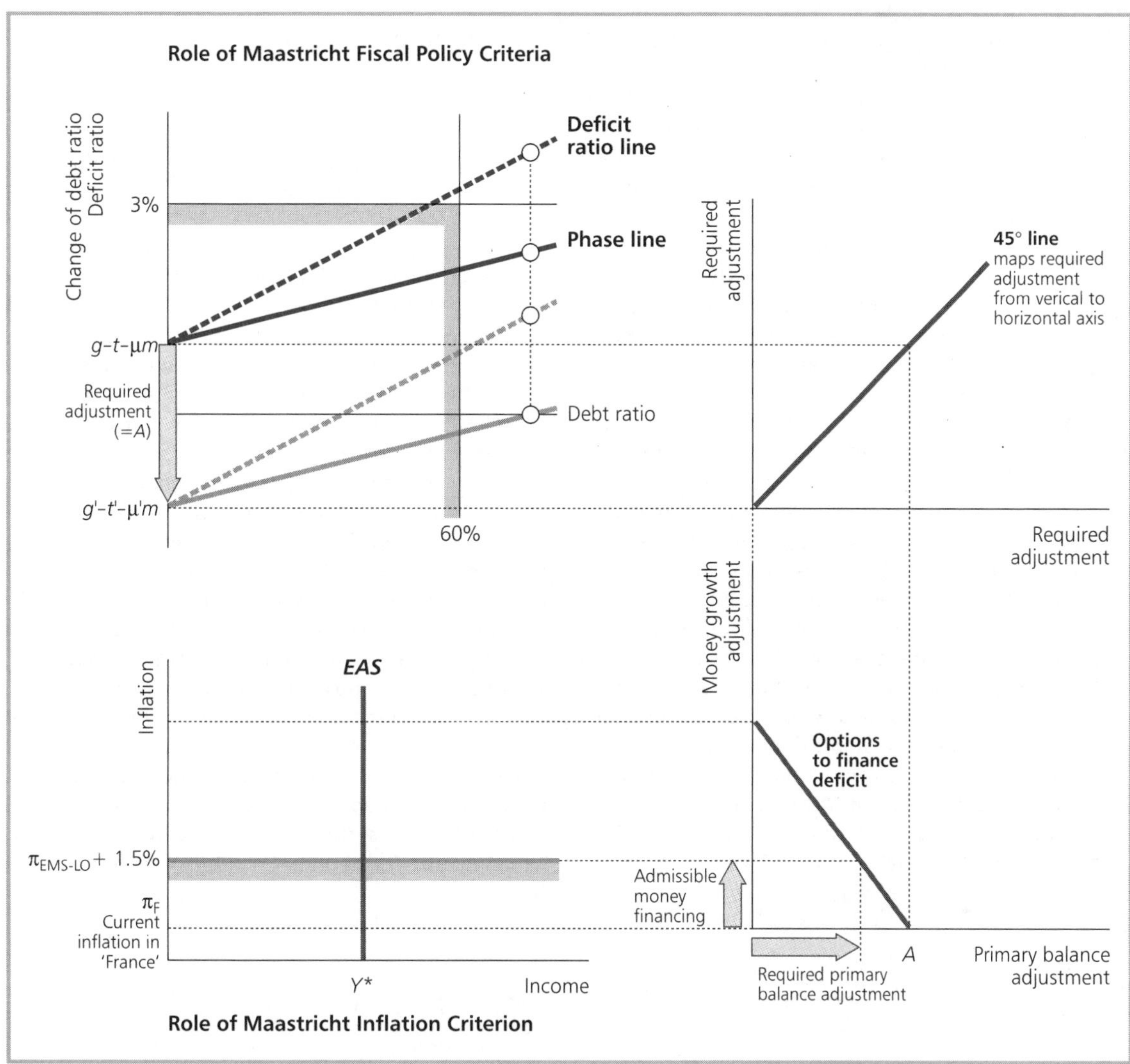

Figure 14.9 In the top left-hand graph the blue arrow indicates the adjustment required to stabilize the debt ratio. The 45° line in the top right-hand panel maps required adjustment onto the horizontal axis. The bottom right-hand panel shows all combinations of primary balance adjustment and money growth adjustment that would achieve the required adjustment. The bottom left-hand panel shows how much inflation and, hence, money growth is permitted by the Maastricht inflation criterion (assuming that income growth is 0). The leeway here equals the difference between France's current inflation and the Maastricht criterion. After marking this 'admissible money financing' in the bottom right-hand panel we can read off how much fiscal adjustment (in terms of the primary balance) is still needed.

would bring about the required adjustment by combinations of primary budget changes and money financing.

Spending cuts and tax increases are politically highly sensitive measures. The preferred option is therefore probably to let the money printing press do most of the adjustment. But here is where the other Maastricht criteria weigh in, particularly the inflation criterion. This states that a country's inflation rate may not exceed the average inflation rate of the three countries with the lowest inflation rates by more than 1.5 percentage points.

CASE STUDY 14.2 Who wanted the euro? The role of government debt

In the mid-1990s not all 15 member states of the European Union welcomed the prospect of a single currency. At one extreme, 70% of Italians welcomed the euro while only 15% rejected it. At the other extreme only 25% of the Danish public wanted the euro while a hefty 60% did not. We saw in Case study 11.1 that part of this difference in attitudes can be attributed to different inflation experiences and, hence, different benefits from the price stability the ECB's monetary policy is expected to bring. We now ask whether fiscal policy experiences play a similar role in public attitudes.

A side effect of the adoption of the euro is that the Treaty of Maastricht disciplines *fiscal policy*. This will affect those countries most which revealed least discipline in government spending in the past. Why should the public care about government budgets? Well, we learned in Chapter 10 that if the government runs deficits, spending mostly on public consumption, there will be less investment, less capital formation and, hence, a steady state that is characterized by a lower capital stock and less income. Since the public debt roughly sums up all past deficits, it is a good indicator of fiscal discipline, or the lack thereof. We may thus postulate a negative relationship between the public debt ratio b and potential income Y^*, say in the form $Y^* = \bar{Y} - \alpha b$, where $\bar{Y}$ denotes maximum potential income to obtain when the government keeps its budget balanced on average. Of course, $\bar{Y}$ differs for each country depending on population size and other parameters.

Figure 1 illustrates the essence of this argument, using Belgium, Italy, Denmark and the UK as examples. The interpretation of the graph is as follows. The EMU dot denotes the hypothetical steady-state income each country can achieve once its spending is disciplined by EMU and the Pact for Stability and Growth. The other dots reflect what each country may expect outside of EMU, based on past debt performance and on the assumption that potential income is negatively correlated with the debt ratio. Britain, for example, could expect to move from the Britain dot into the EMU dot and reap the associated utility gains. Generally, countries like Belgium and Italy (with debt ratios of 135% and 122%, respectively), can expect a relatively large increase in potential income and, if all countries' citizens have the same preferences as indicated by the indifference curves shown, should benefit a lot from adopting the euro. Denmark and Britain, with more moderate debt ratios of 70% and 57%, respectively, would have to settle for much lower benefits. Summing up: *The higher a country's government*

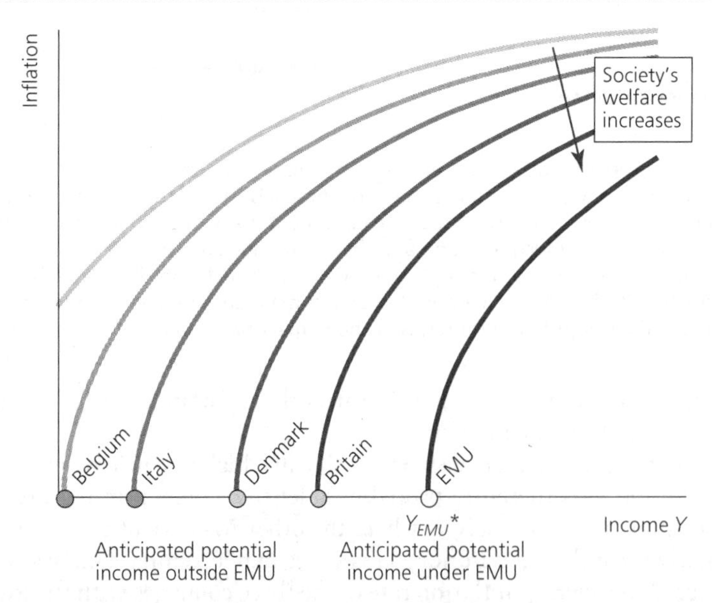

Figure 1

Case study 14.2 continued

deficits (as summed up in the current public debt) were in the past, the more its public should welcome the euro.

Figure 2 allows a detailed examination of this hypothesis. The horizontal axis measures the public debt in 1995 (reflecting the fiscal discipline mustered by independent national governments) for each of the 15 member states. The vertical axis measures the euro acceptance ratio (yes percentage divided by no percentage).

The data support the above hypothesis. Countries like Belgium, Italy and Greece, which had run up very high levels of debt, welcomed the euro a lot. Acceptance ratios ran between 3 and 6. Other countries such as the UK, Denmark and Finland, on the other hand, whose governments had succeeded in keeping the public debt in check even without the euro, bluntly rejected the euro with acceptance ratios around 0.5.

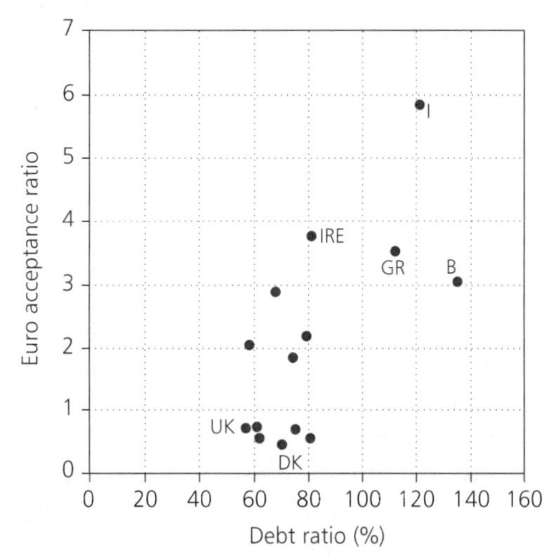

Figure 2

The correspondence between debt and the acceptance ratio suggested by the graph, is not perfect. Italy, for example, has less debt than Belgium, but the acceptance ratio is twice as high. The explanation is that the acceptance ratio depends not only on debt but also on past inflation, and Italy had suffered from much higher inflation than Belgium, as we learned in Case study 11.1. For the same reason, because of pre-euro inflation rates in double figures, Ireland has a rather high acceptance ratio despite a moderate debt ratio.

Tracing the acceptance ratio back to two explanatory variables, inflation and debt, reveals the limitations of graphical data analysis: it cannot properly handle and illustrate relationships between more than two variables. Adequate treatment of more complex relationships requires statistical methods, the kind you are encouraged to use in the 'Your turn' section in this chapter's applied problems. With this reservation, the empirical evidence on how the debt ratio influenced public attitudes towards the euro underscores our previous result (see Case study 11.1) that the public in the EU member states apparently knew quite well why it wanted the euro or why it didn't.

Source and further reading: M. Gärtner (1997) 'Who wants the euro–and why? Economic explanations of public attitudes towards a single European currency', *Public Choice* 93: 487–510.

The bottom left-hand diagram in Figure 14.9 shows the equilibrium aggregate supply curve in the familiar inflation–income diagram. The inflation average of the three low inflation countries is called $\pi_{EMS\text{-}LO}$. So the Maastricht benchmark to be met by France is $\pi_{EMU} = \pi_{EMS\text{-}LO} + 1.5$. Supposing that French inflation so far equalled π_F, the maximum amount of money financing it can afford without violating Maastricht is $\pi_{EMU} - \pi_F$. In the example depicted here this still leaves a sizeable requirement of adjustment in the primary budget balance.

This chapter would not be complete if we ducked two crucial questions. The first, more basic one is: what is wrong with running deficits and accumulating debt? Is it really true that public debt places a burden on future generations, as is often claimed, and therefore is to be avoided? The second question is related to the first but is the more urgent one, given that the world, and Europe with it, appears to be on the brink of a recession in 2002: does EMU, or a monetary union in general, need budget rules as spelled out in the convergence criteria and in the Pact for Stability and Growth? We begin with a brief discussion of the first, more general question.

14.4 WHAT IS WRONG WITH HAVING DEFICITS AND DEBT?

Though this question had not been specifically posed in Chapter 10, we had found the basic answer in section 10.1, where the influence of the government budget on economic growth is discussed in the context of the Solow model. It should suffice here to restate the main insights.

A government budget deficit needs to be financed by credit from the private sector (if we exclude money financing). That means it sucks up private savings, by domestic residents or from abroad, that are then no longer available for capital formation. This reduces the capital stock the country has in the steady state and, therefore, steady-state and potential income.

The insight that repeated budget deficits are bad for income in the long run comes with a few caveats:

- It only applies with full force when the government spends only on public consumption. When the government finances investment projects instead, budget deficits today may even be good for future income levels.
- It needs to be re-evaluated in the context of the Golden Rule of Capital Accumulation. If private savings were excessively high, a government budget deficit might be detrimental for steady-state income, but nevertheless raise present and future consumption.
- If the Ricardian equivalence theorem applied in strict form, the government would not be able to influence national (private plus public) savings. Private savings would simply respond so as to compensate for any changes in public savings. Then budget deficits would not impact on capital formation and steady-state income. While this is a theoretical possibility it appears that this is not the case in reality.

Structural budget deficits run by current generations accumulate debt on which future generations have to pay interest, meaning that this part of their income will not be available for consumption or capital formation. The extent to which this must be considered an unfair burden on future generations depends on whether future generations are compensated by appropriate returns. If today's deficits are due to excessive public consumption, then returns for future generations are zero and the verdict is clear: current generations do place an unfair burden on their offspring. If current deficits are due to investment spending, however, the verdict is open. As a general rule, the interest payment of future generations on government debt must be compared with the returns on investment projects conducted by previous generations before we can judge who is placing a burden on whom.

14.5 DOES MONETARY UNION NEED BUDGET RULES?

You may have noted that the previous arguments were carefully put. Deficits *can* be in the best interest of society, present and future, and *may* be desirable to some extent. It would be naive, however, to downplay or ignore the temptation for governments in today's democracies to direct spending and deficit spending into areas not chosen according to prospective long-run returns for society, but on the basis of short-run political gains. Fiscal policy is driven by incentives similar to those we emphasized while discussing monetary policy in Chapter 11. Just as such incentives may lure monetary policy into generating an inflation bias, fiscal policy may suffer from a **spending bias** that leads to an excessive level of public debt. Having noted those tendencies, the crucial question is whether a monetary union increases the government's temptation to spend or puts a lid on it.

The main argument in support of budget rules in monetary unions focuses on the creation of externalities by one country for other countries. Just as individuals spend more on given products if they can put part of the costs onto the shoulders of others, so will governments. Due to its *n*th currency privileges the Bundesbank made other EU members bear part of the costs of its disinflation efforts after German unification, by raising their interest rates. After the transition to a single European currency each member's fiscal policy action has a smaller effect on domestic interest rates than if the country had retained its own currency and flexible exchange rate. This is due to the open-interest-parity equilibrium condition for the international capital markets. If depreciation expectations are ruled out due to the adoption of a common currency, interest rates should remain the same in all member states at all times. This interest rate externality may undermine fiscal discipline, as we saw when discussing fiscal policy in a currency union in Chapter 12. Hence, budget rules as laid down in the Pact on Stability and Growth need to be put in place to provide for appropriate guidelines.

The advanced argument for fiscal policy rules ignores the possibility that capital markets put a risk premium on countries that run up debt ratios. Since rising debt ratios raise default risk, such countries may only obtain additional loans at higher interest rates than other, more disciplined countries. This would permit interest rates to differ between countries, even though bonds are denominated in the same currency, and thus limit the interest rate externality.

Figure 14.10 looks at two sets of data regarding risk premiums and interest rates. Panel (a) looks at the Fisher equation. In Case study 8.1 we presented evidence for the Fisher equation, which states that in equilibrium the interest rate equals $i = r^{W} + \pi$. In the presence of default and other risk, this equation generalizes to

$$i = r^{W} + \pi + RP \tag{14.11}$$

where RP is the risk premium required for domestic bonds. So home interest rates must be higher, the higher is inflation and the riskier domestic bonds are. The data do support these propositions. First, Russia and Turkey, the countries with the highest inflation rates in the sample, do have the highest nominal interest rates. Second, countries with low inflation, exemplified by some EU

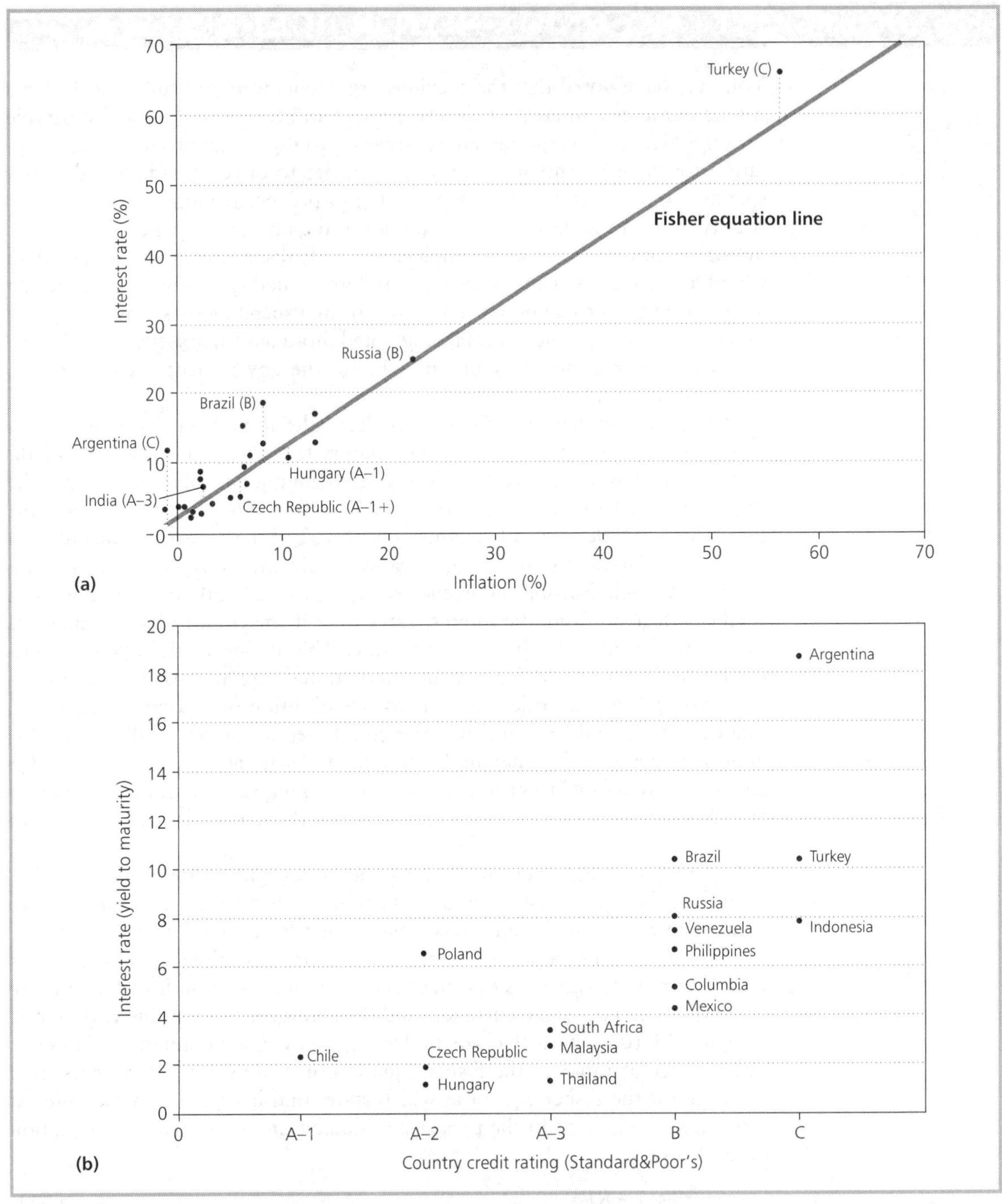

Figure 14.10 This figure looks at the effect of a country's default risk on the interest rate. Panel (a) compares interest rates for loans in national currency. The line shows which interest rates should obtain according to the Fisher equation. In equilibrium, each additional percentage point of inflation should drive up the interest rate by one percentage point. This is indeed roughly the case, but deviations from this line exist. As exemplified by a few countries, these deviations can be partly explained by differences in default risk. Higher than normal interest rates in Turkey, Brazil or Argentina seem to be due to their poor credit rating. Panel (b) looks at interest rates for loans in US dollars. The vertical axis measures differences against the interest rate for US loans. As we move along the horizontal axis to the right, credit risk increases and the interest rate goes up.

members included in the sample, benefit from low interest rates. This one-to-one relationship between inflation and interest rates is represented by the straight line with unity slope.

Most countries are close to this line, but a few are not. The interesting point is, that exactly those countries that are situated quite high above the Fisher line are those that have a poor credit rating according to the Standard&Poor's classification. While the countries positioned close to or below the line typically have an A classification, indicating a 'strong' credit rating, those classified significantly above the line typically have a B rating ('adequate') or even a C rating ('vulnerable') as in the case of Argentina and Turkey. The fit is not perfect, though, since Russia is on the line with a B classification and India is somewhat above the line with an A-3 classification. This is not surprising, however, since the S&P's rating cannot possibly be an all-encompassing measure of risk, and the data shown are short-run data, not long-run averages, and thus are also affected by the business cycle. However, the data illustrate the role of the risk-premium quite clearly.

Panel (b) in Figure 14.10 shows a somewhat different approach. It blends out all other factors that make interest rates differ between countries and currencies by looking at US dollar bonds issued by different countries. Again the vertical axis measures the interest rate (or the yield, to be more precise), and the horizontal axis indicates the Standard&Poor's classification. Again we see that while there is still some variability within risk classes, the risk premium a country has to pay compared with the yield of US bonds grows as a country's credit rating deteriorates.

The empirical evidence suggests that the risk premium may serve to caution fiscal policy. It can only do so if the risk is borne by the country whose policies generate it in the first place. If the market can be confident that some institution – this may be the International Monetary Fund on the world stage, or the other EU members in the case of the euro area – is committed to rescue individual countries that find themselves in financial trouble, there is no country-specific risk and, consequently, no risk premium that drives the domestic interest rate up. To prevent such bailouts, the Maastricht Treaty contains a no-bailout clause that ties the hands of governments and of the European Central Bank. Whether we are prepared to rely on financial markets and the risk premium to tame government spending depends on whether we consider such no-bailout clauses credible. If we do, no additional restrictions on fiscal policy are really needed and we could make do without the rules given in the Pact on Stability and Growth.

Many observers do not consider the no-bailout clause to be very credible, however. In this case, additional constraints are needed. While those specified in the Maastricht Treaty must be considered rather arbitrary, they may have helped to make the launching of the euro less painful. Limiting fiscal policy by rules, as the Pact on Stability and Growth continues to do, has a price. Whether this price is worth paying is difficult to judge on theoretical arguments alone or during normal times. We may obtain an answer when fiscal policy is genuinely needed, which may be during Euroland's first real recession.

CASE STUDY 14.3 Lessons from the Belgium–Luxemburg monetary union

Belgium and Luxemburg formed a monetary union in 1923. The exchange rate between the Belgian franc and the Luxemburg franc was fixed to 1 and Belgian francs were legal tender in Luxemburg. We can draw on the experience of these two countries to shed some light on the issues raised with respect to European Monetary Union in this chapter and in Chapter 12.

Figure 1 looks at inflation rates, interest rates, deficit and debt ratios. The top panel supports the proposition that, since a monetary union does not permit national monetary policies, inflation in the member states will be quite similar. Therefore, the expectation that an ECB commitment to price stability will indeed bring this about for former high-inflation members such as Greece or Italy is warranted.

The second panel in Figure 1 compares deficit ratios as a measure of government spending. The obvious message is that a common currency does not guarantee common fiscal policy. In fact, policies in the two countries could hardly be any different. Luxemburg has followed the most conservative fiscal policy of all in Europe, running budget surpluses regularly. Belgium, in contrast, used to be one of Europe's most generous public spenders. These disparate paths of fiscal policy caused quite divergent developments of the public debt ratio, as shown in the third panel in Figure 1.

Finally, Chapter 12 and the current chapter have argued that because of the possible negative effects of one country's deficit spending on other members, a monetary union may need fiscal policy rules as provided by the Maastricht Treaty and the Pact on Stability and Growth to cap fiscal policy excesses. There is some evidence for such an effect in the data. Belgian interest rates on government bonds have indeed exceeded Luxemburg's by a few percentage points for much of the past 25 years. The size of this premium appears modest, however, given that Belgium's debt ratio at one point approached one and a half year's national income while Luxemburg's debt ratio fell below 10% at the same time (though the premium seemed to be disappearing in the run up to the euro). One way to interpret this is to conclude that the market considers fiscal bailouts even more likely within Euroland than outside. In other words, the no-bailout clause does not seem to be very credible.

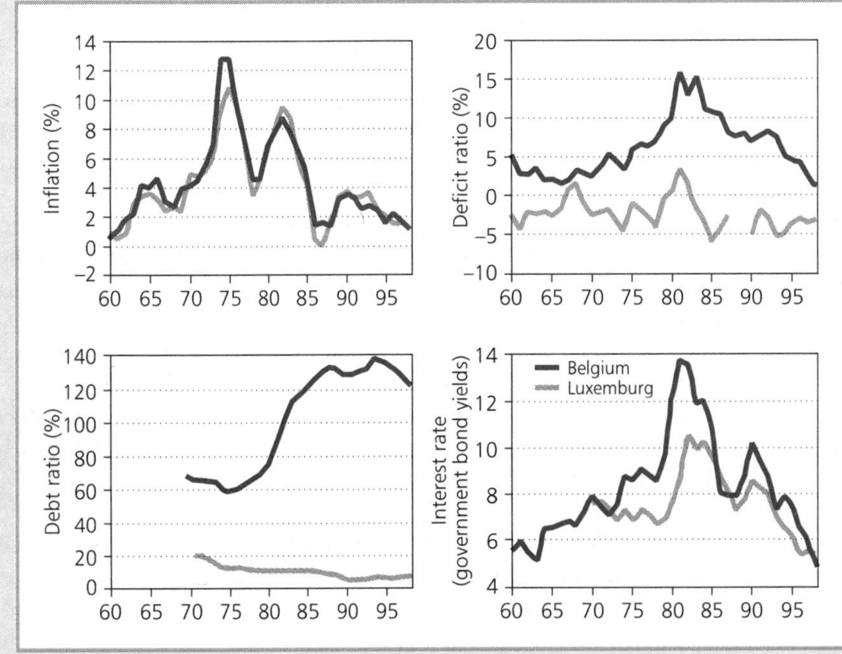

Figure 1

CHAPTER SUMMARY

- Ways of financing a government budget deficit, the difference between expenditures and tax receipts, are to obtain a loan from the public or for the central bank to print money.
- To allow for meaningful comparisons between countries and across time, a country's deficit spending and debt position must be expressed relative to income, in terms of deficit-to-income and debt-to-income ratios.
- Whether a country is a net borrower or a net lender in equilibrium depends on whether the difference between income and the real interest rate and the primary deficit are of the same sign. If they are, equilibrium implies debt. If they are not, equilibrium implies a net lender position.
- Data on income growth and real interest rates suggest that during the past two decades the dynamic interaction between deficits and debt was inherently unstable. In this situation, stabilizing the debt ratio requires appropriate adjustments of non-interest spending by the government.
- The Maastricht Treaty's convergence criteria on deficits and debt force governments to adjust government budgets. The inflation criterion augments these and ensures that governments have little leeway in solving budget problems by recourse to money financing.
- There is nothing inherently wrong with public deficits and debt. Deficit spending and debt accumulation need to be justified, however, either by the higher total investment that results from it, or by the rates of return on public investments that exceed potential rates of return on private projects that are crowded out.
- Monetary unions may undermine budgetary discipline unless the members can commit to a credible no-bailout clause. If that is not feasible, budget rules may be needed.

KEY TERMS AND CONCEPTS

budget deficit
debt ratio (debt-to-income ratio)
deficit financing
deficit ratio (deficit-to-income ratio)
government budget constraint
government debt
Maastricht criteria on deficits and debt
money financing
phase line
primary deficit
public debt
seignorage

EXERCISES

14.1 Table 14.3 presents data on debt and GDP for a number of European countries in 1992. Compute the debt ratios and determine the level of debt that would just meet the Maastricht criterion of 60% of GDP.

14.2 Consider a country with a primary deficit rate of 20%, a growth rate of 5% and a real interest rate of 3%.

(a) What is the equilibrium debt ratio b^*? Is the equilibrium stable?

(b) What is the deficit ratio in the long-run equilibrium?

(c) The government wants to increase the primary deficit to 35% of national income. What is the debt ratio in the new equilibrium? What is the deficit ratio?

(d) Suppose the country wants to meet the Maastricht criterion of a maximum debt ratio of 60%. What would be the primary deficit that would just meet this criterion?

(e) The interest rate rises to 4%, whereas the growth rate decreases to 2%. What is the new equilibrium debt ratio b^*? Starting from a primary deficit of 20%, does the country have a chance of reaching that equilibrium?

14.3 In this chapter, both the interest rate and the growth rate were taken as exogenously given. However, the Solow growth model presented in Chapter 9 provides us with the tools to determine whether, for a given country, the growth rate of income will be higher or lower than the interest rate in the steady state. (Recall that the interest rate equals the marginal product of capital.) Determine the relation between the growth rate of output and the interest rate for the following:

(a) Country A, where the production function is $\hat{y} = \hat{k}^{0.3}$ (where $\hat{y}$ is output per efficiency unit), the savings rate is 20%, the exogenous rate of technological progress is 0.04, the population growth rate is 0.02 and the annual depreciation rate is 10%.

(b) Country B, where the production is $\hat{y} = \hat{k}^{0.1}$ (where $\hat{y}$ is output per efficiency unit), the savings rate is 30%, the exogenous rate of technological progress is 0.05, the population growth rate is 0.01 and the annual depreciation rate is 10%.

14.4 A country's goods and capital markets are isolated from the rest of the world. Consumption out of disposable income is given by $C = 0.8(Y - T)$.

(a) How does steady-state income respond if only government spending is raised while taxes remain unchanged? What happens if taxes are raised while government spending is unchanged?

(b) Let the government raise spending and taxes by the same amount. How does this affect steady-state income? Explain.

(c) How is the result obtained under (b) affected if 50% of government spending is public investment?

14.5 In 1994 British interest rates were $i = 7.83\%$, inflation was $\pi = 2.67\%$ and real GDP growth stood at $y = 4\%$. The primary deficit ratio was 4.3%. What is the equilibrium debt ratio, assuming that i, π, y and $(g - t)$ remain unchanged? Is the equilibrium stable?

14.6 Let debt dynamics follow the familiar equation

$$\Delta b = g - t + (r - y)b$$

The interest rate includes a risk premium RP,

$$r = \bar{r} + RP$$

and the RP increases linearly with the debt ratio:

$$RP = \alpha b$$

Derive the phase line and discuss this country's debt dynamics. Do your results and insights differ from those obtained for the simpler model discussed in the text?

Table 14.3

	D	F	I[b]	GB	B	DK	FIN	GR
Nominal GDP[a]	3076.6	6776.2	1504.0	597.2	7098.4	851.3	476.8	18,238.1
Government debt[c]	1402.5	3076.1	1755.2	284.9	9306.0	627.4	220.3	16,140.7

Notes: [a] generally: in billions of domestic currency; [b] in trillion lire; [c] general government gross financial liabilities.
Source: OECD, *Economic Outlook*

RECOMMENDED READING

A comprehensive guide to the facts and issues of fiscal (and monetary) policy in EMU is Sylvester Eijffinger and Jacob de Haan (2000): *European Monetary and Fiscal Policy*. Oxford: Oxford University Press. See also Barry Eichengreen and Charles Wyposz (1998) 'The stability pact: more than a minor nuisance?', *Economic Policy* 13: 65–113.

APPLIED PROBLEMS

RECENT RESEARCH

Some political economy of government sector size

Nouriel Roubini and Jeffrey Sachs (1989, 'Government spending and budget deficits in the industrial countries', *Economic Policy: A European Forum* 8: 99–132) look at why different countries appear to aim for different levels of government spending. One of their regressions gives the result

$$(G/Y)_{Target} = \underset{(4.90)}{0.26} + \underset{(2.89)}{0.0018}\ LEFT + \underset{(2.28)}{0.047}\ POL$$

$R^2 = 0.49$; cross-section data for 13 countries

where $(G/Y)_{Target}$ is the long-run target ratio of government spending to output derived from another estimate, LEFT is the share of leftist parties in parliament (in %), and POL is an index that goes up if there are more parties in the ruling coalition.

The results suggest that left-wing parties desire a larger government sector. In fact, if the left-wing share in parliament increases from 0 to 100%, $(G/Y)_{Target}$ goes up by 0.18. The positive coefficient of POL indicates that $(G/Y)_{Target}$ rises if more parties stake their claims in a government coalition. The two variables explain 49% of the variation in targeted government spending ratios across countries.

Table 14.4

	Inflation rate π (in %)	Interest rate i (in %)	Sovereign credit rating	Risk dummy RISK
Hong Kong	−1.1	3.55	A−1+	0.125
India	2.5	7.08	A−3	0.750
Indonesia	13.0	17.35	C	2.000
Malaysia	1.5	3.30	A−1	0.250
Philippines	6.8	11.38	A−2	0.500
Singapore	1.2	2.40	A−1+	0.125
South Korea	5.0	5.10	A−1	0.250
Taiwan	0.1	3.90	A−1+	0.125
Thailand	2.2	3.00	A−2	0.500
Argentina	−1.0	12.09	C	2.000
Brazil	8.1	18.89	B	1.000
Chile	3.2	4.46	A−1+	0.125
Colombia	8.1	12.66	A−3	0.750
Mexico	6.6	7.24	A−2	0.500
Peru	2.2	7.90	B	1.000
Venezuela	13.0	13.07	B	1.000
Egypt	2.2	9.00	A−2	0.500
Israel	0.7	4.05	A−1	0.250
South Africa	6.3	9.66	A−2	0.500
Turkey	56.3	66.00	C	2.000
Czech Republic	5.9	5.58	A−1+	0.125
Hungary	10.5	11.00	A−1	0.250
Poland	6.2	15.35	A−1	0.250
Russia	22.2	25.00	B	1.000

Source: Inflation and interest rates from *The Economist*, 11 August, 2001.
Sovereign credit ratings from the Standard&Poor's homepage at www.standardandpoors.com.

WORKED PROBLEM

Interest rates, inflation and the risk premium

A credible no-bailout clause might render fiscal policy rules in a monetary union superfluous. The strength of this argument depends on whether markets do respond to risk strongly enough for risk differences to materialize in interest rate differences. To study this issue econometrically, consider the data in Table 14.4 for interest and inflation rates taken from *The Economist* for a sample of emerging-market economies and the accompanying default risk classification according to the *Standard&Poor's* credit rating.

We begin by regressing the interest rate on inflation to check for support of the Fisher equation (standard errors in parantheses):

$$\underset{(0.89)}{i = 3.56} - \underset{(0.065)}{1.065\pi} \qquad \bar{R}^2 = 0.92$$

The result is strong. With a *t*-statistic of 1.065/0.065 = 16.38 the estimated coefficient is highly significant. Differences in inflation rates explain 92% of observed differences in interest rates. At 1.065 the coefficient of π slightly exceeds the value of 1 which the Fisher equation suggests. To find out if this contradicts the Fisher equation, we can calculate the respective *t*-statistic as (1.065 − 1)/0.65 = 1. So the *t*-statistic says that in this sample 1.065 is not significantly different from 1.

Before we can address the influence of risk on interest rates we need to transform the qualitative Standard&Poor's ratings into numbers. Why? Well, we cannot type ratings such as A − 2 or B into our econometrics program. While other possibilities do exist, and you may want to experiment with some, we assume here that an A rating means no risk so that the RISK dummy variable would be 0. Then B is represented by a RISK value of 1, and C by a RISK value of 2. The subdivisions in the A category carry us in equal steps towards 1, the value for B, so that A–1 = 0.25, A–2 = 0.5 and A–3 = 0.75. A–1+ is assumed to be between A and A–1, that is A–1+ = 0.125. Adding the risk dummy variable to the Fisher equation gives

$$\underset{(0.94)}{i = 1.74} - \underset{(0.065)}{0.9497\pi} + \underset{(1.28)}{4.09\text{RISK}} \qquad \bar{R}^2 = 0.94$$

The key result here is that increased sovereign risk drives up the interest rate. Downgrading a country's credit standing into the next main category, that is from A to B or from B to C, raises the interest rate by 4.09 percentage points. Russia, for example, pays a risk premium of 4.09 × 1 = 4.09%. Turkey's risk premium is even higher at 4.09 × 2 = 9.18%.

A country with no inflation and an A rating would have a (nominal and real) interest rate of 1.74. If this country slips into risk catagory C its real interest rate increases to almost 10% (1.74 + 2 ∗ 4.09 = 9.92).

YOUR TURN

Who wanted the euro? (part II)

One purpose of moving to a common European currency is to discipline *monetary policy* and get inflation under control. In line with this, the worked problem in Chapter 11 showed that those countries whose citizens want the euro most are those that suffered from the highest inflation rates in the past.

A second purpose, or side effect, of moving to a common European currency is to discipline *fiscal policy*. This is spelled out by the Maastricht Treaty's fiscal policy criteria, and is to be made permanent by appropriate disciplinary mechanisms that are currently discussed. These would fine governments whose fiscal policy became too loose as measured against criteria similar to those of the Maastricht Treaty. A natural measure of loose fiscal policy in the past is the accumulated debt. So just as we expected high inflation in the past to pave the way to EMU acceptance, so should a high debt ratio. Use the debt ratio forecasts for 1996 given in Table 14.5, and check whether these are related to the EMUYES variable given in the worked problem in Chapter 8. Check also whether DEBT and AVINFL both determine public attitudes. Look at linear and non-linear influences.

Table 14.5

	A	B	D	DK	E	F	FIN	GB	GR	I	IRL	NL	P	S
DEBT	75	135	61	70	68	58	62	57	112	122	81	79	74	81

To further explore this chapter's key messages you are encouraged to use the interactive online module found at

www.fgn.unisg.ch/eurmacro/tutor/debtdynamics.html

and many other features hosted at **www.fgn.unisg.ch/eurmacro**

CHAPTER 15

UNEMPLOYMENT AND GROWTH

WHAT TO EXPECT After working through this chapter, you will understand:

1 How income growth and unemployment are linked via Okun's law.

2 How the equilibrium component of the unemployment rate, defined as the rate that remains in equilibrium, may be measured by means of the Beveridge curve.

3 How the factors affecting equilibrium unemployment have changed in some European countries.

4 How the two oil price explosions in the 1970s affected unemployment.

5 How temporary shocks to equilibrium unemployment may give rise to long spells of unemployment due to persistence.

6 How persistence affects income dynamics and policy options in the *DAD-SAS* model.

7 Why economists recommend a two-handed approach to solving the unemployment problem, meaning that structural improvements need to be implemented while at the same time attempting to stimulate demand.

This chapter brings us back to income, the most important macroeconomic variable. Closely related to income and income growth is unemployment, indisputably Europe's biggest economic challenge for some time now, and very probably well into this century.

Section 15.1 deals with the empirical link between income growth and movements of the unemployment rate. This link leads us to a discussion of the causes, the prospects and the potential cures for the European unemployment problem, within the EU and beyond. The apparent persistence in the labour market is introduced into the *DAD-SAS* model in Section 15.3 to obtain an even more realistic model of booms and recessions.

15.1 LINKING UNEMPLOYMENT AND GROWTH

Before we move on to the topic of unemployment we need to note that unemployment and growth are closely related. To establish a link between unemployment and growth we proceed from a linearized production function in which output Y is proportional by a factor a to employed labour L:

$$Y = aL \qquad \textbf{Linearized production function} \qquad (15.1)$$

Defining unemployment U as labour force N minus employment, $U \equiv N - L$, equation (15.1) turns into $Y = aN - aU$. Expanding (that is, multiplying and dividing) the last term by N gives $Y = aN - aNU/N = aN - aNu$, where $u \equiv U/N$ is the unemployment rate. This equation holds when the economy is in equilibrium. Then

$$Y^* = aN - aNu^* \tag{15.2}$$

where Y^* is potential output and u^* is the equilibrium (or 'natural') rate of unemployment. It also holds at other times, when Y and u deviate from equilibrium. Then

$$Y = aN - aNu \tag{15.3}$$

Subtracting equation (15.2) from equation (15.3) and letting $a' \equiv aN$ gives

$$Y - Y^* = a'(u^* - u) \qquad \textbf{Okun's law} \text{ (version 1)} \tag{15.4}$$

an equation known as **Okun's law**. It states that deviations of income from its potential level are proportional to the difference between the actual and the natural unemployment rate. Now recall the surprise or short-run aggregate supply curve

$$\pi = \pi^e + \lambda(Y - Y^*) \qquad \textbf{SAS curve}$$

The **Phillips curve** postulates a negative relationship between inflation and unemployment. This relationship is also affected by expected inflation.

Substituting Okun's law into the SAS curve and letting $\lambda' \equiv a'\lambda$ gives the famous **Phillips curve**

$$\pi = \pi^e + \lambda'(u^* - u) \qquad \textbf{Phillips curve}$$

which proposes a negative relationship between inflation and the rate of unemployment, the two foremost economic challenges of modern times.

Figure 15.1 shows the familiar *SAS* curve and the Phillips curve next to each other. The point to note is that the Phillips curve is simply a mirror image of the *SAS* curve. If inflation is as expected, income is at its potential

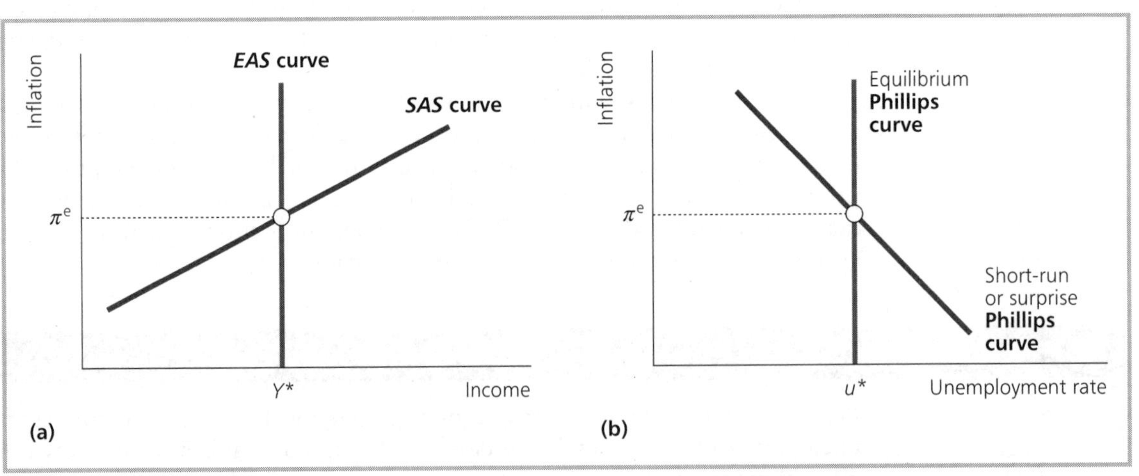

Figure 15.1 The Phillips curve is the mirror image of the *SAS* curve included in our tool-box. If surprise inflation raises income, it reduces unemployment at the same time. Just as the aggregate supply curve comes in a short-run (or surprise) version and in a long-run (or equilibrium) version, so does the Phillips curve.

level and the unemployment rate is at its natural level. Unexpected inflation drives income beyond equilibrium and the unemployment rate below equilibrium.

One version of **Okun's law** states that income growth is negatively related to the change in the rate of unemployment.

A second version of **Okun's law** results after taking first differences on both sides of equation (15.3), letting $a' \equiv aN$ again. This yields $Y - Y_{-1} = -a'(u - u_{-1})$. This formulation is fine in a theoretical context, in which production technology is kept unchanged. However, in empirical work we need to take into account that income growth only drives down unemployment when it exceeds the growth rate of potential income. Denoting potential income growth by b, the second version of Okun's law used in empirical work is $\Delta Y/Y_{-1} - b = -\hat{a}\Delta u$, or, after rearranging,

Note. Since $\hat{a} \equiv aN/Y_{-1}$, treating $\hat{a}$ as a constant is only a first approximation.

$$\Delta Y/Y_{-1} = b - \hat{a}\Delta u \qquad \textbf{Okun's law} \text{ (version 2)} \qquad (15.5)$$

Figure 15.2 documents Okun's law for the United States, the country for which the American economist Arthur Okun first detected the relationship, and for which it holds particularly well. The graph illustrates an important point: equation (15.5) may be rewritten as $\Delta u = (b - \Delta Y/Y_{-1})/\hat{a}$, which shows that unemployment only changes if the economy grows at a rate different from b. In an economy that grows along its potential output path, which assumes the labour market to be in permanent equilibrium, we would not expect the unemployment rate to change. So b is the economy's equilibrium growth rate, or the growth rate of potential output. As in most other countries, US growth has slowed down considerably since 1973, meaning that b became smaller. We would expect this to shift 'Okun's law' line down. As can be seen from the graph this is indeed what happened. The pre-1973 data marked by blue squares and the post-1973 data identified by white squares obviously need to be described by two different lines. Statistical techniques reveal that these two lines have the same slope of $\hat{a} \approx 1.84$, but different constant terms, namely $b_{pre73} = 3.9$ and $b_{post73} = 2.5$.

Now consider (West) Germany's data to illustrate how the experience of a typical European country differs from US experience (see Figure 15.3). Three

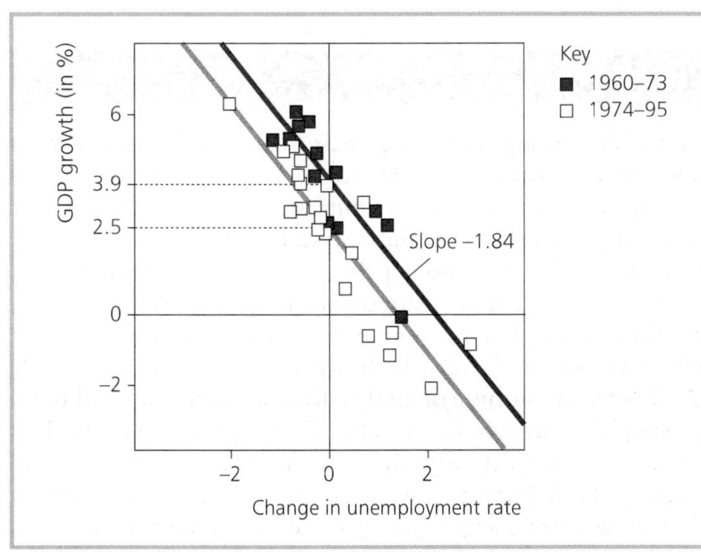

Figure 15.2 Okun's law states that GDP growth and changes in the unemployment rate are negatively related. US data support this claim. It seems that this relationship has shifted down after 1973. While the growth rate that kept unemployment stable was 3.9 before 1973, it was only 2.5 after.
Source: OECD, *Economic Outlook*.

Figure 15.3 These data illustrate Okun's law for Germany. Here the law seems to hold with less precision. Also, while the line shifted down after 1973, it also turned flatter. This means that a given change in GDP growth leads to larger changes in unemployment than before.
Source: OECD, *Economic Outlook*.

observations are important, and hold for most European countries:

1 There is a similarity between the United States and Germany. The 'Okun's law' line for Germany has also shifted down since 1973. Now unemployment is left unchanged by a GDP growth rate of 2.7% instead of the 4.3% growth required before 1973.
2 The fluctuation of the data points about the line is more pronounced than in the United States. So Okun's law holds with less precision. There is more interference from other influences.
3 The line not only moved down after 1973; it also became much flatter. This changes the link between growth and unemployment. Now a given negative shock to income growth pushes up unemployment much more than before 1973. During a recession unemployment deteriorates much more than it did before.

15.2 EUROPEAN UNEMPLOYMENT

While Europe's inflation record during the past two decades is a tale of success, unemployment is causing alarm. Figure 15.4 documents the experience of Western European countries and, for contrast, of Japan and the United States. (When comparing countries, note that the scales differ.)

The experience is quite diverse, although there are some obvious clusters. France, Italy and Spain share a similar pattern (with Japan!). So do Belgium, Germany and the Netherlands. Finland and Sweden suggest a 'Scandinavian' experience, which does not fit Denmark, however, but seems to include Switzerland. What hits the eye in spite of all this diversity, is the upward trend (or shift) of the unemployment rate in virtually all European countries. This observation is important. It conflicts with the view that unemployment fluctuates around some fairly stable ('natural') equilibrium level: if left alone after a disturbance, within a few years unemployment should gravitate back towards

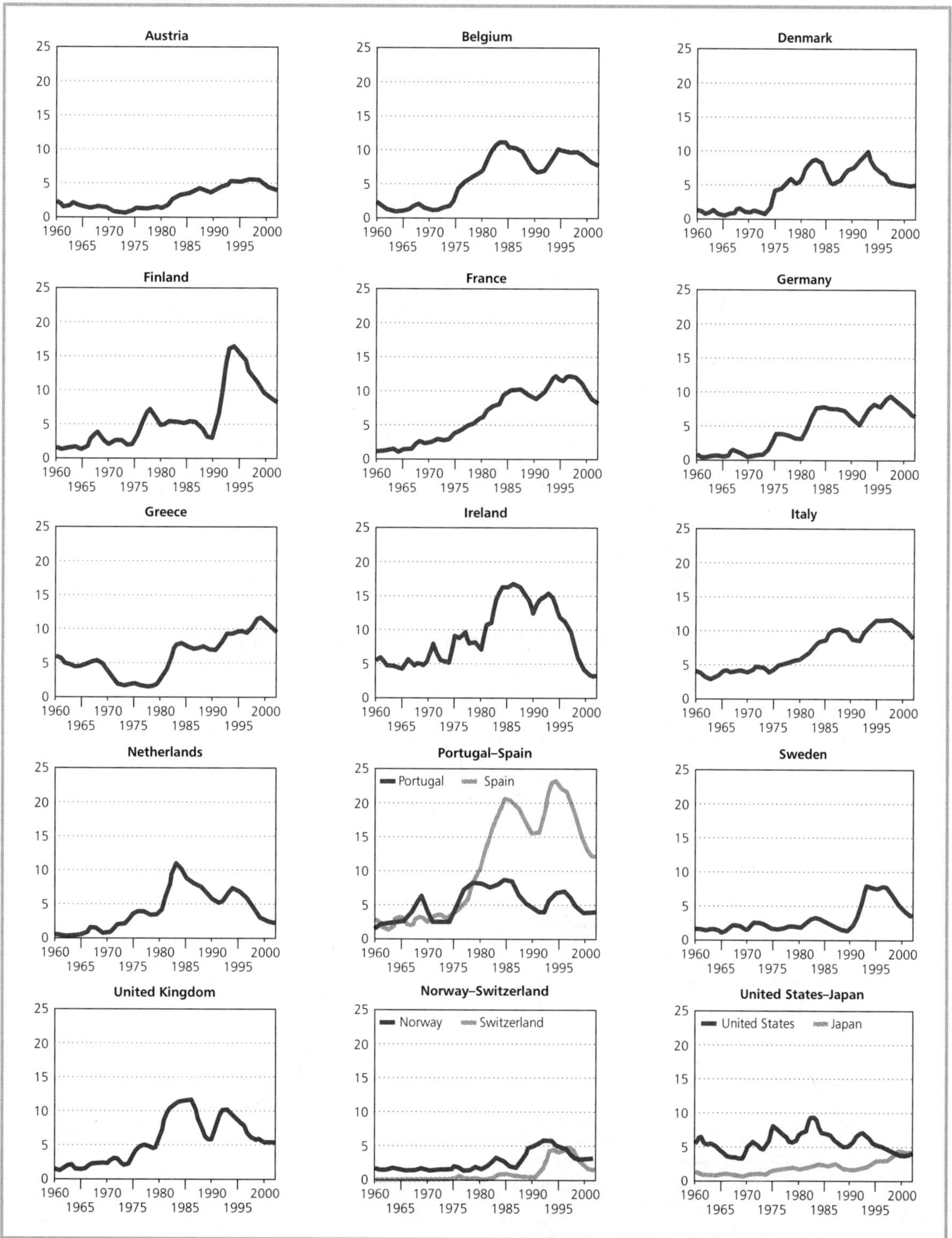

Figure 15.4 Unemployment rates in Europe and the world, 1960–2002.
Source: OECD, *Economic Outlook*; *Eurostat*.

the benchmark provided by the natural rate. Only in the United States are the ups and downs frequent enough and similar enough in magnitude to support the notion of an equilibrium rate that is relatively stable over time.

Why is this presumed upward drift of the natural or equilibrium rate of unemployment so important? Because its causes are very different from what makes unemployment rise during a recession – and so are the remedies. **Cyclical unemployment** eventually takes care of itself. If 'eventually' lasts too long, the government may speed up the adjustment process with the help of fiscal or monetary policy. **Equilibrium unemployment** reflects the institutional characteristics of the labour market and the economy at large. Demand management could camouflage unpleasant structural effects on the rate of unemployment for a while, but could not make them go away.

So first, we need to understand how much of European countries' current unemployment levels may be considered an equilibrium phenomenon and how much must be attributed to cyclical factors.

We bring two concepts to bear on this issue. First, we let data on unemployment and job vacancies speak for themselves and see whether they offer any hints as to changes of the equilibrium rate of unemployment. Whatever change is indicated by the data may then be furnished with an appropriate explanation based on the available theories. Second, we explicitly start from the theories of equilibrium unemployment developed in Chapter 6 and check, one by one, whether these variables account for an upward shift in unemployment.

Equilibrium unemployment vs cyclical unemployment

Unemployment statistics say nothing about what share of unemployment reflects equilibrium and what share reflects the business cycle. To remedy this, economists have developed a battery of approaches to identify equilibrium unemployment. One such concept is the **Beveridge curve**. This curve directly derives from the introduction of imperfections into the labour market diagram shown in Chapter 6 (Figure 6.16), which we reactivate in Figure 15.5.

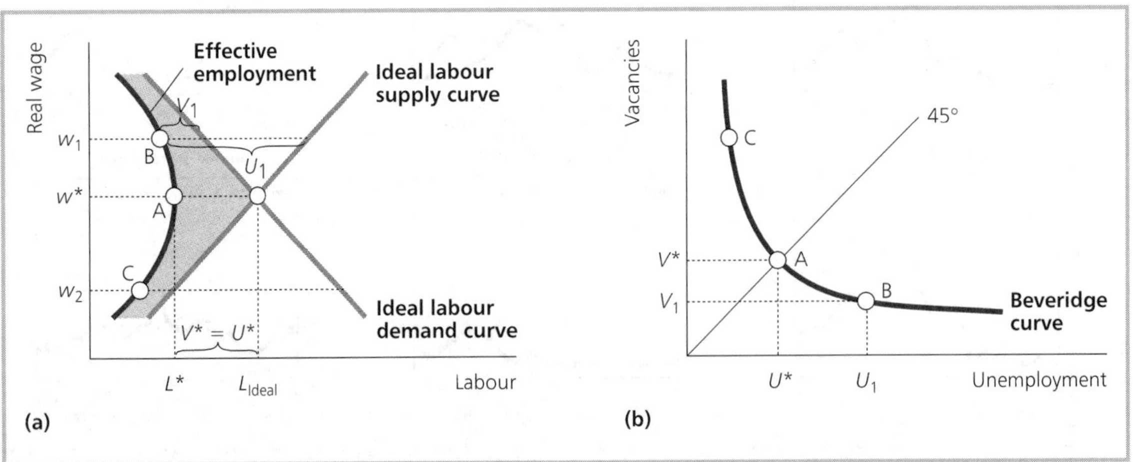

Figure 15.5 Job vacancies and unemployment coexist because of mismatch, friction and information problems. The Beveridge curve shows the ratio between vacancies and unemployment at different real wages.

Panel (a) illustrates the view that in real-world labour markets, informational imperfections or mismatch are responsible for some parts of supply and demand remaining ineffective. So even if the real wage is at its market-clearing level w^*, U^* people are still looking for jobs while firms have the same number of vacancies, V^*, unfilled. Let us take U^* and V^* and identify this combination by point A in panel (b), where vacancies are measured along the vertical axis and unemployment is measured along the horizontal axis.

Now suppose the real wage exceeds its market-clearing level, possibly due to faulty inflation expectations. At w_1 unemployment is at U_1. Vacancies have fallen but, standing at V_1, have not vanished. Take the pair of new unemployment/vacancy observations and mark it in panel (b). This gives point B. To obtain a third point, let the real wage be too low, at w_2. This drives unemployment down to U_2, but boosts vacancies to V_2. Transposing it into panel (b) gives point C. We could perform the same exercise for any other real wage. Lining up the obtained levels of unemployment and vacancies in panel (b) gives the blue line. This line is called the **Beveridge curve**, named after the British economist who first drew attention to it.

The **Beveridge curve** is a negatively sloped line, depicting an inverse relationship between the vacancy rate and the unemployment rate. A boom represents a movement up this line, a recession a slide down the line.

In theory, all we need to do now is add the 45° line to the Beveridge curve diagram, and where it cuts the Beveridge curve (at point A) unemployment is in equilibrium U^* – equilibrium in the sense that in the aggregate the number of jobs matches the number of workers. Outside this equilibrium, say during a recession, real wages rise, as does unemployment, and vacancies become less. Thus we slide down the Beveridge curve to the right. Cyclical unemployment is measured as the difference between U and U^*. Similarly, the economy slides up the Beveridge curve during a boom.

Is the Beveridge curve of use in reality? Yes, very often. An almost textbook example is provided by the Netherlands. Dutch unemployment and vacancy rates, as shown in Figure 15.6, closely match a downward-sloping, convex relationship. Following the argument of the last paragraph, if vacancies and unemployment were affected to the same extent by information problems, mismatch

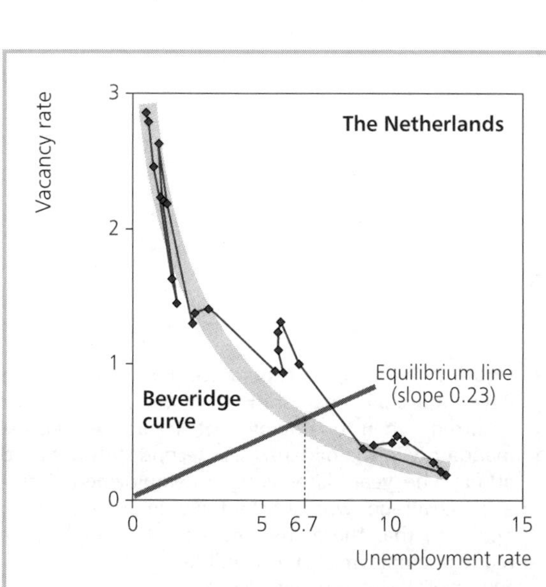

Figure 15.6 Dutch vacancy and unemployment rates seem to behave very much like the Beveridge curve suggests. Lower vacancy rates are accompanied by higher unemployment rates and vice versa. The slope of the straight equilibrium line reflects an estimate of the relative visibility of the two rates. Its intersection with the Beveridge curve suggests an equilibrium unemployment rate of $u^* = 6.7$ during the 1980s.
Source: *Eurostat*; OECD, *Main Economic Indicators*.

and measurement problems, the point of intersection of the Beveridge curve and the 45° line would mark the Dutch labour market equilibrium.

What complicates the use of the Beveridge curve in the real world is that there is no reason to believe that imperfections affect vacancies and unemployment symmetrically. In addition, statistical reporting of unemployment and vacancies is governed by different criteria. To register as being unemployed yields vital rewards in the form of unemployment benefits. So reported unemployment should cover almost 100% of actual unemployment, and is even likely to include some *voluntary unemployment* – people who only pretend to be willing to work at the given real wage in order to reap unemployment benefits. However, reporting a vacancy does not produce any direct pecuniary gains, so revealed vacancies may be just a fraction of actual vacancies. The consequence is that the labour market equilibrium ray through the origin must have a slope much smaller than 1. But how small? The answer is, we don't exactly know. It is quite plausible, however, that the ratio between *average* unemployment and *average* vacancies is a good measure of the relative visibility of the two variables in equilibrium. Following this lead, the ray in Figure 15.6 has slope $v_{\text{average}}/u_{\text{average}} = 0.23$. Consequently, the natural rate of unemployment during the 1980s in the Netherlands is suggested to be around 6.7%.

The Beveridge curve can also be used to identify points in time when labour market characteristics changed, moving the equilibrium rate of unemployment. Consider the Swiss data given in Figure 15.7. From a distance one might have guessed that no Beveridge curve exists at all. On closer inspection, however, it seems that not only one but three different Beveridge curves exist, with the labour market moving rapidly from one to the other. The history of Swiss unemployment insurance provides us with a simple explanation of what went on behind the data:

1 Before 1975 Switzerland did not have mandatory unemployment insurance. As a consequence, less than 20% of the labour force was insured. So the

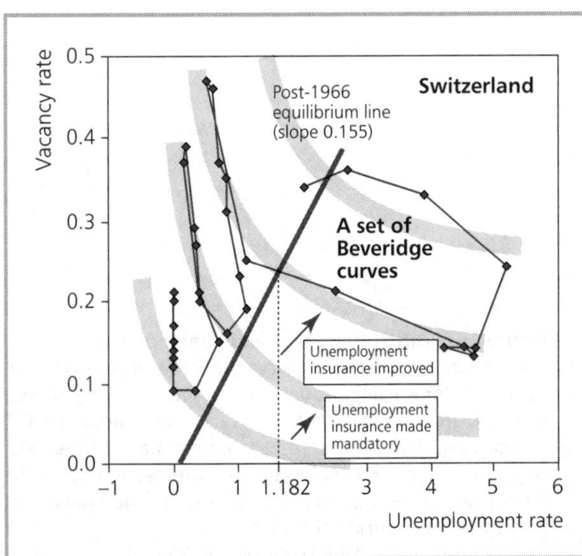

Figure 15.7 The Swiss experience illustrates why the Beveridge curve may shift. A first shift north-east occurred when unemployment insurance became mandatory in the mid-1970s. A second shift occurred about nine years later when unemployment insurance coverage was substantially improved. Note, however, that these changes may also simply have made unemployment more visible.
Source: OECD, *Main Economic Indicators*.

income loss expected from becoming unemployed was very large for most people, resulting in a low equilibrium rate of unemployment. What is more, reporting unemployment was not worthwhile in most cases, causing embarrassment rather than securing help, adding a downward bias to official numbers.

2 Step by step, unemployment insurance became mandatory from 1975 to 1977, resulting in an outward shift of the Beveridge curve due to an increased equilibrium rate. An explanation in the context of the Beveridge curve is that, with the support of good unemployment insurance, workers become more selective when learning about a job opening. This increases job mismatch and shifts the Beveridge curve out.
3 In 1984 the Swiss government introduced a substantial improvement in unemployment insurance coverage. As is to be expected, this seems to have shifted the Beveridge curve out again.
4 Further changes to the unemployment insurance were introduced in the mid-1990s that apparently pushed the Beveridge curve still further out.

The equilibrium line constructed from the post-1985 averages for unemployment and vacancy rates suggests that the Swiss economy ran into a severe slump after 1992. Of the 1995 unemployment rate of 4.2%, less than half (1.8%) is structural (or natural).

The majority of other European countries also seem to have experienced outward shifts of their Beveridge curves – but not all of them, as the Netherlands exemplify. And for those which have, there is usually no unique, clear-cut cause as in the Swiss case.

We now change our perspective and, one by one, look at the variables proposed in Chapter 6 as potential causes for rising unemployment.

Minimum wages

The first individual factor to consider in a search for the cause of rising unemployment is minimum wages. The point to note is that less than half of the current EU member states have a minimum wage set by the the government as a wage floor for the entire country. Figure 15.8 shows the development of these wage floors as shares of average monthly wages.

In most countries this share was lower in 1992 than it was at the beginning of the 1980s. France is the only exception. The upward trend there is not very pronounced, however, and came to a halt in the second half of the 1980s. Spain, being the country with the lowest relative minimum wage and the most pronounced downward trend, has the highest unemployment rate in Europe. So government-administered minimum wages do not appear to be a major cause of Europe's increase in unemployment.

The tax wedge

Taxes drive a wedge between the labour costs incurred by firms and the net wage that workers receive. As taxes rise, either the supply of labour or the demand for labour is reduced (depending on who pays the tax). The result is a drop in employment and, possibly, a rise in *voluntary* unemployment.

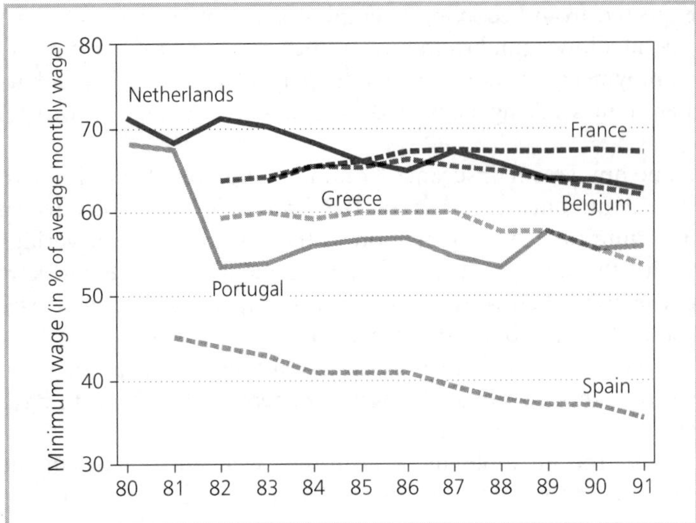

Figure 15.8 Minimum wages in Europe have followed a downward rather than an upward trend. Hence, they do not serve well as a major cause of rising unemployment.
Source: Eurostat.

Figure 15.9 gives a scatter plot of taxes and unemployment rates in some major EU countries, Japan and the United States. The points reflect the proposed positive relationship between the two variables. According to the regression line, as taxes rise from 20% to 50% the unemployment rate doubles from about 6% to 12%. Remember that the tax wedge explanation of unemployment only works if we are prepared to classify Europe's current unemployment as voluntary. Involuntary unemployment needs other explanations.

Are trade unions causing unemployment?

Wages negotiated by trade unions are often binding for large sectors of the economy. They then play a role similar to government-administered minimum

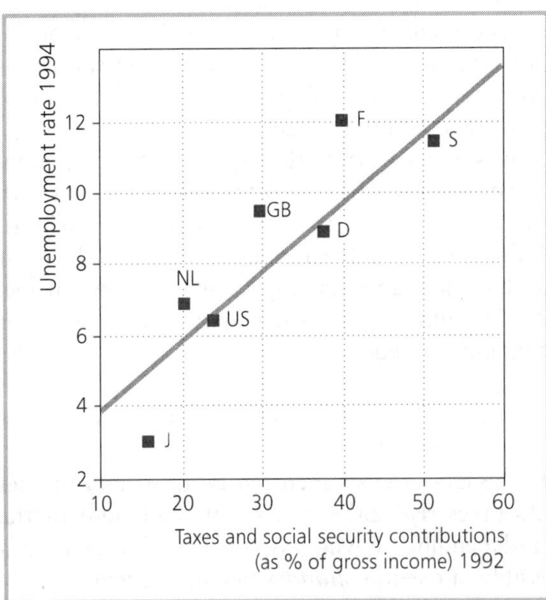

Figure 15.9 According to theory, higher taxes lead to lower employment. As employment falls, voluntary unemployment may rise. The data for this small sample of major industrial countries show such a positive relation between the tax wedge and unemployment.
Source: The Economist, 26 February 1994, p. 75.

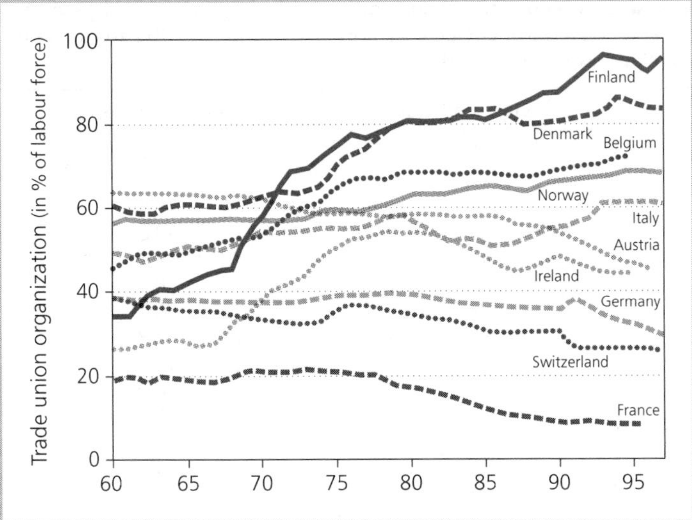

Figure 15.10 Trade union membership rates have not increased in the majority of European countries. At least according to this measure, increased union power does not seem to be a factor behind rising unemployment.
Source: Ebbinghaus and Visser (2000), *Trade Unions in Western Europe since 1945*, New York: Macmillan.

wages. Union coverage (the percentage of the labour force unionized) has been found to explain a (modest) part of inter-country differences in unemployment rates among industrial economies. As an explanation of why unemployment *rose* in Europe during the past two decades, it does not perform well. In most countries, with the United Kingdom being a particularly dramatic example, membership has stagnated or even fallen, and the influence of unions has generally been reduced (Figure 15.10). This obviously clashes with the general trend towards higher unemployment.

It is also hard to explain that rather the weakly represented Spanish trade unions should be a major cause of Spain's 24% unemployment rate. The case of France, however, demonstrates that unionization is an imperfect measure of union power. Despite the lowest union coverage in the entire sample, French unions led by the CGT are among the most visible and, as the December 1995 strikes underscored, most powerful in Europe.

So if unions do play a part in Europe's unemployment problem, it must be more subtle than can be measured by union coverage as a crude indicator of union monopoly power. We will return to this in a moment.

Efficiency wages and unemployment?

Efficiency wage theory proceeds from the assumption that, for a variety of reasons, higher wages may secure higher productivity of labour. If productivity rises faster than the wage, firms may voluntarily pay wages that are higher than really needed to attract the desired number of workers. As a result, part of the labour force remains unemployed involuntarily.

While efficiency wage theories rest on plausible arguments, the variety of factors at work makes it difficult to pin down specific aspects and to confront them with the facts. Consider the shirking version of the theory. Work effort tends to be more difficult to monitor in high-skill categories of employment than in low-skill categories. Therefore we should observe efficiency wages

Table 15.1 General and sectoral unemployment rates. Unemployment rates are given in the second column and unemployment among unskilled workers in the third column. There is no obvious relationship between the two.

	u (all workers)	*u* (unskilled workers)
Austria	4.3	5.6
Belgium	10.3	13.6
Denmark	10.1	14.1
Finland	18.2	14.9
France	12.5	12.1
Germany	6.9	8.9
Greece	9.6	6.1
Italy	12.0	7.3
Ireland	14.7	19.8
Netherlands	7.2	8.0
Portugal	6.8	3.9
Spain	23.8	16.0
Sweden	8.0	4.6
United Kingdom	9.5	12.6
European Union	11.1	10.0
Switzerland	3.8	3.5
United States	6.0	13.5

Source: OECD.

(and the accompanying unemployment) in the higher skill brackets rather than in the lower skill brackets. This conflicts with the fact, observed in virtually all industrialized countries, that unskilled workers are more likely to become and remain unemployed than skilled workers (see Table 15.1).

Other versions of the theory, such as the fairness variant, may be in less obvious conflict with this empirical finding. But they are not supported by it either. Generally, efficiency wage theory seems to play an important role in industrialized labour markets that is substantiated by empirical findings and experimental evidence. However, it does not give any clues as to why European unemployment has drifted up for some time now, or why US or Japanese labour markets seem to adjust better to shocks.

The role of wages

Features such as minimum wages laws, the monopolistic and levelling effects of trade unions, efficiency wage considerations or insider union power keep real wages above their market-clearing level. It is not surprising, therefore, that the most frequently cited cause for unemployment in Europe is that labour is too costly.

A first look at this issue is given in panel (a) of Figure 15.11, where each country's 1995 rate of unemployment is plotted against the same year's labour costs, expressed in dollars per hour. The data certainly do not indicate a positive link between wage costs and unemployment.

It may be argued that the measure of labour costs used in panel (a) does not take proper account of productivity differences and may also be affected by the business cycle. To take care of this, panel (b) uses real wages w relative to labour productivity a. This gives **unit labour costs** w/a. To smooth out the short-run effects of the business cycle, panel (b) plots changes in a country's

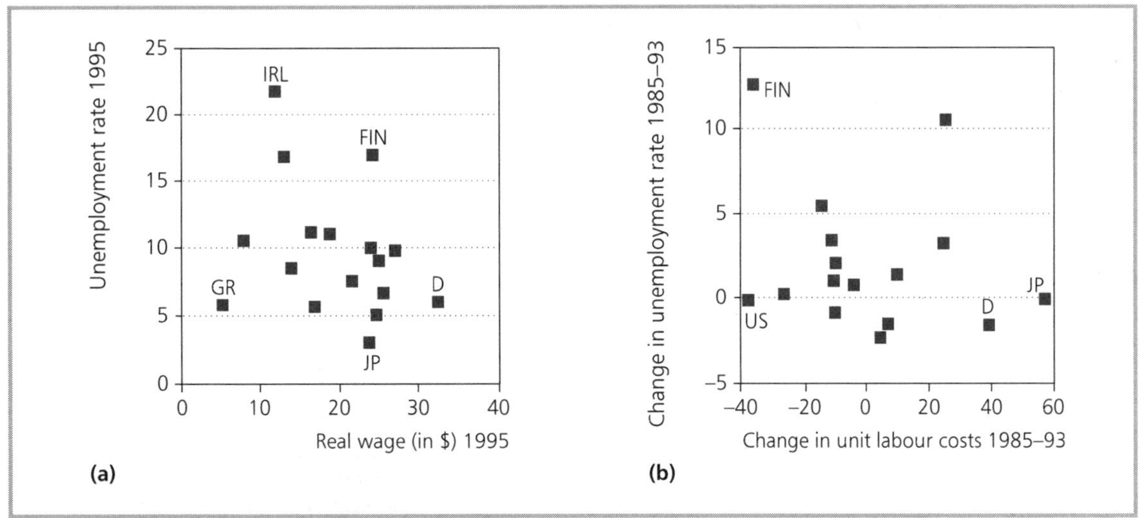

Figure 15.11 Panel (a) plots changes in the economy-wide unemployment rate against changes in unit labour costs (relative to competing economies). There is no evidence that rising wage costs push unemployment up. Panel (b) looks at changes in unit labour costs to control for productivity gains. There is also no positive effect on unemployment.
Source: Swedish Employers' Confederation; IMF, OECD.

unit labour costs relative to unit labour costs of its main competitors between 1985 and 1993 against concomitant changes in the unemployment rate.

These data hardly explain why Europe as a group has performed so unfavourably compared with Japan and the United States. For one thing, Japan and the United States had quite different movements in relative unit labour costs. While US wage costs per unit of output were almost cut in half relative to its competitors between 1985 and 1993, the Japanese economy had to digest a 58.7% increase, the largest among industrialized countries. All European countries had less extreme developments. Germany had to deal with the largest increase of 42.1% in this group. Nevertheless, the West German unemployment rate remains near the lower end of the EU spectrum and has even improved relative to the United States. Switzerland's competitive position improved by 10.4%, but nevertheless records some of the worst deteriorations in the labour market. The same holds for Sweden and, *a fortiori*, for Finland. Altogether, the cloud of unstructured data points certainly does not lend support to the view that changes in labour costs lie at the heart of Europe's unemployment problem.

The International Monetary Fund, the source of the above unit labour cost data, advises that these indexes should be interpreted with considerable caution, mainly due to limited comparability, but also because economy-wide data may conceal some of the things going on in different sectors of the economy. To circumvent this we next look into the low-wage segment of a few OECD economies. Figure 15.12 plots the real wage *change* observed at the lower end of the wage scale against the *change* of the unemployment rate in this sector. While these data points are few, they do illustrate the point that efforts to close income gaps by paying special attention to low-income groups may well backfire, driving a substantial part of this group out of work.

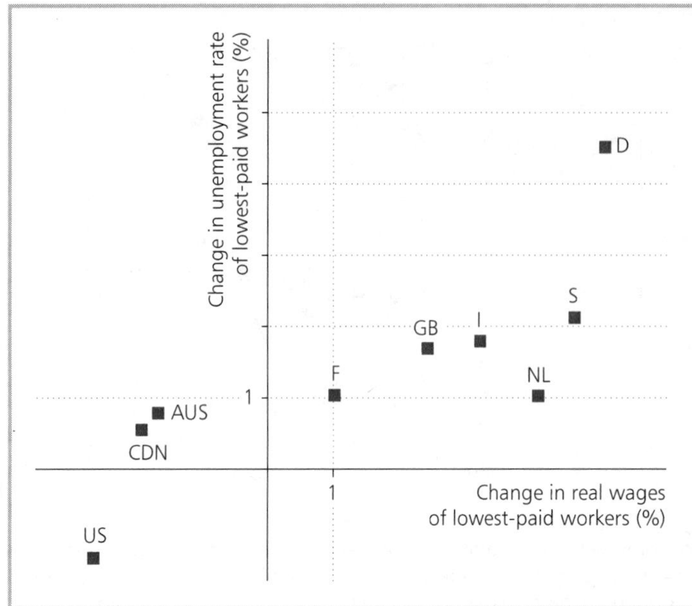

Figure 15.12 Here we consider low-wage categories only. Rising wages go hand in hand with rising unemployment.
Source: 'The employment crisis in industrial countries: Is international integration to blame?' *Regional Perspectives on World Development Report 1995*, The World Bank, 1995.

The price of oil (and other raw materials)

In searching for factors that have pushed European unemployment up so dramatically, it is natural to look at the two major international disturbances during the second half of the twentieth century – the near-quadrupling of oil prices in 1974 and 1979–81. The straightforward explanation is that when oil (or other raw material) prices rise (in real terms) the labour demand curve shifts down. Employment falls, and unemployment rises. If wages are flexible downwards, the increase in unemployment will all be voluntary. In the presence of downward rigidity of nominal wages, involuntary unemployment results which only goes away as inflation erodes real wages.

There are two problems with this explanation:

1 The two oil price shocks were large, but temporary. In the second half of the 1980s real oil prices were back at their pre-1974 levels. So unemployment should also have returned to previous rates.
2 The oil price shocks not only hit the European economies, but Japan, the United States and others as well. US unemployment gives proof of this in the form of a slightly lagged upward jump after each oil price rise. The difference is that in each case this is reversed even before oil prices fell again.

So while the upward effects of rising oil prices on unemployment are almost universally observed, the two features to be explained are why European countries did not digest these shocks as quickly as others, and why they did not even enjoy falling unemployment when oil prices fell back to their old levels.

To obtain answers to these questions, let us discuss the connection between labour demand and oil prices in more detail and then hone the above argument by adding key institutional features to the labour market.

The labour demand curve and the price of oil

The macroeconomic models discussed so far do not really have a channel through which the price of oil or other raw materials could influence the economy. The reason is that we wrote the production function in a highly parsimonious fashion, focusing on two factors of production only, capital and labour. This view is sufficiently general for many purposes. But if we want to analyze the macroeconomic effects of dramatic changes in raw material prices, we need to recognize that raw materials are important inputs in the production of many goods. Highlighting oil as a production input, we may write a Cobb–Douglas production function as

$$Y = K^{\alpha} OIL^{\beta} L^{1-\alpha-\beta} \tag{15.6}$$

where OIL denotes the quantity of crude oil devoured in generating aggregate output, and technology is normalized to $A = 1$. For the same reasons advanced in our treatment of the labour market in Chapter 6, this production function implies a downward-sloping labour demand curve as sketched in panel (a) of Figure 15.13.

What is new here is that this labour-demand schedule is not only determined by the economy's capital stock, but also by the amount of oil put into production. The capital stock is a slow variable, as discussed in the 'growth' chapters (9 and 10). It is fairly constant in the short and medium run. However, firms are much more flexible in their use of oil. How much they use at any point in time is determined by an oil-demand schedule that is also implied in equation

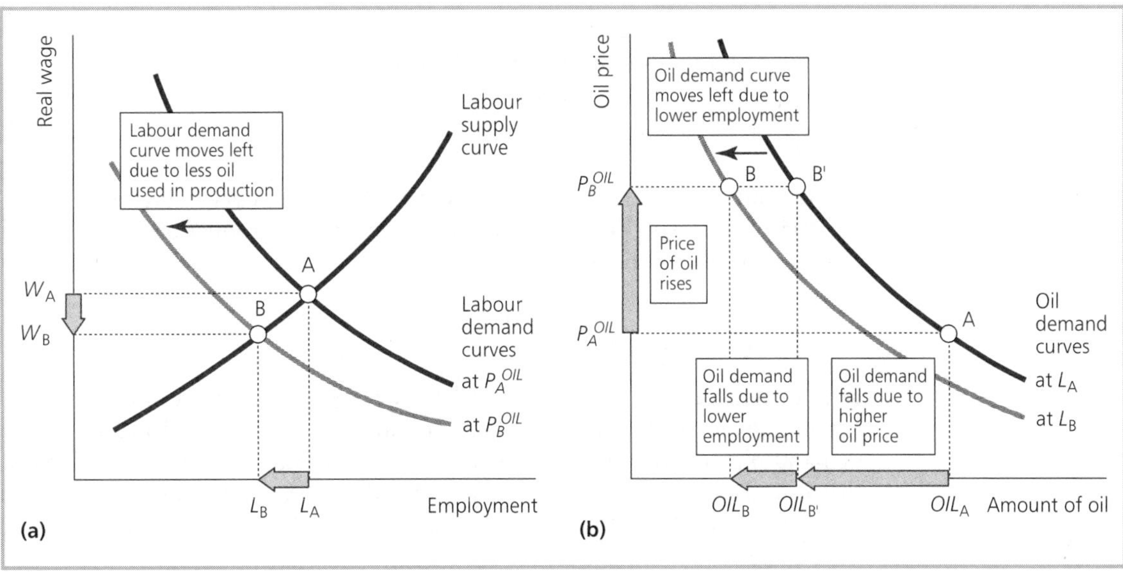

Figure 15.13 The initial equilibrium is given by point A in both panels. When the price of oil increases from p_A^{OIL} to p_B^{OIL} the initial response in panel (b) is a movement up the oil demand curve into B′. This is only a partial, incomplete response, however. With less oil being used, the labour demand curve moves left in panel (a), driving down employment. Since less employment makes oil less productive, this moves the oil demand curve left which in turn moves the labour demand curve further left, and so on. When all this comes to a halt, the labour and oil demand curves are in their respective blue positions and the real wage and employment have fallen. Point B in both panels denote the new equilibria.

Empirical fact. OPEC, the Organization of Petroleum Exporting Countries, the cartel of oil producing countries, controls 40% of the world's current oil production and holds more than 77% of known oil reserves.

(15.6) and this is shown in panel (b) of Figure 15.13. In analogy to our discussion of the labour market, firms employ additional barrels of oil until the marginal product of oil equals the price of oil, p^{OIL}, on the world market. Worldwide this price reflects supply and demand, with a strong influence from **OPEC**, however. For the individual country the price of oil is more or less an exogenous variable to which it can adjust but which it cannot influence to a relevant extent.

When OPEC uses its monopoly power to drive up the price of oil, the following happens. Firms realize that the marginal product of oil is now below its cost. They respond by reducing the amount of oil used until its marginal product equals the price of oil again. This is not the end of the story, however, as this has consequences for the labour market. Combined with the same amount of capital but less oil the marginal productivity of labour falls at all employment levels. This constitutes a downward shift of the labour demand curve and, as long as we are not operating in the vertical section of the labour supply curve, a drop in employment. This is still not the end of the story, however, since this change feeds back into the domestic demand for oil. With less labour to be combined with, the oil demand curve moves down even further, reducing the use of oil, which drives down the labour demand curve still further, and so on. Of course, these effects eventually peter out and the labour demand curve settles into its new position, drawn in light blue.

The algebra of oil prices and labour demand

Given the production function $Y = K^{\alpha} OIL^{\beta} L^{1-\alpha-\beta}$ the labour demand curve is obtained by differentiation with respect to L to obtain the marginal product of labour and require this to equal the real wage:

$$\frac{dY}{dL} = (1-\alpha-\beta)\frac{K^{\alpha} OIL^{\beta}}{L^{\alpha+\beta}} = w \tag{15.7}$$

In the same way, the national economy's oil demand curve obtains by differentiation with respect to OIL to obtain the marginal product of oil and setting this equal to the oil price:

$$\frac{dY}{d\,OIL} = \beta\frac{K^{\alpha} L^{1-\alpha-\beta}}{OIL^{1-\beta}} = p^{OIL} \tag{15.8}$$

Both demand curves are interdependent, since each is influenced by the quantity employed in the other market. To carve out the dependence of labour demand on the price of oil, we solve equation (15.8) for OIL and substitute the result into equation (15.7). This yields the short- and medium-run labour demand curve (in the long run the adjustment of the capital stock would still have to be taken into account)

$$w = (1-\alpha-\beta)\left(\frac{K}{L}\right)^{\frac{\alpha}{1-\beta}}\left(\frac{\beta}{p^{OIL}}\right)^{\frac{\beta}{1-\beta}} \qquad \textbf{Labour demand curve} \tag{15.9}$$

According to this equation, which is curved rather than linear as in our graphical simplification, the labour demand curve moves down and flattens if the price of oil increases. The response of employment and unemployment then depends both on the slope of the labour supply curve and on the stickiness of money wages.

Oil price shocks and unemployment: two stylized scenarios

Returning to our attempt to explain the international experience with unemployment and oil prices, consider the effects of two cumulative oil price increases and their reversal on unemployment in a stylized context. First, assume an 'American scenario', in which nominal wages are flexible except for the length of one-period wage contracts (Figure 15.14).

Labour market equilibrium before 1974 is marked by the intersection between the full blue demand and supply curves. The vertical line over N measures the active population. The difference between N and L_{pre74} gives unemployment as presumably measured by statistics. Some of this is involuntary (if real-wage rigidities exist) and some of it may be voluntary.

The quadrupling of oil prices in 1974 shifts the labour demand curve down to the medium blue position. Initially, as long as nominal wages are stuck in old contracts, employment falls to L_{74}, raising unemployment to U_{74}. After contracts expire, real wages fall to w_1, and employment rises to L_{post74}. This process is repeated in 1979–81, when the price of oil quadruples again. After a temporary large increase of unemployment, falling wages drive it back down to $U_{\text{post79}} \equiv N - L_{\text{post79}}$. Finally, around the mid-1980s, oil prices fall back to their initial level. This shifts the labour demand curve up into its original position, moving wages and unemployment back to their original values as well. The spell of increased unemployment is over.

Unemployment persistence

Next we try to understand what may have made Europe's unemployment so much more persistent than US unemployment. To this effect, consider a

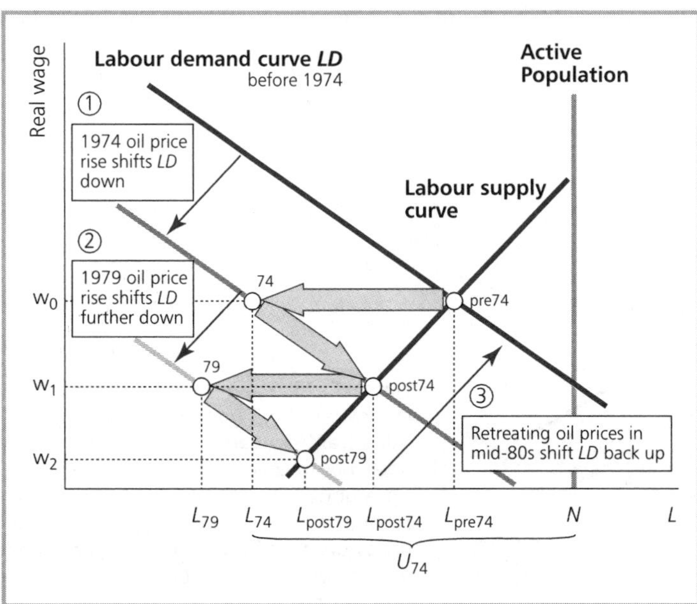

Figure 15.14 The oil price increases of 1974 and 1979 shifted *LD* down in two steps. Each time employment fell sharply (while wages were fixed in contracts negotiated before the shock) but recovered as wages fell. As oil prices dropped and *LD* shifted back up, wages and employment rose back to their initial values.

'European scenario', in which we suppose wages to be negotiated by **labour unions with insider power** (see Figure 15.15).

The point of departure, the pre-1974 equilibrium, is the same as in Figure 15.14, and so are the shifts in the labour demand curve. When the first oil price shock shifts labour demand down, employment falls to $L_{post74} = L_{74}$ (raising unemployment to U_{74}). Catering to employed members (the insiders) only, trade unions prevent the real wage from falling below its current level, despite involuntary unemployment. The second oil price shock replicates the first one, raising unemployment further to $U_{79} = N - L_{post79}$ at an unchanged real wage. Finally, when the oil price eases back to where it started and the labour demand curve shifts back up into the full blue position, unions jump at the occasion by bargaining the real wage up to w_3 for their employed members, leaving a large number of mostly involuntarily unemployed people.

Figure 15.16 shows how unemployment, as measured by the horizontal distance between the active population N and actual employment L, is driven by two oil price shocks and their subsequent reversal in the two stylized scenarios proposed in Figures 15.14 and 15.15. Under the American scenario the two oil price increases give rise to brief bouts of involuntary unemployment. Unemployment may remain somewhat higher after each bout, but only due to voluntary unemployment. Even this effect disappears after oil prices are back to normal.

Under the European scenario the two oil price increases ratchet unemployment up. After each rise, unions keep unemployment where it is. Even after oil prices fall again, there is no tendency for unemployment to fall. This general phenomenon whereby a rise in unemployment may also drag equilibrium unemployment up, and thus may not be reversed even after the initial cause for rising unemployment has disappeared, is known as **persistence**.

Do these stylized stories agree with the data? Not perfectly, but they can explain some essential differences between Europe and the United States. A look at the US unemployment rate in Figure 15.4 above shows the bouts in unemployment after the two shocks in the American scenario. The bouts last

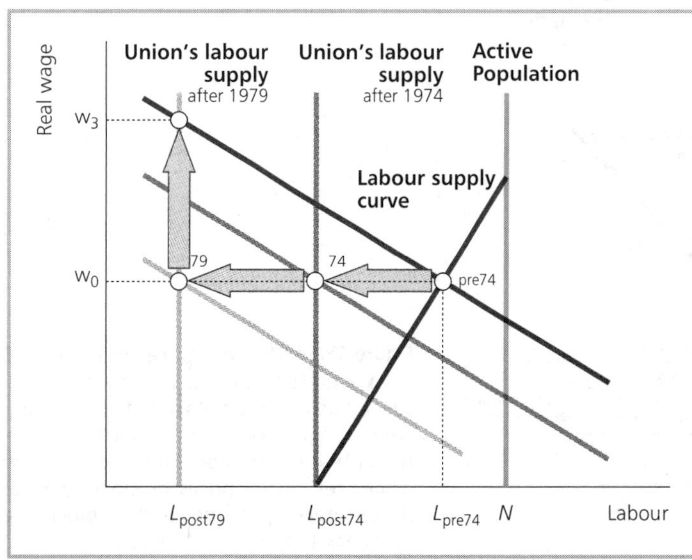

Figure 15.15 Again the oil price rises shift *LD* down twice. Two things differ from the 'American' scenario. First, employment does not recover from the initial drop, since unions do not permit wages to fall. Second, as *LD* shifts up again when oil prices drop, unions seize the occasion by pushing up wages. The employment reduction persists.

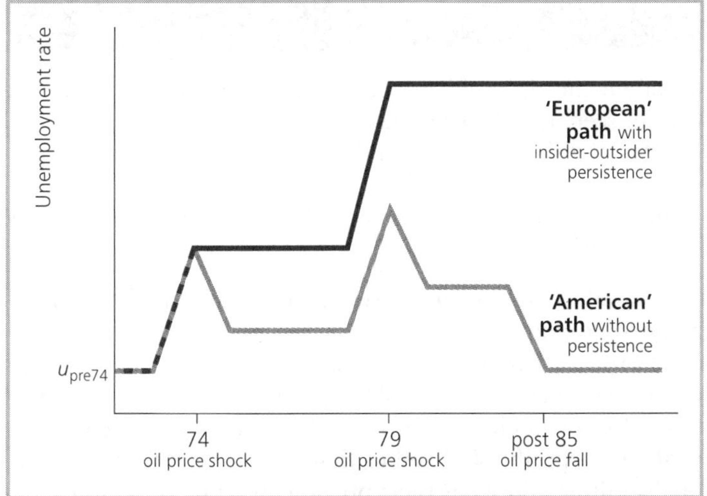

Figure 15.16 In the 'American scenario' the two oil price shocks of 1974 and 1979 cause temporary spells of unemployment. These disappear rather quickly. After oil prices drop to their initial levels, unemployment returns to its initial level. In the 'European scenario' the initial effect of oil price increases is the same as in the American scenario. In Europe the effects persist, however. The eventual fall in oil prices has no effect on unemployment.

a bit longer than in our stylized analysis. But this is easily explained by noting that the majority of wage contracts in the United States are for two and three years.

In contrast, Figure 15.17 shows data from the Netherlands to represent the European scenario. The Dutch unemployment rate is plotted against the Dutch real oil price from the previous year.

From 1973 to 1986 the correspondence between the two series is very close. Each increase in the price of oil pushes unemployment up, and it stays there, just as the stylized analysis suggested. When the oil price falls again, the correlation between the two series breaks down. The unemployment rate does not follow. There is a downward trend, however, but it is a slow one. This suggests that the insider argument points in the right direction, although it overemphasizes the influence of insiders. Nevertheless, even with the presence of falling oil prices substantial persistence is there and this prevents the unemployment rate from falling as quickly as oil prices actually would permit.

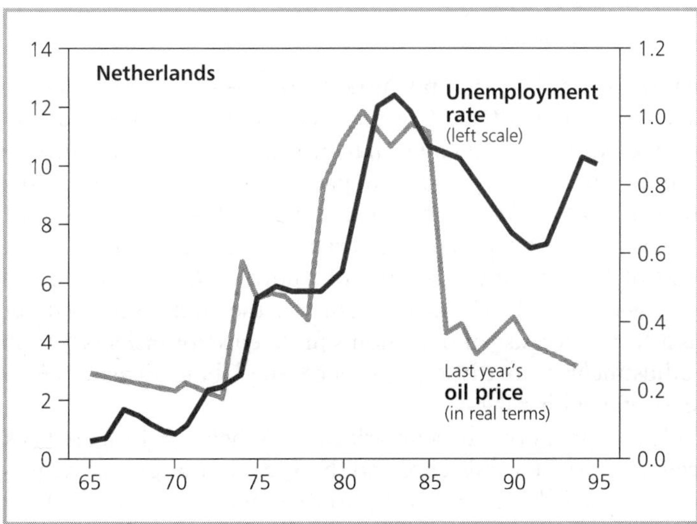

Figure 15.17 The Dutch experience closely matches the behaviour of unemployment in the wake of oil price changes derived above. The two oil price explosions shift unemployment to higher levels in two stages. When oil prices fall, unemployment seems to respond, but very slowly.
Source: IMF, *IFS*.

15.3 PERSISTENCE IN THE *DAD-SAS* MODEL

Hysteresis is the extreme form of persistence, when temporary shocks affect income permanently.

Persistence slows down the dynamics of the economy. In the extreme case labelled the European scenario, the economy would never return to its initial equilibrium, even after the shock has disappeared. This extreme form of persistence is often referred to as **hysteresis**. Hysteresis is probably rare in reality. But milder forms of persistence seem to be the rule rather than an exception. Persistence can have a variety of causes:

- **Trade union monopoly and insider power**, as discussed in the previous sections, is one possible source.
- **Adjustment costs of firms** could cause persistence as employment changes are not costless. It may then be preferable to adjust to a new employment level desired in the longer run in small steps rather than in one big leap.
- **Accumulation of work-specific skills takes time.** If workers become unemployed, their skills fall behind what their previous workplace requires in a dynamic economy with constant innovations and technological progress. When goods demand returns as the economy recovers after a recession, firms might not find the same work-specific and general skills among formerly unemployed that they had before the recession.

All these persistence effects operate on the supply side of the economy and affect the aggregate supply curve. While under the assumption of no persistence used throughout most of this book, surprise inflation influences aggregate output via $Y = Y^* + \frac{1}{\lambda}(\pi - \pi^e)$ and leads to the *SAS* curve

$$\pi = \pi^e + \lambda(Y - Y^*) \tag{15.10}$$

Persistence means that past deviations of income from potential income continue to influence current income. Aggregate output then follows $Y = Y^{**} + \alpha(Y_{-1} - Y^{**}) + \frac{1}{\lambda}(\pi - \pi^e)$, where $0 \leqslant \alpha \leqslant 1$ is the persistence parameter, which may be solved for π to yield the generalized *SAS* curve

$$\pi = \pi^e + \lambda[Y - \underbrace{(Y^{**} + \alpha(Y_{-1} - Y^{**})}_{\text{Potential income } Y^*}] \qquad \textbf{SAS curve with persistence} \tag{15.11}$$

In this formulation Y^{**} is long-run potential income – some super equilibrium income. It only obtains after all persistence effects have petered out. Current potential income Y^*, the income that obtains if there is no surprise inflation, is given by the indicated sum in parentheses. *Current* potential income is determined by *long-run* potential income Y^{**} plus a fraction of last period's deviation of income from Y^{**}. The driving force behind this is that current movements of Y affect either the labour supply or the labour demand curve. In our discussion of oil prices, for example, the trade union labour supply curve was affected because of the union's preference for insiders. Or, to the extent that adjustment costs cause persistence, the labour demand curve follows movements of Y with a lag.

Equation (15.11) comprises two benchmark cases. When $\alpha = 0$ we are back in our normal scenario with no persistence and the *SAS* curve as given by equation (15.10). We discussed this case at length in Chapter 8. When $\alpha = 1$ we have *perfect* persistence or *hysteresis*. Then equation (15.11) simplifies to

$$\pi = \pi^e + \lambda(Y - Y_{-1}) \tag{15.12}$$

This equation implies that when there is no surprise inflation, aggregate output remains where it was last period. In other words, last period's output becomes current potential income. Potential income wanders about without a long-run centre of gravity to which it converges, driven by demand-side shocks via surprise inflation, or by supply-side shocks such as price increases of raw materials. To some extent this corresponds to the 'European' scenario proposed in our discussion of oil prices above.

Hysteresis

Let us discuss the benchmark case of hysteresis first. Consider a reduction in money growth under flexible exchange rates. The *DAD-SAS* model then reads

$$\pi = \mu - b(Y - Y_{-1}) \qquad \textit{DAD} \text{ curve} \quad (15.13)$$

$$\pi = \pi^e + \lambda(Y - Y_{-1}) \qquad \textit{SAS} \text{ curve with hysteresis} \quad (15.12)$$

In Figure 15.18 the economy is in the initial equilibrium at μ_{HI} and Y^{**}. In period 1 the central bank reduces the money supply growth rate to μ_{LO}. Since inflation exceeds money growth, the real money supply falls, shifting the *DAD* curve to the left into position DAD_1. We find the exact position of DAD_1 by following the recipe given in Chapter 8: draw a horizontal line at the current money growth rate μ_{LO}. Draw a vertical line at last period's income, which is Y^*_{HI}. The intersection between the two lines constitutes a construction point through which DAD_1 passes with negative slope.

Unless the labour market had perfect foresight and anticipated the reduction in money growth, inflation does not follow the reduction of money growth instantaneously. When the policy change comes as a surprise, money wages for period 1 were fixed at the end of period 0 based on inflation expectations

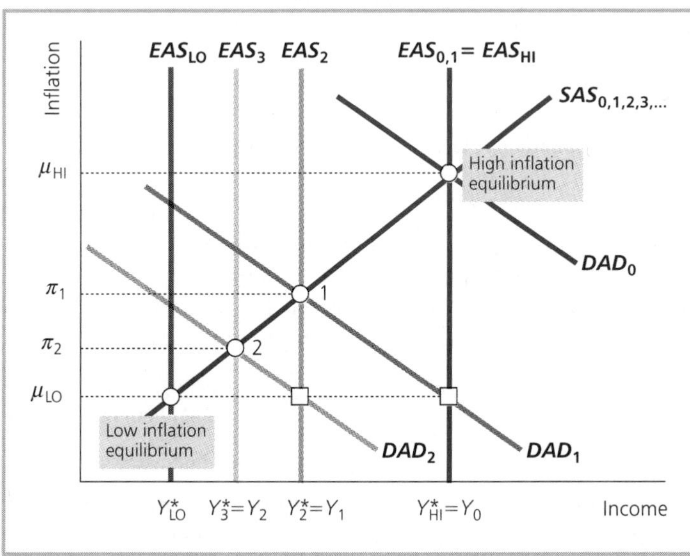

Figure 15.18 Under hysteresis and the specific kind of adaptive inflation expectations assumed here, the *SAS* curve never moves. This is because the effects on potential income (which falls and draws *SAS* to the left) and inflation expectations (which fall and draw *SAS* down) exactly offset each other. Hence the economy moves down *SAS* at a speed determined by the downward shifting *DAD* curve. Under hysteresis a change of monetary policy towards smaller money growth rates causes inflation and income to fall permanently.

$\pi_1^e = \pi_0 = \mu_{HI}$. SAS_0 says how firms respond to a reduction in goods demand, given the current nominal wage. In this case they move down SAS_0, reducing both output and inflation. Equilibrium in period 1 obtains where DAD_1 and SAS_1 (which is identical to SAS_0) intersect. Inflation has fallen to π_1 and income to Y_1.

Having observed this, labour market participants revise their plans. Assume inflation expectations are formed adaptively. Then the first revision is a reduction of inflation expectations to $\pi_2^e = \pi_1$. The second revision concerns potential employment and income. Under hysteresis potential income equals last period's income, that is $Y_2^* = Y_1$. This shifts the vertical *EAS* curve left to Y_1. Having noted this, we can use Chapter 8's construction recipe to identify the position of SAS_2: draw a horizontal line at expected inflation and draw a vertical line at (current) potential income. SAS_2 passes through the intersection of these two lines. Under hysteresis and the kind of adaptive expectations assumed here, this new position coincides with the old one. The *SAS* curve does not shift! The *DAD* curve, on the other hand, does not remain in its previous position. If the real money supply remained unchanged, income could remain at Y_1. This puts the curve into position DAD_2. Equilibrium in period 2 obtains at inflation π_2 and Y_2.

Moving on to period 3, for the same reasons given in the previous paragraph, the *SAS* curve does not change: the leftward shift due to a further reduction in potential income and the downward shift due to the reduction in inflation expectations exactly cancel out. The *DAD* curve moves still further down into DAD_3 (not shown) and income and inflation are π_3 and Y_3, respectively. This process continues in periods 4, 5 and so on, until the economy, in ever decreasing steps, settles into its new long-run equilibrium at $\pi = \mu_{LO}$ and $Y = Y_{LO}^*$.

The important and novel insight arrived at here is that under hysteresis monetary policy affects income permanently. Inflation is still a monetary phenomenon and equals money growth in the long run, but monetary policy exerts a lasting effect on real income. This also applies under rational inflation expectations, though the effect on income would be smaller, as you may easily convince yourself. Only under perfect foresight would monetary policy have no effect on income whatsoever.

Persistence

When persistence is not perfect, effects cannot last for ever, as under hysteresis. But income effects last longer than in the no-persistence scenarios discussed in Chapter 6. As a rule of thumb, we may say that the *DAD-SAS* model with persistence behaves very much like the model of Chapter 6 when the persistence parameter α is small, say 0.2 or 0.3. When α is 0.8 or 0.9, the model behaves very much as if there was hysteresis for a while until income eventually eases back into its original level. Let us now look at an intermediate case assuming $\alpha = 0.5$.

$$\pi = \mu - b(Y - Y_{-1}) \qquad \textbf{\textit{DAD} curve} \qquad (15.14)$$

$$\pi = \pi^e + \lambda[Y - (Y^{**} + 0.5(Y_{-1} - Y^{**}))] \qquad \textbf{\textit{SAS} curve with persistence} \qquad (15.15)$$

Again, the money supply growth rate is reduced unexpectedly in period 1, bringing the economy into the same period-1-equilibrium experienced under

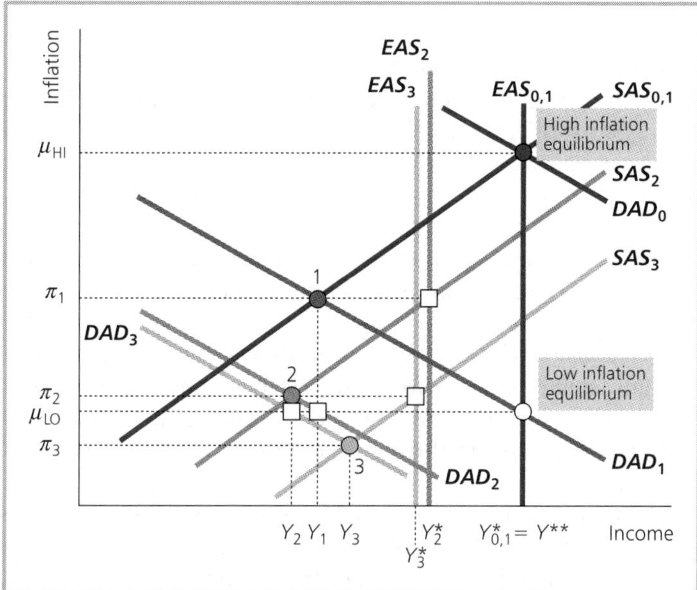

Figure 15.19 Under persistence inflation and income behave in a qualitatively similar way to the way they do in the natural-rate model without persistence, as discussed in Chapter 8. The important difference is that effects of monetary policy on income may last substantially longer. The reason is that when income falls, such as during disinflation as depicted here, temporary drops in income lead to temporary reductions in potential income. This is a drag when income is ready to rise back up towards its long-run potential income Y^{**}.

hysteresis. The difference from the hysteresis-scenario is that potential income does not follow the drop in actual income fully, but only half way: potential income is Y^{**} plus half of last period's deviation of income from Y^{**}. So EAS_2 and current potential income are in the middle between Y^{**} and Y_1. The positions of SAS_2 and DAD_2 are again determined using our recipes. A horizontal line at expected inflation intersects EAS_2 at a construction point for SAS_2. And a horizontal line at μ_{LO} and a vertical line at Y_1 gives a construction point for DAD_2. So income continues to fall in period 2. Period 3 brings the turnaround, beginning to lead income slowly back towards Y^{**}. You may want to compare this path with the path without persistence to see that persistence makes the recession more pronounced and longer lasting.

Less than full persistence does not dramatically change what we learned from the discussion of the *DAD-SAS* model in Chapter 8. There are still the same short-run and the same long-run effects. What does change, though, is the borderline that separates the short from the long run. Short-run effects now may last much longer and can be a lot more pronounced. In general, the implied behaviour fits empirical patterns of booms and recessions much better since policy surprises can affect income for several years even under rational inflation expectations.

15.4 LESSONS, REMEDIES AND PROSPECTS

There is no simple bottom line to our discussion of European unemployment. Nevertheless, putting aside national idiosyncrasies which certainly are essential for a more detailed understanding of labour market experiences, a number of points stand out in the complex picture that has emerged.

Lessons

- *Equilibrium unemployment.* The determinants of equilibrium unemployment discussed in Chapter 6 play their role in certain segments of the labour market and during isolated episodes. They also help to explain why unemployment differs between countries. Their direction or magnitude of change during the past two decades does not explain why unemployment rose so much.
- *Oil price explosions.* The safest thing to say is that unemployment would not be as high as it is, had the two oil price explosions not occurred back in the 1970s.
- *Contractionary monetary and fiscal policy.* Another, more disputed cause, that follows straight from our discussion of disinflations and sacrifice ratios in Chapter 13, is the restrictive monetary and fiscal policy that most European countries have pursued through the 1980s and, in many cases, well into the 1990s.
- *Persistence.* Real oil prices have retreated to former levels. Disinflations have come to a halt (although fiscal policies continue to be contractionary in many countries in pursuit of the Maastricht convergence criteria). Persistence keeps unemployment several percentage points above equilibrium. The presence of persistence complicates the distinction between cyclical and equilibrium unemployment. After an adverse shock that moves unemployment up, unemployment may remain high even if there are no more adverse shocks or after adverse supply shocks have been reversed. This may lead observers to believe, erroneously, that equilibrium unemployment (in the conventional sense, as discussed in Chapter 6) has moved up.

Remedies

Many economists favour what has come to be known as a **two-handed approach** to remedy the current situation:

- *Restructuring the labour market and reforming the welfare state.* A pertinent list of measures would include reforming unemployment insurance and welfare benefits so as to reduce disincentive effects; and increase the flexibility of working time, wages and employment conditions to reflect supply and demand. The purpose of these measures is twofold. First, they are to reduce equilibrium unemployment, which is thought to take part of the blame for the current situation. Second, more flexibility is thought to reduce persistence. Unemployment rates stuck above long-run equilibrium rates could thus be made to fall at a quicker pace – now, and after future adverse shocks.
- *Stimulating demand.* According to the *DAD-SAS* model developed in the first half of this book, expanding demand through fiscal or monetary stimulation can raise income and reduce unemployment – for a while. In the absence of persistence it may be argued that the prospect of a temporary reduction in unemployment is not worth the price of permanently higher inflation. With persistence at work, the benefits from expanding demand may be much larger, or even permanent.

CASE STUDY 15.1 US vs European job growth: cutting the 'miracle' to size

A recurring theme in the business press, in political debates, in textbooks, and in scientific work is that rigid labour markets with powerful trade unions in most of Europe have not only driven up wages, but in the process virtually killed job growth. In stark contrast, US wages have stayed flat, while job growth is the envy of most other industrial countries. This argument is convincingly underscored by graphs like those shown in the four panels of Figure 1, where Britain, Germany and Italy represent the European experience.

The role of real wages and employment appears to be exactly reversed when we compare these (and other) European countries with the United States. Whereas wages remained flat while employment virtually exploded in the US, just the opposite is observed in Europe. (Note that the dividing line really does appear to be the Atlantic, and not whether we compare Anglo-Saxon with non-Anglo-Saxon countries. At least, in the long-run perspective Britain's labour market experience does not differ very much from that of other European countries.)

The standard interpretation of the observed stylized facts is given in Figure 2, which uses the standard labour market diagram. In 1965 the labour demand curve was in the lower position on both sides of the Atlantic. Over time productivity growth raised the demand for labour, gradually moving the labour demand curve up.

In most European economies, strong labour unions and insider power kept their labour supply curves virtually vertical. Thus the upward shift of the labour demand curve drove up real wages while employment remained more or less unchanged. In the United States, unobstructed competition in the labour market made the labour supply curve horizontal. Therefore, as the demand for labour increased, this produced a large increase in employment at unchanged real wages.

The 1996 labour demand curve demonstrates the trade-off the economies seem to face. While exact numbers differ between countries (see Figure 1), we may say that a country's real wage may (at least) have doubled during these three decades (as it did in Britain, Germany and Italy), or

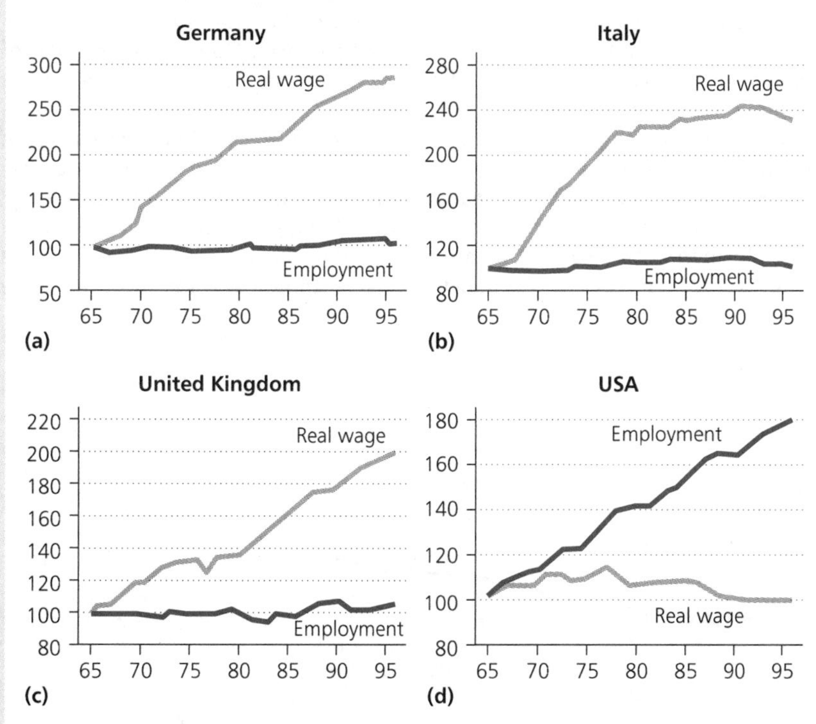

Figure 1

Case study 15.1 continued

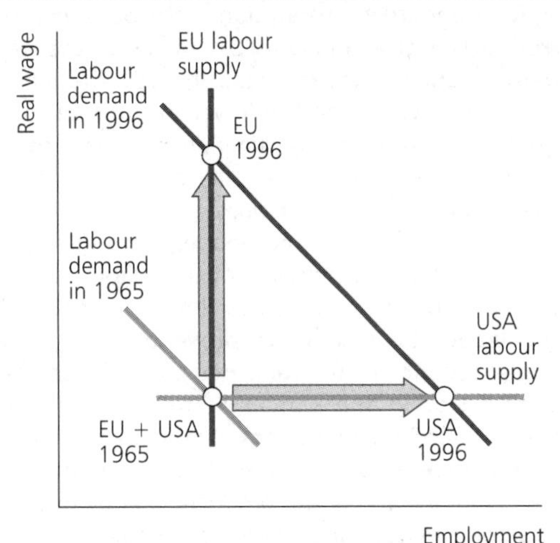

Figure 2

employment may have (almost) doubled (as in the USA). Under either choice (or under intermediate choices), the wage sum about doubles.

Now one has to be careful. Without closer scrutiny, the argument presented here would have about the same validity as the recommendation that the United States should follow China's lead, where wages are but a fraction of US wages, while employment is several times the American employment. Obviously, employment is only meaningful relative to the size of the population, because the size of the population determines the size of the labour market. How far employment can grow is obviously limited by the size of the active population (those aged 15 to 64). So perhaps another factor behind America's job miracle is population growth.

Figure 3(a) repeats Figure 1(d), but adds the active population as an indicator for the development of the labour supply. Figure 3(b) shows the respective time series for France. The graphs reveal two interesting points. First, the active population grew much more in the US than in Europe. US growth is some 50%, twice as much as in France. And France is not even representative of the rest of Europe, since in most of Europe the active population stagnated (see Table 1). And second, the active population goes a long way towards explaining employment growth in the US (and in France). Of the 78.2% increase in employment between 1965 and 1996 almost two-thirds are due to population growth. The rise in net employment (employment relative to the active population) is still impressive, but much less of a miracle than the gross figure suggests.

The graphs suggest an entirely different interpretation why so many more jobs were created in the US compared with Europe, with much less of a role for trade unions and insider power. Consider Figure 4, where we suppose that in 1965 both Europe and the US operated on the vertical part of the labour supply curve. In Europe the labour supply curve stayed close to its original position during the three decades that followed (France is the only European country with a noticeable increase in the active population). Hence, employment could not change very much, and all of the upward shift in the labour demand curve due to productivity gains went into wages. In the US the

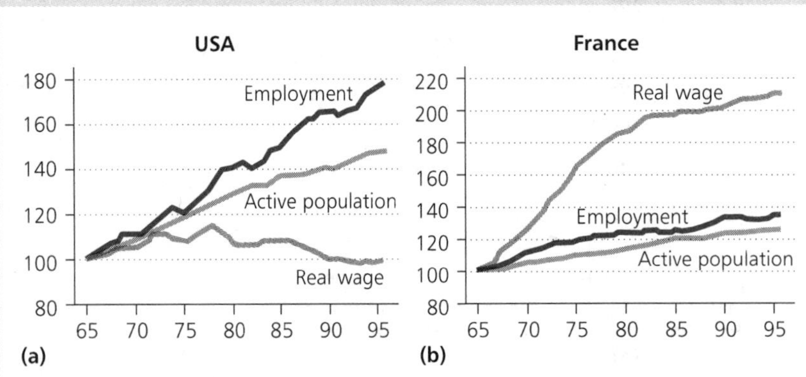

Figure 3

Case study 15.1 continued

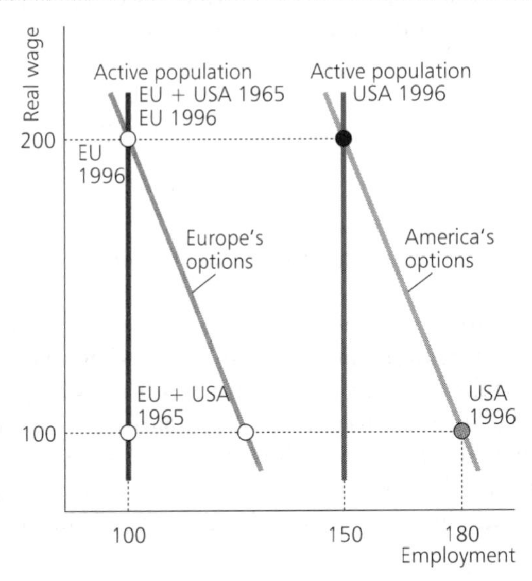

Figure 4

vertical part of the labour supply curve moved to the right by almost 50% due to population growth. Note that this should have shifted the labour demand curve right as well. Why? Well, from the per capita version of the Solow model we know that similar economies should have a similar capital stock per worker in steady state. So when the active population grows the capital stock grows, shifting the labour demand curve to the right just as far as the labour supply curve moved to the right.

Now if this was the whole story, the USA should have ended in the black circle, with wages just as high as Europe's and employment 50% higher. The country, however, ended up in the blue dot instead, at a real wage rate only half as high as Europe's and employment 20% higher than it should be according to its active population. The line passing through the blue dot and the black circle appears to mark the true trade-off between wages and employment. In fact, it is the US labour demand curve. By the same token, the light blue line is Europe's labour demand curve and reveals Europe's options.

Table 1 casts a final glance at changes in the European and US labour markets between 1965 and 1996. East of the Atlantic we observe large real wage growth and small changes in net employment; west of the Atlantic real wages even fell, but net employment rose by as much as 20%. So the trade-off is much less favourable than we had concluded from Figure 1. According to the net wage sum (the change in the wage sum net of changes in the active population) all European countries clearly outperformed the US economy. In Europe net wage sums increased by between 162% in Germany and 92% in Britain, while the US net wage sum only rose by 27%.

Bottom line

Looking at real wages and employment the way we did in Figure 2 gives a wrong impression of how much more employment may be bought by exercising wage restraint. When we correct for changes in the active population, the trade-off becomes much less favourable, as Figure 4 shows. Looking at a summary measure: the net wage sum more than doubled in most European countries, while it grew by a meagre 27% in the US. So the job growth achieved in the US beyond population growth does carry a hefty price tag.

Table 1 Real wages and employment in Europe and the USA (changes between 1965 and 1996 in percentages)

	Britain	France	Germany	Italy	USA
Real wage	100.40	112.40	191.90	135.10	−1.70
Employment	4.30	34.00	4.80	3.00	78.20
Wage sum	109.00	184.60	205.90	139.20	75.20
GDP	94.69	143.37	142.24	159.76	109.90
Active population	8.40	25.70	14.90	14.90	48.60
Net employment	4.10	8.30	10.10	11.90	29.60
Net wage sum	92.20	130.00	162.40	107.10	27.40
Per capita GDP	79.46	103.30	119.24	135.36	53.64

Sources: OECD, *Economic Report of the President*, and IMF.

According to the two-handed philosophy, both types of measures are needed. Structural measures that succeed in reducing equilibrium unemployment may be unable to affect actual unemployment which is being kept up because of insider effects. Demand-side stimulation may succeed in driving unemployment down to its current equilibrium. But this may still be quite high, and there is no firm evidence to suggest that persistence is symmetrical, that is that it also can keep unemployment permanently below equilibrium.

Caveats and prospects

Both groups of measures recommended by the two-handed approach call for comments.

With regard to revitalizing Europe's labour markets and welfare systems, the issue is not whether it should be done, but how far it should go. There is definitely room for 'pruning', as the American economist Paul Krugman put it, for getting rid of unnecessary disincentives without jeopardizing the key purpose of the welfare state, which is to support those in need. The question is whether Europe should go beyond that and 'Americanize'. However, there are lessons that teach us that there are limits to what a deregulation of the labour market can achieve:

- Switzerland in 1975, after the first oil price explosion: with more than 80% of the labour force without unemployment insurance, weak trade unions and one of the most uneven income distributions in Europe, the Swiss economy suffered the worst blow to output among all industrialized countries. As we learned in Chapter 13, the main reason was that the Swiss National Bank did not permit inflation to play a part in reducing real wages. The lesson for the purposes of this section is that the virtual abolition of unemployment insurance, trade unions as weak as they possibly come and having one of the most reluctant governments in Europe as regards engaging in redistribution and taxation, did not suffice as a substitute for monetary accommodation.
- The United States in the 1990s: after two decades of falling real wages, with a minimum wage that peaked at $4.15 in 1991, and a continuously widening income distribution that is in an entirely different league from any European country, the United States still has higher unemployment at the low end of the income scale than most European countries (see Table 15.1), not to mention the nightmare in the inner cities.

Regarding demand stimulation, pertinent recommendations may be rather academic. For countries that are pursuing membership in European Monetary Union and, therefore, have to jump the hurdles of the Maastricht criteria on inflation and fiscal policy, monetary stimulation is not a viable option and fiscal policy will be forced to continue a violently restrictive path. The same holds for Euroland, where monetary policy has been handed over to a European Central Bank with an absolute commitment to price stability, and fiscal policy must remain within the strait-jacket of the Pact for Stability and Growth. With the world standing at the brink of a recession in 2002, however, a less dogmatic handling of some of these guidelines may be called for and observed.

CHAPTER SUMMARY

- Empirically, income growth and unemployment dynamics are linked by Okun's law. The law states that the difference between growth and trend growth is linked to a given change in unemployment.
- The Beveridge curve describes a negative relationship between vacancies and unemployment. Empirical Beveridge curves give a first hint as to which part of current unemployment is due to equilibrium and which part is cyclical.
- Minimum wage laws, trade unionism, efficiency wages, rigid wages and labour market institutions in general (including unemployment insurance) appear to affect unemployment. However, these factors do not seem to be sufficient to account for the large rise in European unemployment.
- Adverse supply shocks in the form of large oil price rises had visible direct effects on unemployment in most industrialized countries. Why these effects have not disappeared even after oil prices sank again can only be explained by reference to persistence, as may be caused by insider-outsider mechanisms.
- Introducing persistence makes the *DAD-SAS* model's behaviour more realistic. Income needs more time to digest shocks, even when expectations are rational.

KEY TERMS AND CONCEPTS

Beveridge curve
efficiency wages
hysteresis
insider–outsider theory
minimum wages
Okun's law
persistence
Phillips curve
replacement rate
tax wedge
two-handed approach
unemployment
union coverage

EXERCISES

15.1 From statistical data, a country's Phillips curve is found to be $\pi = 9 + \pi^e - 0.5u$.

(a) What is the equilibrium rate of unemployment?

(b) By how much does a surprising rise of inflation from 2 to 4% reduce unemployment?

(c) If Okun's law for this country reads $\Delta Y/Y = 0.03 - 0.02\Delta u$, by how much does income grow?

15.2 Suppose your country's Beveridge curve is $v = 4/u$ where v is the vacancy rate.

(a) The current rate of unemployment is 6%. Your task is to reduce unemployment to 2%. Propose appropriate measures. Assume that v and u have the same 'visibility'.

(b) How is your proposal affected if you know that v only has one-fourth of the visibility of u?

15.3 Let the labour market be characterized by the following demand and supply curves:

$$L^s = -10.000 + 5000 \cdot w$$

$$L^d = 40.000 - 5000 \cdot w$$

For five points in time you have data on the real wage and employment.

Observation	1	2	3	4	5
Real wage w	5	7	4	3	6
Employment L	10,000	2,500	7,500	2,500	7,500

Draw the economy's Beveridge curve.

15.4 Suppose that the government levies a proportional tax on labour income.

(a) The government uses the tax revenue for government consumption. What are the effects on potential output?

(b) Suppose that the government uses the tax revenue for public investment, improving the infrastructure and thus labour productivity. What happens to the result you derived in (a)?

15.5 In empirical work the movement of macroeconomic variables over time is often found to follow what statisticians call an autoregressive process. Taking unemployment as an example, such a process may read

$$u_t = \mu + \rho \cdot u_{t-1} + \varepsilon_t$$

ε_t is a random disturbance and the equation is an AR(1) – a first-order autoregressive process. To get a better feel of the economic implications of the parameter ρ, do the following exercise. Suppose that u initially is at its long-run equilibrium level, which is 0. In period 1 the series is hit by a shock of size 5 (i.e. $\varepsilon_t = 5$). There are no further shocks, subsequently. Compute the values of u for periods 1 to 6, letting $\rho = 0.2$, $\rho = 0.9$ and $\rho = 1$, respectively. How does ρ affect the evolution of the time series? Considering Figure 15.16, what estimates of ρ would you expect for unemployment series in the United States and in European countries?

15.6 Suppose that the trade union's insider power is not perfect. By and by, some temporary outsiders regain employment and bid wages down. For concreteness, assume that in the medium run unions only manage to keep real wages in the middle, between where they would want to keep it if they had complete insider power and where wages would go if unions had no insider power at all.

(a) Trace the effects of the two oil price explosions under these new assumptions. Start by modifying Figure 15.15. Then modify the time path given in Figure 15.16.

(b) Does the result provide a better explanation of Dutch unemployment than the assumption of complete insider power?

15.7 Suppose a country with fixed exchange rates reduces government spending G in order to meet the Maastricht convergence criteria. Use the graphical *DAD-SAS* model with persistence ($\alpha = 0.5$) to find out how this affects income

(a) under adaptive expectations ($\pi^e = \pi_{-1}$);

(b) under rational expectations;

(c) under perfect foresight.

15.8 An economy can be represented by

$$\pi = \mu - 0.5(Y - Y_{-1})$$

$$\pi = \pi^e + 2(Y - Y_{-1})$$

Initial income is $Y_0 = 500$. Inflation is 10%. In period 1 the money supply growth rate is reduced from 10% to 5%. What is the new level of income in the long run?

(a) under adaptive expectations ($\pi^e = \pi_{-1}$)

(b) under rational expectations

(c) under perfect foresight.

RECOMMENDED READING

A comprehensive survey of research on European unemployment is Charles R. Bean (1994) 'European unemployment: A survey', *Journal of Economic Literature* 32: 573–619.

More recent studies and discussions are:

- Assar Lindbeck (1996) 'The West European unemployment problem', *Weltwirtschaftliches Archiv* 132: 609–37.
- Stephen Nickell (1997) 'Unemployment and labor market rigidities: Europe versus North America', *Journal of Economic Perspectives* 11: 55–74.
- Horst Siebert (1997) 'Labor market rigidities: at the root of unemployment in Europe', *Journal of Economic Perspectives* 11: 37–54.
- Francesco Daveri and Guido Tabellini (2000) 'Unemployment, growth and taxation in industrial countries', *Economic Policy* 15: 47–104.

A monograph that I recommend is Richard Layard, Stephen Nickell and Richard Jackman (1991) *Unemployment: Macroeconomic Performance and the Labour Market*, Oxford: Oxford University Press. While most of the book is fairly advanced, Chapter 1 provides an excellent highly readable overview of the facts to be explained and what we know. Regular updates on the employment situation in Europe and related policy experiences are provided by publications such as:

- *The OECD Jobs Study: Facts, Analysis, Strategies* (1994) Paris: OECD.
- *The OECD Jobs Study: Implementing the Strategy* (1995) Paris: OECD.
- *Implementing the OECD Jobs Study: Lessons from Member Countries* (1997) Paris: OECD.

APPLIED PROBLEMS

RECENT RESEARCH

Is unemployment persistent?

The simplest way to allow for a shock to the unemployment rate to persist is by writing an equation of the form

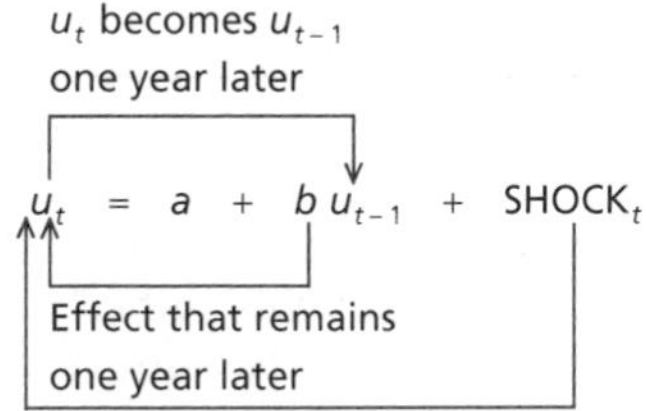

A one-time shock that occurs in period 1 affects u in the same period by the full amount. If $b = 0$ there is no persistence. Since no further shock hits next period, the rate of unemployment falls back to its normal level a. If $b > 0$, a higher unemployment due to a one-time shock in period 1 means a higher u_{t-1} one period later. Part of this, measured by bu_{t-1}, survives as unemployment next period. If $b = 1$ the effects of a one-time shock on u even persist indefinitely.

George S. Alogoskoufis and Alan Manning (1988, 'Unemployment persistence', *Economic Policy* 7: 427–69) try to determine the amount of unemployment persistence in different countries empirically. Remaining more general than in the above equation, they even include up to two lags in the unemployment rate, estimating

$$u_t = a + b_1 u_{t-1} + b_2 u_{t-2} + \text{Random variable}$$

where the shocks to unemployment are assumed to be captured by the random variable.

Estimation results for a few selected countries, based on annual data for 1952–95, are given in Table 15.2 (the constant term is not shown).

Persistence can be measured by the sum of b_1 and b_2. It is strikingly high, ranging from 0.48 in the United States to 1.04 in France. Given in parentheses below, coefficients are not t-statistics in this example, but standard errors. For Germany, for example, the t-statistic of the estimate for b_1 against the null that $b_1 = 0$ is $1.29/0.17 = 7.59$. We may also test whether 1.29 is significantly larger than 1 by computing $(1.29 - 1)/0.17 = 1.71$. Applying usual significance standards, the answer is no.

Table 15.2

	D	F	I	GB	J	USA
b_1	1.29	0.79	1.03	1.29	1.05	0.68
	(0.17)	(0.18)	(0.18)	(0.17)	(0.18)	(0.18)
b_2	−0.35	0.25	−0.08	−0.38	−0.14	−0.20
	(0.17)	(0.19)	(0.19)	(0.18)	(0.19)	(0.17)
$b_1 + b_2$ (persistence)	0.94	1.04	0.95	0.91	0.91	0.48
R^2_{adj}	0.94	0.98	0.95	0.96	0.82	0.64

WORKED PROBLEM

Dutch Beveridge curves

Table 15.3 gives Dutch unemployment and vacancy rates.

A linear approximation of the Beveridge curve introduced in the text gives the estimation equation

$$v = 2.29 - 0.19u \qquad R^2 = 0.84$$
$$(19.40)\ (10.86)$$

While the coefficients are highly significant and the fit of the equation looks OK, the result is not quite satisfactory: the graphical derivation of the Beveridge curve in Figure 15.5 and the data shown in Figure 15.6 suggest that the Beveridge curve is curved and not a straight line. Forcing a straight line through these data points must lead to the result that data points do not deviate randomly from the line. Instead, in the upper left section most points will be way above the line, in the middle section most points will be below the line, and in the lower right section most points will be above the line again. So a straight line systematically misrepresents the data in certain sections. (Technically speaking, the residuals are *autocorrelated*. But we do not address this issue here.)

To obtain a better representation of the data we may want to fit a non-linear curve. How can that work when all equations considered so far were linear and additive? What we can do is transform u, say to $1/u$, and then assume that v is linearly related to $1/u$. The resulting estimate is

$$v = 0.56 + 1.48\,(1/u) \qquad R^2 = 0.82$$
$$(5.87)\quad (10.89)$$

Note that now the coefficient of $1/u$ is positive. This is still as expected, for if u grows, its reciprocal value $1/u$ falls and v falls by $1.48 \times (1/u)$. Note, however, that the fit of the equation is rather worse than the one obtained above.

Since our model only suggests that the Beveridge curve is bent, but does not give a specific functional form, by using $1/u$ we may be 'overbending' the curve. Since we are free to experiment with other functions, let's try a combination of the two above specifications. This gives

$$v = 1.45 + 0.84\,(1/u\ 0.11 - u) \qquad R^2 = 0.95$$
$$(11.03)\quad (7.41)\qquad (7.39)$$

This combined specification seems to match the data much better, boosting R^2 to 0.95. All coefficients are significant, meaning that when unemployment rises, this bears on vacancies via a linear channel $-0.11u$ and via a non-linear channel $0.84/u$. Non-linear relationships are a quite common phenomenon in economics.

Table 15.3

	Unemployment in %	Vacancy rate in %
1964	0.5	2.9
1965	0.6	2.8
1966	0.8	2.5
1967	1.7	1.4
1968	1.5	1.6
1969	1.1	2.2
1970	1.0	2.6
1971	1.3	2.2
1972	2.3	1.3
1973	2.4	1.4
1974	2.9	1.4
1975	5.5	0.9
1976	5.8	0.9
1977	5.6	1.1
1978	5.6	1.2
1979	5.7	1.3
1980	6.4	1.0
1981	8.9	0.4
1982	11.9	0.2
1983	12.1	0.2
1984	11.6	0.3
1985	10.5	0.4
1986	10.2	0.5
1987	10.0	0.4
1988	9.3	0.4

YOUR TURN

Unemployment, unions, replacement rates and taxes

Table 15.4 gives 1994 unemployment rates *u* for some European countries, Japan and the United States. It also gives unionization rates, replacement rates and income taxes plus social security contributions.

Do differences in tax rates, union membership and unemployment insurance benefits (as summed up in the replacement rate) explain differences in the unemployment rate?

Table 15.4

	D	F	I	J	NL	S	GB	US
Unemployment rate in 1994	9.6	12.2	11.3	2.9	7.2	8	9.5	6.1
Taxes and social security contributions as % of gross income, 1992	38	40	51	16	20	44	30	24
Trade union membership as % of labour force, 1992	30	10	35	25	22	80	38	15
Replacement rate (unemployment benefits as % of earnings), 1990	40	n.a.	10	20	75	60	18	35

To further explore this chapter's key messages you are encouraged to use the interactive online module found at

www.fgn.unisg.ch/eurmacro/tutor/DADSASwpersistence.html

and many other features hosted at **www.fgn.unisg.ch/eurmacro**

APPENDIX

A PRIMER IN ECONOMETRICS

WHAT TO EXPECT

Economists relentlessly confront their models, or parts thereof, with real-world data. A soft way to do this is by doing **case studies**. This book makes extensive use of this approach. A harder way makes use of the laws of statistics, and has developed into a discipline of its own, known as **econometrics**.

This appendix tries to introduce you in an informal way to **what econometrics is all about**. After working through this appendix you should be able to do the following:

1 **Read statistical results.**
2 **Ask informed questions** about statistical results.
3 **Start doing statistical work** on matters of interest to you (not just constrained to macroeconomics).

More specifically, you will understand:

4 How econometric methods allow you to **quantify the parameters** of models from real-world data.
5 How you can **tell whether a model or equation fits the data** well or not.
6 **When you have to discard a model** or a hypothesis because of insufficient support from real-world data.

Empirical research links economic theory with the real world. It prevents theory and reality from drifting apart and leading separate lives, by forcing both areas to communicate on a scientific level. Central to empirical research in economics is the methodological discipline called **econometrics**. The two **key tasks of econometrics** are as follows:

1 To **quantify parameters** present in theoretical models. (What is the marginal rate of consumption? What is the interest elasticity of the demand for money? How high is the natural rate of unemployment?)
2 To **test hypotheses** derived from theoretical models. (Does consumption really grow when income grows? Is it true that anticipated increases in the money supply do not affect output? Are exports affected by the real exchange rate?)

This appendix provides a basic understanding of how econometrics approaches these two tasks.

A.1 FIRST TASK: ESTIMATING UNKNOWN PARAMETERS

Suppose you have been elected chairman of Paris Saint-Germain (PSG), and you are planning the budget for next season. A good estimate of your football club's expected receipts is crucial, since it tells you how much leeway you have for buying new players. Of course, you may simply anticipate the same receipts you had last season, or the average of the annual receipts from the last five years. But your manager insists that by investing in better players you may expect a higher ranking in Division 1, which draws more spectators into the home stadium and lets you expect higher receipts in general. While this sounds interesting, it is only useful if you know by how much an improvement of one league table position raises the number of spectators per game. Statistical methods allow us to estimate such a relationship from data on ranking and spectator crowds collected in the past.

Example

You have a red dice and a blue one. In each round you first throw the red dice, then the blue dice. Somebody claims that the number of dots on the blue dice follows the number of dots just observed on the red dice. The proposed 'model' reads

$$\text{dots}_{\text{blue}} = \text{constant} + \text{coefficient} \times \text{dots}_{\text{red}}$$

or, put more formally,

$$b = \alpha + \beta r \tag{A.1}$$

where b represents the number of dots tossed with the blue dice
r represents the number of dots tossed with the red dice
α is a constant term (unknown, and needs to be determined empirically)
β is the regression coefficient (unknown, and needs to be determined empirically)

Equation (A.1) postulates a linear relationship between b and r that can be represented by a straight line; α says where the line cuts the vertical axis, and β indicates the slope. Together α and β identify the unique position of the line, as Figure A.1 shows.

In our artificial example we know, of course, that b and r are not really related, that is, β actually equals zero. Let us pretend that you do not know this true value of β (just as we do not know the true marginal propensity to consume). Therefore, all you can do is throw your dice and check whether the results comply with equation (A.1). After two rounds you may have obtained the results given in Table A.1.

Table A.1 Results from two rounds of dice.

		Colour of dice	
		Red	Blue
Round #	1	4	5
	2	2	3

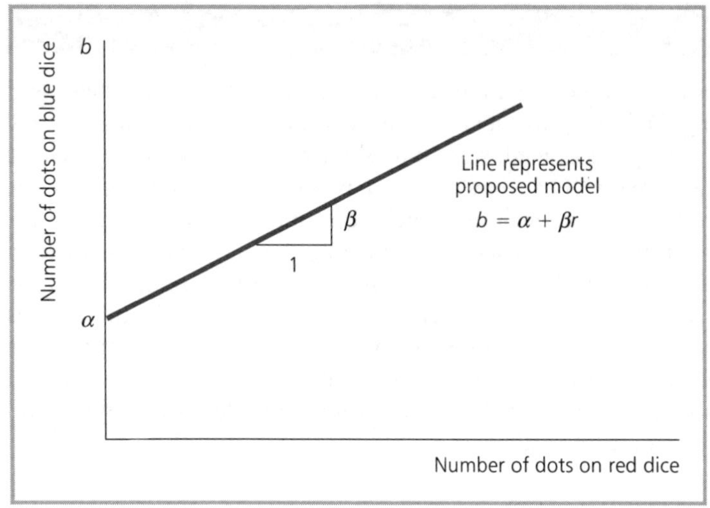

Figure A.1 The model proposed by equation (A.1) has a constant term (or intercept) α and slope β.

Note. If the dice is not 'loaded' the true 'model' is $b = 3.5 + 0 \times r + \varepsilon$, where ε is an unforeseeable (random) impact with expectation zero. ε may assume the values 2.5, 1.5, 0.5, −0.5, −1.5 and −2.5, each with probability 1/6. For example, if we throw a 6, then according to the true model $6 = 3.5 + 2.5$ with $\varepsilon = 2.5$.

Each round's results can be represented by a point in a diagram with b measured along the vertical axis and r along the horizontal axis (Figure A.2). The line passing through both points has a positive slope, apparently indicating that b is indeed higher if r is higher.

The problem becomes more complicated as we add more rounds of dice throws. Suppose we obtain $b_3 = 3$ and $r_3 = 4$. As panel (a) in Figure A.3 reveals, we cannot draw a straight line that passes through all three data points at the same time. The line drawn through points 1 and 2 is off target in round #3. The error committed in explaining b_3 is ε_3. Similarly, any other straight line would have to miss at least one of the three points. And adding yet more data points only compounds the problem. What we need is a new criterion for positioning the straight line (or for determining α and β, which is the same thing).

The most frequently used such method in economics is **ordinary least squares estimation**, or OLS. It is based on the following criterion for positioning

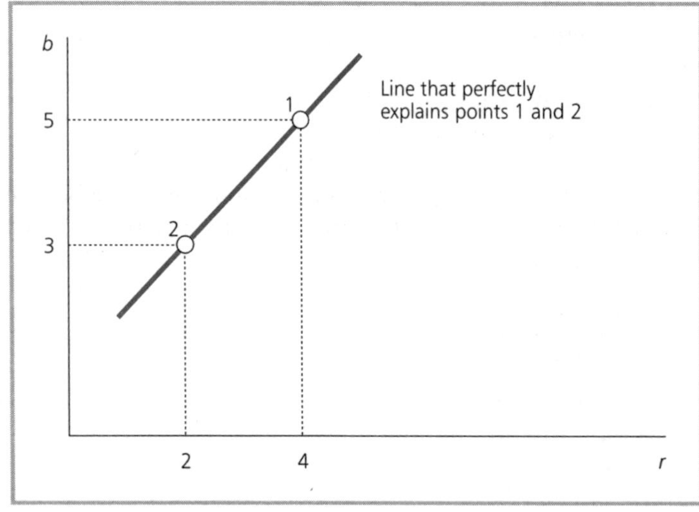

Figure A.2 If we have two observations only, a line drawn through these two points 'explains' both points perfectly.

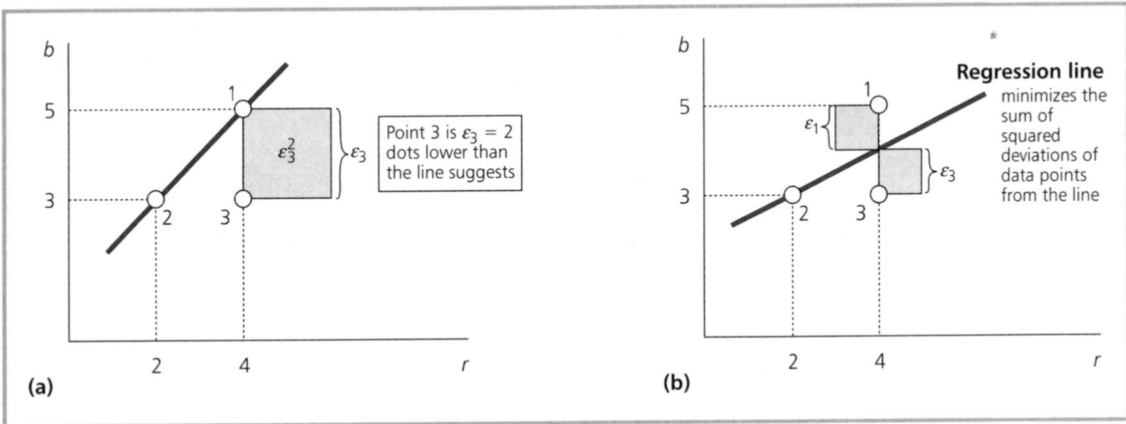

Figure A.3 With three observations, no straight line can pass through all points. The method of ordinary least squares positions the regression line so as to minimize the sum of squared deviations of all points from the line.

the straight line:

> Position the straight line so as to make the sum of the squared deviations of all observation points from the line as small as possible.

Note. In panel (a) of Figure A.3 the sum of squared errors is $2^2 = 4$. If the proposed line divides the distance between points 1 and 3 in half, as in panel (b), the sum of squared errors is $1^2 + 1^2 = 2$.

According to this criterion it is better to have two of our three data points *a little bit* off the line than to have two points on the line but the third one *way* off. Figure A.3 illustrates this: clearly the sum of the squared residuals (or errors) is smaller in the case shown in panel (b) than in the case shown in panel (a).

By squaring the errors we increase the weight of large errors disproportionately. This makes sense if we consider large errors less likely than small ones. In general, OLS has a number of helpful statistical properties.

The fact that our example produced a positively sloped line even though the true line is known to be horizontal highlights one problem clearly: it is possible for statistical methods (OLS or some other method) to indicate a relationship between two variables that does not really exist. Such a relationship obtained in a limited sample of data points could be taken as evidence in support of a false model, or as falsification of a correct model. To prevent economists from doing this and as safeguards against other blunders, estimation results need to be subjected to statistical tests. The following sections elaborate on this.

A.2 SECOND TASK: TESTING HYPOTHESES

Referring again to our Paris Saint-Germain example, after some number crunching with the help of their PCs and a good software package, your staff reports that gaining one place in the league table rankings draws an additional 1,453 people into the Stade de France. That sounds good for a start. But you know very well that this estimate is also influenced by other, random factors that influence the size of the crowd drawn on a given day, such as the weather. Therefore, to be able to gauge the risk you take, you would like to know how reliable the reported result is. Is it possible that it was obtained purely by chance, and that league positions and spectator turnout are not really related? Or what is the probability that each step up the league ladder draws at least 1,000 more spectators? To answer such questions statisticians have developed a whole battery of tests.

Example

It is 1812 and you are living in the Grindelwald Saloon in Yuma, Arizona. You play 'heads or tails' with Bonnie's grandfather, BG. The rules are as follows: BG holds a coin, tosses it up in the air, catches it and smacks it on the back of his other hand. If the coin lands 'tails up' he pays you five dollars; and if it is 'heads up', you pay him five. Asking BG to let you have a look at both sides of the coin is considered a direct accusation of cheating. If you are proved right, you get your money back. If you are proved wrong, he will follow local custom and shoot you. For a similar reason you cannot simply stop playing and walk out.

Since you are a reasonable, but not completely risk averse person, you follow the rule to call an opponent a cheat only if you are 95% sure. In other words, you discard your initial guess (or hypothesis) that BG plays with an untampered coin only if an observed winning streak of BG's could result from an untampered coin with a probability of less than 5%.

The game starts:

- *Round #1*. BG flips tails. While this does annoy you, it can obviously happen with a probability of 50% even if the coin is clean. There is no reason to question BG's integrity.
- *Round #2*. The coin shows tails. Two tails in a row can happen with a probability of 25%. You obviously have bad luck, and ten dollars less.
- *Round #3*. Tails again. Clean coins can produce three tails in a row with a probability of 12.5%. Your anger is rising, and so are your doubts. But you continue to stick to your interpretation that BG is basically an honest fellow and simply in luck.
- *Round #4*. Almost expectedly, BG flips tails again and asks for five more dollars. By now you feel like kicking his shin bone. But since a clean coin could produce five tails in a row with a probability of 6.25%, you are only 93.75% confident that your initial guess that BG is honest is wrong. According to your own limit you do not yet discard your initial presumption.
- *Round #5*. Tails! That's enough. The probability of tossing tails five times in a row with a clean coin is 3.125%. You now feel confident that BG is a crook, and ask him to show you the coin.

The rest of the story contains some more advanced concepts that we do not really need – but you might be curious to know about them.

Version A

BG shoots you in cold blood because you called him a crook without foundation. In statistical terms you committed a **Type I error**: you rejected a hypothesis ('he is honest') although it was correct. You always run this risk when you subject a hypothesis to a statistical test, since perfect confidence cannot be achieved. The risk of committing a Type I error increases if you raise the limit that needs to be reached before you reject your initial hypothesis. With the benefit of hindsight you were right in not rejecting the initial hypothesis (technical term: the **null hypothesis**) after rounds #1, #2, #3 and #4 because the risk of error had not yet fallen below the significance level of 5%. Had we chosen a significance level of 10%, below which we would have discarded the null hypothesis that BG is honest, we would already have committed a Type I error in round #4.

Version B

You get your twenty dollars back, buy yourself a younger horse, and BG goes to jail. You were right in rejecting the null hypothesis in round #5. However, we now know that you committed a **Type II error** after each of the first four rounds. You did not discard the 'he is honest' hypothesis although it was wrong. Type II errors also can never be excluded. The risk of committing one increases if we reduce the required level of significance. A significance level of 1% would have caused you to commit another Type II error in round #5.

Tampering with the significance level always reduces the risk of committing one type of error at the cost of increasing the risk of committing the other type of error. Thus you cannot reduce both risks together. In the face of this trade-off, the selection of a significance level is a compromise that reflects the costs incurred by either type of error. In our example, committing a Type II error costs you another five dollars. A Type I error costs you your life. So it certainly makes sense to set the significance level very, very low, to reduce the risk of committing a Type I error towards zero. When economists test their theories they routinely choose 5% significance levels. Occasionally, significance levels of 10% or 1% are also applied.

A.3 A CLOSER LOOK AT OLS ESTIMATION

Simple and multiple regression

Models are always incomplete. This is because, by definition, models draw simplifying pictures of the real world by omitting factors considered inessential for the problem at hand. Our model for explaining crowds at Paris Saint-Germain home games should therefore correctly read

$$n_i = \alpha + \beta p_i + \varepsilon_i \tag{A.2}$$

where n_i is the size of the crowd at home game #i, the endogenous variable that we want to explain; α is the constant term; β the slope of the regression line; p the current rank of PSG in France's Division 1; and ε combines all the other factors affecting the crowd, such as the weather or the reputation of the visiting team.

According to the artificial data given in Figure A.4 the proposed negative relationship between league table ranking and crowd appears to exist. The negative estimate for β tells us how many spectators we lose if we slide down one place in the rankings. The constant term α simply helps to determine the position of the regression line. Its obviously purely hypothetical interpretation here is how large the crowd would be if PSG held rank 0.

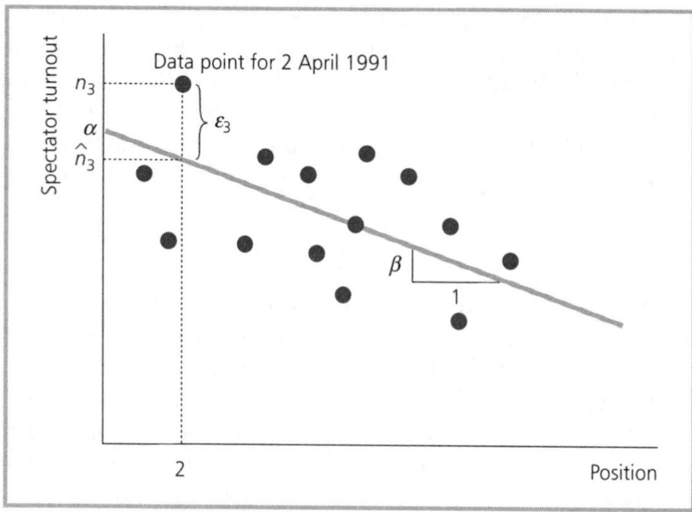

Figure A.4 The hypothetical cloud of data points implies a negative relationship between league position and spectator turnout. Rank 2 gives rise to an expected crowd $\hat{n}_3$.

Note. A hat over a variable indicates that we are dealing with the value suggested by the model, and not with the actual value. We will only use a hat when it is necessary to avoid confusion.

If we want to know the expected turnout when PSG is in second place in the league, we compute $\hat{n} = \alpha - \beta \times 2$ ($\hat{n}$ only gives an average number, an expected value). On 2 April 1991, when PSG was indeed in second place, they actually drew n_3 spectators instead of the $\hat{n}_3$ proposed by the empirical estimate, possibly because of a particularly interesting visiting team.

Up to now we have only tried to quantify relationships between two variables. Such regressions are called **simple regressions**. By contrast, **multiple regressions** involve the relationship between an endogenous variable and two or more exogenous (or explanatory) variables.

Extending what we have learned about simple regressions to multiple regressions is quite straightforward. Suppose we believe that turnout not only depends on the ranking of the home team p_i^{PSG} but on the ranking of the visiting team p_i^{Guest} as well. Then the true model becomes

$$n_i = \alpha + \beta_1 p_i^{\text{PSG}} + \beta_2 p_i^{\text{Guest}} + \varepsilon_i \tag{A.3}$$

Now each game is characterized by three numbers and needs to be represented in three-dimensional space. Marking all observations in such a diagram, we obtain a cloud of data points. Equation (A.3) suggests that this cloud of points may be represented by a plane (or surface) (see Figure A.5).

Again α is the estimated constant term (or intersection with the vertical axis), β_1 measures the detrimental effect of PSG losing one position in the ranking, and β_2 how much it costs in terms of crowd turnout if the visiting team's ranking is also down by one position.

Again, the plane postulated by the model and estimated from the data will not give a perfect account of the data points. Actual numbers will be ε spectators above or below the estimated plane. In comparison to how we proceeded with simple regressions, multiple OLS positions the plane in the cloud of points so as to minimize the sum of squared estimation errors.

This procedure straightforwardly generalizes to more than two exogenous variables, but obviously cannot be illustrated graphically. Because of the direct comparison between simple and multiple regressions, we may illustrate the following concepts by means of easier-to-draw simple regressions.

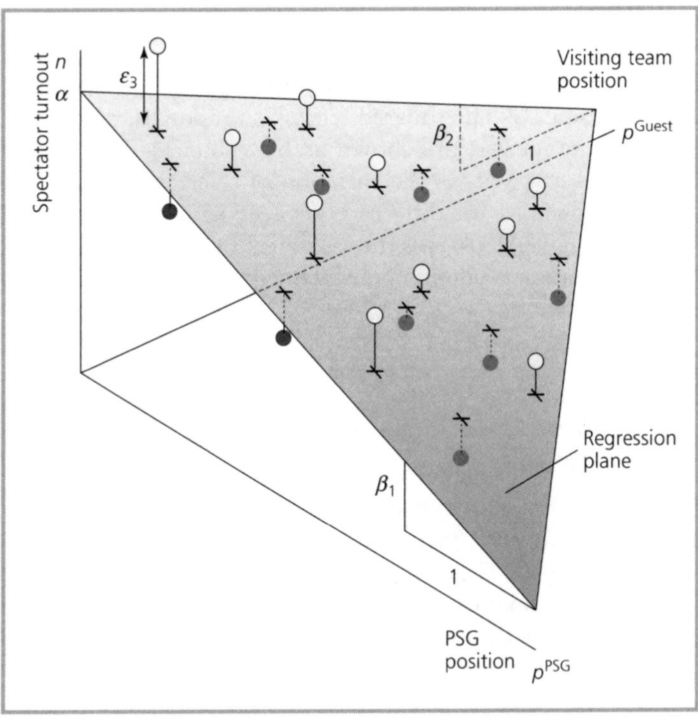

Figure A.5 Multiple regressions do not estimate a line, but a regression plane (or surface). Random influences may put actual observations above or below this plane.

How well does the model explain the data?

Whether we are happy with equation (A.3) depends on how well it explains the variations in turnout. This explanatory power of the equation is measured by the **coefficient of determination.** Figure A.6 provides a hypothetical illustration of what the coefficient of determination does.

The coefficient of determination, denoted by R^2, measures the share of the variation in the variable you want to explain that is actually being explained by your estimation equation. The variation of your endogenous variable is measured as the sum of the squared deviations of the observations from the average

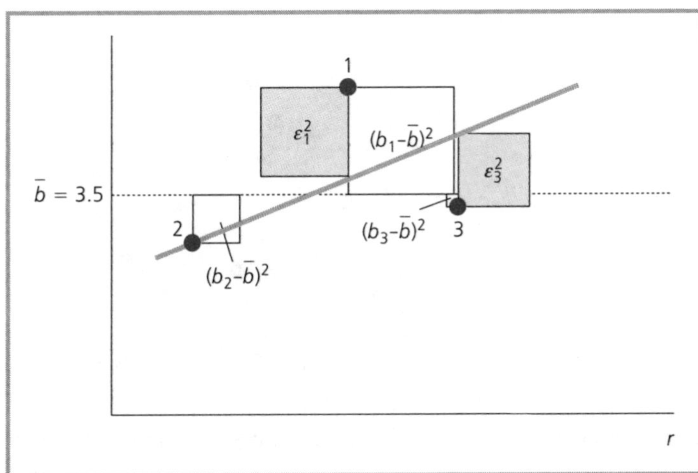

Figure A.6 The coefficient of determination (R^2) is a measure of how close observed data points are to the regression line. Graphically, R^2 first sums up all white squares, then takes away the sum of all grey squares, and finally divides this difference by the sum of all white squares.

value of all observations. Returning to the game of dice, in Figure A.6 we have three observations averaging $\bar{b}$. The squared deviations of b_1, b_2 and b_3 from $\bar{b}$ are represented by white squares. Their sum, $(b_1 - \bar{b})^2 + (b_2 - \bar{b})^2 + (b_3 - \bar{b})^2 = \Sigma_1^3(b_i - \bar{b})^2$, is the **variation** of b. The squared regression residuals, the sum of which the OLS method minimizes, are shown as blue squares. The sum of squares residuals, $\varepsilon_1^2 + \varepsilon_2^2 + \varepsilon_3^2 = \Sigma_1^3 \varepsilon_i^2$ is the variation of b left unexplained by the estimated line. Consequently, the difference between actual variation and unexplained variation, $\Sigma (b_i - \bar{b})^2 - \Sigma \varepsilon_i^2$ is the explained variation of b. Hence, the coefficient of determination is simply the explained variation as a fraction of the total variation of b:

$$R^2 = \frac{\text{explained variation}}{\text{variation}} = \frac{\Sigma (b_i - \bar{b})^2 - \Sigma \varepsilon_i^2}{\Sigma (b_i - \bar{b})^2}$$

$$R^2 = \frac{\text{sum of white squares} - \text{sum of blue squares}}{\text{sum of white squares}}$$

This fraction is limited to the interval between 0 and 1. If all observed data points are exactly on the estimated line (such as point 2 in Figure A.6), there are no estimation errors and, hence, no unexplained variation ($\Sigma_1^3 \varepsilon_i^2 = 0$). Thus the coefficient of determination equals 1, indicating a perfect 'fit' of the model. At the opposite extreme the model does not explain anything. The esti-

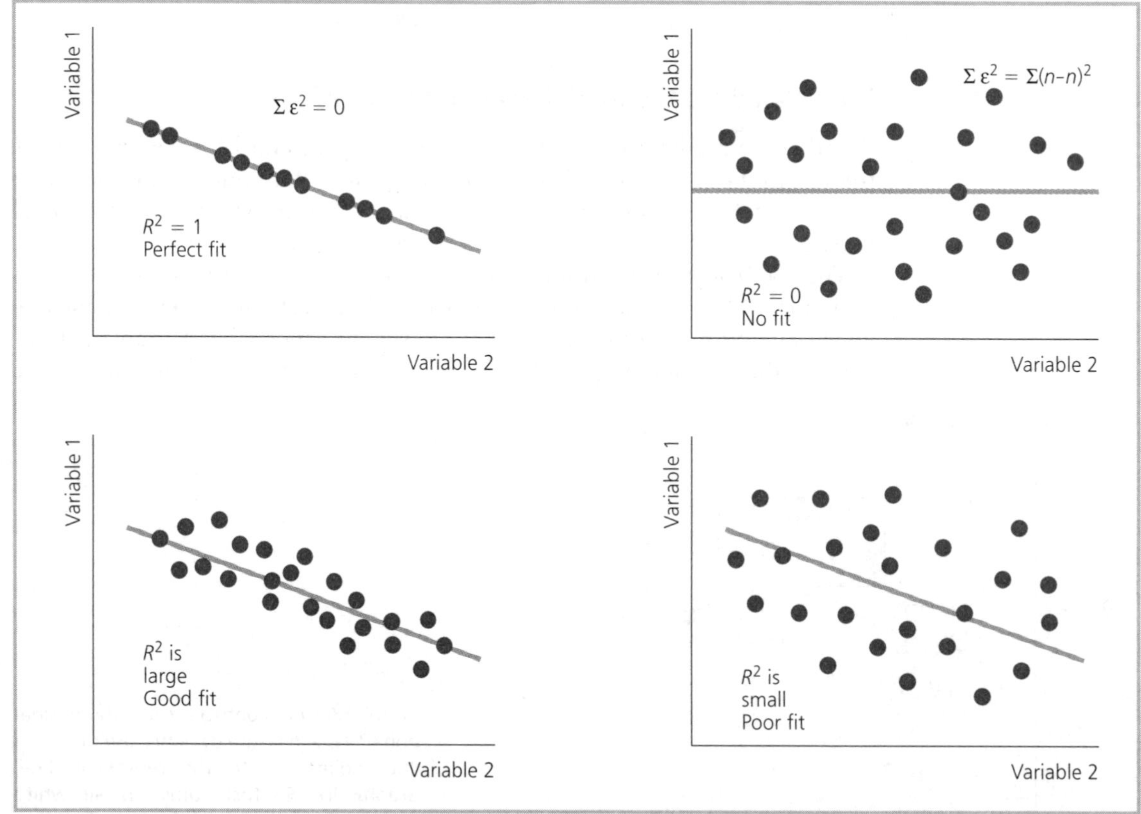

Figure A.7 The top row illustrates coefficients of determination (R^2) of 1 (perfect fit) and 0 (no fit). The bottom row illustrates intermediate cases of a good and a poor fit.

mate of β is zero and the estimate of α equals $\bar{b}$. Now the explained variation is zero, and so is the coefficient of determination. The top two panels in Figure A.7 illustrate the two extreme cases.

Quite dissimilar clouds of data points may yield the same regression line. If, on average, points are close to the line, the coefficient of determination is high, that is close to 1 (see Figure A.7, bottom left-hand panel). If the points are far from the regression line, a low coefficient of determination results (see bottom right-hand panel in Figure A.7).

BOX A.1 The coefficient of determination: R^2

The coefficient of determination, called R^2, takes on values between 0 and 1. It reports the share of the variation of the endogenous variable that is explained by the estimation equation:

$R^2 = 0$ indicates that the estimation equation does not explain anything.
$R^2 = 1$ indicates that the explanation is perfect.

How reliable are the parameter estimates?

We know by now that econometric estimates of parameters are products of chance. If the average height of Italian women over the age of 21 is 165 cm, then the average height of a sample of ten women will usually not match the true value of 165. Similarly, estimates of parameters in a regression equation are influenced by random factors. This calls for the questioning of the reliability and implications of the obtained result. Suppose the true relationship between spectator turnout and league division standing was

$$n_i = 12{,}500 - 500p_i + \varepsilon_i$$

where ε = (number of dots showing when dice is thrown − 3.5) × 1,000. Figure A.8 shows the values that ε can assume and the attached probabilities.

The 3D sketch in Figure A.9 shows how this random variable affects the model. The blue line on the base plane shows the true relationship between n

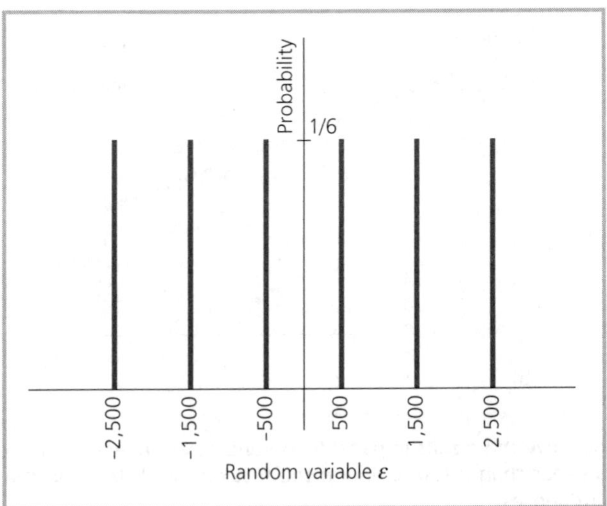

Figure A.8 Here the values of −2,500, −1,500, −500, 500, 1,500 and 2,500 occur with probability 1/6 each. The sum of these probabilities is 1. So no other values may occur.

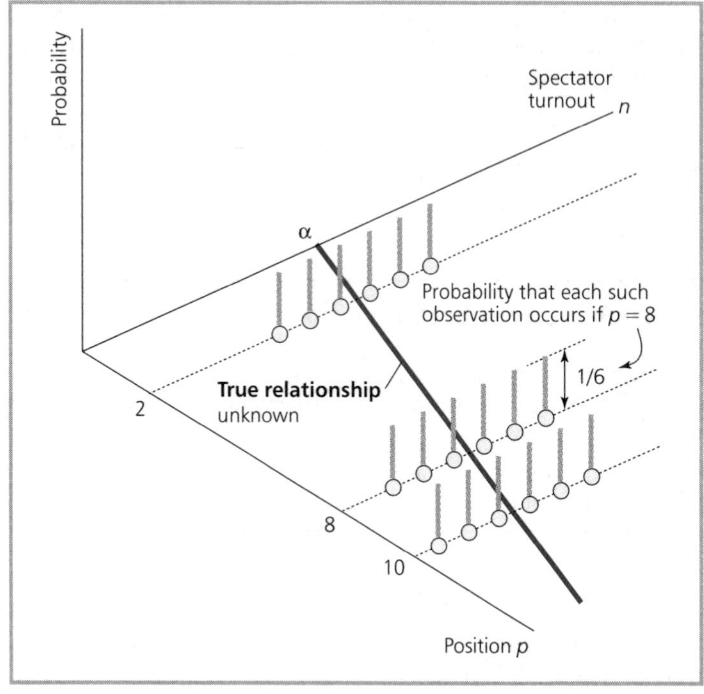

Figure A.9 Due to random influences, if $p = 2$ (or 8, or 10) any of the six white points may result with probability 1/6, making observations scatter around the true relationship given by the blue line.

and p. If PSG is in second place, we may expect a turnout crowd of 11,500, but the actual turnout will be 11,500 – 2,500, 11,500 – 1,500, 11,500 – 500, 11,500 + 500, 11,500 + 1,500 or 11,500 + 2,500, each with probability 1/6. Similar random effects on turnout are at work when PSG is in eighth or tenth place, or in any other position.

Panels (a) and (b) in Figure A.10 transfer the true relationship marked by the straight line and the possible data points onto a plane. Suppose now that

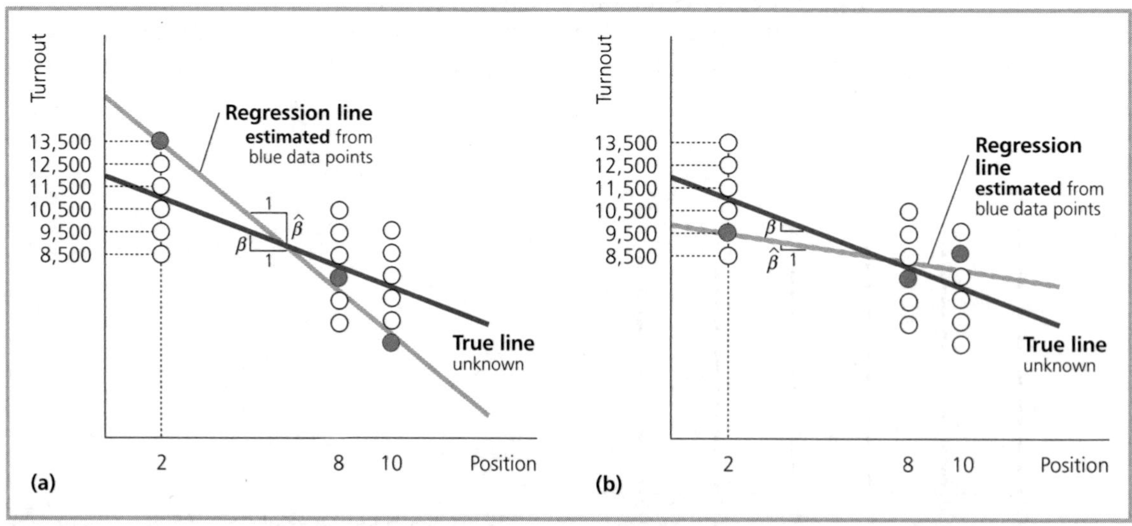

Figure A.10 Random influences on spectator turnout may give the results in panel (a) on one occasion, and those in panel (b) on another. The resulting regression line is steeper than the true line in the first case and flatter in the second. Thus the slope estimate $\hat{\beta}$ is subject to random influences.

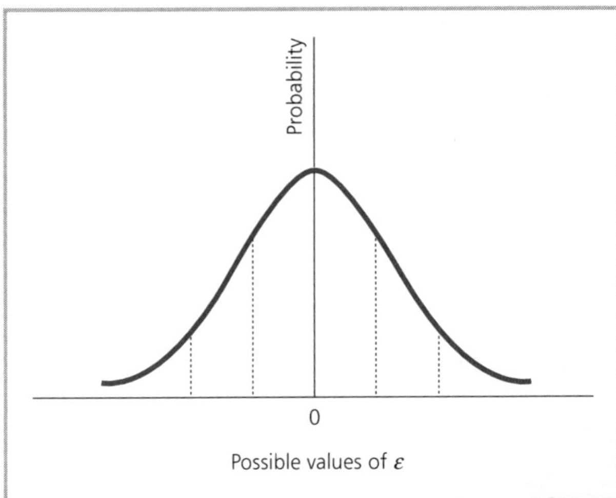

Figure A.11 Econometricians usually assume that random influences ε have a bell-shaped distribution. This means that most frequently disturbances are around 0 or small. Large positive or negative disturbances have a small probability of occurring. One important bell-shaped distribution is the normal distribution.

Note. What is being said *here* about the slope coefficient β and how to test it applies one-to-one to the constant term α.

in this situation two random samples of data are drawn, meaning that we are given two series of three observations of rounds in which PSG was in second, eighth and tenth place. The blue points in panel (a) mark the observations in the first sample and the blue points in panel (b) mark the observations in the second sample.

If a relationship between n and p is estimated from the first sample, the light blue line given in panel (a) of Figure A.10 results. The second sample gives the light blue line in panel (b). The first sample gives a regression coefficient that is larger than its true value of 500 ($\hat{\beta} > \beta = 500$). From the second sample we obtain a regression coefficient that is too small. Although OLS estimation allows us to expect to obtain the true coefficient, this will normally not be the case in a given sample.

Econometricians assume that the random effects that influence the endogenous variable, here on turnout, are not determined by throwing a dice, but are drawn from a **normal distribution** with expectation zero. A normal distribution is a bell-shaped distribution that is uniquely determined by its median (or average value), which determines where the bell sits on a horizontal axis, and by its variance, which determines how wide the bell is. Figure A.11 shows a normal distribution. The bell shape implies that small values (in the region of $\varepsilon = 0$) are much more frequent than large positive or negative values of ε. Now if ε is normally distributed around 0, then the crowd attendance when PSG is in second place in the league is normally distributed around the true value. Figure A.12 illustrates this.

Note. It can be shown that if the error is normally distributed, so is the true distribution of the estimated coefficient. The estimated distribution of the estimated coefficient has a *t*-distribution. If we work with many observations (thirty or more) the *t*-distribution gets close to the normal distribution.

We now come to the important conclusion of the current line of argument: if the crowd attendance figures that result from the true model are superimposed on random disturbances drawn from a bell-shaped distribution, then the regression coefficients estimated from many repeated random samples of observed data will have a bell-shaped distribution around the true coefficient. Figure A.13 illustrates this for the regression coefficient β. Of course, we do not know β, otherwise we would not have to estimate it. We also do not know the true distribution of the estimates around β. What we have is an estimated parameter $\hat{\beta}$ and an estimate of the bell-shaped distribution. For lack of better

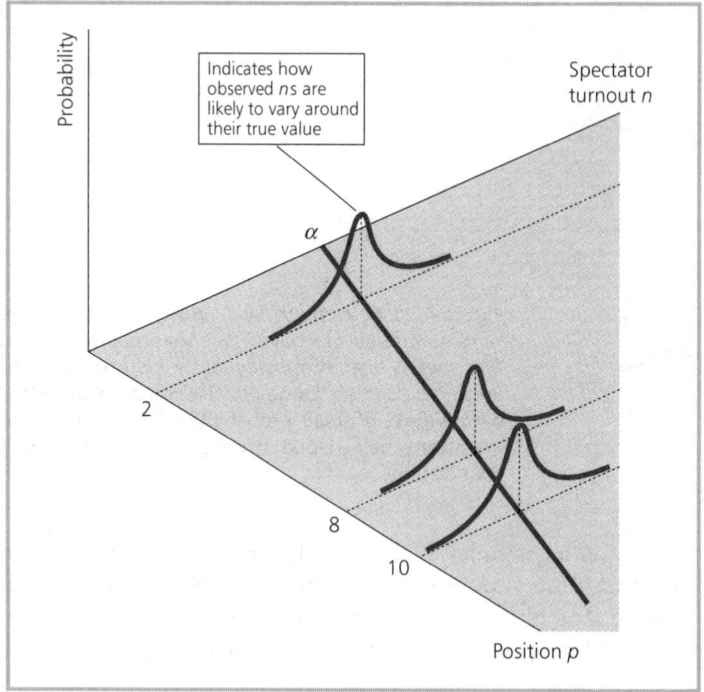

Figure A.12 When disturbances are normally distributed, the endogenous variable is also normally distributed. The graph illustrates this for three different values of the exogenous variable.

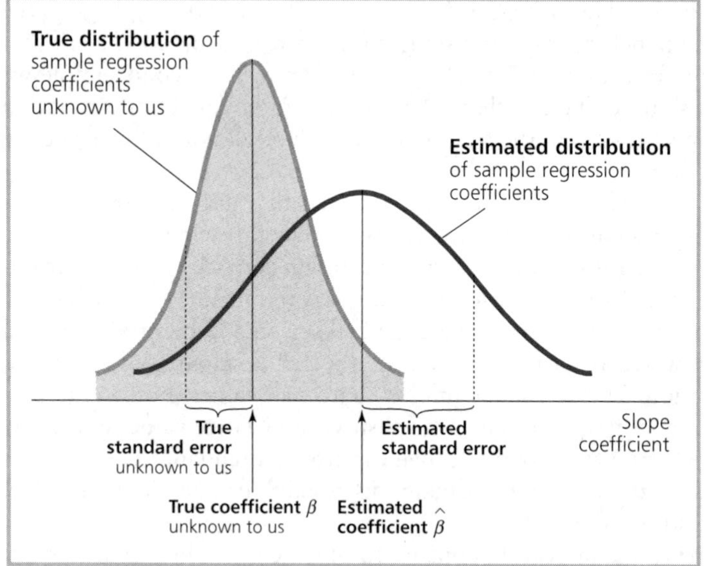

Figure A.13 Neither the true coefficient β nor the standard error of its distribution (left bell curve) is known to us. Instead, from the processed data we obtain a coefficient estimate $\hat{\beta}$ and an estimated standard error (right bell curve).

information we are persuaded that $\hat{\beta}$ is the true parameter and that the estimated distribution is the true distribution.

Two sets of questions are typically raised with the obtained estimates of the parameter and of its distribution. The first set constitutes a refinement of the first task of econometrics discussed in section A.1. It augments the parameter estimate $\hat{\beta}$ with a confidence interval, a range within which the true parameter can be expected to be when having a certain probability. The second set of questions addresses the second task of econometrics, namely that of testing models or hypotheses, which is the theme of this section.

As we will see, both sets of questions are intimately related, but are being asked in different contexts.

Confidence intervals

While the estimate has produced a precise parameter value of 453, we may want to describe the result more cautiously; for instance, the coefficient is approximately 450. While this signals the stochastic or random nature of the result, it is rather vague. Fortunately, despite the uncertainty involved, the results allow us to be more specific. All we need to do is make use of the fact that a specific area underneath the bell-shaped distribution tells us the probability with which parameters in the underlying segment may occur. (The total area underneath the distribution must equal 1, by definition!)

Note. Similar questions can be answered by applying the same principles. For example, what is the probability that the true parameter exceeds 200?

Let us now mark a symmetric interval around the coefficient estimate that excludes 95% of the entire area beneath the distribution curve. In Figure A.14 this is the segment between 253 and 653. The interpretation is as follows. Whenever we draw a new data sample – and the next football season is like a new sample – then the new data will exhibit a relationship between n and p that is between 253 and 653 with a probability of 95%. Since such an OLS estimate is always an unbiased estimate of the true parameter, we may expect that the estimated interval from 253 to 653 includes the true parameter β with a probability of 95%.

Note. The standard error is the square root of the variance. The two standard errors mentioned here are not exact, but good enough as a rule of thumb.

It is easy to determine this 95% confidence interval. It stretches from two standard errors below the parameter estimate to two standard errors above the parameter estimate. Computer programs routinely give the standard error of each regression coefficient. The standard error of β is the square root of the variance of β which, as we know, measures the width of the bell-shaped distribution.

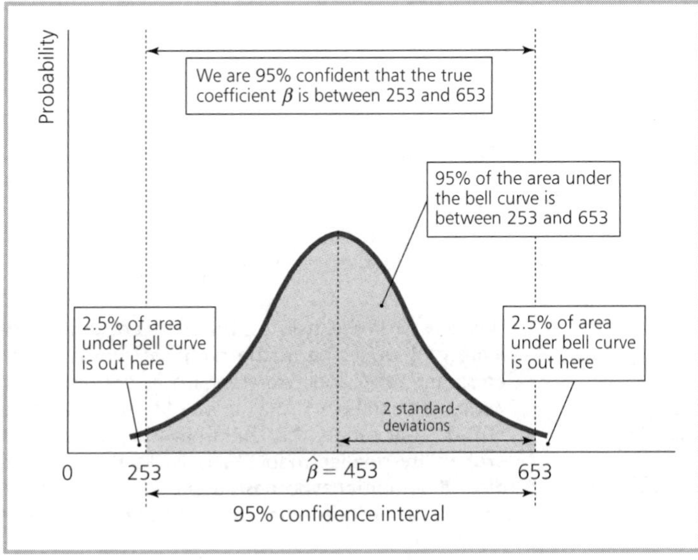

Figure A.14 The estimated distribution of the coefficient provides information as to the probabilities with which the true β is in a certain range. An important rule of thumb is that the true coefficient is between two standard errors left and two standard errors right of β with a probability of 95%. This range is called the 95% confidence interval.

Significance tests

Note the relationship confidence level = 1 – significance level.

Following the line of reasoning used when we played 'heads or tails' in Yuma (in the example above, pp. 438–9) we may phrase the test as follows. Suppose n and p are not really related, so that $\beta = 0$. What is the probability that we still obtain an estimate $\hat{\beta}$ from a random sample of data points? To answer this question, take the estimated distribution bell and slide it to the left so that its peak is directly over the presumed true value $\beta = 0$. Next we fix a significance level, usually of 5%, and then mark the sector within which we expect 95% of the coefficient estimates to be. In this case, this interval reaches from two standard errors below zero to two standard errors above zero. If the estimated parameter is outside this interval (shaded blue in Figure A.15), the probability that it was obtained in spite of the true parameter being zero is less than 5%. In this case we reject the null hypothesis $\beta = 0$. By analogy we could test other initial presumptions (or null hypotheses) such as $\beta = 1$. All we need to do then is check whether the parameter estimate is more than two standard errors away from the presumed value of 1.

Expressed more formally, significance tests are usually performed using the so-called ***t*-statistic**:

$$t = \frac{\text{parameter estimate} - \text{null hypothesis}}{\text{standard error}} = \frac{\hat{\beta} - \beta_0}{\sigma_\beta}$$

If my null hypothesis reads H_0: $\beta_0 = 0$, the t-statistic simplifies to

$$t = \frac{\text{parameter estimate}}{\text{standard error}} = \frac{\hat{\beta}}{\sigma_\beta}$$

If the t-statistic is greater than 2 or less than –2 (or if the *absolute* t-statistic is greater than 2), then the estimated coefficient is said to be significantly different from 0, i.e. from the null hypothesis. This renders the null hypothesis implausible and recommends that it be dropped. Unless stated otherwise, whenever this book's 'Applied problem' sections report t-statistics, these are absolute t-statistics, and they test against the null hypothesis that the true coefficient is zero.

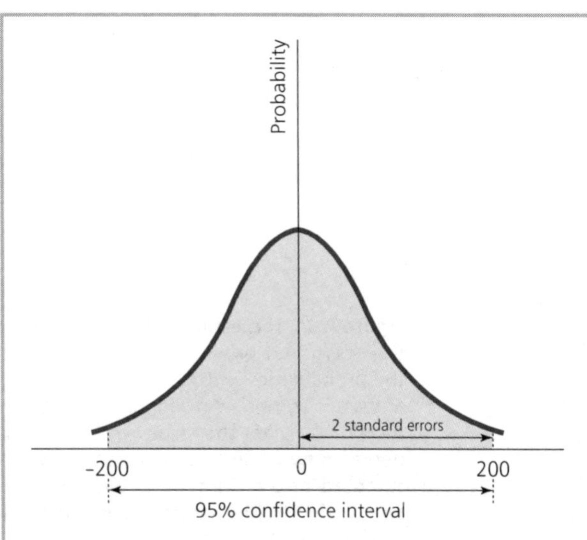

Figure A.15 If the true coefficient were 0, an estimate of $\hat{\beta}$ would be in the range of two standard errors left of 0 and two standard errors right of 0 with a probability of 95%. If we obtain an estimate outside that range, this could have happened with probability smaller than 5% only. In this case we discard our initial hypothesis that $\beta = 0$. The estimate $\hat{\beta}$ is said to be different from 0 at the 5% level of significance.

The above arguments may be condensed into the following formula:

Recipe for parameter tests

Step	What to do	Example
1	Read off the parameter estimate from the computer printout	–469
2	Read off the standard error of this parameter estimate from the computer printout	193
3	Specify a null hypothesis	$H_0: \beta_0 = 0$
4	Determine the interval that reaches from two standard errors below the null hypothesis to two standard errors above	–386 to 386
5	(a) Parameter estimates obtained from random samples fall within the interval identified in step 3 with a probability of 95% if the true coefficient is $\beta = 0$. The probability of obtaining a value outside this interval is only 5%. (b) If the estimated parameter lies outside the ±2 standard-error ~~interval~~ it is said to be significant (or significantly different from zero).	The parameter estimate of –469 is significant

APPENDIX SUMMARY

- Econometrics tries to quantify the relationship between the variables of economic models. It also tests whether presumptions (or hypotheses) about such variables are compatible with the data.
- The method of ordinary least squares (OLS) quantifies the relationship between variables by fitting a (usually linear) model, that is a straight line (or plane), in such a way into the cloud of data points that the sum of squared deviations of the data points from this line is as small as possible.
- The coefficient of determination R^2 indicates how well the model fits the data, that is how closely the data points are positioned to the estimated line. Being defined as the interval between 0 and 1, the larger the coefficient of determination, the better the model explains the data.
- The *t*-statistic usually addresses the question of whether the estimated coefficient is significantly different from zero (or, for short, is significant), that is, whether we may have obtained it by chance, despite the true coefficient being zero. The initial presumption (the null hypothesis) that the true coefficient is zero (that is, the two variables are unrelated) is usually rejected if the absolute *t*-value is larger than 2. Then the null hypothesis is false with a probability of more than 95%.

KEY TERMS AND CONCEPTS

coefficient of determination
confidence interval
estimate
null hypothesis
ordinary least squares (OLS)
regression
sample
significance level
***t*-statistic**

EXERCISES

A.1 The following data have been observed for variables x and y:

x	1	8	8	3	5	5	2	4	7	6
y	2	4	6	2	3	4	1	3	5	5

Show these points in a scatter diagram with y on the vertical and x on the horizontal axis.

Draw a regression line $y = \alpha + \beta x$ through the data points using your hand and your head (do not use formulas). Read α and β off your graph.

A.2 Discuss the O. J. Simpson trial in statistical terms. What is the null hypothesis from which jurors are requested to start? Translate the requirement 'beyond reasonable doubt' into statistical concepts. Do you believe that the jurors committed an error? If yes, was it an error of Type I or of Type II? In the civil law suit subsequently filed against O. J. Simpson the issue is not whether he is guilty 'beyond reasonable doubt' but with a probability of more than 50%. Does this increase the risk of committing an error of Type I or an error of Type II?

A.3 You are engaged in a game of dice. Your opponent throws only fives and sixes. After how many rounds do you discard your initial presumption (your null hypothesis) that the dice is not loaded:
(a) at the 10% level?
(b) at the 5% level?
(c) at the 1% level?

A.4 You would like to check:
(a) whether the quantity theory of money holds. You therefore estimate the equation (in logarithms)

$$\text{Money supply} = a + b \times \text{Price level} + c \times \text{GDP}$$

(b) whether the exchange rate forecasts published biannually in *The Economist* are rational in the sense that they are not systematically wrong. To look into this you estimate

$$\text{Depreciation in period } t = \alpha + \beta \times \text{Depreciation forecast for period } t$$

(c) whether the rate of return in your country's stock market does not really possess any forecasting potential for the rate of return in the next quarter. You estimate

$$\text{Rate of return in period } t = c_0 + c_1 \times \text{Rate of return in period } t - 1$$

(d) that the business cycle in the United States does not affect the business cycle in your country. The estimation equation reads

$$\text{Unemployment rate (your country)} = c + d \times \text{Unemployment rate (USA)}$$

Please formulate one or more appropriate null hypotheses for all of the above questions.

RECOMMENDED READING

There are more than a dozen very good econometrics texts on the market. One outstanding example is Robert S. Pyndick and Daniel L. Rubinfeld (1998) *Econometric Models and Economic Forecasts*, 4th edn, New York: McGraw-Hill. However, this book does include more mathematics than we needed here. If you are looking for a book that makes the most of intuitive reasoning and graphical illustrations, here are three very good choices that you may want to look at:

- Dougherty, Christopher (1992) *Introduction to Econometrics*, New York and Oxford: Oxford University Press.
- Gujarati, Damodar N. (1995) *Basic Econometrics*, 3rd edn, New York: McGraw-Hill.
- Kennedy, Peter E. (1998) *A Guide to Econometrics*, 4th edn, Oxford: Blackwell.

If you do not really want to get into econometrics, but would like to learn more about concepts introduced here while enjoying yourself at the same time, pick up a copy of Larry Gonick and Woollcott Smith (1993) *The Cartoon Guide to Statistics*, New York: Harper Perennial.

To further explore this chapter's key messages you are encouraged to use the interactive online module found at

www.fgn.unisg.ch/eurmacro/tutor/econometrics.html

and many other features hosted at **www.fgn.unisg.ch/eurmacro**

INDEX

Note: Page numbers in **bold** refer to definitions of terms.

absolute convergence hypothesis, 245
active population, 140
actual expenditure, **39**, 40, 44
actual income, 36
adaptive expectations, **182**, **199**, 200
  in *DAD-SAS* model, 208–9
AD-AS model, 176–80
  equilibrium price level, 178–80
  fiscal policy, 180–2
  monetary policy, 182–6
  policy and shocks in, 180–7
adjustment costs of firms, 420
aggregate demand (*AD*) curve, 168–76, 194
  algebra of, 190–1
  fixed exchange rates, 191
  flexible exchange rates, 190–1
aggregate expenditure, **39**, 40, 44, 48
aggregate output, **8**
aggregate supply (*AS*) curve, **16**, **137**, 160–1, 168, 193
  classical, **137**
  linear, 167
  long-run, 178
  non-linear, 167
  real rigidities, 157–8
  short-run, 167–8, 178
AK model, 275–7
  empirical implications, 277–9
algebra
  of *AD* curve, 190–1
  of *DAD* curve, 216
  of *FE* curve, 100–1
  of *IS* curve, 70–3
  of *IS-LM* curve, 82
  of *IS-LM-FE*, 104
  of Mundell-Fleming model, 121–2
  of oil price, 416–17
appreciation, 71
Asia, 1998 crisis, 118–20
autonomous steady states, 262
average income tax rate, **47**

balance of payments, **17**, 18, 91–5
  accounts, 19
  surplus, **95**
Bank of England, 326–7
barter economy, 7
Belgium–Luxemburg monetary union, 396
Beveridge curve, 406–9
big-leap approach, **360**
big push, 268, 269
boom, **34**, 36
Bretton Woods, **312**, 316
budget adjustment requirement, 388
budget constraint, 374, 386
budget deficit, 17, 373
  dynamics of, 374–88
  no money financing and no inflation, 374–86
budget surplus, 12
Bundesbank, 314–16, 345, 352, 374
business cycle, **34**, 36
  synchronization, **366**

capital
  costs, **52**
  human, 271–5, **271**
  per worker, 238
capital account, **18**, 94, 97
Cecchini report, 264
central bank, **17**, 321, 341–3, 352–6, 388–92
  hard-nosed, 351
  independence, 24, **341**, 350–7
  wet, 351
circular flow identity, 14, **252**
circular flow model, 393
  demand categories, 41
  terminology and overview, 38–42
circular flow of income and spending, 7–15
classical aggregate supply curve, **137**
closed economy, **89**, 255, 261
Cobb–Douglas production function, 226–8
  constant income shares, 228
  constant returns to scale, 228
  diminishing marginal products, 228
  mathematics of, 228
coefficient of determination, 441, 443
collective involuntary unemployment, 148
comparative static analysis, **122**, 122–4
conditional convergence, 264
confidence intervals, 447
constant returns to scale, **225**

constraint, **288**, 299, 346–50
  modifying, 299
consumer price index, **346**
consumption function, 43, 47, 50–2, 68
  simple, 68
contingent rule, 345
contractionary monetary and fiscal policy, 424
convergence, 264–7
  conditional, 264
  criteria, 317
crawling peg, **345**
crowding out, 80, **113**
currency board, **345**
currency union, 328
current account, 12, **18**, 94, 97
  Germany, unification and, 12–13
  Italy, before and after 1992 EMS crisis, 98
cyclical unemployment, 406
  vs equilibrium unemployment, 406–9

DAD-SAS model, 195–8, 218
  adaptive expectations, 208–9
  equilibrium in, 196–7
  fiscal policy, 208–10
  genesis of, 216–18
  long-run response in, 204–6
  monetary policy, 201–8
  perfect foresight, 207–8, 209
  policy effectiveness in, 210–14
  rational expectations, 206–7, 209
  short-run response in, 202–4
  synthesis of, 283
debt, public, **374**, 384–5
debt ratio, 375
  dynamics, 375, 387
  in EU member states, 382
  in UK, 255
default risk, 101
deficit
  primary, 373
  ratio, 375
demand, 36
  for labour, 140
  for money, 62, 63
  and supply side, 283
demand-side equilibrium, 40, 44, **168**
depreciation, 71
  expected, 124
devaluation, 71
disinflation costs, 345, 357
  in *DAD-SAS* model, 357–62
  in the real world, 362–4
disposable income, 38, **47**
dynamic aggregate demand (*DAD*) curve, 169, 195, 218, 422
  algebra of, 216
  fixed exchange rates, 216
  flexible exchange rates, 216
  positioning, 197
dynamic analysis, **122**, 122–4
dynamically inefficient, 237

econometrics, 24, 434
economically rational expectations, **201**
economies of scale, **267**
efficiency
  of labour, 240
  units, 241
efficiency wage theory, **149**
efficiency wages, 149–52, **152**
  trade unions and, 411–12
empirical note, **48**
empirical tests, 22–4
endogenous growth, 275–9
endogenous variables, 105
equilibrium, 40
  algebra of *IS-LM-FE*, 104
  condition, 46
  debt ratio, 375
  exchange rate, 104, 121
  with graphs, 102–3
  income, 44, **46**, 47, 48, 82, 104, 121
  interest rate, 82, 104
  long-run, 179
  short-run, 179
  stable, **122**
  unemployment, 406, 424
equilibrium aggregate demand (*EAD*) curve, 196, 197
equilibrium aggregate supply (*EAS*) curve, 196
euro, 302–3, 390–1
Euroland, 309–10
  monetary and fiscal policy in, 328–33
Europe, job growth, 425–7
European Central Bank (ECB), 301, 309, 328–30, 366, 395, 428
European Monetary System (EMS), 309, 312, 317, 324–7
  crisis (1992), 312–16, 324–5
  EMS II, 345
European Monetary Union (EMU), 301, 317, 328, 345, **366**, 428
  shape and future, 365–7
European Union (EU), 6, 263–4
  Pact for Stability and Growth (1996), 275, 331, 332, 392, 393, 395, 397, 428
  Single Markets Acts, 263

exceptional (transitory) income, 52
exchange rate, **61**
  equilibrium, 104, 121
  expectations, 124–6
  fixing, 301
  nominal, 71
  overshooting, 126–7, **127**, 346
  pegging, 356–7
  real, **70**
  target zones, 319–24
  today and the future, 130–2
Exchange Rate Mechanism (ERM), 321
exogenous variables, 105
expected depreciation, 124–6
expected devaluation, **194**
export function, 70
exports, 68–70
extreme Keynesian aggregate supply curve, **137**
E-Y diagram, 103

factors of production, **6**
FE curve, 95–101, **100**, 103, 104, 130
  algebra of, 100–1
Feldstein-Horioka puzzle, 261
financial account, 94
firms, 7
FISC, 388–92
fiscal policy, **78**, **112**
  in *AD-AS* model, 180–2
  constraints on, 331–2
  contractionary, 424
  in *DAD-SAS* model, 208–10
  in Euroland, 328–33
  in *IS-LM* (global economy) model, 77–80
  in monetary union, 330
  in the Mundell-Fleming model, 112–15
Fisher equation, **206**, 211
fixed exchange rates, 105, **114**, 114–15
  in *AD* curve, 191
  in *DAD* curve, 216
  in the Mundell-Fleming model, 116–17, 122–3
  in *SAS* curve, 347
flexible exchange rates, 95, **113**
  in *AD* curve, 190–1
  in *DAD* curve, 216
  in the Mundell-Fleming model, 116, 122
  in *SAS* curve, 347
flow variable, **63**
Ford car plant, 154
foreign exchange market, **95**, 111
foreign exchange market intervention, **321**
France
  EMU and, 318
  GNP, 42, 256
Free Trade Agreement of the Americas (FTAA), 264
frictional unemployment, **155**
Friedman rule, **301**

gain ratios, 364
game, **295**
Germany
  current account, 12–13
  unification, 313
global economy, 310–11
global-economy *IS* curve, 74–5, 82
global economy model, 259
globalization, 88, 89–90, 261, 277
  income and distribution effects, 262
golden rule of capital accumulation, **235**, 253
golden steady state, 236
goods market, 111
government
  budget, **17**, 373–9
  debt, 390–1
  indifference curve, **290**
  purchases, **41**
  reaction function, 353
gradualist approach, **361**
graphs, working with, 22–3
gross domestic product (GDP), 11, 261
  Europe and world (1900–2000), 35
  nominal, 11
  real, 11
gross income, 38
gross national product (GNP), 11, 261
  in France, 42, 256
  in USA, 42, 256–9
growth accounting, 226
  equation, 227
  in Italy, 229
growth rates, 30–1

hard-nosed central bank, 351
high-powered money, 62
horizontal aggregate supply curve, 16, 137, 138
households, 7
human capital, 271–5, **271**
hyperbola, **147**
hysteresis, **420**, 421–2

import function, 47, 70
imports, 38, 68–70
income, 2
  actual, 36
  approach, 8
  disposable, 38, **47**
  distribution, 3, 262
  equilibrium, 44, **46**, 47, 48, 82, 104, 121

income (*continued*)
  gross, 38
  income, 2, 3, 15, 16, 228
  per capita, 222, 234
  permanent, 52, 54
  potential, **34**, 36, 138–43, 232
  regular (permanent), 52, 54
  steady state, **34**, 36, 232
indifference curves, 147
inflation, 4, 193
  bias, **297**, 301
  costs of, 364–5
  expectations, 198–201
  targets, 343
inflation rates, Europe and global, 358
inflation tax, 387, 388
injections, 9
insider power, 420
insiders, 147–9, **148**
institutions, **287**
instrument potency, 299
  eliminating, 300–3
integrated goods markets, 263–4
intensive form, 238
interest control vs money supply, 77–8
interest parity, uncovered, 124
interest rate
  equilibrium, 82, 104
  real, **204**
international capital markets, 24
international monetary arrangements, 308
International Monetary Fund (IMF), 269, 345, 395
international monetary system, 24
intertemporal perspective, 50
investment, **9**
  demand, 8
  function, 68
  planned, 39
  timing of, 52–4
  unplanned, 39
involuntary unemployment, 145, 148
Ireland, public debt, 384–5
IS curve, **70**, 103, 104, 218
  algebra of, 70–3
  global-economy, 74–5, 82
  long-run, 130
IS plane, 71
IS-LM (global economy) model, 73–82
  algebra, 82
  fiscal policy, 77–80
  graphical, 75–6
  Keynesian cross, 79, 80
IS-LM-FE model, 104
  algebra of equilibrium, 104
  long-run response in, 204–6
  short-run response in, 202–4
iso-vote curves, 291
Italy
  current account before and after 1992 EMS crisis, 98
  EMU and, 318
  growth accounting in, 229

Japanese recession, 80–1

Keynes, John Maynard, 49
Keynesian cross, **44**, 49
  with income expectations, 54
  vs *IS-LM* model, 79, 80
Keynesianism, 49

labour
  costs, **145**, 412
  demand curve, **140**, 415–16
  efficiency, 275
  force, 140, 141, 155
  income share, 228
labour market
  classical, 140–3
  flow model of, 155–7
  potential income and, 138–43
labour supply, 141, 142
labour supply curve, **142**
leakages, 9
liquidity trap, 80–1
LM curve, **66**, 69, 82, 103, 104, 218
  semi-logarithmic, 130
logarithmic scales, 31–2
logarithms, 29–30
long-run, 179, 196

Maastricht Treaty, 319, 324–5, 343, 366, 374, 388–92, 395, 397
macroeconomics, **1**
managed floating, **322**
marginal income tax rate, **47**
marginal product
  of capital, **224**, 225
  of labour, 139, **140**, 141
marginal propensity to consume, **43**
market psychology, **194**, 327
mathematical model, **21**
menu costs, 365
microeconomics, **1**
minimum wages, 145–6, 409
mismatch unemployment, 154
model, **20**
monetary base, 62

monetary policy, 66, **76**, 76–7
  in *AD-AS* model, 182–6
  contractionary, 424
  in *DAD-SAS* model, 201–8
  in the Mundell-Fleming model, 115–20
monetary union, 328
  fiscal policy in, 330
  monetary policy in, 328–30
money, **15**, 62, 63
  demand function, 64
  financing, 386–8
  growth rule, 301
  high-powered, 63
  market, 62, 111
money supply
  control, 66
  vs interest control, 77–8
multiple regression, 439–40
multiplier, 45, **47**, 48, 50, 62, 122, 322
  IS-LM government spending, 82
Mundell-Fleming model, **111**, 196, 218
  algebra of, 121–2
  currency union, 338–9
  fiscal policy in, 112–15
  fixed exchange rates, 337
  flexible exchange rates, 336
  monetary policy in, 115–20
  two-country, 336–8
  under capital controls, 115

national economy, 310–11
  model, 259
national income accounts, **14**
natural logarithms, 29
neoclassical growth model *see* Solow growth model
net taxes, **41**
New Keynesian theory of aggregate supply, 158
New Zealand's Reserve Bank Act, 343–4
no-bailout clause, **331**
nominal exchange rate, 71
nominal income, 2, 3, 15, 16
normal distribution, 445
*n*th currency, 311–12
null hypothesis, 439

official reserve account, **18**
oil price, 414
  algebra of, 416–17
  explosions, 350, 424
  labour demand curve and, 415–16
  unemployment and, 417
Okun's law, **402**, 402–4
open economies, **89**, 255, 261
open interest parity, 130
optimum currency area, **366**
ordinary least squares (OLS) estimation, 436
Organization for Economic Cooperation and
    Development (OPEC), **416**
output
  per worker, 238
  potential, 143, 225
outsiders, 147–9, **148**

Pact for Stability and Growth (1996) (EU), 275, 331,
    332, 392, 393, 395, 397, 428
partial production function, 139, 152, 225
peaks, 36
pegging
  the currency, 345
  the exchange rate, 356–7
per capita incomes, 234
  European, 222
perfect foresight, **200**
perfect information, 153
permanent income, 54
permanent shocks, 197
persistence, 418, 422–3, 424
  in the *DAD-SAS* model, 420–3
phase line, **376**, 377–8
Phillips curve, **402**
pivotal role of expectations, 52
planned expenditure *see* aggregate expenditure
planned investment, 39
players, 295
policy games, 295–8
  with two-period horizon, 298
policy-making, **287**
political business cycles, 290–2, **292**
population, 140, 141
potential income, **34**, 36, 232
  labour market and, 138–43
potential output, 143, 225
poverty traps, 267–9
preferences, **288**, 288–90, 299, 341–5
  changing, 299–300
price, oil *see* oil price
primary deficit, 373
producer price index, **346**
production function, 138, 283
  Cobb–Douglas, 226–8
  extensive form, 224
  intensive form, 238
  linearized, 401
  partial, 139, 152, 225
productivity gains, 233
profits, 153
public debt, **374**
  Ireland, 384–5

public support function, 289
purchasing power parity, **70**, 71, 211–13

quantity equation, **16**, 211

random walk, **322**
rate of return, **52**, 53
rational expectations, **200**, 293–5
real exchange rate, **70**
real income, 3, 15, 16
real interest rate, **204**
real wage rigidity, **147**
recession, **34**, 36
regression, 439–40
regular (permanent) income, 52, 54
relative convergence hypothesis, 246
representative agents models, 1
requirement line, 232
revaluation, 71
Ricardian equivalence theorem, **254**, 255
rigidity
  real, 157–8
  real wage, **147**
risk
  neutral individual, **97**
  premium, 101

sacrifice ratio, **360**
secular trend, 33
seignorage, 387, 388
shoe leather costs, 365
short-run aggregate supply curve, 167–8, 178
short-run equilibrium, 179
significance tests, 448
simple regression, 439–40
single European market, 263–4
small open economy, 310
Solow growth model (neoclassical growth model), 230–2
  convergence in, 264–7
  empirical merits and deficiencies, 243–7
  vs endogenous growth models, 279
  poverty traps in, 267–71
  synthesis of, 283
Solow residual, 228, 229
spending
  bias, 393
  plans, changes in, 44–7
stable equilibrium, **122**
steady state, **234**
  with global capital market, 262
  income, **34**, 36, 232
sticky wages, 158–61
stock variable, 63
structural unemployment, **155**
supply of money, 62
supply shocks, 350–7
surprise aggregate supply (*SAS*) curve, **193**, 194, 195, 402
  under fixed and flexible exchange rates, 347
  with hysteresis, 421
  with persistence, 420, 422
  positioning, 197
Swiss National Bank, 352
Swizerland, unemployment, 428

target zones, 323
tax equation, 47
tax wedge, **146**, 409–10
taxation, 253
Taylor rule, **301**, **345**
technological progress, 233
time inconsistency, **297**
trade imbalances, 17
trade unions
  efficiency wages and, 411–12
  monopolistic, 146–7, 420
  unemployment, 410–11
transition dynamics, 124–6, **234**
transitory income, 54
transitory shocks, 197
troughs, 36
t-statistic, 448
twin deficits, 15
two-handed approach, 424
Type I error, 438
Type II error, 439

uncovered interest parity, 99
unemployment, 3
  cyclical, 406–9
  equilibrium, 144–58, 406–9, 424
  European, 404–19
  frictional, **155**
  involuntary, 145, 148
  linking growth and, 401–4
  mismatch, 154
  oil prices and, 417
  persistence, 417–19
  structural, **155**
  voluntary, 145, 408
unit labour costs, **145**, 412
United Kingdom
  actual, potential and steady-state income, 37
  cost of war, 1940, 241–3
  debt ratios, 255

EMU and, 318–19
how to pay for the war, 1940, 49
United States of America (USA)
GNP, 42, 256–9
job growth, 425–7, 428
unplanned investment, 39

variation, 442
vertical aggregate supply curve, 16, 137, 138
voluntary unemployment, 145, 408

wages
efficiency, 149–52, **152**, 411–12
minimum, 145–6, 409
role of, 412–13
sticky, 158–61
sum, 147
wealth, 62
wet central bank, 351
World Bank, 269
world trade, 100
World Trade Organization (WTO), 25